EMPLOYMENT RELATIONS

Sara Miller McCune founded SAGE Publishing in 1965 to support the dissemination of usable knowledge and educate a global community. SAGE publishes more than 1000 journals and over 800 new books each year, spanning a wide range of subject areas. Our growing selection of library products includes archives, data, case studies and video. SAGE remains majority owned by our founder and after her lifetime will become owned by a charitable trust that secures the company's continued independence.

Los Angeles | London | New Delhi | Singapore | Washington DC | Melbourne

SECOND EDITION

CECILIE BINGHAM

EMPLOYMENT RELATIONS

FAIRNESS & TRUST IN THE WORKPLACE

Los Angeles | London | New Delhi
Singapore | Washington DC | Melbourne

Los Angeles | London | New Delhi
Singapore | Washington DC | Melbourne

SAGE Publications Ltd
1 Oliver's Yard
55 City Road
London EC1Y 1SP

SAGE Publications Inc.
2455 Teller Road
Thousand Oaks, California 91320

SAGE Publications India Pvt Ltd
Unit No. 323–333, Third Floor, F-Block
International Trade Tower, Nehru Place
New Delhi 110 019

SAGE Publications Asia-Pacific Pte Ltd
3 Church Street
#10-04 Samsung Hub
Singapore 049483

Editor: Ruth Stitt
Editorial assistant: Charlotte Hegley
Production editor: Martin Fox
Copyeditor: Christine Bitten
Proofreader: Brian McDowell
Indexer: Gary Kirby
Marketing manager: Lucia Sweet
Cover design: Naomi Robinson
Typeset by: C&M Digitals (P) Ltd, Chennai, India
Printed in the UK

Library of Congress Control Number: 2022942241

British Library Cataloguing in Publication data

A catalogue record for this book is available from the British Library

ISBN 978-1-5297-7479-5
ISBN 978-1-5297-7478-8 (pbk)

At SAGE we take sustainability seriously. Most of our products are printed in the UK using responsibly sourced papers and boards. When we print overseas we ensure sustainable papers are used as measured by the PREPS grading system. We undertake an annual audit to monitor our sustainability.

For Nick, James, Ruth and Tom

CONTENTS

List of Case Studies, Case Snippets and News Flashes — xv

Guided Tour — xix

Online Resources — xxi

About the Author — xxiii

Acknowledgements — xxv

About this Book — xxvii

1 Employee Relations: Setting the Scene — 1

2 Employee Relations: The Importance of Context — 31

3 Trust and Getting a Fair Deal at Work — 61

4 Contract Change and the Employment Relationship — 93

5 Employment Relations in Precarious Platform and Gig Work — 123

6 Causes and Expressions of Workplace Conflict — 151

7 Conflict: Reduction, Regulation and Resolution — 187

8 Employee Engagement and the Employment Relationship — 225

9 Sharing Information and Decision-Making: From Employee Involvement to Partnership — 257

10 Employee Voice: Being Heard and Making a Difference — 293

11 Flexibility and Fairness in the Employment Relationship — 333

12 Equitable Reward and the Employment Relationship — 367

13 Fairness in Practice — 399

Glossary — 429

Index — 443

DETAILED CONTENTS

List of Case Studies, Case Snippets and News Flashes   xv
Guided Tour   xix
Online Resources   xxi
About the Author   xxiii
Acknowledgements   xxv
About this Book   xxvii

1   Employee Relations: Setting the Scene   **1**

What to Expect   1
Employee Relations – What Is It?   2
Changes in the UK Employment Market   10
Human Resource Management (HRM)   11
Power Imbalances   12
Frames of Reference   18
Managerial Styles   23
Summary   25
Relevant Articles for Further Reading   26
References   26

2   Employee Relations: The Importance of Context   **31**

What to Expect   31
Context – Is It Relevant?   32
Globalisation and Employment Relations   38
Convergence Versus Divergence   43
Trade Unions   47
Summary   53
Relevant Articles for Further Reading   54
References   55

3   Trust and Getting a Fair Deal at Work   **61**

What to Expect   61
Trust at Work   62
Fairness and Trust   65
Fairness and the Law   67
Equity, Efficiency and Voice   68
Employee Perceptions of Organisational Fairness, Justice and Injustice   70

Psychological Contract   77
Increased Workloads and Levels of Trust   80
Trust and the High-performing Workplace   83
Summary   83
Relevant Articles for Further Reading   85
References   86

4 Contract Change and the Employment Relationship   **93**

What to Expect   93
What Is an Employment Contract?   94
What's in a Name?   94
Employment Contracts and the Power Realities of the Employment Relationship   98
Summary   115
Relevant Articles for Further Reading   118
References   118

5 Employment Relations in Precarious Platform and Gig Work   **123**

What to Expect   123
Platforms and Gigs Explained   124
Precarious Work   125
Insecurity and Platform Work   127
Platform Work   129
Different Types of Platform Work   131
Legislation   133
The Impact of Algorithms on the Employment Relationship   139
Platform Work, Power and Worker Representation   141
Summary   143
Relevant Articles for Further Reading   145
References   145

6 Causes and Expressions of Workplace Conflict   **151**

What to Expect   151
The Causes and Inevitability of Workplace Conflict   152
Academic Perspectives on Conflict   161
Expressions of Conflict   167
Summary   176
Relevant Articles for Further Reading   178
References   179

7 Conflict: Reduction, Regulation and Resolution   **187**

What to Expect   187
A Contested Relationship: Managerial Styles and Their Impact   189

Conflict and Performance Management   192
Conflict Reduction and Strategies Engendering Employee Trust   194
Addressing Conflict   196
Restrictions on Employers That Could Reduce the Incidence of Conflict   203
Examples of Legal Restrictions to Reduce Conflict   204
Procedures and Their Impact on the Employment Relationship   205
Types of Procedures   210
Alternative Dispute Resolution   214
Summary   217
Relevant Articles for Further Reading   218
References   218

8 Employee Engagement and the Employment Relationship   225

What to Expect   225
What Is Employee Engagement?   226
The Engagement Paradox   232
Measures of Engagement   237
Engagement and the Employment Relationship   238
Engagement Trust and Voice   242
Summary   248
Relevant Articles for Further Reading   250
References   250

**9 Sharing Information and Decision-Making: From Employee
Involvement to Partnership   257**

What to Expect   258
Encouraging Commitment Through Involvement and Participation   258
Employee Involvement, Participation and Partnership   262
What Do Employee Involvement, Participation and Partnership Entail?   263
Employee Involvement   266
Employee Networks   270
Employee Participation   272
Categorising Participation   275
Partnership   279
Summary   285
Relevant Articles for Further Reading   286
References   287

10 Employee Voice: Being Heard and Making a Difference   293

What to Expect   293
Voice – Definitions and Their Shortcomings   294
Evidence for the Concept of Employee Voice Within the Employment Relationship   295

Employer Voice   298
Patterns of Voice   299
Direct Voice   301
Indirect Voice   303
Collective Bargaining   307
National v. Local Agreements   310
Collective Bargaining Models   311
Enabling Voice – UK Employers' Legal Obligations   312
Voice and Silence   316
Voice and Diversity   317
Voice, Trust and Fairness   321
Summary   323
Relevant Articles for Further Reading   324
References   325

11 Flexibility and Fairness in the Employment Relationship   333

What to Expect   333
Flexible Work Patterns: What Are They and Who Benefits?   334
Flexibility for the Employee   335
Managerial Styles and Flexibility From the Employers' Point of View   338
Flexible Working and Pluralist Approaches   340
The Flexible Firm   341
Different Types of Flexible Working Patterns   343
Flexibility: Gender and Family-friendly Practices   351
Flexibility: Power, Conflict and Trust   353
Flexibility: Points to Consider for Maintaining an
     Harmonious Employment Relationship   356
Summary   357
Relevant Articles for Further Reading   360
References   360

12 Equitable Reward and the Employment Relationship   367

What to Expect   367
The Value of Reward in the Workplace   368
Employers and Reward   369
Influences Affecting Reward   374
Consensual Methods of Determining Reward   380
Reward and Perceptions of Fairness   382
Different Types of Payment Systems   387
Summary   390
Relevant Articles for Further Reading   393
References   393

13 Fairness in Practice   **399**

What to Expect   399
Fairness in Context   400
Fairness and Power   403
Fairness and Justice at Work: A Recap   406
Injustice, Justice and Conflict   410
Voice Mechanisms and the Perceptions of Fairness   419
Holding the Front Line Via Fairness: The Importance of Line Managers   420
Relevant Articles for Further Reading   422
References   423

Glossary   429
Index   443

4.2 Fairness in Practice

LIST OF CASE STUDIES, CASE SNIPPETS AND NEWS FLASHES

Case Studies

2.1	Union's Fight for Recognition and Reinstatement of Workers in Indian Garment Factory: India	39
2.2	An Employee Relations Academic, Fernando Duran-Palma, Writes to His Students: International Perspective	44
2.3	An International ER Manager, Remy Ligeika, Reflects on His Role: Global	49
2.4	Sodexo Embraces Health and Safety: France	52
3.1	Tesco: UK, Ireland, Hungary, Czech Republic and Slovakia	74
5.1	Platform Work Saved Me From Paying Expensive Childcare: UK and USA	130
5.2	Amazon: Recruiting App Discriminated Against Women: Global	138
6.1	Glasgow Bin Strike During COP26: Scotland	158
6.2	Ireland's Longest Employee Relations Dispute: Ireland	165
7.1	A Metropolitan Council: UK	212
8.1	Kellogg's Reaps Reward From New Online Engagement Hub: Global	235
8.2	Inclusivity Drives Engagement at Auto Trader: Ireland, UK	247
9.1	British Business Bank: UK	269
9.2	Jump on Board (JOB): UK	283
10.1	Law Firm Successfully Promotes Diverse Voices: Global	317
10.2	Silence Voice and Inclusion: USA	319
11.1	Lou's Headache: Lou's Electrical Repairs: UK	350
13.1	Bulgarian Kitchen Hand Physically and Verbally Abused: UK	401

13.2   Sainsbury's Dismissal of Racist Worker Accused of Groping Staff
       Deemed Unfair: UK   402
13.3   In Pursuit of Decency and Fairness in Dunnes Stores Ireland – 30 Years
       and Counting: Ireland   421

Case Snippets

2.1   Female Migrant Labour in Italy Exploited: Italy   40
2.2   Unexplained Migrant Worker Deaths on Qatar World Cup Sites: Qatar   41
2.3   Unilever Instructs Its Suppliers to Pay Living Wages by 2030: Global   46

3.1   Redressing the Balance: USA   64
3.2   Perceptions of Fairness: Universal   71
3.3   Tile Factory Boss 'Drove Car at Workers': UK   81

4.1   Costly Breach of Trust and Confidence: UK   108

5.1   Amazon Defends Itself Against Trade Union Discrimination: UK   140

8.1   Inclusivity Essential for Engagement: Global   243

9.1   Direct Participation – Pringle Crisps: USA   274
9.2   Indirect Participation – Worker Directors, FirstGroup: UK   274
9.3   Indirect Participation – Hewlett-Packard: USA and Europe   275
9.4   Partnership on the Elizabeth Line: UK   281

10.1   Voice at the Go-Ahead Group plc: UK   302

12.1   Paying Everyone the Same Is a Bad Idea: UK   370

13.1   False Accusation: UK   404
13.2   Personal Blackmail: UK   404
13.3   Retaining Good Workers: UK   405
13.4   Inequality (Women's Pensions): UK   411
13.5   Exploitation (Insecure Workers): UK   418

News Flashes

1.1   CBI Calls for at Least One BAME Member on Company Boards   3
1.2   Strike Threatening Johan Sverdrup   6
1.3   The American Jobs Plan   7

1.4   The Shrewsbury Pickets' Struggle for Justice [1972–2021]   14
1.5   Abuse of Power Not Uncommon   15

2.1   Nigerian TUC Demands Government Call Chevron Management and Other
      Multinationals to Order   33
2.2   Alleged Labour Abuses by Dyson in Supply Chain   34
2.3   London Bus Workers Strike Against French-owned RATP   38
2.4   Flowers Rotting on the World's Largest Daffodil Farm Because of Brexit   42
2.5   Global Parental Leave Scheme Introduced by Volvo   43
2.6   Secretly Group Union   48
2.7   Global Campaign to Protect Workers in Garment Factories   49

3.1   Black Men Experience Distrust at Work   65
3.2   East of England Ambulance Service Put in Special Measures   75
3.3   Berlin Brandenburg Airport: Electric Shocks   75
3.4   Trust Must Be Earned   78

4.1   Breaching Levels of Trust and Confidence: Ikea France Spied on at least 400 Workers   99
4.2   Employers' Right to Induce Acceptance of Contract Change Clarified   100
4.3   Spanish Parliament Changes Temporary Contract Regulations   102
4.4   UAE: Contracts of Employment Made More Equitable   103
4.5   10% of Workers Told to Re-apply for Their Jobs on Worse Terms and
      Conditions, says TUC   106
4.6   Water Board Employees Threaten to Go on Strike After Contracts
      Unilaterally Changed   107
4.7   British Gas Workers Sacked Over Contracts Dispute   109
4.8   Ryanair Sacks 'Fake News' Employees   111
4.9   Teacher Fired for Secret Online Profile   114

5.1   Canadian Postal Union Fights for Gig Worker Rights   128
5.2   Low Pay and Spying Lead to Food Delivery Dispute and Demands for Change   133
5.3   Parliamentary Group Proposes New Algorithm Accountability Act   134
5.4   EU Propose Increased Legislative Protection for Gig and Platform Workers   136
5.5   ADCU Fights Against Uber's Use of Racially Discriminatory Facial
      Recognition Systems   137
5.6   Uber Couriers Now Officially Represented by the GMB   142
5.7   A Change in Pay Leads to the UK's Longest Gig-economy Strike   143

6.1   IBM Executives Plan to Eliminate Dinobabies From the Workforce   153
6.2   Workers' Rights Restricted   155
6.3   BrewDog: Toxic Culture Exposed   162
6.4   Better.com: CEO Fires Employees Over Zoom   163
6.5   Sri Lankan Covid-19 Taskforce   164
6.6   Pay Fairness at the Heart of Bus Strike   172

7.1	Thousands of Scottish Workers Subject to Unfair Treatment at Work	188
7.2	Unpaid Work in the United Kingdom	189
7.3	Foreign Office Integrates New HR Model	192
7.4	BrewDog: Increase in HR Resources	195
7.5	Axed for Ambulance Sex	199
7.6	UK Workplaces: Sexual Harassment Duty for Employers	200
8.1	The Loyalty Deficit	228
8.2	Perceptions of Engagement Differ	233
8.3	More Than 10 Million Brits Take Time Off Due to Burnout	236
9.1	Two Thirds of Companies Fail to Capitalise on Direct Employee Involvement	260
9.2	Worker Directors Appointed at JD Wetherspoon	273
9.3	Volkswagen: Further Investments in US Plants Unlikely	276
10.1	'We Don't Want Our Company to Profit Off of Children Being in Concentration Camps'	296
10.2	More Voice for Employees at Wool Mill	299
10.3	'Show Your Face: Raise Your Voice'	300
10.4	Sector Wide Negotiations for London Bus Drivers?	310
10.5	Whistleblowing Costs Include Career Damage and Mental Trauma	314
10.6	Social Media in the Workplace	319
11.1	Homeworking on the Rise	336
11.2	Working Time: Court Imposes Daily Record-keeping Across EU	341
11.3	Hybrid Working Tops-up Flexible Options	344
11.4	Iceland: Four-day Work Week Trial a Success	346
11.5	Zero-hours Contracts	348
12.1	Employees Say Salary Is Their Top Priority	368
12.2	Spain Takes First Step Towards Gender Pay Equality	375
12.3	Ocado Drivers Now Being Paid Way Below the Minimum Wage	377
12.4	Pay: Fairness Creeping up the Agenda Following Black Lives Matter	384
12.5	One in Five Workers Are Banned From Discussing Their Pay	385
13.1	Employees Hiding Reasons for Absence Linked to Mistrust in Employers	406

GUIDED TOUR

By the end of this chapter, you should be able to:

* evaluate the nature of trust at work and analyse its importance for the employment relationship
* provide an overview of the different aspects of organisational justice
* critically analyse the psychological contract
* assess the impact of power realities on the degree of trust and the perceptions of fairness within the employment relationship.

Learning Outcomes Each chapter begins with a handy checklist highlighting the key aims and content covered in the chapter.

British Business Bank

The 100% UK government owned, but independently managed, British Business Bank began operating in 2014. It was specifically designed to help small businesses with a more diverse range of accessible finance options and support the UK's transition to a net zero economy. It neither lends, nor invests, money directly - instead, it works with over a hundred different partner organisations, like banks and leasing companies, to provide finance for enterprises that might otherwise find funding difficult. With

Case Studies Each chapter includes case studies and/or case snippets to help you link theory with practice. Related questions will test your understanding of important topics.

1. Distinguish between each of these terms: employee involvement, employee participation and partnership. To what extent and why might the differences between them be important from the point of view of a) the employer and b) the employee?
2. Which participatory activities do you think managers might need to deploy in order to minimise the incidence of conflict in their organisations? Why did you reach your conclusion?
3. Mellizo et al. (2011) found that individuals who voted to determine their own levels of reward performed better than those who did not vote; evaluate whether you think the findings from this participatory experiment could be applicable to a business organisation.
4. Discuss, with academic justification, whether or not partnership is ever possible in the contested employment relationship.

Review Questions A range of questions provide a starting point for further discussion of important issues.

Teacher Fired for Secret Online Profile

Primary school teacher, Christian Webb, lost his job as soon as it was known that he was the satirical MC Devvo, a foul-mouthed rapper who sang about feeling girls up at the bike sheds, beating up his girlfriend and selling crack. The school governors at King Edward Primary School in Doncaster were outraged to learn that a member of staff had breached their trust by authoring, singing and posting material such as the song 'F**k 'Em Young'. He was summarily dismissed despite the video footage of his 'act' being over a decade old.

Sources: Brown, 2019; Council made, 2019

News Flashes Snappy, thought-provoking extracts from relevant news items contextualise key topics, highlight their relevance in modern working life and encourage you to relate theory to practice.

Revision Exercise 9.2

Critically discuss the following quote in the light of:

* different managerial styles
* employee perceptions of justice.

Involving people varies from informing them of a decision, through to giving citizens full control. The difference between these levels is the relative balance of power and control between the participants and the instigators. (Richards et al., 2004: 3)

Revision Exercises Each chapter contains useful revision exercises designed to check your understanding.

Summary

Whether involvement processes are targeted locally at individual employees or strategically enabling employee representation at higher levels, or whether they comprise single schemes or a mixture of involvement arrangements, both direct and indirect, the degree to which employee involvement contributes to organisational performance will crucially depend on the types of managerial philosophy (and style) in play and on whether the employees want to engage with the involvement processes. A number of factors influence the take-up and operation of EIP schemes, not least whether or not the government encourages or legislates for involvement (e.g., works councils in countries with social democratic traditions), and whether or not intermediary institutions, such as employers' associations, promote involvement activity. The schemes themselves may vary in scope and depth and whether the employer cedes sufficient power to the employees for the

Chapter Summaries Each chapter concludes with a summary of the main issues covered to consolidate what you have learned.

Relevant Articles for Further Reading

Butt, A. N., Rehman, S. and Mushtaq, K. (2019) 'Role of communication and participation in promoting employees' openness to change: Mediating role of trust in supervisor', *Research*, 21(3): 560–75.

Looking at the employee–supervisor relationship in the Pakistan public sector, the authors show how trust in a supervisor, together with enhanced participation, help alleviate resistance to organisational change.

Casey, C. and Delaney, H. (2019) 'The effort of partnership: Capacity development and moral capital in partnership for mutual gains', *Economic and Industrial Democracy*, 43(1): 52–71.

Further Reading At the end of each chapter you will find a suggested list of books and journals to help you explore topics further.

GLOSSARY

Acas Advisory, Conciliation and Arbitration Service. Independent body promoting harmonious employment relationships, providing advice and helping resolve workplace conflict through conciliation, mediation and arbitration.

Acquiescent silence Employees' submissive acceptance of managerial/organisational rules, processes and suggestions.

Affective participation Employee involvement practice that leads to higher levels of personal satisfaction possibly leading to improved productivity.

Glossary Where terms appear in bold within the text this indicates that there is a glossary definition of this term available at the back of the book (pp. 429–442). These easy-to-understand definitions will help you understand any complex terms used.

ONLINE RESOURCES

This second edition of Employment *Relations: Fairness and Trust in the Workplace* is supported by online resources for lecturers to use with students, which are available for lecturers to access at: https://study.sagepub.com/bingham2e.

For Lecturers

Teaching guide outlines the key learning objectives covered in each chapter and provides you with suggested activities and examples to use in class or for assignments.

PowerPoint decks including figures and tables from the book, which can be downloaded and customised for use in your own presentations.

ABOUT THE AUTHOR

Cecilie Bingham is an Emeritus Fellow at Westminster Business School researching, writing and consulting in employment relations. Her main interest is in the field of employment relations and the majority of her current research is on employee relations, trust and diversity. Cecilie encourages the importance of diagnosing the causes of employment problems before ascertaining the most appropriate tools to solve them. Her students in particular have benefitted from classroom discussions around her short news flashes. A fellow of the Higher Education Academy, and an Acas-accredited workplace mediator, her recent research papers have looked at aspects of workplace flexibility and diversity. She is currently researching aspects of bullying in the workplace.

Her experience as chair of the board of trustees for a London-based charity, together with her previous experiences (as the Commissioning Editor for The Work Foundation's bi-monthly journal *Managing Best Practice*, as the principal researcher for the Industrial Society's Best Practice Direct library, together with her work for Incomes Data Services as a journalist and senior researcher) have helped to inform her teaching.

ACKNOWLEDGEMENTS

Thank you to all of the students past and present who have contributed to the knowledge distilled into this book and to my colleagues and family who have borne, with fortitude, my immersion in the writing process. I am indebted, in particular, to Fernando Duran-Palma for his suggestions, ability to turn my sketchy requests for diagrams into reality, and for his 'letter to students' found in Chapter 2. I am also extremely grateful to Remy Ligeika who took time from his busy international work commitments to contribute a case study outlining his experience as an International Employee Relations Director. Thanks too, to the other case study contributors – Kate Boyle, Ronnie Caddow, Ciáran McFadden and Julias Nyiawung – who added to the variety of employment situations depicted in the book. I am, of course, beholden to Ruth Stitt and Jessica Moran, both at Sage, for not only suggesting the second edition and for occasionally tweaking my overlong sentences, but for providing me with an invaluable wealth of advice, support and encouragement.

ABOUT THIS BOOK

> There is something about having a job ... that is good for people ... (although) it's good to have a job, it's better to have a good job. (Mirowsky and Ross, 2003: 275)

This book, like the first edition, is aimed at students of employee relations and is about what goes on in and around work. Employment relations are affected by those who are employed, the people who manage them and the ways in which management skills are deployed; all, of course, influenced by specific contexts, such as legal constraints, historical legacies and prevailing labour markets. This book shows how trust and fairness are crucial, not just for creating good job experiences for employees but for helping organisations to retain staff and create optimum conditions for healthy productive workplaces. It is about power, conflict, gender, diversity and the interrelationship between those who work for money and those who employ them.

Wherever they are based, individuals who are in paid employment, whether temporary or permanent, part-time or full-time, have both subjective and objective perspectives on and about the fairness of their working lives and how they are used and treated by their employing organisation. They have concerns not just about the money they receive (or don't receive) in return for their labour, but also about the conditions in which they work, the ways and means by which they are expected to accomplish their tasks, the tools that they are supplied with, the training they receive and about the future of their employing organisation as it affects their continued employment. Indeed they are likely to compare their own situation with that of others and evaluate it on this basis. How people interact with their employing organisations, and how the organisations treat them, is at the core of this book. It provides the reader with a set of relevant analytical tools, concepts and models to encourage an academic and practical understanding of the employment relationship, with specific regard to the notions of fairness and power.

Throughout this edition a variety of updated and new case studies, case snippets and topical news flashes provide numerous opportunities for students to apply academic theory to practice and critically evaluate and assess a wide variety of employment situations. There are two new chapters: *Employee Relations: The Importance of Context*, which looks at the influences of labour markets, varieties of capitalism, international characteristics, etc. on the employment relationship; while the other, *Employment Relations in Precarious Platform and Gig Work*, explores the ways in which new technologies affect work processes and structures, the worker/workplace interface and management practices. In particular, this chapter looks at algorithmic management and its sometimes discriminatory impact on the employment relationship.

Both practical and academic, each of the 13 chapters is designed to provide the reader with a sound theoretical basis from which to understand the practicalities of managing the employment relationship. Structured to enable the reader to acquire an increasing knowledge about employment relations, it encourages the reader to develop a critical ability to evaluate the causes and outcomes of what is essentially a contested relationship between the employer and employee. Such relationships may be interpreted as harmonious or acrimonious, disputed or consensual, fair or unfair, ethical or unethical, depending upon the perspectives of the parties involved, their culture, the country in which they are operating and on their previous experiences and expectations – and of course these categories are not mutually exclusive. Such critical analysis will, without doubt, depend partly on the readers' own awareness of the perspective from which they are coming and on their own levels of experience.

Features of the Book

Each chapter, written in an accessible and clear way, begins with bulleted learning outcomes and a short indication of what to expect. This is followed by an exploration of the academic research and writings around the topic, explaining current academic thinking and linking this to topical practical examples, thereby encouraging critical analysis and evaluation. All chapters conclude with a summary of what has gone before and a number of revision exercises together with suggestions for further reading and a short explanation of why this reading might be relevant for further study.

Throughout, the book will include a number of case studies (or mini 'case snippets'), designed to illustrate the theoretical explanations in the text. These are often backed by discussion questions designed to encourage critical reflection and analysis, thereby providing a framework for the critical application of knowledge about the subject. Such cases may be used as a basis for seminar questions as well as for personal learning. Numerous thought-provoking News Flashes, providing short extracts of recent news items linked to the text, appear throughout each chapter. Inevitably they will not be completely up to date, but they serve to indicate the 'living' nature of employee relations and provide an immediacy and relevance to the chapters in which they appear. As with the exercises, these thought-provoking short pieces may be used for group discussions. Each chapter ends with revision questions designed to consolidate what the reader has learned and, importantly, to trigger thoughts about the ways in which the employment relationship may be managed in an ethical and fair way, taking account of aspects of diversity, and where relevant, international experiences.

Structure of the Book

The first three chapters provide a strong academic foundation for the rest of the book, introducing crucial theoretical concepts, tools and models that enable the reader to understand (and critically evaluate) aspects of the employment relationship from both academic and practical levels.

Chapter 1 provides an overview of the employment relationship looking at the 'parties' involved together with their interests, both differing and analogous, and the ways in which levels of power – and how it is deployed – can substantially affect what happens at work. Managerial perspectives and styles are explored.

Chapter 2 explains why the contexts in which the employment relationship occurs – international, legal, social and economic – are important. Different varieties of capitalism are explored. The chapter details how context not only shapes what happens at work but how it influences the ways in which workplace activities are viewed by the participants and, indeed, by academic observers.

Chapter 3 critically examines aspects of fairness, trust and organisational justice and the ways in which the perceptions of these affect workplace interactions and behaviours. The ethical behaviour of those within work and the subsequent impact such behaviour has on employee trust and perceptions of organisational justice are considered. Notions of the psychological contract are evaluated in the light of different types of organisational justice.

Chapter 4 concerns contracts of employment, showing how they form the legal basis of an employment relationship, setting out what an employee is expected to do, when and for how much payment. Who is covered by a contract of employment, what happens when the contract needs to be altered, how this is done, the impact on the employment relationship and perceptions of justice related to contracts are all examined alongside the power realities of those involved.

Chapter 5 examines the ways in which precarious work, specifically that linked to electronically enabled work processes, has an impact on employment and the employment relationship. Precarious, insecure work and the reality of working in the gig economy are looked at. In particular, the ways in which such work is regulated (or not) and the power realities behind such forms of employment are explored. The employment relations impact of algorithmic management is discussed as well as some of the ways in which unions are beginning to represent precarious workers.

Chapter 6 elaborates on, and analyses, both the causes behind conflict and expressions of conflict within the employment relationship. The chapter illuminates a number of different academic perspectives about workplace conflict and critically evaluates the ways in which the causes and expressions of individual and collective conflict might materialise. There are, inevitably, links to fairness, trust and the exercise of power. The notion of structured antagonism, introduced in earlier chapters, is elaborated upon and by the end of the chapter readers will have a critical understanding of the causes of workplace conflict. Exercises and case studies enable the reader to develop the skills to evaluate and assess the likelihood of conflict in a given employment relationship.

Chapter 7 explores aspects of conflict resolution and prevention. The different lenses through which both of these aspects might be analysed are examined and both substantive and procedural means of solving conflicts of interest – and conflicts of right – are examined. Readers are helped, by the means of exercises, to develop critical evaluation skills with particular reference to a range of alternative dispute mechanisms designed to resolve workplace conflict.

Chapter 8 takes a critical look at the numerous academic theories defining employee engagement and considers the HR practices that might encourage or discourage employees from engaging. It links engagement with conflict reduction, wellbeing and high-performance workplaces. Claims for and against engagement practices are evaluated.

Chapter 9 extends the theme of engagement by looking at the range of schemes concerned with involving employees in the workplace, from providing information through to participating in decision making. It takes a critical look at the development of employee involvement, participation and partnership (linking these to employers' styles, perspectives and conflict reduction perspectives) as well as exploring employees' reactions to such initiatives and how these might influence their perceptions of justice.

Chapter 10 explores the different forms of voice – direct/individual and indirect/collective, traditional and digital – looking at the ways in which different cultures, laws and organisations ignore or facilitate its operation, together with some of the consequences, intended or otherwise, that arise from its enactment. This chapter also examines collective bargaining and works councils. Importantly, the ways in which employees might choose to remain silent and what this might mean for their organisations is explored. A number of thought-provoking exercises and news flashes help reinforce the learning.

Chapter 11 examines the nature of flexible working. Both employees and employers will have different ideas about the optimum ways of organising their working time (while the law imposes restrictions on how many hours a person can work, or whether or not they are entitled to take maternity or paternity leave); this creates workforces where working patterns are not homogeneous and where, if requests for flexibility are handled inconsistently or in ways that do not conform to statutory requirements, it can cause conflict, low morale and high levels of turnover. Managerial styles, hard and soft approaches, are investigated in the light of their impact on the employment relationship and perceptions of fairness. The impact of technology, for example, as an enabler of remote working is explored. As in other chapters, a range of exercises help the reader to appreciate the difficulties that might arise within the employment relationship when flexibility is requested/required. For intending practitioners a range of different flexible working practices are explored.

Chapter 12 analyses reward practices, payment methods and performance management. The chapter provides readers with the opportunity to critically evaluate the impact of remuneration on the employment relationship. The chapter assesses the impact of different approaches to reward management with reference to notions of distributive and procedural justice. Dysfunctional outcomes of inappropriate payment systems are determined and reviewed, in particular bonus payments, and their impact on working practices and perceptions of justice are explored.

Chapter 13 provides a summary of the salient issues surrounding fairness derived from all of the preceding chapters together with a set of practical exercises linking back to the topics covered previously. This section will be of particular interest to those students undertaking their Chartered Institute of Personnel and Development (CIPD) qualifications because it provides an opportunity to examine some examples of current human resources (HR) practice and looks specifically at redundancy.

The Chartered Institute of Personnel and Development

The book is compatible with the professional standards required by the CIPD Employee Relations modules, both at level 5 (undergraduate) and level 7 (Master's). It also meets many of the requirements for the Employee Experience and Engagement modules. Part of the driving purpose behind the CIPD is to help equip HR practitioners with the knowledge and skills that enable them to provide fair, inclusive, working environments. The fairness emphasis throughout this book meets this purpose.

This book meets many of the requirements outlined in the CIPD Profession Map. Each of the chapters accords with one or more of both the Chartered Associate and Chartered Membership knowledge requirements for Employee Relations (ER), specifically:

- Chapters 1 and 2 cover different types of employee body relationships (e.g., radical, unitarist, pluralist) and how they impact organisations within the UK and internationally.
- Chapter 3 covers aspects of fairness and trust that are applicable for all of the CIPD ER requirements.
- Chapters 4, 7, 11, 12 and 13 cover the different aspects of employment law and how to interpret it into people practices. These chapters respectively cover employment contracts, discipline and grievance, flexible work, pay and redundancy.
- Chapters 7 and 9 look at alternative dispute resolutions and the role that mediation plays within the field of ER.
- Chapters 9 and 10 cover types of employee voice showing the ways organisations can create opportunities for people to have a meaningful voice at work and how this will influence workplace culture. In light of this, different types of working together, from collective bargaining relationships to partnerships, are explored.

In terms of the CIPD requirements for Employee Experience, all the chapters (but particularly Chapter 3) cover the role that trust plays in the employment relationship and Chapter 10 in particular covers the importance of making sure that people are listened to and have a voice about issues that impact them. Chapter 8 looks at employee engagement, focusing on aspects that promote engagement, such as wellbeing, and those that don't, such as situations creating burnout.

Reference

Mirowsky, J. and Ross, C.E. (2003) *Social Causes of Psychological Distress*. Hawthorne, NY: Transaction Publishers/Aldine de Gruyter.

1

EMPLOYEE RELATIONS: SETTING THE SCENE

Learning Outcomes

By the end of this chapter, you should be able to:

- provide an overview of the employment relationship
- be critically analytical about the concepts of unitarism and pluralism
- be aware of changes that have contributed to the rise in individualism and decline in collectivism
- be cognisant of the implications of Human Resource Management (HRM) for the employment relationship
- identify the sources of power and critically assess the impact of power realities in the employment relationship
- evaluate the links between power and differing managerial styles.

What to Expect

This chapter looks at different types of workplace relationships and the ways in which the interactions between the various parties and institutions concerned play a part in that relationship. In particular it explores how the respective, but sometimes diverse, interests of the participants to the relationship might lead to conflict. It highlights the need to be aware of **power**, its sources and its deployment. A number of theoretical perspectives and frames of reference, such as unitarism and pluralism, are considered and the ways in which each affects managerial styles and behaviours is considered.

Employee Relations - What Is It?

The study of employee relations is the study of interactions, behaviours and outcomes based in and around the workplace. It involves those in work, those who employ them, and those who have an impact on their workplace relationships such as legislators and politicians. It is concerned with studying the regulation of the determinants and outcomes of the employment relationship, and sometimes with the breakdown of such regulation. Because workplaces do not exist alone, the economies in which they are based, together with the cultures, philosophies, styles and norms of those working within them, and the desires, wishes and expectations of those reliant on them, all have a bearing on what goes on in the workplace, as indeed does the type of work, the technology used and the levels of competition.

But the relationship between employees (i.e. those who are paid in exchange for work) and employers (i.e. those who pay others in exchange for their labour) is not always straightforward because each has a different set of needs and requirements. Furthermore, not everyone in an organisation is a direct employee as some may be unpaid volunteers or interns, while yet others may be self-employed or working for contractors or sub-contractors. How they work, why they work and their attitudes to one another are crucial. For example, if someone is treated well they are more likely to perform well and stay with an organisation than if they perceive their treatment to be unjust or unfair in some way. As Brewley and Forth say:

> If the balance of power is in favour of the employee, there is a lower likelihood that they will be subject to adverse treatment, since the costs to the employer of treating employees in a way which reduces their productivity or causes them to seek alternative employment is greater. Conversely, where the balance of power favours the employer, there may be less incentive for them to protect their employees against adverse treatment. (2010: ix)

The inherent imbalance of power is such that employees often find it necessary to act collectively, sometimes using external parties to represent their views; such parties may be trade unions, religious groups, pressure groups and so on, and in turn the employers may also use the agency of others, such as Employers' Associations, to represent them.

It is evident from this brief description that the nature of the employment relationship is complex, involving different influences and ideologies. Furthermore, the relationship, which can be both formal and informal, is changeable, often exploitative, and at times contradictory with the potential for cooperation and conflict ever present. In essence then, this is what the study of employment relations encompasses – it seeks to make sense of the formal and informal relationships found at work.

> It concerns the ways in which people interact both with one another and with the jobs they undertake; specifically, it concerns individuals who voluntarily subordinate themselves to the demands of the organisation by exchanging their time, effort and possibly experience and knowledge, for monetary and non-monetary rewards within a regulated environment. (Bingham, 2007: 214)

The Participants

Individuals or groups of individuals who are involved with an organisation, who have an interest in how it operates, performs and interacts with others, are known as **stakeholders**. Employees in particular are often regarded as stakeholders – sometimes for the ways in which they can be used by the organisation and sometimes with regard to the ways in which they are able to behave responsibly for the organisation (Greenwood and Van Buren, 2017; Van Buren and Greenwood, 2011). Low paid individuals without power and whose work is regarded merely as a commodity are known as **dependent stakeholders.** Where stakeholder employees (or groups of employees) have a degree of influence over the organisation it is more likely that they will be treated favourably.

Each employment relationship establishes a set of reciprocal rights and obligations between the **primary parties**, that is, an employee and an employer, within the relationship. This relationship is the main vehicle through which workers gain access to the rights and benefits associated with employment in the areas of labour law and social security. Such rights are underpinned by an informal infrastructure of cultural and ethical values linked to fairness and the subsequent **trust**, or lack of it, between parties (Hyman and Brough, 1975: 229–53; Fox, 1974, 1985). Individual employees have a specific relationship with others in the workplace and with the work itself. This relationship is not static; it has a past and a future both of which affect how the relationship develops – the longer an employee is with an organisation, the more they become socialised to the norms and culture of that organisation, and this affects their perceptions of their treatment and their subsequent workplace behaviours.

The primary parties are not the only participants to have influence on the relationship, others too are involved. These are **secondary parties**, namely union representatives and management. These individuals can be primary parties in their own right but they have an additional role to respectively represent the views of the workforce or of the employers.

A further feature of the employment relationship is the influence of **third parties**. These are often 'agents of the State' and will include the legislature, law enforcers and the courts. Other external third parties that may become involved in the relationship may do so in a lobbying capacity (e.g., Stonewall or the RNIB), while yet others such as **Acas** and the Citizens Advice Bureau may act as advisors, mediators, conciliators or arbiters.

News Flash 1.1

CBI Calls for at Least One BAME Member on Company Boards

Lord Karan Bilimoria, the first BAME president of the Confederation of British Industry (CBI) has declared that, 'The time has come for a concerted campaign on racial and ethnic participation in business leadership. Progress has been painfully slow'. His comments follow the CBI's October 2020 call for UK firms to have at least one BAME (Black, Asian or minority ethnic) member on their board by 2021. The proposal, backed by firms such as Aviva and Microsoft,

(Continued)

asks other UK firms to create, 'clear and stretching targets' in order to diversify their senior management and boards. (In 2020 it was notable that nearly 40% of FTSE 100 companies lacked any ethnic minority board representation.)

The CBI wants companies to make the following commitments:

- Set targets to achieve at least one racially and ethnically diverse board member.
- Increase racial and ethnic diversity in senior leadership by setting targets for black participation at board and senior management levels.
- Publish their progress in the Annual Report or on the company website and disclose ethnicity pay gaps by 2022.
- Create an inclusive culture in which talent from all diversities can thrive.
- Focus on recruitment and talent development to ensure a more diverse pipeline.
- Work with a more diverse set of suppliers/partners and minority owned businesses.

Sources: CBI, 2021; Sharma, 2020

Exercise 1.1

Read the following scenario and then:

- Identify all of the parties and describe each of their respective roles.
- Does your categorisation of the parties show that they are 'mutually exclusive'? Explain how you reached this conclusion.

In 2021 an employment tribunal found against the airline Ryanair following its dispute with 29 pilots following a strike in 2019. In retaliation for the pilots taking union-backed strike action, Ryanair took away some of their workplace benefits. The pilots, members of BALPA - the pilots' trade union - claimed that, by removing the benefits, Ryanair contravened the protective legislation giving workers the right not to be subjected to any detrimental treatment as a direct result of taking part in trade union activities. To strengthen their case the pilots argued that Ryanair contravened the Employment Relations Act 1999 (Blacklists) Regulations 2010 because all 29 were illegally 'blacklisted' by the company when it used a 'prohibited list' to decide which of the BALPA pilots would lose benefits. Following a two-day preliminary hearing, the Employment Tribunal rejected Ryanair's legal submission that the law did not apply in this particular case.

BALPA General Secretary Brian Strutton said,

This is a landmark legal decision, the effects of which go beyond Ryanair and the airline industry to the trade union movement as a whole. ... In particular, by ruling that the claimants were taking part in trade union activities by going on strike, the Tribunal has fired a loud warning shot across the bows of employers who try to punish employees for striking by subjecting them to detrimental treatment. ... The 29 members bringing the claim continue to have the complete and unfaltering support of BALPA and should know that 10,000 BALPA members stand behind them in solidarity.

Sources: BALPA, 2021; Webber, 2021

Trade unions and trade union representatives

One of the ways in which employees have traditionally ensured that their employers have listened and responded to their concerns has been to combine together in groups and to allow representatives to speak for them. As Hyman noted, 'trade unionism has traditionally provided a pooling of resources allowing workers more effectively to defend and advance their personal interests' (1999: 96). The beauty of this system was that it gave individual employees both power and, on occasions, anonymity. The very process of belonging to a group that could speak up for everyone increased the range of influence that individuals could wield over their working conditions and wages, and yet it ensured anonymity if it were desired. This is the philosophy behind trade unions. The member/union relationship is mutually reinforcing: unions help to shape and formulate members' collective interests and identity while the members themselves help shape the focus of union activity. The Webbs (Sidney and Beatrice, who chronicled union activity at the beginning of the twentieth century) described trade unions as 'a continuous association of wage-earners for the purpose of maintaining or improving the conditions of their working lives' (1920: 1). (It is important to note which workers are represented, and how their interests are both articulated and achieved. Union membership is subject to variations within and between sectors and indeed countries.) Trade union membership and organisation began as a way of maintaining and protecting craft standards. During the industrial revolution when Britain moved from an agrarian, rural society to one based on more intensive production in factories, mills and mines, the number of unions grew exponentially. The Union movement is not just a UK phenomenon – it is worldwide, and has a number of different iterations depending upon employer preference, differences in history, culture, legislature, economics and the political climate found in each country. Union membership and subsequent employer and state recognition is not therefore homogeneous. However trade unions do share a number of common aims, namely to:

- act as a countervailing power so members can collectively challenge managerial/political decisions
- improve the pay, conditions and work processes for members
- ensure that members' interests are taken into account by employers when decisions affecting the workforce are made
- act as a lobbying force – voicing members' concerns to government, local councils, etc.
- publicly highlight areas that need addressing, e.g., pension reform
- fight discrimination and promote fair treatment
- educate and inform members about aspects of work such as health and safety.

How such aims are best achieved varies. Some unions cooperate with employers, some are in conflict, some negotiate with state bodies, some, depending on conditions, do all three. For example, in Australia, unions represent their members by promoting better working conditions, lobbying governments for legislative changes and participating in policy formulation – as with the 'Accords' (national agreements between the Australian Labor government and the ACTU, setting goals around wages, industrial relations policy, etc.). Unions operate at national and international levels as well as local ones.

In theory, employee representatives are a means of combating imbalances of power and unfairness at work. Concerns can be raised, wages bargained over, conditions debated and overtime haggled about without, importantly, the process becoming too overtly personal. The act of combining increases the workers' power base and *ipso facto* their voice, influence and impact in the workplace.

From the point of view of the employer, dealing with representatives is often speedier than dealing with strings of individuals. Sometimes obtaining union agreement for changes legitimises those managerial actions required to make the changes, as well as legitimising the changes themselves. The downside is, of course, the ever present and implicit threat of conflict that might escalate into industrial action – such as an overtime ban or a **strike**. (Such action, however, tends to be a last resort – you don't get paid for striking. Sometimes of course the threat of strike action is as important as striking itself and may be used to influence negotiations.)

News Flash 1.2

Strike Threatening Johan Sverdrup

Lundin Energy announced that following a settlement between the Norwegian labour union, Lederne, and the Norwegian Oil and Gas Association (NOROG), the strike which threatened to completely shut down Norway's giant Johan Sverdrup oil field on 14 October 2020, has been called off and operations will now continue as normal. The settlement was timely: had the strike taken place it had the potential to affect a number of other oil fields which in turn may have had to shut down production.

Source: Lundin Energy AB, 2020

Most union behaviour is reactive rather than proactive, responding to the environment in which their members find themselves. Unions simultaneously behave, and are perceived to behave, as if they are in a state of constant opposition and yet, perhaps even because of this, much of their time and energy is actually spent in coming to mutually agreed arrangements with employers. In other words they are involved with making agreements with employers while occupying a position of adversity with them.

The number of people in unions is dependent not just on whether they want a 'voice' within the workplace but upon a range of factors, such as the type of industry they are working in, the political climate of the day, whether or not a union is regularly talked to by their employer, and also the sex, age and education of the employee.

Union membership patterns fluctuate – this can be seen if we look at what has happened in the UK since the Second World War. In the 20 years between 1948 and 1968 the membership of unions grew at a slower rate than the workforce itself. Then in the 10 years between 1969 and 1979 there was a surge in membership, particularly among women, non-manual, service and public sector employees. However, in the years when Mrs Thatcher was Prime Minister the numbers fell as the sectors where unionisation was traditionally high, such as shipbuilding and mining, decreased in size, unemployment was high, legislation was restrictive and, as the unions were perceived to be losing power, fewer people wanted to join their ranks. In 2020, UK union membership rose slightly – as it had for the previous three years – and despite the number of union members in the private sector falling by 110,000 this was off-set by an increase of 228,000 new union members in the public sector (DBEIS, 2021). It will be interesting to see whether the current President Biden's pro-union stance will have an impact on union membership in the US. The fall in the total number of members is known as a fall in **union density** (where density is the ratio of the number of union members to the number of wage and salary earners in the economy). Gross density rates include union members who might be retired or unemployed, whereas net density rates include only those who are in work. Care must be taken when international comparisons are made as the sources of data – and the ways in which figures are compiled – might not be directly comparable. Union membership has fallen across most advanced economies, although, as Crouch says, 'in many cases the membership that remains reflects overall changes in the gender and occupational structure of the economy' (2017: 47). He points out that, despite membership decline, unions remain effective because they are able to act as a political and social voice.

News Flash 1.3

The American Jobs Plan

After 100 days in office President Biden used his first speech to a joint session of Congress to showcase the American Jobs Plan. It is 'a blue-collar blueprint to build America', he said, adding, 'Wall Street did not build this country. The middle class built this country, and unions built the middle class'. The 2021 American Jobs Plan promotes the creation of new 'union jobs', claiming that 'it has never been more important for us to invest in strengthening our infrastructure and competitiveness, and in creating the good-paying, union jobs of the future'.

Sources: Flowers, 2021; Viser and Pager, 2021

Management

Within the context of the employee relationship 'management' refers to the *activities* of managers acting as agents for the employer, but 'management' can also be used as a general term describing the body of people undertaking these activities. Pool (1980) says that management activity is the result of interaction between a number of *constraints* such as economic conditions, government policy and legislation, and of *choices* such as the ways in which activity is undertaken, promoted and communicated. Choices of course may be based on the interests of the organisation, or the interests of individual managers or on ethical/moral values. These three are not mutually exclusive, although in certain circumstances they may be. The role of managers has, over the years, become subject to '**financialisation**' (Knafo and Dutta, 2020; Sisson, 2010). But satisfying shareholders and the market creates managerial pressure to provide short-term results, often with unintended consequences, distorting managerial activities and leading to inconsistent decision making and lack of trust from the workforce. Financialisation is not the only recent influence on managerial choices – increased amounts of legislation affecting employment also constrains, impacts and affects the ways in which managements operate. Not all organisations choose to operate within the law – for example a recent analysis by the TUC shows that on average one in four UK workers are not receiving their legal holiday entitlement (TUC, 2019).

Ethical decision making is complicated, sometimes presenting managers with difficult dilemmas: do they act in the interest of the organisation *or* in the interests of those whom they manage? To a certain extent managers are the squeezed middle and the following extract from Deny illustrates the point very clearly:

> There are a number of times when you know as manager that a particular individual has been identified to be laid off ... and every day, and it may go on for several weeks, you have to come to work and acknowledge the person, deal with them, work with them, knowing that at a given point in time they are going to be out of a job literally. And yet, you can't prepare them, because your job as a manager is to try to get the pieces done, work with the company, and maintain the morale. It's a moral difficulty because I always feel that if I know that a particular individual is going to have something like that happen, that I should tell him ... however I also understand ... that in the business we do need his services for three more months. (1989: 858)

McConville too highlights this dilemma for middle managers, explaining how, particularly now that many personnel functions are undertaken by line managers and not HR/ER specialists, this group find themselves acting like shock absorbers in the buffer zone between organisational demands and employee performance. The added burden of devolved HRM functions both highlight and exaggerate a problem that was previously dissipated by the presence of specialist practitioners (McConville, 2006: 651). Different levels of management have different levels of influence in the workplace. Line managers play a crucial part within the employment relationship; it is they who organise work flows, allocation of tasks, composition of teams, and who are required to control, encourage, facilitate 'voice' and organise the workforce (Townsend and Hutchinson, 2017). It could be said that they are at the cutting edge of the employment relationship – how they interact with their subordinates sets the tone for the way in which the relationship is perceived and develops over time.

Employer associations

The main function of an **employer association** is to support and represent its members. It does this in a number of ways: first, it offers advice on trade, professional and employment matters; second, it acts as a pressure group, lobbying governments and making representation on behalf of its members; third, it takes part in national negotiations setting terms and conditions; and fourth, it may advise about (and possibly become involved in) industrial disputes. In terms of employee relations, those associations concerned purely with trade matters are not relevant here (see Martins, 2020 for a fuller analysis of their functions). Employer associations may be based internationally, nationally or tied to a local region, and membership composition and participation will, in part, be dictated by the culture and size of company concerned. In the USA, for example, the culture is such that companies prefer to operate alone without the benefit of an association. In Europe, with its history of **social partnership**, employer associations are more prevalent (Behrens and Traxler,

2004). The Federation of International Employers (FedEE Global), as its name suggests, operates globally with offices in Asia and Europe. Developing from the Federation of European Employers (which was set up with a grant from the EU), it claims to be the world's leading employers' organisation for multinational employers, offering legal and general HR advice as well as acting as a lobbying body. Sometimes associations come together under an umbrella body – the European Association of Craft, Small and Medium-sized Enterprises (UEAPME), for example, incorporates around 80 member organisations from 34 countries, consisting of national cross-sectorial small and medium-sized enterprise (SME) federations, and is the employers' organisation representing the interests of European crafts, trades and SMEs at EU level. Nationally there are a number of associations that operate both on domestic *and* international fronts – in the UK, for example, the Chemical Industries Association (CIA) provides legal advice to members, participates in national negotiations, represents the views of the industry at national and international levels and, when required, lobbies the government. Sometimes of course there are employers' organisations created specifically to cater for the interests of those in a particular location – for example, the Lancashire Textile Manufacturers' Association concentrates on regional matters but is a member of the UK Fashion and Textiles Association which represents their interests at national level. Within the UK, the number of Employer Associations has, like unions, been declining (Gooberman et al., 2019).

Institutions

Different ways of organising economic activity are likely to be the result of interactions between particular institutional environments (Brewster and Mayrhofer, 2018). The study of employee relations therefore involves the study of institutions, although care needs to be taken as to what exactly the institutional reference means in context. Indeed sometimes the relationship itself is known as an institution (Fudge, 2017). There are three main ways in which the term is used. Firstly it can be as an explicit/implicit reference to an actual organisation such as The Institute of Employment Studies, or, for example, when organisations like the Health and Safety Executive or Acas are regarded as institutions. Secondly, the word may apply to something that is common practice or a recognised process such as the institution of **collective bargaining**. Thirdly, it can refer to a system of control, proscribing the correct ways of behaving, such as rules or directives. In order for organisations to operate effectively they need to interact successfully with a range of institutions, such as trade unions, government bodies and shareholders and in order to do so they must be perceived as operating legally and in good faith – in other words they must be regarded as legitimate (Greenwood et al., 2008).

Exercise 1.2

Keith Sisson, in his paper *Weathering the Storm: The Maturing of British Industrial Relations*, makes the point that 'the employment relationship is a multi-level phenomenon' (2007: 23).

- Explain what you think he means by this.

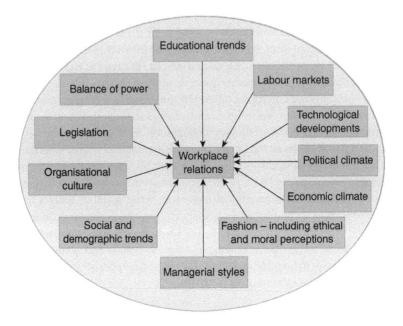

Figure 1.1   Influences on the nature of workplace relations

Changes in the UK Employment Market

Since 1979 there have been a number of changes within the UK employment market. There has been a sharp decline in those sectors such as coalmining and shipbuilding where unionisation was high. Manufacturing has decreased, and the service sector grown. Large nationalised industries have disappeared and there has been a growth in SMEs and multinational enterprises. Within the workplace, job demarcation has diminished and teamwork and matrix working increased. The rise of technology has changed the ways in which many organisations operate. Globalisation has widened markets, created opportunities for labour mobility and facilitated the movement of capital and labour. Digitally enabled remote working, utilising software such as Zoom and Microsoft Teams, alongside algorithmic technology that is able to shape work patterns and processes, has led, in many cases, to increased electronic surveillance and monitoring. Technology has aided the 24/7 economy, hastening the changes to working patterns, some organisations moving to longer operating hours, often with an associated increase in demand for worker flexibility, with employees required to frequently update and utilise new skills and working habits. Such changes in the nature of work have led to decreases in job security and increases in **precarious work, insecurity/redundancy**. More people are working part-time than previously. These changes have had an impact on both employers and employees, in particular on their expectations and needs within the workplace. The impact of these changes has resulted in a drop in the number of people working in organisations that apply terms and conditions negotiated with trade unions. In 1973 there were around 13 million trade union members in the UK but this figure has halved.

During this period there was a corresponding rise in **individualism**. This is a style of management that deploys policies based around the belief in the value of the individual and his or her right to fulfilment, development and advancement at work (Purcell and Gray, 1986: 213; Purcell, 1987). Here there is an emphasis on enabling and managing performance whereby the employer communicates directly with the employee, designs individual contracts and offers financial incentives based on levels of performance and regular training in order to gain an acceptance of personalised performance targets and individual flexibility; such individuality, it is claimed, encourages high levels of commitment to the organisation and sustained productivity.

Individuals are assumed to have interests that are in line with those of the organisation, hence there is no need for them to combine and act together and no requirement for union representation. This has an obvious appeal to managers (Kessler and Purcell, 1995: 31) and is a move away from the more adversarial system of **collectivism**, in which managers communicate with the workforce via union representatives, where pay is set in terms of the job to be done rather than in terms of the individual actually doing it, and where committees and groups negotiate and consult on the terms and conditions for the employees. This approach, defined as 'the recognition by management of the collective interests of groups of employees in the decision making process' (Purcell and Gray, 1986: 213), is useful for employees who find that joining with others increases their levels of power vis-à-vis the employer. The interests of the group are protected and terms and conditions improved in ways that might not have been possible without collective representation. The German system of **works councils** falls into this category.

The two systems, collectivism and individualism, are not, however, mutually exclusive – management often categorise certain employees as members of a specific group and treat them collectively but with individual differences; for example all sales assistants may receive the same basic rates of pay within a retail organisation yet there may be individual bonus payments, commission and targets for individuals within that group. Similarly sometimes where employees are subject to individual levels of pay linked to performance targets, the boundaries for their terms and conditions may have been proscribed following negotiation with representatives. In some organisations, for example those in the banking sector, unions are recognised for bargaining purposes for those employees placed at the lower ends of the salary scales but not for those at the higher ends.

Human Resource Management (HRM)

Alongside the rise in individualism there has been an increase in **Human Resource Management** (HRM). HRM is not just a substitute name for personnel management but refers to an approach to managing an organisation (not just the personnel function) that aligns the resources – human and otherwise – with the business strategy. It is seen as an holistic way of using an organisation's resources to cost-effectively respond to changes in the economic and technical environments. The doctrines of quality management and flexibility are key to the operational effectiveness deployed by HRM strategists. Because everything is geared towards effective use of resources, one of the managerial aims is to ensure that the workforce is not just compliant with organisational demands but also committed to achieving them. This entails using performance management techniques to align employee performance with organisational goals. It is coupled with a management strategy utilising psychological rewards – such as participating in decision making – to encourage employee motivation, engagement, commitment and loyalty. In terms of its relationship with employee relations, HRM is often used as an umbrella term for a set of management practices within the employment relationship, including an increased emphasis on high commitment and greater employee task discretion. Its emphasis on deploying the skills of each employee in the most effective way is individual rather than collective, and unitary rather than pluralist (see below), although in circumstances where the pervading culture is pluralist, such as in Germany, HRM techniques are still deployed.

One of the consequences of the adoption of HRM policies is that many traditional personnel functions have been devolved to line managers, allowing HR managers to concentrate on the strategic aspects of the business. John Storey (1992) defined two different forms of HRM: **hard,** driven by strategic objectives where labour is perceived as just another resource to be treated in a depersonalised way; and **soft,** where labour is regarded as a valued asset and a source of innovation and competitive advantage, and individuals within the organisation are nurtured, well looked after and developed.

Whether the organisation delivers hard or soft HRM, whether or not the line managers are trained in people management and whether the intended delivery of the strategy is the actual strategy that is implemented, all impact on the parties to the employment relationship.

There are problems in analysis if the workforce is regarded as if it is an homogenous group as employees within an organisation have different interests, requirements and perceptions and therefore respond differently to the HRM practices they experience (Kinnie et al., 2005). Therefore a workplace strategy that assumes that one set of policies will be consistently delivered and received in identical ways that suit everyone is unrealistic. Nishii and Paluch (2018) and Wright and Nishii (2004) show that intended policies are not always congruent with actual practices and that such practices may be experienced and acted on differently by employees in the same organisation. **Employee commitment** – a key pillar of the HRM way of managing – may not actually be as high as intended if employees do not perceive their interests to be the same as those put forward by the organisation that they work for; furthermore there may be inconsistencies within an organisation if individualistic targets are advocated simultaneously with those associated with teamwork.

Power Imbalances

To achieve goals within the workplace, the work itself and the processes for achieving and coordinating output must be organised; this, of course, results in divisions of accountability, responsibility and of labour. Such arrangements, of necessity, affect and impact upon the employment relationship. In order to achieve results an employer will direct the workforce who, in return for wages, consents to obey direction, thus entering into a relationship of subordination (Kahn-Freund, 1972).

This inequality is exacerbated by unequal access to resources. The splitting-up of tasks and responsibility means that some individuals will have more control – and others less – either formally or informally, over others: 'The primary purpose of control is to coordinate different organisations' activities in order to achieve the goals for the whole organisation' (Dundon and Rollinson, 2011: 29). The exercise of control affects not just the economic relationship but also social and ethical aspects of the employment relationship; this means that 'the right to manage' must be exercised in a *reasonable* manner (Edwards, 1986: 31–2).

Control over others may be seen in terms of power. Dunlop (1958: 28) thought that power in the workplace was a reflection of power in the wider society, but this does not account for differences in individual workplaces within the same societies; indeed different types of power may be simultaneously wielded in different parts of the same organisation. For example, in Unilever there are different approaches to managing the workforce depending on the country and subsidiary in which it is operating.

Power enables a *few* individuals to minimise the discretion of *many* of the workers by making decisions *deemed by the few to be important* for their purposes and the benefit of the organisation. As Fox so memorably put it:

> It enables the few, in other words, to manifest distrust of the many by imposing upon them work roles and work rules which leave little scope for the important choices – including those determining the whole pattern of rewards, status and privilege. (1974: 14)

The related concepts of 'power' and 'control' are central to the understanding of how the labour process is 'managed'. Yet although the employer has a degree of power, which he or she may or may not choose to exert, employees are not necessarily powerless because the workplace relationship dictates that the employer is dependent upon the services of the employee (Hyman, 1975: 25). The relationship is therefore symbiotic and interdependent, despite the fact that, in the main, the employer has more power than the employee. The power of labour (the employees) is dependent on how much capital (the employer) needs its effort. Such labour power is unlike any other commodity because it is part of a *continuous relationship* that is, in itself, affected by external forces not within its control. As Hyman and Brough (1975: 23) point out, a tight labour market or the possession of scarce skills may militate against the power of the employer; the converse, of course, also holds true. The consequences of the imbalances of power have resulted in the formation of groups, such as trade unions, which act as countervailing forces; governments too have often intervened, in the form of implementing new legislation, to redress real or perceived power imbalances in the workplace. Although inequalities of power do result in conflict, compromise is more often the outcome because it is not simply a matter of (management) control versus (worker) resistance, but more a mixture of dissent and accommodation, conflict and cooperation (Rose, 2008). Indeed Flanders (1970: 172) pointed out that managements often maintain control by sharing it, and Oxenbridge and Brown (2004) and later Bray et al. (2020) showed that within the UK, union influence is no longer as reliant on negotiation, with its concomitant and explicit exercise of power and instead both consultation, and a reliance on procedures, are used to influence the operation of the employment relationship.

Power can be regarded in terms of either the power *to do* something, or in terms of the power *over* someone/something. Both are important within the employment relationship. The power 'to do' may be the result of technical **competence**/skill, or may involve the power to facilitate and enable; used appropriately it can engender respect, loyalty and commitment. The power 'over' refers to the ability of a person or group to dictate what others should or should not be doing and how and when they should be doing it. It relates to the ability to get someone to do something that they would not otherwise do, perhaps including doing so against their will (Lukes, 2005). Lukes divides this category into three:

- *Power in terms of dominance*, for example where an HR manager explicitly tells a line manager he can or cannot do something, or where a trade union calls a strike in opposition to management activity.
- *The concept of power in terms of decision making*, for example setting the parameters for discussion/negotiation.
- *The concept of a more manipulative power*, one which controls the ideology or culture of an organisation, for example at induction, employee expectations are managed and this is reinforced by regular communications from management, perhaps using the intranet, newsletters and so on.

News Flash 1.4

The Shrewsbury Pickets' Struggle for Justice [1972-2021]

It took nearly half a century to get justice but the 24 pickets from Shrewsbury have finally had their criminal convictions overturned.

On Tuesday 23 March 2021, the Court of Appeal overturned the criminal convictions of 24 trade unionists who had been working in the building industry. The men were arrested months after their **picketing** activity during the 1972 national building workers strike against low pay and poor working conditions, They were convicted and - in some cases - imprisoned on charges of unlawful assembly, conspiracy to intimidate, and affray.

Sources: BBC, 2021a; Syal and Evans, 2021

The very actions that management take form part of a pervasive ideology, so for example, if certain behaviours are rewarded, this provides powerful messages about what is, and is not, acceptable behaviour.

French and Raven (1962), in their classic study, delineated five distinct sources of power. Two of these sources, expert and referent power, derive from the holder's individual characteristics. The other three sources – legitimate, reward and coercive power – derive from the holder's position within their organisation.

An individual has **expert power** when they have specific knowledge and expertise that others rely upon – where the sharing or withholding of this specialist knowledge has a direct impact on the organisation. **Referent power** comes not from expertise but from the (sometimes inspirational) personality of the holder. Such people are respected and others want to do their bidding because they want to please them. In terms of the employment relationship, such people are often able to motivate and persuade their colleagues to undertake difficult tasks, stay late at work and perform duties outside their contract merely because they engender loyalty and people don't want to let them down. **Coercive power** is in evidence where threats, explicit or implicit, are used to effect obedience: in employee relations terms this could be displayed by a manager deciding to withhold resources, or perhaps bully colleagues, in order to ensure compliance. The atmosphere created is not one of trust, with people often performing to the minimum rather than the maximum standard required. Sexual harassment and bullying can be regarded as forms of coercive power. The trade union UNISON says that bullying behaviour in the workplace is an abuse of power that is 'persistent offensive, intimidating, humiliating behaviour, which attempts to undermine an individual or group of employees' (2013: 4).

News Flash 1.5

Abuse of Power Not Uncommon

A January 2020 CIPD report on conflict highlights the critical importance of line management in causing and preventing bullying and harassment at work. Four in ten (40%) of *employees* surveyed said their manager was responsible for bullying or harassing them, while 34% of *employers* surveyed said one of the top barriers to effective conflict management was managerial lack of confidence. The findings reveal that bullying and harassing behaviours range across the spectrum from extreme forms of intimidation, like physical violence, to inappropriate joking or ignoring someone. More than half (53%) of the people who said they had been bullied or harassed in the last three years did not report it.

Source: CIPD, 2020

Reward power is where individuals persuade others to do their bidding in exchange for something that they want. In employment terms this is epitomised by the pay–work–bargain (Farnham, 1997: 3), an arrangement whereby employees exchange their labour for monetary reward. The reward, however, may not be monetary – it could be promotion, or the opportunity to work on a prestigious project. The strength of the power that a person holds depends on the perception by others that the 'powerful' can actually deliver (Farmer and Aguinis, 2005). Sometimes, of course, rewards do not match the expectations of the rewarded and conflict may result.

Legitimate power is where someone's position within the organisation gives them the authority to make decisions and control the activities of others. Line managers therefore have the authority to control the work processes of their subordinates merely because of their position in the organisation. Perceptions, too, are important here. If someone is not perceived as being worthy of the position they hold, their power may be diminished. So, for example, if someone with little experience is brought in to manage an existing sales team, the perception of the team may be that the person's inexperience renders them unfit for the job – non-cooperation, conflict and a breakdown in the employment relationship can be the result.

Dawson (2010) extends these sources of power, explaining that *economic position*, in the form of wealth, ownership of resources, and indeed relative pay along with **collective power** (i.e., the ability to combine forces), **personal power** (i.e., an understanding of how the organisation works) and **legal power** all play an important part in the extent to which influence may be deployed. Like Lukes, Dawson refers to **symbolic power** whereby the pervasive ideology is controlled, and like French and Raven she acknowledges *technical power* (expert), *positional power* (legitimate) and *physical* power (similar to coercive power).

Exercise 1.3

In 1920, Carter Goodrich wrote a book entitled *The Frontier of Control: A Study of British Workshop Politics.*

- What do you think is meant by the 'frontier of control'?
- How do you think this relates to the distribution and use of power within an employment relationship?

Eighty years later, Reed wrote that control within the employment relationship refers to:

> a co-ordinating mechanism based on asymmetric relations of power and domination in which conflicting instrumental interests and demands are the overriding contextual considerations. (2001: 201)

- What do you think are the conflicting interests and demands that are found in the employment relationship? Give examples of this.
- What do you think Reed means by the 'asymmetric relations of power'?
- How does Reed's statement relate to the title of the Goodrich book?

In Japan there is a term '*oni joshi*' meaning 'devil boss' and working under such a person can lead to '*Karoshi*', i.e., 'death by overwork' or '*Karojisatsu*', i.e., suicide as a result of workplace pressure. Describe how these three terms relate to the deployment of power.

Interests

The interests of a government or its agents, of the employers and of the employees, do not always coincide. It is, of course, normal for a government to want organisations within its borders to perform effectively, similarly for both employees and employers to want their organisation to succeed; job security is, after all, associated with the success of an organisation and employees are aware that a failing organisation often leads to unwelcome measures, such as pay freezes and/or redundancies. The relationship between employers and employees is symbiotic, that is, each needs the other in order to function. However, the interests of these parties *do differ*. Employees do not just want security of employment, they want the best available in terms of pay, benefits and adequate holidays as well as safe and reasonable working conditions. Many employees also want good promotion prospects and adequate training and development, as well as a say in what they are doing and how they are to do it. Employers, of course, might not want to match these demands (Buzza, 2017; Ciulla, 2000; Cullinane and Dundon, 2014; Kelly, 1998). Individuals in the workplace want to be treated fairly and equitably yet the perceptions of what employees regard as fair and equitable may not match the employers' perceptions of fairness.

Budd (2004; Budd et al., 2010) says that the key employee interests at work are **equity** and **voice.** Equity here refers to fair employment practices in terms not only of *how* employees are treated but also in terms of *what* employees are expected to do, how much reward they receive and the conditions under which employees are expected to work. Voice is the capacity to have *meaningful* input into decisions. Employers, on the other hand, have an interest in efficiency often to the detriment of equity and voice.

Linked to employee interests is the extent to which employees have a degree of autonomy in the way in which they work. Employees like the sense of being trusted to work without supervision, although at the same time they do not want to feel abandoned. This is especially so when they are sufficiently qualified and competent to make decisions about how they undertake their work. Such empowerment does not mean that employees are abandoned to work alone, but instead are offered an environment in which to work where they can be trusted because they are competent to undertake tasks without constant supervision and direction (Greasley et al., 2005). Wilkinson (1998) identified five different types of empowerment – information sharing, upward problem solving, task autonomy, attitudinal shaping and self-management – that are all relevant here.

Employers have different interests as, unlike employees, they would prefer not to pay their workforce more than is necessary to achieve and maintain consistent and sustained productivity. They want the organisation and those in it to perform efficiently and effectively and they would like the freedom to take and implement organisational decisions. Furthermore they would like compliance from employees and commitment to workplace rules and management decisions.

Governments do not just act as employers in their own rights – they have a wider remit and range of interests. Obviously they want to ensure that organisations are contributing to the economy, providing employment, and operating with the minimum amount of conflict. The very nature of employment means that it is incumbent upon the State to oversee and regulate the employment relationship, balancing the rights between shareholders and employees. In most countries laws (and sometimes codes of conduct) define how the relationship should be conducted by setting out the minimum components of the employment contract between an employer and an employee as well as providing an infrastructure for the settling of disputes, the laying down of standards for health and safety, providing standards for the minimum levels of remuneration, and so on. Crucially the State lays down the corporate governance framework, either by legislation or procedure, within which an employment relationship is conducted. In this way, businesses, charities and institutions are regulated so that employees are treated fairly and employers retain a degree of flexibility. Such laws and policies will also impact on workplace representation, encouraging *or* discouraging trade union involvement and, for example, promoting works councils or aspects of codetermination.

─Exercise 1.4─

Unions Oppose Breaking Up Electricity Company EDF

Energy unions in France are fighting against the Government's 'Hercules' plan to split the energy company Electricité de France (EDF) into three separate divisions resulting in its break up and/or part privatisation. Attempting to influence the government the unions have held a number of protests culminating in a day of action in January 2021. The French government wants to separate EDF's capital-intensive nuclear power arm from other parts of the business; however it needs EU clearance to make sure that any new structure does not breach unfair competition rules. The EU has proposed a break-up rather than restructure, splitting EDF into several competing companies.

The four unions – FNME-CGT, CFE-CGC Énergies, FCE-CFDT and FO Énergies et Mines – argue that EDF is a vital national asset, and that its privatisation will remove democratic accountability. In a joint statement, the unions said, 'The dismantling of EDF... would be an economic, industrial and social disaster, [...ending] EDF's very purpose in serving the general interest'. Other European and UK unions have voiced their support for the action.

Sources: IndustriALL, 2021; Mallet and Pineau, 2021

- Who were the primary parties involved – what were their interests?
- Who were the secondary parties involved – what were their interests?
- Who were the third parties involved – what were their interests?

Frames of Reference

A '**frame of reference**' is how one sees the world. The idea of a frame of reference, in terms of the employment relationship, was first mooted by Fox in 1966. He argued that attitudes and subsequent behaviours within workplace relationships can be divided into two mutually exclusive categories: either it is a **unitarist** relationship, that is, one that exists to solely satisfy common interests, or it is a **pluralist** one that exists to satisfy the different interests of separate but interdependent groups. The frame of reference with which an individual views the workplace will affect the ways in which they make assumptions and reach conclusions about events, and this will affect their subsequent behaviour. Fox's frames have been developed a number of times. In his book *Beyond Contract*, Fox (1974) enlarged his theory to incorporate a third frame of reference, **radicalist,** where the employment relationship is perceived as one merely there to satisfy the interests of the dominant party (class). Cradden (2011) has suggested that Fox's categories are rather restrictive and need to be made broader. Indeed Budd and Bhave (2008) did exactly this by adding the **egoist** frame to explain the increasing marketisation and self-interest of employment. While unitarism assumes everyone is on 'the same team', under the egoist frame employers and employees each separately put themselves first. More recently Kaufman et al. (2021) looked for empirical evidence for Fox's theory by mapping his theoretical triage into data from 7,000 non-supervisory employees from Australia, Canada, the US and the UK. They created a 'Relational Quality Index' where high scores indicated common interests and unitary approaches, and low scores indicated a radical approach with pluralism falling between the two. Data for all four countries were similar – the largest group or workplaces fell in the plural-ist camp. It would be interesting to see the investigation conducted in non-western countries to see if similar results occur. Frames of reference are useful analytical devices for divining and categorising the attitudes, perceptions and values behind the management of organisations. Of course within a workplace it is possible to have different groups/individuals with different frames of reference, so, for example, it is possible for a unitarist management to be working alongside employees who hold pluralist perspectives, and vice versa.

Unitarism

A unitarist frame of reference is one where the employer views the workplace from a perspective that assumes *everyone* within the organisation agrees with its common purpose – the success of the organisation – and, importantly, *everyone* agrees with the ways in which management sets about achieving this success. Management, under the direction of the employer, is the only source of authority and has the right to manage; as such this management prerogative is not questioned because *everyone* is part of a team, all pulling in the same direction, all with the same aspirations. This congruence, according to the unitarist perspective, means that there will be no conflicts of interests and therefore no need to have any mechanisms for dealing with conflict. Conflict is regarded as irrational, and even pathological. Certainly, so the view goes, because the workforce is harmonious, unified and behaves as a whole, there is no need for any outside interference. Trade unions are therefore regarded as unnecessary intrusions into a 'happy family'. Where conflict does occur it is rationalised in one of two ways: either it happened because com-munication failed in some way (had everyone understood properly then there would be no disagreement, no misunderstanding of management's intentions) or because the dissenter was some sort of non-conformist, perhaps a rebellious, maverick employee who is best dealt with by dismissal. Such a philosophy has an obvious appeal to managers. It legitimises their decision making and implies that any dissent is not their fault. Here then the employment relationship is perceived as consensual and cooperation is regarded as the norm.

Exercise 1.5

* What are, do you think, the key assumptions behind the unitarist perspective?
* Do you think these assumptions are valid?
* Why did you come to your conclusion?

There are a number of criticisms that can be made about the unitarist perspective, not least the fact that it does not take into account the actual interests of the employees, merely presuming that these coincide with those of management, while the assumption that management decision making is always rational, and in the best interests of everyone, is questionable. By discounting alternative viewpoints as pathological, and not seeing the need for an infrastructure containing mechanisms to deal with conflict, the unitary philosophy may actually engender discontent.

Pluralism

The pluralist perspective, on the other hand, is a framework that assumes workplaces consist of a number of individuals and groups, each with different sets of values, needs, beliefs and loyalties. Such a mixture is unlikely to be homogenous and, as a result, there will be differing expectations and allegiances. Consequently conflict is to be expected, and an organisation will need to find ways of accommodating different viewpoints and managing any potential disagreements by consultation, negotiation or shared decision making. Management's function is therefore to manage by resolving differences and emphasising consensus and consent. Part of this is to take account of alternative viewpoints and have systems in place to listen to representations from the various interested parties. The result is a joint approach to problem solving where trade union representation is not anathema. Indeed to have a system where employee interests are formally represented is a rational response to an awareness of the imbalance of power where employees could, without a voice, be exploited. As Barry and Wilkinson (2021: 115) point out, 'the pluralist frame sees a shared interest in the employer's ability to profitably provide long-term employment, and that this is the basis to bring parties together to negotiate inevitable conflicts that arise from fundamentally differing interests'. There is a recognition that, paradoxically, management maintains control by sharing decision making – as Flanders says, 'The paradox whose truth managements have found it difficult to accept, is that they can only regain control by sharing it' (1970: 172).

Exercise 1.6

- What are, do you think, the key assumptions behind the pluralist perspective?
- Do you think these assumptions are valid?
- Why did you come to your conclusion?

Van Buren et al. (2021: 179) argue, 'that the manner in which the employment relationship is conceptualised and analysed not only reflects an external reality but also has a part in constituting that reality'.

- Explain what this means, giving examples to illustrate your answer.

There are a number of criticisms that can be made about the pluralist perspective, partly because it is a frame of reference that is not relevant for every managerial decision. Managers may seek consensus on a number of fronts, but they do not cede authority for everything; for example, strategic financial or marketing decisions that may have an impact on future employment levels (and hence on the employment relationship) are rarely shared. Furthermore the interaction between those groups of differing interests is not equal: management controls the agendas for discussion and, more often than not, the other interest groups react to management activity and ideas. Crucially there is an assumption that for pluralism to work the groups must actually share a set of social norms – if they were wildly different, the pluralist frame of reference would be untenable.

Bray et al. (2020) argue that the concepts of both pluralism and unitarism need to be elaborated in order to account for, what they term, *collaborative* versus *adversarial pluralism* and *consultative* versus *autocratic unitarism*.

In 2002 Ackers developed the notion of **neo pluralism.** This emphasises the importance of cooperation and of **partnership** between employers and workers, but he combined it with the duty to promote such cooperation for the good of society as a whole. This is interesting because it introduces an ethical dimension (i.e., the morality of social cohesion). Yet it is theoretically lacking because it does not really address elements of power and the interests of different groups. More recently Van Buren et al. (2021) have refined the notion of pluralism by offering two additional core concepts. Firstly **agonism**, as a principle suggesting that the contested nature of the employment relationship is one in which each side has a moral duty to recognise the legitimacy of the other, refuting its ideas *without* wanting to destroy it. Agonism is evidenced by their second core concept **dissensus** (as opposed to consensus) where recognition of the differences between parties is crucial and helps avoid/prevent exploitation.

Radicalism

The **radical perspective** is a frame of reference that accepts that economic inequalities are expressed in social conflict – and at work this is manifest by unrest and conflict within the employment relationship. Under a radicalist perspective such conflict is inescapable; it is class-based and the result of an unequal distribution of power between those who buy labour and those who sell it. This Marxist way of understanding the employment relationship regards conflict as inevitable under capitalist economies.

Paul Edwards offers an alternative, non-Marxist yet radical perspective. He says that employers need to give *discretion* to employees in order to make best use of their skills and talents. Simultaneously, however, they have to *control* the same employees in order to ensure that their work output is maximised. Implicit in the job of managing people is the requirement to instruct subordinates about how to achieve tasks while at the same time allowing them sufficient freedom to choose how they undertake such tasks. The contradiction between these two methods of operation, *discretion* and *control*, creates a tension that he called **structural antagonism**. Unlike unitarism, it recognises that employees have different interests to those of the employer, and unlike pluralism this perspective on the employment relationship permits concurrent conflict and consensus. Edwards states that:

> the key point about the indeterminacy of the labour contract and strategies of labour
> control is that managers and workers are locked into a relationship that is contradictory
> and antagonistic. It is contradictory, not in the sense of logical incompatibility, but

because managements have to pursue the objectives of control and releasing creativity, both of which are inherent in the relationship with workers, and which call for different approaches. The relationship is antagonistic because managerial strategies are about the deployment of workers' labour power in ways which permit the generation of a surplus. Workers are the only people who produce a surplus in the production process but ... they do not determine how their labour power is deployed to meet the objective. (2005: 16–17)

Exercise 1.7

Design a presentation explaining the three different frames of reference: unitarism, pluralism and radicalism.

- Make clear any similarities and differences.
- Include additional information explaining structural antagonism.
- Include the ways in which different frames of reference impact on the balance of power.

In your presentation give examples of separate organisations that fit the categories, and explain why you have classified them in this way.

Exercise 1.8

Below are extracts from two separate job advertisements.

- What does each tell you about the frames of reference for the respective organisations?
- Why did you come to these conclusions?

Advertisement 1

Role: Employee Relations Advisor

Salary: £35,000 to £37,000 pa

Location: Doncaster

Hours: 37 hours per week

The role

The Fxxx Group is a market leading company which is looking for an enthusiastic ER advisor to work in partnership with our fantastic management teams. As the Advisor your ability to influence stakeholders and communicate across all levels of the business will be key to your, and our, success. You will need to manage and prioritise multiple time-sensitive deadlines effectively and to build strong working relationships. You will need excellent written and oral communication skills, and be able to effectively influence at all different levels. Strong coaching and a passion for supporting the Fxxx Group to deliver success through our people is essential. You will be expected to:

- Undertake the full range of generalist HR activities working together with line management.
- Provide advice and guidance on, and manage employee relations issues such as absence, performance management and other key HR areas including restructuring, redundancy, redeployment, disciplinary and grievance matters.
- Promote the wider use and value of Performance Matters and personal development plans, and general learning and development activities. We are looking for a fast paced self-starter who can lead and establish business relationships naturally. The ideal candidate will have integrity and the ability to work autonomously *and* as part of a team.

Advertisement 2

Role: Interim Employee Relations Advisor - 6 month post

Salary: £22.50 - £23.50 per hour

Location: The North East

Hours: 37 hours per week

The role

Immediately available HR Advisor required for a period of initially six months to join this busy generalist HR Team at Sxxx Co. UK. You will be required to hit the ground running, advising all levels of managers on a challenging range of HR issues. This is a heavily unionised environment facing a period of change, so you will have faced similar challenges previously and be confident advising on redundancy, restructure and redeployment. You will be a proactive and can-do person, with strong customer focus and ideally fully CIPD qualified (or equivalent). Good interpersonal and communication skills are essential. This is a great role for someone looking to progress their HR career as you will gain some fantastic exposure to ER and change within a well-known employer.

Managerial Styles

The employment relationship occurs within the employers'/managers' chosen frame of reference, yet within these frames different managerial approaches are deployed. Such alternative ways of doing something (Legge, 1995: 31) are known as '**managerial styles**'. Fox (1974) described six different styles, which were later refined by Purcell and Sisson (1983) into five: **traditionalists**, **sophisticated paternalists**, **standard moderns**, **sophisticated modern consulters**, and **sophisticated modern constitutionalists**.

The *traditionalist style* is one where managers with unitarist perspectives have a strong belief in management's right to manage without any interference from other parties. Trade unions are therefore regarded negatively and with distrust, the workforce is treated in an authoritarian, hard

(Storey, 1992), sometimes exploitative way. Management is the sole source of authority and the managerial prerogative is regarded as a legitimate right. Small family owned businesses often fit into this category, although it is not unknown for larger, better-known organisations, like Amazon, to also fit. The perception that the organisation comprises people with common aims means that conflict is not recognised (why would it be when management knows best) and, if it does occur, this is thought to be either the result of a misunderstanding due to poor communication or the result of a maverick employee.

The *sophisticated paternalists*, on the other hand, are also unitarists but have a soft (Storey, 1992) managerial approach. The key to this approach is the belief that if employees are treated well they will perform well. The managerial prerogative is still regarded as a right, and unions are still seen as an unwelcome intrusion, but employees are treated in an enlightened way with high levels of involvement designed to engender trust, lots of communication and good terms and conditions that are designed to create loyalty and, in part, to eliminate the need for union involvement. Kerr quotes an employee of the Australian company, Australian Abrasives, who epitomised this approach: 'There was no union, nobody wanted a union we had everything we could want. Mr. Miller was a great manager, everybody was happy, we respected him' (2007: 83). Marks and Spencer is a good example, as is Hewlett Packard. In some organisations, such as News International, the fear of external influence from unions leads to the setting up of internal staff associations. Here the staff have representatives, but these are not independent entities. In this way everything is kept 'in house'. (Occasionally a staff association will gradually gain independence from the employer and register as a union; this happened with the Britannia Staff Association, which was formed in 1972, became independent four years later and affiliated to the TUC in 1999.) When workplace representation evolves in this way, the corresponding managerial style will evolve at the same time – albeit sometimes reluctantly.

Those organisations with a *standard modern* style are pluralist, accepting that there are groups with different interests within the organisation and that conflict is likely to occur. Unions are therefore recognised, but not warmly embraced. Union representatives are dealt with 'as and when' necessary, on an adversarial 'fire-fighting' basis. Adversarial bargaining takes place around a fairly narrow range of issues on a win–lose basis and legislation is frequently used in order to enforce compliance with procedures and/or to disrupt union actions. Examples of organisations exhibiting this style would be Carillion, Balfour Beatty, Diageo, Transport for London.

The remaining two groups of *sophisticated modern* managers – the *consulters* and the *constitutionalists* – have strategies, policies and procedures acknowledging that employees will have different perspectives from management and that the processes of employee representation will help contain those differences, maintain stability and reduce/contain conflict. The constitutionalists accept the inevitability of workplace representation but contain it with rules and regulations, and there is a strong emphasis on managerial control and relationships with unions, although cordial, are bounded by procedural regulations. This is found frequently in the manufacturing sectors where competition is high, and in some public sector organisations such as NHS trusts. The consulters, on the other hand, have a much less proscribed relationship with workplace representatives as there is fuller information disclosure, joint problem solving and more of a partnership approach. For example at NPower, a gas and electricity generation and supply company where unions and management work together using problem-solving approaches, there is a very positive employee relations atmosphere. After negotiating and introducing a new capabilities procedure, 'the union reps were heavily involved in the roll-out of training in the new procedure for line-managers' which succeeded in securing high levels of buy-in from these managers (BERR, 2009: 17).

Summary

This chapter has dealt with a large number of issues showing that the employment relationship is affected by the social, economic and legal environment in which an organisation is operating, the culture of its workforce and the ideology and values that the employers and employees bring to the workplace. The study of employee relations has to take all of these influences into consideration in order to analyse and understand the processes and events at work. Such critical realism takes into account the interests and perspectives of the different parties involved, levels of power (and how it is exercised), managerial styles, ethical behaviours and expressions of conflict or cooperation.

Review Questions

1 Do you think conflicts of interest between employees and employers are inevitable? Why did you reach this conclusion?
2 Is cooperation between employees and employers achievable? Why did you reach this conclusion?
3 Do trade unions, representing a 'collective interest' have a legitimate role to play in the workplace? Why did you reach this conclusion?
4 Is it desirable for employers to develop employment policies based on 'individualism' and greater 'employee involvement'? Why did you reach this conclusion?
5 Do you think such an approach is manipulative? Why did you reach this conclusion?
6 What is the significance of power relations and the balance of power in the workplace? Why did you reach this conclusion?
7 How ethical is the use of the traditional hard managerial style? Why did you reach this conclusion?

Revision Exercise 1.1

Read the following case study about Jacobs Douwe Egberts (JDE) coffee factory and then identify:

- the managerial style
- the parties involved
- their respective interests.

(Continued)

UK supermarket deliveries of Kenco, Millicano and L'OR coffee were threatened when, in March 2021, JDE proposed shift changes necessitating the 'firing and rehiring' of nearly 300 coffee workers at its Oxfordshire site. The proposals met with dismay from the workforce - and led to a huge majority voting for industrial action. Unite, the union representing the workers, announced that 96% of its members had voted in favour of a strike in the consultative ballot following company notices of dismissal and re-engagement. Alternative shift proposals made by Unite were, it said, rejected out of hand by JDE. The company, which had very healthy financial results for 2020 also planned to end its final salary pension arrangements with a replacement defined contribution scheme. The union warned that such company decisions would 'damage members' incomes and hit the wider Oxfordshire economy'.

Sources: BBC, 2021b; Lezard, 2021

Relevant Articles for Further Reading

Barry, M. and Wilkinson, A. (2021) 'Old frames and new lenses: Frames of reference revisited', *Journal of Industrial Relations*, 63(2): 114–25.

This is a useful summary, covering the ways in which frames of reference have developed since Fox's early usage.

Demougin, P., Gooberman, L., Hauptmeier, M. and Heery, E. (2019) 'Employer organisations transformed', *Human Resource Management Journal*, 29(1): 1–16.

Here the authors provide an insight into the ways Employer Associations have evolved from the nineteenth century to the current day.

Korczynski, M. (2011) 'The dialectical sense of humour: Routine joking in a Taylorized factory', *Organisational Studies*, 32(10): 1421–39.

This paper provides a good example of the ways in which employees informally react to control, showing workplace solidarity and resistance through the use of humour.

Renwick, D. (2003) 'Line manager involvement in HRM: An inside view', *Employee Relations*, 25(3): 262–80.

This important article provides insight into the ways in which line management (and subsequent subordinate control) impact the employment relationship.

References

Ackers, P. (2002) 'Reframing employment relations: The case for neo-pluralism', *Industrial Relations Journal*, 33(1): 2–19.
BALPA (2021) *BALPA Wins Major Legal Victory Against Ryanair Over 'Blacklisting'*, press release, 15 January. Available at: www.balpa.org/media-centre/press-releases/balpa-wins-major-

legal-victory-against-ryanair- ove#:~:text=balpa%20wins%20major%20legal%20victory%20 against%20ryanair%20over%20'blacklisting'.,-release%20date%3a%2015&text=the%20 pilots%20claim%20the%20threatened,part%20in%20trade%20union%20activities (accessed 12 April 2021).

Barry M. and Wilkinson A. (2021) 'Old frames and new lenses: Frames of reference revisited', *Journal of Industrial Relations*, 63(2): 114–25. doi:10.1177/0022185620983968

Behrens, M. and Traxler, F. (2004) *Employers' Organisations in Europe*. EurWork, European Observatory of Working Life. Available at: www.eurofound.europa.eu/observatories/eurwork/ comparative-information/employers-organisations-in-europe (accessed 13 July 2013).

BBC (2021a) 'Shrewsbury 24: Court of appeal clears picketers' convictions', *BBC News*, 23 March. Available at: www.bbc.co.uk/news/uk-england-shropshire-56494701 (accessed 25 April 2021).

BBC (2021b) 'Talks between Douwe Egberts and coffee workers break down', *BBC News*, 4 March. Available at: www.bbc.co.uk/news/uk-england-oxfordshire-56270971 (accessed 15 May 2021).

BERR (2009) *Reps in Action: How Workplaces can Gain from Modern Representation*. London: HMSO.

Bingham, C. A. (2007) 'Employee relations and managing the employment relationship', in C. Porter, C. A. Bingham and D. Simonds (eds), *Exploring HRM*. Maidenhead: McGraw-Hill, Ch. 12.

Bray, M., Budd, J. W. and Macneil, J. (2020) 'The many meanings of co-operation in the employment relationship and their implications', *British Journal of Industrial Relations*, 58(1): 114–41.

Brewley, H. and Forth, J. (2010) *Vulnerability and Adverse Treatment in the Workplace, Employment Relations Research Series 112*. London: Department for Business Innovation and Skills.

Brewster, C. and Mayrhofer, W. (2018) 'Comparative HRM: The debates and the evidence', in D. G. Collings and G. T. Wood (eds), *Human Resource Management: A Critical Approach*. London: Routledge, pp. 358–77.

Budd, J. W. (2004) *Employment with a Human Face: Balancing Efficiency, Equity, and Voice*. Ithaca, NY: Cornell University Press.

Budd, J. W. and Bhave, D. (2008) 'Values, ideologies, and frames of reference in industrial relations', in P. Blyton, E. Heery, N. Bacon and J. Fiorito (eds), *The SAGE Handbook of Industrial Relations*. London: SAGE, pp. 92–112.

Budd, J. W., Gollan, P. J. and Wilkinson, A. (2010) 'New approaches to employee voice and participation in organizations', *Human Relations*, 63(3): 303–10.

Buzza, J. S. (2017) 'Are you living to work or working to live? What millennials want in the workplace', *Journal of Human Resources*, 5(2): 15–20.

Chartered Institute of Personnel Development (CIPD) (2020) *Quarter of employees believe bullying and harassment are overlooked*, Available at: www.cipd.co.uk/about//media/press/bullying-harassment-overlooked#gref (accessed 14 May 2021).

Ciulla, J. B. (2000) *The Working Life: The Promise and Betrayal of Modern Work*. London: Crown Business.

Confederation of British Industry (CBI) (2021) *British Businesses to Launch New Campaign Aimed at Increasing Racial and Ethnic Participation in Senior Leadership*, press release, 1 October. Available at: www.cbi.org.uk/media-centre/articles/british-businesses-to-launch-new-campaign-aimed-at-increasing-racial-and-ethnic-participation-in-senior-leadership/ (accessed 2 October 2020).

Cradden, C. (2011) *Unitarism, Pluralism, Radicalism... and the Rest?* Geneva: University of Geneva. Available at: https://archive-ouverte.unige.ch/unige:48333 (accessed 11 January 2022).

Crouch, C. (2017) 'Membership density and trade union power', *Transfer: European Review of Labour and Research*, 23(1): 47–61.

Cullinane, N. and Dundon, T. (2014) 'Unitarism and employer resistance to trade unionism', *The International Journal of Human Resource Management*, 25(18): 2573–90.

Dawson, T. (2010) 'Out of sight, out of pocket: Women's invisibility in the British printing industry and its effect on the gender pay gap', *Historical Studies in Industrial Relations*, 29/30: 61–98.

Deny, R. (1989) 'An empirical study of moral reasoning among managers', *Journal of Business Ethics*, 8: 855–62.

Department of Business, Energy and Industrial Strategy (DBEIS) (2021) *Trade union statistics 2020*. Available at: www.gov.uk/government/statistics/trade-union-statistics-2020 (accessed 27 May 2021).

Dundon, T. and Rollinson, D. (2011) *Understanding Employment Relations* (2nd edn). Maidenhead: McGraw-Hill.

Dunlop, J. T. (1958) *Industrial Relations Systems*. New York: Holt.

Edwards, P. (2005) *Industrial Relations Theory and Practice* (2nd edn). Oxford: Blackwell.

Edwards, P. K. (1986) *Conflict at Work: A Materialist Analysis of Workplace Relations*. Oxford: Blackwell.

Farmer, S. M. and Aguinis, H. (2005) 'Accounting for subordinate perceptions of supervisor power: An identity-dependence model', *Journal of Applied Psychology*, 90(6): 1069–83.

Farnham, D. (1997) *Employee Relations in Context*. London: Institute of Personnel and Development.

Flanders, A. (1970) *Management and Unions*. London: Faber.

Flowers, A. (2021) 'Biden talks like the most pro-union president since the New Deal', *Washington Post*, 30 April. Available at: www.washingtonpost.com/business/interactive/2021/biden-on-unions/ (accessed 7 May 2021).

Fox, A. (1966) 'Managerial ideology and labour relations', *British Journal of Industrial Relations*, 4: 366–78.

Fox, A. (1974) *Beyond Contract: Work Power and Trust Relations*. London: Faber.

Fox, A. (1985) *History and Heritage*. London: Allen & Unwin.

French, J. R. P. and Raven, B. (1962) 'The bases of social power', in D. Cartwright and A. F. Zander (eds), *Group Dynamics: Research and Theory*. Evanston, IL: Harper & Row, pp. 607–23.

Fudge, J. (2017) 'The future of the standard employment relationship: Labour law, new institutional economics and old power resource theory', *Journal of Industrial Relations*, 59(3): 374–92.

Gooberman, L., Hauptmeier, M. and Heery, E. (2019) 'The decline of Employers' Associations in the UK, 1976–2014', *Journal of Industrial Relations*, 61(1): 11–32.

Goodrich, C. L. (1920) *The Frontier of Control*. New York: Harcourt, Brace & Howe.

Greasley, K., Bryman, A., Dainty, A., Price, A., Soetanto, R. and King, N. (2005) 'Employee perceptions of empowerment', *Employee Relations*, 27 (4).

Greenwood, M. and Van Buren, H. J. (2017) 'Ideology in HRM scholarship: Interrogating the ideological performativity of "New Unitarism"', *Journal of Business Ethics*, 142(4): 663–78.

Greenwood, R., Oliver, C., Sahlin, K. and Suddaby, R. (eds) (2008) *The SAGE Handbook of Organizational Institutionalism*. London: Sage.

Hyman, R. (1975) *Marxism and the Sociology of Trade Unionism*. London: Pluto Press.

Hyman, R. (1999) 'Imagined solidarities: Can trade unions resist globalization?', in P. Leisink (ed.), *Globalization and Labour Relations*. Cheltenham: Edward Elgar, pp. 94–115.

Hyman, R. and Brough, L. (1975) *Social Values and Industrial Relations*. Oxford: Blackwell.

industriALL (14 01 2021) 'French energy unions plan day of action against energy company', *industriALL*, 14 January. Available at: www.industriall-union.org/french-energy-unions-plan-day-of-action-against-edfs-hercules-project (accessed 6 May 2021).

Kahn-Freund, O. (1972) *Labour and the Law*. London: Stevens.

Kaufman, B. E., Barry, M., Wilkinson, A., Lomas, G. and Gomez, R. (2021) 'Using unitarist, pluralist, and radical frames to map the cross-section distribution of employment relations across workplaces: A four-country empirical investigation of patterns and determinants', *Journal of Industrial Relations*, 63(2): 204–34.

Kelly, J. (1998) *Rethinking Industrial Relations: Mobilization, Collectivism and Long Waves*. London: Routledge.

Kerr, M. (2007) 'Labour management practices in non-union firms: Australian abrasive industry 1945–70', *Labour History*, 92: 75–88.

Kessler, I. and Purcell, J. (1995) 'Individualism and collectivism in theory and practice', in P. Edwards (ed.), *Industrial Relations: Theory and Practice in Britain*. Oxford: Blackwell.

Kinnie, N., Hutchinson, S., Purcell, J., Rayton, B. and Swart, J. (2005) 'Satisfaction with HR practices and commitment to the organisation: Why one size does not fit all', *Human Resource Management Journal*, 15(4): 9–29.

Knafo, S. and Dutta, S. J. (2020) 'The myth of the shareholder revolution and the financialization of the firm', *Review of International Political Economy*, 27(3): 476–99.

Lezard, T. (2021) 'Coffee workers move towards strike ballot over fire-and-rehire', *Union News*, 16 March. Available at: www.union-news.co.uk/coffee-workers-move-towards-strike-ballot-over-fire-and-rehire/ (accessed 15 May 2021).

Legge, K. (1995) *Human Resource Management Rhetorics and Realities*. London: Macmillan.

Lundin Energy AB (2020) 'Strike threatening Johan Sverdrup production called off', *GlobeNewswire*, 12 October. Available at: www.globenewswire.com/news-release/2020/10/12/2106609/0/en/Strike-threatening-Johan-Sverdrup-production-called-off.html (accessed 28 April 2021).

Lukes, S. (2005) *Power: A Radical View* (2nd edn). Basingstoke: Palgrave.

Mallet, B. and Pineau, E. (2021) 'France hopeful for deal with Brussels on EDF overhaul in coming weeks', *Reuters*, 11 March. Available at: www.reuters.com/article/us-edf-restructuring-idUSKBN2B30Z1 (accessed 6 May 2021).

Martins, P. S. (2020) *What Do Employers' Associations Do?*, IZA Discussion Papers No. 13705. Bonn: Institute of Labor Economics (IZA).

McConville, T. (2006) 'Devolved HRM responsibilities, middle-managers and role dissonance,' *Personnel Review*, 35(6): 637–53.

Nishii, L. H. and Paluch, R. M. (2018) 'Leaders as HR sensegivers: Four HR implementation behaviors that create strong HR systems', *Human Resource Management Review*, 28(3): 319–23.

Oxenbridge, S. and Brown, W. (2004) 'Achieving a new equilibrium? The stability of cooperative employer-union relationships', *Industrial Relations Journal*, 35(5): 388–402.

Pool, M. (1980) 'Management strategies and industrial relations', in M. Pool and R. Mansfield (eds), *Managerial Roles in Industrial Relations*. Aldershot: Gower, pp. 40–4.

Purcell, J. (1987) 'Mapping management styles in employee relations', *Journal of Management Studies*, 24(5): 533–48.

Purcell, J. and Gray, A. (1986) 'Corporate personnel departments and the management of industrial relations', *Journal of Management Studies*, 23(2): 205–23.

Purcell, J. and Sisson, K. (1983) 'Strategies and practice in the management of industrial relations in Britain', in G. Bain (ed.), *Industrial Relations in Britain*. Oxford: Blackwell.

Reed, M. I. (2001) 'Organisation, trust and control: A realist analysis', *Organisational Studies*, 22(2): 201–28.

Rose, E. (2008) *Employment Relations* (3rd edn). London: Financial Times/Prentice Hall.

Sharma, M. (Oct 2, 2020) 'Diversity News', *HR Review*, 2 October. Available at: www.hrreview. co.uk/hr-news/racial-diversity-cbi-calls-on-uk-firms-to-have-one-bame-member/127668?utm_ source=rss&utm_medium=rss&utm_campaign=racial-diversity-cbi-calls-on-uk-firms-to-have-one-bame-member&gator (accessed 2 October 2020).

Sisson, K. (2007) *Weathering the Storm: The Maturing of British Industrial Relations*. Coventry: Industrial Relations Research Unit, Warwick Business School.

Sisson, K. (2010) *Employment Relations Matters*. Warwick, Industrial Relations Research Unit. Available at: www2.warwick.ac.uk/fac/soc/wbs/research/irru/erm/ (accessed 30 September 2015).

Storey, J. (1992) *Developments in the Management of Human Resources*. Oxford: Blackwell.

Syal, R. and Evans, R. (2021) 'Shrewsbury 24: How industrial action led to 47-year fight for justice', *The Guardian*, 23 March. Available at: www.theguardian.com/law/2021/mar/23/ shrewsbury-24-industrial-action-47-year-fight-justice (accessed 25 April 2021).

Townsend, K. and Hutchinson, S. (2017) 'Line managers in industrial relations: Where are we now and where to next?', *Journal of Industrial Relations*, 59(2): 139–52.

TUC (2019) '*2 Million Workers Not Getting Legal Holiday Entitlement*' says TUC, press release. Available at: www.tuc.org.uk/news/2-million-workers-not-getting-legal-holiday-entitlement-warns-tuc (accessed 12 May 2021).

UNISON (2013) *Tackling Bullying at Work: A UNISON Guide for Safety Reps*. Available at: www.unison. org.uk/content/uploads/2013/07/On-line-Catalogue216953.pdf (accessed 30 September 2015).

Van Buren, H. J. and Greenwood, M. (2011) 'Bringing stakeholder theory to industrial relations', *Employee Relations*, 33: 5–21.

Van Buren, H. J., Greenwood, M., Donaghey, J. and Reinecke, J. (2021) 'Agonising over industrial relations: Bringing agonism and dissensus to the pluralist frames of reference', *Journal of Industrial Relations*, 63(2): 177–203.

Viser, M. and Pager, T. (2021) 'Biden, in speech to Congress, offers sweeping agenda and touts democracy', *Washington Post*, 29 April. Available at: www.washingtonpost.com/politics/biden-speech-congress/2021/04/28/f33615ac-a7a2-11eb-bca5-048b2759a489_story.html (accessed 7 May 2021).

Webb, S. and Webb, B. (1920) *The History of Trade Unionism*. London: Longman.

Webber, A. (2021) 'Ryanair pilots' trade union detriment case over first hurdle', *Personnel Today*, 20 January. Available at: www.personneltoday.com/hr/ryanair-pilots-trade-union-detriment-case-over-first-hurdle/ (accessed 26 April 2021).

Wilkinson, A. (1998) 'Empowerment: theory and practice', *Personnel Review*, 27(1): 40–56.

Wright, P. and Nishii, L. (2004) 'Strategic HRM and organizational behaviour: Integrating multiple level analysis', paper presented at the What Next For HRM? Conference, Rotterdam, June.

2

EMPLOYEE RELATIONS: THE IMPORTANCE OF CONTEXT

Learning Outcomes

By the end of this chapter, you should be able to:

- provide an overview of why context is important when studying the employment relationship
- be critically analytical about the concepts of convergence and divergence in the context of the employment relationship
- be aware of global changes that have impacted the employment relationship
- be cognisant of the challenges when studying comparative international employee relations
- identify why studying international variations in employee relations is useful.

What to Expect

This chapter looks at the importance of context, giving a brief overview of the ways in which globalisation affects the employment relationship. In particular it explores why context is so important when comparing different employee relations practices, especially when they have evolved from within constituencies holding different philosophical and political values. It highlights the need to be aware that blanket comparisons, without awareness of context, can be misleading and on occasion erroneous. A number of theoretical perspectives such as convergence and divergence, varieties of capitalism, human capital, and varieties of union strategies are considered.

Context - Is It Relevant?

In the previous chapter we saw that the employment relationship is a complex contested one and that it concerns those in work, those who employ them, and those who have an impact on their workplace relationships, such as legislators and politicians. The relationship, however, does not occur in isolation, it takes place within specific contexts ranging from the local to the national, international and the global – none of which are mutually exclusive. In all these relationships there is an ongoing struggle between capital and labour (that is, between those who pay for work and those who get paid for doing it). The tension between these two opposing forces, and the ways in which this 'tension' is managed and regulated by rule making, negotiation, consent or coercion, is the essence of what we are analysing and evaluating in the relationship. When we compare the employment relationship in different countries we must be aware that each relationship will be subject to different cultural and institutional influences, different legislative restrictions, different power imbalances, different economic constraints and different attitudes to trade unions; such differences make comparisons problematic but not impossible. Awareness is crucial for meaning-ful understanding. So, for example, if we look at – and compare – how different academic studies approach the ways in which unions operate, it becomes clear that the concept of union strategy has, on occasion, been explored without being put into context and has sometimes been 'molded' in order to allow for 'easy' cross-national comparisons and academic ethnocentrism (Gasparri et al., 2019; Hyman, 2004). The more aware we are of differences and context the more accurate our perceptions and relevant our analysis. Accurate and insightful comparisons allow academics (and organisations) to learn valuable lessons from successful outcomes and, importantly, from mistakes. As Frege and Kelly say:

> cross-national comparative methodology is in many ways the fundamental laboratory
> for employment relations. Without the ability to compare across countries it is virtually
> impossible to understand and explain the scientific importance of findings in one
> particular economy. Moreover, one of the core functions of comparative research is
> to link conceptually micro – and macro – levels of analysis (for example, employees'
> job happiness with collective representation systems) and to compare across different
> national settings. (2020: 10)

In the years since the Second World War many significant changes in, and to, the ways in which work – and the ways it can be organised – have occurred. There has been more internationalisation of economic activity and an increase in international labour mobility. The predominant Western neoliberal philosophy, promoting free trade (and relatively unrestricted, liberalised, integrated markets) has exacerbated these trends. Howell (2021) argues that impact on employment relations, through the spread of neoliberal work practices, has been enhanced and assisted by the central role played by *active* state involvement. Such an interventionist approach is particularly evident, he says, with regards to the accelerating shifts towards individual employment regulation away from collective regulation, and by the increased promotion of permeable boundaries between work and non-work. This state 'activity' becomes apparent if you look at the amount of legislation enacted over the last 35 years. For example, in Ireland there were six different tripartite Social Partnership

Programmes and in the same period Germany enacted the Hartz labour market reforms and New Zealand enacted both the Employment Contracts Act and the Employment Relations Act. Similarly in England and Wales there has been a steady stream of individualist 'enabling' employment legislation since the Thatcher era. Yet Howell (2021: 4) argues that these approaches are, in large part, pragmatic responses to, 'national institutional legacies and obstacles to liberalization more than ideological proclivities' towards an espoused neoliberal philosophy.

All of these changes have occurred alongside huge technological and economic transformation around production processes, investment and, indeed, the ownership of employing organisations. These changes have impacted the ways in which work processes are regulated and managed and hence the ways in which employment relationships have developed. The predominance and power of multinational corporations (MNCs), operating globally, have become increasingly important, particularly since MNCs are able to pressure governments, lobby for legislative changes and dominate markets by standardising and moving production processes to where they are the most cost effective and by selling their goods worldwide (Reiche and Minbaeva, 2019; Wailes et al., 2020).

News Flash 2.1

Nigerian TUC Demands Government Call Chevron Management and Other Multinationals to Order

In October 2020 the Trade Union Congress of Nigeria (NTUC) urged the Nigerian Federal Government to take action against the multinational oil company, Chevron.

It strongly condemned the management of Chevron (and other multinationals) claiming Chevron was replacing Nigerians in its establishments with its own nationals, as well as scheming to relocate some jobs to its home countries.

The Nigerian TUC is unhappy because Chevron management recently notified 2,000 of its employees that their services are no longer required and that those still interested in working with them should apply afresh for a new job.

The NTUC says that this runs contrary to Nigeria's laws regulating the Oil and Gas industry, as it does not protect Nigeria's national interest.

Source: http://tucnigeria.org.ng/call-chevron-management-other-multinational-companies-to-order-now/ (accessed 6 April 2012).

It is within this globalised, interconnected context that the **BRICS** countries (Brazil, Russia, India, China and South Africa) have become as important as those previously dominant within the Western economies such as the US and the UK (Dicken, 2015). The growth and increasing dominance of the BRICS countries in the global marketplace disrupted Western domestic markets and helped precipitate a deceleration in Western industrial work and production with an inevitable impact on the employment relationship. Indeed China was the only major economy to show positive growth in 2020 when its share of the world economy rose from 3.6% in 2019 to 17.8% in 2020. Interestingly, Xiao and Cooke (2020) have shown that over the last half century, employment in the Chinese economy shifted from the state (78% of total urban employment in the late 1970s) to the private sector (15% in 2016). In its annual league table, the UK-based think tank, the Centre for Economics and Business Research (CEBR), expected the value of China's economy (when measured in dollars) to exceed that of America by 2028 (CEBR, 2020:70–1).

Context is crucially important. The general economy, the political complexion of the government concerned, and the state of the market in which an organisation is operating, will all have an impact on employment patterns either indirectly or directly. For example, at national and local levels education policies influence the attainment of skills, and therefore have an impact on the suitability of job seekers for employment. At an international level, there are a similar range of influences; for example, Article 4 of the European Convention on Human Rights prohibits *forced* labour, aiming to ensure that workers are not illegally coerced into employment. Similarly, the International Labour Organisation (ILO), comprising governments, employers and workers from 187 member states, sets labour standards and policies. It produced a *Declaration on Social Justice for a Fair Globalisation* (Kaufman, 2008) that promoted 'decent work' through four strategic objectives: employment, social protection, social dialogue, and fundamental principles and rights at work. Similar impacts of legislative requirements are seen throughout the EU where the EU European employment strategy requires minimal working standards in all member states. The UK too is influential, the Modern Slavery Act restricting exploitation in supply chains at home and abroad. (It is worth noting, however, that the existence of legislation does not necessarily mean that all workplaces are free from exploitation – the February 2020 policy document, by Vicky Xu and her colleagues from the Australian Strategic Policy Institute, connected 83 well-known worldwide brands with the illegal and abhorrent mistreatment of Uyghur Muslims.)

News Flash 2.2

Alleged Labour Abuses by Dyson in Supply Chain

In February 2022 the UK Labour MP Bill Esterson tweeted, 'Reports of forced labour in Dyson's supply chain - 12 hours a day, 7 days a week, 30 days a month - are awful. Big companies have a massive responsibility to prevent modern slavery in their supply chains. Dyson have serious questions to answer'.

The tweet followed the news that 12 Malaysia-based workers who had made components for Dyson were taking legal action over alleged labour abuses by a Dyson supplier, ATA Industrial. Apparently, the workers were under persistent threats of punishment by the factory management if they didn't adhere to the stringent company requirements. The workers who were allegedly denied annual leave had worked without taking a break for over a year and a half, and moreover, they were compelled to live in unsanitary and crowded accommodation.

Dyson said the claims were 'false and defamatory'.

In November 2021, following an independent audit at ATA Industrial, uncovering issues around forced labour and excessive working hours Dyson ended its contract with ATA.

Source: McCulloch, 2022.

Wars and natural disasters have an impact on and skew levels and types of employment. The Ukraine–Russia conflict in 2022/23 resulted in economic consequences (rising levels of inflation, shortage of petrol and grain, for example) that had an impact on the cost of living across Europe, with subsequent pressures on wages and employment levels. The period covering the 2020/21 Covid pandemic had huge implications for both trade and employment because national borders and many workplaces worldwide were closed, affecting the movements of labour and of goods. Across Europe the numbers of people employed (and the remuneration they received) were badly affected. Levels of work and income were negatively impacted in a number of ways: workers were made redundant; employment contracts were not renewed; workers remained employed but were **furloughed** (temporarily laid-off) – this sometimes led to eventual job losses; workers remained working, but for a fraction of their usual hours; workers took temporary jobs, such as delivery driving, in order to boost their income. The reduction in wages and loss of income disproportionately affected the young and those in precarious employment (see Figure 2.1). Across Europe those who lost their jobs also lost income (unless they were in Denmark). The most marked decreases in income were in Portugal and Spain (–3.5 % and –4.3 % respectively), while the lowest decreases were registered in the Netherlands and Hungary (less than –0.1 % for both) (Eurostat, 2020).

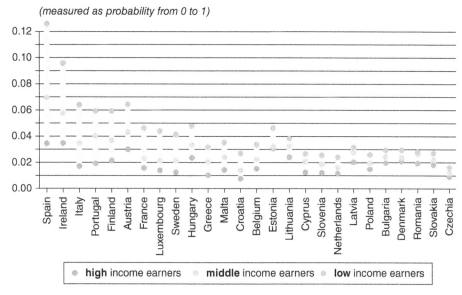

Figure 2.1   Risks of job loss for different income groups across Europe in the second quarter of 2020

Source: https://ec.europa.eu/eurostat/web/products-eurostat-news/-/DDN-20201027-2 (accessed 11 March 2021)

Covid, however, is not the only way in which unfortunate events can have negative repercussions on an international scale. The recent war in Ukraine has had an impact on fuel prices – resulting in increases in the cost of food and transport. Those dependent on cars for work have to evaluate whether or not to leave the labour market, change jobs, or ask for more money; those organisations reliant on fuel are having to decide whether to absorb the additional costs or pass them on, both with possible consequences for employment. It is not just recent events that have global repercussions. For instance, the foot and mouth outbreak in Britain in 2001 had a devastating impact on the Turkish sheepskin coat industry, resulting in job losses in both Turkey and the UK. The 2011 Japanese tsunami and earthquake had an impact on the infrastructure of Japan that was felt more widely across the globe, particularly in terms of car manufacture (see Todeschini, 2011, for an interesting discussion on the impact of the tsunami on Japanese management). A more positive example can be seen in Haiti, when in January 2011, a year after the devastating earthquake worsened the country's 70% high unemployment rate (causing the number of people without work in the capital Port-au-Prince and its outskirts to quadruple), the South Korean company SAE-A signed a deal to give Haiti $78m of sewing machine equipment, undertaking to train and employ 20,000 jobless Haitians. Simultaneously, the American government spent millions of dollars constructing an industrial park, power plant and housing for 5,000 Haitian workers. Both the disastrous earthquake and the subsequent foreign help had an impact on employment levels and impacted the employment relationships.

Global employment was badly affected by the banking crisis and recession (for 2007 onwards see Della Porta and Portos, 2020; Macdonald, 2019). Some countries have fared better than others. Australia with its well-regulated banks (and as a supplier of raw materials to China) was one of the few nations to escape recession, and its employees largely remained unaffected. The UK, on the other hand, with its steady decline in manufacturing, coupled with an increase in service sector jobs has, post-2007, found it more difficult to maintain a level of growth; while Germany, with its emphasis on manufacturing, initially fared better, although its links with other countries within the Euro Zone (particularly Greece, Spain and Italy, where debts and austerity measures prevailed) resulted in a detrimental impact on its economy. In order to aid exports and stimulate growth, the Chinese government felt compelled to devalue its currency three times in August 2015, bringing subsequent falls in the international stock markets. Such global turbulence results in a knock-on effect on employment levels and workplace behaviours. If we look at the impact of the Covid pandemic (the results are, of course, atypical and global output and production will improve once the infection rates come down and the vaccination rates go up), in the last quarter of 2020 China was the only country to experience a rise in GDP growth (4.9%) while the UK's growth rate was –9.6 % and India was similarly affected with –7.5% (Statista, 2021). The global economic environment therefore has a direct impact on employment (see Table 2.1) and hence on employee conditions and on workplace relationships.

Exercise 2.1

- What does Table 2.1 tell you about the levels of employment for men in the Netherlands compared to the men in Spain?
- Are women in Mexico as likely as women in Turkey and Germany to be employed?
- What do you think accounts for these differences?
- Looking at the employment figures for each separate country, how much bargaining power do you think female employees are able to exert? Why did you reach your conclusions?

Table 2.1 Labour market statistics showing employment rates (percentage)

	April 2009			April 2010			April 2011			Jan 2012		
	Men 15-64	Women 15-64	All 15-64	Men 15-64	Women 15-64	All 15-64	Men 15-64	Women 15-64	All 15-64	Men 15-64	Women 15-64	All 15-64
Norway	78.9	74.6	76.8	77.4	73.5	75.5	76.9	73.3	75.1	77.9	73.6	75.8
Netherlands	82.6	72.3	77.0	80.0	69.2	74.6	79.4	69.8	74.7	80.3	70.2	75.3
New Zealand	79.3	67.3	73.2	78.2	66.7	72.3	78.1	67.3	72.6	78.5	67.5	72.9
Germany	75.2	65.2	70.2	76.0	66.1	71.0	77.2	67.6	72.5	77.4	67.6	72.6
UK	74.7	64.9	69.8	74.5	64.6	69.5	74.6	64.5	69.5	74.6	64.4	69.5
USA	72.2	49.0	67.9	71.1	62.5	66.8	71.1	62.0	66.5	72.1	62.1	67.0
France	68.4	60.0	64.1	68.0	59.8	63.8	68.2	59.7	63.9	67.8	59.9	63.8
Japan	80.1	59.6	69.9	79.9	59.8	69.9	80.7	61.0	71.0	80.2	60.4	70.4
Chile	69.7	41.9	55.8	71.9	46.1	58.9	73.8	49.3	61.5	73.8	49.8	61.7
Turkey	63.7	23.7	43.6	66.8	26	46.2	68.9	27.6	48.1	68.8	28.3	48.5
Spain	66.8	52.9	59.9	64.8	52.2	58.6	63.7	52.9	58.3	61.3	51.1	56.2
Greece	73.7	49	61.4	71.2	48.5	59.9	66.7	45.5	56.1	62.6	43.1	52.9
Italy	68.7	46.5	57.6	67.7	46.2	56.9	67.6	46.5	57.0	66.8	47.0	56.9
Mexico	77.6	42.9	59.4	78.5	43.7	60.2	77.8	43.3	59.8	78.1	44.3	60.4

Source: http://stats.oecd.org/Index.aspx?DatasetCode=STLABOUR# (accessed 4 June 2013)

Globalisation and Employment Relations

According to Steger, globalisation, with its worldwide increase in interconnectivity and interdependence, enabling the ease of movement of goods, services, people, knowledge and capital across the globe, is one of the defining issues of the twenty-first century (2017). Globalisation involves the three Ps – Project, Process and Practice. The project element refers to the ways in which trade and labour are organised, e.g., neoliberalisation. Process, on the other hand, concerns the ways in which the labour market and economic growth are facilitated and enabled. Practice relates to the activities of individuals and collectives, such as unions, in direct response to the globalised environment (Amoore, 2002). Manufacturing, and indeed production in the service sector, often involves many different organisations from a range of different countries, sectors and institutional settings, all relying on decreasing trade barriers and ease of transportation. The resulting growth in international trade (supported by institutions such as the World Trade Organisation [WTO] and bolstered by the General Agreement on Tariffs and Trade [GATT]) is a phenomenon enabled and made possible by advanced technology, creative software and improved transport infrastructure. Within this framework of fluidity, national borders have lost some of their importance and, in effect, the world has become 'smaller' and more interconnected, serving as one big marketplace.

Globalisation bears on the employment relationship in a number of ways. The increasing drive towards profitability has led companies to devote more time to 'playing the market' than in investing in production and labour. Managers have become more answerable to shareholders and the owners of private equity firms who, removed from the day-to-day running of an organisation, often have little regard for employee welfare and actively work to suppress trade unions because these are seen as a threat, likely to constrain and impede organisational profit-making processes. The dislike of union and state interference is bound up with neoliberal philosophy, the adherents of which resent any mechanisms that might hamper the ways in which they operate, particularly when, for example, union activity or state-imposed protection for employees and the manner in which they should be treated is imposed on them (Lakhani et al., 2013).

News Flash 2.3

London Bus Workers Strike Against French-owned RATP

Following a ballot of London bus drivers, the Unite union called 2,000 members to strike for three days from 22 February 2021, in protest against worsening pay and conditions demanded by the French company RATP. (RATP, headquartered in France, operates in 13 different countries and is responsible for around 1,000 buses in London.) According to Transport for London the strike will affect around 80 bus routes across the west of the capital stretching to both the north and southwest of London. The Union accused the RATP bosses of using the Covid pandemic as 'a convenient smokescreen' to permanently change contracts in order to facilitate wage cuts of up to £2,500 a year, taking wage levels back to their 2015 levels.

Sources: www.ratp.fr/en/groupe-ratp; www.ratp.fr/groupe-ratp/bus/bus-associer-economie-et-performance; www.standard.co.uk/news/uk/london-bus-drivers-strike-2021-tfl-pay-b920697.html; https://unitetheunion.org/news-events/news/2021/february/london-bus-bosses-accused-of-using-pandemic-as-a-smokescreen-for-attacks-on-pay-as-2-200-drivers-set-to-strike-next-week/

Alongside this there has been a general waning of trade union density (Brady et al., 2009) associated with a reduction in union power and the ability for employees to bargain collectively for better terms and conditions of employment. The global marketplace for goods and labour has not quite displaced the more piecemeal national and domestic markets but it has certainly had a transformative impact. Organisations seek to maximise their profits by outsourcing where appropriate and by utilising the cheapest source of appropriate labour, often from abroad. The need for profit maximisation has led many organisations to diversify their income streams, a number choosing to invest capital in the financial markets. This is often at the expense of their own workforces, employers squeezing their labour costs by opting, wherever possible, for the cheapest appropriate source of labour. This strategic drive towards achieving a competitive advantage results in such companies developing business models that drive down labour costs, often by contracting-out services and manufacturing to countries where costs are comparatively low and the legal restrictions around employment less onerous (Batt, 2018; Cushen and Thompson, 2016; Gittell and Bamber, 2011; Wills and Linneker, 2014). This process was neatly encapsulated by Barnet and Muller who pointed out that:

> ... the essential strategy of the global corporation is based on the international division of labour. Top management continues to be recruited from rich countries: workers increasingly come from low-wage areas [...] wage differentials are becoming more critical in maintaining competitive profit margins. (1974: 29)

The process makes union organising across national boundaries problematic, and, as Streeck says,

> ... the sweated workers of today and the middle class workers in the countries of 'advanced' capitalism, being so remote from each other spatially that they never meet, do not speak the same language and never experience together the community and solidarity deriving from joint collective action. (2016: 25)

The globalisation process, however, does not prevent local and domestic trade and production occurring, but it does mean that smaller local business and trades people have to work in an environment impacted by competitively priced goods and services originating from elsewhere.

Case Study 2.1

Union's Fight for Recognition and Reinstatement of Workers in Indian Garment Factory

Gokaldas Exports, producing clothing for a number of prominent European brands familiar on the high street, such as H&M, has lost its fight with the Garment and Textile Workers' Union (GATWU) which successfully won its eight-month campaign to reverse discriminatory, anti-union activity against its members in February 2021. Managers at the company had removed site machinery and shut down the factory illegally firing 1,257 employees. The company had proactively tried to break the union and prevent GATWU activity at one of its factories. This occurred despite H&M being a signatory to a global

(Continued)

framework agreement guaranteeing freedom of association within its supply chains. H&M threatened to stop all orders from Gokaldas if it continued to prevent union activity and failed to respect the right for its workers to remain in the union and take part in collective action.

The Union signed an agreement with Gokaldas Exports recognising it as the sole bargaining agent for three years in any factory with more than 20% membership. Furthermore the sacked 1,257 employees were offered work at two other sites owned by the company with Gokaldas providing transport should it be necessary.

IndustriALL General Secretary Valter Sanches said the deal was a 'tremendous victory for GATWU against almost impossible odds'. He added it also showed the importance of its global framework agreements.

Source: www.industriall-union.org/union-wins-reinstatement-of-1257-workers-in-india

---

The strong economic imperative lying behind many business cases has led to distinct ways of treating employees. The highly skilled and those regarded as integral to the success of any business (i.e., those people who are capital assets to the business) are treated with **soft HRM** techniques, with emphasis placed on wellbeing, teamwork, empowerment and personal development. Employees who are deemed to be expendable, easily replaceable resources, are treated with **hard HRM**. The assumption that labour markets are accessible for all workers, with firms hiring the most productive at the cheapest cost to them, is known as **Human Capital theory**. This advocates that individuals' wages are provided in direct proportion to their productivity, which in turn is linked directly to their capabilities, knowledge, skill, education and relevant experiences, in other words their human capital (Aliaga, 2001; Barney, 1991; Becker, 1962; Brown et al., 2020; Schultz, 1961). The moving of work processes, particularly manufacturing, to less well developed countries, while developed countries experience an escalating growth of higher skilled jobs, particularly in the service sector, has led to imbalances in national and domestic labour markets. One of the unfortunate consequences of the neoliberalisation, endemic in countries keen to promote globalisation, is the rise in higher levels of precarious work. There has been an increase in part time, flexible, temporary work fuelling the threat of insecure employment, under-employment and unemployment (Heintz and Razavi, 2015; Standing, 2011). Rubery has pointed out that employers have a choice about who they choose to employ, how work is organised and which work or shift patterns they offer. Consequently, she says, they often opt to adopt the least expensive labour unless there is an alternative need to act differently. In situations such as these, workers without a voice are vulnerable, but where there is a strongly unionised workforce, employees have a voice and conditions tend to be better (Rubery, 1988, 2007). In-work poverty in the twenty-first century is on the increase, leading Richards and Sang (2019) to talk about the emerging trend of **socially irresponsible HRM**.

Case Snippet 2.1

Female Migrant Labour in Italy Exploited

In 2015 in Italy, 42% of irregular farm workers were migrant women (frequently overrepresented in unpaid and seasonal work).

Women migrant farm workers often labour under the same harsh conditions as men: 10 or 12-hour days in unsafe and inadequate conditions for a daily wage of EUR 15 to 25. They face additional risks, because agricultural workers usually live on the farms, in contexts of isolation and poorly maintained housing. These conditions are often accompanied by sexual harassment and abuse. (ILO, 2020)

Case Snippet 2.2

Unexplained Migrant Worker Deaths on Qatar World Cup Sites

In 2021 it was reported that an average of 12 migrant workers from five south Asian nations had died each week in Qatar since it won the right to host the World Cup just over a decade ago in 2010. In total at least 6,500 migrant workers from India, Bangladesh, Nepal, Pakistan, and Sri Lanka had lost their lives working on sites connected to the World Cup.

Qatar is culpable, failing to protect its migrant workforce, or investigate the unexplained causes of sudden death amongst the migrant workforce. The authorities circumvent the provision of legitimate medical explanations for the underlying causes of workplace deaths, omitting to say, for example, whether they are linked to heat stroke or an accident, etc. Deaths are often merely classified as 'natural' and without an autopsy – it is difficult to prove otherwise.

Sources: www.theguardian.com/global-development/2021/feb/23/revealed-migrant-worker-deaths-qatar-fifa-world-cup-2022; www.business-humanrights.org/en/latest-news/qatar-unexplained-death-of-world-cup-stadium-worker-one-of-hundreds-dismissed-as-natural-by-authorities-fifa-responded/

The movement of labour (migration) has become politically sensitive and occasionally controversial in the Western economies. Yet Autor and Dorn (2013) have shown that a rise in low-skilled migration had less influence than technological factors around the expansion of low-skilled occupations, while Andersson et al. (2019: 1), looking at refugees, discovered that their 'migration has a small but positive and statistically significant impact on the growth of low-wage occupations in the EU 15 as a whole', affecting particularly the economies of Southern Europe, the UK and Ireland, with little impact on Continental Europe and the Nordic economies. Ian Fitzgerald and Jane Hardy argued, in a conference paper, that there are three structural conditions that 'underpin migration: uneven development within (and outside Europe), an intensification of competition and the drive towards flexibility' (2008: 2). It is not uncommon for unskilled migrant labour to be used as a cheap source of labour – often undertaking jobs that the domestic population would not undertake for the wages offered. In agriculture, for example, different countries facilitate the movement of labour in ways that are temporary but allow for the peaks and troughs of food production. Within the European Union the movement of labour is controlled by both the EU Seasonal Directive and by the free movement provisions covering the EU countries themselves. America allows temporary labour though its H2-A programme and Canada has a Seasonal Agricultural Workers Programme. In Italy over 250,000 additional people are needed annually to maintain vineyards, while Germany deploys around 300,000 additional people to work in agriculture, and in France 80% of the agricultural labour force is foreign (ILO, 2020). Where the skills of migrants are seen as complementary to the resident workers it is likely that local wages and productivity will go up. If, on the other hand, the migrant skills are similar to the prevailing workforce, it is probable that wage levels will go down – the newcomers displacing their more expensive counterparts.

News Flash 2.4

Flowers Rotting on the World's Largest Daffodil Farm Because of Brexit

The world's largest daffodil grower, Varfell Farms based in Cornwall, has been forced to let hundreds of thousands of pounds worth of flowers rot in the fields. The farm needs 700 workers to pick the flowers but, since Brexit and the Covid pandemic, migrant labour has dried up and the farm is at least 300 pickers short.

Recruitment drives for local pickers have been ineffective as the work, undertaken outdoors in wet and cold conditions, is tough. Those locals actually recruited for picking tasks, lasted for less than a week before resigning. The government seasonal worker pilot scheme, whereby workers from outside Europe, such as those from Ukraine and South America, are eligible to work in the UK harvesting *edible* crops, does not include eligibility for harvesting the inedible poisonous daffodil! (The ornamental crop industry annually contributes £150 million to the UK economy.)

Sources: Trewhela, 2021; Zorzut, 2021

Exercise 2.2

Donaghey et al. (2014: 229) highlighted the ways in which reliance on overseas contractors will, on occasion, dilute the government oversight of labour regulations with the consequence that the standards of workplace terms and conditions slip.

- Read the following quote and explain, firstly, what it means and, secondly, why you think that governance and union influence might be linked.

  As companies have moved production offshore, their supply chains have become supranational, with complex ownership structures and chains of control, a development that has been accompanied by questions related to the ability and desire of the state to regulate labour across borders. This tension is exposing the failure of the traditional tripartite model of labour governance in relation to supply chains, where labour, state and employers collectively produce labour governance (Dunlop, 1958). The result is a lack of meaningful labour regulation across the globe which is creating a global governance gap.

Convergence Versus Divergence

It is often thought that the increase of globalisation, together with the prevalence of multinational companies, has led to a gradual erosion of the differences between diverse employee relations practices and the associated shift towards an increasing similarity of work processes and procedures. Following this train of thought MNCs are depicted as rationalising their processes, harmonising their ways of working across national boundaries. For example, Schneider Electric, the automation and energy management organisation, launched a global paid family leave policy across 100 geographically diverse locations from the autumn of 2017. Smaller organisations are deemed to be following the same converging path, having, in effect, absorbed and adopted what they deem as the prevailing 'best practice' employment practices. As Tayfur (2013: 634) states, 'Undeniably, globalization, competitive pressures, and Western management-style practices promoted as universal truths make organizations and their practices more alike'. Baccaro and Howell (2011, 2017) have argued that it appears that national systems of employment are converging, becoming more liberal over time (**convergent employment practices**). They demonstrate that, over the last 40 years or so, **neoliberalism** has resulted in cross-national convergence, specifically benefitting employers rather than employees. In particular they show that, in Europe certainly, employers' powers have evolved giving them higher degrees of discretion around recruitment and termination, setting remuneration levels and organising work. Yet the trend for such convergence does not eliminate the differences between nations, which, although moving in similar neoliberal directions, have chosen a variety of different ways to express this, depending on their national culture and the power realities of their industrial relations actors.

News Flash 2.5

Global Parental Leave Scheme Introduced by Volvo

Following a successful pilot scheme in Africa, the Middle East and Europe, Volvo Cars has introduced a global paid parental leave policy. All of the 40,000+ Volvo employees who have been with the company for a year or more, and who are parents (including those who are adoptive or surrogates), are eligible to take up the provisions in the gender-neutral scheme that provides 80% of pay for a period of 24 weeks. To help embed the scheme, Volvo will communicate the policy as a 'pre-selected' option for new joiners, so that it becomes the 'default' choice of staff.

'This is more than a new parental leave policy for our employees – it is the embodiment of our company culture and values', said Hanna Fager, head of corporate functions. 'We want to lead change in this industry and set a new global people standard. By opting all our employees into paid parental leave we narrow the gender gap and get a more diverse workforce, boosting performance and strengthening our business'.

Sources: Crush, 2021; Volvo Cars, 2021

It is true that in times of economic crisis companies tend to adopt similar cost-cutting measures, but it is also true that different organisations are operating under, and subject to, a variety of different local, national and cultural constraints that work against convergence. National interests, dictated by governments and enshrined in legislation, prevent the overall indiscriminate adoption of some practices. Similarly the different power balances within organisations will impact on whether some things are adopted and/or others jettisoned or shaped for specific needs. Where there is a strong union presence and voice this, too, often prevents a standardised lowering of employment terms and conditions. Management practices do indeed vary from one country to another and each environment is likely to impose constraints on the ways in which employers determine their own employee relations structures. Dalton and Bingham (2017), for example, were able to show how often, in Romania (after it transitioned from communism to a democratic republic), prospective new HRM employment practices from the West were not adopted wholesale, but tweaked, ignored or partially adopted, depending on underlying historical and cultural influences. The process, of the present being viewed through the lens of the past and hence affecting the future is referred to by Xiao and Cooke (2020). They explain how traditional Chinese state-owned companies were subject to what was known as the 'iron rice bowl' system up until 1978. Under this regime, work was planned centrally, jobs were for life with worker welfare a concern and remuneration regarded as fair. After this date, the Chinese government introduced a set of policies designed to encourage the marketisation of **state-owned enterprises (SOEs)**. HR practices were adopted, contracts of employment introduced, performance management linked to pay was adopted and central planning was jettisoned in favour of market-based hire and fire practices, thereby converging towards Western managerial practices (Akhtar et al., 2008). The switch was not without problems; the state still occasionally controlled who held certain top work positions and, in particular, absorption of the new system was not always welcomed. Thus convergence was 'patchy' and the evolving system was a pragmatic hybridisation of HRM and the iron rice bowl. As Xiao and Cooke say,

> Taken as a whole, HR practices in Chinese SOEs consist of a mix of the market-based HRM model found in the western countries and elements of the socialist 'iron rice bowl' regime, which may differ from the non-SOE and non-Chinese contexts. (2020: 53)

Case Study 2.2

An Employee Relations Academic, Fernando Duran-Palma, Writes to His Students

One of the most frustrating sides to teaching is that students seem to switch off at the mere mention of the word 'theory'. Not you personally, of course, but everybody else;-). Problem is, theory is the key to the advancement of knowledge and therefore unavoidable if you want to *understand*, as opposed to merely describe, what is going on around you. Indeed, as this chapter has made abundantly clear, there are significant similarities and differences in employment relations across countries but, how can these be explained? Here is where theory comes in. I hope that this brief letter will stimulate your interest!

Let's consider the following example:

Trade unions, workers' representative organisations, vary greatly across countries in all sorts of ways: ideological orientation, structure, strength, membership, etc. Indeed, while in countries such as Germany, they are powerful, encompassing organisations able to influence state and employer policy, in others, such as the USA, they are, *relatively speaking*, weak, fragmented associations struggling to make their members' voice heard.

How can these differences be explained? As you would expect, there are numerous possible explanations and while it is impossible to include them here, every student of employment relations should be at least aware of two largely competing sets of explanations: cultural and institutional.

Is it the people..? Cultural explanations are perhaps the better known and easiest to grasp. You are probably familiar with the work of Geert Hofstede but there are many other culturalists. Very simply put, they argue that people across cultures – typically, but not exclusively, countries – see the world, and 'think, feel, and act' in different ways and that these are reflected in differences in employment relations. From this perspective, you would try and explain cross-national differences in union strength by looking at cultural factors like 'individualism' or 'collectivism' or the way in which interests, orientations and behaviours are based on predominantly group or predominantly individual reference points and involve competition or cooperation respectively with other members of that group (adapted from Peetz, 2010). If you went to www.hofstede-insights.com you'd see that, actually, the USA scores higher in individualism than Germany – 91 vs. 67 – and you could provisionally hypothesise that 'unions seem to be weaker in countries with higher levels of individualism' (or stronger in countries with higher levels of collectivism).

... or the rules? In contrast, institutional explanations point at countries' specific institutional arrangements. Note that by 'institutions', I do not mean 'organisations' but, instead, 'humanly devised constraints that structure political and social interaction which can be formal (constitutions, laws, rights) and informal rules (sanctions, customs, traditions, codes of conduct)' (after North, 1991: 97). In other words, the institutional approach focuses not on the mind of the people as the place where differences reside, but on the wider 'rules of the game'. From this point of view, differences in union strength are due to the relative presence or absence of supportive regulative, normative and cognitive supports. If you look at Germany's 'co-determination' institutions, you will quickly realise that the position of workers and their unions in relation to employers is far more favourable than in the US. At workplace level, workers in companies with at least five employees are legally entitled to elect a works council, which employers must consult on a number of issues; at company level, the law mandates that workers in companies with more than 2,000 employees elect up to half the supervisory board, which monitors the actions of management; in addition to this, unions and employers engage in collective bargaining at industry level, setting terms and conditions of employment for whole sectors. Given that none of these institutional supports exist in the US, you could reasonably conclude that the stronger position of German unions in relation to that of their American counterparts is due to the presence of German co-determination institutions and its systems of statutory employee representation.

... or both? But these two sets of explanations do not have to be mutually exclusive. Although I have over-simplified these approaches (I haven't even mentioned different schools of thought within them), both culture and institutions point to key elements of the environment of employment relations. There are, in fact, commentators who argue we should adopt a 'societal' approach that integrates cultural and institutional approaches ...

(Continued)

Let's think of another, linked, example.

Unions across countries have experienced a general decline in power and influence in recent years. How can we explain this? Again, there are many possible explanations but thinking in terms of cultural or institutional factors can yield rather interesting insights. If we think in terms of cultural factors then we could say that unions are declining because the collectivism of labour is in fundamental decline. We have become more and more individualistic and, as a result, we are less likely to join organisations such as trade unions. But if we think in terms of institutional factors, then we are forced to think not in terms of individualistic *attitudes or values* but, as Peetz (2010: 1) argues, in relation to attempts by employers and governments to individualise the employment relationship by the reduction, or removal, of *concrete collective mechanisms* to determine terms and conditions of employment such as anti-union legislation, weakening of collective bargaining rights, etc. Or is it both, as we have become more individualistic, we have elected politicians who have undermined collective rules? After all, not only do the rules rule over the people, but the people also write the rules ...

What do you think?

Best wishes
Fernando

Exercise 2.3

- Think of *any* employment relations issue, either within one country or between two countries.
- Try and explain it using the cultural and institutional approaches.

Case Snippet 2.3

Unilever Instructs Its Suppliers to Pay Living Wages by 2030

Unilever, the UK-based multinational, known for producing brands such as Marmite, Dove, Domestos, and Flora, has made a public undertaking that *all* of its suppliers will pay their employees a living wage by the end of the decade. That is, a wage that gives people sufficient money to cover food, water, clothing, transport and housing, with enough left over to cover emergencies. It has stipulated that all workers for companies directly supplying it with goods and or services must receive a living wage by 2030. But, because the cost of living varies around the world, the company is working with suppliers to help establish agreed living wage rates for the 190 countries in which it operates.

Sources: Narwan, 2021; Unilever, 2021; Webber, 2021

Different societal influences, together with robust and historically established systems and institutions, work against complete convergence, resulting in degrees of cross-national differences (Wailes et al., 2020). Such differences are apparent when one evaluates the types of institutions, philosophies and importantly the varieties of capitalism (VOC) that influence and control national economic arrangements. Capitalism, by its very nature, does not demonstrate a homogenous front. Although labour is bought (discarded and sold) in order to add value, there are two main and distinct approaches to how this is achieved. Firstly, there are **coordinated market economies** (CMEs) where it is usual for employers to consolidate and arrange employment activities by non-market mechanisms, such as multi-employer collective bargaining, with a stakeholder-based framework of social dialogue – as in Germany, Japan and Denmark. Secondly there are **liberal market economies** (LMEs), for example found in the US and the UK, in which employers depend upon market forces to influence the levels of remuneration and encourage the acquisition of appropriate skills (Frege and Kelly, 2020; Hall and Soskice, 2001). Globalisation actually accentuates the differences between LMEs and CMEs, i.e., companies (and states) endeavouring to maximise their comparative advantages (that paradoxically originate from the capitalist model under which they are operating) (Hall and Gingerich, 2009). Dibben and Williams (2012) argue for a third VOC, that of an *informally dominated market economy*, pointing out that informal employment, as a contemporary and prominent feature of the global economy, is widespread, citing an OECD report showing that out of a global working population of 3 billion, around two-thirds (1.8 billion) work in the informal sector. Wailes et al. (2020: 18) suggest that the VOC approach to international employment relations analysis, although limited, provides a 'promising framework' within which to explore different national and international systems and approaches.

Trade Unions

In the last few decades unions have experienced drops in membership density, restrictions placed on their ability for taking controversial, sometimes provocative, action and diminished power resulting from the decentralisation of collective bargaining coupled with governments' austerity policies (Kelly, 2015; Lehndorff et al., 2017). Organisational factors, found within different national contexts, sectoral contexts and trade unions' resources, all constrain activities and have an impact on how effectively unions can operate and the strategies they adopt in order to achieve their aims. Hyman (2001) distinguished between three different types of union: social partnership, class and business based, depending on the context in which they were operating. However further contextual analysis is necessary when making comparisons. There are three broad ways of looking at (and analysing) the ways in which trade unions strategically undertake their work, ensuring they maintain high levels of both membership and influence. These different approaches are important when taking into account the contexts within which unions are operating, particularly if different activities are being compared. Firstly, following Murray (2017) and Frege and Kelly, 2004, there is the '**varieties of unionism**' (VOU) approach (similar to the 'varieties of capitalism' perspective propounded by Hall and Soskice). Each of these two perspectives (VOU and VOC) suggests that analogous institutional conditions lead to parallel strategic responses from the relevant parties. Unions look for, and invest time in, those strategies that promise the most suitable fit with the types of institutional contexts within which they are operating. Consequently, institutionally strong unions endeavour to gain advantage by relying on collective bargaining to embed themselves within appropriate institutions; institutionally weak unions on the other hand attempt to improve their political power via rank-and-file activism. As Frege and Kelly point out (2004: 6–7) there are differences 'between labour movements that focus revitalization efforts on mobilization, and those that focus on institutional position'.

The second approach looks at the ways in which unions have reacted to the impact of increasing employer control under neoliberalism (Clawson, 2003; Milkman, 2013; Voss and Sherman, 2000) and is known as **'social movement unionism'** (SMU). Here unions consciously begin to fight injustice, mobilising their resources against unacceptable terms and conditions (Baccaro and Howell, 2011; Dörre et al., 2009; Ibsen and Tapia, 2017). Often their success is due to their combining with other like-minded social groupings such as community, welfare or faith groups. In the UK this was evident where unions, faith groups and local communities combined to fight for the London Living Wage. The SMU approach is evident not just in anti-union environments, such as the US, but also where unions are regarded in a more favourable light such as in Germany and parts of Central and Eastern Europe (Bernaciak and Kahancovà, 2017; Ost, 2011).

The third perspective is one of pragmatically converging divergence as it integrates the two previous approaches, suggesting that conscious and invigorated union activity occurs when unions act as both institutions in their own rights and as socially mobilising movements. Heery exemplifies this dual approach with his argument that the labour movement in the USA, 'is handicapped by a weak institutional inheritance and needs not just to reverse the decline but to create new institutions, including new forms of unionism' (2001: 307).

Care needs to be taken however as there are exceptions to these three broad distinctions. Exceptions to the rule are not uncommon. Gasparri et al. (2019) looked at trade union strategies in the fashion retail industry and discovered that in the US, neoliberal employers, with a propensity to exploit labour, engendered a union strategy of institution building; conversely in Italy with its more institutional approach, the unions evolved a strategy based on grass roots **mobilisation**.

News Flash 2.6

Secretly Group Union

In the USA, the indie-music company Secretly has recently recognised the newly formed Secretly Group Union, bucking the industry trend. Here, in order to address the exploitation endemic in the creative industries, the employees mobilised to form a union which has now gained recognition. In a statement the employer said,

> Just as we work to empower our artist and label partners, we want to empower our employees: collaboratively, openly, in full recognition of our competing priorities and our shared goals ... More to the point, our employees have taken this progressive step to empower themselves in partnership with us. We applaud this effort and we welcome this renewed opportunity for that partnership ... we are also confident that this is a positive step for our company and the industry writ large, and it is with this in mind that we look forward to recognition and collective bargaining with the Secretly Group Union.

Source: Kelly, 2021

It is within the context of globalisation and that of the varieties of capitalism and unionism, that analysis of the employment relationship occurs. When evaluating and comparing particular ER arrangements it is imperative, in order to make sense of the similarities and differences that, where appropriate, we look at, and contrast, the national, international, multinational and sectorial influences and variations, noting parallels, connections and disparities – and these, of course, may well change over time. National differences that are crucially important in one decade may well be less so in future decades. For example, if we look at a comparison of wage rates, one can see that in the last quarter of a century there has been *increasing* earnings inequality among both LME and CME countries such as the US, and Denmark respectively, while places like Ireland and the UK have seen *diminishing* earnings inequality. Yet these results do not readily fit with the VOC patterns where one would expect to see – as was evident in the half century prior to this – managerial prerogative under LMEs facilitating increasing wage inequality and collective responses to wages within CME areas, showing a decline in wage inequality (Baccaro and Pontusson, 2016). It is essential therefore to put any evaluation of different employment relations systems into context and to be mindful of the differences – are these cultural, structural, philosophical, or down to the production processes themselves? It is only by such vigilance that meaningful evaluation and comparison can be made.

News Flash 2.7

Global Campaign to Protect Workers in Garment Factories

A worldwide day of action, organised by the IndustriALL global union on 4 September 2020, demanded an end to union-busting activities in the textile and garment industries; for example, four workers in Cambodia were recently fired after they organised a union at Greenfield Industry which produces garments for Irish retailer Dunnes Stores.

According to UNI Global Union, which also supported the campaign, there has been a rise in activities such as harassing union organisers and threatening to sack workers who are also trade union members.

UNI General Secretary, Christy Hoffman, said that brands (including Adidas, Gap, H&M, M&S and Walmart), 'need to take off their blinkers and recognise there is a union-busting problem at many of their suppliers [where they have] the power to influence and improve conditions'.

Sources: www.uniglobalunion.org/news/4-september-global-action-day-stop-union-busting-garment-sector; www.industriall-union.org/global-day-of-action-on-4-september-to-end-union-busting-in-the-textile-industry

Case Study 2.3

An International ER Manager, Remy Ligeika, Reflects on His Role

Being an ER Manager in a multinational organisation means providing services 24/7. It's a unique role within the HR function where one must balance the business's needs and, at the same time, act as an employee champion. My current organisation operates in about 40 countries, so naturally,

(Continued)

the ER team must keep a close eye on any incoming queries from all over the world. The geographical structure allows the team members to support assigned locations, and we always have strong links with senior managers and legal counsel. This is to ensure that our responses are legally compliant for whichever country we are operating in as well as consistent across all business units.

My typical day always begins with catching up with colleagues' queries based on different time zones and finishes with a heavy project-based workload. But, because the job involves international experience, it's always about dealing with matters that I haven't seen before. So, it's a lot more about research and transferrable skills rather than actual technical knowledge. However, I think three reappearing themes significantly affect ER policy beyond borders: power, local regulations, and employee voice.

Power and authority

One of the exciting things I've observed over time is how employees connect with, and show trust in, their organisation and leadership. It stems from a natural human susceptibility to working out where power is coming from. For example, when the central management decisions originated from the UK, the rest of the global workforce resisted and demanded local practices to be followed. This was seen when the US staff insisted on finishing Fridays early because that's how things are done on Wall Street. Reflecting on that situation now, I can see that for the US colleagues, 'work hard, play hard' seemed to be a deal-breaker. They fought for what they considered to be an acceptable practice.

Likewise, as soon as the power moved to the USA, employees in the UK asked to elect local leadership to address cultural differences. On this occasion, the UK-based employees challenged the lack of consultation. They complained that all new initiatives were American-centric, causing overall job intensification. A consequence of this insensitive managerial approach affected their psychological contracts and impacted staff motivation and engagement. As the ER Manager, you get involved in change management projects, where people do anything to show their resistance and opposition. This is the case not only for employees but managers and even HR colleagues too!

Fortunately, I have the opportunity to see a variety of managerial styles and witness how different styles affect employees' cooperation, compliance, and productivity. People are swift to recognise when managers start to act as 'masters', bringing new ideas and attempting to change the 'normal'. Therefore, my job is to advise and guide both managers and employees through these transitions. The change can be achieved in many ways but often involves drafting a new policy or going through information and consultation. A good example here could be the Global Leave of Absence policy, necessitating harmonisation of time-off entitlements in different business units. It takes a lot of time and effort to bring the majority to consent without being overly coercive, so people understand the need to change and accept it.

Local and national practices

In the ideal world, I wish we had a set of global work practices playbook. However, when it comes to managing employment internationally, it's tough to navigate complex local and national labour laws, work practices, cultural norms, and foreign languages. Understandably, it's not feasible to have ER resources in all locations, so I always try to learn more about every country where the business operates. Some countries, like Singapore, are clear on what good employers need to do to ensure compliance is in place; however, others such as Germany and France have complex regulatory labour frameworks. You also learn about countries like the USA – although they have 'employment-at-will', there are many unique local and state regulations. Nothing is ever easy or straightforward; it takes time to understand philosophical and practical differences. To illustrate the contrasting systems, a dismissal procedure could be looked at at a national level:

- Under **German** labour law, employment terminations are severely restricted. There are multiple legal procedural steps to ensure employers act appropriately, such as consultation with works councils, provision of written notice to employees (oral notices and emails are invalid), lengthy statutory notice periods, and restrictions around who can sign-off letters on behalf of the employer. After a six-month probation period, an employer can only initiate employment termination based on three reasons: personal (e.g., illness), conduct, or operational justifications. Also, special employee categories have additional protections, such as disabled workers, pregnant women, employees on maternity leave, and works council members. As the laws in Germany governing dismissals are very descriptive, it leaves little room for employer's interpretations. Therefore, this results in negotiating directly with an employee and attempting to settle on mutually acceptable terms to end employment. This means that any employer-proposed changes, including dismissals, go through a thorough consultation process with both workers' representatives and employees directly.
- When it comes to dismissal reasons and procedures in **Singapore**, a common law is at the centre. Here, it's imperative to follow what is spelt out in actual terms and conditions. Employers must adhere to anything that was agreed in contractual terms, both expressed and implied, as long as the agreed provisions are equal to or above the minimum detailed in the Employment Act. So, it's relatively risk-free to end employment without cause if that is what the contract allows. Of course, employers need to be mindful and ensure dismissals aren't based on age, race, gender, religion, marital status, family responsibilities, or disability. Although Singaporean labour law is more 'employer friendly' compared to continental European countries, the legislators have been gradually increasing workers' protections. There are severe penalties for businesses that are found to have breached the Employment Act.
- Finally, the **US** is well-known for the 'employment-at-will' provision, which means employment can be terminated at any time without any reason, explanation, or warning. This provides enormous power to employers, reducing the risk of being sued by disobedient or rebellious employees. As in most other countries, federal anti-discrimination provisions apply; therefore, dismissal may be litigated if an employee suspects unfavourable treatment because of age, disability, genetic information, national origin, pregnancy, race or skin colour, religion, or sex. However, it's worth noting that there are vast differences between progressive and Southern states on how much protection employees receive. Shockingly, some states prevent employees from forming unions that might be supportive during the dismissal process, or, for example, employers aren't required to pay accrued but untaken annual leave on termination.

These substantial variations between cultural norms, legislation and benefits create a degree of tension between colleagues based in different countries. Because it's the same company, people would like to be given equal treatment and be subject to the same practices and policies, yet the domestic provisions often supersede. As such, it isn't easy to ensure equity for employees globally. A good example could be maternity leave provisions, where some countries offer, e.g., 32 weeks of fully paid leave and others only 12 weeks. Consequently, as an ER Manager, I need to make sure people across the board feel there is organisational justice, and the way to do it is to maintain open and transparent policies.

(Continued)

Voice and engagement

Traditional ER is all about employees' participation in the decision-making process. Although the medium of how employee voice reaches management continuously changes, it is even harder to manage it in a multinational firm. Because of local norms, the business needs to accommodate direct versus indirect employee representation. As mentioned before, every new proposal to *standardise* policy or practice often fails because people don't want to be instructed by 'alien' powers, or feel that the new policy is making them worse off.

Overall, it's hard to define international ER due to its ambiguity and application in practical terms. Managing the employment relationship is not a simple process in one country, let alone in a multinational group. This is because people perceive employment very differently in all countries, so one size fits all is never applicable.

Exercise 2.4

Read the following case study about Sodexo and the IUF.

- Using the concepts found in this chapter what can you say about the company and the ways in which it operates?
- Is it possible to compare different situations, in different countries where the same company is involved?
- Explain why you reached your conclusions for each of these questions.

Case Study 2.4

Sodexo Embraces Health and Safety

Sodexo, headquartered in Paris, is a French food services and facilities management company, with 428,237 employees and a presence in 80 different countries. In March 2021 it signed a 'Declaration of Intent on Health and Safety' with the Global food and farming union IUF. The declaration commits the company and the union to regularly review the risks to - and the protection of - workers from both accidents and occupational illnesses. Importantly it encourages ongoing and regular negotiation to implement the appropriate relevant corrective and preventative processes at local and national levels. This is the first of its kind in the industry and builds on the already strong relationship between Sodexo and the IUF. The IUF has a history of successfully negotiating agreements to improve the working lives of the Sodexo employees. Previous agreements include the 2017 joint commitment to preventing sexual harassment and the 2011 international framework agreement on fundamental rights for human beings.

Denis Machuel, chief executive officer for Sodexo Worldwide, said:

> The declaration of intent is a critical step towards collectively restating that ensuring our employees' health and safety is pivotal to everything we do and the way we work at Sodexo. Together with the IUF, we are committed to partner with unions, employee representatives

and clients to raise the bar on health and safety standards and help drive improvements across the industry.

Sue Longley, IUF general secretary, said:

> Health and safety has always been a priority for workers, but the Covid-19 pandemic has underlined its fundamental importance and the need for joint union-management action. This agreement represents a real opportunity for unions to strengthen their representation on safety and health. We will be working with our affiliates to give it life at all levels – local, national and international.

Yet, despite this pro-union rhetoric, Sodexo does not have an unblemished record when it comes to harmonious employment relations. It has had unhappy relationships with unions in both the US and the UK. In America, in the run up to the 2020 Presidential election, the Democrats were hoping to hold a convention meeting at Loyola Marymount University. This looked as though it would be cancelled because 150 workers, employed by Sodexo, threatened strike action in support of their claim for 'liveable' wages and affordable healthcare. The dispute, which had dragged on for months prior to this, was quickly settled following negative national publicity spotlighting Sodexo and pressure from the Democrats. The threatened action at an opportune time, together with public exposure and the Democratic intervention, prompted a change of heart by Sodexo and brought the negotiations to a successful conclusion. Sodexo acceded to the employees' demands and signed a three-year agreement giving the workers a 25% pay increase and reducing their healthcare costs by half. Prior to the deal many of the workers had previously received an hourly rate of less than $15.

In the UK and Ireland, Sodexo's involvement with university catering, providing food for students and university staff at nearly 50 university sites (and 1,600 sites globally) is not always smooth. At the University of London's Birkbeck College, for example, there have been a series of problems between it and Unison, the union representing the catering staff. In 2020 Sodexo announced that it wanted to make half of these staff redundant despite Birkbeck having no plans to reduce the amount of catering on site. According to the union the consultation process had been inadequate. The Unison 'Justice for Workers at Birkbeck' campaign also pointed out that:

> before the pandemic, the workers had received assurances that they would be brought in-house at Birkbeck before the contract with Sodexo ends in 2022, as part of UNISON's campaign to end outsourcing at the college. If this had taken place, they would not be exposed to the vagaries of a profit-hungry multinational corporation but would be firmly part of the Birkbeck community.

Sources: www.iuf.org/news/iuf-and-sodexo-commit-to-safer-workplaces-in-breakthrough-global-declaration/;www.lamag.com/citythinkblog/loyola-marymount-labor-dispute/

Summary

This chapter has shown how analysis of employment relations events is aided by knowledge about the context in which those events happen. There are a number of theoretical tools and concepts that aid the analytical processes. In particular it is helpful to know about the impact that globalisation has on a situation, about the type (or types) of capitalism that is (are) prevalent and whether or not the events being analysed are undertaken in a collective or individual setting. Multinational companies are influential in standardising processes and aiding the convergence of employment practices, although such convergence is influenced by culture, history, and individual state legislation. How labour is used and the effects of shifting labour patterns, including migration from one state to another, impact the employment relationship.

Review Questions

1   Do you think that the convergence of employment practices and processes is inevitable? Why did you reach this conclusion?
2   Is the accurate and meaningful comparison between different systems of employment relations achievable? Why did you reach this conclusion?
3   Are the different ways in which capitalism varies useful when analysing the employment relationship? Why did you reach this conclusion?
4   In what way might the adherence to neoliberal perspectives hinder trade union activity? Why did you reach this conclusion?

Revision Exercise 2.1

In the context of the employment relationship explain the following terms, giving at least one example for each term:

- Informally dominated market economy
- Human capital
- Coordinated market economies
- Academic ethnocentrism
- Divergence
- Liberal market economies
- Globalisation

Relevant Articles for Further Reading

Benassi, C., Dorigatti, L. and Pannini, E. (2019) 'Explaining divergent bargaining outcomes for agency workers: The role of labour divides and labour market reforms', *European Journal of Industrial Relations*, 25(2): 163–79.

Cross-national comparisons are, as we have seen, difficult, but this article successfully looks at the ways in which unions in the German and Italian metal sector reacted to precarious employment. Highlighting the different approaches taken to similar problems it examines the interaction between the trade unions' institutional and associational power resources and shows how these are affected both by employers' divide-and-rule strategies as well as by the unions' rebuilding strategies.

Lakhani, T., Kuruvilla, S. and Avgar, A. (2013) 'From the firm to the network: Global value chains and employment relations theory', *British Journal of Industrial Relations*, 51(3): 440–72.

This article is interesting because it develops a framework explicitly addressing the employment relations' implications of the connections within and between firms in the global economy. The authors argue that different value chain configurations will give rise to different employment relations patterns.

References

Akhtar, S., Ding, D. Z., and Ge, G. (2008) 'Strategic HRM practices and their impact on company performance in Chinese enterprises', *Human Resource Management*, 47(1): 15–32. doi:10.1002/hrm.20195

Aliaga, A. O. (2001) *'Human capital HRD and the knowledge organisation'*, in A. O. Aliaga, Academy of Human Resource Development 2001 Conference Proceedings. Baton Rouge, LA: AHRD, pp. 427–34.

Amoore, L. (2002) *Globalisation Contested: An International Political Economy of Work*. Manchester: Manchester University Press.

Andersson, L. F., Eriksson, R. and Scocco, S. (2019) 'Refugee immigration and the growth of low-wage work in the EU15', *Comparative Migration Studies*, 7(1): 1–19.

Autor, D. H. and Dorn, D. (2013) 'The growth of low-skill service jobs and the polarization of the US labor market', *American Economic Review*, 103(5): 1553–97.

Baccaro, L. and Howell, C. (2011) 'A common neoliberal trajectory: The transformation of industrial relations in advanced capitalism', *Politics & Society*, 39(4): 521–63.

Baccaro, L. and Howell, C. (2017) *Trajectories of Neoliberal Transformation: European Industrial Relations Since the 1970s*. Cambridge: Cambridge University Press.

Baccaro, L. and Pontusson, J. (2016) 'Rethinking comparative political economy: The growth model perspective', *Politics & Society*, 44: 175–207.

Barnet, R. J. and Muller, R. E. (1974) *Global Reach: The Power of the Multinational Corporations*. London: Jonathan Cape.

Barney, J. (1991) 'Firm resources and sustained competitive advantage', *Journal of Management*, 17(1): 99–120.

Batt, R. (2018) 'The financial model of the firm, the "future of work", and employment relations', in A. Wilkinson, T. Dundon, J. Donaghey, A. J. S. Colvin (eds), *The Routledge Companion to Employment Relations*. London: Routledge, pp. 465–79.

Becker, G. S. (1962) 'Investment in human capital: A theoretical analysis', *Journal of Political Economy*, 70 (5): 9–49.

Bernaciak, M. and Kahancovà, M. (2017) *Innovative Union Practices in Central-Eastern Europe*. Brussels: ETUI.

Brady, D., Fullerton, A. and Moren Cross, J. (2009) 'Putting poverty in political context: A multi-level analysis of adult poverty across 18 affluent democracies', *Social Forces*, 88: 271–99.

Brown, P., Lauder, H. and Cheung, S. Y. (2020) *The Death of Human Capital?: Its Failed Promise and How to Renew it in an Age of Disruption.* Oxford: Oxford University Press.

Centre for Economics and Business Research (CEBR) (2020) *World Economic League Table 2021: A World Economic League Table with Forecasts for 193 Countries to 2035.* Available at: https://cebr.com/wp-content/uploads/2020/12/WELT-2021-final-29.12.pdf (accessed 5 March 2021).

Clawson, D. (2003) *The Next Upsurge: Labor and the New Social Movements.* Ithaca, NY: Cornell University Press.

Crush, P. (2021) 'Volvo unveils global paid parental leave policy', *Personnel Today*, 1 April. Available at: www.personneltoday.com/hr/volvo-unveils-global-paid-parental-leave-policy/?ID=zzrzf~qthrqj~n9hxj~W4ik~Ky0gk&utm_campaign=PTELD-PT-AWARDS-090421-DE&utm_medium=email&utm_source=newsletter&utm_content=newsletter (accessed 9 April 2021).

Cushen, J. and Thompson, P. (2016) 'Financialization and value: Why labour and the labour process still matter', *Work, Employment and Society*, 30(2): 352–65.

Dalton, K. and Bingham, C. (2017) 'A social institutionalist perspective on HR diffusion: Historical and cultural receptivity to HRM in a post-communist context', *The International Journal of Human Resource Management*, 28(6): 825–51.

Della Porta, D. and Portos, M. (2020) 'Social movements in times of inequalities: Struggling against austerity in Europe', *Structural Change and Economic Dynamics*, 53: 116–26.

Dibben, P. and Williams, C. C. (2012) 'Varieties of capitalism and employment relations: Informally dominated market economies', *Industrial Relations: A Journal of Economy and Society*, 51: 563–82.

Dicken, P. (2015) *Global Shift: Mapping the Changing Contours of the World Economy* (7th edn). New York: Guilford Press.

Donaghey, J., Reinecke, J., Niforou, C. and Lawson, B. (2014) 'From employment relations to consumption relations: Balancing labor governance in global supply chains', *Human Resource Management*, 2(53): 229–52.

Dörre, K., Holst, H. and Nachtwey, O. (2009) 'Organizing: A strategic option for trade union renewal?', *International Journal of Action Research*, 5(1): 33–67.

Dunlop J. (1958) *Industrial Relations Systems.* New York: Henry Holt.

Eurostat (2020) *Impact of COVID-19 on Employment Income: Advanced Estimates.* Available at: https://ec.europa.eu/eurostat/statistics-explained/index.php?title=Impact_of_COVID-19_on_employment_income_-_advanced_estimates#E2.80.A6and_skewed_towards_the_left_of_the_distribution_with_low_wage_earners_having_losses_3_to_6_times_larger_for_half_of_the_countries (accessed 11 March 2021).

Fitzgerald, I. and Hardy, J. (2008) *Cross Border Trade Union Collaboration in the Context of Competition and Arbitraging Labour in an Enlarged Europe.* Available at: https://researchportal.northumbria.ac.uk/en/publications/cross-border-trade-union-collaboration-in-the-context-of-competit (accessed 5 January 2021).

Frege, C. and Kelly, J. (eds) (2020) *Comparative Employment Relations in the Global Economy* (2nd edn). London: Routledge.

Frege, C., Kelly, J. and Kelly, J.E. (eds) (2004) *Varieties of unionism: Strategies for union revitalization in a globalizing economy.* Oxford: Oxford University Press on Demand.

Gasparri S., Ikeler P. and Fullin, G. (2019) 'Trade union strategy in fashion retail in Italy and the USA: Converging divergence between institutions and mobilization?', *European Journal of Industrial Relations*, 25(4): 345–61.

Gittell, J. and Bamber, G. (2011) 'High- and low-road strategies for competing on costs and their implications for employment relations: International studies in the airline industry', *The International Journal of Human Resource Management*, 21: 165–79.

Hall, P. and Gingerich, D. (2009) 'Varieties of capitalism and institutional complementarities in the political economy', *British Journal of Political Science*, 39(3): 449–82.

Hall, P. A. and Soskice, D. (eds) (2001) *Varieties of Capitalism: The Institutional Foundations of Comparative Advantage*. New York: Oxford University Press.

Heery, E. (2001) 'Learning from each other: A European perspective on American labor', *Journal of Labor Research*, 22(2): 307–19.

Heintz, J. and Razavi, S. (2015) *Social Policy and Employment: Rebuilding the Connections*. Available at: http://unrisd01.bsky.net/UNRISD/website/document.nsf/ (httpPublications)/7BF762F250A4C055C1257AE200307048?OpenDocument (accessed 11 August 2022).

Howell, C. (2021). Rethinking the role of the state in employment relations for a neoliberal era. *ILR Review*, 74(3), 739-772.

Hyman, R. (2001) *Understanding European Trade Unionism: Between Market, Class and Society*. London: Sage.

Hyman, R. (2004) 'Is industrial relations theory always ethnocentric?', in B. Kaufman (ed.), *Theoretical Perspectives on Work and the Employment Relationship*. Champaign, IL: IRRA, pp. 265–92.

Ibsen, C. and Tapia, M. (2017) 'Trade union revitalisation: Where are we now? Where to next?', *Journal of Industrial Relations*, 59(2): 170–91.

International Labour Organisation (ILO) (2020) *Seasonal Migrant Workers' Schemes: Rethinking Fundamental Principles and Mechanisms in light of COVID-19*. Available at: www.ilo.org/wcmsp5/groups/public/---ed_protect/---protrav/---migrant/documents/publication/wcms_745481.pdf (accessed 26 February 2021).

Kaufmann, C. (2008). ILO, Declaration on Social Justice for a Fair Globalization. *ILO* Available at: www.ivr.uzh.ch/institutsmitglieder/kaufmann/archives/fs13/iel/text46.pdf (accessed 21 October 2022)

Kelly, J. (2015) 'Trade union membership and power in comparative perspective', *Economic and Labour Relations Review*, 26(4): 526–44.

Kelly, K. (March 25, 2021) 'Secretly Group: Workers at indie-music company begin efforts to unionize', *Rolling Stone*, 25 March. Available at: www.rollingstone.com/pro/news/secretly-group-union-employees-1145334/ (accessed 5 April 2021).

Lakhani, T., Kuruvilla, S. and Avgar, A. (2013) 'From the firm to the network: Global value chains and employment relations theory', *British Journal of Industrial Relations*, 51(3): 440–72.

Lehndorff, S., Dribbusch, H. and Schulten, T. (2017) 'European trade unions in a time of crises: An overview', in S. Lehndorff, H. Dribbusch and T. Schulten (eds), *Rough Waters: European Trade Unions in a Time of Crises*. Brussels: ETUI, pp. 7–35.

Macdonald, D. (2019) *Under-employment: A Crisis Hangover, or Something More?, OECD Social, Employment and Migration Working Papers*. Available at: www.oecd-ilibrary.org/social-issues-migration-health/under-employment_47123848-en (accessed 1 March 2021).

McCulloch, A. (2022) 'Dyson faces supply chain labour abuse claim', *Personnel Today*, 11 February. Available at: www.personneltoday.com/hr/dyson-faces-supply-chain-labour-abuse-claim/ (accessed 4 May 2022).

Milkman, R. (2013) 'Back to the future? US labour in the new gilded age', *British Journal of Industrial Relations*, 51(4): 645–65.

Murray, G. (2017). Union renewal: what can we learn from three decades of research?. *Transfer: European Review of Labour and Research*, 23(1), 9-29.

Narwan, G. (2021) 'Unilever promises living wage to its supply chain', *The Times*, 21 January Available at: www.thetimes.co.uk/article/unilever-promises-living-wage-to-its-supply-chain-98jlr57kp#:~:text=Millions%20of%20people%20around%20the,the%20living%20wage%20by%202030 (accessed 7 March 2021).

North, D. (1991) 'Institutions', *Journal of Economic Perspectives*, 5(1): 97–112.

Ost, D. (2011) '"Illusory corporatism" ten years later', *Warsaw Forum of Economic Sociology*, 2:1(3): 19–49.

Peetz, D. (2010) 'Are individualistic attitudes killing collectivism?', *Transfer: European Review of Labour and Research*, 16(3): 383–98.

Reiche, B. S. and Minbaeva, D. (2019) 'HRM in multinational companies', in A. Wilkinson, N. Bacon, S. Snell and D. Lepak (eds), *The SAGE Handbook of Human Resource Management*. London: Sage, pp. 541–56.

Richards, J. and Sang, K. (2019) 'Socially responsible human resource management? Conceptualising HRM practice and philosophy in relation to in-work poverty in the UK', *The International Journal of Human Resource Management*, 32(10): 2185–212.

Rubery, J. (ed.) (1988) *Women and Recession*. London: Routledge and Kegan Paul.

Rubery, J. (2007) 'Developing segmentation theory: A thirty years perspective', *Economies et Sociétés*, 41(6): 941–64.

Schultz, T.W. (1961) 'Investment in human capital', *American Economic Review*, 51: 1–17.

Standing, G. (2011) *The Precariat: The New Dangerous Class*. London: Bloomsbury.

Statista Research Department (2021) *GDP Growth Rate of the World's Seven Largest Economies as of 3rd Quarter of 2020, by Country*. Available at: www.statista.com/statistics/1207780/gdp-growth-rate-of-the-world-s-seven-largest-economies-by-country/ (accessed 5 March 2021).

Steger, M. B. (2017) *Globalization: A Very Short Introduction* (4th edn). Oxford: Oxford University Press.

Streeck, W. (2016) *How Will Capitalism End?: Essays on a Failing System*. London: Verso Books.

Tayfur, O. (2013). Convergence or Divergence? Evaluation of Human Resource Practices in Turkey. *Journal of Economics and Behavioral Studies*, 5(9), pp. 625-638. https://doi.org/10.22610/jebs.v5i9.436

Todeschini, M. M. (2011). "Webs of engagement": Managerial responsibility in a Japanese company. *Journal of Business Ethics*, 101(1), 45-59.

Trewhela, L. (2021) 'World's largest daffodil farm letting flowers rot in fields because of Brexit', *Wales Online*, 24 February. Available at: www.walesonline.co.uk/news/wales-news/worlds-largest-daffodil-farm-letting-19905422 (accessed 6 March 2021).

Unilever (2021) *Unilever Commits to Help Build a More Inclusive Society*, press release. Available at: www.unilever.com/news/press-releases/2021/unilever-commits-to-help-build-a-more-inclusive-society.html (accessed 7 March 2021).

Volvo Cars (2021) *Volvo Cars Family Bond gives all Employees 24 Weeks Paid Parental Leave*, press release, 3 March. Available at: www.media.volvocars.com/global/en-gb/media/pressreleases/280244/volvo-cars-family-bond-gives-all-employees-24-weeks-paid-parental-leave (accessed 9 April 2021).

Voss, K. and Sherman, R. (2000) 'Breaking the iron law of oligarchy: Union revitalization in the American labor movement', *American Journal of Sociology*, 106(2): 303–49.

Wailes, N., Wright, C. F., Bamber, G. J. and Lansbury, R. D. (2020) 'Introduction: An internationally comparative approach to employment relations', in R. D. Lansbury, G. J. Bamber and N. Wailes (eds), *International and Comparative Employment Relations: National Regulation, Global Changes*. London: Routledge.

Webber, A. (2021) 'Unilever to require all suppliers to pay living wage', *Personnel Today*, 21 January. Available at: www.personneltoday.com/hr/unilever-to-require-all-suppliers-to-pay-living-wage/ (accessed 7 March 2021).

Wills, J. and Linneker, B. (2014) 'In-work poverty and the living wage in the United Kingdom: A geographical perspective', *Transactions of the Institute of British Geographers*, 39: 182–94.

Xiao, Q. and Cooke, F. L. (2020) 'Towards a hybrid model? A systematic review of human resource management research on Chinese state-owned enterprises (1993–2017)', *The International Journal of Human Resource Management*, 31(1): 47–89.

Xu, V. X., Cave, D., Leibold, J., Munro, K. and Ruser, N. (2020) *Uyghurs for Sale: 'Re-education', Forced Labour and Surveillance Beyond Xinjiang*. Canberra: Australian Strategic Policy Institute.

Zorzut, A. (2021) 'World's largest daffodil farm forced to let flowers rot in fields due to Brexit staffing issues', *The New European*. Available at: www.theneweuropean.co.uk/brexit-news/westminster-news/varfell-farm-radio-4-brexit-issues-daffodils-7657614 (accessed 6 March 2021).

3

TRUST AND GETTING A FAIR DEAL AT WORK

Learning Outcomes

By the end of this chapter, you should be able to:

- evaluate the nature of trust at work and analyse its importance for the employment relationship
- provide an overview of the different aspects of organisational justice
- critically analyse the psychological contract
- assess the impact of power realities on the degree of trust and the perceptions of fairness within the employment relationship.

What to Expect

This chapter explores the impact that levels of employee trust and perceptions of fairness have on the employment relationship. It examines the behavioural implications that high and low levels of trust have on workplace behaviours. Theoretical explanations and the associated evidence behind the employee/employer trust relationship, including **social exchange theory**, **organisational justice** and the **psychological contract** are addressed.

Trust at Work

Where employees perceive the employment relationship to be fair, they are more likely to trust the employer. Trust is not only something that an employee invests in the employer, employers too exhibit different degrees of trust in their employees – and importantly the *perceptions* of whether or not they are trusted by an employer have an impact upon employees' attitudes, behaviour and performance and therefore on the overall employment relationship.

Trust is a crucial element within the employment relationship. Lewis and Weigert point out that 'when we see others acting in ways that imply that they trust us, we become more disposed to reciprocate by trusting them more. Conversely we come to distrust those whose actions appear to violate our trust or to distrust us' (1985: 971). Trust within the employment relationship is an important element in determining how employees behave – greater levels of trust result in higher workplace commitment. Where employees trust their employers they perform tasks more willingly and are more cooperative; where trust is absent employees may have to be coerced to undertake their normal employment tasks. Sometimes, especially when transient work projects require people who are new to one another to mix, trust needs to be established early on. Such 'swift trust' is often established on the basis of known qualifications and experience. Here individuals are trusted (until events might prove otherwise) because of the role they undertake and their presumed levels of expertise (Kroeger et al., 2021; Meyerson et al., 1996). Managers who are perceived by their subordinates to be fair and supportive tend to have fewer (and less severe) workplace incidents of employee misbehaviour (Everton et al., 2007). This finding indicates the importance of perception. Managers who want to encourage their teams to perform to the best of their abilities should behave in ways that ensure their subordinates feel respected and treated fairly, thereby promoting affective commitment to the work processes and to the employing organisation (Allen and Meyer, 1997; Innocenti et al., 2011; Safari et al., 2020). Trust is not just engendered by face-to-face interactions; it can also be fostered (or indeed diminished) by the ways in which organisations use (or abuse) technology. Iqbal et al. found that 'technology-enabled HRM supports organisations by enhancing organisational trust and productivity outcomes' (2019: 879).

Lewicki and Benedict Bunker (1996) suggest that there are degrees of trust; trust in one's co-workers apparently grows as one becomes more familiar with them. The first stage in trust development they call '**calculus-based trust**'. Here individuals analyse one another's behaviour to establish levels of trust and any negative events detrimentally influence burgeoning feelings of trust. The second more stable stage occurs when individuals have a greater familiarity with one another and can predict and anticipate behaviours. They call this '**knowledge-based trust**' and it is less easily influenced by minor negative events occurring in their working environment. The third stage they label '**identification-based trust**'. Here the individuals identify with one another's intentions and have developed complete mutual understanding and trust one another.

The development and subsequent maintaining of levels of trust between those employed and their employer, require a degree of congruence between the values promoted by the organisation and the adherence to these values in practice. That is to say, as Avolio and Walumbwa point out (2006), the management within an organisation has to actually behave in ways that match its words and statements of intent. So, if for example a company website claims that the organisation values diversity, then the employees will expect this to be the case and to be treated accordingly. This is borne out by the work of Macey et al. who, in 2009, suggested that in order for employees to be engaged at work it is essential for them to trust their employer – because trust and fairness are, they say, the foundation behind employees feeling and acting in an engaged way. Those managers who fail to inspire trust because of their unfair or inconsistent practices are likely therefore to have a disengaged workforce that may 'misbehave' in disrespectful and/or subversive ways. Such behaviour was evidenced by Kate Mulholland (2004: 716) when she examined workplace resistance in an Irish call centre where she discovered that managerial responses 'considered to be disproportionate and arbitrary' by their subordinates exacerbated antagonistic responses from the workforce including ways in which to cheat the employer, such as logging 'fake' sales, increased absenteeism and sickness as well as a predisposition towards leaving work before the official end of a shift. None of these resulting negative behaviours improved the employment relationship, nor indeed were the levels of workplace productivity enhanced. A study of 575 French public sector workers by Neveu and Kakavand (2019) found a direct link between corrupt behaviour (such as accepting bribes) and perceptions of being treated unfairly.

Hughes and Bozionelos too found levels of worker resistance when they studied male bus drivers and their perceptions of a poor **work–life balance** stemming from managerial unfairness. Such perceptions of unfairness led, on occasions, to feigned sickness:

> Work–life imbalance relates not only to job turnover and genuine sick leave, but also to absence from work due to faked illness. And this is certainly an area of importance for organisations and managers. It also emerged that work–life balance issues can be a source of negative attitudes towards the management of the company. … In turn, the perceived lack of management willingness to consider work–life balance and to accommodate even minimal pertinent requests, as well as their perceived lack of ability to exert influence upwards, seemed to seriously undermine drivers' morale and organisational commitment. This is corroborated by the job turnover rate in the company, which runs at three times the rate in the sector it belongs to. (2007: 151)

Indeed perceptions of unfairness and/or untrustworthiness sometimes lead to employees disengaging with the work process – with the associated tendency to lower their performance and become less productive or leave the organisation altogether (Duan et al., 2010; Reyhanoglu and Akin, 2020). Disengaged behaviour can lead to increased levels of conflict influencing the ways in which the employment relationship is managed. Poor trust can lead to a downward spiralling of employee–employer interactions that have subsequent repeated negative influences on the employment relationship. Searle and Rice found that when employees *perceive* promises to have been broken, it reduces the overall trustworthiness they have for their employing organisation. This then,

> changes the explanations employees make for events that have occurred in the past, those in the present and for the future. Consequently, individuals become more cynical towards the organisation … This cynicism then triggers their moral disengagement towards work tasks and work colleagues; individuals who morally disengage from their

work environment identify less with their role and organisation, which lowers their organisational citizenship behaviours. [… Some] individuals can retaliate through uncivil behaviours, such as anti-social behaviour and aggression, and through passive responses such as withdrawal of cooperation and depleted investment in resources. (2018: 9)

Case Snippet 3.1

Redressing the Balance

Cheating the employer, or 'redressing the balance', within the workplace environment when something has been done to diminish employee trust can range from minor acts of grumbling to more obvious acts of insubordination through to leaving the organisation. Karen Wollard provides a number of graphic examples of such employee behaviour including that of an elderly woman employee with 20 years of seemingly faithful employment for a jewellery company being handcuffed after nearly half a million dollars in jewellery was found in shoeboxes under her bed, in her closet, and buried in her backyard. When questioned, she told security that every time her manager was mean to her, … she would pocket 'a little something', and then put it in the shoeboxes. This store had fired several managers and associates over the years due to the persistent inventory shortages, but no one had ever dreamed that the real culprit was one elderly and seemingly loyal employee (Wollard, 2011: 527).

Trust, as noted earlier, is a concept that can be viewed from the perspective of the employee *and* from that of the employer. Tzafrir (2005) looked at 104 HR managers in leading Israeli companies and found that HR managers were more likely to offer training to subordinates where levels of trust were high. Similarly, and unsurprisingly, he found that internal systems for promotion were also linked to higher levels of trust – as were higher levels of organisational performance. In his work with Dolan (Tzafrir and Dolan, 2004), albeit from a rather unitarist perspective, he points out that within the employment relationship trust is three dimensional, comprising harmony, reliability and concern. Here **harmony** represents a collective identity and a set of values shared by those within the workforce, while **reliability** is an indication that employees can expect management to show consistency between what it says it is going to do and what it actually does, whereas **concern** is where there is evidence of self-interest being balanced against the interest of another.

Exercise 3.1

- Which of Lewicki and Benedict Bunker's three different sorts of trust is in evidence in the following case study?
- Identify the areas in the case study below where Tzafrir and Dolan's notions of harmony, reliability and concern might be missing.

Victim Support (Northern Ireland) is a charity that was set up in 1981 to provide practical and emotional assistance to people affected by any type of crime. It receives around £2m a year from Stormont's Department of Justice. In 2014 members of staff complained that the chief executive, Susan Reid, who had been employed by the charity for 10 years, was expecting too much of them at work – she had, it was claimed, created an atmosphere of fear where bullying was the norm and unreasonable and unfair demands were frequently placed on the staff. Following the resignation of an employee, Tony Barkley, who emailed the charity's board of trustees about her alleged unprofessional behaviour, an investigation was undertaken and Reid's **contract of employment** terminated. She took the case to a tribunal. During the hearing in 2015 it became apparent from the evidence of those employed by the charity that Reid had exhibited a combative management style, sometimes using the phrase 'FIFO' ('Fit in or f*** off') and using derogatory language to the employees, referring to one particular member of staff as a 'fat bastard'. On one occasion a staff member complained that while she was outside smoking a cigarette someone had spat on her shoe, to which Reid had allegedly responded that it was a sign that she should give up the smoking habit. The case was withdrawn following an out-of-court settlement.

Sources: Rutherford, 2015; Woodhouse, 2015

Fairness and Trust

Whether something is fair or not is, however, in the eye of the beholder. Fairness within the sphere of work is a concept that means different things to different people. Notions of fairness as outcomes of levels of perceived trustworthiness are inevitably subjective and often comparative. Such notions are not static but change over time, so in the UK, for example, types of behaviour that were perceived by many to be fair and acceptable – such as lighting fires under small boys when they were actually working inside chimneys (it speeded them up), to prohibiting female teachers from working once they had married (it kept them at home) – are no longer so.

Perceptions of what is, and what is not, fair are culturally dependent; attitudes are formed by social expectations, but the interpretation of such attitudes in relation to the workplace necessitates judgement – and that judgement is subject to the ways in which an individual interprets and construes a situation. When, for example, does something that is considered to be fair become something that is viewed as exploitative and unfair? An individual's experience at work, coupled with the culture of the workplace, managerial frames of reference and their own values, and expectations will influence the degree to which work colleagues, supervisors and the employer are to be trusted. The consistency with which employees are treated and the workplace regulation imposed, impact here.

News Flash 3.1

Black Men Experience Distrust at Work

Black men feel the least trusted and Black women the least empowered in UK offices according to an Engaging Works survey recording the responses of 10,000 employees.

The results show Black men aged 35-44 feel the least trusted to make decisions in the workplace. They are also the least happy and enjoy their job less. In contrast, white employees feel more positive about their views being heard at work and feel more trusted to make decisions.

Source: McQuaid, 2020

Within some workplace cultures, particularly where the managerial style is hard, managers may well rely on disciplinary measures rather than trust to encourage compliance and commitment. Indeed sometimes the imposition of rules, maybe inconsistently, will have an impact on perceptions of fairness, crucially depending upon whether or not the employees regard the rules as legitimate. As Edwards points out, 'Punishment-centred rules are imposed and the group on whom they are imposed may well feel that they are unfair, and may react by trying to evade them, supporting those who are punished, and questioning their relevance' (1994: 575).

Results from the 2017 UK Skills and Employment Survey, based on face-to-face interviews with workers aged 20 to 60, found, that over one in twenty were very concerned that their working hours could change unexpectedly in terms of duration and/or scheduling. This, the authors say, equates to 1.7 million employees. Many interviewees working insecure hours were anxious about ill treatment, insecure hours, and changes in job status. Trust in an employer in such situations is minimal. According to the 2019 Edelman 'Trust Barometer' (a survey of 33,000 people in 28 countries), one in three people distrust their employer. That trust decreases from the top positions to the lowest: 64% of executives trust their organisations, while 51% of managers and just 48% of other staff stated they trust their organisations. Employees said they trusted their peers more than the CEO and upper-level executives (Edelman, 2019). These findings imply that it is critically important to build organisational trust from the top down. In 2007, Tae-Yeol and Kwok compared cross-cultural reactions about employee perceptions of fairness from America, China, Korea and Japan. The transactional ways in which pay and resources were allocated were seen to be strongly related to perceptions of overall fairness for the Chinese and Koreans. In contrast, the Americans and Japanese were more likely to show perceptions of overall fairness linked to *interpersonal relational behaviours*. Moreover perceptions of overall fairness and trust in the employer had an impact on whether an employee expressed an intention to stay or leave an organisation, with the Americans more likely to say they were going to leave the organisation than the Chinese and Koreans (Tae-Yeol and Kwok, 2007).

The fact that fairness is interpreted in different ways often leads to damaging levels of mistrust and expressions of conflict within organisations and has repercussions for managing the employment relationship.

The notion of structural antagonism (covered in Chapter 1) is important here. As we saw, implicit in the managerial function is the requirement to tell others what to do while simultaneously allowing them sufficient freedom to choose how they undertake their tasks (Edwards, 2003). This contradictory tension between managerial *discretion* and *control* occasionally means that employees feel that the balance between being told what to do and being allowed to make their own decisions is being exercised in an unfair way, leading to perceptions that they feel that those in authority do not trust them. Pressures from globalisation, competition and technology can impact on the workplace in potentially detrimental ways. Sometimes the interminable struggle for perpetually improving efficiency causes a 'drip-feeding' erosion of working conditions. Such performance management has, in some instances, led to lower levels of employee discretion, increasing levels of surveillance and subsequent lack of trust and damaged employment relationships. Yet Thompson and Ackroyd (1995: 629) argue that, despite increasing levels of managerial innovations extending surveillance over employees, employees will continue to devise ways of retaining some control over their own working time.

As we saw in Chapter 1 the employment relationship is *not* one in which the parties involved hold equal amounts of power. The employer is the one who dictates the relationship, setting the terms and conditions of employment. This of course has links to managerial style. Managerial styles impact on the ways in which organisations operate. A hard, traditionalist way of managing is much more authoritarian, allowing minimum employee discretion, implying lower levels of trust in employees, while a softer approach, facilitating wider levels of employee decision making, may, providing it is applied consistently, enhance perceptions of trust and commitment. However, which styles promote and which hinder levels of workplace trust and fairness is open to debate. Can, for example, the unitary style of management, with its blanket denial of dissenting views and an assumption that everyone thinks in the same way, ever be regarded as completely fair? Do employees under such a regime feel trusted? Managerial behaviour, even if unfair, is often regarded as legitimate if it is justified by the pursuit of company goals. The pressure on business is such that a cavalier disregard for workplace justice if not inevitable is certainly a latent possibility. Indeed as Ackers (2001: 386) points out, 'management culture may become a major obstacle to the full realisation of an ethical workplace' particularly when there is a mismatch between the goals of an organisation (profit) and the ethical – sometimes regarded as self-indulgent and unnecessarily costly – treatment of the workforce.

Fairness and the Law

To ensure a modicum of fairness and limit the opportunities for exploitation, the imbalance in power between an employer and an employee is addressed in part, if not redressed, by third-party intervention. Such intervention may come from lobbying bodies but certainly comes from the state, together with the legislation designed to regulate (and in many cases make more equitable) the employment relationship. Statutory intervention is therefore an imperative ingredient in the underpinning of equity within the workplace. Different cultures regard legislating to control the workplace differently. In the UK there was a tradition of voluntarism where the main parties to the employment relationship reached voluntary agreements without any state intervention. The laws, policies and codes that govern the relationship between a workforce and an employer can be:

- prohibitive (e.g., employers cannot treat some employees less well than others because of their ethnicity)
- enabling (e.g., employers and unions have the option of using Acas for **conciliation**)
- instructional (e.g., the minimum wage/the working time directive)
- advisory (e.g., the various Acas codes, such as the code on settlement agreements or the one for time off for union duties).

Perceptions of legislative restrictions are often dependent on an individual's political philosophy. For example, each UK Government, dependent upon its own philosophy, has, since the late 1960s, endeavoured to regulate the employment relationship in different ways – they are not alone. Since the 1980s whenever right wing governments have been in power (for example in the US, Australia or the UK) they have endeavoured to increase employer (and employee) flexibility and strengthen the employers' control of the employment relationship, shifting the balance of power by, for example:

- loosening employment regulations
- removing some wage regulation
- restricting union power.

The perception of fairness is subjective and linked irrevocably to the question 'fairness for whom?'.

Exercise 3.2

- In what ways do you think that some legislative restrictions on employer behaviour, curbing the employers' power to operate unilaterally, were a result of a) employers and b) governments being unconcerned with trust within the employment relationship?
- Why did you come to this conclusion?

Equity, Efficiency and Voice

Budd (2004, 2010) argues that the objectives of the employment relationship should be equity, efficiency and voice, and that a good employment relationship should aim at striking a *balance* between the three (see Figure 3.1). **Efficiency,** or the effective use of scarce resources, is an important objective of the employment relationship because of the clear implications for economic prosperity. However, because work is a human activity, employees are entitled to equitable, fair, treatment together with opportunities to **voice** their opinions and to be listened to by their employer. On the one hand, **equity** is how employees are unilaterally treated by the employer, entailing fairness in both the distribution of economic rewards (e.g., wages) and the management of employment policies (e.g., how work is allocated, how people are promoted/dismissed, etc.). On the other hand, *voice* is the ability to make meaningful employee input into decisions both individually and collectively (e.g., via focus groups, employee surveys, grievance procedures, trade union representation, etc.). Crucially, Budd maintains that equity and voice are critical objectives of the employment relationship, even when they do *not* improve efficiency. What matters therefore is striking a balance between all three of the objectives. Where employees are treated in ways that they perceive to be equitable and fair then the levels of trust in management and commitment to the organisation are correspondingly high.

Exactly where individuals within the same organisation would place themselves within the triangle would depend on their own perceptions, which, of course, will be influenced by their position in the organisation and their type of employment contract – those employed on a temporary basis are likely to have different expectations and experiences within the workplace from those working full-time.

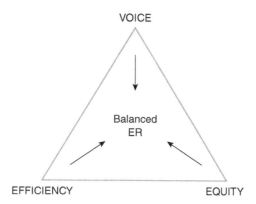

Figure 3.1 The balance between efficiency, equity and voice creates an employment relationship with a human face

Source: Reprinted from *Employment with a Human Face: Balancing Efficiency, Equity and Voice* by John W. Budd. Copyright © 2004 by Cornell University. Used by permission of the publisher, Cornell University Press. All rights reserved.

Budd's framework has, unsurprisingly, been criticised in several ways. For example, in a dysfunctional organisation where there is poor efficiency, no equity and no voice, it could be argued that there is still a balance, even though none of the ideal objectives of the employment relationship are met. Similarly one of the ingredients in the employment relationship is the use and restraint of power, yet this remains unspoken in Budd's triad and consequently the ways in which power might influence each of the three categories to differing degrees is not addressed. Hyman (2005: 128) points out that for much of the time an employer's idea of efficiency contrasts with that of the employee and therefore 'it is impossible to speak of the "objectives of the employment relationship" as if these were common to both parties'. He also argues that Budd's pursuit of even-handedness – a 'balance' between competing principles – offers little prospect of a stable equilibrium.

Significantly Dietz and Fortin (2007) argue that voice is increasingly important within knowledge-based workplaces where the giving and sharing of information, some of which will be sensitive, allowing organisations to function effectively; and trust, of course is a central component in this relationship. Kim and Beehr (2020: 109) emphasise the importance of voice-enabling procedures, suggesting that,

> … managers should pay attention to the level of formal procedural justice in the organisation by sharing information and offering feedback on decision-making processes transparently. This entails managers and immediate supervisors listening to employees' opinions and involving employee groups from various work positions and departments in the process of making decisions to help improve and maintain procedural justice.

While Le et al. (2021: 14) support this, arguing that justice-based voice practices are crucial and that when they are fairly implemented (and *discussed with all employees*), perceptions of fairness and subsequent levels of trust are higher. When used in conjunction with other HRM policies and practice, **employee voice** measures have been linked to improved organisational performance (Boxall and Purcell, 2011). Boxall and Purcell (2011) argue that exactly which type of voice practices are implemented are less important than the levels of managerial sincerity accompanying them and the employee perceptions that such sincerity induces. Different types of voice activities will be underpinned by different levels of managerial sincerity. Holland et al. (2012) say that it follows, therefore, that in order for such improved organisational effectiveness to occur the voice mechanisms used must, *ipso facto*, induce perceptions of trust.

Employee Perceptions of Organisational Fairness, Justice and Injustice

> People do care about outcomes … they also care about the processes that produce those outcomes. They want to know that they have had their say – that their point of view was considered even if it was rejected. Outcomes matter, but no more than the fairness to the processes that produce them. (Kim and Mauborgne, 2003: 127)

Not all employees will perceive the same workplace environment in identical ways – to some the culture and values of the organisation will appear intrinsically unfair, while to others the same culture will seem quite acceptable. How employees view themselves – indeed whether they have basically happy or sad predispositions – will impact on how the workplace is perceived, and hence on how employees act and interact at work.

Adams (1965) talks about the concept of **organisational justice**, which he said was based on employees' perceptions of fairness at work – this need not, of course, be merely about how employees see themselves as being treated but also about whether they perceive their colleagues and co-workers to be treated in a fair way. For example, those remaining in employment following a badly handled redundancy may have an altered view of their organisation. Mistreatment from peers can reduce the effects of respectful treatment from an employer and vice versa (Bendersky and Brockner, 2020). Where employees find the allocation of resources unfair (e.g., perceiving a mismatch between what they think they are worth and what they are actually paid), it is known as **distributive justice/injustice**. Employees regard pay inequality as fair when it is linked to higher skill levels and greater responsibility (Schulz et al., 2021). Stecher and Rosse (2005) found that there was a significant relationship between distributive injustice and negative emotion, intent to leave a job and intent to reduce efforts. Yet it is not quite this simple. Employee views on the fairness of resource distribution may be tempered by how they feel their manager treats them (e.g., are they valued or disregarded), and this is known as **interactional justice/injustice** (Bies and Moag, 1986). So for example the manner in which decisions are explained, or not explained, could be regarded as unfair. Here the quality of interpersonal processes and the treatment of individuals (i.e., were they spoken to with sincerity and sensitivity and was the reasoning behind any outcomes sufficiently explained) all link to interpersonal justice, which in turn links with structural antagonism and managerial styles (see Chapter 1). Roch and Shanock (2006) found that levels of interactional justice can predict the quality of supervisory relationships at work and thus impact on the employment relationship. Where employees perceive interactional injustice, their relationships with supervisory staff tend to be poor, and vice versa. The amounts of information which employees are given, or not given, will affect the ways in which they perceive their managers. If they are given sufficient information to undertake a task well, understand why the task is necessary and how it fits into the overall scheme of things, this is known as **informational justice** (Colquitt, 2001). Where information is deliberately withheld, or perhaps where an employer makes decisions without fully briefing the workplace, this is known as **informational injustice** and it leads directly to employee disquiet and lack of trust.

There is yet another category of injustice. John Thibaut and Lauren Walker (1975) discussed the ways in which employees perceived the ways in which decisions are made within their organisations and if the processes of decision-making and organisational administration are perceived to be unfair then this is known as **procedural injustice**. Perceptions of procedural justice/injustice may impact on turnover and a whole range of employment issues. Where promotions are concerned, for example, if the decision-making process is perceived to be unfair it affects the organisational commitment of employees (see Arvey and Sackett, 1993: 186).

Exercise 3.3

* Folger and Bies (1989) have said that there are seven stages necessary in order for procedural justice to effectively operate in a positive way within the employment relationship. Think of an organisation that you know well – do Folger's following seven stages apply to the ways in which the employment relationship operates there?

    1　Identifying and effecting managerial responsibilities that promote procedural justice.
    2　Giving adequate and public consideration of employees' viewpoints.
    3　Suppressing biases.
    4　Operating consistently when applying decisions affecting employees.
    5　Giving clear and timely feedback to employees following a decision.
    6　Communicating to employees in a truthful way.
    7　Treating employees with courtesy and civility.

Employee perceptions of fairness are also affected by the different rationales that employers provide for work situations. For example, steelworkers in a 2001 study by Bacon and Blyton understood that redundancies had to be made when there was a business downturn and therefore did not view this as unfair. It was a different matter, however, when redundancies were the result of company outsourcing policies – here the company policy *was* regarded as unfair. This perception of unfairness had a detrimental impact on employee relations and the levels of trust within the steel plant (Bacon and Blyton, 2001).

Case Snippet 3.2

Perceptions of Fairness

Researchers looking at organisational fairness tend to focus on organisational outcomes and why fairness matters, rather than looking at what triggers initial perceptions of fairness and how these

(Continued)

develop/change over time. Jordan et al. (2022) specifically addressed this omission in two studies and found that those starting new jobs rely on combinations of previous workplace justice-related experiences to formulate their views on (un)fairness. They then use these experiences to anticipate their new employer's behaviour. Their research showed that perceptions of injustice are subjective, strongly associated with prior experience, and linked to 'the eye of the beholder'.

Where there is an element of workplace change that is perceived as unfair then employee resistance is greater than when it is perceived as fair (this is hardly surprising!). If management behaviour during the change process is perceived to be unfair then employee resistance is considered to be legitimate by the employees resisting and those observing the resistance. 'Withdrawing effort is only one behavioural response to inequity. Other behaviours might include theft, sabotage and even violence' (Folger and Skarlicki, 1999: 36). This catalogue of responses is all at an individual level. The authors do not point out that the response could be at a collective level and that industrial action could ensue. When, for example, there is a change that affects a number of unionised employees, a strike or go-slow is often the response to perceived unfairness. The British Airways employees who, in 2003, did not trust their employer because they feared that the introduction of swipe-cards requiring them to 'clock in and out' might be put to an unfair use, went on strike, causing chaos at Heathrow Airport. While also in 2003 members of the GMB and Amicus unions working for the chemical company Rhodia went on strike, not to protect *themselves* from unfairness but to protect *future employees* who would be denied entry to a final-salary pension scheme. Similarly it is not unknown in China for those employees who perceive workplace conditions to be unjust to attempt to draw attention to their plight by a variety of means ranging from holding their employer hostage to posting pictures of their offspring carrying signs demanding that the working conditions and pay for their parents change for the better.

Exercise 3.4

Read the scenario below and then answer the following questions:

- In which ways, if any, was the treatment of Mr Starnes legitimate?
- Did those employees remaining at Speciality Medical Supplies think that the ways in which the redundancies were managed complied with organisational justice? Give the reasons, with academic justification, for your answer.
- Evaluate whether the final outcome was fair for those who only received severance pay but no longer had a job.
- How does holding someone a prisoner until they meet your demands fit with the model proposed by Budd?

In June 2013, Chip Starnes, a co-owner of Florida-based Specialty Medical Supplies, visited the company's Huairou, Beijing, factory to oversee the redundancies of some staff from the plastics section of the factory together with the transferring of some work to India. It was not as straightforward as he had hoped. Mr Starnes lost nine pounds in weight and was unable to leave the factory for nearly a week as the employees held him as an on-site prisoner, blocking all exits and depriving him not just of freedom but of sleep by banging doors and shining bright lights. They were demanding additional payments to match the severance pay of those workers who had, according to some reports, received payments worth two months' salary when they had lost their jobs. A negotiated settlement was eventually reached whereby the workers' demands were met and Mr Starnes freed. Although ostensibly a kidnapping, the police declined to intervene to rescue the owner as they said it was a civil matter and that such instances were not uncommon in China.

Sources: Watt, 2013; BBC News, 2013a,b

Perceptions of distributive, procedural and interactional justice are strongly related to the perceptions of one's co-workers and workgroup. Salamon and Robinson (2008) contend that when employees perceive that they are trusted by management, they are likely to develop greater responsibility for organisational outcomes. The distribution of rewards, organisational policies and procedures, and interpersonal treatment by supervisors show strong links to co-worker trust and overall morale (Forret and Love, 2007). These results are important in terms of the employment relationship, given that lack of co-worker trust and poor morale are associated with many negative outcomes such as low organisational commitment, decreased productivity and higher intentions to leave the organisation (Ocampo et al., 2018).

> To promote healthy co-worker relationships, organisations need to consider how justice perceptions are related to the ability of employees to work well with one another. Employees who are busy 'keeping score' as to how they are treated and the rewards they receive are unlikely to be thoughtful, resourceful contributors for their colleagues. (Forret and Love, 2007: 254)

There is a dichotomy within managerial practice. The emphasis on empowerment and trust sometimes sits uncomfortably with that of performance management systems that allow little employee discretion in target setting and the processes of achieving these targets. Where an organisation has policies encouraging trust but proceeds, regardless of these, to allow employees little say in what they are doing and how they are doing it, the result is one of perceived procedural injustice – and sometimes perceived interactional injustice.

The resulting cynicism of the workforce leads to low commitment and may lead to low productivity and weak morale. In a survey of 19 separate organisations, Kim and Mauborgne pointed out that 'managers who believed the company's processes were fair displayed a high level of trust and commitment that, in turn, engendered active cooperation. Conversely when managers felt fair process was absent they hoarded ideas and dragged their feet' (2003: 128).

Lemons and Jones found that:

> … one may infer that the perception of fairness or unfairness in promotion-decision systems is a strong predictor of employee attitudes for most employees regardless of demographic variables. Thus, to avoid costly discrimination cases, as well as turnover

and other negative organisational outcomes, employers need to address the problem of perceptions of unfairness regarding promotion procedures. With the importance of organisational commitment well established ... this study presents an additional relationship that deserves more attention. (2000: 277)

One of the ways that commitment can be gained is by the organisation having procedures that promote a better working environment and show **transparency** and consistency in the ways in which employees are dealt with.

In the UK, Leeds Council, for example, introduced a 'violence at work' policy that showed the employees that the authority took their fears seriously – the result was a rise in commitment and decrease in unrest. Similarly the retail employer Selfridges introduced a gift policy to ensure that it not only behaved in a just way but was also seen by everyone to do so.

Exercise 3.5

• Read Case Study 3.1 and then discuss with a friend how the implementation of this policy fits with notions of the different types of organisational justice.

Case Study 3.1

Tesco

Tesco, a multinational retailer operating in the UK, Ireland, Hungary, the Czech Republic, and Slovakia has more than 360,000 employees. It is committed to ensuring a safe environment for all of its prospective and current employees, temporary and agency workers, and anyone else working directly for Tesco on a permanent or temporary basis. Consequently bullying, harassment and victimisation of any kind are not condoned. An up-to-date UK policy making this explicit was introduced in March 2021. It defines victimisation, bullying and harassment (including sexual harassment), clearly showing the steps that employees need to take if they wish to complain and how the company will then respond.

Managers *must* take action on complaints of harassment, etc. that are raised with them *or that they witness*. They are then compelled to discuss the incident with the person concerned in order to understand if they wish to raise a complaint - then subsequently act on that complaint. When a complaint is not made, but a manager is aware of the problem, or if the complainant expresses a wish for no further action, the policy allows for Tesco to act providing the seriousness of the allegations cannot be ignored, thereby ensuring Tesco upholds its responsibility (and legal obligations) to provide a safe working environment. Should this happen Tesco undertakes to inform the 'aggrieved' person and assure them that all reasonable steps will be taken to ensure they do not face victimisation as a result.

Importantly the policy details external organisations that offer support and makes it clear that if complaints are made in good faith but not then upheld there will be no repercussions for the complainant.

The policy should reassure employees that Tesco will:

- help prevent incidents
- respond rapidly if an incident does occur
- provide support to employees should they need to overcome any problems.

The ways in which differing perceptions of organisational justice/injustice interact go to the very heart of the employment relationship because they influence workplace behaviour, expressions of conflict, perceptions of the psychological contract, workplace productivity, levels of morale and labour turnover.

Employers Have a Duty of Care

Linked to the notion of a fair and equitable workplace is the employers' *duty of care* to those who work for them: this notion means employers have a duty to protect employees from physical *and* mental danger. Consequently high levels of workplace-based stress caused by work, colleagues or by the physical environment are as unacceptable as hazardous conditions. Fair employers, cognisant with the 'duty of care', will ensure that workplaces are physically safe, and the work that people are required to do is of minimum risk to their wellbeing.

News Flash 3.2

East of England Ambulance Service Put in Special Measures

Former staff have spoken of a 'toxic work environment' at the NHS Trust for the East of England Ambulance Service that serves Bedfordshire, Cambridgeshire, Essex, Hertfordshire, Norfolk and Suffolk. After serving for over 20 years, a former senior paramedic, who wished to remain anonymous, said staff were 'not supported by a management structure' and the 'endemic culture of bullying' would change only after 'the removal of the management team'.

When it visited the Trust between 25 June and 15 July 2020, the Care Quality Commission found a string of failures, including sexual misconduct, bullying and concerns over how the Trust failed to act. The Trust says it is 'taking urgent action to address challenges'.

Source: www.bbc.co.uk/news/uk-england-beds-bucks-herts-54602729

News Flash 3.3

Berlin Brandenburg Airport: Electric Shocks

Since the new Berlin Brandenburg Airport opened at the end of October 2020 sixty baggage handlers have suffered electric shocks from the scanners. According to Benjamin Roscher, the

(Continued)

regional head of the trade union, Verdi, every luggage inspection scanner in Terminal 1 produces the shocks and should not be operated until the problem is rectified. Verdi says workers have complained of dizziness, pain, and numbness and on several occasions the affected staff have been taken to hospital by ambulance.

The airport management acknowledges that the electric shocks have been happening – but has said it sees no reason to close the terminal, suggesting instead that employees operating the scanners wear shoes capable of conducting electric charges away. The airport has been urged to ensure that its cleaners mop the floors more frequently, and anti-static key rings have also been distributed.

Sources: Connolly, 2021; Klisauskaite, 2021; Neuman, 2021

There are of course (rare) occasions when the employer is put in a position of having to protect an employee who does not want to be protected. This will range from wearing a safety hat on a hot day on a construction site to the atypical occasions when an employee's need for paid work outweighs any safety considerations: 'despite the employee's desire to remain at work notwith-standing his recognition of the risk he runs, the employer will nevertheless be under a duty in law to dismiss him for his own good so as to protect him against physical danger' (*Coxall* v. *Goodyear GB Ltd* [2002] IRLR 742). In this case Coxall, an asthmatic, continued to work as a paint operator despite being advised against this by the works' doctor – he collapsed at work and claimed personal injury. Technically the implications of this ruling mean that employers must evaluate the health risks posed to each employee by their continuing in their present job, and then ensure that the risks are minimised to an acceptable level, perhaps by offering alternative work after consultation with the affected employee. Dismissal would, of course, be a last resort.

An intensive pace of work and the battery of measurement techniques used to assess performance may lead employers to neglect their duty of care, and hence create an employment relationship that is low on trust and loyalty. Just-in-time work processes coupled with regimes of continuous improvement can lead to intense managerial pressures on a workforce, which may go against the spirit, if not the letter, of Human Rights legislation and, of course, some health and safety legislation. For example, some employees are subject to stressful invasive surveillance, measuring every component they produce. Any faults in the product can be tracked back to identify the perpetrator, who is then publicly identified. Similarly, good producers are examined closely so that any good practice in their performance can be identified and promulgated by the company. Within such organisations individual co-workers and team members may also police and subsequently chastise anyone whose performance is not up to scratch.

Of course different employees have different perceptions of the ways in which they are monitored: sometimes such measurement and associated surveillance is regarded as a legitimate managerial activity, carried out in an impartial way and undertaken in order to serve the interests of all within the organisations by exposing poor performance practices, while others see the process as intrusive and an invasion of privacy. The ways in which managers exert authority within the workplace, and the discretion with which they choose how to, and indeed whether to, exercise their power, has links to Edward's notion of structured antagonism.

Psychological Contract

One of the concepts used to explain employee perceptions and subsequent behaviours within the workforce is that of the psychological contract. This construct, based on exchange theory, maintains that individuals at work are not affected solely by economic constraints but are also influenced and affected by their social environment (Blau, 1964; Lambert et al., 2008). It is, according to David Guest (2004a, 2004b, 2016; Guest and Clinton, 2011), a model that addresses the core issues found within the employment relationship of trust, exchange and control. Individuals in the workplace, following this concept, hold a number of unwritten, sometimes unspecified, implicit expectations about the work process, and freely exchange their commitment, loyalty and hard work in exchange for these expectations to be met by the employer, for example by the provision of a safe place of work and adequate and appropriate training.

Under the psychological contract both the employer and the employee will hold differing sets of expectations about the behaviour (and obligations) of the other, but the key is reciprocity. (The use of the word 'contract' is something of a misnomer here as parties to an employment contract know what they are signing up to and here they don't – as the requirements and commitments from one another are all inferred!) Of course, as the expectations and corresponding obligations are not written down, and on occasions not even articulated, there is a large arena in which misunderstandings can occur. Levinson et al. describe the construct as 'a series of mutual expectations, of which the parties to the relationship may not themselves be dimly aware, but which, nonetheless, govern their relationship to each other' (1962: 21). Each individual has their own psychological contract linked to their different perceptions of organisational justice. As careers, jobs and family experiences change, so too does each individual's psychological contract. Morgan and King (2012), in a study of first-time mothers, showed how the mothers thought their psychological contracts had been breached if their supervisors treated them as they did prior to their maternity leave, rather than in a new way, taking into account their altered domestic circumstances.

Rousseau (1989, 1990) delineated two types of psychological contract: the **relational** and the **transactional**. A relational contract is one based on loyalty and commitment in return for job security, while a transactional one is more materialistic and 'hard-nosed' with employees expecting tangible rewards in return for increased effort, accommodating flexible approaches to work and long, sometimes antisocial, hours. Tomprou and Lee (2022) found that individual employees managed by 'human' rather than algorithmic processes, were more likely to react badly to breached transactional arrangements suffering consequential damage to their psychological contracts, while those organisations using algorithmic methods for relational aspects were more likely to encounter mistakes in employee perception causing damage to the psychological contract. During periods of recession the transactional concept seems to describe the processes in many workplaces, particularly where there is an individual rather than collective approach to managing employment. The changing ways of working, with unremitting production pressures, intensive and different, more stressful working patterns may have resulted in a switch from relational aspects to concerns about remuneration and an emphasis not just on financial rewards but also on aspects of the work that may be improved. Guest (2004b) says that where flexible work practices and individual contracts abound, reciprocal promises that deliver the expectations of both parties lead to perceptions of fairness and increasing levels of trust, resulting in a healthy psychological contract with higher levels of performance and job satisfaction.

Trust Must Be Earned

Research from The Workforce Institute at UKG shows that,

> trust in employees must be earned is (a belief) most prevalent in India (90%), the US (68%), the UK (67%), Australia and New Zealand (64%), Canada (64%), and France (64%). Comparatively, employees and business leaders in Mexico (63%) are more likely to presume trust starting day one than any other country. ... Nearly two-thirds (64%) of employees say trust has a direct impact on their sense of belonging at work, including 4 out of 5 employees in India (79%) and two-thirds of employees in the US (68%), Canada (65%), and Mexico (63%).

The findings are based on a global survey in June 2020 of nearly 4,000 employees and business leaders in 11 different countries.

Source: Business Wire, 2020

When the psychological contract is violated in some way because expectations are unfulfilled or obligations unmet, individuals may take action to redress the imbalance. This could take a number of forms: affected employees could decide to reduce their efforts, take industrial action or even change jobs. Sometimes such dissatisfaction is not articulated clearly and instead the expressions of discontent are channelled into more explicit and tangible issues such as complaints about pay and working conditions. In this respect the construct of the psychological contract as a stand-alone concept can be confusing: employees switching from an unspecified relational psychological relationship to an unspecified transactional one, and then finally to an explicit one linked to the employment contract itself.

Where a workplace is perceived as unfair this will impact upon the levels of commitment to the organisation exhibited by those who work there, and, as a consequence, the psychological contracts will be less positive. Gallie et al. found consistent evidence that organisational support has a positive impact on attitudes and that the degree of personal participation, autonomy and control helps to maintain positive perceptions towards and about the employing organisation (2001). Those organisations that were less supportive, particularly those with tight control and surveillance, encouraged negative attitudes from employees – with a resulting damaged psychological contract.

If, as a result of perceived unfair work practices, the employee regards the psychological contract as damaged, it leads to diminishing trust and commitment levels. Downsizing and restructuring are particular areas where this is a problem:

> The neglect of procedural justice – granting employees involvement in determining decisions about change, giving input during objective setting and performance evaluations – has been a serious weakness in reshaping the performance management

processes and employees feel disenfranchised by the change process ... consequently holding less trust in the firm's senior management. ... As a consequence, morale and commitment have suffered. (Stiles et al., 1997: 65)

The literature is clear: fair and transparent work practices lead to commitment and trust – it does not matter whether the processes are to do with performance management, employee voice or something as routine as promotion. It also shows that the converse is seen to be true: where employees perceive either their managers or the system to be unfair, commitment and trust diminish to the detriment of the employment relationship.

Because employees' trust in management is higher where management supports union membership, Bryson (2001) argues that managerial support for a union may signal employer interest in the concerns of workers, leading to more positive attitudes towards management and, he argues, better managerial decision making. (Union membership does not however, according to Bessa et al. [2020: 25], have a causal impact on job satisfaction.) Certainly the presence of a recognised trade union increases the levels of perceived fairness and consequently improves workplace commitment; indeed Guest and Conway (1998, 2002) found that where there was a union presence the psychological contract was stronger.

This, however, is not always so. For example, when Cadbury embarked on a long-term restructuring and change programme with full union cooperation in the early 1990s, productivity went up in a number of ways. Then company documents emerged showing that the new strategy was not just a means of increasing productivity but also of weakening the Transport and General Workers Union. Part of the document said:

The role of the union needs to be marginalized by greater focus on direct communication and consultation, but without an overt statement to this effect. Employee support for the trade union should therefore decrease over time. (Partnership at Work, 2001)

Without prompting, the union members withdrew support and the company suffered. Company behaviour was perceived as hypocritical, and regarded as unfair. Commitment from the workforce, which had risen, plummeted. The psychological contracts were weakened and there was a lack of what Tzafrir and Dolan (2004) would call 'reliability'.

Exercise 3.6

Read the scenario below and then answer the following questions:

- Analyse the managerial style at Amazon and indicate the likely impact this has on the psychological contract of those 300 staff working there.
- Kelly (1998, 2005) suggested that joining a union is likely to be triggered by a number of factors including a sense of injustice, a breach of legal rights and a breach of social values. Identify and categorise any such breaches epitomised in the case study and analyse the likely impact such breaches would have on the perceptions of organisational justice.

(Continued)

- From the evidence in the case study, evaluate whether or not you think the behaviour of Amazon is ethical.

Amazon working conditions are gruelling and unfair, said witness Jennifer Bates to a USA Senate committee listening to evidence for its enquiry into the 2021 Income and Wealth Inequality Crisis in America. Bates' comments were made before 1,798 (out of 5,800) workers at Amazon's centre in Bessemer, Alabama, voted against unionising, compared to 738 in favour. In her evidence, Bates said Amazon thinks 'you are another machine' and that her workday felt like a nine-hour intense workout, where her every move was tracked.

Bates claimed that Amazon made a concerted effort to convince the Alabama workers that a union was unnecessary by sending anti-union messages to workers' phones and posting anti-union signs in workplace toilet stalls. In addition she said, 'We were forced into what they call "union education" meetings. We had no choice but to attend them, not given an opportunity to decline. ... They would last for as much as an hour, and we'd have to go sometimes several times a week'. If an employee spoke up disagreeing with what the company was saying, 'they would just shut the meeting down', she said.

RWDSU - the Retail, Wholesale and Department Store Union - representing the workers said it would challenge the vote by filing unfair labour practice charges with the National Labor Relations Board alleging that Amazon broke the law with anti-union activity prior to the election.

Sources: Arcieri, 2021; Solon and Kaplan, 2021

Increased Workloads and Levels of Trust

Increased workloads, pressures to complete more and more tasks in shorter timeframes, coupled with sustained levels of workplace monitoring, can increase levels of stress and decrease levels of trust. In the UK, Deutsche Bank had to pay compensation to Helen Green, a secretary who suffered severe depression following incidents of workplace bullying and a manager who arbitrarily increased her workload to unacceptable levels (*Green* v. *DB Group Services* (UK) Ltd EWHC 1898 (QB2006)).

Some enlightened employers, who are aware of the unpleasant side-effects of concentrated techniques used to 'encourage' continuous, pressurised, performance improvement, have introduced dignity-at-work policies and developed **family-friendly policies**, often emphasising greater job autonomy as a means of recruiting and retaining staff. An article by Roper et al. illustrates this. They use the WERS data to show how some employers have utilised family-friendly policies which resulted in benefits that 'included happier staff (50%), improved retention rates (36%) and "other improvements" such as reduced absence (24%)' (2003: 215). Arguably such workplaces are fairer environments than those without such policies. Wherever they occur in an organisation, high stress levels may lead to bullying. Hoel and Cooper (2000) suggested that 47% of UK employees have been witness to some form of bullying at work, 10% claiming to have been bullied in the six months prior to their survey. Given such widespread stress levels within the UK, they unsurprisingly believed that 68% of employees identified that *managers* had been the source of the bullying. (See Einarsen et al. [2020] for a European historical perspective on this.) Bullying may not, of course, just be the result of increasing workplace pressures as it may also be used tactically to weed out 'unnecessary' employees.

For example, Capita plc, which provides a range of white-collar, professional support services on long-term contracts across the private and public sector, has grown over the last few years following a number of aggressive takeovers. Those staff subject to TUPE regulations presumed their jobs to be safe. (TUPE is the Transfer of Undertakings (Protection of Employment) Regulations that protect employees' terms and conditions of employment when one business, or part of a business, is transferred from one owner to another. Employees who are transferred with the business automatically become employees of the new employer but, crucially, on the same terms and conditions that they had previously worked under.)

Capita staff were safe for a time, but after a period some of the employees felt aggrieved, explaining to this author that, as far as they could tell, rather than finance redundancy payments the Capita group adopted a tactic of harsh and aggressively applied performance management to purge anyone considered to be unnecessary from the organisation. They insisted that not only was this practice intrinsically unfair – denying people their redundancy payments – but that the levels of stress that this induced in the remaining staff, who felt they dare not put a foot wrong, were probably illegal under health and safety legislation and certainly fell short of Capita exercising its 'duty of care'.

Ishmael and Alemoru (1999: 308) provide a strategic example of how employers can set about combating some of those workplace practices that induce perceptions of organisational injustice resulting in low levels of trust and reduced commitment. They suggest that organisations continuously monitor their workplace cultures in order to evaluate and review policies and practices so that they meet the needs of the organisation. They propose that organisations:

- set standards of behaviour that appreciate differences in the workplace
- acknowledge the place of empowerment in creating a positive working environment
- encourage leaders, managers and strategists to be visible role models
- be tough on perpetrators of injustice, while helping them to change their behaviour
- educate and develop the workforce, networking with other organisations that are taking on the challenge of tackling abusive behaviour
- never underestimate the effects of not taking harassment, bullying and violence seriously.

Edwards (2007) is not quite so prescriptive in his approach, suggesting that in order to promote a fairer more just workplace employers should strengthen the reality – and hence the perceptions of fairness and equity – by adopting consultation arrangements and/or negotiation with employee representatives.

Case Snippet 3.3

Tile Factory Boss 'Drove Car at Workers'

The boss of Marley Tiles Ltd (a roof tile manufacturer), that faced complaints over Covid safety, drove his car at workers during a 2020 Christmas strike, the union GMB has said. The union also claimed that the same manager also instructed a lorry driver to head straight for the picket line. Both incidents were

(Continued)

reported to the police. The GMB expressed dismay that the company, rather than act against the manager, suspended five long-standing workers. The union said victimisation of workers for taking industrial action and defending themselves against serious and dangerous actions by management is 'a disgrace'. The union said that during the strike, a number of workers were brought from a higher Covid risk tier into Reading, allegedly in just one vehicle, breaking Covid laws and other regulations. GMB national organiser Nikki Dancey said, 'Marley's treatment of the workforce has been nothing short of appalling and has led to a complete breakdown of trust with management. Victimisation of workers for taking industrial action and defending themselves against serious and dangerous actions by management is a disgrace'. She added, 'GMB will back the Marley Five to the hilt. We hope that members of the public will support the campaign to get justice for these workers and return them safely to their jobs'.

Source: GMB, 2021

Exercise 3.7

- After reading the following case scenario, compose an email (or blog) to a student new to studying employee relations, explaining how an employer's duty of care and employees' perceptions of justice relate to what happened at France Télécom. You may want to include information about the psychological contract and something about the impact that workloads have on levels of employee trust and commitment.

Leave 'by the Window or the Door'

In December 2019, three top executives from France Télécom (Orange) were convicted of 'institutional moral harassment'. The criminal court in Paris said the men, who put in place a conscious scheme to worsen employees' work conditions in order to 'speed up departures', were responsible for creating an atmosphere of fear leading directly to the suicides and attempted suicides of numerous employees.

They were accountable for 35 workplace-linked suicides between 2008-10 associated with a change management programme, 'NEXT', that was designed to reduce the number of employees while simultaneously catering for the upsurge in demand for mobile phones. The programme, introduced after privatisation, altered both workplace policies and practices and was implemented with a rigour and efficiency which was difficult for some of the employees to adjust to, particularly where they had to retrain to work in call centres, change location and, for some, suffer the indignity of demotion. The chief executive at the time Mr Lombard told company officials that employees would have to leave 'by the window or the door'.

The company's reputation suffered as it became known for its brutal regimes and management by terror. Eventually, of course, action was taken and managers were trained to deal with 'sensitive issues', job transfers became voluntary and no longer mandatory, while decision making became more local and not dictated centrally from the head office. The union, however, has claimed the changes were too little too late and failed to deal with psychosocial risks associated with intensive work patterns. The French Labour Code (Code du Travail) makes it mandatory for employers to protect their workforces, yet clearly this did not happen.

Workplace suicides are not unusual – there are instances of them occurring in the UK, Italy, the USA and Australia, to name a few. Where employees have expectations of work and trust their employer to provide safe working conditions, manageable workloads and reasonable hours, it sometimes creates unbearable tension when these expectations are violated.

Sources: BBC News, 2019; Jolly, 2010; Reuters, 2012

Trust and the High-performing Workplace

Theoretically high-performance workplaces (HPWs) (where the ways of working promote, incentivise, provide opportunities for and develop the capabilities of employees) ensure the maximisation of all workplace resources, effecting optimum organisational performance. Here employees are often encouraged to use their skills and expertise collaboratively, embracing teamwork and problem-solving forums, sharing knowledge and working closely with one another. Trust is a crucial ingredient for this type of working. Indeed Schulz et al. (2020: 274) discovered

> … that individuals with supervisors who withheld support for some HPW practices responded with greater perceptions of procedural injustice committed against their interests by the supervisor, impressions of lessened managerial support and trust, and a heightened proclivity to behave counterproductively towards the supervisor.

Gambetta (1988) suggests that trust enables, and hence engages, employees in cooperation. Trust, therefore, is seen as the basis from which quality relationships, cooperation and stability arise.

Such HR policies and subsequent practices are central in developing what Fox (1974) describes as high-trust informal employment relationships (ER) and low-trust formal ER. In this high-performance context the increased levels of employee commitment that are integral to this way of working are inextricably linked to high levels of employee trust; consequently, trust is the necessary ingredient for increased organisational performance leading to competitive advantage (Abuelhassan and AlGassim, 2022; Searle et al., 2011). Not all organisations of course adopt the high-performance route – many adopt versions of HRM where individuals are treated merely as units of resource and here, as mentioned earlier, such hard HRM exacerbates feelings of organisational injustice and a lack of trust (see, e.g., Webb and Palmer, 1998: 611–27).

Summary

We have seen that:

- perceptions of fairness differ between cultures and from individual to individual
- employers have to exercise a duty of care towards their employees, ensuring a safe physical and mental environment
- different countries promote fairness at work to differing degrees with some enacting legislation and providing codes of practice designed to inhibit/prevent unfairness
- individuals' perceptions of fairness fall into a number of categories:

- ○ procedural
- ○ interactive
- ○ distributive
- ○ informational

● the interaction between these perceptions is important and impacts on the employment relationship
● the degree of employee voice within the workplace has an impact on levels of trust
● perceptions of trustworthiness will affect levels of employee commitments and loyalty, and hence productivity.

Review Questions

1   Do you think perceptions of organisational justice are the same for employers and employees? Why did you reach this conclusion?
2   Is Budd's model (equity, efficiency and voice) all that is required for achieving a balanced employment relationship? Why did you reach your conclusion?
3   Evaluate whether trust is important within the employment relationship. Justify your answer with reference to academic sources.
4   Analyse, in a critical way, the relationship between structural antagonism, levels of trust and the psychological contract.

Revision Exercise 3.1

Peace of Mind Insurance Co. is a growing insurance company based in a small tower block in the centre of a new town in the South East of England. It employs some 506 staff - 253 of these are on flexitime and most of them are concerned with front-line selling activities such as pet, accident and travel insurance. In the past year the company has expanded its portfolio of services to cover commercial insurance and has seen a corresponding growth in profits, profile and people. Recent incidents in the town, coupled with a risk assessment around the security of the company, have led the CEO to decide to introduce 'active badges'. These credit-card sized badges are worn on the clothing of employees – not only do they act as photo identification, but they also emit soundless electrical signals that are picked up by sensors placed in the corridors and rooms of the workplace, ensuring that the employees, who will each have their own individual electronic code, are tracked wherever they are.

The CEO has sent the following memo to the HR Director:

Dear Chirag,

As you know we have been concerned about the levels of security in our building for some time and I have decided that one of the ways of tackling this is to introduce active badges for all staff from next April. This fantastic invention means that we will know where anyone is at any given time. Given our experiences following the introduction of CCTV cameras at the exits/entrances to the building, when all of the smokers overreacted and were up in arms about us spying on their smoking breaks – to say nothing of the local union getting wind of what was going on and having the cheek to offer to mediate even though no one here is in a union – I want us to introduce the change as smoothly as possible.

Please could you give me a short presentation, say next Wednesday at 2 pm, about the employee relations implications around the introduction, suggesting how we might prepare the ground so that the badges are introduced with the minimum of fuss. I have booked the electricians; they will be on site, installing the sensors, over the annual shut down at the end of December, so we have about two months to get things organised.

Regards,

Roger.

Your task is to imagine that you are the HR director, Chirag, and produce a set of no more than six PowerPoint slides (together with their notes that include academic references), showing why you think the introduction of the badges might be counterproductive. The slides will be aimed at the CEO and the Board of Directors and worded accordingly, while the notes must show the reasoning behind and justification for your thinking, with links to academic sources.

Your answer should draw on your knowledge of the interests of the parties, managerial styles, the psychological contract and notions of trust and fairness at work.

Relevant Articles for Further Reading

Fortin, M., Cropanzano, R., Cugueró-Escofet, N., Nadisic, T. and Van Wagoner, H. (2020) 'How do people judge fairness in supervisor and peer relationships? Another assessment of the dimensions of justice', *Human Relations*, 73(12): 1632–63.

Here the authors explore and enlarge on the four main concepts of justice in relation to supervisory relationships and develop 14 new justice rules.

Ghimire, B. (2019) 'The mediating role of trust in management on job satisfaction and organisational commitment', *Pravaha*, 25(1): 43–52.

Looking at nursing, this paper shows that organisational justice alone will not improve job satisfaction – trust is the key mediating factor that makes the difference.

Vatcha, A. (2020) *Workplace Surveillance Outside the Workplace*. Available at: https://ischannel.lse.ac.uk/articles/abstract/170/ (accessed 24 May 2021).

This paper looks at the increasing (and excessive) use of surveillance methods on employees, exploring the subsequent erosion of trust and how this might be avoided by using performance rewards.

References

Abuelhassan, A. E. and AlGassim, A. (2022) 'How organizational justice in the hospitality industry influences proactive customer service performance through general self-efficacy', *International Journal of Contemporary Hospitality Management*. Available at: www.emerald.com/insight/content/doi/10.1108/IJCHM-10-2021-1238/full/html (accessed 11 May 2022).

Ackers, P. (2001) 'Employment ethics', in T. Redman and A. Wilkinson, *Contemporary Human Resource Management*. London: FT/Prentice Hall, Ch. 12.

Adams, S. J. (1965) 'Inequity in social exchange', in L. Berkowitz (ed.), *Advances in Experimental Social Psychology*, Vol. 2. New York: Academic, pp. 267–99.

Allen, N. J. and Meyer, J. P. (1997) *Commitment in the Workplace: Theory, Research, and Application*. London: Sage.

Arcieri, K. (2021) 'Amazon employee testifies about "grueling" working conditions amid union battle', *S&P Global Market Intelligence*, 17 March. Available at: www.spglobal.com/marketintelligence/en/news-insights/latest-news-headlines/amazon-employee-testifies-about-grueling-working-conditions-amid-union-battle-63210649 (accessed 15 May 2021).

Arvey, R. D. and Sackett, P. R. (1993) 'Fairness in selection: Current developments and perspectives', in N. Schmitt and W. Borman (eds), *Personnel Selection in Organisations*. San Francisco, CA: Jossey-Bass, p. 186.

Avolio, B. J. and Walumbwa, F. O. (2006) 'Authentic leadership: Moving HR leaders to a higher level', in J. J. Martocchio (ed.), *Research in Personnel and Human Resources Management*, Vol. 25. Oxford and Greenwich, CT: Elsevier Science/JAI, pp. 273–304.

Bacon, N. and Blyton, P. (2001) 'Management practices and employee attitudes: A longitudinal study spanning fifty years', *The Sociological Review*, 49(2): 254–74.

BBC News (2013a) 'Workers hold US boss in China factory over dispute', *BBC News*, 25 June. Available at: www.bbc.co.uk/news/world-asia-china-23042461 (accessed 2 October 2015).

BBC News (2013b) 'US boss Chip Starnes released from China factory', *BBC News*, 27 June. Available at: www.bbc.co.uk/news/world-asia-china-23063829 (accessed 30 October 2015).

BBC News (2019) 'France Télécom suicides: Three former bosses jailed', *BBC News*, 20 December. Available at: www.bbc.co.uk/news/world-europe-50865211 (accessed 15 February 2021).

Bendersky, C. and Brockner, J. (2020) 'Mistreatment from peers can reduce the effects of respectful treatment from bosses, and respectful peers can offset mistreatment from bosses', *Journal of Organizational Behavior*, 41(8): 722–36.

Bessa, I., Charlwood, A. and Valizade, D. (2020) 'Do unions cause job dissatisfaction? Evidence from a quasi-experiment in the United Kingdom', *British Journal of Industrial Relations*, 59(2): 251–78.

Bies, R. J. and Moag, J. S. (1986) 'Interactional justice: Communication criteria of fairness', in R. J. Lewicki, B. H. Sheppard and M. Bazerman (eds), *Research on Negotiation in Organization*, Vol. 1. Greenwich, CT: JAI, pp. 43–55.

Blau, P. (1964) *Exchange and Power of Social Life*. New York: Wiley.

Boxall, P. and Purcell, J. (2011) *Strategy and Human Resource Management* (3rd edn). Basingstoke: Palgrave Macmillan.

Bryson, A. (2001) 'The foundation of "partnership"? Union effects on employee trust in management', *National Institute Economic Review*, 176(1): 91–104.

Budd, J. W. (2004) *Employment with a Human Face: Balancing Efficiency, Equity, and Voice*. Ithaca, NY: Cornell University Press.

Budd, J. W. (2010) 'Theorizing work: The importance of conceptualizations of work for research and practice', presentation at the 25th Cardiff Employment Research Unit Annual Conference, Cardiff Business School, 13–14 September. Available at: www.legacy-irc.csom.umn.edu/faculty/jbudd/research/cardiff2010.pdf (accessed 24 February 2013).

Business Wire (2020) *Trust is the Foundational Imperative of 2021: Global Research by The Workforce Institute at UKG Explores Why Trust is Hard to Find at Work.* Available at: www.businesswire.com/news/home/20201215005273/en/Trust-is-the-Foundational-Imperative-of-2021-Global-Research-by-The-Workforce-Institute-at-UKG-Explores-Why-Trust-is-Hard-to-Find-at-Work (accessed 4 February 2021).

Colquitt, J. A. (2001) 'On the dimensionality of organizational justice: A construct validation of a measure', *Journal of Applied Psychology*, 86(3): 386.

Connolly, K. (2021) 'Berlin airport's baggage handlers suffer electric shocks in latest mishap', *The Guardian*, 14 January. Available at: www.theguardian.com/world/2021/jan/14/berlin-airport-baggage-handlers-electric-shocks?CMP=Share_iOSApp_Other (accessed 12 August 2022).

Duan, J., Lam, W., Chen, C. and Zhong, J. A. (2010) 'Leadership justice, negative organizational behaviours, and the mediating effect of affective commitment', *Society for Personality*, 38(9): 1287–96.

Dietz, G. and Fortin, M. (2007) 'Trust and justice in the formation of joint consultative committees', *The International Journal of Human Resource Management*, 18(7): 1159–81.

Edelman (2019) *Return to Largest-Ever Inequality of Trust Driven by Spike Among Informed Public.* Available at: www.edelman.com/news-awards/2019-edelman-trust-barometer-reveals-my-employer-most-trusted-institution (accessed 4 May 2021).

Edwards, P. K. (1994) 'Discipline and the creation of order', in K. Sisson (ed.), *Personnel Management: A Comprehensive Guide to Theory and Practice in Britain.* Oxford: Oxford Blackwell Publishers, pp. 562–92.

Edwards, P. K. (2003) 'The employment relationship and the field of industrial relations', in P. Edwards (ed.), *Industrial Relations: Theory and Practice.* Oxford: Blackwell.

Edwards, P.K. (2007) *Justice in the Workplace: Why it is Important and Why a New Public Policy Initiative is Needed.* Work Foundation. Available at: www.theworkfoundation.com/assets/docs/publications/67_justice%20in%20the%20workplace.pdf (accessed 1 October 2015).

Einarsen, S. V., Hoel, H., Zapf, D. and Cooper, C. L. (2020) 'The concept of bullying and harassment at work: The European tradition', in S. V. Einarsen, H. Hoel, D. Zapf and C. L. Cooper (eds), *Bullying and Harassment in the Workplace.* London: CRC Press, pp. 3–53.

Everton, W. J., Jolton, J. A. and Mastrangelo, P. M. (2007) 'Be nice and fair or else: Understanding reasons for employees' deviant behaviors', *Journal of Management Development*, 26(2): 117–31.

Folger, R. and Bies, R. J. (1989) 'Managerial responsibilities and procedural justice', *Employee Responsibilities and Rights Journal*, 2(2): 79–90.

Folger, R. and Skarlicki, D. (1999) 'Unfairness and resistance to change: Hardship as mistreatment', *Journal of Organisational Change Management*, 12(1): 35–50.

Forret, M. and Love, M. S. (2007) 'Employee justice perceptions and co-worker relationships', *Leadership & Organization Development Journal*, 29(3): 248–60.

Fox, A. (1974) *Beyond Contact: Work, Power and Trust Relations.* London: Faber & Faber.

Gallie, D., Felstead, A. and Green, F. (2001) 'Employer policies and organisational commitment in Britain, 1992–97', *Journal of Management Studies*, 38(8): 1081–21.

Gambetta, D. (1988) 'Can we trust?', in D. Gambetta (ed.), *Trust, Making and Breaking Cooperative Relations.* Oxford: Blackwell, pp. 213–37.

GMB (2021) *Tile Factory Boss 'Drove Car at Workers' During Christmas Strike*, news release, 4 February. Available at: www.gmb.org.uk/news/tile-factory-boss-drove-car-workers-during-christmas-strike (accessed 12 August 2022).

Guest, D. (2004a) 'Flexible employment contracts, the psychological contract and employee outcomes: An analysis and review of the evidence', *International Journal of Management Reviews*, 5/6: 1–19.

Guest, D. (2004b) 'The psychology of the employment relationship: An analysis based on the psychological contract', *Applied Psychology*, 53(4): 541–55.

Guest, D. (2016) 'Trust and the role of the psychological contract in contemporary employment relations', in P. Elgoibar, M. Euwema and L. Munduate (eds), *Building Trust and Constructive Conflict Management in Organizations*. Cham.: Springer. doi:10.1007/978-3-319-31475-4_8

Guest, D. and Conway, N. (1998) *Fairness at Work and the Psychological Contract*. London: IPD.

Guest, D. and Conway, N. (2002) *Pressure at Work and the Psychological Contract*. London: CIPD.

Guest, D. and Clinton, M. (2011) 'Human resource management, the psychological contract and trust', in R. Searle and D. Skinner (eds), *Trust and Human Resource Management*. Cheltenham: Edward Elgar, pp. 87–108.

Hoel, H. and Cooper, C. L. (2000) *Destructive Conflict and Bullying at Work*. Manchester: Manchester School of Management, UMIST.

Holland, P., Cooper, B. K., Pyman, A. and Teicher, J. (2012) 'Trust in management: The role of employee voice arrangements and perceived managerial opposition to unions', *Human Resource Management Journal*, 22(4): 377–91.

Hughes, J. and Bozionelos, N. (2007) 'Work-life balance as source of job dissatisfaction and withdrawal attitudes: An exploratory study on the views of male workers', *Personnel Review*, 36(1): 145–54.

Hyman, R. (2005) 'Striking a balance? Means, ends, and ambiguities', *Employee Responsibilities and Rights Journal*, 17(2): 127–30.

Innocenti, L., Pilati, M. and Peluso, A. M. (2011) 'Trust as moderator in the relationship between HRM practices and employee attitudes', *Human Resource Management Journal*, 21(3): 303–17.

Iqbal, N., Ahmad, M. and Allen, M. M. C. (2019) 'Unveiling the relationship between e-HRM, impersonal trust and employee productivity', *Management Research Review*, 42(7): 879–99. doi:10.1108/MRR-02-2018-0094

Ishmael, A. and Alemoru, B. (1999) *Harassment, Bullying and Violence at Work*. London: The Industrial Society.

Jolly, D. (2010) 'France Télécom needs "radical change" after suicides, report says', *New York Times*, 8 March. Available at: www.nytimes.com/2010/03/09/technology/09telecom.html?hpw&_r=0 (accessed 2 October 2015).

Jordan, S. L., Palmer, J. C., Daniels, S. R., Hochwarter, W. A., Perrewé, P. L. and Ferris, G. R. (2022) 'Subjectivity in fairness perceptions: How heuristics and self-efficacy shape the fairness expectations and perceptions of organisational newcomers', *Applied Psychology*, 71(1): 103–28.

Kelly, J. (1998) *Rethinking Industrial Relations: Mobilisation, Collectivism and Long Waves*. London: Routledge.

Kelly, J. (2005) 'Social movement theory and union revitalisation in Britain', in S. Fernie and M. Metcalf (eds), *Trade Unions: Resurgence or Demise?* London: Routledge, pp. 62–82.

Kim, M. and Beehr, T. A. (2020) 'Making the case for procedural justice: Employees thrive and work hard', *Journal of Managerial Psychology*, 35(2): 100–14.

Kim, W.C. and Mauborgne, R. (2003) 'Fair process: Managing in the knowledge economy', *Harvard Business Review*, 81(1): 127–36.

Klisauskaite, V. (2021) 'Berlin Airport (BER) staff suffer electric shock', *Aviation News*, 15 January. Available at: www.aerotime.aero/26969-Berlin-airport-staff-suffers-electric-shock (accessed 12 August 2022).

Kroeger, F., Racko, G. and Burchell, B. (2021) 'How to create trust quickly: A comparative empirical investigation of the bases of swift trust', *Cambridge Journal of Economics*, 45(1): 129–50.

Lambert, E. G., Jiang, S. and Hogan, N. L. (2008) 'The issue of trust in shaping the job stress, job satisfaction, and organizational commitment of correctional staff', *Professional Issues in Criminal Justice*, 3(4): 37–64.

Le, H., Johnson, C. P. and Fujimoto, Y. (2021) 'Organizational justice and climate for inclusion', *Personnel Review*, 50(1): 1–20.

Lemons, M. and Jones, C. (2000) 'Procedural justice in promotion decisions: Using perceptions of fairness to build employee commitment', *Journal of Managerial Psychology*, 16(4): 268–80.

Levinson, H., Price, C. R., Munden, K. J. and Solley, C. M. (1962) *Men, Management and Mental Health*. Cambridge, MA: Harvard University Press.

Lewicki, R. J. and Benedict Bunker, B. (1996) 'Developing and maintaining trust in work relationships', in R. M. Kramer and T. R. Tyler (eds), *Trust in Organizations*. Thousand Oaks, CA: Sage, pp. 114–39.

Lewis, J. D. and Weigert, A. (1985) 'Trust as a social reality', *Social Forces*, 63: 967– 85.

Macey, W. H., Schneider, B., Barbera, K. M. and Young, S. A. (2009) *Employee Engagement: Tools for Analysis, Practice, and Competitive Advantage*. Malden, WA: Wiley-Blackwell.

McQuaid, D. (2020) 'Black women feel the least empowered in UK offices', *HRreview*, 11 September. Available at: www.hrreview.co.uk/hr-news/121000/121000 (accessed 15 March 2021).

Meyerson, D., Weick, K. E. and Kramer, R. M. (1996) 'Swift trust and temporary groups', in R. M. Kramer and T. R. Tyler (eds), *Trust in Organizations: Frontiers of Theory and Research*. London: Sage, pp. 166–95.

Morgan, W. B. and King, E. B. (2012) 'Mothers' psychological contracts: Does supervisor breach explain intention to leave the organisation?', *Human Resource Management*, 51(5): 629–49.

Mulholland, K. (2004) 'Workplace resistance in an Irish call centre: Slammin', scammin'smokin'an'leavin'', *Work, Employment & Society*, 18(4): 709–24.

Neuman, P. (2021) 'What's electrocuting security staff at BER airport?', *Berliner*, 11 January. Available at: www.berliner-zeitung.de/en/whats-shocking-employees-at-ber-li.131833 (accessed 17 January 2021).

Neveu, J.-P. and Kakavand, B. (2019) 'Endangered resources: The role of organizational justice and interpersonal trust as signals for workplace corruption', *Industrial Relations*, 74(3): 498–524. doi:10.7202/1065170ar

Ocampo, L., Acedillo, V., Bacunador, A. M., Balo, C. C., Lagdameo, Y. J. and Tupa, N. S. (2018) 'A historical review of the development of organizational citizenship behavior (OCB) and its implications for the twenty-first century', *Personnel Review*, 47(4): 821–62.

Partnership at Work (2001) Available at: www.partnership-at-work.com/cgi-bin/webdata_ipapaw.pl?fid=1043406901.27 (accessed 20 June 2003).

Reuters (2012) 'France Telecom investigated over spate of staff suicides', *Reuters*, 6 July. Available at: www.reuters.com/article/2012/07/06/us-france-francetelecom-idUSBRE8650XB20120706 (accessed 2 October 2015).

Reyhanoglu, M. and Akin, O. (2020) 'Impact of toxic leadership on the intention to leave: A research on permanent and contracted hospital employees', *Journal of Economic and Administrative Sciences*. doi:10.1108/JEAS-05-2020-0076

Roch, S. G. and Shanock, L. R. (2006) 'Organizational justice in an exchange framework: Clarifying organizational justice distinctions', *Journal of Management*, 32: 299–322.

Roper, I., Cunningham, I. and James, P. (2003) 'Promoting family-friendly policies: Is the basis of the government's ethical standpoint viable?', *Personnel Review*, 32(2): 211–30.

Rousseau, D. (1989) 'Psychological and implicit contracts in organizations', *Employee Responsibilities and Rights Journal*, 2: 121–39.

Rousseau, D. (1990) 'New hire perceptions of their own and employer's obligations: A study of psychological contracts', *Journal of Organizational Behaviour*, 11: 389–400.

Rutherford, A. (2015) 'Victim Support NI chief sack row settled: Unfair dismissal case ends as organisation and former boss strike a deal', *Belfast Telegraph*, 31 January. Available at: www.belfasttelegraph.co.uk/news/northern-ireland/victim-support-ni-chief-sack-row-settled-unfair-dismissal-case-ends-as-organisation-and-former-boss-strike-a-deal-30951660.html (accessed 10 August 2015).

Safari, A., Barzoki, A. S. and Aqagoli, P. H. (2020) 'Exploring the antecedents and consequences of impersonal trust', *International Journal of Organizational Analysis*, 28(6): 1149–73.

Salamon, S. D. and Robinson, S. L. (2008) 'Trust that binds: The impact of collective felt trust on organizational performance', *Journal of Applied Psychology*, 93(3): 593–601.

Schulz, E. R., Pandey, A. and Camp, R. R. (2020) 'Broken promises: Supervisors and high performing work practices', *Editorial Policy*, 32(3).

Schulz, F., Valizade, D. and Charlwood, A. (2021) 'The effect of intra-workplace pay inequality on employee trust in managers: Assessing a multilevel moderated mediation effect model', *Human Relations*, 75(4): 1–29.

Searle, R. H. and Rice, C. (2018) *Assessing and Mitigating the Impact of Organisational Change on Counterproductive Work Behaviour: An Operational (Dis) Trust Based Framework*. Available at: https://eprints.gla.ac.uk/158525/1/158525.pdf (accessed 21 May 2021).

Searle, R., Den Hartog, D. N., Weibel, A., Gillespie, N., Six, F., Hatzakis, T. and Skinner, D. (2011) 'Trust in the employer: The role of high-involvement work practices and procedural justice in European organizations', *International Journal of Human Resource Management*, 22(5): 1069–92.

Solon, O. and Kaplan, E. (2021) 'Amazon warehouse workers vote not to unionize in Bessemer, Alabama', *NBC News*, 9 April. Available at: www.nbcnews.com/tech/tech-news/early-vote-counts-show-amazon-warehouse-workers-not-likely-unionize-n1263558 (accessed 15 May 2021).

Stecher, M. D. and Rosse, J. G. (2005) 'The distributive side of interactional justice: The effects of interpersonal treatment on emotional arousal', *Journal of Managerial Issues*, 17(2): 229–46.

Stiles, P., Grafton, L., Truss, C., Hope-Hailey, V. and McGovern, P. (1997) 'Performance management and the psychological contract', *Human Resource Management Journal*, 7(1): 57–66.

Tae-Yeol, K. and Kwok, L. (2007) 'Forming and reacting to overall fairness: A cross-cultural comparison', *Organizational Behavior and Human Decision Processes*, 104(1): 83–95.

Thibaut, J. W. and Walker, L. (1975) *Procedural Justice: A Psychological Analysis*. Hillsdale, NJ: Erlbaum.

Thompson, P. and Ackroyd, S. (1995) 'All quiet on the workplace front? A critique of recent trends in British industrial sociology', *Sociology*, 29(4): 615–33.

Tomprou, M. and Lee, M. K. (2022) 'Employment relationships in algorithmic management: A psychological contract perspective', *Computers in Human Behavior*, 126: 106997.

Tzafrir, S. S. (2005) 'The relationship between trust, HRM practices and firm performance', *The International Journal of Human Resource Management*, 16(9): 1600–22.

Tzafrir, S. and Dolan, S. (2004) 'Trust me: A multiple item scale for measuring managers "employee trust"', *Management Research*, 2(2): 115–32.

Watt, L. (2013) 'Chip Starnes, US boss held hostage in Chinese factory, freed after reaching deal with workers', *HuffPost*, 27 June. Available at: www.huffingtonpost.com/2013/06/27/chip-starnes-free_n_3509707.html (accessed 2 October 2015).

Webb, M. and Palmer, G. (1998) 'Evading surveillance and making time: An ethnographic view of the Japanese factory floor in Britain', *British Journal of Industrial Relations*, 36(4): 611–27.

Wollard, K. K. (2011) 'Quiet desperation, another perspective on employee engagement', *Advances in Developing Human Resources*, 13(4): 526–37.

Woodhouse, C. (2015) 'Victims' charity boss called colleague "fat b*****" and "Castle Catholic", tribunal told', *Belfast Telegraph*, 26 January. Available at: www.belfasttelegraph.co.uk/sunday-life/news/exvictims-charity-boss-called-colleague-fat-b-and-castle-catholic-tribunal-told-30937204.html (accessed 10 August 2015).

4

CONTRACT CHANGE AND THE EMPLOYMENT RELATIONSHIP

Learning Outcomes

By the end of this chapter, you should be able to:

* evaluate the importance of contracts of employment *within* the context of the employment relationship - with specific reference to the UK
* provide an overview of the reasons why contracts of employment change and critically analyse the implications of any such changes on the employment relationship
* link what you have read about employment contracts with managerial styles, power realities, degrees of trust and the perceptions of fairness within the employment relationship.

What to Expect

This chapter, although dealing with a legal construct, does not delve into the intricacies of the law surrounding contracts of employment. Instead it discusses why the employment contract forms the basis of the employment relationship, and evaluates how the ways in which the contract is managed impact upon the employment relationship. It explores what happens when the contract needs to be altered by looking at how the act of making changes at work – and hence to the contract – sometimes affects the perceptions of fairness and notions of mutual trust and confidence. There will be links with the preceding chapters (managerial style, perceptions of fairness, **balance of power**, psychological contract, etc.) and the importance of communication will be emphasised – leading naturally into the next chapters looking at precarious work, workplace conflict, **flexible work patterns**, **employee involvement** and participation.

What Is an Employment Contract?

What an organisation can require from its workforce is predominantly regulated by the individual employee's contract of employment. The contract defines what an employee can expect to be asked to do by the employer, and therefore influences the employee's perceptions of what really happens, day to day, in the workplace. Each employee has a contract of employment that embodies an agreement between two parties: the *employer* who guarantees to pay wages in return for the *employee* agreeing to work; that is, to provide their time, effort and expertise to be deployed in ways dictated by the employer (this exchange is the essence of what is known as the 'pay-work-bargain' – Farnham, 1997: 3). In effect it is a **contract of service** stipulating the tasks to be undertaken and the remuneration that an individual can expect in return for their labour. The essential ingredients to such an agreement/contract are:

- an *offer* of work
- *acceptance* of that offer
- an element of *consideration* – something that is valuable to the employee, usually pay, by which the employer can induce the employee to be ready, willing and able to work (Wiley, 2009: 43).

It is important that there is clarity about what the employee is expected to be doing and what they will receive in return. Poorly communicated terms of an employment contract can lead to misunderstandings and subsequent conflict, damaging the employment relationship and perhaps leading to perceptions of organisational injustice.

As soon as an offer of employment is accepted the contract comes into play (Acas, 2013). By starting work the employee indicates that they have accepted the terms and conditions offered by the employer. If, however, any one or more of the three essential ingredients (offer, acceptance and consideration) is missing then there is no contract of employment. This is important, since many statutory employment rights apply only to employees with a contract of employment, rather than, for example, the self-employed or to someone who has a contract *for* rather than *of* service. (A contract *for* service is one where there is no question of employment – it is usually one where a specific task is required to be undertaken by another organisation or by, for example, a freelance worker, who will have sole responsibility for the satisfactory completion of a specific function, as is seen, for instance, when an organisation outsources some of its operations.)

What's in a Name?

On occasions the word 'worker' is used rather than 'employee'. This seeming insignificant change in wording may have a huge impact because, although under EU legislation the term 'worker' is synonymous with 'employee', under UK legislation there are fewer rights accorded to workers than to employees. Recent UK legal cases – for example, Pimlico Plumbers (*Smith v. Pimlico Plumbers Ltd* UKEAT/0211/19/DA.), Uber (*Uber BV & Ors v Aslam & Ors* [2021] UKSC 5) and Adison Lee (*Addison Lee Ltd v Lange & Ors* [2021] EWCA Civ 594) – have centred on the distinctions between being an employee, self-employed, or a worker. The terms are important as employers, historically, did not provide holiday or sick pay to those classed as self-employed. In theory when someone is classed as a worker they receive at least the minimum wage, are covered by the working time directive and can choose to refuse or take up work that is offered to them. They are, however, unable to claim for unfair dismissal or redundancy.

Exercise 4.1

A worker is defined as someone who personally undertakes work, or service, for another party whether or not there is an explicit/implicit contract of employment or indeed a different type of contract. But this rather loose definition is causing problems. The Edinburgh Employment Appeal Tribunal has now ruled that foster carers are entitled to employment rights and should be regarded as council workers. Recently a barrister, undertaking an 'independent chair' role for the Midwifery Council, claimed to be a worker and therefore entitled to holiday pay pro rata for the time he spent chairing a panel (*Nursing and Midwifery Council v Somerville* UKEAT/0258/20/RN).

- With these two cases in mind discuss whether the term 'worker' is too loosely defined when it comes to enabling employment protections and rights. What do you think are the implications for:
  - ○ 'volunteers' who work for charities and for those who manage them
  - ○ school age children who regularly babysit
  - ○ a waiter in a sea-front café that only opens when the weather is fine
  - ○ a group of Sikh volunteers who routinely provide afternoon tea for the elderly?

The employment contract, like the employment relationship, does not occur in a vacuum. It is a product of history, echoing the shifts in the economic and social realities of the workplace. Each contract is affected not only by the type of work required and the skills that a potential employee might bring to the job, but by a mixture of other factors such as the culture of the country in which the work is to be undertaken, the social mores of the region, and legislative restrictions and requirements imposed on the parties to the contract. Contracts therefore are a combination of the interactions between culture, custom and practice, common law and different pieces of legislation introduced at different times. Within this overarching context an employee's perceptions of fairness and fair treatment are emphatically important.

In the UK, legislation that has influenced and affected the employment contract ranges from the Statute of Artificers in 1563, through a series of Master and Servant Acts – some of which sanctioned up to three months' imprisonment for breaches of the employment contract – and the Employers and Workmen Act 1875, to the Contracts of Employment Act 1963 and finally to the present Employment Rights Act 1996. Similarly other industrialised nations, such as Canada, Japan and Germany, have enacted legislative restrictions (both collective and individual) on the employment contract over time (Roehling, 2004: 67). In essence, however, it is critically important to recognise that the key issue affecting the operation of the contract is that it remains based on property rights, as evident from the (sometimes implicit) notions of 'master and servant'. The philosophy behind this prescribes that an employer has the right to do what he likes with his property. In relation to employment this means that the employers' agents, their managers, have this right by proxy. Yet the demands a manager can actually make from the employer's 'property' are not without restrictions. Managers have to contend with the reality that the contract can only specify certain terms, such as hours, pay, holidays and so on, but it cannot decree exactly how much *effort* and/or *enthusiasm* an employee will put into their work. Such effort is not theirs to control. This has become particularly important as managers increasingly seek greater **discretionary behaviour** or *beyond contract working* from employees. Much of the flexibility that managers seek when trying to enforce an employment contract stems from this basic problem which is part of the hinterland behind many employment tribunal cases where questions determining the fine line between efficiency and exploitation become all important.

In the UK, the concept of a contract *of* employment only became the norm following the National Insurance Act 1946. This importantly established the distinction between the two different types of wage earners: those employed under a contract *of* service, as opposed to those employed on their own account under a contract *for* service, who under the Act were ineligible for unemployment benefits. This distinction was deemed useful and so applied both for the calculation of income tax and then later, in the 1960s, it was adopted within new employment protection legislation. These changes had the effect of harmonising the workforce by removing the old distinction between manual and non-manual workers; all employees with a contract *of* employment were now treated equally in the eyes of the law. (For a good account of the development and history of the contract of employment, see Deakin, 2001.)

One of the current issues that can sometimes lead to confusion around the employment relationship is the variety of contracts that exist, for example, contracts for permanent full-time or part-time staff, temporary or fixed-term contracts, zero-hours contracts and those for the self-employed. (See Chapters 5 and 11 for discussions about the variety of contract types linked to a flexible workforce and why they might be used.)

With the increasing demands from employers to have a flexible workforce, the nature of the contract of employment has become more contentious, particularly since one of the ways of achieving flexibility involves a departure from the 'typical' or 'standard' contract (i.e., a contract for permanent full-time or part-time work), thereby creating different forms of employment status covering those, for example, on fixed-term contracts such as 'bank staff', agency workers, zero-hour contracts and so on. A zero-hours contract is one where an employee has been hired even though there is no guarantee of work for them. Such contracts allow employers to deploy the individuals on these contracts as and when they are needed, often at short notice. Their pay therefore depends on how many hours they actually work. Zero hours contracts often receive negative publicity where unscrupulous employers choose to cynically abuse these forms of contract, treating those subject to them in a cavalier manner. When an organisation employs a number of people who are on a variety of different terms and conditions, yet ostensibly undertaking the same tasks, it may lead to perceptions of organisational injustice and discontent amongst the employees, resulting in poorly motivated staff and lower levels of productivity. The majority of employees do, however, work under permanent contracts that have no termination date (although these contracts usually specify the notice periods that either party is required to give, should they wish to end the contract).

In the UK approximately 1.5 million employees were employed under temporary contracts between October and December 2021 although this number has decreased slightly (ONS, 2022).

Guest (2004) suggested that where employees themselves deliberately choose a flexible contract of employment their psychological contracts are positive, and their levels of commitment and innovation are similar to those on permanent contracts. Storey et al. (2002) examined the part played in enhancing innovation by the use of flexible employment contracts – the theory being that such contracts encouraged a reduction in workplace rigidity, promoting an influx of new ideas – but they found that, although flexible contracts often occurred in tandem with innovative practices, there was no direct link. Two decades on from this research it is apparent that many employees do not actively choose temporary contracts but accept that this may be the only work available to them. Analysis by the Trades Union Congress (TUC 2013, Collinson 2020) shows that within the UK involuntary temporary work – people on temporary contracts of employment because they are unable to find permanent work – has been growing sharply for a number of years and that Black and minority ethnic workers (BME) are far more likely to be trapped in temporary and insecure work (see also Rubery and Rafferty, 2013). Garcia-Pérez et al. (2019) echoed these findings when they looked at the use of temporary contracts in Spain. Here temporary contracts were a great help for the young trying to get a foothold on the employment ladder. Yet such employment often did not, as hoped, lead to better paid alternative employment and those on such contracts remained there. Kiersztyn (2021) too noted that, in Poland, such contracts were more of a trap than a stepping stone in terms of moving to alternative forms of employment.

The most common form of contract enabling temporary work is for a fixed contractual period, but casual work (e.g., someone who is not part of the permanent workforce but supplies work on an *irregular* basis) has been the fastest growing form of temporary work. Prevailing economic conditions impact both the levels of employment and the types of work available, with the subsequent effect of affecting the numbers and types of contract in use. Guest and Isaksson (2019: 166) suggest that employers prefer to use temporary work contracts because they provide more control, allowing them to manipulate the numbers employed in line with their current requirements:

> As legislation in many European countries provided greater protection against dismissal for permanent staff, organizations began to use temporary employment contracts as a means of maintaining employment flexibility, enabling them to adjust their workforce numbers as demand rose and fell. This tendency was more marked in countries such as Spain, where legislation made it more difficult to remove labour compared with the UK, where it was less of a problem.

This all indicates that, as Menegatti has suggested,

> … we are witnessing a growing number of work relationships that fall outside the scope of labour law, where supposedly independent contractors are functionally, and quite often even economically, dependent on a single main client. (2020: 27)

Such casual forms of employment do not have the same protection as that given to those on contracts of employment where the employee has an ongoing relationship with the employer. Table 4.1 shows clearly how the numbers of temporary workers fluctuate, although of course the figures do not show the numbers who work 'off the books' and therefore remain unrecorded.

Table 4.1 Employees who are on temporary employment contracts as a percentage of the total number of employees

	2016	2017	2018	2019	2020	2021
European Union - 27 countries (from 2020)	12.3	12.5	12.3	11.9	10.7	11.2
Denmark	10.9	9.5	8.2	8.3	8.7	8.8
France	13.4	13.9	13.7	13.3	12.4	11.9
Ireland	6.5	6.7	7.4	7.2	6.7	6.9
Spain	21.5	22.1	22.3	21.9	20.1	29.9
UK	4.5	4.3	4.2	3.8	-----	-----

Source: data taken from: Euro Stat (LFSI_PT_A) https://ec.europa.eu/eurostat/databrowser/view/
tesem110/default/table?lang=en%20%20%20(updated%2002%2F06%2F2021)https://ec.europa.eu/
eurostat/databrowser/view/tesem110/default/table?lang=en

It is not just in the UK where difficult economic circumstances have had an impact on employment patterns. Elsewhere temporary fixed-term types of contract are becoming more prevalent, and different governments have enacted legislation 'freeing-up' labour markets in order to encourage non-traditional types of employment and economic growth. (See Wass, 2008, for an account of such legislative loosening occurring in Germany prior to the 2008 financial crisis.) In Italy labour law reforms in 2013 provided for fixed-term contracts to be extended for up to 12 months, and crucially employers no longer have to state exactly why the contract is fixed-term rather than permanent (Ashurst, 2013). Other countries too have experienced a loosening of restrictions around fixed-term contracts with the aim of introducing greater flexibility into the labour market. In Germany, until late 2012, an employer could enter into a fixed-term contract just once with each separate employee during that employee's working life; this is no longer the case since the Federal Labour court revoked this 'lifetime' restriction and now employers can offer fixed-term contracts to employees (provided that they have held no other employment contract with that employee in the previous three years).

Employment Contracts and the Power Realities of the Employment Relationship

The problem with contracts of employment, whether temporary or fixed, is that the parties who agree to the contractual terms are not equal. This inequality is affected by a number of internal and external factors, such as the state of the labour market, the employer's need for specific skills or an employee's need for money. So, for example, if there are high levels of unemployment and someone is desperate for work they are more likely to accept employment terms that, in other circumstances, they might not. On the other hand, if the employer is looking for someone with specific skills that are in short supply, employees with those skills are in a stronger, though not yet equal, position and may be able to negotiate contractual terms that are more to their liking. Even when the labour market is buoyant the employee/potential employee has less power and influence over a contract than the employer who will be able to dictate the type of work required, the place of work, the pace of work and the requisite hours:

[T]he relation between an employer and an isolated employee or worker is typically a relation between a bearer of power and one who is not a bearer of power. In its inception it is an act of submission, in its operation it is a condition of subordination, however much the submission and subordination may be concealed by that indispensable figment of the legal mind known as the 'contract of employment'. (Kahn-Freund et al., 1983: 18)

This power imbalance – and the ways in which this is managed – has a direct impact on employee perceptions of organisational justice and hence on levels of trust, and on the psychological contract and consequently on the employment relationship. On occasions it may lead employees to see the benefits of trade union membership, particularly if they feel that collective action may provide them with greater protection (Kelly, 1998).

News Flash 4.1

Breaching Levels of Trust and Confidence: Ikea France Spied on at Least 400 Workers

In June 2021 Ikea was fined €1 million (roughly £860,000) following its conviction for spying on its French employees and Jean-Louis Baillot, the former CEO of Ikea France, was given a two-year suspended prison sentence and fined €500,000 for storing personal data. A further 15 people including several HR employees, police officers, private investigators and store managers, are also facing allegations, while the company is bracing itself to cope with potential damages from separate lawsuits filed by unions and 74 employees. Worker representatives said the information collected was used to target union leaders. Such activities affect the levels of trust within the company.

The court heard how the company illegally obtained information about its staff, collecting and storing information on and about them by scrutinising their bank records and paying for access to police records. A number of dubious means were deployed in order to gain information - for example, a senior member of staff pretended to be an airline worker in order to ascertain whether an employee, who travelled to Morocco, was faking a year-long illness. In addition to its own sleuthing Ikea used private investigators (the annual bill for this running to as much as €600,000). Once it knew about the allegations IKEA fired several managers and overhauled its internal policy.

Similarly, in 2020, H&M was fined €35 million following its monitoring of hundreds of German employees in the previous six years.

Sources: BBC, 2021; Pailliez and White, 2021

Evidence for some of the ways that this power imbalance affects employees can be seen by looking at the number of people who are dissatisfied with their contractual conditions of work. A TUC survey of 3,000 working people in 2008 highlighted the discrepancy between employee expectations and the realities of work, giving some idea of the strength/weakness of the respective levels of power held by employers and employees. It found that the commonest problems that people report at work fall into three groups:

- Pay – just under half the workforce say that their contractual pay has not kept up with the cost of living (42%) and significant proportions say that their workplace has unfair pay structures (26%) or that they do not get the same pay as people doing similar jobs for other organisations (31%).
- Workloads, stress and hours – the biggest complaint is of an increased workload (46%), with 39% complaining of increased stress levels and 23% of longer working hours. Often excessive working hours are outside of the original contractual terms agreed between the employer and employee.
- Training and progression – 30% complain of poor promotion prospects and 27% say they lack training. (TUC, 2008: 2)

Sometimes of course there is an extreme imbalance of power. This can be seen, for example, when employees are so desperate to make a good impression that they subjugate themselves to the will of the employer to a degree that is potentially harmful. This desire for work, counter-balanced by possible exploitation, is graphically illustrated by the behaviour of student interns working in parts of the finance sector in the City of London. The overworking of junior employees coupled with the suicide of a (possibly overworked) German student working for Merrill Lynch in the summer of 2013 led to demands to overhaul the long-hours culture, prevalent in the City. Here, regardless of the terms within the contract of employment, the student interns felt obliged to work for what they perceived to be the standard working week of six and a half 15-hour days. Interns, desperate to convert to a full-time role, did whatever it took to appear committed and worthy of a future as a full-time employee, epitomising the powerlessness of those who are desperate for work. Recent cases against Merrill Lynch in the USA have indicated that there is still a long-hours problem for the firm – staff claim they are required to work long hours, exceeding their contractual obligations, without receiving appropriate payment (Braswell, 2019).

News Flash 4.2

Employers' Right to Induce Acceptance of Contract Change Clarified

In October 2021, when hearing *Kostal UK vs Dunkley*, the five members of the UK Supreme Court explicitly clarified the details of an employer's rights when bargaining with trade unions. Despite Kostal (the employer) losing the case, the majority of the Supreme Court importantly agreed that, should negotiation with a union fail and the collective bargaining process end, then *trade unions do not have the right to reject changes to employee terms and conditions.*

Once collective bargaining processes have been exhausted employers can therefore legitimately bypass a union and make direct offers to employees. Ultimately this means that unions cannot rely on the existing status quo and prohibit proposed changes to terms and conditions when negotiations have failed.

Source: Jackson, 2021

Contract Terms

A contract of employment sets out the terms and conditions that the parties agree to. Contract terms can be *express*, this is where the terms are clearly stated, and may either be written down or orally explicit. An express term cannot remove or override a statutory right by imposing less favourable terms. So for example in the UK, if the employer states that a full-time employee's holiday entitlement is a mere 10 days a year this is an express term that would be superseded by the current legislation; however, if the contract stipulated that the holiday would be 45 days per year then this would be allowable as an express term that exceeds the legislative requirements. Theoretically neither the employer nor the employee can alter the **express terms** without the agreement of the other, so if for example the employer wanted to make a change to the number of days' leave this could not be done without the agreement of the employee; neither can the employee act in a way that changes the contract without the express specific agreement from the employer. However, employees can agree to waive their rights to work no more than 48 hours per week. In 2013 the UK Government introduced a scheme allowing employees to waive employment protection, such as the rights to claim unfair dismissal, or ask for flexible work, in return for at least £2,000 worth of shares in the company, causing Lord Pannick to declare, in a House of Lords' debate, that employment rights must not become tradable, 'because the inequality of bargaining power between employee and employer means that freedom of contract is quite insufficient to protect the employee'. This should be considered in the light of the discussion of power realities, above.

Express terms are not just terms that enable activities as they can also, on occasion, restrict the behaviour of an employee and specify behaviours that the employee is prevented from undertaking, such as talking to the press, working for a competitor and so on. It is usual for express terms within a contract to be explicit about where an employee is expected to work and what work they are supposed to undertake. However this may, on occasion, be much broader than a specific workplace address and range of specific tasks. For example, a clause could be so broad that it specifies that an employee would be required to work 'anywhere within the United Kingdom undertaking whatever tasks are deemed necessary as and when required', although such clauses must be 'reasonable' (see below).

Some terms, however, are not explicit but can be implied. Brodie quotes Lord Steyn, who made the point that,

> … the implied obligation … is apt to cover the great diversity of situations in which a balance has to be struck between an employer's interest, in managing his business as he sees fit, and the employee's interest in not being unfairly and improperly exploited. (2001: 85)

Such **implied terms** exist in any employment contract because they cover issues so fundamental to the notion of an agreement or contract that without them there would never have been an agreement in the first place. Collins and Mantouvalou (2016: 205) have proposed an additional implied term for employers, suggesting that they need to respect both the dignity and autonomy of their employees. This addition arises because, they say, there will be occasions when an employee may be required to undertake something or behave in a way that goes against their dignity. Implied terms, of course, will be influenced by the culture of the organisation and the country in which the work is being undertaken. Such implied terms arise through custom and practice and/or from the conduct of the parties.

News Flash 4.3

Spanish Parliament Changes Temporary Contract Regulations

In order to change the extensive use of temporary jobs in the Spanish labour market (over 26%) and prevent some of the exploitative practices associated with temporary work contracts, the Spanish Parliament has revised the use of temporary contracts. There are now two types – structural and training – where structural refers to unexpected short term cover, such as providing cover for an absent worker. The new regulations cap the total length of *consec utive* temporary contracts at one year, rather than four. For those who previously worked for the same company, under a temporary contract, for 18 out of the previous 24 months, it will automatically be converted to a permanent arrangement.

Sources: Carreño, 2022; Cook, 2022

In the UK, 'custom and practice' refers to a term in the contract that can be said to be implied as a result of work being undertaken in a particular way over a prolonged period of time. To achieve the status of a recognised term within the contract the custom must be reasonable (fair), notorious (well-known to everyone concerned) and certain (well established, clearly understood and not discretionary). Implied terms are not written down but can be divined by looking at the circumstances that are pervasive in the workplace and/or by looking at what may have been intended when the contract was initially formed. Implied terms, despite not being explicit, are still *binding* on the parties to the contract, especially in the following circumstances:

- *Employees' binding terms* include obeying lawful orders and instruction, exercising reasonable care and skill, loyalty and good faith, adapting to reasonable changes in work practices, and, importantly, maintaining the relationship of mutual trust and confidence.
- *Employers' binding terms* include paying wages, providing a safe system of work, informing employees of important entitlements, taking reasonable care, maintaining the relationship of mutual trust and confidence and not stigmatising employees. In some countries there are terms which bind the ways in which an employer must behave, whether or not they are explicitly included in the written contract. In China, for example, regardless of what is written into a contract, legislation dictates the grounds upon which a contract may be terminated and specifies severance pay.

Both the employer and the employee have a duty to the other that expects mutual reciprocity of trust and confidence. The principles underpinning European and UK contract law make explicit that there is a duty on the parties to operate the contract in good faith with fair dealing (Nogler, 2008). Brodie (2001: 86) points out that those implied obligations linked to mutual trust are exactly what distinguishes the employment contract from a commercial one and quotes the views of two of the UK Law lords concerned in the Malik case where 'Lord Steyn saw it as having a role in preventing exploitation of workers' and 'Lord Nicholls regarded it as a tool to prevent employers mistreating employees by "harsh and oppressive behaviour or by any other form of conduct which is unacceptable today as falling below the standards set by the implied trust and confidence term"' (*Malik* v. *BCCI* [1998] AC 20 at 37).

The term *mutual trust and confidence* is not explicit and is open to the subjective interpretation of the parties to the contract, and of course any court to which it is referred. Mutual trust and confidence are concepts that, although not universal, do figure in the fabric of employment contracts across the majority of different national legal systems. For example, employers and employees in Mexico have mutual duty of trust and confidence towards one another, while in an Australian case (*CBA* v. *Barker* [2013] FCAFC 83) the Australian Full Federal Court concluded that there is an implied term of mutual trust and confidence in *all* Australian employment contracts and that any contravention of this can lead to the wronged party claiming breach of contract. (In this particular case the court decided that the Commonwealth Bank breached its implied duty of mutual trust and confidence by removing phone and email access and failing to take positive steps to consult with an employee of 20 years' standing about the possibility of redeployment.)

News Flash 4.4

UAE: Contracts of Employment Made More Equitable

On 2 February 2022 new laws covering employment contracts used by private sector employers in the United Arab Emirates (UAE) came into force. Compliance with the new regulations must be made by February 2023. It is hoped that the changes, designed to boost competitiveness, will encourage more people to work and stay in the UAE. The new law creates a more flexible approach, enabling part-time and flexible working arrangements. (Historically, only full-time employment was permitted.) Unlimited contracts must be abolished and replaced with new contracts for a fixed term (for a period of three years), which may be renewed on the same conditions with the consent of both parties for a similar period or less. Women are to get **equal pay** and improved maternity leave provision. Different modes of working such as full, part-time, flexible and temporary work are now permitted as is job sharing and remote working. Employees on fixed term contracts can now be dismissed with notice as normal, with no additional compensation being payable as in the past, but it is now unlawful to dismiss an employee for filing a complaint against the employer.

Source: SHRM, 2021

Exercise 4.2

After reading the piece below answer the following questions:

- Write a list of the implied terms in the injured employee's contract of employment that you think have been breached.
- Say what impact you think this accident had on the employment relationship of the work colleagues of the injured man; in particular, how do you think it affected their perceptions of organisational justice?
- Why did you come to your conclusions for Question 2?

In March 2021 a Nottingham-based mattress manufacturer Dreamtouch Mattresses Ltd., was fined £66,000 and ordered to pay costs of £4,835.20 following a nasty accident when an employee suffered multiple injuries to his arm, shoulder, ribs and neck after he was dragged into a mattress rolling machine. There were no guards on the machine to prevent workers from accessing dangerous moving parts and, frighteningly, it was common practice at the site for employees to use their hands and arms when feeding and pressing mattresses onto the unguarded rotating winding reel. The company had no documented safe system or training in place for the use of that machine and allowed the process of hand feeding the mattresses.

Source: Health and Safety Executive, 2021

As we have seen, some express terms within a contract may be negotiated by the parties, but others can originate from a number of different sources. Within each contract therefore terms may be:

- *Express* – that is, those specifically stated in the contract
- *Implied* – these are fundamental but not made explicit within the contract
- *Statutory* – that is, the law requires this (employers can offer better terms, but not legally those that are less favourable). Such terms are a statutory requirement (e.g., payment of the minimum wage, maternity pay, redundancy pay, right not to be discriminated against) and will differ from country to country – across Europe employment legislation tends to be harmonised but many of these areas are universal.
- *Incorporated* – that is, present because they are included in the employer's rules or procedures or have been negotiated with a trade union or staff association and the relevant parts of the collective agreement have been incorporated into contracts. In the UK few employees outside the public sector are covered by collective agreements and, as a consequence, fewer employees have terms incorporated from collective agreements although many are affected by handbooks, health and safety legislation and employer regulations being wholly or partially incorporated. In Europe, where works councils cover a greater proportion of employees, incorporated terms stemming from collective agreements are more prevalent. In Finland, for example, a collective agreement is deemed to be binding on all employers and employees within the sector covered by that agreement – whether or not the parties concerned are actually signatories. This consequently has a knock-on impact on the contracts of everyone within that sector (Hietanen, 2000).

While in the UK there is *no* legal obligation on the part of the employer to put *all* the terms of a contract in writing, workers and employees now have the same right to a written statement of their employment particulars when they start work or before their first day, regardless of how long they are to be employed.

The written statement must include details about:

- the job title and a description of the work required
- the hours and days of the week the worker or employee is required to work, and whether they may be varied and how
- where the work will take place
- entitlements to any paid leave
- any other benefits such as holidays and holiday pay, sick pay and pension arrangements
- any probationary period
- any training provided by the employer
- details of the **discipline** and **grievance** procedures or where they may be found. (s1 of the Employment rights Act 1966 (amended by the Employment Act 2002 and the Employment Rights [Miscellaneous Amendments]Regulation 2019 that came into effect from April 2020)

However, the statement is not a contract. Any changes to the written particulars must be detailed, in writing and *agreed* by the parties to the employment contract. Often employers wanting agreement will notify employees of a change and ask them to sign and return a form indicating their agreement – this saves time, is administratively simple and ensures that a written record is kept. In Russia verbal agreements are forbidden as the Labour Code here stipulates that an employment contract *must* always be in writing, while in Turkey some terms are implied within each employment contract because they are not specifically part of employment regulation but fall under the Turkish Code of Obligations under which, for example, employers have a duty to protect their employees from physiological and sexual harassment.

Changing contract terms and the impact on the employment relationship

Working practices and requirements are *not* static – contracts, however, are. Changes in technology, product details and market requirements all dictate that the work employees undertake alters over time – as do their wages, holiday entitlements and so on. Yet a contract is more like a photograph than a film; it is a snapshot of an employee's terms and conditions at the beginning of the relationship with the employer, yet the relationship is ongoing. Indeed Commons (1924: 285) suggests that the employment contract is a *continuing implied series of contracts*. Because work and its rewards change over time, so the contract needs to change too. In terms of managing the employment relationship in a positive – and legally compliant – way, such changes, allowing for the terms and conditions of the contract to evolve over time, should be managed without alienating an employee while simultaneously allowing the employer to achieve the levels of work required. The concept of an evolving contract is unknown in law so changes can only be made through the same process that created the contract in the first place, that is, with the agreement of both the parties to the contract. If an employer changes the terms of an employee's contract unilaterally this breaches the contract and, depending on the change, may have a negative impact on the employee's perceptions of organisational justice, and influence whether or not the employee trusts the employer. Thus any changes proposed by the employer should be discussed with the employees concerned. Such a conversation must be genuine; the employer must respond in a way that considers and takes into account any views expressed by the employee. The consultation can be with trade union representatives, non-trade union representatives or with individual employees. Where it leads to an agreement to change the terms and conditions, this is known as a *consensual variation*.

News Flash 4.5

10% of Workers Told to Re-apply for Their Jobs on Worse Terms and Conditions, says TUC

An online survey of 2,231 employed people in England and Wales in November 2020 found 1 in 10 workers were subject to 'hire and fire conditions'.

The TUC General Secretary Frances O'Grady said: 'Everyone deserves to be treated with dignity and respect at work. Forcing people to re-apply for their jobs on worse terms and conditions is plain wrong. Fire and rehire tactics have no place in modern Britain and must be outlawed'.

The TUC found the practice of 'firing and rehiring' workers (where redundancy is the only alternative for those refusing to sign up) is most commonly used for younger workers and those from Black, Asian and minority ethnic backgrounds. Almost a fifth (18%) of 18- to 24-year olds said their employer had tried to rehire them on inferior terms during the Covid pandemic. Almost twice as many BAME (15%) as white employees (8%) had been subject to the same treatment. Those from lower socio-economic groups were almost twice as likely to have been told to reapply for their jobs than those on higher socio-economic grades.

Source: TUC, 2021

The employment contract can, however, be changed or varied by any of the following:

- A formal agreement between employer and employee to the change.
- Periodic changes in the law affecting statutory rights – so, for example, if the legislation surrounding hours of work, or minimum wage levels, alters, this will impact on those contracts where the existing terms and conditions have become illegal because they no longer comply with the law. Changes are required to ensure compliance with the law – there does not have to be agreement between the parties for this to happen.
- Where the contract allows for the terms and conditions to be updated by the negotiation of a collective agreement between the employer and a representative party, the new collective agreement alters the existing terms and newly negotiated terms are incorporated into the contract without the express agreement of the individuals concerned.

- The contract itself allows for a change, for example if it contains a mobility or flexibility clause. These clauses tend to use words like 'as and when necessary' and are sufficiently broad to allow the employer to perhaps dictate a new place of work or range of tasks. It is not uncommon for a contract to say, for example, that an employee has to work anywhere where the organisation is based. In theory this would mean that if someone worked for an organisation with sites across the UK they might be required to relocate from say Glasgow to Exeter. Requests to move, however, must be 'reasonable' and this usually means the employer has to give sufficient notice of the change. Where this does not happen it damages the employment relationship, leading to perceptions of organisational injustice and possible litigation.
- The employer attempts to impose a change unilaterally. As above, this too can result in a poorer employment relationship and possible litigation.
- Working methods that 'evolve' over time, changing the basis of some of the contract terms.

Clearly where there is consensual variation, that is where both parties agree to the changes, the implications for the employment relationship are very different from when an employer chooses to impose a change unilaterally. Any attempt by the employer to do so will almost always amount to a breach of contract. Breaches of contract are not only restricted to breaches of express terms as they also cover breaches of implied terms, especially the need to maintain a relationship where there is mutual trust and confidence between the parties to the contract. Acting in a way that indicates that the employer no longer has confidence in the employee (or vice versa) will amount to breach of contract, for example, singling out one employee for different treatment, or publicly reprimanding an employee, could irrevocably change the relationship of trust between the two and result in a breakdown in the relationship – here a breach of contract is almost inevitable.

News Flash 4.6

Water Board Employees Threaten to Go on Strike After Contracts Unilaterally Changed

In April 2021 Workers at a South African water utility, Rand, threatened to strike after it unilaterally changed their contracts, withdrawing incentive bonuses (which had been paid for the last 17 years according to the South African Municipal Workers Union) and altering some of their employment conditions with no consultation. The judge at a hearing in the Labour Court lambasted the employer for failing to meet with the union to solve this issue as a matter of urgency and urged both sides to meet and reach an amicable settlement.

The Commission for Conciliation Mediation and Arbitration (CCMA) is to arbitrate on the matter.

Sources: https://ewn.co.za/2021/04/21/samwu-postpones-rand-water-strike-to-allow-ccma-intervention; http://mediadon.co.za/2021/04/21/samwu-vindicated-by-labour-court-postpones-strike-at-rand-water/

Case Snippet 4.1

Costly Breach of Trust and Confidence

An Employment Tribunal has said that the charity, Age Concern, as an employer,

> ... was in fundamental breach of [the employment] contract in respect of the implied term
> that an employer will not, without reasonable cause, act in a way which is calculated, or likely
> to destroy, or seriously damage, the trust and confidence between employer and employee.

This was said in relation to Gillian Smith who had worked for the charity from 2014 until August 2019. She resigned after the Board of Trustees overturned several of her decisions, breaching the implied term of trust and confidence making her continued employment untenable. She explained her grievances in a letter to the Board – but it did not respond.

The tribunal heard about three areas where Gillian Smith felt unsupported and undermined by the board:

1   After warning employees that if their bullying behaviour continued it would lead to disciplinary action, one of them shouted, 'shove your job up your arse'. Smith interpreted this as a resignation and informed the Trustees. Later the Trustees dealt with a complaint from the 'shouting x-employee' without informing Smith. Furthermore this complaint was raised at her 2019 appraisal.

2   Smith confronted an employee who lied about owning a car (a prerequisite for a promotion she wanted). This employee complained to the Board about Smith saying that it was Smith who had lied about the car and that Smith had only offered her statutory sick pay not full pay while she was off sick. The Board dealt with the aggrieved employee without involving Smith and merely informed her of the outcome.

3   When Smith decided to suspend an employee, pending an investigation into hostile behaviour, the Board supported this then – without her knowledge – reversed its decision, so the employee returned to work. This, Smith felt, humiliated her and damaged both her authority and reputation.

The Tribunal found that Smith was subject to cumulative breaches of trust and confidence from the Board and awarded her £26,578.88 in compensation, including awards for loss of earnings, ongoing future loss and loss of statutory rights.

Source: Ms G Smith v Age Concern Exmouth & District: 1404736/2019 (2 October 2020). Available from: www.gov.uk/employment-tribunal-decisions/ms-g-smith-v-age-concern-exmouth-district-1404736-2019

In many cases employers sometimes impose the change and wait for the employee to either consent by conduct (i.e., by actually working in the new way without formally protesting) or to commence legal proceedings.

When a contract is amended to take account of new term(s), Section 4 of ERA 96 says that a new statement incorporating the change must be issued within a month of the agreement.

In 2021 the Scottish Fair Work Convention recognised that

> ... fair work is a journey that individual employers are making at different paces, we are also aware that some practices are almost always incompatible with fair work. 'Fire and rehire', in our view, fits this definition. Its use flies in the face of normal contractual relations, which require genuine agreement to any contractual change; it undermines the need for constructive dialogue within workplaces as well as good workplace relationships, and may well undermine employee trust and commitment long beyond its immediate use, harming businesses along the way.

- With this quote in mind analyse the implications for the employment relationship of an employer changing the terms of the employees' contracts a) without talking to them first b) by operating a hire and rehire. Give the reasons for your answer, using the concepts and models discussed in the previous chapter.

Source: Scottish Fair Work Convention, 2021

Implications for the employment relationship of a poorly handled contract change

A poorly handled contract change can have an adverse impact on employee commitment, motivation, levels of trust and the psychological contract. It can create the potential for increased numbers of grievances and the potential for damaging legal claims and cases going to employment tribunals. This can be time consuming, costly and damaging to the organisation's reputation. It might also lead to higher levels of staff turnover, lowered productivity and increased membership of a trade union, with subsequent demand for recognition. Where a union is already recognised, there could be industrial action – damaging both the output and the reputation of the organisation. For example, Yvonne Roberts (2015), writing in the *Observer*, documents the case of hotel room assistants who, despite assurances that their terms and conditions of work would not change when their employer switched from one cleaning services company, Hotelcare, to another similar company, WGC, discovered that they were expected to clean more rooms over the same period of time and for the same amount of money.

British Gas Workers Sacked Over Contracts Dispute

Around 500 British Gas engineers (2% of the workforce) have been sacked after they refused to sign new contracts introducing inferior terms and conditions and reducing their pay by 15%.

(Continued)

Workers who had been in dispute with the company had been given until 14 April 2021 to sign the contract or be dismissed. Following 43 days of strike action in protest against the changes, the GMB union warned the sackings would not be the end of the dispute and that action against the company would continue. Justin Bowden, GMB Regional Secretary said: 'British Gas doesn't give a toss for either customers or staff (this) is shown by the mass sackings of engineers it needs so badly for customer services (and by its suspension of) the sale of boiler insurance cover'.

Sources: www.bbc.co.uk/news/business-56746656; www.gmb.org.uk/british-gas-bosses-push-ahead-with-sackings-of-engineers-140421

Advice for employers seeking change to contracts of employment

Clearly the approach taken by the employer will vary with the organisation involved and the types of employee representation in place. It will be influenced by factors such as the aim and nature of the change. Changes are often introduced to reduce headcount and costs, thus worsening the employment rights for some employees. Other influential factors affecting the ways in which contracts are altered will be the different management styles and frames of reference; the power relations between the employer and employee, including whether or not there is a trade union presence; the nature and the importance of the change to the business itself; legal advice; existing procedures; and the perceived need to maintain harmonious employee relations. It would be illegal for an employer to alter a contract in such a way that the terms offered fall below the statutory minimum.

Since it is possible to bring about change by consent, employers are advised to pursue this avenue first. In this case an employer should:

- *talk* to the employees (in good time) about the changes and seek their views and subsequent agreement
- *explain* the reasons behind the change if not all employees are affected, and *justify* the choice
- provide sufficient *time* before the change – this notice period is essential if the start and end times of work or the location are altering
- explain the benefits to the employees of the change and if necessary use appropriate *discretionary benefits*; that is, offer an incentive to undertake the change – this does not have to be money, it could for example be an additional half day holiday tacked onto the Christmas break
- consider, if necessary, the availability of *alternative work* for those employees not wishing to change
- consider building into any contract of employment, *express mobility and flexibility clauses*. Phrases like 'as and when necessary' become useful tools in this process, although of course changes introduced via this method must be 'reasonable'.

News Flash 4.8

Ryanair Sacks 'Fake News' Employees

Six Ryanair cabin crew members from Portugal were dismissed on Monday 5 November 2018 for breach of contract on grounds of gross misconduct. Their behaviour was deemed to have damaged Ryanair's reputation and caused a breach of trust considered irreparable.

Four Ryanair planes diverted to Malaga following Hurricane Leslie, left staff spending the night in an office as hotel accommodation was fully booked. The six had apparently staged a photograph to back-up a false claim that they were forced to sleep on the floor of the Malaga crew room. (The photograph and accompanying story went viral and were widely reported on a variety of international media outlets.) The Portuguese union SNPVA disputes Ryanair's summary of events saying that between 1.30 a.m. and 6 a.m. 24 staff members were put in the crew room where there were 'minimum rest facilities' and no food or drink. The group moved to a VIP lounge at 6 a.m. to sleep on shared sofas, before flying back to Porto the following day.

Sources: Griffith, 2018; Jasper, 2018

Organisations can enhance the possibility of consensual change by adopting appropriate long-term strategies, for example: developing appropriate organisational cultures by using effective workplace communications systems; ensuring that there are effective employee involvement and participation mechanisms, including, on occasion, trade union representation; and negotiation encouraging functional flexibility and providing extensive training and development.

Many of these strategies fit with the Budd (2004; Budd et al., 2010) model of a balanced employment relationship encompassing equity, efficiency and voice. In the UK since the case of *United Bank Limited* v. *Akhtar* [1989] IRLR 507 EAT employers have been more mindful of the need to be aware of the likely impact that any changes may have on the employee, so even when there is an express clause in the contract allowing for an employee to move location, this has to be done in a *reasonable* way. In this particular case a clerical worker from Leeds was required to relocate to Birmingham with just six days' notice. The Employment Appeals Tribunal (EAT) said that the mobility clause, although an express term, was subject to three implied terms, namely: the duty of mutual trust and confidence; the duty for the employer to give reasonable notice of the move; and, importantly, the duty not to deploy an express term in such a way that it makes it impossible for the employee to comply with the contract. It is not just in cases of relocation where an employer wishing to change the work practices, and hence the contract of employment, has to behave in a reasonable way. For example, it is important for an employer who wants to retain the power to alter the hours of work, or perhaps the timing of shift patterns, to ensure that the contract expressly allows for these changes and that sufficient notice is given prior to the implementation of different work practices.

Exercise 4.4

Read the following press extracts about the dispute between USDAW and Tesco then answer the following questions.

- What do you think are the interests of:
  - Tesco management
  - the employees on the Livingstone Distribution site
  - other employees working at the three distribution centres in England
  - those Tesco employees not currently receiving retained pay?
- Consider the contract change that Tesco wanted to make.
  - Do you think this was an equitable change in the contract of employment for the distribution centre employees?
  - Evaluate the possible employee perceptions around the organisational justice of the proposed alterations to their employment contract.
- How would you assess the balance of power between Tesco management, the employees and USDAW? Give reasons for your answers.

The Introduction of 'Fire and Rehire' at Tesco's Distribution Centres Subject to Court Decisions

In February 2021, USDAW, the shop workers' union, won a Scottish High Court case temporarily stopping Tesco from moving staff at its Livingston, West Lothian, distribution centre onto new contracts.

The argument centred around a Retained Pay clause in the contract that was offered a number of years ago as an incentive; in return staff agreed to remain in Tesco's employment, to transfer to new work sites when appropriate, and not to participate in industrial action. At the beginning of 2021 Tesco no longer had a staff retention problem so took the decision to phase out Retained Pay, by seeking agreement from the affected employees. To 'encourage' this agreement, it offered, as an incentive, a 'buyout' of about 18 months' worth of the benefit. But it made it clear that, in the absence of agreement, the company would terminate the Retained Pay contracts, offering new ones containing identical terms and conditions but excluding the right to Retained Pay. USDAW claimed that the arrangement would have resulted in workers losing between £4,000 and £19,000 per year. Currently the company has 16,000 employees working in distribution centres, the vast majority of whom do *not* receive this top-up pay. The Scottish Court judgement temporarily prevented Tesco from terminating employment contracts giving staff Retained Pay.

A court case in England, in May of the same year, heard the case brought against Tesco by USDAW in respect of the warehouse staff based at three separate Tesco distribution sites in England, who still faced the threat of being moved on to new contracts.

Neil Todd of Thompsons Solicitors said: 'Tesco has used the uncertainty of job security in the pandemic to manipulate its workers into taking worse terms because they are so scared of losing their jobs'. A Tesco spokesperson said, 'We will continue to engage with USDAW and the very small number of colleagues who are affected by this'.

Sources: Express & Star, 2021; Webber, 2021

Terminating the contract

A contract of employment may come to an end in a variety of ways: perhaps the two most common of these occur where someone resigns, perhaps to take on a new role elsewhere, or when a fixed-term contract reaches its natural end. Neither of these endings is usually problematic. Sometimes, of course, the contract ceases to exist either because both the employee and the employer agree, by mutual consent, that the contract should terminate, or it ceases by virtue of redundancy. Here the impact on the employment relationship is not always positive. Those left behind following a redundancy often feel damaged by the experience of seeing their colleagues lose their jobs and, depending on how the redundancy has been handled, may experience a loss of trust in the management, with a subsequent damaging impact on their psychological contract and perceptions of organisational justice. Often those employees who have been retained following a redundancy experience a negative response towards their organisation, mirroring those reactions felt by their redundant colleagues (Eze et al., 2021; Hargrove et al., 2012; Hopkins and Weathington, 2006). This occurs especially when their own contracts have changed, exposing them to increased workloads and greater responsibility.

Different countries, of course, impose different legislative requirements around the creation – and operation – of contracts of employment. In the USA for example there is an **'at-will' employment principle** allowing an employer to end a contract of employment at any time, without reason and without notice providing it is not for an unlawful reason. Similarly, the employee has the right to end their contract of employment at any time and for any reason. Unless a contract has been specifically worded otherwise, US employees can be sacked without notice or payment in lieu. In reality although the 'at-will' provisions apply to *both* employer and employee; employees in the USA work *at the will of the employer*. The 'at-will' rule is not, however, interpreted in the same way across all of the states, and some have restricted its application and legislated for additional worker protection.

In Japan, on the other hand, there is a cultural expectation of lifetime employment – employees remaining with their employer indefinitely. More recently this expectation has been eroded and temporary contracts have become more commonplace, although they are tightly regulated by the Ministry of Health, Labour and Welfare. It is possible, however, to terminate a Japanese contract of employment on the grounds of the employers' economic necessity, or of the employees' mental or physical incapacity, lack of cooperation, poor work attitude and poor performance.

In China there is no 'at-will' provision; here employees can normally resign following a month's notice, although the employer may terminate the contract without notice and severance pay *only* if specific grounds are met. These reasons for dismissal are fairly universal, and similar to those operating in Japan, that is that the employee:

- fails to reach the required standards during a probationary period
- breaks company regulations
- acts in such a way to harm the organisation
- is prosecuted for a criminal offence
- produces work that is negatively affected because they are in a relationship with another employer
- the employee suffers ill health.

In the UK and elsewhere contracts cease when an employee is dismissed. The dismissal can be for conduct that is unacceptable (e.g., for inappropriate behaviour such as theft or sabotage), or incapability (where the employee is unable to complete tasks to the appropriate standard). Where an employee has behaved in ways that bring the organisation into disrepute, this breaches the implied term of 'mutual trust and confidence' and the employer terminates the contract ostensibly because the employee can no longer be trusted to show loyalty towards the employer and behave in ways that guarantee organisational commitment. For example, employees initiating derogatory YouTube clips or adverse social networking comments or remarks critical about the organisation and/or those in contact with it that are publicly available are likely to provide adequate grounds for their employers to claim that they have brought the organisation into disrepute – with the consequent disciplinary action possibly ending in contract termination. The behaviour may not be such that it directly mentions the organisation concerned in a negative way. For example in 2003, the European Court of Human Rights (ECHR) confirmed that employers may regard parts of an employee's life away from their workplace as relevant to their employment provided they are injurious to the employer's reputation and relevant to the employee's role. In the UK an employee of the Lancashire Probation Service (Mr Pay), whose job required him to work with sex offenders, was dismissed because it became known that outside of his work with the Probation Service he performed shows of an explicit sexual nature at fetish clubs and was also a director in a company selling bondage, domination and sadomasochistic materials. The employee felt the dismissal to be unfair and took his case to the ECHR but lost because, amongst other things, the ECHR took into account the potential damage to his employer's reputation given the nature of his workplace role (Mantouvalou and Collins, 2009).

News Flash 4.9

Teacher Fired for Secret Online Profile

Primary school teacher, Christian Webb, lost his job as soon as it was known that he was the satirical MC Devvo, a foul-mouthed rapper who sang about feeling girls up at the bike sheds, beating up his girlfriend and selling crack. The school governors at King Edward Primary School in Doncaster were outraged to learn that a member of staff had breached their trust by authoring, singing and posting material such as the song 'F**k 'Em Young'. He was summarily dismissed despite the video footage of his 'act' being over a decade old.

Sources: Brown, 2019; Council made, 2019

Employees do not have to behave in outrageous ways to be dismissed. Contracts may be terminated because the employees are not capable of undertaking the tasks set, or perhaps because they have received too many formal warnings about certain unacceptable aspects of their behaviour, such as persistent unexplained lateness. Here the employer consciously takes action to end the contract, but where an employee is asked to undertake a task, or range of tasks, that they feel for one reason or another to be impossible they, not the employer, may terminate the contract by resigning and claiming constructive dismissal. Terminating the contract of employment in this way occurs because the workplace activity expected under the original contract of employment, has been altered or fails to live up to the original expectations and, in effect, a new set of terms and conditions that the employee finds intolerable, has been imposed, irrevocably damaging the employment relationship. For example, an employee of a fruit and vegetable wholesaler found the racist nicknames and banter at the workplace intolerable and, when nothing was done to rectify the situation (e.g., a delivery driver was not disciplined when he suggested that 'Black people should be burnt at the stake like Jews'), he resigned and claimed constructive dismissal. The Bristol Employment Tribunal found in his favour and awarded him £14,286 for lost earnings as a result of the constructive dismissal and a further £13,427 for racial harassment and injury to his feelings (Evans, 2013).

Sometimes circumstances dictate that the contract legally comes to an end. Occasionally the contract ceases because it has been *frustrated* as it can no longer operate due to unforeseen circumstances making it impossible for work to continue in the way originally envisaged. The type of frustration can vary from war breaking out, to a driver losing his licence – making it impossible for him to work legally – through to a workplace being destroyed by fire. Frustration can occur, for example, when one of the parties is imprisoned or is suffering a debilitating illness with no prospect of recovery, making it impossible for them to continue undertaking the same type of work.

Summary

The contract of employment is an agreement between the employer and employee that may be written or oral, its contents explicitly expressed or implied: 'The employment contract is the outcome of a transaction that encompasses both the *entitlements* and the *obligations* of the employee and employer' (Brown et al., 2000: 616). The terms of the contract derive not just from this agreement between the employer and the employee but may also include terms dictated by statute or incorporated from another source, such as a collective agreement between the employer and a union. Different cultures, legislatures, contexts, managerial styles and, importantly, the balance of power between the parties to the contract will have an impact on the content, execution and termination of each employment contract which in turn will influence employees' perceptions of justice and their corresponding levels of trust within the employment relationship.

Review Questions

1   Explain, with examples, what you think Lord Wedderburn meant when he said that the contract of employment 'exhibits an individualism which necessarily ignores the economic reality behind the bargain. The parties are not equal, even in their ability to go to law' (1986: 142).

2   Employees at a large retail outlet have, for the last 11 years, been able to finish work at lunchtime on Christmas Eve. The HR manager has sent them all a letter saying that this custom is ending and that they will be expected to work a full day on Christmas Eve in the future.

(Continued)

Do you think there is a contractual right for these employees to leave work at lunch time? Give reasons for your answer. What impact do you think the letter will have on the employment relationship at the outlet?

3   A global software company with operations in South Asia, Australia, the USA and Europe has given one week's notice to its UK team of risk assessors that they will be relocated to Germany. Their contract says they are required to work anywhere that the organisation is based. What advice would you give the risk assessors? What reasoning lay behind your offering this advice?

4   Following redundancies and a difficult trading period a company making bespoke stained-glass windows for luxury hotels has told its remaining employees that, for the foreseeable future, they will no longer be offered overtime. In the past irregular overtime has boosted wages but never before has the company said it would no longer be offered. What do you think the employees' contractual position is, and why did you reach this conclusion?

5   Is it ethical to dismiss an employee for an activity that they undertake outside of work? Give reasons for your answer.

Revision Exercise 4.1

Read the case scenario below. Assume that you are the HR director at Thompson's Further Education College and are aware that the Head is keen to introduce more cost-effective working arrangements. Advise the Head on the options open to her and specify the one you would recommend and why.

Delia's Dilemma

Delia Crisp is in charge of Student Counselling at Thompson's Further Education College in Essex. When she was employed nine years ago it was as a sociology lecturer; however, 20 months ago she was invited to apply for a transfer to be in charge of Student Counselling and agreed to the change so long as she retained her academic terms and conditions of employment. This request was agreed to.

Following a reduction in public funding the newly appointed Head of Student Services reviewed the College staffing and explained to Delia that it might not be possible to let her continue on her existing academic terms and conditions of employment because she was no longer employed in an academic post – and that the working practices and terms and conditions of employment were being reviewed throughout the College. If Delia wanted to retain her academic terms and conditions she would have to be transferred back into an academic role.

Delia was not happy with this; she was really pleased with her current role and did not want to re-vert to an academic one, particularly as there were no current vacancies for sociology teaching. She said that the College should stick to the agreement made 20 months ago and filed a grievance, to be heard by the Head of Thompson's, about the proposal to either put her on non-academic terms and conditions or transfer her back to an academic post.

Other relevant facts are:

1   The key difference in terms and conditions of employment relates to the leave arrangements. The academic vacation is 11 weeks per annum while that for non-academic staff is just 22 working days (excluding Bank holidays) per annum.

2   Delia takes her main vacation from the end of June until mid-August. She does this in order to be available to comfort distraught students who have not done as well as expected in their exams and to answer student queries when A-level results are announced and students want to discuss the options regarding further courses or jobs they should apply for. July is a traditionally slack period for the services.

3   There is no current opening for a lecturer in Sociology.

4   Delia is a single parent with a one-year-old child.

Revision Exercise 4.2

Read the case scenario below and then complete the tasks.

Brochure and Team Briefing Notes on Contract Change

Following a merger with another call-centre company, Caliente Calls, your organisation, Person to Person, is seeking to standardise leave arrangements for everyone. Caliente Calls' 170 full-time staff have 22 days paid annual leave, based on a January to December leave year arrangement. A maximum of 15 days leave can be taken in one block. The 190 part-time staff have a pro-rata leave entitlement. Person to Person's 195 full-time staff have 20 days paid annual leave, rising to 23 days after five years' service – with no more than 10 working days to be taken at any one time. Their leave year runs April to April. For the past six years, it has been company policy to close down the business between Christmas and New Year, with all staff required to take three days of annual leave during this period. Any remaining working days are seen by all as taking place during the 'annual closure' (it has been Person to Person practice to close completely between 25 December and 1 January inclusive. This practice has never been ratified). The 125 part-time staff have pro-rata leave entitlement.

The management proposal, in the interests of business efficiency and harmonisation of terms and conditions, is for *all* full-time staff to have 23 days of paid annual leave, with a leave year running January to December. No more than ten working days are to be taken at any one time, and three days of the annual leave entitlement has to be during the Company's annual closure period from 25 December to 1 January inclusive.

There is no trade union recognition in the company, but the management is aware that Unite have been successfully recruiting members among Person to Person staff. It is therefore possible that at some stage there will be an approach for recognition by the Union.

The company is anxious to get all staff to agree to this change and to avoid conflict. It has embarked on an information and persuasion exercise.

You work in the HR Department of Person to Person and have been asked to produce a brochure and team briefing notes. (Remember that these will have to link to the correct managerial style. The words used will not be for an academic audience so will have to persuade and influence without using academic phrases like 'psychological contract' and 'organisational justice', although these concepts should underpin both the brochure and set of notes.) Produce the following documentation:

(Continued)

1   *An information brochure, of around 500 words,* which can be circulated to all staff outlining:

- the nature of the proposed change
- why it is necessary
- advantages of the change
- the company's desire to maintain harmonious relations with all staff
- actions an employee should take in the event of a problem with the changes
- a section posing and answering frequently asked questions (FAQs).

2   *Team briefing notes, of around 1,500 words* for line managers providing the information needed to answer employees' questions on the contents of the brochure. This should include a section providing FAQs and answers, and provide useful sources of additional information to which the line managers can refer.

Relevant Articles for Further Reading

Deakin, S. (2001) 'The contract of employment: A study in legal evolution', Working Paper No. 203. Cambridge: ESRC Centre for Business Research, University of Cambridge.

This article does what it says on the tin, providing an historical legal perspective of the ways in which contracts of employment have evolved.

Farina, E., Green, C. and McVicar, D. (2020) 'Zero hours contracts and their growth', *British Journal of Industrial Relations*, 58(3): 507–31.

A useful look at the growth of zero hours contracts and the demographics of those subject to them.

Golding, G. (2020) 'The origins of terms implied by law into English and Australian employment contracts', *Oxford University Commonwealth Law Journal*, 20(1): 163–91.

This comparative article examines the origins and use of implied terms and gives readers an insight into the historical development, usage and relevance of such terms within the employment contract.

References

Acas (2013) *Contracts of Employment.* Available at: www.acas.org.uk/index.aspx?articleid=1577 (accessed 1 August 2013).

Ashurst (2013) 'Italy seeks economic boost through employment law reforms', *Ashurst's World@ Work*, February. Available at: www.ashurst.com/publication-item.aspx?id_Content=8807 (accessed 22 October 2013).

BBC (2021) 'Ikea France fined €1m for snooping on staff', *BBC News*, 15 June. Available at: www.bbc.co.uk/news/world-europe-57482168 (accessed 25 June 2021).

Braswell, M. (2019) 'Merrill reaches half-million-dollar settlement in overtime class-action suit', *AdvisorHub*, 13 November. Available at: www.advisorhub.com/merrill-reaches-half-million-dollar-settlement-in-overtime-class-action-suit/ (accessed 21 June 2021).

Brodie, D. (2001) 'Commentary: Mutual trust and the values of the employment contract', *Industrial Law Journal*, 30(1): 84–100.

Brown, E. (2019) 'MC Devvo sacked as primary school teacher after parents found out his identity', *Unilad*, 8 August. Available at: www.unilad.co.uk/news/primary-school-teacher-sacked-after-being-outed-as-rapper-mc-devvo/ (accessed 25 June 2021).

Brown, W., Deakin, S., Nash, D. and Oxenbridge, S. (2000) 'The employment contract: From collective procedures to individual rights', *British Journal of Industrial Relations*, 38(4): 611–29.

Budd, J. W. (2004) *Employment with a Human Face: Balancing Efficiency, Equity, and Voice*. Ithaca, NY: Cornell University Press.

Budd, J. W., Gollan, P. J. and Wilkinson, A. (2010) 'New approaches to employee voice and participation in organizations', *Human Relations*, 63(3): 303–10.

Carreño, B. (2022) 'Spanish labour reform passed in knife-edge vote, opposition blames error', *Reuters*, 3 February. Available at: www.reuters.com/world/europe/spanish-labour-reform-goes-knife-edge-vote-eu-funds-stake-2022-02-03/ (accessed 22 February 2022).

Collins, H. and Mantouvalou, V. (2016) 'Human rights and the contract of employment', in M. Freedland, *The Contract of Employment*. Oxford: Oxford University Press.

Commons, J. R. (1924) *Legal Foundations of Capitalism*. New York: Macmillan.

Cook, A. (2022) 'Spain unveils labour legislation reforms', *IR Guru*, February. Available at: https://irguru.online/news/spain-unveils-labour-legislation-reforms/ (accessed 22 February 2022).

Collinson A (2020) *Work Your Proper Hours Day – let's stop working for free Trades Union Congress* available from www.tuc.org.uk/blogs/work-your-proper-hours-day-lets-stop-working-free (accessed 31 October 2022)

Council Made (2019) 'Devvod! Primary school teacher sacked after his YouTube alter ego "Devvo" is outed', *Council Made*, 9 August. Available at: https://councilmade.wordpress.com/2019/08/09/devvod-primary-school-teacher-sacked-after-his-youtube-alter-ego-devvo-is-outed/ (accessed 25 June 2021).

Deakin, S. (2001) 'The contract of employment: A study in legal evolution', Working Paper No. 203. Cambridge: ESRC Centre for Business Research, University of Cambridge.

Evans, M. (2013) 'Black worker awarded £27,000 after hearing colleague referred to as golliwog', *Daily Telegraph*, 4 August. Available at: www.telegraph.co.uk/news/uknews/law-and-order/10221339/Black-worker-awarded-27000-after-hearing-colleague-referred-to-as-golliwog.html (accessed 28 August 2013).

Express & Star (2021) 'Usdaw begins High Court "fire and rehire" fight with Tesco', *Express & Star*, 5 May. Available at: www.expressandstar.com/news/uk-news/2021/05/05/usdaw-begins-high-court-fire-and-rehire-fight-with-tesco/ (accessed 24 June 2021).

Eze, S. C., Uchenna, C. O. and Chinedu-Eze, V. C. (2021) 'Psychological impact of downsizing on survivor-managers in a developing economy', *European Journal of Business and Innovation Research*, 8(8): 53–70.

Farnham, D. (1997) *Employee Relations in Context*. London: Institute of Personnel and Development.

García-Pérez, J. I., Marinescu, I. and Vall Castello, J. (2019) 'Can fixed-term contracts put low skilled youth on a better career path? Evidence from Spain', *The Economic Journal*, 129(620): 1693–730.

Griffith, J. (2018) 'Ryanair fires crew members who allegedly staged photo sleeping on airport floor', *NBC News*, 7 November. Available at: www.nbcnews.com/news/world/ryanair-fires-crew-members-who-allegedly-staged-photo-sleeping-airport-n933531 (accessed 3 March 2020).

Guest, D. (2004) 'Flexible employment contracts, the psychological contract and employee outcomes: An analysis and review of the evidence', *International Journal of Management Reviews*, 5(1): 1–19.

Guest, D. E. and Isaksson, K. (2019) 'Temporary employment contracts and employee well-being during and after the financial crisis: Introduction to the special issue', *Economic and Industrial Democracy*, 40(2).

Hargrove, M. B., Cooper, C. L. and Quick, J. C. (2012) 'Individual outcomes resulting from downsizing related stress', in C. L. Cooper, A. Pandey and J. C. Quick (eds), *Downsizing: Is Less Still More?* Cambridge, UK: Cambridge University Press, pp. 293–325.

Health and Safety Executive (2021) 'Mattress Manufacturer Fined After Employee Dragged Into Machine', press release, 9 March. Available at: https://press.hse.gov.uk/2021/03/09/mattress-manufacturer-fined-after-employee-dragged-into-machine/ (accessed 10 June 2021).

Hietanen, J. (2000) 'Dispute over Employment Contracts Act resolved', *EurWORK, European industrial relations observatory online*. Available at www.eurofound.europa.eu/eiro/2000/09/feature/fi0009161f.htm (accessed 5 September 2013).

Hopkins, S. M. and Weathington, B. L. (2006) 'The relationships between justice perceptions, trust, and employee attitudes in a downsized organisation', *The Journal of Psychology*, 140(5): 477–98.

Jackson, B. (2021) 'Supreme Court confirms employers' right to change contracts if negotiation fails', *HR Magazine*, 28 October. Available at: www.hrmagazine.co.uk/content/news/supreme-court-confirms-employers-right-to-change-contracts-if-negotiation-fails (accessed 18 February 2022).

Jasper, J. (2018) 'Ryanair sacks six cabin crew after "staged" photo sleeping on airport floor', *The Guardian*, 7 November. Available at: www.theguardian.com/business/2018/nov/07/ryanair-sacks-six-cabin-crew-after-staged-photo-sleeping-on-malaga-airport-floor (accessed 3 March 2020).

Kahn-Freund, O., Davies, P. L. and Freedland, M. R. (1983) *Kahn-Freund's Labour and the Law*. London: Stevens.

Kelly, J. (1998) *Rethinking Industrial Relations: Mobilisation, Collectivism and Long Waves*. London: Routledge.

Kiersztyn, A. (2021) 'Who moves from fixed-term to open-ended contracts? Youth employment transitions in a segmented labour market', *Acta Sociologica*, 64(2): 198–214.

Mantouvalou, V. and Collins, H. (2009) 'Private Life and Dismissal Pay v UK Application No 32792/05, [2009] IRLR 139 (ECtHR)', *Industrial Law Journal*, 38(1): 133–8.

Menegatti, E. (2020). Taking EU labour law beyond the employment contract: The role played by the European Court of Justice. *European Labour Law Journal*, 11(1), 26-47.

Nogler, L. (2008) 'Why do labour lawyers ignore the question of social justice in European contract law?', *European Law Journal*, 14(4): 483–99.

Office of National Statistics (ONS) (2022) *Temporary Employees*. Available at: www.ons.gov.uk/
    employmentandlabourmarket/peopleinwork/employmentandemployeetypes/datasets/
    temporaryemployeesemp07 (accessed 5 May 2022).
Pailliez, C. and White, S. (2021) 'IKEA fined $1.2 mln for spying on French employees', *Reuters*, 15
    June. Available at: www.reuters.com/business/retail-consumer/ikea-found-guilty-fined-12-mln-
    french-employee-spy-case-2021-06-15/ (accessed 25 June 2021).
Pannick, D. (2013) House of Lords Debate, 6 February, vol. 743, col. 265.
Roberts, Y. (2015) 'Britain's hotel workers – bullied, underpaid and with few rights', *Guardian*,
    30 May. Available at: www.theguardian.com/business/2015/may/30/hotel-workers-bullied-
    underpaid-few-rights-uk (accessed 9 August 2015).
Roehling, M. V. (2004) 'Legal theory: Contemporary contract law, perspectives and insights for
    employment relationship theory', in J. A-M. Coyle-Shapiro, L. M. Shore, N. S. Taylor and L.
    E. Tetrick, *The Employment Relationship: Examining Psychological and Contextual Perspectives*.
    Oxford: Oxford University Press.
Rubery, J. and Rafferty, A. (2013) 'Women and recession revisited', *Work, Employment & Society*,
    27(3): 414–32.
Scottish Fair Work Convention (2021) *'Fire and Rehire' – A Test for Scotland's Fair Work Principles*.
    Available at: www.fairworkconvention.scot/fire-and-rehire-a-test-for-scotlands-fair-work-
    principles/ (accessed 2 February 2021).
SHRM (2021) *The New UAE Labor Law – What You Need to Know*. Available at: www.shrm.org/
    resourcesandtools/hr-topics/global-hr/pages/new-uae-labor-law.aspx (accessed 5 May 2022).
Storey, J., Quintas, P., Taylor, P. and Fowle, W. (2002) 'Flexible employment contracts and their
    implications for product and process innovation', *International Journal of Human Resource
    Management*, 13(1): 1–18.
Trades Union Congress (2008) 'Trades Union Congress – What workers Want – Fair Pay, Great
    Workmates and the Chance to Get On', August, *Trades Union Congress*.
Trades Union Congress (2013) 'Trades Union Congress – Involuntary temporary jobs driving
    rising employment', *Contract*, 248(257,026): 264–48.
Trades Union Congress (2021) *Fire and Rehire Tactics Have Become Widespread During the Pandemic -
    Warns TUC*, press release, 25 January. Available at: www.tuc.org.uk/news/fire-and-rehire-tactics-
    have-become-widespread-during-the-pandemic-warns-tuc (accessed 2 February 2021).
Wass, B. (2008) 'Labour policy and fixed-term employment contracts in Germany', paper, Goethe
    University, Frankfurt. Available at: www.jil.go.jp/english/reports/documents/jilpt-reports/
    no.9_germany.pdf (accessed 25 October 2013).
Webber, A. (2021) 'Tesco prevented from using "fire and rehire" tactics at Livingston warehouse',
    Employee Benefits, 17 February. Available at: https://employeebenefits.co.uk/tesco-prevented-
    fire-and-rehire-tactics-livingston-warehouse/ (accessed 17 February 2021).
Wedderburn, K. W. (1986) *The Worker and the Law* (3rd edn). Harmondsworth: Penguin.
Wiley, B. (2009) *Employment Law in Context: An Introduction for HR Professionals*. Harlow: Pearson.

5

EMPLOYMENT RELATIONS IN PRECARIOUS PLATFORM AND GIG WORK

By the end of this chapter, you should be able to:

- understand the terms precarious employment, platform working, gig worker
- critically examine the impact of precarious platform and gig work
- describe the levels of workplace power experienced by platform workers
- understand some of the legislation surrounding gig and other precarious workers
- evaluate the effectiveness of the protective role of trade unions for precarious workers
- discuss precariousness and workforce diversity.

What to Expect

This chapter examines the ways in which precarious work, specifically that linked to electronically enabled work processes, has an impact on employment and the employment relationship. Since the end of the last century, employment conditions in wealthy countries have been transformed by digital technologies that facilitate a 'virtual marketplace' for the on-demand buying and selling of short-term labour. This has resulted in inhibiting trade union influence, the increased international mobility of workers (and capital), and the weakening of legislative social protections. There has been a burgeoning of new ways of working that are far removed from the traditional standard employment relationship. For many, working in non-standard ways is precarious, making them socially and financially vulnerable and prone to ill health. Precarious, insecure work and the reality of working in the gig economy are looked at, and the ways such work is regulated (or not) and the power realities behind such forms of employment are explored. The chapter looks at the employment relations impact of **algorithmic management** and discusses some of the ways in which unions are beginning to represent precarious workers.

Platforms and Gigs Explained

Technological changes have resulted, for some, in new ways of organising both work processes and working people, affecting the interaction between the two and of course the employment relationship. In 2020 The World Economic Forum estimated that organisational investments in digital technologies and artificial intelligence could create such efficient cost savings that the use of algorithms could disrupt 85 million human jobs worldwide by 2025. (Although, of course, a cost-linked strategy does not automatically mean that is effective [De Cremer and Kasparov, 2021]; reducing costs may well have an adverse impact on productivity, quality and morale.) If this prediction is accurate the workforce in the coming decades could be unrecognisable.

Platform work is a form of non-standard employment that has appeared over the last decade (Berg et al., 2018, 2021). Online, virtual, platforms act like digital notice boards or 'clearing' organisations, facilitating the matching of a flexible workforce with available work (gigs). They are perhaps one of the most important economic changes and challenges of the last few decades (Kenney and Zysman, 2016; Van Dijck et al., 2018; Williams et al., 2022).

Definitions of the gig economy are many and varied. The UK Department for Business, Energy and Industrial Strategy (BEIS, 2018: 4) says that:

> The gig economy involves the exchange of labour for money between individuals or companies via digital platforms that actively facilitate matching between providers and customers, on a short-term and payment by task basis.

Such work is,

> characterised by uncertainty, unpredictability, insecurity and instability of both schedules and income. Gig workers are likely to work for multiple platforms and/or employers' with much, if not all, of their work activity controlled digitally by algorithms and apps. (Hafeez et al., 2022: 3)

Gig work, however, does not include those who use digital platforms for things that are not directly related to labour, for example buying goods online, nor does it include those who find short term or permanent work by using an agency. The TUC says that the number of gig workers in England and Wales in 2021 was 4.4 million, three times as many as in 2016, and the number working as delivery or private hire drivers quadrupled in that time. It points out that, by November 2021, 22.6% of workers had engaged in platform work at some time, up from 11.5% in 2016 (TUC, 2021).

Much of this gig work is facilitated by a range of increasingly sophisticated algorithms. These computer-generated formulas automatically make decisions and predictions based on data sets, models, and simulation, *without* any human intervention. They can be tweaked and recalibrated relatively rapidly ensuring a speed and flexibility of process that was traditionally absent from workplace scheduling and organisation. Their agility allows them to problem solve and utilise existing data to rejig their own programmes in real time (Eurofound, 2018) rapidly enabling the movement of labour, or tweaking work processes to quickly fit areas of need. In this way they are capable of rapidly managing and creating complicated business processes (Mann and O'Neil, 2016). Gig work now covers a growing variety of jobs, including on-demand delivery, domestic and care work, taxi driving, freelancing and **crowdwork** (Woodcock and Graham, 2019). (Crowdwork occurs where a large number of people each contribute a small amount of work to complete a larger task, for example, all simultaneously analysing different parts of a large data set.)

Precarious Work

Precarious work is distinguished by the uncertainty, insecurity, and instability suffered by those experiencing it. Sometimes referred to as '**contingent work**' (USA) or 'atypical' or 'nonstandard' forms of employment (EU), precarious work is where those undertaking it are marginalised, vulnerable, and for whom there is little certainty, because the duration of the job is unknown and employment unpredictable (Sverke et al., 2002). Hours of work may well be scheduled in seemingly erratic ways, which leads to volatile income levels and makes budgeting difficult or impossible. Job holders, in such circumstances, usually lack social power and access to few, if any, resources that might enable them to challenge their working conditions (Bosmans et al., 2016). Precarious workers often have to spend disproportionate amounts of time looking for work, or travelling to and from work, leading to additional strains on health and finances (Premji, 2017). Those working in precarious environments are likely to be from socially disadvantaged groups. There is evidence that recent migrants experiencing precarious work need to take jobs that do not match their education and are often underemployed (Ndiuini and Baum, 2021; Noack and Vosko, 2011). Precariousness therefore is related to both employment structures and to individual experiences, encompassing low levels of control over how and when work is performed and paid for, fears about imminent job loss, and insecurity about future employment (Heyes et al., 2018). Precarity *at* work is linked to a volatile, perhaps unsafe, environment where standard workplace rights are unprotected, occupational injury is a risk, and harassment and discrimination may occur (Allan et al., 2021). Dependence on their employers for continuous work can render precarious workers vulnerable and powerless. They may experience organisational injustice particularly in the form of abuse, social rejection, bullying and harassment (Perry et al., 2020). Precarity *from* work results from having a job that fails to meet one's basic needs. For example, one in which there is a low level of distributional justice where the amount of pay is inadequate, often irregular, and requires long hours in order for basic needs to be met (Allan et al., 2021; Kreshpaj et al., 2020). Precarious work is damaging to the physical and mental health and wellbeing of workers and their families.

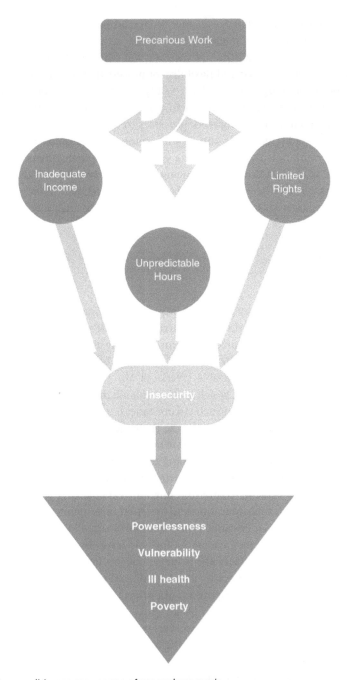

Figure 5.1 The possible consequences of precarious work

Platform businesses operate across a variety of sectors throughout the global economy. The work they promote and facilitate is often concentrated within lower skilled sections of the labour market, where formal qualifications are often not necessary, and they attract a disproportionate number of people from disadvantaged groups. Those individuals who traditionally have struggled to gain well paid employment (women, ethnic minorities, disabled) are likely to be overrepresented in forms of employment linked to precariousness (Tan et al., 2021; Zyskowski et al., 2015).

An exploration into the precariousness of the lives of migrant workers by Premji in (2018) exemplifies the pattern shown in Figure 5.1. Interviewing 27 migrant workers, originally from 11 different countries and now all based in Toronto, she found that in order to survive, they had to work for multiple employers. Their precarious employment caused economic insecurity as their needs drove them to take work with nonstandard and unpredictable schedules and hazardous working conditions, which resulted in feelings of powerlessness. Overall, the workers had little access to workplace benefits and protections, and they were often subject to bullying and degrading treatment, which had a negative impact upon their physical and mental health together with that of their families.

Insecurity and Platform Work

Over the centuries employment for many workers has not always been secure. Indeed, the formation and success of trade unions over many decades exemplified the need for workers to combine in order to achieve a degree of power, economic independence, and job security. As the different varieties of capitalism evolved, so too did forms of work, and the ways of using and exploiting labour. In liberal and coordinated market economies, like the USA and the UK, for example, working life for many has become less secure than under economies where social protectionism provides workers with more security, such as those in the European Union (Hall and Soskice, 2001: see also Chapter 2 for a discussion on the varieties of capitalism). Over the last 20 years there has been a proliferation of work organised by platforms, whereby most of the human work is not performed by the owner of the platform but by those operating elsewhere. Millions of jobs across the globe have now been outsourced to platforms (Srnicek, 2017). The more people connected with a platform (i.e., the platform owners, customers and the various service providers), the more it increases in value (Florisson and Mandl, 2018). Over the last few years platform-based multinationals have expanded their reach and profit levels at prodigious rates. Companies founded just a few years ago are valued in the millions and have become household names, such as Uber (Moore and Joyce, 2020). The ubiquity of developing technology along with the speed and flexibility of algorithmic decision making means 'that platforms transcend both markets and firms: they provide functions of both but can do even more than either (they facilitate economic transactions that neither markets nor firms could coordinate)' (Eurofound, 2018:10).

The organisations for whom gig and platform workers ultimately work, and their 'real' employing organisations, are often obscure and or hidden; while the work itself, the methods of control, and workplace isolation results in workers being marginalised. Digital technologies have ensured efficient communication of information, reducing transaction costs, influencing economic processes, and infiltrating and impacting employment practices. Such processes have led to significant growth in the outsourcing of some operations and tasks to other companies without regard to national boundaries (Eurofound, 2018). The gig business model bypasses many standard employment practices, legal responsibilities and costs, resulting in widespread legal ambiguity, leading to challenges as to whether workers should, in fact, be classified as employees (Collier et al., 2017; Fabo et al., 2017; Srnicek, 2017). Such workers on non-standard work contracts experience high levels of job insecurity involving uncertain income levels and unpredictable working times and periods (Doellgast et al., 2018; Keune and Pedaci, 2020). Not all non-standard working arrangements lead to insecurity, however, and some arrangements may suit certain individual lifestyles and preferences. It is not unknown, for example, for people in full time employment to supplement their income by taking on additional gig work (Gupta et al., 2022).

News Flash 5.1

Canadian Postal Union Fights for Gig Worker Rights

On 25 February 2021, the Canadian Union of Postal Workers (CUPW) launched a new campaign for *all* delivery workers working for delivery apps, claiming they all face similar conditions and many of the same health and financial risks. The express aim of the campaign - Gig Workers United - was to establish workers' rights and respect within the Canadian gig economy. The delivery workers, said CUPW, are calling on employers and legislators to make fundamental changes in an industry where apps control workers' lives and create unsafe and unliveable conditions.

Source: Uniglobal, 2021

The incidences of precarious, or insecure, work have increased since the beginning of the century due to a number of factors:

- The widespread use of personal computers and smart phones has created many jobs based outside the traditional workplace. Technological changes and digitalisation have enabled increasing numbers of people to work unencumbered by geographical location.
- The global and widespread use of computers in many workplaces, for example in the finance sector, has replaced the requirement for a significant proportion of the labour-intensive processes with the subsequent loss of jobs.
- The diminution of trade union influence has emboldened employers to introduce lower, non-standard, employment practices.
- The ways in which resources (capital and people) can move around the globe, both physically and virtually, has exacerbated the reduction in permanent employment and increased job insecurity.

Chen et al. (2020:1) show how these elements impacted patterns of labour management of work within two Chinese cities, stating that:

The traditional employment relationship, characterized by written contracts with clearly defined entitlements and obligations for employers and employees, have been increasingly substituted by new, volatile, fluid and fragile employment forms, softening the labour rights and social rights of 'digital employees' and strengthening social control over them through online evaluation systems supported by smart phones and apps.

Awareness about the increasing prevalence of work insecurity is widespread. Bauman (2000: 160–1) describes how the phenomenon of precariousness has been studied, under different guises, particularly in developed and affluent countries. He relates how,

> The French theorists speak of précarité, the Germans of Unsicherheit and Risikogestellschaft, the Italians of incertezza and the English of insecurity – but all of them have in mind the same aspect of the human predicament, experienced in various forms and under different parts of the planet.... The phenomenon which all these concepts try to grasp and articulate is the combined experience of insecurity (of position, entitlements, and livelihood), of uncertainty (as to their continuation and future stability) and of unsafety (of one's body, one's self, and their extensions: possessions, neighbourhood, community).

International and, indeed sectoral, comparisons are however, problematic: data is not always collected systematically or comprehensively, while different categories of worker may be classified as precarious; for example, some countries include part-time and temporary work in the precarious category while others do not (Bechter et al., 2012; Grimshaw et al., 2016; Keune, 2015). Moreover, many platform workers hold more than one job simultaneously. Huws et al. (2017) found, in their study of over 2,000 European gig workers, from seven different countries, that over half were in additional full-time employment. This 'employment plus' pattern echoed that found in the US by Smith (2016) whose study of 4,000 platform workers showed 44% were also engaged in full-time work. The numbers of people holding a patchwork of multiple jobs, together with incidence of double counting and differences in worker categorisation, mean that a meaningful analysis of platform and/or precarious worker statistics is challenging if not impossible.

Exercise 5.1

Discuss the following quotation using your academic knowledge:

There is some debate about whether platforms really enable a more efficient organisation of production, or just simply facilitate the exploitation of labour and competitors. (Eurofound, 2018: 19)

Platform Work

Fernández-Macías (2017) suggests that platforms are, in effect, digital networks that use algorithms to coordinate transactions. Codagnone et al. (2016) distinguish between *online labour markets*, either local or global, that enable the remote delivery of electronically transmittable services (i.e., Amazon Mechanical Turk, Upwork, etc.) and *mobile labour markets* that are locally based and offer digitally enabled administrative matching systems that are coupled with physical service delivery requiring direct local interaction: for example, domestic help. Certainly, digital platforms are a result of technological advances; they mediate the relationships between those who buy and sell labour and are often regarded as 'disrupters', undermining the ways traditional work had previously been allocated and undertaken. Labour platforms, because of a) their reach, b) evasion of employment regulation, and c) ability to split and re-organise work into small fragments or tasks that can be completed by a large number of people simultaneously (rather like **Taylorism**), can result in significant changes to the ways in which production and employment are managed. This system of organising work creates a power imbalance between the platform owners and the individual platform workers. Pesole et al. (2018) suggest that this 'unbundling of tasks', is a radical deepening of the division of labour, and Srnicek describes this type of activity, particularly where companies profit from seemingly altruistic activities (e.g., Uber and Task Rabbit) as platform capitalism (2017).

Digital labour platforms include:

- web-based platforms, where work is outsourced through a general appeal for providers of work (who could be based anywhere)
- location-based applications (apps) that assign work to individuals based in a particular area.

The web-based platforms enable businesses, etc. to have access to a large crowd of flexible, cheap labour. Individuals making up the crowd are able, on demand, to undertake small, mostly clerical tasks, that can be completed remotely using a computer and internet connection. Once a task has been completed the organisation has no further obligation to those who have completed the work. This means, more often than not, that microtask platforms categorise those who undertake such tasks as self-employed – and this of course removes the safety net of legislative employee protection (Berg et al., 2018). For example, Uber successfully achieved a share of the traditional taxi market with its innovative use of apps, competitive pricing and disregard of some safety checks and balances.

Case Study 5.1

Platform Work Saved Me From Paying Expensive Childcare

With two children under school age I needed to work, but the cost of childcare was prohibitive. I searched online forums and discovered two companies, Appen and Lionbridge, that offered online working opportunities for someone in my position. Lionbridge, in particular, wanted someone with analytical skills and geographical awareness. I applied online, was sent a non-disclosure agreement to sign before the next stage in recruitment (this was a bit of a surprise) and then had to complete a technical test, the guidelines for which came in a separate email. Preparing for the test was all a bit time consuming - I did it over a weekend - unfortunately it was unpaid. The test obviously originated from America, but I found the process interesting and could afford to take the risk on time. I passed and was offered work online. I was paid a flat-rate per task and, although the time for completing each task varied (some tasks were much quicker than others) it worked out that I was getting around the minimum wage so I did not feel exploited. My work was quality assessed and it was obviously OK as, to my surprise, I was promoted to 'moderator' and asked to check other people's work as well as doing my own. This increased my rate of pay, so I was pleased. At the same time, as a one-off, I was asked if I would like to write a couple of training documents (I assumed they wanted to water down the American aspects) and was pleased to get additional money for this. Extra, *unpaid*, training webinars were offered, but I chose not to do these. The good thing about working like this was that I could fit the tasks in around my daily activities. It was good to know that, unlike a regular day job, I could always turn down tasks, turn the computer off and walk away; only working when *I* found it convenient. I scheduled my days without taking the employer's needs into account, working between seven to fifteen hours a week. The work was interesting, mentally stimulating and there were no office politics. Their paperwork was good, I received regular payslips, etc, although, unlike my previous full-time employment, I had to become a self-employed contractor. There were other downsides to the process: I would have liked to have known upfront, before I spent time preparing for (and taking) the test, how much I would be earning. I had no idea whether others were getting more, less or the same rate as me. There was no personal interaction with others in the same role, and I never knew who was making decisions and why they were made; but, overall, it was a good experience.

The children are now in school and I am back working full-time for a local organisation.

Source: interview with platform worker, Southwest England, April 2022

Different Types of Platform Work

As discussed, the downside to some platform work includes long hours, little if any job security, unpredictable – often low – income, being 'controlled' by an app rather than an individual, lack of training, and lack of access to protective employment regulation. Platform work can also improve work–life balance, by allowing flexibility of time and place of work as well as providing an income for those who might not otherwise be able to work for health, caring, or lifestyle reasons. Such work allows for innovative solutions, often enabling large numbers of potential workers to connect with suitable job providers. In Ireland, for example, Bowsy, a start-up platform that launched in 2020, connects third year students with suitable employers offering remote work experience – a venture that helps both students and employers and exposes employers to potential talent.

Duggan and his colleagues (2020: 117–8) differentiate between the types of platform work that comprise gig working, i.e., where this type of work is marked by short-term work relationships (without long term obligations from either party), flexible working hours, payment for the task and, on occasion, project work. They split the unwieldy category of the gig economy into three key areas of activity.

Firstly, they discuss capital platform work – this is more like e-commerce than an employment relationship and occurs when customers are brought into contact with someone selling a service, e.g., eBay, Airbnb.

Secondly, they talk about **crowdwork**, which is where an amorphous online group of separate individual workers remotely undertakes and completes tasks (see Case Study 5.1) via the internet. If the task is further divided into smaller units with each person receiving the same payment for each individual task Duggan and his colleagues call this *micro-tasking crowdwork*. If, however, the work is not split into smaller sections but undertaken simultaneously by a large group of individuals, with only one result used and paid for, they term it **contest-based crowdwork**. As can be seen from this last category of crowdwork not all versions of this type of employment are paid in equitable ways. There is little distributional justice for those undertaking contest-based crowdwork as not everyone gets paid for their time, effort and output. Huws et al. in their extensive study of European crowdworkers found that:

> Many crowdworkers appeared to be using crowdwork as part of a strategy to piece together an income from whatever sources are available rather than adopting it as a freely chosen lifestyle choice … [T]here were complaints about many aspects of work organisation and working conditions. Particular sources of stress and grievance included difficulty in communicating with platform personnel, arbitrary terminations, perceptions that platforms always take the side of clients against workers and frequent changes to payment and other systems. (2017: 10)

Lastly, Duggan and his colleagues distinguished **app-work** whereby algorithms, controlled by go-between platform organisations, use apps to identify the requirements for labour and offer the work to an appropriate individual. Such work concerns at least three different parties: the enabling platform, the customer and the workers (sometimes more parties are involved, particularly if the workers have to pick up goods for delivery). The use of apps means that the process of hiring and commissioning work can be almost instantaneous, although prospective workers have to agree online, prior to undertaking any work, to the terms and conditions set by the platform. Often this undertaking is required for each individual task and may involve the worker providing proof of identity and relevant skills on each separate occasion. Apps are crucial to this type of work because they control and direct each stage of the work arrangement, thereby functioning as a centralised go-between and regulator, dictating the employment relationship, albeit electronically removed from each individual worker (Wood et al., 2018). Using algorithmic management to control and sometimes penalise workers began in the gig economy, as platforms needed to spot and eliminate any attempts to 'game' their systems. For example systems evolved so that drivers who rejected lower paid work for that paid at a higher rate were disciplined, sometimes by removing them from the app either permanently or for short periods of time (Doug, 2016). This denial of free choice is a strong argument for those claiming that the self-employment label is bogus, as when a worker is constrained from choosing certain jobs in favour of others, it indicates that they do not have the freedom of choice available to a self-employed person.

Many gig workers earn their living by driving, and it has been customary for them to be classified as self-employed. This important categorisation relieves proprietors of a number of expenses associated with employees. Self-employed drivers have to maintain their own vehicles and pay for their own fuel. Those delivering items are often paid for the actual drop off rather than the journey to and from the drop destination and waiting time between tasks is, more often than not, unpaid. The result is that, despite working long hours, take-home pay often fails to reach minimum wage levels when expenses are taken into account. In 2021 Mellino et al. analysed pay and journey data from around 12,000 journeys of 318 UK Deliveroo riders, which totalled 34,000 hours. They found that a third earned, on average, less than the national minimum wage for their overall time per session. Some earned less, with one cyclist logged in for 180 hours paid the equivalent of £2 per hour.

News Flash 5.2

Low Pay and Spying Lead to Food Delivery Dispute and Demands for Change

Delivery drivers from Just Eat, Deliveroo and Uber Eats, based in Belfast, took action against their 'insufficient' pay in a dispute which resulted in a public protest at McDonalds on Boucher Road and a six-hour strike on 23 March 2022, with drivers – who work 12- to 16-hour shifts for as little as £100 (€120) – demanding their operating costs be covered and that they receive a guaranteed £10 per hour.

The App Drivers and Couriers Union (ADCU) pointed out that since last year vehicle maintenance costs have increased by a third while fuel costs have risen by over this amount. However, this was not their only complaint as the drivers also objected to increasingly unreasonable intrusive on-the-job electronic surveillance and excessive levels of algorithmic control, both of which have resulted in what they consider to be unfair pay deductions and summary dismissals without the right of appeal or representation.

A Just Eat spokesperson said the company, 'takes any concerns raised by our couriers seriously. Our delivery payment model has been designed to give couriers the flexibility to work when they choose. We continue to offer a competitive base rate to self-employed couriers and pay is reviewed regularly'.

Sources: Graham, 2022; Wickens, 2022

Legislation

A report from the prestigious European Economic and Social Committee stated that,

> The digital platform business model is increasingly seen as a key driving force contributing to the ongoing erosion of labour standards and social protections. This is because domestic legal systems and national courts are providing different legal solutions regarding this type of work, and because platform work has specific features that place the workers employed in this field in a particularly vulnerable position. (2021: 8)

This nicely highlights the advantage to employers and disadvantage to employees of working on a digital platform. Firms are able to adopt business models whereby the use of a labour force is unfettered by legal obligations such as equal pay, minimum wages, pension provision, and supply of safe equipment, while at the same time their workforce is working without a legal safety net that ensures basic employment standards and practices. The need for a source of income often means that these workers have little or no choice other than to accept the work when offered.

Over the years different legal systems have adopted a range of protective measures for those in work. Across Europe there are disparities around the ways in which similar workers are regarded; thus a platform worker in one Member State might be covered by social protection and collective bargaining, yet if they moved state, they might be outside the remit of collective bargaining and regarded as self-employed. At the end of 2021 the European Commission proposed a directive addressing such differences.

News Flash 5.3

Parliamentary Group Proposes New Algorithm Accountability Act

Following investigations, from May to July 2021, looking at the use and implications of surveillance and other artificial intelligence (AI) technologies used at work, the All-Party UK Parliamentary Group showed how this form of work is out-pacing existing regulations so made a number of recommendations including:

1. **An Accountability for Algorithms Act** – this would establish a new corporate and public sector duty to undertake, disclose and act on pre-emptive Algorithmic Impact Assessments (AIA).
2. **Updating digital protection** – the Act would plug the specific gaps in protection from adverse impacts of powerful but invisible algorithmic systems.
3. **Enabling a partnership approach** – to boost a partnership approach and recognise the collective dimension of data processing, some additional collective rights are proposed for unions and specialist third sector organisations to exercise new duties on members or other groups' behalf.
4. **Enforcement in practice** – the joint Digital Regulation Cooperation Forum (DRCF) should be expanded with new powers to create certification schemes, suspend use or impose terms and issue cross-cutting statutory guidance, to supplement the work of individual regulators and sector-specific standards.

Source: APPG, 2021

Where legal action has been taken, safeguards usually relate to the definition of an employee. We saw in the previous chapter how employment status, defined by an employment contract, gives employees a range of rights and imposes a number of requirements on employers. When a company argues that someone working for them is *not* an employee, and instead is a contractor, or self-employed, these rights evaporate. The advent of digital platforms has affected the standard definitions of an employee and a significant amount of legal case law has been devoted to unravelling just how much autonomy a so-called independent worker actually has before they are classed as an employee. Some platform organisations, for example, regulate work activity in detail dictating exactly what workers are expected to do and how much time they should take to complete a task. In certain circumstances turning down work more than a couple of times means that the worker is no longer used, in effect forcing them to take work that is unprofitable. In such cases it is difficult to argue that they are truly independent of the organisation using them. In the UK, a number of cases have resulted in 'workers' obtaining legal rights to holiday pay and the minimum wage; for example, the Supreme Court ruling on Pimlico Plumbers in 2018. Although not regarded as part of the gig economy, this ruling is important because it clarified some of the uncertainty around the permissibility of calling someone self-employed which has an impact on gig workers and those they work for. In this particular case Mr Smith worked for Pimlico Plumbers for a number of years. Following a heart attack, he asked for a reduction in his 40-hour working week, which was denied and the case went to an employment tribunal. Eventually after several appeals it came before the Supreme Court which confirmed that although Mr Smith's contract called him self-employed he was, in fact, a 'worker'. This was evident because Mr Smith did not operate independently and was in effect controlled by Pimlico and integral to its operation. Additionally, Mr Smith's independence from Pimlico was also in doubt as Pimlico was quite stringent about who Mr Smith could use as a replacement if he was unable to undertake a shift – the substitute had to be an accredited Pimlico operative. A year later, in February 2021, the Supreme Court also ruled that Uber drivers must be thought of as 'workers', rather than self-employed. In a later 2022 case, Pimlico were once again thwarted – the Court of Appeal ruled that the company had to recognise that annual leave should be paid to Mr Smith, who had been denied the right to paid annual leave on the basis that he was not a 'worker'. This latter case also strengthens the case for gig workers, who following the European Court of Justice judgement on *King v Sash Windows Workshop*, are able to carry over any untaken portion of their four-weeks' leave each year, and should they leave the organisation, obtain full compensation for it. Those employers now using 'self-employed' contractors who, in reality, have 'worker status' could, possibly, face financial liability for unpaid holiday pay. Of course, where workers are unaware of their rights it does not necessarily mean that they will now have them instated by corrective employer action. Some employers may continue to operate on 'the windy side' of the law. (Pimlico Plumbers Ltd and another v Smith [2018] UKSC 29; Pimlico Plumbers Ltd v Smith [2021] UKEAT 0211_19_1703; *King v The Sash Window Workshop Ltd*. ECLI:EU:C:2017:914.)

The position in other parts of Europe is not dissimilar. In France, the Cour de Cassation (Supreme Court) has made two similar recent rulings. For both Take Eat Easy and Uber, it clarified that workers were in relationships of subordination and should properly be classified as employees rather than self-employed contractors. It pointed out, in the Uber case, that the criteria for self-employment includes the possibility of building one's own clientele and the freedom to set one's own terms and conditions (Goury, 2020). Similarly in the Netherlands, the court ruled in favour of the Dutch union, Federatie Nederlandse Vakbeweging (FNV) and against Uber, finding that its drivers were not self-employed but instead met all the necessary characteristics of employees. Here the Amsterdam court also found that the drivers were covered by the national taxi drivers' collective bargaining agreement that sets pay and benefits such as sick pay. Uber now has to abide by this, and in some cases was required to pay its drivers back pay (Lomas, 2021).

News Flash 5.4

EU Propose Increased Legislative Protection for Gig and Platform Workers

In December 2021 the European Union proposed new conditions enabling fair treatment for platform workers. The proposals will be an improvement because the Union recommends standardising the legal protection for about 4 million gig workers by *altering* their classification from self-employed to employee, provided that two out of the following five criteria are met:

- the platform determines the pay
- the platform requires workers to follow rules regarding appearance, conduct toward clients or performance of the work
- the platform uses electronic means to supervise and assess job performance
- the platform restricts work times or the freedom to turn the app off
- the platform requires exclusivity or non-competition.

Gig workers newly reclassified as employees would have the right to a minimum wage, (in the countries where it exists), safety protections, paid leave, unemployment benefits and the right to collectively bargain for their terms and conditions. Platforms will be able to challenge the reclassification; however the legal burden of proving that there is *no* employment relationship rests on them.

Importantly, the proposed Directive increases transparency around digital labour platforms' use of algorithms and gives the right to contest automated decisions. These new rights will be granted to both workers and the genuine self-employed.

If it's passed, EU member countries have two years within which to incorporate the regulations into their own legislative systems – this means that the guidelines may well be applied differently in different countries. It is interesting that the EU has adopted a binary approach, unlike in the UK where there is no separate 'worker' category.

Source: European Union, 2021

There have been legal challenges too around the ways that algorithms might regulate a workplace. Automatic regulation can, and occasionally does, lead to a lack of transparency, leaving those individuals subject to its demands without any means of voicing their concerns. Moreover, Bigman and Gray found that people have a strong dislike to the involvement of algorithms in moral decisions (2018). It is not uncommon for algorithms to affect perceptions of organisational justice, inhibiting procedural and interactional justice. In two recent experiments, De Cremer and McGuire (2022) considered 201 and 601 individuals, and were able to show that people regarded working with decision making, independent, self-directed algorithms to be so unfair that they would be happy to take a financial hit in order to prevent becoming involved. People were, however, not completely opposed to algorithms, and regarded a 60–40 human–algorithm partnership as fair.

The digital observation and recording, both of worker personal data and task performance, may lead to legitimate feelings that privacy is being compromised, affecting levels of trust and engagement with the employing organisation. Data protection legislation goes some way to ensuring that personal information is not abused, but this is not a guarantee of privacy and does not affect the day-to-day monitoring of task activity. Algorithms may also inadvertently discriminate against certain sectors of society – hiring algorithms, for example, can determine who has access to certain jobs and their future levels of remuneration (Yam and Skorburg, 2021). The use of such technology is becoming more widespread; for example, LinkedIn claim that 64% of employers use AI systems and data analytics as part of their talent strategy (LinkedIn Talent Solutions, 2018). If an algorithm excludes certain people due to age, ethnicity, gender, or postcode, this may sometimes perpetuate discrimination and deny economic opportunities for specific categories of people (Arneson, 2015). Pauline Kim pointed out that,

> Algorithms built on inaccurate, biased, or unrepresentative data can produce outcomes biased along lines of race, sex, or other protected characteristics. Data mining techniques may cause employment decisions to be based on correlations rather than causal relationships; they may obscure the basis on which employment decisions are made; and they may further exacerbate inequality because error detection is limited, and feedback effects compound the bias.

She goes on to say that when,

> … automated decisions are used to control access to employment opportunities, the results may look very similar to the systematic patterns of disadvantage that motivated antidiscrimination laws. What is novel is that the discriminatory effects are data-driven. (2016: 857, 86)

News Flash 5.5

ADCU Fights Against Uber's Use of Racially Discriminatory Facial Recognition Systems

Since March 2020, Uber has been using a facial recognition system, incorporating Microsoft's FACE API. In 2021 the App Drivers and Couriers Union took Uber to an Employment Tribunal over the unfair dismissal of two workers, a driver and a courier, claiming that the company's biometric identity checks discriminate against people of colour and that its facial recognition system failed to correctly identify the dismissed workers. Uber had defended the dismissals, pointing out that at least two people reviewed the evidence prior to a dismissal.

Sources: ADCU, 2021; Booth, 2021

Case Study 5.2

Amazon: Recruiting App Discriminated Against Women

Growing, and knowing it was going to need to recruit a large number of people, in 2015 Amazon set up a team to develop, trial and introduce, a new recruiting algorithm. The developed application worked by looking for patterns in all of the CVs that had been submitted to Amazon over the preceding decade. Unfortunately, this did not take into account that the majority of CVs had been submitted by men, and by using this information the app 'believed' that male candidates were preferable. Certain CVs were disregarded or downgraded if they referred specifically to women's schools or clubs. The programmes were tweaked to ensure they were more gender neutral, but bias was still evident. The algorithms assigned less significance to skills, such as the ability to write computer codes, which were commonplace across applicants, instead concentrating on certain words and phrases. This turned out to be problematic, firstly because it became evident that certain words, such as 'execute' and 'captured' were less likely to be used by women and, secondly, because the removal of common IT skills from the system meant that the algorithms sometimes picked people who were not qualified for the work required.

The project was scrapped at the end of 2017 and a new team set up to work on automated employment screening with focus on diversity. Vestiges of the old version remain, but only for undertaking basic tasks like removing duplicate candidate profiles from databases.

Source: Dastin, 2018

Another legal challenge relates to labour platforms using algorithmic systems to replace, at least in part, the organisational functions that managers traditionally performed, for example, there have been lawsuits challenging the fairness of algorithms used to evaluate teachers (*Houston Federation of Teachers v. Houston Independent School District* 2017 – see *Houston Public Media*, 2017). Algorithmic management diffuses the ways in which a workforce is managed, not just absolving managers of responsibility, but removing them from the process altogether. Algorithms are control mechanisms, concentrating employer control by diffusing responsibility to electronic activities. Legally this raises questions as to who should be liable if a worker raises a complaint – the employer, the designers of the software, or an electronic training provider? As with the legal questions around who is or is not an employee, the use of apps to hire, manage, control and sometimes terminate a worker's employment leaves open to question who is responsible when things go wrong and there is a detrimental impact on the working conditions.

Exercise 5.2

Suggest how algorithmic management could:

- bring a risk of bias and discrimination
- hinder workers' understanding of work organisation
- prevent the effective exercise of the right of trade unions and work councils to information and consultation.

The Impact of Algorithms on the Employment Relationship

Algorithms are increasingly making decisions that have been the prerogative of managers and HR specialists. Duggan et al. define such algorithmic management as:

> … a system of control where self-learning algorithms are given the responsibility for making and executing decisions affecting labour, thereby limiting human involvement and oversight of the process. (2020: 119)

Extensive use in gig and platform work means that algorithms replace the human element of much of the organisational day-to-day people management, removing the need for face-to-face interaction, therefore helping to keep costs down (Lee et al., 2015). In effect, algorithms replace human supervisory roles based on social exchange and subjective feelings (see, e.g., Wang and Varma, 2020), with electronic systems of checks and balances based on 'objective' electronic surveillance. A combination of constant data collection, coupled with machine-learning analysis, allows employers to monitor and direct their workforces on a continuous basis, in effect allocating the day-to-day managerial responsibilities to algorithms. An 'algorithmic manager' augments personal/human decision-making by digitally hovering over each worker, rather like a virtual personalised drone, recording and controlling each aspect of a worker's day, from initial recruitment and setting expectations, to assigning tasks, controlling how work is done and paid for, scrutinising and sanctioning substandard performance – and, in some circumstances, terminating the employment relationship without any recourse to remedy. Where gig couriers are concerned, the algorithms work in conjunction with the workers' own smart phones using GPS data to track when and where they are at any given time. All of such managerial algorithmic monitoring and organising is frequently accomplished without any trace of transparency or accountability, making 'managerial' decisions difficult to explain. This is a case, not so much of devolving decisions and power to line managers, but to devolving decisions and accountability to an app with the employer retaining power.

These digitally created, controlled and managed work environments create an imbalance in the working relationship. The worker is without a meaningful voice and may therefore become discouraged, disaffected and disengaged. The lack of personal autonomy and inability to control their working day, often with complete absence of influence over the work process, reduces people to little more than cogs in their working environment. The perceptions of injustice and the drip-feeding of powerlessness create an environment ripe for unionisation: however, the isolation of many platform and gig workers mitigates against mobilisation. Möhlmann and Henfridsson's (2019) research into Uber drivers from New York and London showed how the impact of algorithm management left the drivers 'feeling … lonely, isolated, and dehumanized'. These feelings were exacerbated because, 'they don't have colleagues to socialize with or a team or community to be part of. They lack the opportunity to build a personal relationship with a supervisor'. Their research uncovered driver attitudes to algorithmic management that was so frustrating that their resentment led to subversive behaviour. The workers resented the constant surveillance, control and system of customer ratings, and this, rather than improving productivity, decreased it. The research revealed that the drivers found,

> … the lack of transparency of the underlying logic of the complex algorithms frustrating, believing it to be an unfair system which manipulates them subtly without their knowledge or consent. (Möhlmann and Henfridsson, 2019: 3)

All this led to the drivers gaming the system, switching between employers, and influencing pricing. They also began to use online networks to communicate with one another and join workers' rights groups such as Working Washington, which actively fights for couriers for on-demand services. (Sometimes of course resistance to workplace practices arises without recourse to union help. In China, for example, as Chen (2018) explains, drivers for the taxi app, Didi Chuxing, used several software packages that allowed them to refuse allocated jobs *without* incurring penalties. Drivers were observed to be using up to six smart phones simultaneously to identify the most lucrative jobs.) Yet not all gig-based drivers feel discontent, or a need to game the system. For example, in a study comparing Chicago-based Uber drivers with traditional taxi drivers – albeit with a very small sample size – Norlander et al. (2021) discovered that, although there was a higher level of surveillance for gig workers, this had no perceivable negative impact on either enjoyment of the job or on motivational levels.

Overall it can be said that the algorithmic management has a negative impact on those being managed in such a detached way. Such forms of impersonal management are sometimes derided and receive a degree of negative publicity. Amazon regularly receives a 'bad press' for its rather impersonal, somewhat brutal electronic dismissal practices. It remains unabashed however, and, on occasion uses such electronic decision making as a cover for bad practice.

Case Snippet 5.1

Amazon Defends Itself Against Trade Union Discrimination

When Amazon defended itself against a claim that it discriminated against a trade union employee, its defence relied on the fact that the management had no *active* part in the dismissal. Instead, it declared that a *neutral* algorithm dismissed the claimant using information based purely on its measurement of the claimant's lack of productivity. Amazon stressed that the local warehouse management had had no input, control, or understanding of the details of the system used to sack the claimant.

Source: Lecher, 2019

Being managed by an app creates conditions of frustrated powerlessness. Ravenelle (2019) argues that the seemingly random elements of control experienced by workers managed by apps may well damage their psychological contract. Workers, whether they are technically employees or not, are likely to have expectations about their work (and those they work for) and expect a reciprocal arrangement. Yet the transactional nature of much gig work militates against this. Apps that use hard rather than soft management techniques, perhaps incentivising different workers with fluctuating rates of pay, and sometimes removing workers from the system altogether, are likely to endanger a healthy respect for the employer and damage the psychological contract. It is not just gig workers whose transactional work experiences engender negative feeling as platform crowdworkers too are liable to feel that the employment relationship with their employer is less than reciprocal. In an explorative study of 266 German crowdworkers Pfeiffer and Kawalec found that, in relation to their work environment, 'crowdworkers perceive injustices in four specific areas: planning insecurity, lack of transparency in performance evaluation, lack of clarity in task briefings and low remuneration' (2020: 483). These findings indicate that the crowdworkers experienced a damaged psychological contract and strong perceptions of organisational injustice, particularly procedural, informational and distributional injustice (Bies and Moag, 1986; Colquitt, 2001).

Levels of trust experienced by those working under algorithmic control are likely to be low; the harmony, reliability and concern highlighted by Tzafrir and Dolan (2004) are all likely to be missing. Where workers feel an organisation treats them in an unfair way this leads to a drop not just in trust, but may also result in a downward shift in productivity (Chen, 2018; Duan et al., 2010; Möhlmann and Henfridsson, 2019). It is the very precariousness of those in gig and platform employment that often renders them unable to look for alternative employment.

Platform Work, Power and Worker Representation

Digital platform workers in the gig economy have limited power and are often exploited. As we have seen, they are easily replaced, work in isolation, and are often completely reliant on the digital platform for the amount of work and remuneration that they receive. The levels of control exercised by the platforms, algorithmically scrutinising work and monitoring worker activities, often pressurising those under their control to work exclusively for them, not only renders the workers defenceless, but makes resistance difficult and taking collective action against their employers seemingly impossible. Furthermore, any efforts towards collective representation are actively resisted by some platform organisations. Yet management can never fully eliminate the resistance of workers to whatever form of managerialism is in place, digital or otherwise (Moore and Joyce, 2020: 927).

Traditionally trade unions have not taken into membership those classified as employers or self-employed. The labelling of gig workers as self-employed, independent contractors, however erroneous, therefore weighed heavily against the unions representing such workers. However, as the intention behind categorising such workers as self-employed is nothing more than an expedient cost-cutting strategy to reduce access to regulatory employment protection, this creates a dilemma for unions. Clearly self-employed platform personnel are not, in the main, independent contractors but rather, vulnerable workers in need of protection. Alongside the conceptual difficulty of representing the self-employed, unions also face the physical difficulty of reaching – and then organising – platform workers, as many work in isolation and, because platform-based work often involves triangular relationships, making it difficult to identify the employer, and consequently, the bargaining counterpart.

Effective collective representation is, however, as essential in the arena of platform work as it was, and is, in traditional forms of employment. In both, union involvement moderates the risks faced by workers and acts towards improving the terms and conditions of work by rebalancing the lack of transparency and power asymmetries between the organisations and their workers. The Budd (2004) tripartite requirements for a healthy employment relationship – equity, efficiency and voice – are as relevant in platform organisations as in any other work situation, and both equity and voice can and should be provided by union engagement with platform workers and their organisations. Interestingly, France, unlike the USA, the UK and other European countries, explicitly recognises the right of platform workers to unionise and their right to take industrial action. Academic opinion analysing the union response to precarious workers is divided, some authors suggesting that the unions, by concentrating on protecting the terms and conditions of employment for their members in traditional employment, have promoted the segmentation of workforces and disregarded the needs of insecure workers that fall outside of their constituencies (Hassel, 2014; Palier and Thelen, 2010). Others, like Doellgast and her colleagues, have disagreed pointing out that trade unions do engage with and help precarious workers improve their pay and working conditions (2018). Keune and Pedaci suggest that such union activity,

> … is more inclusive and aimed at bridging the gap with regular workers, often explicitly targeting non-standard workers, both to improve the position of precarious workers and to protect the standards of regular workers. (2020: 145)

There have been some successful forays into representation for platform workers. In May 2017 Airtasker, an Australian platform connecting task seekers (domestic and commercial) with individuals willing to perform tasks, concluded an agreement with Unions New South Wales (UNSW). The agreement establishes working conditions compliant with health and safety standards, ensures pay levels stay above the stipulated minima, gives provision for insurance compensation, establishes an independent dispute resolution system overseen by the Fair Work Commission and makes an undertaking to continue engaging with UNSW (Minter, 2017; Taylor, 2017). While in the city of Vienna, app-based couriers with Foodora, have, with the support of Vida, the Austrian union representing workers in the transport and services sector, succeeded in establishing a works council (WC). In Germany, the small Freie ArbeiterInnen-Union union is marshalling delivery workers together under the #deliverunion campaign, and the Food, Enjoyment and Restaurants Union, Gewerkschaft Nahrung-Genuss-Gaststätten (NGG), is attempting to set up a works council for its local couriers (EWC 2017).

News Flash 5.6

Uber Couriers Now Officially Represented by the GMB

Uber has agreed to recognise the UK GMB union for its 70,000 private hire drivers.

Under the deal (agreed on the 26 May 2021), the union will meet quarterly with Uber management to discuss driver issues and concerns, such as health and safety, and also have regular access to drivers' meeting hubs in order to offer support and advice. Drivers are able to join the union if they wish to do so but it is not obligatory. The hard-won agreement follows the company's gradual softening of its cost-efficient approach to managing drivers; it had already agreed to pay the minimum hourly wage and provide pensions, although paying for all the time drivers are actually logged on remains a contentious issue.

Mick Rix, national officer of the GMB, said: 'When tech private hire companies and unions work together like this, everyone benefits - bringing dignified, secure employment back to the world of work. We now call on all other operators to follow suit'.

The agreement does not apply to delivery riders for the Uber Eats food service.

Source: Butler, 2021

News Flash 5.7

A Change in Pay Leads to the UK's Longest Gig-economy Strike

Between December 2021 and the spring of 2022 takeaway food outlets, like Greggs, McDonalds and Just Eat, in cities as widely dispersed as Sunderland, Sheffield, Blackpool and Leicester, have been the subject of three-hourly strikes across the lunch period and picketing by members of the Independent Workers Union of Great Britain (IWGB). The strike is unusual, organising freelance workers is difficult, and only around a fifth are members of the IWGB. In addition many drivers do not want to take part in the action against their employer, partly because they are grateful to be able to earn a living and partly because some are new immigrants who feel insecure and don't want to jeopardise their income and current standing in the UK. Taking action is not easy as not only do the drivers miss out on pay, but cancelling a booked delivery, via the company app, is time consuming, and occasionally the drivers have to submit pictures of the picket line they are refusing to cross - something that probably breaches the privacy of the picketers and clearly identifies them to Stuart, the platform used by the food company.

The action is not intended to impact customers who use the outlets on foot, but to deter delivery couriers who are working for Stuart. Stuart is a company that claims to be Europe's leading on-demand logistics platform able to link retail and hospitality businesses with local, independent, couriers.

The strike started because Stuart changed the pay structure for its UK delivery drivers. Before the change couriers had earned £4.50 for all journeys of up to 2.499 miles rising to £7.50 if they were required to go further. Under the new scheme the rates dropped to £3.40 for the shortest trips (up to half a mile) increasing to £7.20 for journeys of 4.5 miles or more. Stuart denies the changes are a pay cut, and points out that average courier earnings are higher than the real living wage.

Source: Pidd, 2022

Summary

Electronically enabled work processes have become prevalent in the last few decades resulting in a proliferation of work patterns and employing organisations that create work opportunities that are far removed from the traditional standard forms of employment. There has been a rise in platforms – organisations that match a flexible workforce with available work – and a dramatic increase in gig employment. Such work is often precarious, unpredictable and poorly paid leading to insecurity and vulnerability for the workers involved. The advent of self-learning algorithms that are able to monitor, control and command workers digitally has had an impact on the employment relationship, on occasion harming the psychological contract, creating negative perceptions of organisational justice and disrupting traditional ways of collective representation.

Review Questions

1   Define the terms;

    a   Platform work

    b   Gig economy

    c   Precarious work

2   Describe the differences between the types of platform work that Duggan and his colleagues categorise (Duggan et al., 2020: 117-8).

3   Analyse the pros and cons of platform work.

4   Explain why gig workers might feel vulnerable at work.

5   How might algorithms discriminate against certain sectors of society?

6   Explain, with academic justification, why platform workers might find digital monitoring, feedback, ranking and rating systems unfair.

7   Using your knowledge of international employee relations, critically assess at least two different legal approaches used to categorise gig workers.

8   Explain why it is difficult for unions to organise and represent platform workers.

9   Evaluate any variations found between the employment relationship for platform work and work under a traditional contract of employment.

Revision Exercise 5.1

Moore (2018) discusses how digitally based and controlled work (within the platform-based labour market) generates working conditions leading to worker alienation and precarity, with considerable risks of physical violence and harassment to those workers involved. Using academic argument explain why Moore might be either right or wrong.

Revision Exercise 5.2

Tom Slee, in his book *What's Yours is Mine: Against the Sharing Economy*, argues that systems using management algorithms taking customer feedback then using it to rate workers, are iniquitous. He likens the apps themselves to a 'boss from hell: an erratic, bad-tempered and unaccountable manager that may fire you at any time, on a whim, with no appeal' (2015: 100-1).

Research to find examples of companies that use algorithms in a way that Slee describes. How might this form of algorithmic management impact on the employment relationship, and perceptions of fairness, in the organisations you have identified?

Relevant Articles for Further Reading

Campbell, I. (2002) 'Platform work and precariousness: Low earnings and limited control of work', forthcoming in V. De Stefano, I. Durri, C. Stylogiannis and H. Wouters (eds), *A Research Agenda for the Gig Economy and Society*. Available at: https://ssrn.com/abstract=4071315 (accessed 5 June 2022).

This chapter examines recent research on precarious work, in particular it looks at research describing the different experiences of those on low earnings with limited job control.

Duggan, J., Sherman, U., Carbery, R. and McDonnell, A. (2020) 'Algorithmic management and app-work in the gig economy: A research agenda for employment relations and HRM', *Human Resource Management Journal*, 30(1): 114–32.

This article is useful in two different ways: firstly it categorises different types of work within the gig economy, partitioning this heterogenous field into three separate and distinct areas. Secondly it explores the pros and cons from an employee relations point of view, of app-based management practices.

Gandini, A. (2019) 'Labour process theory and the gig economy', *Human Relations*, 72(6): 1039–56.

While exploring labour process theory within the gig economy this article sheds light on emotional labour and the importance of monitoring, ratings and customer feedback on worker control.

Premji, S. (2018)' "It's totally destroyed our life": Exploring the pathways and mechanisms between precarious employment and health and well-being among immigrant men and women in Toronto', *International Journal of Health Services*, 48(1): 106–27.

An interesting article that provides lots of quotes from those experiencing precarious work. It provides a good sense of the levels of insecurity and powerlessness felt by Canadian migrant workers.

References

ADCU (2021) *ADCU Initiates Legal Action Against Uber's Workplace Use of Racially Discriminatory Facial Recognition Systems*. Available at: www.adcu.org.uk/news-posts/adcu-initiates-legal-action-against-ubers-workplace-use-of-racially-discriminatory-facial-recognition-systems (accessed 19 April 2022).

Allan, B. A., Autin, K. L. and Wilkins-Yel, K. G. (2021) 'Precarious work in the 21st century: A psychological perspective', *Journal of Vocational Behavior*, 126: 103491.

APPG (2021) *MPs Call on the UK Government to Take Urgent Action on AI Accountability*, press release, 11 November. Available at: www.futureworkappg.org.uk/news/zownl0mx4t4n6smrk4dmzor0oz4djg (accessed 5 May 2022).

Arneson, R. (2015) 'Equality of opportunity', in E. N. Zalta (ed.), *The Stanford Encyclopedia of Philosophy*. Metaphysics Research Lab, Stanford University.

Bauman, Z. (2000) *Liquid Modernity*. Cambridge: Polity Press.

Bechter, B., Brandl, B. and Meardi, G. (2012) 'Sectors or countries? Typologies and levels of analysis in comparative industrial relations', *European Journal of Industrial Relations*, 18(3): 185–202.

Berg, J., Hilal, A., El, S. and Horne, R. (2021) *World Employment and Social Outlook: Trends 2021*. Geneva: International Labour Organization.

Berg, J., Furrer, M., Harmon, E., Rani, U. and Silberman, M. S. (2018) *Digital Labour Platforms and the Future of Work: Towards Decent Work in the Online World*. Available at: www.ilo.org/global/publications/books/WCMS_645337/lang--en/index.htm (accessed 15 August 2022).

Bies, R. J. and Moag, L. S. (1986) 'Interactional justice: communication criteria or fairness', in R. J. Lewicki, B. H. Sheppard and M. Brazerman (eds), *Research on Negotiation in Organizations*, Vol. 1. Greenwich, CT: JAI, pp.43-55

Bigman, Y. E. and Gray, K. (2018) 'People are averse to machines making moral decisions', *Cognition*, 181: 21–34.

Booth, R. (5.10.2021) 'Ex-Uber driver takes legal action over 'racist' face-recognition software', *The Guardian*, 5 October. Available at: www.theguardian.com/technology/2021/oct/05/ex-uber-driver-takes-legal-action-over-racist-face-recognition-software (accessed 19 April 2022).

Bosmans, K., Hardonk, S., De Cuyper, N. and Vanroelen, C. (2016) 'Explaining the relation between precarious employment and mental well-being: A qualitative study among temporary agency workers', *Work*, 53(2): 249–64.

Budd, J. (2004) *Employment with a Human Face: Balancing Efficiency, Equity, and Voice*. Ithaca, NY: Cornell University Press.

Butler, S. (2021) 'Uber agrees union recognition deal with GMB', *The Guardian*, 26 May. Available at: www.theguardian.com/business/2021/may/26/uber-agrees-historic-deal-allowing-drivers-to-join-gmb-union (accessed 18 April 2022).

Chen, B., Liu, T. and Wang, Y. (2020) 'Volatile fragility: New employment forms and disrupted employment protection in the new economy', *International Journal of Environmental Research and Public Health*, 17(5): 1531.

Chen, J. Y. (2018) 'Thrown under the bus and outrunning it! The logic of Didi and taxi drivers' labour and activism in the on-demand economy', *New Media & Society*, 20(8): 2691–711.

Codagnone, C., Abadie, F. and Biagi, F. (2016) *The Future of Work in the 'Sharing Economy'. Market Efficiency and Equitable Opportunities or Unfair Precarisation?* Institute for Prospective Technological Studies, JRC Science for Policy Report EUR 27913 EN. doi:10.2791/431485

Collier, R. B., Dubal, V. B. and Carter, C. (2017) Labour Platforms and Gig Work: The Failure to Regulate. *Institute for Research on Labour and Employment*, Working Paper 106–17.

Colquitt, J. A. (2001) 'On the dimensionality of organizational justice: A construct validation of a measure', *Journal of Applied Psychology*, 86(3): 386–400.

Dastin, J. (2018) 'Amazon scraps secret AI recruiting tool that showed bias against women, *Reuters*, 11 October. Available at: www.reuters.com/article/us-amazon-com-jobs-automation-insight/amazon-scraps-secret-ai-recruiting-tool-that-showed-bias-against-women-idUSKCN1MK08G (accessed 4 April 2022).

De Cremer, D. and Kasparov, G. (2021) 'AI should augment human intelligence, not replace it', *Harvard Business Review*, 18 March. Available at: https://hbr.org/2021/03/ai-should-augment-human-intelligence-not-replace-it (accessed 6 April 2022).

De Cremer, D. and McGuire, J. (2022) 'Human–algorithm collaboration works best if humans lead (because it is fair!)', *Social Justice Research*, 35: 33–55.

Department for Business, Energy & Industrial Strategy (BEIS) (2018) *The Characteristics of Those in the Gig Economy*. Available at: https://apo.org.au/sites/default/files/resource-files/2018-02/apo-nid244361.pdf (accessed 6 April 2022).

Doellgast, V., Lillie, N. and Pulignano, V. (eds) (2018) *Reconstructing Solidarity: Labour Unions, Precarious Work, and the Politics of Institutional Change in Europe*. Oxford: Oxford University Press.

Doug, H. (2016) 'Fired from Uber: Why drivers get deactivated, and how to get reactivated', *Ride Sharing Driver*, 21 April. Available at: www.ridesharingdriver.com/fired-uber-drivers-get-deactivated-and-reactivated/ (accessed 4 April 2022).

Duan, J., Lam, W., Chen, C. and Zhong, J. A. (2010) 'Leadership justice, negative organizational behaviours, and the mediating effect of affective commitment', *Society for Personality*, 38(9): 1287–96.

Duggan, J., Sherman, U., Carbery, R. and McDonnell, A. (2020) 'Algorithmic management and app-work in the gig economy: A research agenda for employment relations and HRM', *Human Resource Management Journal*, 30(1): 114–32.

Eurofound (2018) *Automation, Digitisation and Platforms: Implications for Work and Employment*. Luxembourg: Publications Office of the European Union. Available at: www.eurofound.europa.eu/sites/default/files/ef_publication/field_ef_document/ef18002en.pdf (accessed 14 April 2022).

European Economic and Social Committee (2021) *The Definition of Worker in the Platform Economy: Exploring Workers' Risks and Regulatory Solutions*. Available at: www.eesc.europa.eu/sites/default/files/files/qe-05-21-286-en-n_0.pdf (accessed 12 April 2022).

European Union (2021) *Commission Proposals to Improve the Working Conditions of People Working Through Digital Labour Platforms*, press release, 9 December. Available from: https://ec.europa.eu/commission/presscorner/detail/en/ip_21_6605 (accessed 12 April 2022).

EWC (2017) *Austria: The Foodora Platform Sets Up its First Works Council*. Available at: https://ewcdb.eu/node/241548 (accessed 13 March 2022).

Fabo, B., Karanovic, J. and Dukova, K. (2017) 'In search of an adequate European policy to the platform economy', *Transfer: European Review of Labour and Research*, 23: 163–75.

Fernández-Macías, E. (2017) *Automation, Digitization and Platforms: Implications for Work and Employment*, Eurofound Working Paper. Available at: www.eurofound.europa.eu/sites/default/files/wpef17035.pdf (accessed 10 April 2022).

Florisson, R. and Mandl, I. (2018) *Platform Work: Types and Implications for Work and Employment: Literature Review*. Dublin, Ireland: Eurofound. Available at: www.forschungsnetzwerk.at/downloadpub/wpef18004.pdf (accessed 10 April 2022).

Goury, R. (2020) *Uber: The Cour De Cassation Reclassify the Contractual Relationship Between Uber and a Driver as an Employment Contract*. Available at: www.mayerbrown.com/en/perspectives-events/publications/2020/03/cour-de-cassation-reclassify-the-contractual-relationship-between-uber-and-a-driver-as-an-employment-contract (accessed 12 April 2022).

Graham, R. (2022) '"Gig economy" workers strike in Belfast over pay and conditions', *The Irish Times*, 23 March. Available at: www.irishtimes.com/business/work/gig-economy-workers-strike-in-belfast-over-pay-and-conditions-1.4834542 (accessed 19 April 2022)

Grimshaw, D., Johnson, M., Rubery, J. and Keizer, A. (2016) *Reducing Precarious Work: Protective Gaps and the Role of Social Dialogue in Europe*. Manchester: European Work and Employment Research Centre, University of Manchester.

Gupta, A., Tewary, T. and Gopalakrishnan, B. N. (2022) *Sustainability in the Gig Economy*. Cham.: Springer.

Hafeez, S., Gupta, C. and Sprajcer, M. (2022) 'Stress and the gig economy: It's not all shifts and giggles', *Industrial Health*. doi:10.2486/indhealth.2021-0217

Hall, P. A. and Soskice, D. (eds) (2001) *Varieties of Capitalism: The Institutional Foundations of Comparative Advantage*. New York, NY: Oxford University Press.

Hassel, A. (2014) 'The paradox of liberalization: Understanding dualism and the recovery of the German political economy', *British Journal of Industrial Relations*, 52(1): 57–81.

Heyes, J., Moore, S., Newsome, K. and Tomlinson, M. (2018) 'Living with uncertain work', *Industrial Relations Journal*, 49(5-6): 420–37.

Houston Public Media (2017) 'Federal lawsuit settled between Houston's teacher union and HISD', *Houston Public Media*, 10 October. Available at: www.houstonpublicmedia.org/articles/news/2017/10/10/241724/federal-lawsuit-settled-between-houstons-teacher-union-and-hisd/ (accessed 18 April 2022).

Huws, U., Spencer, N., Syrdal, D. S. and Holts, K. (2017) *Work in the European gig economy: Research results from the UK, Sweden, Germany, Austria, the Netherlands, Switzerland and Italy*. FEPS, UniGlobal and University of Hertfordshire.

Kenney, M. and Zysman, J. (2016) 'The rise of the platform economy', *Issues in Science and Technology*, 32(3): 61–9.

Keune, M. (2015) 'Trade unions, precarious work and dualisation in Europe', in W. Eichhorst and P. Marx (eds), *Non-Standard Employment in Comparative Perspective*. Cheltenham: Edward Elgar, pp. 378–400.

Keune, M. and Pedaci, M. (2020) 'Trade union strategies against precarious work: Common trends and sectoral divergence in the EU', *European Journal of Industrial Relations*, 26(2): 139–55.

Kim, P. T. (2016) 'Data-driven discrimination at work', *Wm. & Mary L. Rev.*, 58: 857.

Kreshpaj, B., Orellana, C., Burström, B., Davis, L., Hemmingsson, T., Johansson, G., Kjellberg, K., Jonsson, J., Wegman, D. H. and Bodin, T. (2020) 'What is precarious employment? A systematic review of definitions and operationalizations from quantitative and qualitative studies', *Scandinavian Journal of Work, Environment & Health*, 46(3): 235–47.

Lecher, C. (2019) 'How Amazon automatically tracks and fires workers for productivity', *The Verge*, 25 April. Available at: www.theverge.com/2019/4/25/18516004/amazon-warehouse-fulfillment-centers-productivity-firing-terminations (accessed 4 April 2022).

Lee, M. K., Kusbit, D., Metsky, E. and Dabbish, L. (April 2015) 'Working with machines: The impact of algorithmic and data-driven management on human workers', in *Proceedings of the 33rd Annual ACM Conference on Human Factors in Computing Systems* (pp. 1603–12). Available at: https://dl.acm.org/doi/abs/10.1145/2702123.2702548 (accessed 20 April 2022).

LinkedIn Talent Solutions (2018) *LinkedIn Global Recruiting Trends 2018*. Available at: https://business.linkedin.com/content/dam/me/business/en-us/talent-solutions/resources/pdfs/linkedin-global-recruiting-trends-2018-en-us2.pdf (accessed 17 February 2022).

Lomas, N. (2021) *Dutch Court Finds Uber Drivers are Employees*. Available at: https://techcrunch.com/2021/09/13/dutch-court-finds-uber-drivers-are-employees/?guccounter=1&guce_referrer=aHR0cHM6Ly93d3cuZ29vZ2xlLmNvbS8&guce_referrer_sig=AQAAALu3U6gH_O6WFOc8Y-AojjpsOOrYifDnxjM6geoqTkNZtMzKjuwJk7k-kLTU7pqSmn_lqycoJld-WU8Uzei2H TV4GnnuUByBg2sDeckn35xn2GbXnITAZdgu9NOoEDALpdMzll5yy7zuyZIiv1Hipb6BYQMpgm 6bONNu-KwURBLP (accessed 12 April 2022).

Mann, G. and O'Neil, C. (2016) 'Hiring algorithms are not neutral', *Harvard Business Review*, 9.

Mellino, E., Boutaud, C. and Davies, G. (March 25 2021) 'Deliveroo riders can earn as little as £2 an hour during shifts, as boss stands to make £500m', *Bureau of Investigative Journalism*, 25 March. Available at: www.thebureauinvestigates.com/stories/2021-03-25/deliveroo-riders-earning-as-little-as-2-pounds (accessed 17 February 2022).

Minter, K. (2017) 'Negotiating labour standards in the gig economy: Airtasker and Unions New South Wales', *The Economic and Labour Relations Review*, 28(3): 438–54.

Möhlmann, M. and Henfridsson, O. (2019) 'What people hate about being managed by algorithms, according to a study of Uber drivers', *Harvard Business Review*, 30 August. Available at: https://hbr.org/2019/08/what-people-hate-about-being-managed-by-algorithms-according-to-a-study-of-uber-drivers (accessed 10 April 2022).

Moore, P. V. (2018) *The Threat of Physical and Psychosocial Violence and Harassment in Digitalized Work*. Geneva: International Labour Office. Available at: www.ilo.org/actrav/events/WCMS_616826/lang--en/index.htm (accessed 18 April 2022).

Moore, V. P. and Joyce, S. (2020) 'Black box or hidden abode? The expansion and exposure of platform work managerialism', *Review of International Political Economy*, 27(4): 926–48.

Ndiuini, A. and Baum, T. (2021) 'Underemployment and lived experiences of migrant workers in the hotel industry: Policy and industry implications', *Journal of Policy Research in Tourism, Leisure and Events*, 13(1): 36–58.

Noack, A. M. and Vosko, L.F. (2011) *Precarious Jobs in Ontario: Mapping Dimensions of Labour Market Insecurity by Workers' Social Location and Context*. Toronto, Canada: Law Commission of Ontario.

Norlander, P., Jukic, N., Varma, A. and Nestorov, S. (2021) 'The effects of technological supervision on gig workers: Organizational control and motivation of Uber, taxi, and limousine drivers', *The International Journal of Human Resource Management*, 32(19): 4053–77.

Palier, B. and Thelen, K. (2010) 'Institutionalizing dualism: Complementarities and change in France and Germany', *Politics & Society*, 38(1): 119–48.

Perry, J. A., Berlingieri, A. and Mirchandani, K. (2020) 'Precarious work, harassment, and the erosion of employment standards', *Qualitative Research in Organizations and Management: An International Journal*, 15(3): 331–8.

Pesole, A., Brancati, U., Fernández-Macías, E., Biagi, F. and Gonzalez Vazquez, I. (2018) *Platform Workers in Europe*. Luxembourg: Publications Office of the European Union.

Pfeiffer, S. and Kawalec, S. (2020) 'Justice expectations in crowd and platform-mediated work', *The Economic and Labour Relations Review*, 31(4): 483–501.

Pidd, H. (2022) '"Snoop Dogg is advertising Just Eat, but it is me that has to deliver it": The courier leading the UK's longest gig-economy strike', *The Guardian*, 16 March. Available at: www.theguardian.com/society/2022/mar/16/snoop-dog-is-advertising-just-eat-but-it-is-me-that-has-to-deliver-it-the-courier-leading-the-uks-longest-gig-economy-strike?CMP=Share_iOSApp_Other (accessed 16 March 2022).

Premji, S. (2017) 'Precarious employment and difficult daily commutes', *Relations Industrielles/Industrial Relations*, 72(1): 77–98.

Premji, S. (2018, Jan). '"It's totally destroyed our life": Exploring the pathways and mechanisms between precarious employment and health and well-being among immigrant men and women in Toronto', *International Journal Health Services*, 48(1): 106–27.

Ravenelle, A. J. (2019). '"We're not uber:" control, autonomy, and entrepreneurship in the gig economy', *Journal of Managerial Psychology*, 34(4): pp. 269–285.

Slee, T. (2015)*What's Yours is Mine: Against the Sharing Economy*. New York: O/R Books.

Smith, A. W. (2016) 'Shared, collaborative and on demand: The new digital economy', *Pew Research Center*, 19 May. Available at: www.pewresearch.org/internet/2016/05/19/the-new-digital-economy/ (accessed 15 August 2022).

Srnicek, N. (2017) *Platform Capitalism*. Cambridge: Polity Press.

Sverke, M., Hellgren, J. and Näswall, K. (2002) 'No security: A meta-analysis and review of job insecurity and its consequences', *Journal of Occupational Health Psychology*, 7(3): 242.

Tan, Z. M., Aggarwal, N., Cowls, J., Morley, J., Taddeo, M. and Floridi, L. (2021) 'The ethical debate about the gig economy: A review and critical analysis', *Technology in Society*, 65: 101594.

Taylor, D. (2017) 'Airtasker agrees to minimum working conditions for "gig economy" contractors', *ABC News*, 1 May. Available at: www.abc.net.au/news/2017-05-01/airtasker-agrees-tominimum-working-conditions-for-contractors/8484946 (accessed 17 March 2022).

TUC (2021) *Platformisation and the Pandemic: Changes in Workers' Experiences of Platform Work in England and Wales, 2016-2021*. Available at: www.tuc.org.uk/news/gig-economy-workforce-englandand-wales-has-almost-tripled-last-five-years-new-tuc-research (accessed 13 April 2022).

Tzafrir, S. S., Baruch, Y. and Dolan, S. L. (2004) 'The consequences of emerging HRM practices for employees' trust in their managers', *Personnel Review*, 33: 628–47.

Uniglobal (2021) 'Canada's app-based delivery workers organizing with CUPW', *Uniglobal*, 1 March. Available at: https://uniglobalunion.org/news/canadas-app-based-delivery-workers-organizing-with-cupw/ (accessed 14 April 2022).

Van Dijck, J., Poell, T. and De Waal, M. (2018) *The Platform Society: Public Values in a Connective World*. Oxford: Oxford University Press.

Wang, C. H. and Varma, A. (2020) 'Supervisor subordinate relationships', in A. Varma and P. Budhwar (eds), *Performance Management Systems: An Experiential Approach*. London: Sage.

Wickens, Z. (2022) 'Belfast food delivery staff strike over pay demands', *Employee Benefits*. Available at: www.employeebenefits.co.uk/belfast-food-delivery-staff-strike-over-pay-demands/ (accessed 19 March 2022).

Williams, P., McDonald, P. and Mayes, R. (2022) 'The growing gig economy', in P. Brough, E. Gardiner and K. Daniels (eds), *Handbook on Management and Employment Practices*. Cham.: Springer, pp. 769–85.

Wood, A. J., Graham, M. and Lehdonvirta, V. (2018) 'Good gig, bad gig: Autonomy and algorithmic control in the global gig economy', *Work, Employment and Society*, 33(1): 56–75.

Woodcock, J. and Graham, M. (2019) *The Gig Economy. A Critical Introduction*. Cambridge: Polity Press.

World Economic Forum (2020) *The Future of Jobs Report 2020*. Available at: www.weforum.org/reports/the-future-of-jobs-report-2020 (accessed 18 March 2022).

Yam, J. and Skorburg, J. A. (2021) 'From human resources to human rights: Impact assessments for hiring algorithms', *Ethics and Information Technology*, 23(4): 611–23.

Zyskowski, K., Morris, M. R., Bigham, J. P., Gray, M. L. and Kane, S. K. (2015) 'Accessible crowdwork? Understanding the value in and challenge of microtask employment for people with disabilities', in Proceedings of the 18th ACM Conference on Computer Supported Cooperative Work and Social Computing, pp. 1682–93.

6
CAUSES AND EXPRESSIONS OF WORKPLACE CONFLICT

Learning Outcomes

By the end of this chapter, you should be able to:

- have a critical understanding of the causes of conflict in the employment relationship
- critically evaluate the nature of conflict in the employment relationship in the light of different academic perspectives
- analyse the links between power and conflict in the relationship and its impact on both individual and group behaviours
- have an ability to assess the likelihood of conflict in a given employment relationship.

What to Expect

Conflict in the workplace is the outcome of contested incidents leading to workplace exchanges resulting in disagreement. This chapter looks at the causes and expressions of conflict arising from workplace interactions. Whether they arise from clashes between operational and strategic activities (Marchington, 2015), from interpersonal differences, or from perceptions of injustice (Boodoo et al., 2020), tensions within the employment relationship abound. In particular the chapter examines the ways in which conflict is engendered, the myriad of ways, both collective and individual, in which it is expressed and the impact that such expressions might have on the employment relationship. As Brown et al. have made clear, 'the workplace of the early twenty-first century has changed radically from that of a quarter century earlier' (2009: 354), with a decline in union membership and subsequent decline in union activity and collective bargaining. This of course has impacted on how conflict is expressed and dealt with in the workplace. The chapter explores a variety of definitions and perspectives relating to conflict and gives due weight to individual expressions of conflict that are now more prevalent than their collective counterparts. Importantly it examines the different critical assumptions behind the analysis of workplace conflict and how such perceptions influence subsequent conflict analysis.

The Causes and Inevitability of Workplace Conflict

Workplace conflict is unavoidable and inevitable (Egerová and Rotenbornová, 2021). The employment relationship itself arises from a contested workplace and the inherent nature of paid work. Disagreements at work and expressions of conflict are integral to the employment relationship. As Bélanger and Edwards point out, 'the employment relation is distinct because antagonism is inscribed into it' (2013: 8), and as Kolb and Putnam say:

> Conflict is seen as a perennial feature of organisations, always present in the crevices and crannies and just below the surface, bubbling up occasionally as disputes in certain places are enacted according to particular conventions and rule, across cultures and across diverse populations. (1992: 315)

Hebdon and Noh elaborate on this, suggesting that

> … workplace conflict should inherently be thought of as a phenomenon for which individual motivation, working conditions and labour-management relations combine to shape its dynamic character within an organisation. (2013: 27)

The employment relationship is therefore one where the relationship between employers and employees

> … is innately hostile, the status and self-respect of both groups rest(ing) on their ability to outwit or control the other. Consequently, workplace conflict emerges from the power struggles due to the suppression or diversion of worker dissatisfaction and to worker resistance to control and domination. (2013: 29)

The existence of conflict may be damaging to both interpersonal workplace relationships and to the employer/employee relationship. Conflicts may stem from the work process itself, from interpersonal differences, from perceptions of injustices and unfairness or from unequal access to resources. As such, conflicts may stem from entrenched class, cultural, gender, ethnicity or racial perspectives. Conflict occurs at work because of differing interests, inappropriate uses of power, divergent concerns, and differences in perception and attitudes resulting in workplace friction. Workplace tension that develops into antagonism and disagreement can arise at a number of levels, for example it may occur between:

- those disputing changes to their patterns of work or to the ways in which they are being managed
- groups of employees, teams, or sections that have complaints about pressures of work, allocated pay grades and inconsistent treatment relative to others

- groups of employees vying with one another over resource allocation
- interpersonal differences between employees arising from inappropriate behaviour such as bullying
- employees with different levels of authority and/or power – so, for example, senior and middle managers may express strongly held differences of opinion
- mistrust.

It is also possible for conflict around workplace issues to take place at more macro levels where, for example, expressions of conflict between the state (acting as an influential third party affecting the employment relationship) and groups of concerned workers may occur. In recent years, for example, action directed against the state has been seen in terms of employees protesting against austerity measures or changes in pension provisions (Bélanger and Edwards, 2013: 8; Chenoweth, 2020). In 2015, for example, there was a 24-hour strike by thousands of Greek workers protesting against the Government-imposed austerity measures. The General Confederation of Greek Workers accused the government of pursuing punishing austerity policies leading to poverty and wretchedness. As a result of the strike, public services were closed, public transport disrupted and there were violent demonstrations in Athens. When there is economic hardship – whether precipitated by a pandemic or for example by austerity measures – the lines separating economic dissatisfaction from social unrest and sporadic outbreaks of violence often become stretched to breaking point. Sometimes, of course, the State strives to avoid getting involved with disputes. During the 2022 and 2023 cost of living crisis, unions from the UK rail and health services laid the blame for their repeated bouts of industrial action firmly on the UK government. In response, the government endeavoured to remain at arm's length, declaring that it was the employers, not the state, who were responsible for the fractious negotiations and inability to settle on acceptable new terms and conditions of employment.

News Flash 6.1

IBM Executives Plan to Eliminate Dinobabies From the Workforce

Recently released documents from a US age-discrimination court case against IBM, apparently show top management discussing the need to oust older employees in favour of younger ones, along with reducing the number of mothers on the pay roll.

The tranche of emails is revealing: one mentions a plan to 'accelerate change by inviting the "dinobabies" (new species) to leave' making them an 'extinct species'. Another discusses IBM's 'dated maternal workforce', saying, 'This is what must change. They really don't understand social or engagement. Not digital natives. A real threat for us'.

The emails appear to bear out the 2020 findings from the Equal Employment Opportunity Commission. It found evidence of senior IBM executives directing managers to engage in aggressive approaches to significantly reduce the head count of older workers although the evidence was not made public at the time.

Sources: Clarey, 2022; Scheiber, 2022

Exercise 6.1

Paresashvili et al. say that, 'The six basic sources of conflict are: incompatible goals; difference; interdependence; scarce resources; vague rules and bad relationships' (2020: 458).

- Explain what you think they mean by 'interdependence' and provide at least three examples of how this might be one of the causes of workplace conflict.

The essence of the employment relationship is one of balance between the competing interests of the parties involved in the relationship and their inherent expressions (implicit and explicit, restrained and unrestrained) both of powerlessness and of power. As we saw in Chapter 1, the interests of an employee differ on occasions from those of an employer. Generally in the employment relationship conflict arises from:

- unequal power relationships
- feelings of discontent and job insecurity
- employee opposition to management policies and practices
- management opposition to employee practices
- perceptions of organisational injustice particularly that of distributional injustice
- expressions of solidarity and support for individuals or groups perceived to have been wronged
- inconsistent treatment of employees
- lack of trust in management by employees or vice versa
- attitudes that interfere with the attainment of organisational goals.

Richard Hyman, in his seminal book *Strikes* (1972: 109), postulates that within capitalist economies there are four sources of conflict: inequalities of income; fears around job security; insufficient or negligible control over work processes; and imbalances of power between employees and employers.

As we have seen, workers place themselves under the control of an organisation, following instructions and providing their skill, knowledge and labour in return for payment, training and so on. They are therefore expected to abide by the organisation's requirements; conflict arises when such requirements – or the returns on the effort to meet those requirements – are perceived to be inadequate or unfair. When conflicts surface they fall into two distinct categories: *conflicts of right*, for example conflicts around health and safety violations or discrimination; and *conflicts of interests* that usually occur when resources are finite and groups compete to 'win' a larger share for their members, as seen for example in conflicts about wage increases. Such conflicts of interest are best resolved through the parties discussing their differences and negotiating an outcome satisfactory to both, whereas conflicts of rights are often best resolved through independent adjudication by a third party such as a mediator or court. The distinction between rights and interests is not, however, always clear-cut – sometimes what are regarded as rights in one country are not regarded as rights elsewhere. In the USA, for example, workers for Zara (part of Inditex, a company that recognises and negotiates with the representatives from UNI Global Union) are *denied* certain rights around anti-discrimination although the company actually provides these rights for their employees working outside the USA (LabourStart, 2014a). Sometimes agreements made between employees and employers explicitly acknowledge both the interests and rights of the parties. In the summer of 2019 an agreement between the finance section of the UNI Global Union and international bank Crédit Agricole SA (which operates across 47 different counties) is an example of this stating that, 'The provisions of this agreement are designed to ensure a balance between the strategic interests of the entities, respect for the fundamental rights of the Group's employees, the practice of social dialogue and the quality of life at work'.

News Flash 6.2

Workers' Rights Restricted

Workplaces are less safe, trade union activity more restricted and the surveillance of workers increasing says the 2021 ITUC Global Rights Index that details breaches of employees' rights and interests. The ten worst countries for working people in 2021 are, it claims, Bangladesh, Belarus, Brazil, Colombia, Egypt, Honduras, Myanmar, the Philippines, Turkey and Zimbabwe.

The eighth edition of the ITUC Global Rights Index ranking 149 countries on the degree of respect for workers' rights found that:

- 87% of countries violated the right to strike.
- 79% of countries violated the right to bargain collectively.
- 74% of countries excluded workers from the right to establish and join a trade union.
- The number of countries which denied or constrained freedom of speech increased from 56 in 2020 to 64 in 2021.
- Workers were exposed to violence in 45 countries.
- Workers had no or restricted access to justice in 65% of countries.
- Workers experienced arbitrary arrests and detention in 68 countries.
- Trade unionists were murdered in six countries: Brazil, Colombia, Guatemala, Myanmar, Nigeria and the Philippines.

Source: www.ituc-csi.org/2021-global-rights-index (accessed 27 October 2021)

Expressions of power and impact of divergent and convergent interests

The very nature of work itself dictates that those who are employed are subject to, and required to, meet the demands and interests of those doing the employing – yet within these constraints employee workplace interests are many and varied, and fall along a spectrum, where at one end some coincide with the interests of the employer while at the other their interests diametrically oppose those of the employer.

The employment relationship is complex; it is not merely concerned with transactional interactions – relational aspects are at play too. Employers running an organisation need to control and direct the workforce while simultaneously eliciting its cooperation. This can be achieved via pay (transactional) and by providing an environment in which employees feel comfortable, and are able to have a say in, the work process (relational). Employers require specific workplace behaviours and oblige their employees to abide by the organisational procedures, yet at the same time they would like the workforce to participate in work activities to the best of their abilities and to engage in discretionary behaviour. It is not uncommon for employers to expect their staff to display behaviours at odds with their true feelings. Workplace requirements for publicly aligning emotions with employer expectations (for example a nurse being nice to a difficult patient), can take its toll on employees. Such emotional labour, particularly in the service sectors can create dissonance and **burnout** (Davis and Stazyk, 2021; Grandey and Gabriel, 2015; Song, 2021). Often employees have little or no say in what they are required to achieve and the time and manner in which they are to achieve it, yet they are expected to willingly cooperate with work processes. This is exemplified by Bolton and Boyd's (2003: 301) study of aircraft cabin crew who were expected to deliver an enhanced customer service while at the same time their working conditions, over which they had no control, deteriorated. Here the workforce found itself in the invidious position of having to operate under worsening conditions while being expected to deliver an improved level of customer care, resulting in their increased perceptions of organisational injustice. Hannah Cooke's (2006) study of the nursing profession found a similar contradiction between increased levels of managerial control coupled with higher levels of discretionary care demanded from employees. Employee perceptions surrounding such demands and expectations of cooperative compliance may trigger feelings of frustration and expressions of conflict and dissent. This of course echoes Goodrich's 1920 thoughts about the 'frontier of control' referred to in Chapter 1. The dialectical tension between the subjugators and subjugated is at the heart of the employment relationship. As Richard Hyman memorably expressed it:

> the function of labour control involves both the direction, surveillance and discipline
> of subordinates whose enthusiastic commitment to corporate objectives cannot be
> taken for granted; and the mobilization of the discretion, initiative and diligence which
> coercive supervision, far from guaranteeing, is likely to destroy. (1987: 41)

The relationship, with its dual elements of cooperation and conflict, is one of finely balanced opposition. The interplay between parties at the boundary of control was explored in a study comparing British and Irish control mechanisms in public transport. The importance of gaining employee cooperation (thereby ensuring optimum operational functioning) is always going to be finely balanced. Here the authors found that, at the frontier of control, the Irish employment relations mechanisms were more cooperative than those of the British (Hughes and Dobbins, 2020).

The employment relationship, a product of the workplace environment, is therefore affected by the degree of power that each party has and subsequently *chooses* whether or not to deploy. It is at this crucial intersection between the degree of controlling activity, together with the perception of the person subject to such control, that the interests of the parties collide and may be contested, resulting in expressions of conflict. Conflict therefore occurs when there is a perceived divergence of interest that, if unresolved, is likely to escalate (Pruitt et al., 1997). For example, the employees of Wizz Air, a unitarist company with a hard, traditionalist style, were the recipients of such escalation. Following dissatisfaction with their working environment they set up a union; however, the union's leadership were specifically targeted by management, its president was dismissed while both the vice president and secretary of the union were suspended because, according to Wizz Air, their close involvement with the union specifically made them a safety hazard. Following this, a further 19 union members were sacked at the end of 2014. Here the employer, threatened by the *potential* increase in employee power – expressed by union membership – exerted *actual* power and sacked the 'offending' employees, thereby intimidating other employees into not joining the union (LabourStart, 2014b).

Power may be exerted by either party. The employer, for example, might wield power in a coercive way, threatening site relocation or disadvantageous contract changes if certain terms are not agreed to. Such a threat became reality at British Gas when it exerted coercive power dismissing hundreds of engineers who, unlike some of their colleagues, refused to accept lower wages and longer working hours (Walker, 2021). Such tactics and overt visible expression of power is not a new phenomenon. In the USA, for example, Kate Bronfenbrenner, when researching for the North American Commission for Labor Cooperation, discovered that:

> Where employers can credibly threaten to shut down and/or move their operations in response to union activity, they do so in large numbers. Overall, over 50 percent of all employers made threats to close all or part of the plant during the organizing drive. The threat rate is significantly higher, 62 percent, in mobile industries such as manufacturing, transportation, and warehouse/distribution, compared to a 36 percent threat rate in relatively immobile industries such as construction, health care, education, retail, and other services. (1996: 2)

The threat of relocation is, however, sometimes empty. Ron Edwards, when he looked at multinational corporations in Australia, found that not all of them had the ability to relocate – despite threatening that they might do so (Edwards, 2003). Jalette (2011) added to the research around employer threats to relocate when she found that unions were sometimes able to prevent relocation by conceding issues linked to manpower flexibility – yet, importantly, where wages were concerned employers often realised their relocation threats.

Employees, on the other hand, may express dissatisfaction by exerting their power, (either as individuals or in groups) by, for example, activities such as taking excessive sick leave, sabotage, writing negative comments on social media, striking, **working to rule**, or as a last resort, resigning. Sometimes employees exert levels of power when particular (and often unique) circumstances facilitate this, putting them into conflict with management. For example, when the 2021 Climate Change conference (Cop26) was being held in Glasgow, transport workers, represented by the RMT and Unite unions, threatened to strike in an attempt to get Abellio Scot Rail to address issues of pay, service cuts and inadequate investment (Brooks, 2021a). At the same time the Glasgow bin men confirmed a week-long strike to coincide with the running of the conference (Brooks, 2021b). It was at this time when they were at their most powerful (with the vulnerable employers dependent upon their cooperation) that the unions were able to make demands on the employer.

Exercise 6.2

In an article for the *GlobalPost*, Kraft (2015) quotes a 2008 Canadian study into workplace conflict that surveyed 357 HR professionals and found 'that work-related conflict is most often linked to competing egos, personalities and values, or a lack of strong leadership'; she also pointed out that dishonesty and stress contribute to increased incidence of workplace conflict.

- Analyse how employee perceptions around different types of organisational justice might be linked to this list of issues.
- What issues do you think might be missing from this list?

Source: Psychometrics, 2009

Case Study 6.1

Glasgow Bin Strike During COP26

In October 2022, Cosla – the voice and pay negotiating body of Local Government in Scotland – attempted to resolve a long running dispute about pay and conditions with employees from 32 local councils by proposing a pay rise of 5.8% for the lowest paid local government workers as part of a £1,062 rise for all staff earning below £25,000. GMB Scotland, Unison and Unite all suspended planned strikes by local government workers while consultation on the offer took place. All three unions had previously called for a £2,000 pay rise.

Glasgow City Council cleansing department workers, however, decided to continue action with backing from GMB Scotland who were bargaining for a Glasgow-specific deal. A Glasgow City Council spokesperson at the time expressed that it was 'very disappointing they have reneged' on their agreement to halt industrial action.

The UN climate change summit was due to take place in Glasgow between 31 October and 12 November 2021 with over 20,000 people expected to descend on Glasgow amidst Covid-19 lockdown restrictions. Uncollected rubbish had the potential to create a public health hazard. While the GMB denied the timing was a political stunt, over 1,000 Glasgow City Council cleansing department workers represented by GMB Scotland commenced industrial action from 1 November.

The action included an all-out strike, relevant picketing of depots, the use of social media to publicise the dispute and a rally in the City's George Square on the last day of action on 8 November. The rally was addressed by Jeremy Corbyn, the ex-leader of the Labour Party who told BBC Scotland:

> I take my hat off to them. I think they've done an amazing job of educating the public about how important refuse collection is, about explaining that they are getting lower pay than other people working in other neighbouring refuse collection areas and their heads are held high. They've stood up and achieved some changes … I think it's very important that the eyes of the world are on Glasgow and therefore it's very important that workers in Glasgow, such as refuse workers, are properly paid and treated properly.

The dispute has since been resolved; however, some of the staff concerned are affected by the threatened industrial action over equal pay in March/April 2022 that was called off after the council maintained that a deal over interim payments will be delivered by October 2022.

Authors: Dr K. Boyle and R. Caddow, GCU

Sources: www.bbc.co.uk/news/uk-scotland-glasgow-west-59113839; www.bbc.co.uk/news/uk-scotland-glasgow-west-59206306; www.heraldscotland.com/politics/19732302.glasgow-bin-strikes-return-snp-council-deal-ignored-workers/

Trust, Conflict and the UK Expressions of Workplace Conflict

When the data from the Workplace Employee Relations Surveys (WERS) (e.g., DBIS, 2013) is examined, it is evident that, within the UK, employers and employees differ in their interpretations of their workplace interactions. The data from each survey gives a clear impression of the problems that employees face, their perceptions of the workplace and the demands that work places upon them and gives an indication of incipient conflict that may lead to employees challenging managerial decisions and activities. For example, the WERS surveys from 2004 and 2011 looked at responses from 22,451 and 21,981 employees respectively (for workplaces with five or more employees) and discovered that in many cases just under half of the total number of employees felt their employers could not be trusted to deal with them in an honest manner, nor did they feel the employers made a serious attempt to take their views into account, and furthermore the employees thought that the employers were unlikely to keep their promises to their workforce (see Table 6.1).

Table 6.1 Data from WERS showing employee perceptions of management trustworthiness

Measuring three different dimensions of employee trust in their managers, WERS showed that employees felt that managers:	Private sector		Public sector		Total	
	2004	2011	2004	2011	2004	2011
Deal with employees honestly	58	60	52	51	56	58
Are sincere in their attempts to understand employees' views	56	59	52	51	55	57
Keep their promises	51	53	44	42	49	50

Source: DBIS, 2013

Moreover, it is clear that smaller businesses are less prone to resort to taking disciplinary action when employees behave in ways that are, from the organisation's point of view, less than desirable (Forth et al., 2006). Arguably this is because the size of smaller organisations makes it easier to resolve issues quickly and informally before the parties become entrenched in opposition, although as Moore and Read say,

> the nature of social relations in micro and small firms … inhibits the articulation of injustice. This is not least because the framing of grievances is a high-risk strategy with a potential to shatter the informal social relationships upon which work is based. (2006: 357)

Yet the picture is complicated. Disciplinary action might not be taken, but in smaller organisations the absence of adequate procedures and processes to deal with conflict does mean that smaller companies are disproportionately represented in the number of cases going to employment tribunals (Hayward et al., 2004). There are gender, age and sectoral differences too in the ways that conflict is expressed and dealt with. Older workers and women, for example, are less likely to be involved in conflict linked to workplace discipline (Antcliff and Saundry, 2009) while unskilled non-white employees are more likely to be subject to disciplinary action. Trade union presence too has an impact. Where a union is active in the workplace there are less likely to be as many incidents of disciplinary action, at least in the UK; in France, for example, Tanguy points to the opposite conclusion, stating that 'the occurrence of collective disputes, including both strikes and non-strike disputes, significantly and strongly reduce the likelihood of Employment Tribunal claims in French workplaces' (2013: 131). In contrast collective disputes are found to significantly increase the likelihood of disciplinary action in the form of written warnings.

Exercise 6.3

Manifestations of conflict at work, particularly incidents of individual conflict, are common. In 2020 a CIPD report looking at responses from 2,211 employees and 1,016 senior HR professionals and decision makers found that there was what it termed as a 'serious perception-reality gap' where employers' confidence about dealing with conflict was not matched by those employees experiencing it. Overall the findings showed:

26% of employees and 20% of employers said conflict was a common workplace occurrence.

35% of employees had experienced interpersonal conflict at work over the preceding year.

4% of employees had experienced sexual harassment (8% other forms of harassment).

15% of employees experienced bullying. (Suff, 2020)

Subsequently, the CIPD found that*, in the year prior to being questioned, over 40% of LGBT+ workers experienced a work-based conflict (typically around being personally undermined/humiliated) rising to 55% among trans workers. This was compared with the 29% of heterosexual workers who also experience conflict (Fletcher, 2021).

- What does the information above tell you about conflict in the employment relationship in general and for LBGT+ individuals in particular? Explain why you reached your particular conclusions.

* Respondents = 15,620 UK workers, of whom 13,733 are heterosexuals and 1,357 are LGBT+ (530 did not state a sexual orientation).

Academic Perspectives on Conflict

The ways in which workplace conflict is regarded and analysed is dependent upon the perspectives – and hence the underpinning assumptions – of the person(s) undertaking the analysis. Managers will view conflict in ways that are congruent with their overall values and beliefs underpinning their managerial styles; academics too will have different ways of looking at and interpreting incidents of conflict within the workplace. Because of these differences the myriad of perceptions and assumptions surrounding conflict analysis are not always in accord. Over the years a number of different academics undertaking research in the employment relation have provided a range of different explanations behind the causes and expressions of workplace-based conflict. Tjosvold (2008), for example, sees conflict (in a positive way) as a socialised praxis whereby diverse individuals narrow their differences in order to achieve organisational goals. Wajcman, on the other hand, points out (in a less than positive way) that the main body of industrial relations' academic literature fails to provide 'any sustained attempt to explain why sex segregation comes about and how it is maintained', pointing out that 'the tendency in industrial relations studies to overlook the masculinity of their usual subjects means that aspects of employment … remain hidden' (2000: 184, 186). From her feminist perspective therefore any analysis of conflict in the employment relationship *not* taking aspects of gender and its impact into account would be inadequate. Feminism and positive perceptions of conflict are not of course the only lenses through which to view the contested labour relationship. Godard (2014: 31–6) suggests that conflict analysis falls into six different categories, dependent upon the perspective of the individual undertaking the analysis:

1   The evolutionary perspective
2   The neoliberal perspective
3   The managerial perspective
4   The industrial pluralist perspective
5   The neo-corporatist perspective
6   The radical perspective

The evolutionary perspective

This rather simplistic **evolutionary perspective** assumes that the process of industrialisation over the years created environments in which the workforce was disengaged from the products of its labour, subject to hazardous working conditions and prone to insecurity; conflict was therefore endemic in the workplace. Over time, however, employers in the post-industrial era have become less exploitative and, as conditions improve and employees rely less on work as an expression of their identity, conflict decreases.

This Western linear perspective is rather too general and too simplistic to be useful. Legislation, technology and fashion have indeed all played a part in improving the workplace; however, evidence of enlightened employers operating at the same time as exploitative employers is available for both the industrial and post-industrial periods, as is evidence of both contested and non-contested workplace relations. The linear progression of exploitative to fairer workplace conditions is not a given, as Elliott opines, during the Cold War fear of the East was a restraint on the West; however, as this fear receded employment conditions, rather than improving, have worsened (Elliott, 2014: 22).

The neoliberal perspective

The **neoliberal perspective** is one whereby events are interpreted as if any form of workplace dissent, or resistance to managerial control, is against the economic welfare of an organisation and morally wrong – employers can therefore legitimately ignore dissenting employee opinions and discipline or sack employees who do not comply with their wishes. Crowley and Hodson (2014) examined 217 work groups within organisations where a neoliberal perspective was prevalent and found that the pressures on organisations to compete and optimise performance led to increasing neoliberal work practices with subsequent decreases in wellbeing, diminishing levels of effort and high labour turnover. Employees, according to the neoliberal perspective, are powerless apart from their ability to leave an employer – this though is rather one-dimensional and naive, as individual employees *are* able to resist and express their resistance to employer control in a number of ways, not all of which are as overt as leaving the organisation. Fleming and Spicer, for example, suggest that cynicism is a way of employees 'dis-identifying' with systems of managerial control (2007: 83), while, Wieslander (2021), Taylor and Bain (2003, 2007) and Ackroyd and Thompson (1999) discuss the importance of employee humour as a form of resistance that contests the status quo of the employment relationship.

News Flash 6.3

BrewDog: Toxic Culture Exposed

In the summer of 2021 60 ex-employees of the brewery company, BrewDog, posted an open letter on Twitter to their former bosses, claiming the company, which has breweries in Aberdeenshire, Berlin, Brisbane and Columbus, Ohio, was guilty of presiding over a toxic, fear-inducing culture. The letter said they had suffered from 'fear to speak out about the atmosphere we were immersed in, and fear of repercussions even after we have left'. The ethos of 'growth at all costs', they asserted, was damaging to the mental health of employees and they called for a company apology for 'treating people like objects, harassing, assaulting, belittling or gaslighting them'. (See Revision exercise 6.2, Point 4.)

Sources: BBC News, 2021a; Benton, 2021

The managerial perspective

This unitarist **managerialist perspective** is one that assumes that conflict is not inherent but rather that workplace relationships can be managed successfully by the adoption of the correct managerial policies and practices. It is at the heart of Western HRM thinking and is the ideology behind initiatives linked to employee involvement and empowerment. The assumption here is one of a single source of workplace authority, whereby conflict, if it occurs, is a result of poor policies or poor work design and can be solved by adopting different practices and procedures, from recruiting the right employees to aligning their specific work practices with the goals of the organisation. Expressions of conflict that interrupt the work processes are regarded as examples of mismanagement and inappropriate work processes. Godard points out that when the state has an ideology based on these assumptions the inference is that industrial unrest may be avoided by a 'combination of the appropriate macroeconomic (especially monetary) polices and dispute resolution systems (e.g. conciliation, arbitration)' (2014: 33). Of all of the perspectives identified, this is the only one that does not regard employee interests as inimical to those of the employer, and therefore presumes that the existing distribution and deployment of power is uncontested.

News Flash 6.4

Better.com: CEO Fires Employees Over Zoom

Vishal Garg, the boss of the US mortgage company Better.com held an online Zoom meeting for 900 of his staff and told them, 'If you're on this call, you are part of the unlucky group that is being laid off. Your employment here is terminated, effective immediately'. He went on to explain that everyone would be contacted by the HR department with the details of their individual redundancy benefits and conditions. The announcement came as a surprise as in the previous week the company had received around £565 million in investment.

Source: ITV News, 2021a

The industrial pluralist perspective

The **industrial pluralist perspective** recognises that the imbalance of power between the parties to the employment relationship can, provided that there are appropriate mechanisms facilitating independent collective representation, be offset by common interests, dialogue, negotiation and enabling procedures (Budd, 2004; Budd et al., 2010; Clegg, 1975). It recognises that power is not static and can shift from one party to another depending upon fluctuating economic and business cycles. Conflict between parties may be manifest in a variety of ways such as strikes or, for example, overtime bans, but such expressions of conflict can usually be resolved by negotiation. Failing settlement, however, conflict may become apparent in a variety of alternative ways ranging, on the employees' part, from absenteeism, increased labour turnover or even sabotage, or in the case of employers, by lockouts, relocation and termination of employment contracts.

The neo-corporatist perspective

The **neo-corporatist perspective**, deriving from political exchange theory, assumes that the intensity, degree and frequency of conflict will be in direct response to the amount of power that the labour movement can exert in relation to the amount of restraint that the state and associated institutions are able to bring to bear against it. Here national policies are designed to ensure that sources of conflict are resolved via political exchange through institutions representing labour, capital and the state.

Neo-corporatism is based on voluntary, tripartite, social partnerships where agreement between labour unions, employer/business associations and the state promote the main goal of economic prosperity, restraining costs and inflation so that domestic living standards are high and international trade competitive. Such a tripartite partnership should ensure that there is sufficient institutional infrastructure to address and deal with sources of conflict. An example of the way in which tripartism operates was evidenced by the Irish Haddington Road Public Service Agreement, where the Irish government negotiated with the public sector unions and employer representatives, reaching a deal giving a 1% pay increase (or €500, whichever was the greater) from both 1 October 2021 and 1 October 2022.

News Flash 6.5

Sri Lankan Covid-19 Taskforce

A three-party Sri Lankan Covid-19 taskforce – that included representatives from the Employers' Federation of Ceylon (EFC), the trade unions, including IndustriALL and the Ministry of Skills Development, Employment and Labour Relations – was committed to ensuring the interests of workers *and* employers throughout the period of the Covid pandemic.

This tripartite body agreed that workers would not be excluded from work due to lockdown measures and that employees would be given, through rotation, equal numbers of shifts, thereby protecting their interests while respecting health and safety measures such as social distancing. Those employees unable to work during May and June would be eligible for 50% of their basic wages.

Anton Marcus of IndustriALL affiliate Free Trade Zone & General Services Employees Union, and one of the members of the taskforce said,

> Given the difficult circumstances we are facing with Covid-19, this tripartite agreement is an instrument to safeguard workers' interests. Now we are working to create more awareness among workers about this agreement to ensure that large number of companies implement it.

Source: IndustriALL, 2020

The radical perspective

The **radical perspective** is a theory that assumes that conflict is ever present within the capitalist employment relationship due to the paid work nature of the association between an employer and employee. Worker accession to, and participation in, expressions of work-initiated conflict can take a variety of forms, ranging from the collective strike through to individual acts of defiance such as absenteeism. Conflict seen from a radical perspective is an expression of the central, fundamental differences between capital and labour, where the employers are committed to extracting as much value as possible out of their workforces and where reactive employees disagree with, and resist, such pressures in order to achieve a greater degree of control over their workplace experiences. Employers attempt to manage the contested workplace, and erode the will to resist (Hyman, 1989: 212) both by coercion and/or by eliciting consent though the deployment of sophisticated management techniques (Burawoy, 1979, 1985). As Hyman has said:

> Certainly there are many employers whose handling of labour relations has become more sophisticated, and whose preference is to achieve change through agreement; reciprocally, more trade union representatives than in the past see strikes as a last resort. The priority of survival in an ever more competitive world reinforces the pursuit of peaceful solutions. (Hyman, 1999)

Exercise 6.4

- Critically evaluate whether or not the six different categories of perspective are mutually exclusive. Justify your answer using examples from different organisations and the ways in which they regulate the employment relationship.

Case Study 6.2

Ireland's Longest Employee Relations Dispute

The longest employee relations dispute in Irish history came to an end in May 2021 when the Mandate union accepted a €3m training and wellness fund instead of the two weeks' redundancy pay per year of service, that it had been fighting for.

The dispute began in April the previous year when Debenhams Retail Ireland informed its 950 direct employees and 550 concessionary staff that it was liquidating its Irish operations and closing all stores. The affected staff opposing the closures began a number of protests, including marches, picketing and sit-ins. They were often joined by local people who supported their cause (indeed former workers from Vita Cortex* joined the picket on the 161st day of the dispute to mark the day the strike became the longest running industrial dispute in Irish history). There was huge dissatisfaction with and scepticism about the ways in which the workforce had been treated by both Debenhams and the Irish Government. In September the workers increased the pressure on the company by a march on the Taoiseach's Cork office to demand Government support as opposed to the way it had been acting up until that time. The Taoiseach finally met with the workers in November and later that month it was agreed that the chair of the Labour Court would act as a mediator between the parties. Summing up in his final report to the court the chair, Kevin Foley, said:

(Continued)

It has been my role to explore comprehensively all aspects of this matter with representatives of the workers, with the joint liquidators and with representatives of Government so that I might be able to identify the maximum possible set of measures which could be put in place as a response to this situation which has been made exceptional by the longevity of the dispute and the incapacity of the liquidator to complete the liquidation over a long period.

Mobilising support and fighting the closure decision had been a steep learning curve for local strike leaders Valerie Conlon and Madeline Whelan – the length of the dispute coupled with the unwavering strength of public support meant they went from serving customers to managing a large team of protestors, dealing with Mandate officials, meeting ministers from the Dáil and becoming adept at talking to and using the media.

By Christmas 2020 the dispute had lasted 260 days and remained unsolved. In January a workforce vote rejected a government deal offering a €3m training fund. In the following months the picketing continued and there were store-based struggles as strikers tried to prevent stock from being removed by the appointed liquidators, KPMG. There was a victory of sorts when in May 2021 the companies (Protection of Employees' Rights in Liquidations) Bill 2021 aiming to make workers preferential creditors in a liquidation was brought to the Dáil.

At the end of May the workforce finally voted to accept the €3m training fund bringing the dispute to an end.

*Previous holders of this record.

Sources: Dunphy, 2020, 2021; Labour Court, 2020

Collective acts of workplace defiance, regardless of the perspectives and assumptions of those undertaking the analysis, are clear expressions of discontent designed to influence the behaviour of an employer or employers in order to persuade them to behave differently towards those they employ. However, individual acts of defiance may or may not be regarded as fundamental expressions of conflict depending upon the perceptions of either, or both, the employee and employer. When, for example, is a bad back a medical problem or a way of 'getting back at' a manager or a way of absenting oneself from a situation that one finds unpleasant? In this instance absence could be taken at face value by either party, or it could be regarded, by either or both, as an act of defiance and as means of the employee asserting a modicum of control and influence over a workplace situation.

Exercise 6.5

Read the case study below about Egyptian steel workers, and then critically analyse the action taken by the workers from these perspectives:

- industrial
- managerial
- radical

How did each analysis differ?

In January 2021, at the headquarters of the State-owned Egyptian Iron and Steel company, based in Greater Cairo, around 4,000 of 7,500 steel workers began a 'responsible', permanent sit-in (continuing to work on site during their protest). This action, along with marches, demonstrations and social media posts, was used to denounce the plant's planned closure and publicise their plight. The workforce disputed the Government's intention to close the company following, it claimed, years of loss making. The employees rejected the closure plans, saying that they should not be made to pay with their jobs for years of mismanagement and lack of investment. The Egyptian Ministry of Public Enterprise said that each worker would receive a retirement payment of at least around £10,000, but the workers countered this saying the money would affect just a quarter of those affected as the others were not eligible.

The decision to liquidate the company came after a series of failed negotiations between representatives and shareholders, the government asserting that a glut of steel forced the shutdown. Yet a factor contributing to the saturated steel market was the amount of steel production from the Suez Steel factory controlled by the Egyptian army and benefitting from subsidised energy and transport costs.

Not only was the closure disputed but the way in which the final decision was ratified was also contested, the workers saying they would *never* have agreed to the proposals. The liquidation was *apparently* agreed by an extraordinary General Assembly meeting. (The General Assembly is composed of the company's senior management team, the unions, comprising a workers' syndicate, and the workers.)

Sources: Mada Masr, 2021; Meena Solidarity Network, 2021; Middle East Eye, 2021

Expressions of Conflict

Where aspects of the employment relationship are contested, the subsequent expressions of conflict may be individual or collective, and either obvious or hidden. Consequently, expressions of conflict range from individual manifestations of disquiet, such as frequent periods of unexplained absence, through to deliberate incivility and lack of cooperation, through to those incidents where employees finally leave the organisation. On the other hand, collective expressions of group dissatisfaction with employers range from a mass withdrawing of discretionary effort and working to rule through to overtime bans and strike action. Some collective disruptive acts are designed to send a message to the government of the day rather than to employers. It is rare for individuals to act alone against a political or legislative dictat or intention, whereas group expressions of conflict, often in the form of demonstrations or strikes, are more prevalent at this level.

An *individual* act of defiance in terms of 'sickness' absence is *covert*, as would be, for example, deliberately misleading customers or an act of undiscovered theft that has been undertaken specifically to 'punish' an employer. Gossiping, blogging in a negative way, taking out grievances and leaving the organisation, however, are markedly different individual acts as these are *overt* and explicit public individual expressions of dissatisfaction. There has been some research looking at acts of individual employee incivility which, although seemingly insignificant, can cost organisations in terms of reputation, repeat business and staff turnover (De Clercq et al., 2020; Johnson and Indvik, 2001a). Sabotage, often embarked on individually, is undertaken in a covert way; however, the consequences may be very public and overt. For example, in 1980 Associated Biscuits had to withdraw from sale thousands of biscuit tins when it was realised that the idyllic Edwardian tea party scene depicted (see Figure 6.1) on the lids contained explicit images of a human couple copulating, and a pair of dogs behaving in a similar fashion; the designer of the lid, Mick Hill, acting alone, successfully disrupted sales – and, in the eyes of management, brought the good name of the organisation into disrepute.

Figure 6.1   The sabotaged biscuit tin

Exercise 6.6

In 2022, in order to limit strike action, the British Transport Secretary, Grant Shapps, was said to be in favour of reversing a legal restriction preventing employers from hiring agency workers as temporary cover for striking staff. His proposed legal modification would apply to employers in all sectors. The proposed changes received widespread publicity in the weeks leading up to a national rail strike in June 2022, although any legislative changes could not have been put in place in time to affect this particular strike.

- Evaluate the pros and cons of this proposal in the light of what you know about aspects of organisational justice.
- How practical is it, do you think, for agency workers to be used as replacement cover in the rail industry? Give reasons for your answer.

Recent examples of individuals behaving in equally disruptive ways, but without such public displays of displeasure, include Laurn Arafat who, when dismissed after just two days in her post as a receptionist, caused irreparable damage by logging into the company booking system from her iPhone and deleting 211 appointments which could not be restored (Corcoran, 2022). Edward Sobolewski was also an employee who took revenge on his employer. He was an accounts controller for the market research company Frost & Sullivan. Unhappy because he did not receive a pay increase, he regularly sprayed a cleaning fluid (Cillit Bang – renowned for its advertising catchphrase 'bang and the dirt is gone') into the company's servers and computers in order to bring the firm's IT systems to a halt. His activities routinely brought the company's IT systems down and cost the company thousands of pounds for 'downtime', repairs and lost work. When eventually caught and confronted, following CCTV footage which showed him spraying server grills with Cillit Bang and pouring a container of liquid into one of the servers, he said he was merely cleaning them. This defence did not impress the authorities and he was imprisoned for eight months and fined (Leach, 2013; Nimmo, 2013).

Individual acts such as these have an impact on the ways in which the employment relationship is perceived by both the employer and the employee, but typically they remain individual and without a collective consciousness of political awareness to give them wider significance. Lone and uncoordinated acts of rebellion against an organisation may, however, develop into collective acts of defiance. Johnson and Indvik, for example, point out that 'workplace incivility is not violent or harassment or even open conflict, although it can build up to any of those things' (2001b: 706), and John Kelly (2012) describes a process of mobilisation whereby employees with a common sense of grievance can combine together to act collectively to confront an employer. Kelly's mobilisation theory suggests that seven things are prerequisite for any sort of collective consciousness and subsequent action to occur:

1   Employees should see their grievances as *specific injustices*.
2   Employees feel entitled to have such grievances discussed and addressed at the appropriate managerial level.
3   Employees attribute the problem to the employer or to a force beyond the employer's control.
4   Employees feel there is a possibility of a collective approach rectifying the issue.
5   A collective sense of the problem arises as a shared interest is generated.
6   Union organisation representing interests is enabled by structural factors or via social networks and processes.
7   The presence or absence of workplace leadership stimulates the articulation and representation of employee concerns.

Hughes et al. (2022) provide comprehensive evidence of mobilisation across two separate unions in a dispute around competitive tendering affecting a bus company in the Republic of Ireland. Blyton and Jenkins show the occurrence of mobilisation to good effect in their paper on workers in the Burberry factory in South Wales where for the employees, prior to the announcement of a decision to relocate production to China, conforming to managerial control was customary and 'where resistance … tended to be individualised and unorganised, mainly in the form of absence and turnover' (2012: 30). Following a poorly organised meeting called by very unsympathetic management to announce the closure, the collective sense of injustice and grievance against a management blamed for such injustice was high and was a major contributor in uniting the workforce:

What united them was not only their initial sense of injustice, or their attribution of blame towards the employer, but crucially their vocabularies of motive around the future of their community, sustained by leadership and enormous organisational effort. (Blyton and Jenkins, 2012: 41)

These four mutually supporting components of mobilisation (feelings of injustice about a blame-worthy employer, shared feelings around the fate of the community, strong sustained leadership and effective organisation) were crucial to the ways in which the workforce acted in a sustained and collective way.

Figure 6.2 shows how expressions of dissent can be expressed individually and/or collectively, and how individual actions may move from covert to overt behaviours and from individual to collective acts against an employer.

Figure 6.2   Individual and collective expressions of dissent

Dissatisfaction with an employer does not always lead to a collectively mobilised workforce. Forret and Love found that when perceptions of procedural and interactional injustice were high it was not unusual for employees to spend disproportionate amounts of time distrusting their co-workers. Rather than the emergence of a common sense of grievance, individuals spent time checking and keeping score of how others were treated in comparison to themselves (2007: 254). Such behaviours inhibit effective teamwork, lead to cultures of mistrust, result in lower levels of productivity and increase individualistic behaviours. Where supervisors consistently exhibit fair and procedurally just behaviour towards their subordinates this is likely to lead to increased levels of trust within the organisation (Fulmer and Ostroff, 2017) and a diminution of conflictual activities. Nelson et al. (2019) looked at a number of different school settings and found that the justice behaviours of those at the top of an organisation trickled down – impacting co-worker levels of trust and the ways in which workplace matters were communicated and dealt with. (Interestingly they found that 'respect' was best treated separately from trust, with its own processes of development with the organisation. Such findings have clear implications for levels of conflict and prejudice – visible and hidden within the employment relationship.) Where procedural justice is endemic within an organisation it is probable that this will promote collegiate helpfulness and trust, moderating some of the causes of conflict.

Individual responses can be contrasted to obvious *overt collective* expressions of dissent in the form of protests, strikes, explicit working to rule and so on (although collective working in an excessively slow manner – known as **ca'canny** in Scotland – or for example mass 'sick taking', as when the employees on the same shift at British Airways all reported in sick on the same day, are ostensibly individual and not collective acts of defiance). Not all collective acts of dissention are undertaken as *conscious* acts of solidarity, some are the result of individuals banding together for a specific act, for example, in a London-based office of company X, a particular supervisor was rather overbearing. This man had a hat of which he was inordinately fond. Some of his subordinates clubbed together and bought two identical hats – identical that is apart from the size, one was slightly smaller and one slightly larger. Over the course of weeks they took it in turns to swap these hats for the original. Sometimes the supervisor would leave the office with a smaller hat perched on his head and at other times with the larger hat loosely sitting on his eyebrows. After a week or so the supervisor took sick leave – convinced that his head was changing shape, expanding and contracting on a daily basis. This rather cruel joke was a way in which the members of his team were able to vent their feelings of dissatisfaction without actually addressing the nature of their complaints in an overt way. Generally, however, collective overt action is more directive and designed to alter the employment relationship in some way. Strikes are an obvious way of conveying frustration with an existing situation and exerting power in order to change a given situation; protests too have the same aim. On occasion collective action is designed not in furtherance of a dispute but more as an expression of solidarity against an organisation, for example, the author is aware of an engineering machine shop in the Midlands where one of the machines was hardly ever used, but when the organisation decided to decommission and replace it the workforce protested. This went on for some time, and the management declared the machine to be a 'white elephant' (i.e., no use to anyone). Eventually the machine was disconnected, but before it could be removed, the workforce formed a 'funeral' procession and paraded the 'white elephant', in a solemn procession, around the factory and nearby car park. This action irritated management and stopped production for an hour – it was an overt expression of solidarity and a symbolic reaffirmation of power for the workforce who had felt powerless over the decision to remove the machine. The act of defiance reinforced the group identity of the workers concerned, binding them together in a collective expression of revolt against the employer.

The increasing use of robots/machinery within the workplace is often regarded as contentious because employees feel their livelihoods to be threatened. Bricklaying, for example can now be done more speedily by robots, than humans. Hadrian X, developed by Fastbrick Robotics, an Australian company, can lay 1,000 standard bricks in an hour – something that would take two people around 12 hours. Estimates from the Office of National Statistics (2019a) suggest that 1.5 million workers in Britain risk losing their jobs to automation, with women and those in part-time work most affected. Such job insecurity can lead to conflict as Jessica Sorenson points out in her conference paper:

> Workers have disabled, abandoned, and destroyed robots in response to tensions over lost wages, decreased task complexity or changing workflows, and violations of personal privacy/security. (2019: 1)

Collective protests are not always based around one organisation. The GMB union, unhappy with construction companies blacklisting some of its members, held a number of protest demonstrations called a 'Crocodile Tears Tour'. This was designed to shame 63 HR managers, from different organisations, into admitting their blacklisting and apologising for their actions (GMB, 2014). More recently Romanian unions representing a variety of workers in the health service acted collaboratively to obtain better terms and conditions (Adascalitei and Muntean, 2018). Occasionally unions will operate collaboratively across national boundaries, as when the steel unions worked together around the effect of the EU Emissions Trading System (Thomas, 2021).

The impact of technology, particularly the ways in which it has improved the speed and reach of instant means of communication, has meant that mobilisation as a response to conflict has become easier. The success of the Black Lives Matter movement shows how effective such communication might be. Unions are increasingly using such 'non-traditional' methods for contacting and mobilising their members and this often happens alongside spontaneous clusterings of discontent. Pasquier et al. talk about '**flashmob' unionism** and distinguish between traditional forms of **collectivism** and the newer, technologically enabled, more spontaneous, **connectivism** characterised by decentralised, but coordinated, local groupings (2020: 340). In further research, with Hennebert, he shows how technological forms of communication have four enabling advantages: visibility, intensification, aggregation and addressability, for union organisers wishing to mobilise against adversity (Hennebert et al., 2021).

News Flash 6.6

Pay Fairness at the Heart of Bus Strike

Hundreds of North Wales bus drivers, employed by Arriva, voted to take strike action in the run up to Christmas 2021. Their action followed a breakdown in negotiations about what the drivers said was an unfair pay disparity between them and drivers employed by the same company but based in the Northwest of England. Drivers in the Northwest receive £1.81 an hour more than those in Wales and on average work a 37- rather than 39-hour week like their Welsh colleagues.

Sources: BBC News, 2021b; ITV News, 2021b

Expressions of conflict can, on occasions, be costly for both the employer and employee. In the UK, for example, workplace conflict costs around £28.5 billion each year – more than £1,000 per employee (Acas, 2021). In 2018, 39,000 workers were involved in labour disputes resulting in 273,000 working days lost (ONS, 2019b). As a consequence of these expressions of conflict, employees lost pay and employers lost productivity. The UK is not alone, e.g., in Australia the number of days lost due to strikes over wages rose to 32% from 18% during 2012–2013 (Bailey and Peetz, 2014), while in the USA, although the numbers are smaller, 27,000 workers were involved in major work stoppages that began in 2020 (Bureau of Labor, 2021). It is notable that during the Covid pandemic the number of strikes (resulting in working days lost) declined. In Poland, for example, 41,900 working hours were lost in 2020 compared to 8.6 million hours lost to strike action in the previous year. Similarly strike activity and days lost declined in Sweden, Portugal, Spain and Denmark (Kinnunen and Gustafsson, 2021).

Aggregate international comparative statistics should be treated with caution for two reasons. First, it is difficult to compare data from one country with another as the processes for recording and measuring days lost are likely to vary, so comparisons are not looking at like-for-like data. For example, some countries, such as the UK and the USA, discount political strikes while others do not. Similarly the length of the dispute is important as some countries, such as Denmark, record only those strikes resulting in more than 100 days lost (so, for example, a strike by 99 employees for one day would not be recorded), while countries such as Spain will record a dispute if it lasts for an hour or more (Blyton and Turnbull, 2004: 332). Second, the ways in which the figures are collated rely on a variety of measures and are likely to under-report the numbers of days lost due to industrial conflict – management don't always record or report the incidents of inactivity resulting from workers striking. There are some international comparisons of strike activity, for example Godard (2011) provided evidence of strike activity across a number of different Western countries comparing days lost through strike activity in liberal market economies with their social market counterparts (USA, UK, Canada, Germany, Netherlands and Sweden) and showed how strike activity in general has declined. Recent analysis by Kelly has shown that 'strike activity, measured by frequency, days lost or workers involved, has declined significantly in most countries during the past 50 years although the rates of decline differ between countries and sectors' (2015: 729).

Sapsford and Turnbull (1994) have argued that within a capitalist environment, where the employment relationship is *ipso facto* contested and where conflict is therefore inevitable, the amount of conflict is constant. It is just the expressions of conflict that change, becoming diverted from strike activity into alternative, perhaps less overt, expressions of conflict. They liken this to an inflated balloon where if one part is constricted another part bulges, the volume if not the shape of the balloon remaining constant. Thus if the expression of conflict can, for whatever reason, no longer take a particular form, it will be expressed in another way.

This, however, does not seem to be the case, certainly in the UK, as there were just 81 stoppages in 2018, the second-lowest figure since records for stoppages began in 1930 (ONS, 2019b). Such a decline in strike activity (a possible consequence of both declining union membership and strike-prone industries, combined with rigorous strike-limiting legislation and employers more willing to go to court) seems *not* to have been replaced by an equal increase in alternative expressions of collective discontent, such as working to rule or restrictions on overtime working. (The collation of data and evidence for such activity is, however, difficult.) It may be that by unions using the threat of holding a strike ballot, or indeed of holding a strike ballot in order to put pressure on recalcitrant employers is, in part, taking the place of strike action, but again this is difficult to prove. Gall and Cohen, in their analysis of strike activity using the Sapsford and Turnbull analogy, posit that 'the balloon is losing air' (2013: 104) and that it is possible that strikes and other forms of collective action against employers are declining overall.

Table 6.2   The number of working days lost and workers involved in stoppages, UK, 2017 and 2018

	2017	2018
Working days lost through stoppages	276,000	273,000
Workers involved in stoppages	33,000	39,000
Stoppages	79	81
Mean number of WDL per stoppage	3,499	3,367
Median number of WDL per stoppage	345	400

Source: ONS, 2019b

A strong union presence at work is linked to fewer incidents of conflict reaching formal levels of disciplinary activity (Edwards, 2000). This is due in part to unions interceding at an earlier informal level but also to the restraining influence of union activity on the unrestricted wielding of managerial power. Where expressions of conflict are not collective it is useful to consider the demographics of the working population. Data from WERS repeatedly show that skilled employees, older workers and women are less likely to be involved in disciplinary incidents (Antcliff and Saundry, 2009; Knight and Latreille, 2000), while non-white or younger employees are more likely to be subject to higher levels of disciplinary activity (Casebourne et al., 2006). Andy Charlwood and Anna Pollert (2014), in a survey of non-unionised low wage UK employees, discovered that where employees experienced problems at work, particularly problems concerned with rights violations, they were often resolved in a way that left the employees, if not their employers, dissatisfied with the outcome. Where there were good informal relationships between staff and their line managers some conflict was resolved, but where the employee relationship lacked any opportunities for employees to have their say there was much less likelihood of the conflict being sorted out to the employees' satisfaction. Where there were perceptions of rights violation, employees managed the conflict by leaving the organisation.

Conflict and the tribunal system in the UK

There has been a huge rise in the number of recorded individual disputes in the UK over the last half century. During this time employment rights have burgeoned (over 70 at the time of writing) and the numbers of claims (both individual and multiple) registered with tribunals has risen exponentially from below 20,000 in 1972 to more than 100,000 by 1999 (Dix et al., 2008).

Since the period of austerity, marked by the beginning of the recession in 2008, there has been an increase in conflict expressed by industrial action, as well as a corresponding rise in employment tribunal claims, particularly those for unfair dismissal, redundancy and breach of contract. It is possible that workplaces under pressure are more prone to stricter workplace control and that this has led to the increase in disputed incidents of fairness. Writing a report for the **CIPD**, Suff (2020: 2) pointed out that 'conflict is very much part of organisational life, and a common occurrence at work according to a significant proportion of both employees (26%) and employers (20%)'. Managing conflict is time-consuming. Employers spend an 'average of six days of management time dealing with each individual disciplinary case and five days dealing with a grievance case' (ibid.: 12). The time and costs increase when unresolved cases are no longer dealt with in-house but move to Acas or are lodged with the courts (see Table 6.3).

Table 6.3 ETI cases received for conciliation by Acas from the employment tribunal service by all grounds of complaint

Major jurisdictions by volume		2020-21		2019-20		2018-19	
Jurisdictions	Volume	% of cases	Volume	% of cases	Volume	% of cases	Volume
Unfair dismissal	18,320	52%	17,397	42%	18,571	26%
Wages Act	11,718	33%	14,464	35%	14,809	26%
Breach of contract	9,972	28%	11,633	28%	12,200	12%
Working time (annual leave)	8,270	23%	10,232	25%	9,490	10%
Disability	6,356	18%	7,474	18%	7,119	9%
Discrimination	3,782	11%	3,761	9%	3,618	6%
Redundancy pay	3,329	9%	4,012	10%	3,514	5%
Race discrimination	3,277	9%	4,329	11%	3,841	3%
Sex discrimination	2,698	8%	2,796	7%	2,543	2%
Public interest disclosure	2,076	6%	2,286	6%	1,633	3%
Age discrimination	8,325		357		9,041	
Other	77,968		88,741		86,379	
Total jurisdictions	35,274		40,978		36,531	
Total cases						

Source: Acas, 2021: 25

Exercise 6.7

- Look at Tables 6.2 and 6.3. What do they tell you about the levels and expressions of workplace conflict within the UK?
- Research the recent strike data (e.g. over the last two years) from a country of your choice. Has the incidence of strike activity increased or decreased? Why do you think this might be the case?

Summary

This chapter has examined the ways in which conflict arises in the workplace and in particular how such conflict is articulated. The different ways of regarding the employment relationships and how these perspectives affect the perspectives of both management and academics was explored, while examples and patterns of both individual and collective expressions of conflict have been investigated. The following review exercises provide practical examples of conflict within workplaces together with questions designed to encourage analytical reflection around the topic. The next chapter should be read in conjunction with this one as it deals with the ways in which conflict is managed.

Review Questions

1   To what extent and why do you think that some people regard conflict within the employment relationship as inevitable?
2   Discuss how mobilisation theory applies to the actions of the Burberry workers who resisted the closure of their plant. You will need to read the Blyton and Jenkins (2012) article in order to do this.
3   In January 2023, the UK government proposed legislation to ensure that, during strikes, the operation of minimum core activities in essential public services would be safeguarded. Explain how and why this measure could either increase or decrease conflict?

Revision Exercise 6.1

Evaluate the causes of a workplace conflict that you are familiar with in relation to Goddard's six different ways of analysing conflict.

Revision Exercise 6.2

For each of the eight examples of different expressions of conflict below work out:

- the interests of the parties
- the cause of the dispute

- the levels of power exercised by the protagonists
- whether there are perceptions of organisational injustice, and if there are, which categories these might fall into
- the likely impact of the action being taken.

1   At a Manchester-based factory making lorries, the planners made a mistake with one of the part sizes. The workers said nothing even though they were aware of the mistake and, importantly, knew it would cause problems with the subsequent manufacturing process. 'They said they had tried to talk to management before and had never got anywhere. If a company assumes people only work for money and treats them as such, it becomes a self-fulfilling prophecy' (Spillius, 1996).

2   'Campaigners Amazon Anonymous, which protests the fact that online retailer Amazon does not pay staff the living wage, ... [used the] organisation's website and published a spoof book titled *A Living Wage for All Amazon Workers*. The book appeared on the site on 11 June priced at £7.65' (Crawford, 2014).

3   Fifty-five biomedical employees at Northampton General Hospital were locked out of work, for over a week, following a 24-hour strike against the Hospital's proposed changes to their terms and conditions. When the strikers returned to work at the pathology laboratory they discovered that all of the entrances were barred against them unless they signed new contracts which, according to their Unite union representative, could mean doubling their night shifts with a corresponding out-of-hours reduction in pay of up to £6,000 a year. The strikers, many of whom had long service with the hospital, continued to turn up for work until a final deal, protecting pay for all staff, was brokered under the auspices of Acas. The new contract began in March 2015 (*Northampton Herald & Post*, 2014a, 2014b).

4   In the summer of 2021 former employees of Scottish brewery, BrewDog, took to Twitter to write an open letter to its owners highlighting – and complaining about – the toxic and hypocritical culture of the company and asking for an apology. They requested 'a genuine apology from anyone and everyone who has worked for BrewDog and treated people like objects; harassing, assaulting, belittling, insulting or gaslighting them. It's the absolute minimum we should expect from you, and yet we still don't actually expect to see one. We hope we're wrong.' BrewDog responded with a public apology, although at the time of writing there is no public evidence of culture change. (Makortoff and Davies, 2021; for the original letter see: www.punkswithpurpose. org/dearbrewdog/)

5   In 2005 the Canadian broadcaster CBC locked out 5,500 workers after failing to reach an agreement over the introduction of more flexible temporary employment contracts with their union, the Canadian Media Guild. Despite the lockout, CBC continued to operate by running a different schedule of programmes and deploying the 10% of its employees who were not union members (*BBC News*, 2005).

6   When she was dismissed, Diane Kuprewicz took revenge on the School of Visual Arts in New York by posting, on appropriate websites, two job advertisements for a Director of Human Resources at the school. In addition, she registered the work email address of the HR director on a number of pornographic websites. Unsurprisingly the director's inbox was inundated with a large number of job applications, sexually explicit emails and unwanted catalogues of pornographic material. The school sued Diane because her actions had depleted the hard drive disk space, drained processing power and taken up valuable staff time (Lewis, 2004).

(Continued)

7   In July 2021 the GMB union announced an end to its protracted dispute with British Gas after workers voted 3 to 1 in favour of an improved pay and pensions deal. The eventual agreement followed some weeks after a lengthy strike (44 days) and the dismissal of 500 of the 7,000 engineers who chose not to agree to proposed changes to their terms and conditions. The new deal improved overtime rates, unsocial hours payments, and limited unsocial working hours. Importantly it reversed the decision to close the defined benefit pension scheme to new starters and 'opened the door' for those who were dismissed to return to work (GMB, 2021).

8   A gym assistant invoked the grievance procedure at her organisation following a number of incidents whereby the gym manager appeared to overlook her skills when allocating dance classes to be held in the studio attached to the gym. Assistants taking the classes received a higher level of remuneration than assistants overseeing the use of gym equipment, and furthermore they worked to a fixed rather than *ad hoc* weekly schedule. During the grievance hearing it was alleged that the manager had called the assistant 'smelly like all black people'. Records showed that the assistant's amount of sick leave had escalated. The grievance hearing, following unsuccessful mediation, found against the gym manager, who appealed.

Relevant Articles for Further Reading

Hughes, E., Dobbins, T. and Merkl-Davies, D. (2022) 'Moral economy, solidarity and labour process struggle in Irish public transport', *Economic and Industrial Democracy*, 43(1): 146–67.

This article examines the ways in which two rival Irish unions built collective worker solidarity during a dispute over competitive tendering and marketization. Aspects of mobilization and structured antagonism are explored.

Gupta, A. and Kumari, P. (2020) 'Incivility: A menace to workplace', *Haryana School of Business*, 217.

A useful, clear exposition of the causes and impact of workplace incivility, helping to place low level expressions of conflict in the context of the hotel industry.

Blyton, P. and Jenkins, J. (2012) 'Mobilizing resistance: The Burberry workers' campaign against factory closure', *The Sociological Review*, 60(1): 25–45.

This is an interesting case study showing how the processes of mobilization are important for articulating and channelling conflict within a contested arena.

Kelly, J. (2015) 'Conflict: Trends and forms of collective action', *Employee Relations*, 37(6): 720–32.

This paper reviews the knowledge we have about the ways in which strikes and collective action are occurring.

Nayak, S., Budhwar, P., Pereira, V. and Malik, A. (2021) 'Exploring the dark-side of E-HRM: A study of social networking sites and deviant workplace behavior', *International Journal of Manpower*.

A topical look at electronic and digital HR systems, particularly those that use social networking mechanisms, and their impact on employees. The systems themselves may provide employees with the impetus to behave badly, resulting in conflict-ridden underperforming organisations.

Pasquier, V., Daudigeos, T. and Barros, M. (2020) 'Towards a new flashmob unionism: The case of the Fight For 15 movement', *British Journal of Industrial Relations*, 58(2): 336–63.

Ways of expressing workplace dissatisfaction, via collective and connected action are explored through the lens of the USA Fight For 15 minimum wage campaign, initiated by the Service Employees International Union.

References

Acas (2021) *Annual Report and Accounts 2020-21*. London: HMSO.

Ackroyd, S. and Thompson, P. (1999) *Organisational Misbehaviour*. London: Sage.

Adascalitei, D. and Muntean, A. (2018) 'Trade union strategies in the age of austerity: Evidence from the Romanian public sector', *European Journal of Industrial Relations*, 25(2).

Antcliff, V. and Saundry, R. (2009) 'Accompaniment, workplace representation and disciplinary outcomes in British workplaces – just a formality?', *British Journal of Industrial Relations*, 47: 100–21.

Bailey, J. and Peetz, D. (2014) 'Australian unions and collective bargaining in 2013', *Journal of Industrial Relations*, 56(3): 415–32.

BBC News (2005) 'Canada's CBC locks out employees', *BBC News*, 15 August. Available at: http://news.bbc.co.uk/go/pr/fr/-/1/hi/world/americas/4153850.stm (accessed 20 January 2015).

BBC News (2021a) 'Ex-BrewDog staff allege culture of fear at brewer', *BBC News*, 10 June. Available at: www.bbc.co.uk/news/business-57428258 (accessed 21 July 2021).

BBC News (2021b) 'North Wales buses: Arriva drivers back five-week strike', *BBC News*, 13 November. Available at: www.bbc.co.uk/news/uk-wales-59264939 (accessed 15 November 2021).

Bélanger, J. and Edwards, P. (2013) 'Conflict and contestation in the contemporary world of work: Theory and perspectives', in G. Gall (ed.), *New Forms and Expressions of Conflict at Work*. Basingstoke: Palgrave Macmillan, pp. 7–25.

Benton, L. (2021) *The Toxic Culture Brewing Inside BrewDog*. Available at: https://libertymind.co.uk/the-toxic-culture-brewing-inside-brewdog/ (accessed 21 July 2021).

Blyton, P. and Jenkins, J. (2012) 'Mobilizing resistance: The Burberry workers' campaign against factory closure', *The Sociological Review*, 60(1): 25–45.

Blyton, P. and Turnbull, P. (2004) *The Dynamics of Employee Relations* (3rd edn). Basingstoke: Palgrave Macmillan.

Boodoo, M. U., Frangi, L., Gomez, R. and Hebdon, R. (2020) *How do Employees Respond to Workplace Injustice? New Insights from Ranked Ordinal Employee Preferences*. Available at: https://ssrn.com/abstract=3634539 (accessed 16 August 2022).

Bolton, S. C. and Boyd, C. (2003) 'Trolley dolly or skilled emotion manager? Moving on from Hochschild's Managed Heart', *Work, Employment & Society*, 17(2): 289–308.

Bronfenbrenner, K. (1996) 'Final report: The effects of plant closing or threat of plant closing on the right of workers to organize', *International Publications*, 1.

Brooks, L. (2021a) 'ScotRail engineers plan strikes during Glasgow climate summit', *The Guardian*, 5 October. Available at: www.theguardian.com/uk-news/2021/oct/05/scotrail-engineers-plan-strikes-during-glasgow-climate-summit (accessed 28 October 2021).

Brooks, L. (2021b) 'Glasgow bin workers to strike during Cop26 climate summit', *The Guardian*, 19 October. Available at: www.theguardian.com/environment/2021/oct/19/glasgow-bin-workers-to-strike-during-cop26 (accessed 28 October 2021).

Brown, W., Bryson, A., Forth, J. and Whitfield, K. (eds) (2009) *The Evolution of the Modern Workplace*. Cambridge: Cambridge University Press.

Budd, J. W. (2004) *Employment with a Human Face: Balancing Efficiency, Equity, and Voice*. Ithaca, NY: Cornell University Press.

Budd, J. W., Gollan, P. J. and Wilkinson, A. (2010) 'New approaches to employee voice and participation in organizations', *Human Relations*, 63(3): 303–10.

Burawoy, M. (1979) *Manufacturing Consent*. London: Verso.

Burawoy, M. (1985) *The Politics of Production*. London: Verso.

Bureau of Labor (2021) *Work Stoppage Summary*, US Department of Labour Statistics press release, 19 February.

Casebourne, J., Regan, J., Neathey, F. and Tuohy, S. (2006) 'Employment rights at work – survey of employees 2005', DTI Employment Relations Research Series No. *51*. London: Department of Trade and Industry.

Charlwood, A. and Pollert, A. (2014) 'Informal employment dispute resolution among low-wage non-union workers: Does managerially initiated workplace voice enhance equity and efficiency?', *British Journal of Industrial Relations*, 52(2): 359–86.

Chenoweth, E. (2020) 'The future of nonviolent resistance', *Journal of Democracy*, 31(3): 69-84.

Clarey, K. (2022) 'IBM exec referred to older workers as "dinobabies", suit says', *HRDrive*, 18 February. Available at: www.hrdive.com/news/ibm-exec-referred-to-older-workers-as-dinobabies-suit-says/619046/ (accessed 19 February 2022).

Clegg, H. A. (1975) 'Pluralism in industrial relations', *British Journal of Industrial Relations*, 13(3): 309–16.

Cooke, H. (2006). Seagull management and the control of nursing work. *Work, Employment and Society*, 20(2), 223-243.

Corcoran, S. (2022) 'Former Batley spa owner speaks out after receptionist took revenge for being fired', *Yorkshire Live*, 12 May. Available at: www.examinerlive.co.uk/news/local-news/former-batley-spa-owner-speaks-23932924 (accessed 15 May 2022).

Crawford, R. (2014) 'Spoof book used in Amazon pay protest', *Employee Benefits*, 13 June. Available at: www.employeebenefits.co.uk/news/spoof-book-used-in-amazon-pay-protest/104903.article (accessed 4 October 2015).

Crowley, M. and Hodson, R. (2014) 'Neoliberalism at work', *Social Currents*, 1(1): 91–108.

Davis, R. S. and Stazyk, E. C. (2021) 'Ambiguity, appraisal, and affect: Examining the connections between goal perceptions, emotional labour, and exhaustion', *Public Management Review*, 1–22.

Department for Business, Innovation & Skills (DBIS) (2013) *The 2011 Workplace Employment Relations Study (WERS) Transparency Data*. London: DBIS. Available at: www.gov.uk/government/publications/the-2011-workplace-employment-relations-study-wers-transparency-data (accessed 5 October 2015).

De Clercq, D., Haq, I. U. and Azeem, M. U. (2020) 'The relationship between workplace incivility and depersonalization towards co-workers: Roles of job-related anxiety, gender, and education', *Journal of Management & Organization*, 26(2): 219–40.

Dix, G., Forth, J. A. and Sisson, K. (2008) *Conflict at Work: The Pattern of Disputes in Britain since 1980*. London: Acas.

Dunphy, L. (2020) 'Special Report: Debenhams strikers won't back down', *The Irish Examiner*, 7 September. Available at: www.irishexaminer.com/news/spotlight/arid-40044209.html (accessed 22 November 2021).

Dunphy, L. (2021) 'Debenhams debacle: Reflecting on the longest industrial relations dispute in Irish history', *The Irish Examiner*, 29 May. Available at: www.irishexaminer.com/news/spotlight/arid-40300472.html (accessed 22 November 2021).

Edwards, P. (2000) 'Discipline towards trust and self discipline', in S. Bach and K. Sisson (eds), *Personnel Management: A Comprehensive Guide to Theory and Practice* (3rd edn). Oxford: Blackwell, pp. 317–39.

Edwards, P. K. (2003) 'The employment relationship and the field of industrial relations', in P. K. Edwards (ed.), *Industrial Relations: Theory and Practice*. Oxford: Basil, pp. 1–36.

Egerová, D. and Rotenbornová, L. (2021) 'Towards understanding of workplace conflict: An examination into causes and conflict management strategies', *Problems of Management in the 21st Century*. doi:10.33225/pmc/21.16.07

Elliott, L. (2014) 'As the Berlin Wall fell, checks on capitalism crumbled', *The Guardian*, 3 November: 22.

Fleming, P. and Spicer, A. (2007) *Contesting the Corporation*. Cambridge: Cambridge University Press.

Fletcher, L. (2021) *Inclusion at Work: Perspectives on LGBT+ Working Lives*. London: Chartered Institute of Personnel and Development.

Forret, M. and Love, M. S. (2007) 'Employee justice perceptions and co-worker relationships', *Leadership & Organization Development Journal*, 29(3): 248–60.

Forth, J., Bewley, H. and Bryson, A. (2006) *Small and Medium-sized Enterprises: Findings from the 2004 Workplace Employee Relations Survey*. London: Routledge.

Fulmer, C. A. and Ostroff, C. (2017) 'Trust in direct leaders and top leaders: A trickle-up model', *Journal of Applied Psychology*, 102(4): 648–57.

Gall, G. and Cohen, C. (2013) 'The collective expression of workplace grievances in Britain', in G. Gall (ed.), *New Forms and Expressions of Conflict at Work*. Basingstoke: Palgrave Macmillan.

Gallie, D., Felstead, A., Green, F. and Inanc, H. (2013) *Fear at Work in Britain: First Findings from the Skills and Employment Survey 2012*. London: Centre for Learning and Life Chances in Knowledge Economies and Societies, Institute of Education.

GMB (2014) 'Blacklist "Crocodile Tears Tour" launched', *Newsroom*, 15 October. Available at: www.gmb.org.uk/newsroom/blacklist-crocodile-tears-tour-launched (accessed 17 October 2014).

GMB (2021) *British Gas Fire and Hire Dispute Over After GMB Members Back Improved Pay Deal*, press release, 20 July. Available at: www.gmb.org.uk/news/british-gas-fire-rehire-dispute-over-after-gmb-members-back-improved-pay-deal (accessed 1 December 2021).

Godard, J. (2011) 'What has happened to strikes?', *British Journal of Industrial Relations*, 49(2): 282–305.

Godard, J. (2014) 'Labour-management conflict', in W. K. Roche, P. Teague and A. J. Colvin (eds), *The Oxford Handbook of Conflict Management in Organizations*. Oxford: Oxford University Press.

Goodrich, C. L. (1920) *The Frontier of Control*. New York: Harcourt, Brace & Howe.

Grandey, A. A. and Gabriel, A. S. (2015) 'Emotional labor at a crossroads: Where do we go from here?', *Annual Review of Organizational Psychology and Organizational Behavior*, 2(1): 323–49.

Hayward, B., Peters, M., Rousseau, N. and Seeds, K. (2004) *Findings from the Survey of Employment Tribunal Applications 2003*, Employment Relations Research Series No. 33. London: DTI.

Hebdon, R. and Noh, S. C. (2013) 'A theory of workplace conflict development: From grievances to strikes', in G. Gall (ed.), *New Forms and Expressions of Conflict at Work*. Basingstoke: Palgrave Macmillan, pp. 26–47.

Hennebert, M. A., Pasquier, V. and Lévesque, C. (2021) 'What do unions do … with digital technologies? An affordance approach', *New Technology, Work and Employment*. doi:10.1111/NTWE.12187

Hughes, E. and Dobbins, T. (2020) 'Frontier of control struggles in British and Irish public transport', *European Journal of Industrial Relations*, 0959680120929137.

Hughes, E., Dobbins, T., and Merkl-Davies, D. (2022). Moral economy, solidarity and labour process struggle in Irish public transport. *Economic and Industrial Democracy*, 43(1), 146–167.

Hyman, R. (1972) *Strikes*. London: Fontana.

Hyman, R. (1987) 'Strategy or structure? Capital, labour and control', *Work, Employment & Society*, 1(1): 25–55.

Hyman, R. (1989) *Strikes* (4th edn). London: Macmillan.

Hyman, R. (1999) 'Strikes in the UK: Withering away?', *European Observatory of Working Life – EurWORK*. Available at: http://eurofound.europa.eu/observatories/eurwork/articles/other/strikes-in-the-uk-withering-away (accessed 23 November 2014).

IndustriALL (2020) *Tripartite Agreement to Protect Sri Lankan Workers*. Available at: www.industriall-union.org/tripartite-agreement-to-protect-sri-lankan-workers (accessed 5 November 2021).

ITV News (2021a) '"If you're on this call, you are part of the unlucky group": Boss fires 900 employees over Zoom', *ITV News*, 6 December. Available at: www.itv.com/news/2021-12-06/you-are-part-of-the-unlucky-group-boss-fires-900-employees-over-zoom (accessed 6 December 2021).

ITV News (2021b) '"Enough is enough": North Wales Arriva bus drivers who feel "undervalued" strike due to pay gap', *ITV News*, 15 November. Available at: www.itv.com/news/wales/2021-11-15/north-wales-arriva-bus-drivers-take-strike-action-feel-undervalued-due-to-pay (accessed 16 August 2022).

Jalette, P. (2011) 'Relocation threats and actual relocations in Canadian manufacturing: The role of firm capacity and union concessions', *American Behavioral Scientist*, 55(7): 843–67.

Johnson, P. R. and Indvik, J. (2001a) 'Rudeness at work: Impulse over restraint', *Public Personnel Management*, 30(4): 457–65.

Johnson, P. R. and Indvik, J. (2001b) 'Slings and arrows of rudeness: Incivility in the workplace', *Journal of Management Development*, 20(8): 705–14.

Kelly, J. E. (2012) *Rethinking Industrial Relations: Mobilization, Collectivism, and Long Waves*, Vol. 1. London: Routledge.

Kelly, J. (2015) 'Conflict: Trends and forms of collective action', *Employee Relations*, 37(6): 720–32.

Kinnunen, A. and Gustafsson, A-K. (2021) 'Relative calm on the industrial action front in 2020', *Eurofound*. Available at: www.eurofound.europa.eu/it/publications/article/2021/relative-calm-on-the-industrial-action-front-in-2020 (accessed 26 November 2021).

Knight, K. G. and Latreille, P. L. (2000) 'Discipline, dismissals and complaints to employment tribunal', *British Journal of Industrial Relations*, 38: 533–55.

Kolb, D. M. and Putnam, L. L. (1992) 'The multiple faces of conflict in organizations', *Journal of Organizational Behavior*, 13(3): 311–24.

Kraft, D. (2015) 'An example of conflict in the workplace', *GlobalPost*. Available at: http://everydaylife.globalpost.com/example-conflict-workplace-2460.html (accessed 23 January 2015).

Labour Court (2020) *Outcome of Engagement by Kevin Foley, Chairman of the Labour Court, on Matters Associated with the Liquidation of Debenhams Ireland*. Available at: www.labourcourt.ie/en/useful-information/latest-news/debenhams-ireland/ (accessed 27 November 2021).

LabourStart (2014a) 'USA: Zara must respect workers' rights', 29 October. Available at: www.labourstartcampaigns.net/show_campaign.cgi?c=2564 (accessed 29 October 2014).

LabourStart (2014b) 'Wizz Air stop union busting now', 26 November. Available at www.labourstartcampaigns.net/show_campaign.cgi?c=2580 (accessed 26 November 2014).

Leach, A. (2013) 'BANG and the server's gone: Man gets 8 months for destroying work computers', *The Register*, 4 February. Available at: www.theregister.co.uk/2013/02/04/cillit_bang_server_attack_prison_sentence/ (accessed 17 August 2014).

Lewis, B. (2004) 'Disgruntled former employees may use the internet for revenge', *Workforce*, 10 May. Available at: www.workforce.com/articles/disgruntled-former-employees-may-use-the-internet-for-revenge (accessed 27 January 2015).

Mada Masr (2021) 'Egyptian iron and steel workers stage sit-in to protest liquidation: "Here you have a house, outside you have a house, but outside you'll reside in humiliation"', *Mada Masr*, 18 January. Available at: www.madamasr.com/en/2021/01/18/feature/politics/egyptian-iron-and-steel-workers-stage-sit-in-to-protest-liquidation-here-you-have-a-house-outside-you-have-a-house-but-outside-youll-reside-in-humiliation/ (accessed 28 October 2021).

Makortoff, K. and Davies, R. (2021) 'Former BrewDog staff accuse craft beer firm of culture of fear', *The Guardian*, 10 June. Available at: www.theguardian.com/business/2021/jun/10/brewdog-staff-craft-beer-firm-letter (accessed 27 November 2021).

Marchington, M. (2015) 'Human resource management (HRM): Too busy looking up to see where it is going longer term?', *Human Resource Management Review*, 25(2): 176–87.

Meena Solidarity Network (2021) '"We will not leave it to the thieves!": Egyptian steel workers battle for justice after plant slated for closure', *Meena Solidarity Network*, 7 March. Available at: https://menasolidaritynetwork.com/2021/03/07/we-will-not-leave-it-to-the-thieves-egyptian-steel-workers-battle-for-justice-after-plant-slated-for-closure/ (accessed 28 October 2021).

Middle East Eye (2021) 'Egypt: In shuttering a national icon, the government has unleashed rare public anger', *Middle East Eye*, 22 January. Available at: www.middleeasteye.net/news/egypt-steel-iron-company-wind-up-public-anger (accessed 28 October 2021).

Moore, S. and Read, I. (2006) 'Collective organisation in small- and medium-sized enterprises – an application of mobilisation theory', *Human Resource Management Journal*, 16: 357–75.

Nelson, J. L., Hegtvedt, K. A., Haardörfer, R. and Hayward, J. L. (2019) 'Trust and respect at work: Justice antecedents and the role of coworker dynamics', *Work and Occupations*, 46(3): 307–38.

Nimmo, J. (2013) 'Cillit saboteur is banged up', *Oxford Mail*, 2 February. Available at: www.oxfordmail.co.uk/news/10202588.Cillit_saboteur_is_banged_up/ (accessed 17 August 2014).

Northampton Herald & Post (2014a) 'Biomedical staff at Northampton General Hospital locked out of work for a fifth day', *Northampton Herald & Post*, 30 June. Available at: www.northampton-news-hp.co.uk/Biomedical-staff-Northampton-General-Hospital-locked-work-fifth-day/story-21678321-detail/story.html#ixzz3Q766uA00 (accessed 12 December 2014).

Northampton Herald & Post (2014b) 'Industrial action is over after 27 days as Acas brokers a deal between Northampton General Hospital and the biomedical staff', *Northampton Herald & Post*, 24 July. Available at: www.northampton-news-hp.co.uk/Industrial-action-27-days-ACAS-brokers-deal-Northampton-General-Hospital-biomedical-staff/story-22029963-detail/story.html#ixzz3Q77xUcDQ (accessed 12 December 2014).

Office of National Statistics (2019a) *Which Occupations are at Highest Risk of Being Automated?* Available at: www.ons.gov.uk/employmentandlabourmarket/peopleinwork/employmentandemployeetypes/articles/whichoccupationsareathighestriskofbeingautomated/2019-03-25 (accessed 5 November 2021).

Office of National Statistics (2019b) *Labour Disputes in the UK*. Available at: www.ons.gov.uk/employmentandlabourmarket/peopleinwork/workplacedisputesandworkingconditions/articles/labourdisputes/2018#annual-changes (accessed 17 November 2021).

Paresashvili, N., Gurbanov, N., Gechbaia, B., Goletiani, K. and Edzgveradze, T. (2020) *'Significant issues of organizational conflict management'*, paper presented at 55th International Scientific Conference on Economic and Social Development, Baku, 18–19 June.

Pasquier, V., Daudigeos, T. and Barros, M. (2020) 'Towards a new flashmob unionism: The case of the Fight for 15 movement', *British Journal of Industrial Relations*, 58(2): 336–63.

Pruitt, D. G., Parker, J. C. and Mikolic, J. M. (1997) 'Escalation as a reaction to persistent annoyance', *The International Journal of Conflict Management*, 8(3): 252–70.

Psychometrics, (2009), Warring Egos, Toxic Individuals, Feeble Leadership, A Study Of Conflict In The Canadian Workplace. Edmonton: Psychometrics, Canada

Sapsford, D. and Turnbull, P. (1994) 'Strikes and industrial conflict in Britain's docks: Balloons or icebergs?', *Oxford Bulletin of Economics and Statistics*, 56(3): 249–65.

Scheiber, N. (2022) 'Making "dinobabies" extinct: IBM's push for a younger work force', *New York Times*, 12 February. Available at: www.nytimes.com/2022/02/12/business/economy/ibm-age-discrimination.html (accessed 19 February 2022).

Song, J. (2021) 'Emotional labour and professional development in ELT', *ELT Journal*, 75(4): 482–91.

Sorenson, J. (2019) 'Robot sabotage: Resisting technological transformations in the workplace', AAA/CASCA Annual Meeting, 20–24 November, Vancouver, BC.

Spillius, A. (1996) 'Sabotage their systems and steal their stationery', *Independent*, 10 March. Available at: www.independent.co.uk/life-style/sabotage-their-systems-and-steal-their-stationery-1341182.html (accessed 4 October 2015).

Suff, R. (2020) *Managing Conflict in the Modern Workplace*. Available at: www.cipd.co.uk/Images/managing-conflict-in-the-workplace-1_tcm18-70655.pdf (accessed 26 October 2021).

Tanguy, J. (2013) 'Collective and individual conflicts in the workplace: Evidence from France', *Industrial Relations*, 52(1): 102–33.

Taylor, P. and Bain, P. (2003) '"Subterranean worksick blues": Humour as subversion in two call centres', *Organization Studies*, 24(9): 1487–509.

Taylor, P. and Bain, P. (2007) 'Humour and subversion in two call centres', in S. Fleetwood and S. Ackroyd (eds), *Critical Realist Applications in Organisation and Management Studies*. London: Routledge, pp. 274–97.

Thomas, A. (2021) '"Heart of steel": How trade unions lobby the European Union over emissions trading', *Environmental Politics*, 1–20.

Tjosvold, D. (2008) 'The conflict-positive organization: It depends upon us', *Journal of Organizational Behavior*, 29(1): 19–28.

Wajcman, J. (2000) 'Feminism facing industrial relations in Britain', *British Journal of Industrial Relations*, 38(2): 183–201.

Walker, P. (2021) 'Anger as ministers block fire and rehire bill in Commons', *The Guardian*, 22 October. Available at: www.theguardian.com/law/2021/oct/22/anger-as-ministers-block-fire-and-rehire-bill-in-commons (accessed 27 October 2021).

Wieslander, M. (2021) 'Challenging and destabilizing official discourses: Irony as a resistance resource in institutional talk', *Culture and Organization*, 27(1): 16–32.

7

CONFLICT: REDUCTION, REGULATION AND RESOLUTION

Learning Outcomes

By the end of this chapter, you should be able to:

- analyse the impact that different managerial styles have on conflict reduction and resolution
- evaluate perceptions of organisational justice in relation to the reduction and resolution of conflict
- critically review a range of alternative dispute mechanisms
- analyse and evaluate different methods of resolving conflict at work
- be cognisant of a range of employment procedures designed to process incidents of conflict.

What to Expect

Conflict at work is expensive. Acas estimates that it costs UK employers £28.5 billion every year, which is around £1,000 for each employee (Saundry and Urwin, 2021). Badly handled conflict management can result in low productivity and increased levels of employee stress and anxiety/depression. It is imperative therefore that employers create workplace cultures in which the opportunities for conflict are diminished and, should they occur, be dealt with swiftly and appropriately. This chapter looks at the ways in which conflict is managed; in particular it covers the ways in which different management styles impact the incidence of, and perceptions about, workplace dissention, with the concomitant attempts to contain, reduce and deal with manifestations of conflict. Dix et al. (2009) differentiate between conflicts, expressed or otherwise, that develop from *perceived* differences of interests and disputes that are *visible, and clear expressions* of that discontent. From the employee relations perspective these differences are important because the ways in which conflict – expressed or otherwise – and disputes are managed depends on the perceptions of the parties about the nature and type of the contested incident. A range of various conflict management techniques, both collective and individual, will be examined in this chapter together with aspects of formal and informal alternative dispute mechanisms.

The ways of addressing, ignoring or attempting to prevent conflict are key elements in any employment relationship and provide a barometer of the nature of the relationship and the ways in which management and employees both perceive one another and interact within the workplace environment in which they find themselves. While employers may have much to gain from cooperation with employees, this does not diminish the fact that employers would like to utilise (to the full) their employees' efforts in order to make their employment worthwhile for the organisation. Such utilisation may be constricted by legal obligations. Importantly, the ways in which employers manage a workforce may lead to differences of interest with, and perhaps between, their employees that subsequently lead to levels of workplace conflict.

The occurrence of conflict and the incidences of disputed events are not, however, always an indication of an unhealthy employment relation. It may be, for example, that a high number of employee grievances are a result of an enabling workplace allowing employees a voice across a wide range of issues, rather than a disabling workplace, that is, one that inhibits voice and restricts complaints, thereby engendering higher incidents of conflict. Many organisations, particularly in the UK and EU, where it is a legal requirement, will have procedures that facilitate the processing of grievances and disciplinary matters; however, it is important to remember that regardless of legal requirements the mere existence of a procedure does not mean that it is followed, or even that its existence is 'public knowledge' within an organisation.

News Flash 7.1

Thousands of Scottish Workers Subject to Unfair Treatment at Work

Citizens Advice Scotland (CAS) said it saw more than 46,500 instances of unfair treatment at work in 2014, an increase of 5.5% on 2013. Its report, *Fair Enough?*, cites examples of unfair dismissal, refusal to pay sick pay, non-payment of wages - in one case for six months' full-time work - cancellation of holidays, dismissals linked to pregnancy, bullying and racism, including exploited migrant workers made to work excessive hours, and paying below the minimum wage. The report recommends the removal of Tribunal fees and the creation of a statutory Employment Commission to promote fair employment practices and ensure compliance with the law.

A CAS spokesman, Rob Gowans, said,

... it is in the interests of government and society as a whole that fair employment is promoted. Workers in low quality, stressful jobs have poorer general health, and poor daily quality of life than other groups - even those who are unemployed. It is also important to ensure that unscrupulous employers who wilfully undermine their employees' basic rights do not gain an unfair advantage over fair employers.

Source: BBC News, 2015a; Citizens Advice Scotland, 2015

A Contested Relationship: Managerial Styles and Their Impact

We have seen from the preceding chapters that the ways in which employers and employees view the employment relationship are not necessarily congruent. Employers too are not a homogenous group. Depending on their perspectives they will have different attitudes towards dealing with their workforces that may be individual, collective, hard or soft, or a pragmatic mixture of these. The managerial perspective, whether unitarist or pluralist, together with the managerial style, will have an impact on the ways in which workplace conflict is perceived, and hence how it is managed. How an organisation chooses to respond to real, or potential, incidents of conflict will depend too on the country, culture of the organisation, and the operative employment legislation at the time. Whatever the type of style deployed, or legislation in play, managers attempt to reduce the potential for conflict by the careful recruitment and selection of staff and many couple this strategy with endeavouring to ensure adequate communication pathways to, and from, their employees.

Fox (1985) identified two distinct and separate strategies that managements could choose to adopt in order to persuade employees to observe and conform to their regulations and workplace requirements. The first of these was via *coercion*. Here employers insist on conformity with their own plans, methods and processes of work by the use of force, or the intimidatory threat of force. For example, when workplace productivity is affected by an employee habitually arriving late for work, an employer who threatens to disproportionately dock the employee's pay for the time lost, is exerting coercive power. For example, it is not unknown in Japan for employee workplace infringements to be punished by reductions in pay (Muzaffar, 2021); similarly, some airlines such at Ryanair and Emirates behave in coercive ways towards those cabin crew found to 'violate' in-flight sales or body weight codes (Noyen, 2022; *The Irish Times*, 2017). The UK Conservative government as an employer exerted coercive power when, in 1984, it unilaterally withdrew trade union recognition from its employees working within the security service at GCHQ in Cheltenham – although this decision was later rescinded in 1996 by the Labour government. On occasions employers exert coercive power by expecting (insisting) their employees undertake tasks that are 'outside' their contracts of employment, often in the form of unpaid overtime. Unpaid overtime rose from 7.3 to 9.2 hours per week on average between 2020 and 2021, according to the ADP Research Institute that surveyed 32,471 workers in 17 countries between 17 November and 11 December 2020. The findings were particularly striking for North America where the average amount of unpaid overtime doubled from four hours per week to nearly nine (Richardson and Klien, 2021: 15).

News Flash 7.2

Unpaid Work in the United Kingdom

Over five million UK employees worked for a total of 2 billion unpaid hours in 2019 according to TUC analysis of official statistics published in February 2020.

(Continued)

It reported that five million people averaged 7.6 hours a week in unpaid overtime during 2019, the equivalent of having £6,828 taken from individual pay packets. TUC General Secretary, Frances O'Grady, said:

The government needs to crack down on Britain's long hours culture. Too many bosses are getting away with stealing their workers' time. Overworking staff hurts productivity, leaves workers stressed and exhausted and eats into time that should be spent with family and friends.

Source: TUC, 2020

Coercive management practices tend to be found where the managerial style is either traditionalist or standard modern, where the employees are dealt with in a hard rather than soft manner. Employees who are not central to the operational requirements of an organisation are more likely to be managed by coercive, hard methods.

In many jobs the use of employer power in a coercive way leads to drift, or creep, in the amount of time employees are required to spend at work and the number of tasks that they are required to accomplish in that time. In such situations the employees are likely to exert their countervailing power by adjusting their effort, taking time off work or otherwise getting 'their own back'. Such retaliative action increases the levels of conflict and often escalates the ways in which managers attempt to coerce 'offenders' to work harder. In situations like these, employees may resort to legal means to help redress wrongs. In the USA, Wall-Mart had, following a court case in 2009, to pay $35m to around 80,000 current and former Washington State employees in order to settle allegations that it had forced them to 'work off-the-clock' (i.e., work at times when they were not officially signed in as working), as well as denying them meal and rest breaks (Greenhouse and Rosenbloom, 2008; US Department of Labor, 2012; *Barnett* v. *Wal-Mart* [Case No. 01–2–24553–8, King County Superior Court for the State of Washington]). This, of course, is rather an extreme example, but non-payment of wages or paying below the minimum wage are both examples of coercive behaviour, as are, for example, changing someone's shift times without adequate consultation and agreement, or deliberately allocating unpleasant tasks to someone regarded as problematic. Not all employees resort to the courts for a solution to coercive employer behaviour. Hughes and Bozionelos (2006) discovered that male bus drivers, unhappy with the lack of work–life balance and faced with an inflexible management unwilling to alter shift patterns, took matters into their own hands by feigning illness and taking sick leave, thereby ensuring a more 'favourable' work–life balance despite managerial opposition. Where coercive management leads to perceptions of injustice, the psychological contract is damaged and the 'normal' reciprocity between employer and employee breaks down. Harris and Ogbonna (2012) said that 85% of employees are possibly linked to revenge-led sabotage, while Hongbo et al. (2020) found a direct link between coercive abusive supervisors and retaliative acts of sabotage. Here the studied Chinese supervisees, powerless to retaliate directly, did so indirectly, by 'misbehaving' towards customers.

Greenberg (2006) provides an example of coercive power when he shows how nurses in two, out of the four researched, hospitals reacted when their employer notified them about a change to the way in which they were to be paid, moving from an hourly rate to a monthly salary, reducing their overall remuneration. The way in which the change was made, in particular where it was introduced by managers untrained in aspects of interactional justice, led to high levels of discontent, stress and insomnia and led the nurses into conflict with the management. Yet for nurses who received an explanation from those supervisors who had been trained in interactional justice, insomnia was less pronounced not just in the period immediately after training but even six months later.

Exercise 7.1

Some proponents of coercive power say that it is an effective way of addressing, correcting and inhibiting employee insubordination.

- Explain, using Budd's model of a balanced employment relationship, together with theories of organisational justice (see Chapter 3), why this assumption might be incorrect.

Coercive acts of 'unfettered' employer power provoke conflict, damage psychological contracts and lead to employee perceptions of organisational injustice and reduced levels of trust and discretionary effort. Where the use of power is perceived by employees to be unjust this has a corrosive impact on the employment relationship, leading to lower levels of productivity and higher levels of employee turnover (Galai, 2022; Håvold and Håvold, 2019).

The second category identified by Fox is that of *compliance*. It is more usual in the workplace for an employer to persuade employees to comply with workplace requirements voluntarily (see Chapter 4 on contract), and in order to do this it is essential that a degree of communication occurs (Galai, 2022). Typically, this form of managerial control occurs where the managerial style is either sophisticated paternalist or sophisticated modern, with a soft rather than hard approach. Where a sophisticated modern approach is adopted employees may encourage compliance by using either *constitutional* (i.e. regulatory) mechanisms or *consultative* ones, whereby employees are encouraged to actively communicate their views to management (Purcell and Sisson, 1983). Sometimes of course a pragmatic combination of both constitutional and consultative mechanisms will be deployed. Early work by Folger and Greenberg (1985) showed that where employees were involved in their own **performance appraisal** process and where, for example, they had some say in the ways in which their total benefits package was arranged, there were consequently higher positive employee perceptions of organisational justice, lower levels of workplace dissent and fewer expressions of conflict. Discussions with employees led directly to their subsequent 'buy-in' to organisational requirements. Management by consent led to a less conflicted employment relationship. Where employees know what is expected of them, and why, it is more likely they will comply with workplace requirements, even though they might disagree with them (Laundon et al., 2019; Salam, 2020; Tyler and Bies, 1990). Where supervisees regard their managers as fair, and know what is expected of them, there are fewer conflictual incidents, such as time wasting and violent behaviour (Everton et al., 2006). The implications of this for the employment relationship are self-evident: utilising managerial methods centred around compliance rather than coercion will, theoretically, limit the explicit incidence of conflict within the employment relationship. Where employees regard managerial behaviour as fundamentally fair (rather than accidentally fair) they are more likely to comply willingly with supervisory requests (Matta et al., 2020).

News Flash 7.3

Foreign Office Integrates New HR Model

The UK Foreign and Commonwealth Office (employing 15,000 staff from more than 150 nationalities) has reinvented its HR model so that all of its employees feel integrated into one organisation. The new model ensures that policies and procedures for overseas and UK staff are now aligned: there is to be a single performance management system; career development has been enhanced, and new openings are now advertised rather than staff being allocated to fill vacancies; a Diplomatic Academy and language centre have been created to aid skill development; gender diversity is being enhanced (40% of board members are women) and recruitment processes designed to attract suitable candidates irrespective of gender or background; a slimmed down HR function now operates centrally, thereby promoting consistence of treatment for staff.

Source: Phelan, 2015

The managing of employees whereby they are informed, and importantly can contribute to decisions that affect the work process, results in greater levels of trust, higher perceptions of organisational justice and more positive discretionary behaviour, leading to greater organisational effectiveness; this in turn reduces the potential for conflict, resulting in a self-perpetuating spiral of effective organisational behaviours minimising the potential for conflict (Men and Yue, 2019). Part of the range of conflict-reducing strategies open to management is therefore to facilitate open dialogue between the workforce and its managers. This can be seen quite clearly in cases of redundancy. Brockner et al. (1994) found that where the procedures were deemed by employees to have been fair (and applied in a fair manner) it was apparent that whether people were made redundant, expected to be next in line for redundancy, or whether they had a reasonable chance of remaining in secure employment, then the fairer their perception of the management processes the more positive the impact on the employment relationship – and the less contested it was for those employees remaining in work. (See Chapter 13 for more information on redundancy procedures.)

Conflict and Performance Management

Over the last couple of decades there has been a shift in emphasis away from controlling employees towards encouraging their engaged commitment, that is, a move from coercion towards encouraging compliance and willing cooperation. Greater competitive demands increasing the pressures on quality, coupled with the impact of technology, have encouraged a number of changes within the employment relationship. Employees are now given greater discretion about the ways in which they organise and perform their work (see Avgoustaki and Frankort, 2019; Bird, 1999: 63) yet, paradoxically this means they are often subject to greater scrutiny in the form of performance management and performance measurement, reinforcing the potential for conflict (see comments on structural antagonism in Chapters 1 and 3; also Edwards, 2003; Edwards and Wajcman, 2005). Continuous task monitoring, according to Gallie et al. (2001), has led to organisations adopting a system of devolved control away from the centre, with line managers moving from supervisory roles to ones with a greater involvement in the personnel function, such as recruitment and disciplining. Such organisations need well-developed regulatory procedures for involving line managers in wider decision making (Lawless and Trif, 2016). There are, of course, concomitant outcomes: line manager decisions are expected to show consistency of employee treatment while simultaneously creating environments that are legally compliant, without prejudice yet still enabling and encouraging employee discretion. Accordingly, employee activity will be subject to some sort of checking; often this is achieved by a range of performance management and monitoring/surveillance techniques (Ravid et al., 2020; Saundry et al., 2021; Stanton and Julian, 2002). Sewell and colleagues (Sewell and Barker, 2006; Sewell et al., 2012) in their work on call centres point out the dichotomy in performance management used to monitor and measure employee activity in order to assess whether it meets with, or diverges from, expected standards of performance. Employees are, they say, happy that the poor performance (of others) is picked up but less happy when it becomes an intrusive tool serving the interests of the employer at their own expense. They suggest that monitoring (intended to pick up on behaviour for the good of all, i.e., preventing 'freeloading' from some employees) can be seen as *caring*, but where it is used to increase and intensify the subordination of employees it can be regarded as *coercive*, thereby echoing both Fox's categorisation (compliance v. coercion) and the tensions found within structural antagonism. How performance is monitored and the subsequent perceptions of the workforce are, as previously noted, linked to managerial perspectives and styles. Sewell et al. say that:

> … the legitimacy of performance measurement depends on which side of the employer/ employee fault line you stand. If you are an employer it is almost always good because it serves your interests by ensuring you get what you think you rightfully deserve: the full and undivided efforts of your workforce. If you are an employee, however, it is almost always bad because you consider it to militate against your interests by intensifying work, reducing autonomy, increasing stress and undermining solidarity by putting worker against worker. (Sewell et al., 2012: 191)

See Figure 7.1 for an overview of care and coercion in performance management.

Coercion			Care		
Management and employees have divergent interests and behaviours ➞	Managers require maximum effort ➞ Employees restrict output	Increased likelihood of perceptions of injustice and expressions of conflict	Management and employees have a mutual interest in ensuring 'good' workplace behaviours ➞	Managers ensure transparency, encouraging effort from everyone ➞ Employees are happy to put in the effort required	Increased likelihood of perceptions of justice and fewer expressions of conflict

Figure 7.1   Performance management: Care or coercion

Exercise 7.2

Reflect on an example known to you of a workplace where employees are given greater discretion in how they perform and organise their work and yet paradoxically are under greater surveillance (you will find examples in Chapter 3 if you cannot think of one).

- Is the subsequent impact on the employment relationship positive or negative from the employee's perspective?
- Why did you reach this conclusion? Justify your reasoning with reference to academic sources (such as the work by Edwards and by Fox) and include some references that concern organisational justice.

Exercise 7.3

Discuss the reasoning and efficacy behind the following two statements:

- 'The imposition and use of various ... monitoring technologies in the workplace erodes employment relationships and contributes to the increased feeling of powerlessness for employees' (Indiparambil, 2019: 90).
- 'coercive control assumes that surveillance is needed to expose and coerce unruly or deviant employees to constantly work hard' (Watkins Allen et al., 2007: 174-5).

Conflict Reduction and Strategies Engendering Employee Trust

The nature of an employment relationship is influenced by, and contingent upon, the perspectives and experiences brought to that relationship by the employee. Where employees can see that the organisation operates with procedural justice they will be more likely to trust the employer and subsequently assume they will be treated in an open and honest way; consequently there will be fewer expressions of conflict. Supervisors who engender trust and fairness by the ways in which they manage, encounter lower levels of conflict (Ehlers, 2013; Strom et al., 2014). The US National Bureau of Economic Research postulated, rather surprisingly, that for employees a 10% increase in trust around managerial actions has the equivalence of an increase in just over one-third of salary (Helliwell et al., 2009).

More trusting relationships indicate to the parties involved that they are valued (Kramer and Tyler, 1995), and according to Allan Lind such perceptions 'lead to a shift from responding to a social situation in terms of immediate self-interest ... to responding to social situations as a member of the larger social entity' (2001: 66). In other words, the research indicates that where the parties trust one another it is probable that they will work towards organisational rather than individual goals, notwithstanding the fact that parties may well have different interests and requirements from the employment relationship. Bray and his colleagues looked at aspects of 'working together towards the same end' when they examined workplace cooperation (2020: 118), framing it within unitarism and pluralism. Their typology (Table 7.1) is useful because it enables a greater depth of analysis around the concept of cooperation; however, they do not address aspects of trust and fairness nor the impact that these might have on their various categories.

Table 7.1   The Six Perspectives of Cooperation in the Employment Relationship

Perspective	Cooperation means
Critical perspective/ Radicalism	Acquiescence by employees to employer-established goals and practices.
Adversarial Pluralism	Employers, employees and their representatives pursuing their separate goals and compromising with each other in ways that respect the legitimacy of each party's interests.
Collaborative Pluralism	Employers, employees and their representatives working together on mutual goals and compromising on conflicting goals in ways that respect the legitimacy of each party's interests.
Consultative Unitarism	Employers and employees working together on organizational goals, in ways that are established by management through consultation.
Autocratic Unitarism	Employees following managerial directives for serving organizational goals, that in turn also are assumed to benefit employees.
Market perspective/ Egoism	Employers and employees complying with freely entered contractual obligations in self-interested ways.

Source: Bray, M., Budd, J. W., and Macneil, J. (2020) The many meanings of co-operation in the employment relationship and their implications. *British Journal of Industrial Relations*, 58(1), 114-141. John Wiley & Sons Ltd.

News Flash 7.4

BrewDog: Increase in HR Resources

Scottish craft beer giant BrewDog has committed to a major increase in HR resources in response to a review into its allegedly 'toxic' work culture (see News Flash 6.3).

Two new heads are to be appointed. One in leadership and development, tasked with introducing leadership and management development training across the business. The other will be a head of HR operations to cover the company's many sites. Career development reviews are to be introduced alongside new career framework guidelines to make it easier to progress through the company and to build experience.

Source: McCulloch, 2021

Differing interests have an impact on workplace relationships. Information from the 2011 Workplace Employee Relations survey shows that 96% of managers reported good employee relations with their employees, while just 64% of corresponding employees claimed that their relationships with managers were good. Although their loyalty to the organisations they worked for was up from 60% in 2004 to 65% in 2011, it was noticeable that less than half of the employees surveyed felt that managers were good at responding to suggestions and allowing employees to influence workplace decisions (DBIS, 2013). In some organisations, where there has been an attempt to introduce and train staff in **mediation** techniques in order to deal with issues of dissent promptly and informally, increased levels of trust and decreased levels of adversity have been found (Gardner and Cooper-Thomas, 2021; Saundry and Wibberley, 2014; Saundry et al., 2014). Employers wishing to reduce the potential for workplace conflict may choose strategically to introduce measures that enhance **employee engagement** and give employees a degree of voice within the organisation (see Chapters 8, 9 and 10).

Exercise 7.4

'It's Not What You Do It's The Way That You Do It'

Vishal Garg, the CEO of Better, an American digital mortgage company, terminated the employment of around 900 employees during a Zoom call the week before the Christmas break in 2021. Mr Garg told employees they were an 'unlucky group' and, wishing the news were better, he stated that, 'This is the second time in my career I'm doing this, and I do not, do not wanna do this. … The last time I did it, I cried, this time I hope to be stronger'. This isn't the first time Mr Garg has acted in a less than tactful way. In the year prior to this, in a leaked email he sent to staff, he wrote: 'You are TOO DAMN SLOW. You are a bunch of DUMB DOLPHINS … SO STOP IT. STOP IT. STOP IT RIGHT NOW. YOU ARE EMBARRASSING ME' (Khan, 2021).

●   Discuss the first statement, together with Mr Garg's actions, in relation to what you know about trust and conflict within the contested employment relationship.

Addressing Conflict

Incipient, potential and real, expressions of conflict may be addressed in a number of different informal and formal ways ranging from the training of managers to hold 'difficult conversations' through to a raft of different regulatory procedures, some individual, some collective, some leg-islative. Farnham (2000) distinguishes between a range of different conflict-reducing, regulating and solving methods, namely: *managerial action* such as rule making, direct communication with employees, employee involvement and so on; *joint action* between managers and unions such as negotiating, bargaining and consulting; *state regulation for individuals* such as employment protection rights for individual workers, contract of employment requirements and so on; and *state regulation covering collective issues* such as redundancy consultation and restrictions around industrial action.

The degree of power held by an employer influences the ways in which workplace conflict is managed. It is management who set the strategic objectives for the organisation and this will include the ways of managing a workforce, the types of policies and rules, and which managerial style to adopt. Where unions are recognised by an employer they too have an important regulatory impact – for example, they can act as legal regulators (cops), legal advisors or 'entreprunal' problem solvers (Nelson and Nielsen, 2000). On occasion small unions deal with conflict by publicly calling for a judicial review. This occurs particularly when they are faced with a stubborn management and are unwilling to strike against the public (Guillaume, 2018; Guillaume and Kirton, 2017). A trade union workplace-based representative will be knowledgeable about the organisation, know the employees and their likes, dislikes and requirements, and consequently would be able to broker solutions, contributing to conflict management by:

- processing employees' grievances
- representing employees in grievance and disciplinary cases
- discussing planned changes in working arrangements
- passing on management information concerning state of business
- negotiating, interpreting and implementing collective agreements.

Organisational rules, policies and procedures are designed, in part, to diminish conflict by informing the workforce about the behaviours expected of them and encouraging consistency of treatment from managers. Such regulatory constructs are supplemented by employers using a range of communication tools designed to inform their workforces about what is expected from them and, on occasions, allowing employees a degree of voice around workplace issues that affect them (see Table 7.2). The combination of communication plus regulation ensures the interests of the employer are known to the employee and, if utilised appropriately, guarantee that **natural justice** (sometimes known as 'due process') occurs.

Natural justice, a concept that has evolved through case law, imposes a duty on employers to act in a timely way, fairly and without bias, ensuring that their employees have:

- knowledge of expected/required standards/behaviour
- the right to be told if someone has made an allegation against them and what it is
- an opportunity to state their case before a decision is reached
- been informed in good time of their right to appeal.

It is not uncommon to find the principles of natural justice, whether enshrined in statute or embedded in common law, evident in most democratic countries. In Malaysia, for example, where there is no legal process stipulating how to undertake an investigation into misconduct at work, the courts system depends on the common law rules of natural justice (Rajan et al., 2021). In England and Wales, the Employment Rights Act 1999 stipulates that workers have the opportunity to be accompanied to relevant disciplinary meetings by a friend/colleague/union representative and to be given the outcome of the hearing in writing. Folger and Bies (1989) point out that managers have a number of responsibilities when dealing with staff that reinforce and echo the requirements of natural justice, suggesting that managers should:

- give adequate consideration to employee's viewpoints
- suppress biases

- consistently apply decision-making criteria
- provide employees with timely feedback following decisions
- provide justification for the decision
- be truthful when communicating with employees
- treat employees with courtesy and civility.

Information Box 7.1

Avoiding Accusations of Unfair Dismissal

In order to safeguard against accusations of breaching the rules of natural justice employers should, where there is a suspicion of wrongdoing:

- Conduct a reasonable and thorough investigation, collecting all relevant evidence prior to any decision being made before taking any formal action. Anyone involved in the investigation should be reminded not to discuss the allegations with others. (It is prudent to ask the employee to attend an investigation meeting.)
- The employee's invitation to the disciplinary hearing should be in writing, clearly and explicitly delineating the exact allegations together with all evidence to be relied upon. The letter should highlight any likely sanctions should the employee be found guilty.
- Tell the employee of the right to be accompanied at the hearing.
- Allow the employee sufficient time to prepare for the hearing.
- Follow the company procedure/Acas code of practice on discipline and grievance as any deviation could lead to accusations of unfairness.
- It is wise to suspend an employee on full pay pending a full investigation if the allegations against them are for potential gross misconduct because, if they are found guilty, it may be difficult to argue that the employee committed a fundamental breach of contract justifying their dismissal.
- All evidence that the employer intends to rely upon at the disciplinary hearing should be given to the employee in advance of the hearing so that they can prepare a defence.
- Where possible each of the investigation, disciplinary hearing and appeal hearing should be conducted by different people.
- Provide the employee with an opportunity to appeal the disciplinary sanction. (The employee should be advised of the right of appeal in the disciplinary outcome letter.)
- The appeal hearing should be unbiased.
- The outcome should not be a foregone conclusion.
- A full written record should be made of the whole process. If notes are *not* taken, it leaves the details of the meetings open to challenge. All information gathered in relation to the employee should be stored in their personnel file.

News Flash 7.5

Axed for Ambulance Sex

Following sex with a male colleague in an ambulance while it was parked at Portsmouth FC's Fratton Park car park, near to where a blood donation bank was operating, Emma Croydon, an emergency worker, and the male ambulance driver were sacked for inappropriate use of NHS property, conduct likely to damage the reputation of the trust and actions likely to offend patients and other employees. Although she initially denied the charges an investigation revealed CCTV footage showing the ambulance 'swaying from side to side' and evidence from the security guards who found the couple in a 'state of undress' with the man's trousers undone and shoes off. Although both Emma and the male driver were sacked for gross misconduct in April 2019, she appealed the decision, arguing that the South Central Ambulance Service NHS Foundation Trust's procedures were 'flawed' and 'dishonest'. Her dismissal, however, was upheld, the tribunal saying the Trust had followed sound and fair procedures, undertaken a reasonable investigation and that the decision to terminate was within the law.

Source: Croydon v. South Central Ambulance Service NHS Foundation Trust, ET 1403233/2019. Available at: https://assets.publishing.service.gov.uk/media/611baee6e90e070540bae171/Miss_E_Croydon_v_South_Central_Ambulance_Service_NHS_Foundation_Trust_-_1403233.2019_-_Written_Reasons.pdf

The implications of natural justice are far-reaching. Employees have to know the rules and regulations governing the workplace as they cannot be disciplined for behaviour which breaches those rules when they are unaware of the rules in the first place. This is why induction is such an important part of the employment process – it lets new employees know what is required of them – and it is also why many procedures are not just included in staff handbooks but are specifically alluded to by managers when an employee starts a new job. Greenberg (1996, cited in Allan Lind et al., 2000) makes the point that employees need to know what is, and what is not, expected of them because this can affect any subsequent disciplinary actions and, importantly, may also influence perceptions of an organisation's *injustices*, the most negative of which are linked to several forms of inappropriate, difficult or antagonistic organisational behaviour, such as stealing from the organisation. Where employers want to encourage ethical behaviour from their employees, and by doing so help to promote perceptions and levels of trust, it is essential that senior management clearly understand what exactly constitutes wrongdoing and injustice, and the penalties the organisation may suffer if the conduct continues (Markowitz et al., 2021; Near and Miceli, 2008).

The type of organisation, the sector in which it is found, and the make-up of the workforce are all crucial ingredients affecting the extent and types of problems encountered by people at work. These factors in turn help determine how employers organise and regulate their workforce and whether or not managers are likely to find their decisions being challenged. The data from WERS consistently provides evidence for this, for example, larger rather than smaller organisations are more likely to impose disciplinary actions, such as dismissal, on recalcitrant employees (Forth et al., 2006). (This may indicate a greater propensity to resolve things informally in smaller organisations, reflecting the more personal nature of their employment relations – Harris et al., 2008.) Size is not the only factor influencing the ways in which expressions of conflict are dealt with – younger workers are more likely to face some sort of disciplinary action (Casebourne et al., 2006), while those in more skilled occupations, women and older workers have a lower incidence of disciplinary activity (Antcliff and Saundry, 2009; Knight and Latreille, 2000). Workplaces with high proportions of non-white employees have higher rates of disciplinary activity including dismissals and applications to employment tribunals.

News Flash 7.6

UK Workplaces: Sexual Harassment Duty for Employers

A report from the Women and Equalities Committee recommends that the UK government introduce a 'duty' on employers to help prevent sexual harassment in the workplace.

The report's findings show that employers' internal sexual harassment procedures (as well as the employment tribunal system), are insufficiently robust. Additionally, it found that some employers – and legal professionals – unfairly use non-disclosure agreements to silence sexual harassment victims. The Committee concluded that, despite the prevalence of workplace sexual harassment, little has been done to tackle unlawful behaviour. Furthermore, it found that the lack of appropriate support for victims, where the burden falls unacceptably on the individual to hold harassers and employers to account, is unacceptable.

Maria Miller MP, chair of the Women and Equalities Committee, said, 'It is utterly shameful that … unwanted sexual comments, touching, groping and assault are seen as an everyday occurrence and part of the culture in many workplaces'.

Source: House of Commons Women and Equalities Committee, 2018

In the UK, as the number of organisations recognising trade unions has diminished, and as collective representation has declined, the collective mechanisms for containing and dealing with conflict have also declined. This has been coupled with the devolving to line managers a number of additional conflict-solving responsibilities that, in some circumstances, create workplaces with risk-averse cultures where the use of formal, rather than informal, ways of coping with conflict have escalated. This shift to the line has significant consequences for the way that conflict is managed – if line managers are insufficiently experienced in employee relations matters they may lack the confidence and skills required to address 'difficult issues' (Jones and Saundry, 2012, 2016). Light touch, discretionary managerial behaviours tempering employee behaviours are less in evidence, creating what Saundry and Dix call the 'resolution gap' (2014: 465, 485), particularly noticeable where the culture of the workplace results in line managers who are so wary about getting something wrong that they rigidly adhere to the organisation's rules (Saundry et al., 2015).

Increasingly regulatory in nature, procedures could be regarded as unnecessary red tape, yet, when applied, they do ensure consistency and allow managers – and those they manage – to know how to behave in certain circumstances. Lynette Harris, talking at the Fourth Conference on Ethical Issues in Contemporary HR Management, warned that increased opportunities for and incidents of litigation would make employers more defensive: 'the rules of the game becoming more important than the justice of the final outcomes' (CIPD, 2001). She made the point that HR practitioners using a heavily proceduralised approach miss out on investing in interpersonal relationships that are likely to lead to a positive employment relationship and feelings of organisational justice (Deeks, 2001).

Table 7.2   Methods designed to reduce conflict

Methods of downward communication designed to reduce conflict in the ER	Methods of upward communication created to reduce conflict in the ER	Methods of consultation designed to reduce conflict in the ER	Methods of negotiation designed to reduce conflict in the ER
• Induction • Job descriptions • Contract of employment • Team briefing • Company magazine or newsletter – this can be via the intranet or paper based • Appraisals • Total quality management (TQM) • Self–tailored remuneration packages • Employee recognition programmes designed to encourage workplace engagement • A range of procedures to enhance fair processes at work	• Attitude survey • Suggestion scheme • Appraisals • TQM • Teamwork • Self–managed teams • Open–door policies	• Attitude survey • Self–tailored remuneration packages • Local consultation • Joint Consultative Committee (JCC) • Quality circles • Joint working party • Focus group	• Recognition of and negotiation with trade unions and/or works councils • Individual negotiation • Departmental negotiation • Local collective bargaining • National collective bargaining

Some contested workplace behaviour has the potential to be regulated by UK laws, regulations and codes

The last quarter of a century has seen a burgeoning of UK employment legislation, much originating from Europe. The intention behind much of the regulation is to make the employment arena safer and fairer. This has resulted in the encouragement of a range of employment practices that have the potential to reduce some of the conflict between the parties. For example, the UK's Information and

Consultation of Employees Regulations 2004 (dealt with in Chapter 9) and the European Works' Council requirements (covered in Chapter 10) both encourage discussions between employee representatives and employers – the very acts of consulting designed to foster cooperative partnership working rather than adversarial, conflict-ridden, wrangling. Employers and employees are under a regulatory umbrella from the moment an employer composes a job advertisement through to organising retirement. Within the UK there are a number of pieces of legislation that impact on the ways in which the employment relationship is managed: for example, inhibiting excesses of power from either the employer or employee, controlling individual and collective behaviour, outlawing unsafe work practices and, particularly in the financial sector, restricting unethical behaviour. Information Box 7.2 shows a brief outline of a few examples of the legislation that, if followed, is designed to damp down explicit expressions of conflict in the contested workplace. The examples are by no means exhaustive but are intended to give you some idea of some of the relevant restrictions imposed on the parties to the employment relationship that, if followed correctly, should constrain the potential for conflict. For a more detailed look at the legislation, readers are advised to consult Briane's report on key employment rights for the House of Commons Library (2022).

Information Box 7.2

The Main UK Acts Impacting the Employment Relationship

The Health and Safety at Work Act 1964

The Trade Union and Labour Relations (Consolidation) Act 1992

The Pensions Act 1995

The Employment Rights Act 1996

The Human Rights Act 1998

The National Minimum Wage Act 1998

The Employment Relations Act 1999

The Employment Act 2002

The Gangmasters (Licensing) Act 2004

The Work and Families Act 2006

The Employment Act 2008

The Equality Act 2010

The Enterprise and Regulatory Reform Act 2013

Trade Union Act 2016

When legislation is introduced it is often divisive. The alteration of the law by the Coalition government that changed the length of time during which an individual had to be employed before they were entitled to claim unfair dismissal is a case in point. By lengthening the period from one to two years the change was hailed by some as a welcome strengthening of the employers' hand, while others regarded it as a retrograde step that would lead to increased unfairness.

Restrictions on Employers That Could Reduce the Incidence of Conflict

The Equality Act 2010 disallows gender, race, disability and religious discrimination, from advertising vacancies, designing and implementing workplace activities, schedules, programmes and so on, through to terminating employment. An employer is not permitted to discriminate in an unlawful way. Such restrictions are designed to ensure fairness and, if followed, should reduce potential levels of conflict and enhance perceptions of organisational justice.

Similarly, the Employment Rights Act 1996 provides a range of safeguards for employees, imposing restrictions on the ways in which employers can act. We saw in Chapter 4, for example, how the ways in which contracts of employment are drawn up (and executed) are influenced by this particular piece of legislation. Contract law is designed to ensure that an employee is aware of, and has agreed to, the terms and conditions of their employment. This means that before they start work there should be no confusion about what they will be doing, where they will be doing it, the hours that are required and the remuneration they are to receive. Such clarity is designed, in part, to regulate the relationship and, importantly, to reduce the potential areas of contestation: employees, for example, are expected to undertake the work that they have agreed to do and employers are not expected to ask their workforce to undertake tasks outside the remit of the contract. However, because the nature of work undertaken evolves over time, it is apparent that although such measures may inhibit conflict they are no guarantee of its prevention. Under the implied contract terms employers have a duty of care towards their employees and this too, in an ideal environment, will help to promote a workplace that is safe, both mentally *and* physically, for the workforce, thereby once again reducing the opportunities for some areas of work to be contested and conflictual.

This Act stipulates that each employee has to receive a written statement of their terms and conditions and that this must include information about the organisation's disciplinary and grievance procedures and where they might be found. Although not overtly reducing conflict, this provision 'encourages' employers to put such procedures in place and to follow them, thereby institutionalising the ways in which conflicts can be managed, reducing the opportunity for inconsistent treatment and enhancing perceptions of procedural justice. Acas (2015, 2020) provides guidance and a Code on disciplinary and grievance procedures; it is not obligatory for employers to adhere to its recommendations; however, failure to do so will be taken into consideration in any subsequent tribunal hearing or appeal, although this is not so in Northern Ireland. The Code reinforces the requirement under the Employment Relations Act 1999 (s.10), which obliges employers to allow someone being disciplined to be accompanied by a trade union representative or work colleague at a disciplinary hearing, a measure designed to help redress power imbalances and create a fairer, less conflictual environment when differences are being discussed.

Fitzner (2006: 16) has pointed out that every year 'technically' about a million and a half employees have their employment terminated. Of course, many of these terminations are quite legal, but some are not, because they have been conducted in an unfair way. This act allows those employees who feel their contracts have been unfairly terminated to take a case to an employment tribunal. By regulating what is – and what is not – lawful, the existence of the

Act helps to constrain unfair unilateral acts of dismissal by employers. This Act also (ss.139(1)) makes provision for employers to make employees redundant providing that the organisation or workplace is closing or if there is a reduced requirement for employees to carry out the work that they have been doing. The legislation restricts the ways in which employers behave and stipulates the requirements for consulting with employee representatives. The aim of the legislation is to redress the balance of power so that the employee is not completely voiceless and without rights. In this way it regulates some of the expressions of dissent that always surround redundancy situations.

Health and safety legislation and its associated regulations prohibit and constrain the ways in which many industrial chemicals and processes may be used, additionally setting standards and controls for the use of equipment and manpower. In terms of employment this obviously fosters workplaces that are less hazardous for those who work in them and *ipso facto* less exploitative. Specifically, the Health and Safety at Work Act 1964 places a duty on employers to provide for, as far as practical, the health, safety and welfare of those whom they employ, and since 1992 employers have been required to consult with workplace representatives about the health and safety implications of any changes that they might want to introduce – this arrangement, giving representatives a voice, is designed to diminish, not increase, workplace conflict. The Working Time Regulations 1998 discourage employers from imposing lengthy periods of working and requires them to provide adequate numbers of breaks and holidays. These regulations provide workers who feel aggrieved about the time spent at work with a means of redress should their employer require them to work additional hours when they have not signed a waiver.

The Work and Families Act 2006 extends some of the provisions in the Employment Act 2002. It extends parental leave for parents of children up to the age of 18, gives the right to ask for flexible working to all employees, requires employers to provide paid shared maternity (and paternity) leave and give unpaid time off to parents for ante-natal appointments (the Children and Families Act 2014 also makes provision for shared parental leave). In April 2020, employed parents were given the right to two weeks' bereavement leave following the death of a child. The introduction of these provisions may not have explicitly reduced areas of conflict within the employment relationship, but their enabling impact allows employees to feel more comfortable about taking something that is a 'right' rather than a discretionary favour.

Examples of Legal Restrictions to Reduce Conflict

In June 2021 the European Court of Human Rights made it clear that the right to strike takes precedence over the 'economic freedoms' of the single market, thereby confirming that striking workers' rights take precedence. In the UK however there is no legal right to strike (it would be a breach of the contract of employment) unless the striking individual is a member of a trade union taking action in 'contemplation or furtherance of an industrial dispute' (The Trade Union and Labour Relations (Consolidation) Act 1992: s.219). This immunity is null and void if the strike is unofficial; that is, if it has not been called in accordance with the procedures set out in the sections 226A to 239 of the Act. These sections lay down quite a complicated formula for union behaviour, ensuring that their proposed strike action is 'official' and proscribing behaviour during the dispute. Prior to any strike activity the members involved in the dispute must be balloted (by post). The ballot for industrial action must:

- be held before the union asks members to take or continue taking action
- be open to all members the union wants to take action
- be supervised by a qualified independent person if over 50 members are being balloted
- return the postal vote in a prepaid envelope
- include information on what the ballot is about and provide information about the deadline for voting
- give the employer one week's notice of the start of the ballot – and tell them the result as soon as possible afterwards.

The processes are time-consuming and ensure that the strike action takes place some time after the cause of the dispute, the delay intended to 'take the heat' out of a situation. Furthermore the process of postal voting is expensive – something designed to make unions think twice before calling for action. This Act (s.220) also gives protection to a limited number of peaceful pickets (six) who, because they are acting in connection with an industrial dispute at or near their workplace, are permitted to tell others why they are striking and attempt to persuade them to abstain from working.

These restrictions, designed to inhibit explicit acts of collective conflict, have evolved and changed over the years, recurrently constraining and reducing the power of collective labour and, many would argue, ensuring that the balance of power lies with the employer and not the workforce.

Procedures and Their Impact on the Employment Relationship

In order to achieve consistency of treatment and to guide line managers along the right routes for dealing with those under their charge – in an equitable and fair way – many organisations develop a range of policies and codes of behaviour often backed up by rules and regulations (known as 'procedures') that are designed to channel the processing of behaviours (such as poor performance), requests (for such things as maternity/compassionate/annual leave) and complaints (such as staff grievances) in ways that are relatively even-handed, standardised and managed without bias.

Procedures are exactly what they say they are: processes for moving forward. Within the employee relations arena they detail the ways in which managers and employees ought to behave, indicating what is and what is not acceptable and laying down the ways in which people are expected to act at particular stages in certain situations and, naturally enough, what will happen if they do not and how they might appeal a decision with which they are unhappy. Such processes work towards helping managers in a variety of ways, from record keeping to ensuring consistent treatment of employees. As such they are one of the main mechanisms for containing, controlling and channelling employee expressions of conflict within the contested relationship, fundamentally helping to maintain a balance of power.

Expectations, obligations, pathways and sanctions are all outlined and defined within procedures, rather like board games that dictate 'you have failed to accomplish A, go to square X'. Procedures set out the ways of applying the rules that govern the employment relationship. They dictate the processes of behaviour – what is expected, who does what to whom and when – and are, in effect, a part of each organisation's 'constitution', comprising sets of regulatory mechanisms dictating how policies and codes must be implemented in the workplace. Procedures, importantly, inform the parties of their rights and obligations while making clear the sanctions that they may expect if regulations have been breached. Employees are given a number of rights – such as the right to raise a grievance – as well as a number of responsibilities such as not to bring the organisation into disrepute. Where there are potential issues of conflict, procedures will indicate the route to follow in order to gain resolution.

As with much of employee relations, field procedures are a by-product of the process of power regulation. Statute, of course, plays a part here but, even under the umbrella of legal constraints constricting employer/employee behaviour, workplaces use procedures to encourage and promote voluntary restraints of power, and hence behaviour, in order that anarchy does not ensue.

Modern employee relations procedures are a product of:

- historical precedent
- unilateral managerial action
- legal requirements and the need to avoid legal sanctions
- negotiation between secondary parties to the employment relationship
- an agreement between an organisation and an insurance company covering employee relationship matters
- off-the-peg solutions provided by consultancy companies
- publicity and fashion (for example it has become 'on trend' to produce menopause procedures following an increased awareness campaign)
- the desire to ensure consistency of treatment across the workplace, particularly now that so much has been 'devolved to the line'
- an awareness that the ways in which people perceive that they have been treated has an impact upon organisational performance
- previous results of collective bargaining agreements
- a history of industrial unrest, past strike activity and tribunal claims
- a pre-emptive strike by employers to ensure that when the employment relationship enters difficulties managers will know how to respond appropriately
- a desire to incorporate the principles of fairness and natural justice into the processes of employment
- a desire to show corporate social responsibility and thereby attract and retain staff; for example, Adecco Alfred Marks Ltd approached and then invited the union CWU to represent its staff – the subsequent recognition agreement between the company and union was cited by the company as an example of its fair processes
- the need to comply with conditions imposed by service level agreements with other organisations; for example, it is not unknown for organisations tendering for work with public sector organisations to provide evidence that they use a range of policies and procedures covering such things as diversity, flexibility and so on.

Inevitably procedures reflect the mores of the country, culture and time in which they operate. Any shifts from organising the workforce collectively to individually, as well as moves away from legally imprecise regulation towards the more legally precise, are echoed in the ways that workplaces are regulated and the procedures that underpin such regulation. The procedures that are in use today are a product of what has gone before, some enshrining, some eschewing, habits, values, processes and regulations that were relevant in previous employee relations eras – often each generation tries to redress and address the problems of the one before. This can be seen, for example, by the ways in which equal opportunity procedures have, over time, morphed into those advocating inclusivity, intersectionality and dignity at work, or by the ways in which alternative ways of resolving disputes, such as mediation, have been incorporated into the processes of domestic dispute resolution. Procedures, by their very nature, have an impact upon the ways in which employees interact and upon the employment relationship. Procedural efficacy goes to the heart of the ways in which individual workplaces operate and organise the employment relationship, with a consequent effect on perceptions of fairness, employee morale and productivity.

Historically, employers could treat employees pretty much as they wanted, often demanding long hours and hard work in unsafe conditions with very little remuneration. There were, for example, in the UK, Europe, the USA and Australia a number of responses to this situation:

* The law intervened in order to control recognised excesses (the Factory Act 1961 in England and Wales, for example, placed restrictions on the types of work that could be done by women and children, while currently the European Working Time Directive restricts the numbers of hours that people may legally be required to work over specified periods). Employers now endeavour to comply with the law by not behaving in a range of discriminatory ways, ranging from racial prejudice to sacking someone merely because they belong to a union, while the act of whistleblowing is protected from retribution by employers – perpetrators are protected both from victimisation and dismissal. Such legal protection does not just encompass a list of prohibitions. Sometimes, rather than inhibit behaviour, the law encourages it by requiring employers to act in ways that promote a fairer, safer environment. Such positive legal requirements impacting on the employment relationship include the requirement to consult representatives when collective redundancies, or transfers of undertakings, are likely and the creation of workplace health and safety committees. Organisations in the UK and Europe are legally required to ensure that they have in place fair grievance and disciplinary procedures that comply with the rules of natural justice.
* Trade unions negotiated with the employers for better working arrangements for their members, reaching deals that were usually enshrined in written agreements. Such agreements were either procedural (the 'how' of the arrangements delineating bargaining groups, frequency of meetings, topics to be talked about, which employees were affected, what to do when the parties to the negotiations could not agree, etc.) or substantive (the 'what' of the arrangements, recording the outcomes of the negotiations – defining pay, hours, conditions, benefits, etc.). Such agreements, regarded as the cornerstone of collective bargaining by Jenkins and Sherman (1977), are commonplace in organisations where unions are recognised for collective bargaining and consultative purposes.

- Employers saw consistency and fairness as a way of gaining and improving employee engagement, commitment and hence productivity, while conversely, unfair practices and inconsistency were seen as demotivating, leading to higher levels of employee turnover and potential litigation – both costly to the organisation.
- The realisation that treating people well had a direct impact on the bottom line led to an adoption of HRM and high-commitment workplace practices.
- The introduction into the workplace of a number of procedures (regardless of whether a union was recognised or not) to ensure that conflict was minimised and that production maximised in ways that did not incur costs.

The belief that procedures curb unrest is, in many ways, rather simplistic: the assumption that if procedures are introduced then the numbers of disputes would automatically decrease is open to criticism. It is rather like assuming that by increasing the availability of checkouts in a store shoplifting would decrease.

Where there are differences of interest, despite the presence of robust procedural agreements, there are likely to be incidents of disagreement that could result in expressions of conflict leading to disputes. For example, despite following the negotiating procedures agreed between Transport for London (TfL) and the four rail unions – RMT, ASLEF, TSSA and Unite – from the summer of 2015 until the time of writing (spring 2023) there were regular tube strikes in London. The unions concerned were extremely unhappy with, amongst other things, the proposals to bring in an all-night tube service on some lines. The proposed plans changed shift patterns, something the unions considered detrimental to the work–life balance of their members. The commencement date for the new service, announced by the London Mayor, allowed insufficient time for negotiation, but was advantageous to the unions enabling pressure to be exerted on the employer who was, because of the public announcement, under tight time constraints. The strike activity encouraged TfL to continue talks, with the help of Acas.

Despite the presence of procedures there can still be expressions of conflict ranging from individual grievances to strike activity. Not all strike activity is over collective issues, sometimes collective action can be used to put pressure on an employer to alter the way in which an individual has been dealt with. The RMT union, for example, called two strikes in 2014 against Transport for London (December and the following March) in support of one of its tube drivers, a diabetic, who had shown an unacceptable level of alcohol in his blood, and was subsequently dismissed. The case exhausted the disciplinary procedure, going through all appropriate stages, including appeals, as well as a separate independent director's review, but the union remained unhappy with the result. As the RMT Regional Organiser explained, hand-held machines can give false positive readings: 'The current system is unfair because it doesn't offer safeguards to those with disabilities or who are on certain diets' (*BBC News*, 2015b). Those who voted for the strike were aware that the procedure had been followed, but feelings of procedural injustice were invoked despite adherence to the procedures because of the 'unfair' way in which the original matter was not addressed to their satisfaction. As Kim and Mauborgne point out,

> When employees don't trust managers to make good decisions or to behave with integrity, their motivation is seriously compromised. Their distrust and its attendant lack of engagement is a huge, unrecognized problem in most organizations (2003: 126)

There is some evidence to show that employees perform better, with higher productivity and morale, when they know that the regulatory procedures deployed at their specific workplace are fair, indicating that, in many ways, procedures are more than the sum of their parts. That is, where procedures are in place – and importantly, are *seen* to be fair – the resulting effect at the workplace is not just one of an environment in which everyone is treated with consistency in a just way, but one in which the perceptions of fairness have a direct and real influence on the ways in which people interact and hence on the productivity of the organisation. Procedures therefore play an important part in establishing a favourable psychological contract.

Exercise 7.5

- Discuss the following statement: 'People care about the decisions you make, but they care even more about the process you used along the way'. Say why you think this is important within the employment relationship.
- Justify your answer by using academic concepts.

The struggle for control of the workplace has the effect of promoting the use of procedures – both unions and management often regarding them as a check on the power of the other while simultaneously ensuring that all employees are aware of the workplace rules and what would happen if they were flouted. Gospel and Palmer (1993: 212) argue that union representatives like procedures because the arrangement legitimises their position and increases their effectiveness. Yet following procedures is sometimes not enough to redress the balance of power and further action occurs.

Just having a procedure, however, does not mean that it is always followed, or always followed in the same way. In the 1960s, for example, negotiators at Ford UK used to have a blue book of rules to which both sides were supposed to adhere. Often negotiations would begin by one side or the other asking, 'Is the blue book on, or under, the table?'. The answer would dictate whether the ensuing negotiations were 'played by the book' or whether negotiators cut corners in order to reach a deal acceptable to all parties. Currently in many organisations where line managers are responsible for ensuring that procedures are followed it is not unknown for different managers to have different interpretations of the same set of regulations, leading to inconsistent treatment of employees and instances of unfairness. There is evidence that the existence of workplace anti-bullying policies is no guarantee of a proactive managerial approach towards prevention, or of actually prioritising the lack of tolerance towards bullying (Rayner and Lewis, 2020). Indeed, it is not unheard of for HR managers to have different 'understandings' of the contents of an anti-bullying policy from its actual substance.

In a study of Canadian workplaces, Colvin (2004) found that where managements initiated workplace voice mechanisms and encouraged employee involvement there were lower incidences of formal grievances in unionised workplaces, yet where these mechanisms were absent the levels of formal workplace grievances were unaffected by either the presence or absence of a union. Pollert and Charlwood's 2009 research in the UK looking at grievance handling for low-waged, non-unionised workers found that informal methods of settlement were largely ineffectual, with just under one-third of respondents saying that their problem had been resolved, and only half of these actually satisfied with the outcome. In 2014, Charlwood and Pollert found that informal methods for resolving less serious grievances and complaints, where voice mechanisms were present, led to greater levels of satisfaction with the outcome and lower levels of intention to leave, thus indicating a higher level of perceived organisational justice (Charlwood and Pollert, 2014).

Exercise 7.6

- What are, do you think, the employee relations implications for those organisations where procedures are non-existent, poorly written or applied in an *ad hoc* fashion?
- Why did you reach these conclusions?

Types of Procedures

Procedures are many and varied, some stand alone and others are integrated into organisational policies and agreements. All should adhere to the principles of natural justice, although occasionally they do not.

The most common procedures are those concerned with the ways in which discipline and grievances are dealt with. Such procedures stand alone but may be referred to by other policy documents. So, for example, where an organisation has policies concerned with dignity at work or whistleblowing, there are often provisions included so that when breaches occur there is a direct link to the company's disciplinary or grievance procedures. Indeed, many grievance procedures now echo this trend and include sections specifically setting out the pathways in the event of specific complaints – sexual harassment by an immediate superior, for example, will often have a separate section detailing to whom the complainant should go for help.

Many organisations will have a separate procedure that they follow in case of redundancies, and often where unions are recognised there will be a procedure that is used to control patterns of behaviour prior to and during a dispute. There will be procedures concerning the amount of information to be given to a union and how it will be disseminated and how collective bargaining will be undertaken. All of these are designed to ensure consistency of treatment for the workforce and to reduce the inflammatory nature of conflicts of interest, channelling the disputants towards a solution.

Some procedures are designed to help wellbeing and good health and, when applied appropriately, these aid perceptions of procedural justice. But sometimes good intentions have a negative impact, allowing some, but not all, employees behavioural leeway that may create perceptions of distributional injustice. The Spanish Government has just (2022) introduced a draft bill making provision for several days paid menstrual leave per month, for women suffering period pain, etc. (To some this may seem revolutionally but countries like Japan and Indonesia have had laws in place facilitating menstrual leave since the middle of last century and Zambia introduced similar legislation in 2017.) If the Spanish proposals become law, it remains to be seen whether there will be an outcry from those unable to take such leave.

Information Box 7.3

The following list shows some of the types of procedures operating within organisations. Sometimes such procedures will stand alone and at others be incorporated into a separate policy or code.

Discipline/dismissal
Grievances
Redundancy
Collective disputes, industrial action
Bargaining/negotiating/consulting arrangements with a union or staff association
Consultation and the dissemination of information
Mediation
Whistleblowing
Data protection
Email/social media/telephone use
Accepting gifts and gratuities
Seeking and granting flexible work
Leave arrangements that are not covered by annual leave
Training
Health and safety issues
Workplace security
Surveillance of employees
Internal promotions, secondments, transfers
Use of company facilities
Lone working
Absence
Smoking, substance abuse
Bullying
Violence, whether perpetrated by a fellow employee or a customer/client
Workplace-related stress
Sexual relationships between members of staff/competitors/customers
Procedures to do with reward:
    Timing and frequency of changes
    Job evaluation/re-evaluation
    Flexible benefit allocation and claims
Recruitment
Resignations
Relocation

(Continued)

Financial organisations will have tight procedures linked to fraud, confidentiality and insider trading.

Health related organisations will have numerous procedures detailing patient care, treatment of 'spare' body parts, drug use and so on. (Where such procedures are regarded as unnecessary, or perhaps too lax, this will have an impact upon the psychological contract with a consequent influence on employee relations and possibly on retention and recruitment.)

Defence and armaments-related organisations will have tight procedures to do with health and safety, confidentiality and data security.

It is apparent that organisations are converging in matters of conflict management (Carroll et al., 2019), in particular tightening up on regulating employee behaviour, ensuring legal compliance and using methods such as non-disclosure agreements to maintain secrecy about their actions. Many organisations in the UK protect themselves by following Acas codes and guidance and by using at least three formal stages within the disciplinary and grievance processes.

Exercise 7.7

Read Case Study 7.1 and analyse how the Council:

- might move forward, taking into account both its need to maintain its reputation while continuing to provide a positive employment relationship for its employees
- might respond to UNISON, and in particular what its bargaining strategy might entail
- tackles its employees' perceptions of organisational justice
- avoids 'survivor syndrome' should redundancies occur.

Case Study 7.1

A Metropolitan Council

Affected by government-imposed austerity measures, this Metropolitan Council reached (what it regards as) a regrettable decision to make cuts in some of its services. This is not popular. The Council serves an area of severe deprivation where unemployment – particularly youth unemployment – is high, where there is an aging population, which has a disproportionate impact on the local health services, and where there are acute housing shortages. The Council prides itself on its innovative practices and ability to deliver quality services on a 'shoe string', yet its 'shoe string' approach seems now to have left it with little alternative other than to outsource some functions and cut others entirely from its portfolio of offerings. It is more than likely that there will be redundancies. The need to make cuts has therefore come as an unwanted, if not unexpected, response to government demands.

How the Council makes the cuts is yet to be decided. The way forward seems to be to outsource a number of functions, particularly those to do with some of its day-to-day functions such as refuge collection alongside the services connected to health and wellbeing. These functions are grouped under what the Council calls 'The Hub', and it is apparent that no less than 80 jobs will have to be shed from at least two of the largest departments within The Hub. There have been fierce discussions in the Council chamber and back offices around the degree of job losses necessary, and the departments from which they are to be shed. Whether a single department can be outsourced, or whether jobs and functions can be rationalised and redundancies spread across the board, leaving all departments in-house but with depleted staff, has been hotly debated. No one wants their area or department to be targeted. The staff have, in the main, been left in the dark. Some supervisors, fearing that they might have to account for the ways in which they resource their departments, have begun to take more of a hands-on approach, monitoring their staff closely and imposing stringent constraints on their departmental budgets. Discretionary effort has become non-existent. The mood of uncertainty has affected morale and a disproportionate amount of time seems to be spent on discussing 'what might happen' rather than actually getting on with the day-to-day Council work. This, of course, increases the pressure on supervisors who are becoming frustrated, tightening up on control while understanding the reasons behind the drops in productivity.

UNISON, the union representing the majority of the staff, has begun to mobilise them against the cuts, even though, as yet nothing has been finalised. The union is talking to local community groups to gain their support - it hopes that, should strike action become necessary, the community will put pressure on councillors to ignore the government strictures. It fears that wholesale cuts will decimate local services, that once lost to the Council these functions will never be resumed, and that any redundancies will leave many of its members unemployed and unable, in the current job market, to get alternative work. It has made representations to the Council and insisted that talks about alternative ways of dealing with government pressure take place immediately. So far it has not had a response.

Exercise 7.8

* Read the scenario below and make an assessment, taking into account the 'points to consider', about whether Joseph Green was treated with due process. Justify your reasoning with academic sources.

Out of the Frame

Joseph Green, a 36-year-old administrative assistant with a history of mental health problems, worked for a small photographic processing company, In the Picture, based in a small Staffordshire town. In general he was regarded as a productive member of the team running the general office – although colleagues sometimes found him a little odd.

Over the past 18 months his attendance pattern at the office had been slightly erratic and on a number of occasions his abrupt manner upset some of the women in his department. His supervisor had had 'informal chats' about these instances, along with those of loud and intrusive humming, especially when he was concentrating, but nothing formal was ever put in motion – colleagues were aware of his history and made allowances.

One morning last February he arrived at work with an assortment of sharp-bladed knives that he ostentatiously arranged next to the PC on his desk. He was dismissed on the spot and sent home immediately.

(Continued)

Later that day his colleagues cleared his desk, sorting the personal belongings from those that belonged to In the Picture. During this process they came upon an unlabelled CD-Rom. Unsure of whether it belonged to the company or to Joseph, they inserted it in the PC and played it. It was apparent that it contained explicit pornographic images, upon which an image of the head of his supervisor had been superimposed.

Mr Green claimed he was dismissed unfairly and that discovering and running the CD was a breach of his privacy and Human Rights. Not only this, he claimed that bringing knives to work was normal and even if it hadn't been, the company should have made allowances under the Equality Act 2010.

Points to consider

Contents of CD:

- No evidence (yet) that the contents had been downloaded, manipulated or displayed on the company machine – is this important?
- Would the outcome rest on whether the company had a dignity at work or an anti-harassment and bullying policy?

Unfair dismissal:

- Was the procedure fair?
- Was he given the opportunity to take the knives home?
- Was he given the opportunity to answer allegations before he was told to leave the building?
- Did the previous warnings carry any weight?

Legislation such as the Equality Act 2010 and the Human Rights Act:

- Had the company made sufficient allowance for his disability?
- Was his behaviour linked to his disability?
- Was the company correct in looking at the CD contents?

Alternative Dispute Resolution

In many organisations, increasing attention has been given to trying to solve issues of work-place conflict by deploying informal, **alternative dispute resolution** (ADR) methods prior to embarking on recognised procedures. (In the USA, atypically, ADR clauses have often been included in employment contracts, since the 1990s – Jagtenberg and de Roo, 2018.) Systems of ADR (e.g., mediation and conciliation) are used in particular to diminish the confrontational, and often explicitly adversarial, aspects of grievance and disciplinary procedures. Adherence to traditional regulatory processes sometimes leads to the participants becoming locked into win–lose scenarios, occasionally ending in litigation. Under ADR the participants engage in activities that concentrate less on apportioning blame and more on the promotion of techniques that repair impaired workplace relationships (Acas, 2011). Moreover such processes tend to be confidential and allow solutions to be tailored to individual requirements without 'precedent setting' for the rest of the organisation (Cooper et al., 2005). Feng and Xie (2020) found, unsurprisingly, that, in China, employees were more likely to opt for mediation when they trusted the organisation to choose its mediators in a fair way. There is evidence for a global increase in ADR usage – see surveys by Acas, 2011 and 2012. Its increasing prevalence can be seen in, for example, Ireland (Roche, 2021; Teague et al., 2020), Wales (Hann et al., 2019), Northern Ireland (Nash and Hann, 2021), the USA (Stipanowich and Lamare, 2013) and Australia (McKenzie, 2012).

Oni-Ojo et al. (2014: 66) describe a number of different alternative dispute mechanisms; in particular they look at:

- **Facilitation**: where a third party attempts to enable smoother emotion-free communication between the disputants in order that they might reach a resolution acceptable to them both.
- **Conciliation**: where a neutral third party acts as a conduit, passing relevant information between the disputing parties in order to establish common ground so that they re-establish direct communication with a view to solving their differences.
- **Mediation**: where a third independent party helps the parties to reach their own agreed solution to their differences by guiding discussion and making appropriate suggestions.
- **Peer review**: whereby a panel of employees, often with someone from HR to facilitate, listen to the disputed parties and make a ruling on, or recommendation about, the conflicted issue. Such systems are more likely to occur in the USA than the UK and are often used as a way of signposting to employees and managers that the organisation operates in a procedurally just way – knowing that contested decisions will go before the panel encourages managers to perform to the required standards and acts as a check on unorthodox behaviours. However, the decision-making powers of a review panel are often limited to *strictly* interpreting existing organisational regulations – reinforcing that the balance of power lies with the employer – nevertheless employees perceive them to be fair while managers approve of the system because it reinforces managerial actions but creates an environment whereby employees are apt to blame the panel, and not managers, for the imposition of any disciplinary actions (Cooper et al., 2005; Wilensky and Jones, 1994).
- **Arbitration**: whereby a neutral third party hears evidence from both sides about the contested activity and makes a decision that in most cases is not only the final decision, with no opportunity to appeal, but binding on the parties. (Oni-Ojo et al. do not discuss pendulum arbitration whereby the arbitrator hears the evidence but the subsequent decision has to come down on the side of one or other of the contestants, with no opportunity to make a decision that is mid-way between the parties to the dispute.) Arbitration is often the last resort when collective disputes have reached an impasse.
- **Negotiation**: this process of bargaining between the parties, or more often between the representatives of the parties, is the usual way of settling collective disputes where trade unions are recognised for bargaining purposes. Ridley-Duff and Bennett point out that in the UK 'as collective cultures are eroded, there is an increased likelihood that collective grievances will have to be expressed through individualised forms of action, and that

management control will be exercised through disciplinary actions against individuals'
(2011: 1), with the consequence that incidents of negotiation as a form of ADR will decline
and those of mediation and conciliation in particular will increase. This view is echoed by
Acas (2014), who note that it is the channels through which conflict is managed, resolved
and dealt with that have become more individual over recent years, while Antcliff and
Saundry (2009) show a clear association with falling union density and increased rates of
disciplinary activity and dismissals.

In the UK the government has, since the Gibbons Review in 2006, placed additional emphasis on
workplace mediation and conciliation, in part to try to take pressure off the increasingly congested
and expensive employment tribunal system. Since April 2014 it has been a legal requirement for
Acas to provide pre-tribunal conciliation for parties who are intending to be involved in a tribunal
claim; thereby providing the opportunity to settle disputes in a cheaper, faster way. (The Acas
2020–21 annual report clearly indicates the success of such conciliation: in the period covered by
the report over 500 collective conciliation cases and nearly 115,000 requests for individual conciliation were dealt with. Roughly 1,860 of its weekly 2,000 cases were settled, or not progressed,
only 7% resulting in an ET hearing – Acas, 2021:2.)

Mediation too is being encouraged by the government, influenced in part by academic evidence indicating that it is cheaper and less disruptive to time and workplace relationships than
traditional adversarial methods for settling disputes, and in part because of evidence of how effective mediation techniques are for reconciling the parties to workplace disputes in the USA and
Australia. Despite such encouragement, the data from the last Workplace Employment Relations
Survey (DBIS, 2013) shows that during the 12 months prior to the survey being undertaken, only
6% of workplaces had deployed mediation techniques to help settle conflict (van Wanrooy et al.,
2013). Bennett, in his 2013 research in the North of England, found important differences in the
take-up of this form of dispute resolution across different sectors. Pluralist organisations, such as
cooperatives and public sector organisations, were more likely to use mediation than unitarist private sector ones. Yet the very act of mediation often individualises conflict, emphasises the individual and at times sits more comfortably within the unitarist perspective. The evidence of 'successful'
mediation within the UK is sparse and raises the questions about 'success for whom?' and what
success actually means in this context. Is it regarded as successful by management, for example,
because it has saved time, or circumvented a court case, or individualised a more collective generic
problem? There are dangers in regarding workplace mediation as a cure-all solution.

ADR is regarded as a particularly useful tool for maintaining a healthy employment relationship because not only does it offer cheaper, and frequently speedier, solutions but, according to
Blackard (2001), such systems also help build trust by exposing the possibility that, on occasions,
management too is vulnerable and willing to cede power in order to achieve an effective resolution of the contested issues. Blackard also points out that where organisations are known to
operate ADR, this can be connected with perceptions of enhanced, and positive, diversity management which in turn are linked to positive perceptions of fairness and organisational justice,
employees and prospective employees assuming that the employing (ADR operative) organisation must value the expression of different viewpoints since it has ensured there are processes
whereby employees can work out their differences in a safe respectful way. This suggests that
ADR helps foster workplace cultures where women and minorities prefer to work because they
feel that any contested issues will be managed in an appropriately fair way.

- Given that ADR takes into account differing viewpoints, is it practical for a unitary management to adopt ADR?
- Justify your answer using academic arguments and practical examples.

Summary

It is clear that employers and employees operate within a contested relationship because they have different interests, expectations and objectives (**divergent employment practices**). Divergent interests can lead to discontent and expressions of conflict that need to be regulated within the workplace. The managerial perspectives and styles in operation will have a significant impact on the ways in which this is done, as will the balance of power within an organisation. Legislation, codes and workplace rules, regulations and procedures, together with the degree of voice and engagement, play a part in conflict reduction, regulation and resolution. The processes, systems and mechanisms for dealing with conflict and the ways in which they are deployed are crucial components to the ways in which employees perceive organisational justice and may, if deployed incorrectly, exacerbate rather than reduce dissent.

Review Questions

1 What do you think managers need to do in order to minimise the incidence of conflict in their organisation?
2 What contribution could a) HR, b) unions and c) legislation make to both the avoidance and resolution of conflict?
3 What skills do you think HR and line managers need to develop in order to deal with conflict in the workplace?
4 How might an ethical workplace contribute to minimising expressions of workplace conflict? Justify your answer with reference to academic concepts and models.

Revision Exercise 7.1

Read the paragraph below and then decide, with reasons:

- whether the employer's laissez-faire attitude was appropriate and ethical, or not, in the circumstances
- how the employer might have ensured organisational justice when dealing with the situation
- How the employer should have dealt with the situation.

(Continued)

A report from a West of Scotland Citizens Advice Bureau documented the case of a lone female, with three years continuous employment at a garage, taking sick leave due to work-related stress triggered by workplace bullying, harassment and persistent humiliation by the mechanic and apprentices at the garage who repeatedly commented on her appearance and weight in a disparaging way. Despite frequent complaints to her employer nothing changed, her employer insisting that the individuals concerned sort their differences out between them, making it clear that if she remained unhappy she would be the one to leave employment as the mechanic was crucial for the success of the business. (Later it became apparent that her employer paid half her wages in cash, and did not pay her income tax or National Insurance, which affected her entitlement to Statutory Sick Pay.)

Source: Citizen's Advice Scotland, 2015

Relevant Articles for Further Reading

Acas (2014) 'Managing conflict at work'. Available at: www.acas.org.uk/media/pdf/i/d/Managing-conflict-at-work-advisory-booklet.pdf (accessed 5 October 2015), together with
Acas (2014) *Reframing Resolution – Managing Conflict and Resolving Individual Employment Disputes in the Contemporary Workplace*, Acas Policy Discussion Paper. London: Acas.

Both of these practitioner documents give a good grounding in the ways in which conflict can best be dealt with at work.

Doherty, L. and Teague, P. (2012) 'Conflict management systems in subsidiaries of non-union multinational organizations located in the Republic of Ireland', *International Journal of Human Resource Management*, 22(1): 57–71.

Looking at 83 non-unionized multinational companies based in Ireland, the authors examine the proliferation of HRM practices and the less adversarial ways of managing workplace dissent.

Saundry, R., Fisher, V. and Kinsey, S. (2021) 'Disconnected human resource? Proximity and the (mis) management of workplace conflict', *Human Resource Management Journal*, 31(2): 476–92.

This is an interesting article looking at the ways in which conflict management has become that much more bureaucratic and formalised as a direct result of increased functional specialization.

References

Acas (2011) *Acas Mediation 2010/11: Responses From Participants and Commissioners*. London: Acas.
Acas (2012) *Acas Individual Mediation 2011/12: Responses From Participants and Commissioners*. London: Acas.
Acas (2014) *Reframing Resolution – Managing Conflict and Resolving Individual Employment Disputes in the Contemporary Workplace*. London: Acas.

Acas (2015) *Code of Practice 1 – Disciplinary and Grievance Procedures*. Norwich: The Stationery Office. Available at: www.acas.org.uk/media/pdf/f/m/Acas-Code-of-Practice-1-on-disciplinary-and-grievance-procedures.pdf (accessed 6 October 2015).

Acas (2020) *Discipline and Grievances at Work: The Acas Guide*. Available at: www.acas.org.uk/sites/default/files/2021-03/discipline-and-grievances-at-work-the-acas-guide.pdf (accessed 2 February 2022).

Acas (2021) *Annual Report and Accounts 2020-21*. Available at: https://assets.publishing.service.gov.uk/government/uploads/system/uploads/attachment_data/file/1002534/acas-ara-2020-2021-accessible.pdf (accessed 4 January 2022).

Allan Lind, E. (2001) 'Fairness heuristic theory: Justice judgments as pivotal cognitions in organizational relations', in J. S. Greenberg and R. Cropanzano (eds), *Advances in Organizational Justice*. Redwood City, CA: Stanford University Press, pp. 56–88.

Allan Lind, E., Greenberg, J., Scott, K. and Welchans, T. D. (2000) 'The winding road from employee complaint: Situational and psychological determinants of wrongful termination claims', *Administrative Science Quarterly*, *45*(3): 556.

Antcliff, V. and Saundry, R. (2009) 'Accompaniment, workplace representation and disciplinary outcomes in British workplaces – just a formality?', *British Journal of Industrial Relations*, *46*(1): 100–21.

Avgoustaki, A. and Frankort, H. T. (2019) 'Implications of work effort and discretion for employee well-being and career-related outcomes: An integrative assessment', *ILR Review*, *72*(3): 636–61.

BBC News (2015a) 'Thousands of Scots "unfairly treated at work"', *BBC News*, 5 February. Available at: www.bbc.co.uk/news/uk-scotland-scotland-business-31138150 (accessed 19 October 2015).

BBC News (2015b) 'Tube drivers vote to go on strike over colleague sacking', *BBC News*, 10 February. Available at: www.bbc.co.uk/news/uk-england-london-31362269 (accessed 8 March 2015).

Bennett, T. (2013) 'Workplace mediation and the empowerment of disputants: Rhetoric or reality?', *Industrial Relations Journal*, *44*(2): 189–209.

Bird, F. P. (1999) 'Empowerment and justice', in J. J. Quinn and P. W. Davies (eds), *Ethics and Empowerment*. West Lafayette, IN: Purdue University Press.

Blackard, K. (2001) 'Assessing workplace conflict resolution options', *Dispute Resolution Journal*, February/April: 56–62.

Bray, M., Budd, J. W. and Macneil, J. (2020) 'The many meanings of co-operation in the employment relationship and their implications', *British Journal of Industrial Relations*, *58*(1): 114–41.

Briane, P. (2022) Key *Employment Rights*. London: House of Commons Library. Available at: https://researchbriefings.files.parliament.uk/documents/CBP-7245/CBP-7245.pdf (accessed 16 January 2023).

Brockner, J., Konovsky, M., Cooper-Schneider, R., Folger, R., Martin, C. and Bies, R. J. (1994) 'Interactive effects of procedural justice and outcome negativity on victims and survivors of job loss', *The Academy of Management Journal*, *36*(2): 396–409.

Carroll, T., Gonzalez-Vicente, R. and Jarvis, D.S. (2019) 'Capital, conflict and convergence: A political understanding of neoliberalism and its relationship to capitalist transformation', *Globalizations*, *16*(6): 778–803.

Casebourne, J., Regan, J., Neathey, F. and Tuohy, S. (2006) 'Employment rights at work — survey of employees 2005', *DTI Employment Relations Research Series No. 51*. London: *Department of Trade and Industry.*

Charlwood, A. and Pollert, A. (2014) 'Informal employment dispute resolution among low-wage non-union workers: Does managerially initiated workplace voice enhance equity and efficiency?', *British Journal of Industrial Relations, 52*(2): 359–86.

CIPD (2001) 'God knows the value of tea and sympathy', *People Management*, 3 May. Available at: www.cipd.co.uk/pm/peoplemanagement/b/weblog/archive/2013/01/29/858a-2001-05.aspx (accessed 6 October 2014).

Citizens Advice Scotland (2015) *Exposed: The Dismal State of Workers' Rights in Scotland.* Available at: www.cas.org.uk/news/exposed-dismal-state-workers-rights-scotland (accessed 6 October 2015).

Colvin, A. J. S. (2004) 'The relationship between employee involvement and workplace dispute resolution', *Relations Industrielles, 59*: 681–704.

Cooper, L., Nolan, D. and Bales, R. (2005) *ADR in the Workplace.* St. Paul, MN: West Publishing.

Deeks, E. (2001) 'Good HR knows the value of "tea and sympathy"', *People Management, 6*(9): 10.

Department for Business, Innovation and Skills (2013) *The 2011 Workplace Employment Relations Study (WERS) Transparency Data.* Available at: www.gov.uk/government/publications/the-2011-workplace-employment-relations-study-wers-transparency- data (accessed 3 October 2014).

Dix, G., Forth, J. and Sisson, K. (2009) 'Conflict at work: The changing pattern of disputes', in W. Brown, A. Bryson, J. Forth and K. Whitfield (eds), *The Evolution of the Modern Workplace.* Cambridge: Cambridge University Press.

Edwards, P. (2003) *Industrial Relations Theory and Practice* (2nd edn). Oxford: Blackwell.

Edwards, P. and Wajcman, J. (2005) *The Politics of Working Life.* Oxford: Oxford University Press.

Ehlers, L. I. (2013) 'A typology of desirable employment relationship conditions in supervisory relationships', *South African Journal of Labour Relations, 36*(2): 48–68.

Everton, W. J., Jolton, J. and Mastrangelo, P. (2006) 'Be nice and fair or else: Understanding reasons for employees' deviant behaviour', *Journal of Management Development, 26*(2): 116–31.

Farnham, D. (2000) *Employee Relations in Context.* London: CIPD.

Feng, J. and Xie, P. (2020) 'Is mediation the preferred procedure in labour dispute resolution systems? Evidence from employer–employee matched data in China', *Journal of Industrial Relations, 62*(1): 81–103.

Fitzner, G. (2006) *How Have Employees Fared? Recent UK Trends,* Employee Relations Research Series 56. London: Department Business Enterprise Regulatory Reform.

Folger, R. and Bies, R. J. (1989) 'Managerial responsibilities and procedural justice', *Employee Responsibilities and Rights Journal, 2*(2): 69–90.

Folger, R. and Greenberg, J. (1985) 'Procedural justice: An interpretive analysis of personnel systems', in K. Rowland and G. Ferris (eds), *Research in Personnel and Human Resources Management*, Vol. 3. Greenwich, CT: JAI Press, pp. 141–83.

Forth, J., Bewley, H. and Bryson, A. (2006) *Small and Medium-sized Enterprises: Findings from the 2004 Workplace Employment Relations Survey.* London: Department of Trade and Industry.

Fox, A. (1985) *Man Mismanagement* (2nd edn). London: Hutchinson.

Galai, D. (2022) 'The relationship between managers' formal sources of power and open-book management practices: An applied study on workers of special centers and units at Mansoura University', *Scientific Journal for Financial and Commercial Studies and Research*, Faculty of Commerce, Damietta University, *3*(1): 235–84.

Gallie, D., Felstead, A. and Green, F. (2001) 'Employer policies and organizational commitment in Britain 1992–97', *Journal of Management Studies*, *38*(8): 1081–2002.

Gardner, D. and Cooper-Thomas, H. D. (2021) 'Addressing workplace bullying: The role of training', *Dignity and Inclusion at Work*, Handbooks of Workplace Bullying, Emotional Abuse and Harassment: 85–107.

Guillaume, C. (2018) 'When trade unions turn to litigation: "Getting all the ducks in a row"', *Industrial Relations Journal*, *49*(3): 227–41.

Guillaume, C. and Kirton, G. (2017) 'NAPO, un cas exemplaire des difficultés rencontrées par les syndicats britanniques du public', *Sociologie du Travail*, *59*(1).

Gospel, H. F. and Palmer, G. (1993) *British Industrial Relations*. London: Routledge.

Greenberg, J. (1996) *The Quest for Justice on the Job: Essays and Experiments*. Thousand Oaks, CA: Sage.

Greenberg, J. (2006) 'Losing sleep over organizational injustice: Attenuating insomniac reactions to underpayment inequity with supervisory training in interactional justice', *Journal of Applied Psychology*, *91*(1): 58–69.

Greenhouse, S. and Rosenbloom, S. (2008) 'Walmart settles 63 lawsuits over wages', *The New York Times*, 24 November. Available at: www.nytimes.com/2008/12/24/business/worldbusiness/24iht-24walmart.18903928.html (accessed 17 August 2022).

Hann, D., Nash, D. and Heery, E. (2019) 'Workplace conflict resolution in Wales: The unexpected prevalence of alternative dispute resolution', *Economic and Industrial Democracy*, *40*(3): 776–802.

Harris, L., Tuckman, A., Snook, J., Tailby, S., Hutchinson, S. and Winters, J. (2008) *Small Firms and Workplace Disputes Resolution*, Acas Research Paper No. 1 (08). London: Acas.

Harris, L. C. and Ogbonna, E. (2012) 'Motives for service sabotage: An empirical study of front-line workers', *Service Industries Journal*, *32*(13): 2027–46. doi:10.1080/02642069.2011.582496

Håvold, J. I., & Håvold, O. K. (2019). Power, trust and motivation in hospitals. *Leadership in Health Services*.

Helliwell, J. F., Huang, H. and Putnam, R. D. (2009) 'How's the job? Are trust and social capital neglected workplace investments?', in V. O. Bartkus and J. H. Davis (eds), *Social Capital: Reaching Out, Reaching In*. Camberley: Edward Elgar, pp. 86–144.

Hongbo, L., Waqas, M., Tariq, H., Nana Abena, A. A., Akwasi, O. C. and Ashraf, S. F. (2020) 'I will hurt you for this, when and how subordinates take revenge from abusive supervisors: A perspective of displaced revenge', *Frontiers in Psychology*, *11*: 503153. doi: 10.3389/fpsyg.2020.503153

House of Commons Women and Equalities Committee (2018) *Sexual Harassment in the Workplace*, Fifth Report of Session 2017–19, House of Commons. Available at: https://publications.parliament.uk/pa/cm201719/cmselect/cmwomeq/725/725.pdf (accessed 29 January 2022).

Hughes, J. and Bozionelos, N. (2006) 'Work-life balance as a source of job dissatisfaction and withdrawal attitudes: An exploratory study on the views of male workers', *Personnel Review*, *36*(1): 145–54.

Indiparambil, J. J. (2019) 'Privacy and beyond: Socio-ethical concerns of "on-the-job" surveillance', *Asian Journal of Business Ethics*, *8*(1): 73–105.

Jagtenberg, R. and de Roo, A. (2018) 'Employment disputes and arbitration: An account of irreconcilability, with reference to the EU and the USA', *Zbornik Pravnog Fakulteta U Zagrebu*, *68*(2): 171–92.

Jenkins, C. and Sherman, B. (1977) *Collective Bargaining*. London: Routledge & Kegan Paul.

Jones, C. and Saundry, R. (2012) 'The practice of discipline: Evaluating the roles and relationship between managers and HR professionals', *Human Resource Management Journal*, *22*(3): 252–66.

Jones, C. and Saundry, R. (2016) 'A crisis of confidence? Front-line managers and the complexities of conflict', in R. Saundry, J. Latreille and I. Ashman (eds), *Reframing Resolution*. London: Palgrave Macmillan, pp. 105–25.

Khan, F. (2021) 'US boss fires 900 workers on the same zoom call', *HR Review*, 7 December. Available at: www.hrreview.co.uk/hr-news/mass-firing-on-zoom/139569 (accessed 19 December 2021).

Kim, W. C. and Mauborgne, R. (2003) 'Fair process, managing in the knowledge economy', *Harvard Business Review*, *81*(1): 126–36.

Knight, K. G. and Latreille, P. (2000) 'Discipline, dismissals and complaints to employment tribunals', *British Journal of Industrial Relations*, *38*(4): 533–55.

Kramer, R. M. and Tyler, T. R. (eds) (1995) *Trust in Organizations: Frontiers of Theory and Research*. London: Sage.

Laundon, M., McDonald, P. and Cathcart, A. (2019) 'Fairness in the workplace: Organizational justice and the employment relationship', in K. Townsend, K. Cafferkey, A. McDermott and T. Dundon (eds), *Elgar Introduction to Theories of Human Resources and Employment Relations*. London: Edward Elgar Publishing.

Lawless, J. and Trif, A. (2016) 'Managing interpersonal conflicts at work by line managers', *Irish Journal of Management*, *35*(1): 74–87.

Markowitz, D. M., Kouchaki, M., Hancock, J. T. and Gino, F. (2021) 'The deception spiral: Corporate obfuscation leads to perceptions of immorality and cheating behavior', *Journal of Language and Social Psychology*, *40*(2): 277–96.

Matta, F. K., Sabey, T. B., Scott, B. A., Lin, S. H. J. and Koopman, J. (2020) 'Not all fairness is created equal: A study of employee attributions of supervisor justice motives', *Journal of Applied Psychology*, *105*(3): 274–93.

McCulloch, A. (2021) 'BrewDog to expand HR in response to work culture allegations', *Personnel Today*, 23 December. Available at: www.personneltoday.com/hr/brewdog-to-expand-hr-in-response-to-work-culture-allegations/?ID=zzrzf~9fztt9~n9hxj~W4ik~K y0gk&utm_campaign=PTPR-WORKHUMAN-040122-DE&utm_medium=email&utm_source=email&utm_content=newsletter (accessed 8 January 2022).

McKenzie, D. (2012) 'The impact of mediation on workplace relationship conflict and return to work outcomes: A snapshot review', *International Journal of Law and Psychiatry*, *39*: 52–9.

Men, L. R. and Yue, C. A. (2019) 'Creating a positive emotional culture: Effect of internal communication and impact on employee supportive behaviors', *Public Relations Review*, *45*(3): 1–12.

Muzaffar, M. (2021) 'Japanese civil servants punished for leaving work two minutes early', *The Independent*, 19 March. Available at: www.independent.co.uk/asia/east-asia/japan-civil-servants-work-early-pay-cut-b1819538.html, (accessed 22 January 2022)

Nash, D. and Hann, D. (2021) *Disputes and their Management in the Workplace: A Survey of Employers in Northern Ireland*. London: Acas.

Near, J. and Miceli, M. (2008) 'Wrongdoing, whistleblowing and retaliation in the US government: What have researchers learned from the Merit Systems Protection Board (MSPB) survey results?', *Review of Public Personnel Administration*, *28*(3): 263–81.

Nelson, R. L. and Nielsen, L. B. (2000) 'Cops, counsel, and entrepreneurs: Constructing the role of inside counsel in large corporations', *Law and Society Review*, *34*(2): 457–93.

Noyen, M (2022) 'Some former Emirates employees say officers known internally as "weight police" monitor and punish cabin crew members deemed to be heavy', *Insider*, 21 January. Available at: www.insider.com/former-emirates-staff-say-cabin-crew-monitored-weight-police-2022-1 (accessed 22 January 2022).

Oni-Ojo, B. E., Iyiola, O. O. and Osibanjo, A. O. (2014) 'Managing workplace conflicts in business environment: The role of alternative dispute resolution (ADR)', *European Journal of Business and Management*, 6(36): 64–82.

Phelan, T. (2015) 'Foreign Office rethinks its HR Model', *HR Review*, 23 February. Available at: www.hrreview.co.uk/hr-news/strategy-news/foreign-office-rethinks-hr-model/55666 (accessed 24 February 2015).

Pollert, A. and Charlwood, A. (2009) 'The vulnerable worker and problems at work in Britain', *Work, Employment and Society*, 23(2): 343–62.

Purcell, J. and Sisson, K. (1983) 'Strategies and practices in the management of industrial relations in Britain', in G. Bain (ed.), *Industrial Relations in Britain*. Oxford: Blackwell.

Rajan, R. U. D. R., Jamaluddin, S. Z. and Mohamed, A. A. A. (2021) 'Pre-dismissal right to be heard in the private sector in Malaysia: Lessons from England and India', *Journal of Legal, Ethical and Regulatory Issues*, 24(1): 1–7.

Ravid, D. M., Tomczak, D. L., White, J. C. and Behrend, T. S. (2020) 'EPM 20/20: A review, framework, and research agenda for electronic performance monitoring', *Journal of Management*, 46(1): 100–26.

Rayner, C. and Lewis, D. (2020) 'Managing workplace bullying: The role of policies', in S. Einarsen, H. Hoel, D. Zapf and C. Cooper (eds), *Bullying and Harassment in the Workplace*. Boca Raton: CRC Press, pp. 497–519.

Richardson, N. and Klien, S. (2021) *People at Work 2021: A Global Workforce View*, ADP Research Institute. Available from: www.adpri.org/wp-content/uploads/2021/04/23084556/WFV-Global_2021_US_Screen_697691_162389_FV.pdf (accessed 21 January 2022).

Ridley-Duff, R. and Bennett, A. (2011) 'Towards mediation: Developing a theoretical framework to understanding alternative dispute resolution', *Industrial Relations Journal*, 42(2): 106–23.

Roche, W. K. (2021) 'The genesis of private dispute resolution in Irish industrial relations', *Industrial Relations Journal*, 52(1): 82–106.

Salam, A. (2020) 'Organizational justice as a predictor of organizational citizenship behaviour', *International Business Education Journal*, 13.

Saundry, R. and Dix, G. (2014) 'Conflict resolution in the United Kingdom', in W. K. Roche, P. Teague and A. J. S. Colvin (eds), *The Oxford Handbook of Conflict Management in Organizations*. Oxford: Oxford University Press, pp. 465–93.

Saundry, R. and Urwin, P. (2021) *Estimating the Cost of Workplace Conflict*. Available at: www.acas.org.uk/estimating-the-costs-of-workplace-conflict-report (accessed 3 February 2022).

Saundry, R. and Wibberley G. (2014) *Workplace Dispute Resolution and the Management of Individual Conflict*, Acas Research Paper. London: Acas.

Saundry, R., Latreille, P., Dickens, L., Irvine, C., Teague, P., Urwin, P. and Wibberley, G. (2014) *Reframing Resolution: Managing Conflict and Resolving Individual Employment Disputes in the Contemporary Workplace*, Acas Policy Discussion Papers. London: Acas.

Saundry, R., Jones, C. and Wibberley, G. (2015) 'The challenge of managing informally', *Employee Relations*, 36(4): 428–41.

Saundry, R., Fisher, V. and Kinsey, S. (2021) 'Disconnected human resource? Proximity and the (mis)management of workplace conflict', *Human Resource Management Journal*, 31(2): 476–92.

Sewell, G. and Barker, J. R. (2006) 'Coercion versus care: Using irony to make sense of organizational surveillance', *Academy of Management Review*, 31(4): 934–61.

Sewell, G., Barker, J. R. and Nyberg, D. (2012) 'Working under intensive surveillance: When does "measuring everything that moves" become intolerable?', *Human Relations*, 65(2): 189–215.

Stanton, J. M. and Julian, A. L. (2002) 'The impact of electronic monitoring on quality and quantity of performance', *Computers in Human Behavior*, 18(1): 85–101.

Stipanowich, T. and Lamare, J. R. (2013) *Living with 'ADR': Evolving Perceptions and Use of Mediation, Arbitration and Conflict Management in Fortune 1,000 Corporations*. Available at: http://papers.ssrn.com/sol3/papers.cfm?abstract_id=2221461 (accessed 6 October 2015).

Strom, D. L., Sears, K. L. and Kelly, K. M. (2014) 'Work engagement: The roles of organizational justice and leadership style in predicting engagement among employees', *Journal of Leadership & Organizational Studies*, 21(1): 61–82.

Teague, P., Roche, W., Currie, D. and Gormley, T. (2020) 'Alternative dispute resolution in Ireland and the US Model', *ILR Review*, 73(2): 345–65.

The Irish Times (2017) 'Passengers see our Ryanair uniforms and think we are out to screw them', *The Irish Times*, 26 September. Available at: www.irishtimes.com/news/consumer/passengers-see-our-ryanair-uniforms-and-think-we-are-out-to-screw-them-1.3234310 (accessed 21 January 2022).

TUC (2020) *More than 5 Million UK Workers put in a Total of 2 Billion Work of Overtime Last Year – TUC Analysis*, press release, 28 February. Available at: www.tuc.org.uk/news/workers-uk-put-more-ps35-billion-worth-unpaid-overtime-last-year-tuc-analysis (accessed 20 March 2020).

Tyler, T. R. and Bies, R. J. (1990) 'Beyond formal procedures: The interpersonal context of procedural justice', in J. S. Carroll (ed.), *Applied Social Psychology and Organizational Settings*. Hove: Psychology Press, pp. 66–98.

United States Department of Labor (2012) 'US Department of Labor recovers $4.83 million in back wages, damages for more than 4,500 Wal-Mart workers', Press release, 5 January. Available at www.dol.gov/opa/media/press/whd/WHD20120801.htm (accessed 1 November 2015).

van Wanrooy, B., Bewley, H., Bryson, A., Forth, J., Freeth, L. and Wood, S. (2013) *Employment Relations in the Shadow of Recession*. Basingstoke: Palgrave.

Watkins Allen, M., Coopman, S. J., Hart, J. L. and Walker, K. L. (2007) 'Workplace surveillance and managing privacy boundaries', *Management Communication Quarterly*, 21(2): 172–200.

Wilensky, R. and Jones, K. (1994) 'Quick response key to resolving complaints', *Human Resources Management*, 39: 42–6.

8

EMPLOYEE ENGAGEMENT AND THE EMPLOYMENT RELATIONSHIP

Learning Outcomes

By the end of this chapter, you should be able to:

- identify and evaluate the concept of employee engagement
- examine engagement in the light of different managerial styles and frameworks
- analyse the impact and influence that employee engagement programmes might have on employee perceptions of trust within the employment relationship
- critically evaluate the notion that 'too much engagement is bad for you'.

What to Expect

This chapter (which should be read in conjunction with Chapters 9 and 10, looking at employee involvement and voice) takes a critical look at what constitutes employee engagement and explores a number of the claims made about it. It naturally follows from Chapter 7 (concerned with managing dissent) because many managers assume that the creation of an engaged work-force helps reduce both labour turnover and incidences of workplace conflict (Alfes et al., 2010; Kaur and Randhawa, 2020). When they do occur, incidences of conflict are likely to *disengage* employees (John-Eke and Akintokunbo, 2020; John-Eke and Gabriel, 2019). Yet the study of engagement raises more questions than answers. Does employee engagement, for example, always have positive outcomes – is it possible for everyone employed in an organisation to be actively and positively engaged? The chapter looks at whether or not employee engagement is affected by perceptions of organisational justice, by national culture and by levels of reciprocal communication. The strategic implications of deploying employee engagement mechanisms, and the effects that these might have on the employment relationship, are also explored.

What Is Employee Engagement?

Trying to define employee engagement accurately is like trying to grasp, and hold on to, a handful of fog: 'you know what it is when you see it' say managers, but often they can only define it in terms of who is *not* engaged. A UK government-initiated report *Engaging for Success*, by David MacLeod and Nita Clarke (2009: 8) discovered around 50 different definitions of the term, some looking at engagement in terms of behaviour, some in terms of what is required to produce engaged employees, others in terms of employee attitudes, yet still others defined engagement in terms of results, such as lower absence levels, increased retention, greater productivity and enhanced innovation. Much of the work academics have done around the area stems from exchange theory (Blau, 1964). This depicts engagement as part of an exchange between the employer and the employee. In this context engagement is regarded rather like the psychological contract where the employee is actively using positive discretionary behaviours at work because they are comfortable with the tasks they have been set and the way in which the organisation treats them. MacLeod and Clarke themselves saw

> ... employee engagement as a workplace approach designed to ensure that employees are committed to their organisation's goals and values, motivated to contribute to organisational success, and are able at the same time to enhance their own sense of well-being. (2009: 9)

They declared that there were four key areas: management integrity; leadership; employee voice; together with engaged (and therefore engaging) managers that were crucial in engendering engagement within a workforce.

> Employee engagement is business critical. There is a commercial link between employees being engaged and profitability. A more engaged workforce is likely to have a lower absence rate, a lower turnover and a higher productivity rate which all has an impact on bottom line. There is a very strong link between profitability and employee engagement. (Brownhill, 2013)

This quote from Louise Brownhill, from when she was Head of Experience and Engagement at PwC, epitomises the way in which employee engagement is regarded by some practitioners; that is, as the 'philosopher's stone' in the range of tools available to managers wanting to deploy and motivate staff in order to ensure maximum organisational success. Optimising employee performance through engagement is, they hope, the answer to increasing the competitive edge, retaining happy staff and delivering the subsequent sustained success of the organisation. Whether or not employees respond to being manipulated in this way is, however, a moot point! Things are not quite as linear, or as simple as some of the definitions might suggest. Briner (2014: 54) explicitly addressed this when he said:

> Some definitions focus on employee behaviour (eg, discretionary effort), some on employee attitudes (eg, commitment), some on employee feelings (eg, enthusiasm), some on the conditions of work and what the organisation does (eg, provides support), some on various combinations of these, and yet others define engagement as a situation in which one of these things, such as attitudes, causes another, such as behaviour. In other words, when it comes to defining engagement it appears that almost anything goes.

Guest importantly pointed out that,

> the quality of the evidence for the academic approach focussing on work engagement remains less than wholly convincing while the consultancy approach with its focus on organisational engagement is deeply unconvincing. (2014: 230–1)

Many of the academic explanations of engagement tend to define it in relation to aspects of an individual's engaged behaviour, using words and phrases such as 'enthusiastic', 'dedicated', 'pro-active', 'focused', 'zealous', 'absorbed in the work', 'innovative', 'prepared to go the extra mile'. So, for example, Schaufeli et al. looked at engagement in terms of three interrelated but separate factors, defining it as 'a positive, fulfilling, work-related state of mind that is characterised by *vigour, dedication* and *absorption*' (2002: 74). Shuck and his colleagues (2017) pointed out that engagement has been defined as the maintenance, intensity and direction of cognitive emotional and behavioural energy – direction, energy and intensity are, of course, all concepts that are less than precise and open to subjective interpretation. Employees who are deemed to be 'engaged' are thought to work harder because they derive enjoyment from what they do (Zeijen et al., 2018; Van Wijhe et al., 2013) unlike those who fall into the workaholic category who work because they feel compelled or driven to do so. (Although of course it is not unknown for a workaholic to also be engaged with what they are doing!) Further definitions of engagement make a distinction between employee engagement and work engagement; so, for example, an employee might well be fully engaged with their work but less so with the organisation that they work for. In the health service, for example, many nurses enjoy and are passionate about the aspects of their day-to-day undertaking of their own professional tasks but are much less enamoured with the NHS trust for whom they are working. Kahn, who is often credited with being the first to suggest that engagement was a separate construct worthy of study, viewed it as very much an aspect of an employee's *behaviour at* work rather than an employee's *attitude to* work, saying that engagement was

> ... the simultaneous employment and expression of a person's "preferred self" in task behaviours that promote connections to work and to others, personal presence (physical, cognitive and emotional) and active full performance. (1990: 700)

This concentration on behaviour rather than attitude is not always helpful. What employees actually 'think' (i.e., their attitude) while they are working may, or may not, impact their performance; indeed someone could really enjoy what they are doing and still perform badly and vice versa.

There is an assumption that creative and innovative workplace behaviours arise both from an individual's natural traits, but also from their *attitudes to* the work itself. Engagement is regarded by some as an essential ingredient arising from and continually shaping such attitudes. Yet engagement is a vague and abstract concept that (apparently) motivates individuals to achieve higher levels of performance (Katili et al., 2021: 199). For managers, the ways and means of channelling and nurturing engagement is sometimes speculative and frequently elusive.

> Employee engagement remains an elusive success factor given that global reports state how only a quarter to a third of employees feel engaged, while the rest are to some extent fed up or disillusioned with the experience of conducting their work. (Direction, 2020)

News Flash 8.1

The Loyalty Deficit

A 2019 employee engagement report from Tiny Plus looked at data from over 25,000 employees across 20 industries from January to December 2018. The results showed that giving recognition for excellent work encourages and sustains employee engagement. The authors questioned employees in a range of organisations employing 10 to 10,000 employees, with companies spread across Northern America, Europe, Asia, and Australia. They concluded that employee recognition programmes improved employee engagement, retention and affinity with their organisation.

However the main findings from the report showed that:

- Employee loyalty is decreasing. 43% of workers would be willing to leave their companies for a 10% salary increase, and weak company cultures are to blame.
- Leadership teams lack self-awareness. While 39% of managers strongly agree that management within their organisation is transparent, only 22% of employees feel the same way.
- Workers need better direction. Less than half of employees feel that their promotion and career path is clear to them. Furthermore, a staggering 44% of employees don't feel they have sufficient opportunities for professional growth in their current positions.
- Employees aren't getting the recognition they deserve. Only a third of workers received recognition the last time they went the extra mile at work and just a quarter feel highly valued at work.
- Employees care deeply about their co-workers. 91% of people rate their co-workers positively, and yet just 9% of people think their average coworker is very happy.
- Most cultures are decidedly mediocre. Less than one third of people believe they have a strong culture.
- Only two in five people strongly agree that their managers have clearly defined their roles and responsibilities, and how they contribute to the success of the organisation. Furthermore, only one in four employees strongly agree with the statement, 'My company takes my feedback and suggestions seriously and effectively' (2019: 3)

Source: Tiny Pulse, 2019

Macey and Schneider, in an influential paper (2008) and then later book (Macey et al., 2009: 7), said that 'engagement is an individual's sense of purpose and focused energy evident to others in the display of personal initiative, adaptability, effort, and persistence, directed toward organisational goals', explaining that 'engagement happens when (a) employees have work that interests them and aligns with their values; and (b) employees are treated in a way that reinforces the natural tendency to reciprocate in kind' (2008: 12), such that 'persistence, proactivity, role expansion and adaptability are all features of engagement behaviour that, in the aggregate, connote performance above and beyond typical or normal expectations' (2008: 35). They split such engaged behaviours into three different types:

- trait (e.g., found when someone has a naturally positive outlook)
- state (e.g., found when someone is involved and satisfied with their work)
- behavioural (e.g., found when someone engages in a positive way with the tasks being undertaken).

Saks (2008: 40), however, was scathing about this approach, arguing that employee engagement defined in this way was too imprecise, amalgamating a 'little bit of this, a little bit of that', and as such it covered whatever Macy and Schneider wanted it to. He pointed out that actively doing one's job in a manner that was expected was indeed engagement but that although any additional activity, such as innovation, could well arise from an employee being engaged with work, this activity was *not* necessarily, in itself, engagement. Shuck et al. (2021) showed how job satisfaction was an antecedent of employee engagement, rather than the other way round. This research together with previous work on job satisfaction, demonstrates that the antecedents, expressions and outcomes of engagement are so intertwined that it is difficult to disentangle which workplace activities occur as a result of engagement or whether the engagement is a result of the activities themselves – sometimes, inevitably it will be a mixture of both.

It is clear then that employee engagement is an amorphous concept with numerous definitions – some relating to outcomes, others to the behaviours that contribute towards those outcomes. Yet although more research is required to refine the concept, it is apparent that employers are positively seeking to create environments in which employees are so involved with their work that they happily perform at their best and in so doing achieve a sense of fulfilment and wellbeing that ensures they remain with the employing organisation and continue to contribute in a positive way towards organisational goals.

Exercise 8.1

Compare and then list the similarities and differences between the Macey and Schneider definitions of engagement - trait, state and behavioural - with three of the engagement elements defined in a recent CIPD report (Gifford and Young, 2021: 6):

- *Personal role engagement*, where employees are able to express their favoured self through their work, emotionally, cognitively and physically. By so doing they are energised, alert and feel a connection to colleagues.

(Continued)

- *Work engagement* occurs when, psychologically, employees experience vigour, dedication and absorption in relation to their work.
- *Multidimensional engagement* incorporates cognitive, emotional and behavioural experiences by employees. It distinguishes job-focused engagement from organisation-focused engagement.

How do you think the CIPD approach might be specifically attractive to managers? Why did you reach this conclusion?

Engagement is by its very nature discretionary and experienced *by* employees – it is not something that is done, or given to them. Aran Caza (2012) has shown that there are a variety of types of discretionary behaviour (he found 46 in his literature review), and to simplify things he developed a model showing eight different domains of discretionary behaviour:

1   Effort discretion
2   Goal discretion
3   Technical discretion
4   Staffing discretion
5   Support discretion
6   Interpersonal style discretion
7   Civic virtue discretion
8   Buffering discretion.

These eight domains of discretionary behaviours are complicated because individuals at work not only decide on their own discretionary behaviours but also are influenced by and, importantly subject to, the discretionary behaviours of those around them, not just their co-workers but also their supervisors and managers, all of whom will have an impact on their levels of engagement. The employment relationship can therefore be influenced in both positive and negative ways by the deployment of discretion. It is not unknown for employees to deliberately use their own discretion to shape their specific work tasks in order to provide themselves with the maximum amount of work-based satisfaction. Where this happens engagement is high, conversely where this is attempted and fails engagement is likely to be somewhat diminished (Baghdadi et al., 2021; Kooij et al., 2020; Kuijpers et al., 2020).

Where supervisors and managers show high levels of engagement then their teams too exhibit higher levels of engaged workplace behaviours. This is, however, slightly double-edged: a team led by a highly engaged manager who demands the same high level of zeal from subordinates is likely to produce a stressed team in which individuals are likely to resent the additional pressures heaped on them and look for alternative work.

Exercise 8.2

Read the quotes below from both Hearn and Macey et al.

- Analyse and evaluate the relationship between managers and their subordinates with regard to engagement.

- Keeping both of these quotes in mind, discuss the importance of employees' perceptions of organisational justice on their own potential engagement. Explain why you reached your conclusions.

Macey and his colleagues said,

> most executives unfortunately think it is the job of management to motivate when it is really the job of management to promote conditions under which employees display the motivation and energy that they have at their discretion. (2009: 166)

While, in 2020, Hearn used the results of a Gallup survey to point out that the management of employee engagement is not the sole responsibility of the HR function, but of everyone in the organisation:

> According to Gallup, managers account for over 70% of the variance in employee engagement. Employees with highly engaged managers are 59% more likely to be engaged than employees supervised by actively disengaged managers. Managers play an integral role in ensuring employee engagement because they have a closer relationship with employees than senior leaders and HR. They understand their employees' day-to-day work and should have some responsibility in ensuring that they feel motivated. It's important for managers to create an environment in which employees can openly discuss their work and how they are feeling.

Sources: Hearn, 2020; Macey et al. 2009; Gallup 2021

Engagement is something about which there is a growing managerial concern. Studies by Gallup (2021) and Robertson and Cooper (2010) suggest that this concern is global. Indeed Gallup (2021: 3,5) suggests that levels of global employee engagement have decreased by 2%, from 22% in 2019 to 20% in 2020. In other words less than a quarter of the total of those surveyed were engaged at work. The percentage of engagement differed between nations, so for example 11% of employees were engaged in Western Europe and 21% in Eastern Europe, the engagement percentage for the Middle East, and North and Sub Saharan Africa was 16% while that from Australia and New Zealand stood at 20%. The USA had 34% of engaged employees and Canada 19%. From its East Asian research it was apparent that 17% of Chinese employees said they were engaged (Gallup, 2021: 36, 57, 66, 81, 90, 126,,169). Different cultural expectations will have, of course, impacted these findings.

Whether or not engagement attitudes (and behaviours) are task – rather than job – induced, and are as a consequence time sensitive, has also been subject to academic scrutiny. Can absorption in, and immersion with, a task be defined as engagement even if it occurs for relatively short periods of time, fluctuating from hour to hour or week to week? Different aspects of a job may capture the attention and result in an individual's enthusiastic, involved, workplace behaviour that is transient and hence sustained only for as long as the individual remains absorbed. Sonnentag et al. labelled such sporadic bursts of engagement, sustained for short surges of activity, as '**state work engagement**' (2010). The CIPD study (Alfes et al., 2010: 6) found that just 18% of their respondents were engaged on a daily basis, while nearly 60% claimed to be engaged 'once a week', with 22% reporting engagement a few times a year. States of permanent workplace engagement therefore appear to be an unrealistic managerial expectation. Costa et al. (2017: 206) discovered that a diet of permanent engagement is not optimal and that 'it is fundamental to alternate more excit(ing) and fun moments with more task focused ones and collective interaction moments with individual work' in order to achieve engagement and organisational success. Because work engagement is regarded as a win–win phenomenon – organisations benefitting simultaneously with those engaged employees who find higher levels of workplace satisfaction and enjoyment – there has been an effort to discover the optimum conditions necessary to induce workplace engagement. The CIPD (2010) suggest that organisations can engender engagement by providing:

- appropriate matching of individuals to jobs
- meaningful work, so that employees can see the link between what they are doing and broader organisational aims
- supportive work environments where employees are unafraid to share information and are able to express themselves freely
- transparency and clearly communicated vision about the direction and values that senior management want the organisation to follow; MacLeod and Clarke (2009: 33) also found that such espoused values need to be seen to be 'lived' by senior management, resulting in a culture of trust and a sense of integrity
- approachable senior management
- relationships with line managers that are regarded in a positive way by employees
- the opportunity for employees to be 'vocally involved'; having a say in work processes has a direct positive link with engagement.

Work by Jabeen and Rahim (2021), specifically looking at the effects of despotic management in Malaysia, reinforces the findings from the CIPD and MacLeod and Clarke studies that trust is vitally important in helping to create a workplace atmosphere that engenders engagement ultimately improving performance. They point out that under despotic self-serving and aggrandising leadership, employees lose trust in management, conserve their resources and decrease their work engagement behaviours.

The Engagement Paradox

Indeed if all these 'ideal' antecedents are present there is good reason to assume that at least some members of the workforce will be engaged and experiencing, as the IES survey said, 'a blend of job satisfaction, organisational commitment, job involvement and feelings of empowerment' where engagement 'is a concept that is greater than the sum of its parts' (Robinson, 2008, cited in MacLeod and Clarke, 2009: 9).

There is such a multitude of different definitions and ways of looking at employee engagement that Welbourne (2011: 86) has indicated that it could be viewed not as a construct but as a field of study in its own right, perhaps even an industry. She had her own way of looking at engagement, not in terms of a definition but with regard to the question 'Engaged with what?', making the important point that there are only a limited number of hours available for work and that if someone is engaged by actively pursuing one aspect of a job then other aspects might well suffer. She says that it is crucial to look at the number of roles an individual undertakes at work and that, for managers specifically, it is imperative to decide which roles and activities are core to the business and which are less so. The impact of misplaced engagement resulting in too much, or too little, time spent on essential activities could be damaging and dysfunctional to an organisation rather than enabling it to achieve higher levels of productivity. For example, if an employee spends a disproportionate amount of time working on researching competitor products at the expense of essential day-to-day activities, that employee may well be 'fully-focused', 'engaged' and 'working above and beyond' certain requirements of their job, to the detriment of other aspects of their work which, because they are neglected, reduce the organisation's overall productivity. This might not matter for the individual concerned, who will have a positive attitude to work and a healthy psychological contract, but will be a problem for the employing organisation and perhaps for the individual's colleagues. Attempts to redress the balance may lead to conflict and subsequent lack of engagement that may benefit the organisation if not the individual concerned.

There are of course other downsides to engagement. It is not unknown for work to be too engaging and too challenging, for someone to become so wrapped up in their workplace activities that they lose a degree of perspective, spend a disproportionate amount of time and energy working and, as a consequence, lose their zeal, become psychologically exhausted, disillusioned, less engaged and 'burnt out'. This effect can be likened to having too much of a good thing – food, for example is good for you, but too much food can lead to obesity and severe health problems. Macey et al. suggest that the paradox of engagement is that 'you have to be on fire to burn out' (2009: 152), while Maslach et al. (2017) argue that burnout is the polar opposite of engagement (i.e., disengaged employees exhibit characteristics such as exhaustion and cynicism rather than energy, positivity and enthusiasm).

News Flash 8.2

Perceptions of Engagement Differ

Employers making efforts to bring people together and foster a sense of belonging and engagement find their culture has benefitted. This was one of the findings from an August 2020, Chartered Management Institute survey of around 2,300 senior executives, managers and employees to discover how they found work during the Covid 19 pandemic.

Some of the results, however, were not quite so clear cut. In some organisations just under half of the senior leaders (49%) believed they were successfully placing employees at the heart of their businesses and enabling more participatory decision making, yet this was contradicted by the responses from some of their employees; just under three quarters of whom did not agree. There were other disconnects, too, for example 40% of managers felt job satisfaction had improved while only 23% of employees felt the same way. The CIM pointed out that leaders must ensure that their employees are part of their 'company journey' and genuinely feel listened to.

Source: Chartered Management Institute, 2020: 14-16

Not everyone, however, thinks that there is a clear and progressive engagement continuum, ranging from the severely burnt out to the vigorously and enthusiastically engaged. Schaufeli (together with Salanova, 2011) changed his original view and claimed that rather than being on a continuum, engagement and burnout are two distinct and separate states of being where one does not bleed into the other. Importantly Richard Peccei (2004) does not discuss this continuum, but he does distinguish between *job demands* and *job resources*. Job demands are linked to parts of a job that 'require sustained physical, mental or emotional effort and are therefore associated with certain physiological and psychological costs'; for example, where there is excessive pressure, and maybe role ambiguity, this is a cost to the individual and inhibits active engagement. Poor job demands, resulting from ineffective leadership causing lack of direction and role clarity are associated with burnout (Conte and Landy, 2019; Leary and Miller, 2021) and hence with subsequent perceptions of procedural injustice. Weak managerial leadership is therefore inimical to employee engagement. Peccei categorises job resources, as opposed to demands, as being more enabling, reducing job demands, stimulating 'personal growth and development and functional in achieving work goals'. Examples of such job resources would be high levels of social support, a degree of job control and performance feedback with opportunities for development. These resources, he claims, satisfy an individual's need for workplace autonomy and may therefore augment an individual's willingness to actively engage with the work processes (2013: 347). There is certainly a positive link between Peccei's job resources and employees' perceptions of organisational justice. Where job demands are 'just about' attainable, albeit with a degree of effort, employees may deem such demands as a challenge and therefore regard a mix of reasonably high demands and high resources to be ideal, perceiving tasks with low demands and high resources as boring and unworthy of engagement (Eldor, 2017). Certain circumstances, such as redundancy, may result in a redistribution of job demands without the associated resources to accompany them; here those left employed by the organisation may find that their workloads and responsibilities have increased. If these changes are viewed negatively by the employees, as is often the case following restructuring after redundancy, it may lead to lower levels of job satisfaction, and perceptions of distributional and procedural injustice. Mishra and Spreitzer (1998) point out that involvement with workplace tasks, productivity and enthusiasm may all wane in such circumstances, leading to cynical, demotivated and on occasion overworked and burnt out employees. (See also Laulié and Morgeson [2020] who examine both voluntary and involuntary employee turnover and discuss the implications for those that remain. It follows, from their examples, that should a toxic person leave an organisation the engagement of those remaining could well improve. The converse, of course, is true, so when a trusted colleague leaves, then engagement is likely to decrease.) Jabutay's (2018) study of nearly 700 call centre workers in the Philippines supports the notion that job demands can be discouraging and inimical to engagement. Here the workers, subject to frequent and abusive callers, suffered emotional dissonance and were less engaged with their work.

What seems apparent is that engagement and job resources, rather than job demands, are mutually reinforcing, resource-rich jobs leading to engagement that in turn leads to the allocation of further job resources that further engender more engagement and so on. The *assumption* here is that employees will exhibit increased levels of discretionary behaviour, engagement and organisational commitment in a direct response to the job resources available to them.

Case Study 8.1

Kellogg's Reaps Reward From New Online Engagement Hub

Kellogg, a global food company, renowned for its breakfast cereals, operates from 43 sites based across a range of different countries. Its 33,000 staff span several generations, a multitude of cultures and a diverse mix of race, gender and ethnicity, so encouraging, rewarding and engaging them in a consistent and holistic way is no easy task. Prior to 2018 the company's main way of 'recognising' staff was top-down and monetary. This process usually involved a number of separate, personal transactions between managers and their subordinates and any monetary reward was often forgotten by the following year. The company wanted to change this and make the process global and more employee centric, encompassing wellbeing, social health, community involvement, as well as the usual Kellogg-specific work activities. The scheme had to deliver not just annually but throughout the year so that it was always in the minds of employees.

To this end it introduced a new online global platform where a social hub allowed people to see what others in the company were doing and specifically how they were succeeding across a variety of areas. The scheme was designed so that it would:

- engender engagement through recognition
- enhance the visibility of staff accomplishments
- ensure employees receive public (and frequent) recognition
- enable easy peer-to-peer acknowledgement of successes
- empower employees with a choice of rewards – redeemable monthly on a 'use it or lose it basis'.

The roll out of the scheme began in 2018 in North America. In the spring of 2019 it was introduced to South America and to Europe in the autumn of that year; by January 2020 it had expanded to Africa, the Middle East and Australia. Although global in reach and appearance the scheme caters for individual country differences because each region can set its own recognition values and criteria. All employees are able to use the hub to 'post' comments about those who have helped them, or who have excelled in some way, however small. On average each employee now receives at least 40 recognition moments throughout the year. The programme has helped change the culture and make it more inclusive. It has increased Kellogg's overall recognition scores, decreased staff turnover, improved engagement and helped drive operational outcomes.

The system is a useful engagement tool, employees log on daily, managers can get and give instant feedback. It has improved internal networking and social connections; for example one of the aspects of the scheme allows employees to opt for a virtual coffee chat – where, rather like a blind date for those who want to participate, the system randomly fixes up coffee dates between people from different parts of the company. Health issues can be addressed and the scheme helps to drive changes in behaviour, employees receiving recognition (and therefore reward points) for participating in healthy activities or helping others to get recognition by publicly acknowledging those who have encouraged them to act healthily. Such activities could be taking part in a virtual 5K or just making sure they drink eight glasses of water a day. Overall the new way of appreciating and recognising employees in such an holistic way has delivered benefits not just for them but for the business.

Sources: https://discover.resources.achievers.com/kellogg/kellogg-achievers-_h; https://discover.resources.achievers.com/kellogg/o2amvbjg6yu

Exercise 8.3

The argument that workplace resources are antecedents to engagement has ties with notions of the psychological contract in which employees and employers make assumptions about their reciprocal obligations.

Saks said that 'managers need to provide employees with resources and benefits that will *oblige* them to reciprocate in kind with higher levels of engagement' (2008: 614).

- Discuss the quote from Saks in relation to job demands, job resources, perceptions of organisational justice and the psychological contract, and critically analyse whether an *obligatorily* engaged employee is a truly engaged employee.

What is clear is that engagement at work, with work itself, is an important facet of employment and that under the right conditions (i.e., with sufficient time and the right resources) employees who find what they are doing engrossing are likely to do it well and that this in turn *may* benefit their organisation and have a positive impact on their own wellbeing, their perceptions of organisational justice and on their psychological contracts.

News Flash 8.3

More Than 10 Million Brits Take Time Off Due To Burnout*

This headline announced new findings from MetLife UK, who surveyed 1,428 UK part- and full-time workers between 1 - 3 February 2022. It found that:

- Businesses across the UK are losing more than 80 million hours per year due to sick days from burnout.
- This could be costing businesses more than £700m as more than two in five (44%) UK adults admit to calling in sick feeling exhausted, stressed, depressed, overwhelmed and unmotivated.
- Women were much more likely than men to call in sick due to feeling burnt out (54% vs 35%).
- A further third (34%) of 'Brits' admitted that they have, or would, call in sick because they felt they needed to take a break from work, indicating potentially gruelling workloads.

Amy Tomlinson, Head of HR at MetLife UK, said,

Stress, declining productivity and a lack of engagement are all common signs of employee burnout ... Our research shows that employees are having to call in sick in order to take a break and recover from burnout, a worrying sign that could lead to greater issues such as absenteeism. Employers have a social responsibility to their employees to identify and manage the main causes of stress at work and put checks in place to ensure that it doesn't start to impact their mental and physical health.

*UK workforce, as of November 2021, 24,391,000. See: www.statista.com/statistics/1119783/full-time-workers-in-the-uk/

Source: MetLife UK, 2022

Measures of Engagement

There are different ways of measuring employee engagement, none of which is particularly accurate, in part because the definitions of what engagement actually is are problematic and in part because engagement is not necessarily a static state but can fluctuate from task to task, day to day, month to month and so on. Some of the measures look specifically at attitudes to work, others at behaviours in evidence at work. Care has to be taken when looking at studies to note which aspects are actually being investigated under the overall engagement umbrella. Organisations sometimes measure engagement, not by examining attitudes and behaviours but by looking at absence, retention and productivity figures; yet these will not necessarily reflect and measure real levels of engagement, particularly as other influences impact upon the data. Consultancy firms have developed a range of measurement techniques specifically targeting engagement, but most just look at the elements that are necessary pre-conditions for the encouragement of engagement. The Gallup Q^{12} employee engagement scale (Schaufeli and Backer, 2010), on the other hand, measures engagement by asking employee respondents 12 questions that are directly linked to their performance. Larger organisations will, on occasion, use targeted questions within a staff opinion survey to gauge engagement levels, but again this data might not be completely accurate. Sometimes what is *not* said in these surveys is more important than what is. The author once asked someone if they had filled in their staff satisfaction survey and was told 'I'm not satisfied so I don't see why I should fill it in', illustrating the dangers of making assumptions about, and relying too heavily on, some of the data collected.

Academic data collection in this area too is beset with problems about accuracy; for example, do questions about taking initiative, or working unpaid overtime, actually measure engagement, or are they picking up on other aspects of the employment relationship that may not have anything at all to do with whether or not an employee is engaged with their work? One most often cited – and internationally deployed (Shimazu et al., 2010) – method of measurement is the Utrecht work engagement scale (UWES): here engagement is perceived as a relatively stable state and examines different dimensions of *vigour, dedication* and *absorption* (Schaufeli et al., 2002: 74–5). There are two different versions of this scale, the fuller one measuring 17 aspects of engagement and the slightly shorter version that compresses these 17 into nine key elements. Both look at the different extents of employee vigour, dedication and absorption by providing statements such as 'At my work I feel as if I am bursting with energy' or 'I am proud of the work that I do', to which the respondent employee is required to indicate their degree, or not, of agreement across a range of seven options (Schaufeli et al., 2006: 714). The assumption is that employees in an engaged condition will provide a number of positive answers that correlate to engagement, but no account is taken of the fact that an employee might have fluctuating emotions about their work – the scale merely measures what the respondents *report* having felt/ experienced over the preceding year. The scale has been used and tested across a range of different contexts (and indeed continents) and, according to Halbesleben (2010), predicts levels of employee wellbeing and performance.

There have been several very large studies of engagement and its antecedents and outcomes (Christian et al., 2011; Cole et al., 2012; Tran et al., 2020; Wang et al., 2021) which point out that the construct of engagement, as a concept when measured by the UWES, measures attitudes about work that are insufficiently distinct from other areas of study, such as job satisfaction, making it difficult to view employee engagement as a stand-alone phenomenon. Newman et al. observe that in terms of attitudes 'employee engagement as measured by the UWES is largely redundant' (2010: 55).

It is clear that the terms of reference and the ways of looking at engagement data are subjective interpretations of antecedents, attitudes, behaviours and outcomes that are not time-sensitive and should therefore be used with care.

Engagement and the Employment Relationship

In the middle of the last century, Douglas McGregor (1960) suggested that managers fell into two different categories depending upon the ways in which they saw their staff. Those who thought their staff needed to be pressed into working hard and who were induced to work solely by money he labelled '**Theory X managers**', while those who saw their staff as motivated, enthusiastic and willing to work hard he called '**Theory Y managers**'. These basic and diametrically opposed visions of employee types are often the unacknowledged ancestors behind some of the thinking embedded in the vast engagement literature. Those employees deemed to be engaged correspond to the Theory Y version of actively motivated participants in the workforce, while the disengaged would fit the expectations of Theory X managers. With regard to employee engagement, in terms of managerial styles these two reductionist ways of perceiving the workforce have similarities with Storey's (1987) concepts of hard and soft management and with the Purcell and Sisson (1983) typology of managerial styles. Under a unitarist frame of reference, the traditionalist way of managing, with its authoritarian, hard approach towards the workforce, would neither encourage employees to behave in actively engaged creative ways nor recognise and reward such behaviour when it occurred. In such situations, conflict may occur and if it is not dealt with appropriately it can lead to reduced confidence levels, stress, frustration and employee disengagement. On the other hand, sophisticated paternalist managers are more likely to listen to employee ideas and encourage enthusiasm and independent employee innovation. Here conflict is less likely – the managerial style enabling employee enthusiasm, absorption and engagement (John-Eke and Akintokunbo, 2020: 302; John-Eke and Gabriel, 2019). Research by Shantz et al. (2013) exemplifies this: they surveyed nearly 300 employees in two working environments – construction and consultancy – and found that engaged employees were those allowed to work with high levels of discretion and autonomy with varied tasks, while conversely those with little engagement were more likely to exhibit deviant behaviours, bringing them into conflict with their organisations. The design of job-related tasks and the resources allocated to those entrusted to carry out such tasks are therefore crucial elements in encouraging engagement and discouraging conflict. It may be of course that this research merely reflects the type of jobs and therefore the types of employee found in each of the different specified sectors and is not a reflection of engagement *per se*. It is, however, apparent that where there is open dialogue combined with higher levels of trust within an organisation then there are more likely to be increased employee engagement and correspondingly lower levels of conflict within the employment relationship. Conversely where there are lower levels of trust there are likely to be lower levels of engagement and higher levels of conflict and a poor employment relationship. Yet, whether or not it is deliberately fostered by an employer, or is the result of employees actively enjoying their tasks, there is no escaping the fact that positive expressions of employee engagement do not eradicate, but only mask, the inbuilt tensions at work that derive from managerial styles (influencing job demands and job resources) and found around manifestations of managerial power and jurisdiction, between supervisory levels of control and degrees of employee commitment, echoing what Delbridge (2007) labels '**conflicted collaboration**' and Edwards' 'structural antagonism' (2003: 16–17) (see Chapter 1).

There are a number of factors that are precursors (antecedents) to the ways in which employees behave at work and consequently help to determine whether or not they are engaged with what they are doing. If the employment relationship is such that the employees find that they have:

- sufficient resources to meet the not unrealistic demands of their jobs
- have meaningful work
- encouragement to voice their opinions
- sufficient time to complete their tasks

and are:

- not subject to unrealistic managerial expectations
- able to identify with, and enjoy, their work

then their psychological contracts are likely to be healthy, they are likely to trust their manager, and the workplace relationship will be positive. If this is the case absence rates and turnover are likely to be low and productivity probably higher. As the authors of the 2010 CIPD report found, when they analysed 5,291 questionnaires (supplemented with 180 separate interviews), the main impetuses for engagement were 'meaningful work, voice, senior management communication style and visions, supportive work environment, person–job fit and line management style' (Alfes et al., 2010: 3).

The converse of these incentivising engagement conditions can occur where there are unrealistic managerial expectations, insufficient time in which to complete tasks, a hard managerial style, poor line-manager relationships and work that has little meaning for the employees. Then there is likely to be little employee engagement and higher absence and turnover with a potentially detrimental impact on productivity (see Figure 8.1). In such environments not only will the levels of engagement be low but there is also likely to be a proportionally higher level of conflict – this of course can be expressed individually, with employees perhaps doing the bare minimum and being disparaging about the employer outside work, or it may be expressed collectively in a number of ways ranging from high levels of grievances being processed by the relevant union, to overtime restrictions and perhaps ultimately by strike activity. Indeed, as Rees et al. point out, there is a danger that 'engagement can drive work intensification, with employers coming to *expect* employees to "go the extra mile" as a matter of course, overtime becoming normalized and only over-performance being rewarded' (2013: 2793, emphasis in the original).

The regular Workplace Employment Relations Survey (WERS) has, since 1998, examined, amongst other things, the levels of employee commitment in the workplace as well as the relationship between managers and those they supervise. The 2011 survey (van Wanrooy et al., 2013: 163) showed that one in ten employees regarded workplace relations to be poor, or very poor, yet their managers thought they were good. The latest survey also looked at commitment but, additionally, tried to capture the level of workplace engagement when it asked recipients the extent to which they agreed with the statement 'Using my own initiative (I) carry out tasks that are not required as part of my job' (2013: 167). The results for this are shown in Table 8.1. Just over a quarter of respondents said that they did not use their initiative in this way, but the higher proportion who did may be an indication of greater engagement; it may, on the other hand, have little bearing on engagement but be linked to other factors such as role expectations and an enabling managerial style.

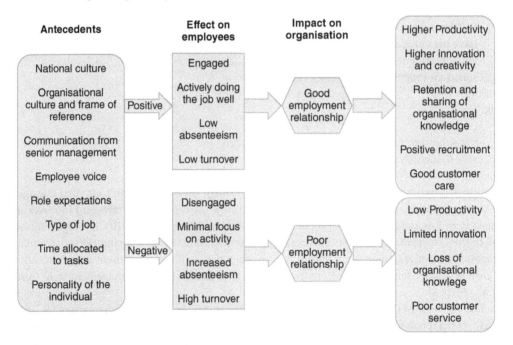

Figure 8.1 Processes of engagement

Table 8.1 WERS data showing percentage of employees who agreed that initiative taking was part of their job

| | Small private enterprise | Medium private enterprise | Large private enterprise | | |
	(<50 employees)	(50-249 employees)	(250+ employees)	Public sector	Total
	%	%	%	%	%
Agree or strongly agree	75	71.2	69.7	69.6	70.8
Neither agree nor disagree	19.2	20.6	20.3	20.5	20.2
Disagree or strongly disagree	5.8	8.2	10	9.9	9
Total	100	100	100	100	100
Base: All employees	2,833	2,244	8,120	8,191	21,388

Source: DBIS, 2013

Exercise 8.4

Read the scenario below and then answer the following questions:

- What aspects of Lucy's experience lead you to think that she was engaged, or otherwise, with her work?
- What aspects of Lucy's experience lead you to think that she was engaged, or otherwise, with her organisation?
- From the little information available, what can you say about the employment relationship at the charity?
- Do you think Lucy's resignation was appropriate behaviour in the circumstances? Why did you say this?

Lucy had worked for a small London charity since 2000. She was a general administrator and because she had been with the organisation for 20 years was able to undertake a range of tasks. Due to increasing financial pressure in 2017 the charity moved premises and made a number of people redundant. The new workplace was very different. Lucy described it as 'characterless' - not only was the building 'just another square box' but a number of her friends and close colleagues had left the organisation. She felt the atmosphere in the new location was very different, as did a number of others who, over the next half a dozen years, either resigned or were placed on stress-linked long-term sick leave.

(Continued)

Lucy found she was having to do more and more work to cover for missing staff. She resigned and explained in her exit interview that she was,

> thinking about work all the time. I can't switch off. It is so frustrating, nothing seems to work properly or be in place, too many people have left. I thought about contacting the union, but what was the point? We no longer have a rep, no one wants to do it and I don't suppose the main union office would be interested. Last week I had a lot of customer facing things to do, nothing was right, the computer system is c**p, it's too slow and awkward, there is no one to help me, I'm doing three people's jobs as it is; it takes ages to sort out queries - people get cross and don't come back. I worry about work all the time and can't switch off, I stay late and start early to get things done, but still have too much work. I can't see it getting any better and that's really upsetting. I am not sleeping and it is making me ill. I'm sorry I am letting you down but it is making me ill.

Engagement Trust and Voice

When discussing engagement, Kahn highlighted the importance of trust, pointing out that feeling safe at work meant an individual was 'able to show and employ one's self without fear of negative consequences to self-image, status or career' (1990: 708). Employees, he said, allowed themselves to become personally engaged in situations where they trusted that they would not suffer. In such an environment, therefore, employees are able to become actively involved with their tasks without fear of this being career limiting and detrimental to their interpersonal relationships at work. Over time the workplace relationship between an employee and an employer, if it is successful, becomes mutually rewarding and creates and fosters levels of trust (Cropanzano and Mitchell, 2005: 890; Sharma, 2021), enabling higher levels of engagement. Where there are high levels of perceived procedural justice that engender high levels of trust within an organisation (particularly when the employer exhibits discretionary behaviour that promotes employee wellbeing), this can prompt improved levels of role performance and extra-role activities that benefit the organisation, just as Tremblay et al. (2010) discovered when they sampled just under 1,300 Canadian health workers. Where employees perceive the resources of an organisation to be allocated in fair ways it links to distributional justice. This is particularly important in organisations where employees feel included and welcome. Here levels of trust and engagement for LGBT+ and ethnic minorities are significantly higher than where distributional *in*justice occurs (Collins and Rocco, 2018; Downey et al., 2015; Victor and Hoole, 2017). Brandl (2021), looking at workers across Europe, has shown that 'mutual trust' is important for maintaining and improving productivity – and engagement along with the psychological contract are, of course, part of this picture. Thus trust is an essential antecedent to employee engagement. If an employee does not trust their line manager, colleagues or employer there is likely to be no engagement with the workplace, although, perhaps, there might be some engagement with the work itself; in such situations it is, however, unlikely that creative and innovative risk taking will occur, employees being wary of the reception such activity might receive. Trust and engagement are inextricably linked; if employees trust their co-workers and supervisors it leads to effective collaboration and higher productivity (Choia and Chobc, 2019; Kaltiainen et al., 2018; Yildiz et al., 2017).

If organisations want to encourage an engaged workforce then the culture must be one that engenders and sustains trust. Individuals with high levels of trust in an organisation are likely to have a positive psychological contract, positive perceptions of all aspects of organisational justice and are therefore more likely to actively engage both with their work and with the organisation itself. Trust, as we have seen in Chapter 3, has direct links with fairness and perceptions of organisational justice – if employees 'perceive their organisation to be unfair because it uses unfair procedures for resource allocations, employees will develop negative attitudes towards the organisation' (Cohen-Charash and Spector, 2001: 287). Such negativity is the antithesis of engagement and has links with Peccei's notion of job resources, that is, where resources are perceived to be inadequate, it leads to lower engagement and perceptions of organisational injustice.

Mentari and Ratmawati (2020) showed, in their study of employees in an Indonesian chemical company, that there is a positive correlation between both distributive and procedural justice and employee engagement. However, when an individual perceives that their treatment in the workplace has been unfair, possibly due to perceptions of distributional, procedural, interactional or informational injustice, it is likely that they will infer that, compared to others in the workplace, they are neither valued nor respected by the organisation (Allan Lind and Tyler, 1988); such perceptions inhibit engaged behaviours and may of course lead to the individuals either leaving the organisation or behaving in ways that are counterproductive. Where there are few, or no, perceptions of distributional and procedural justice this may result in employees adjusting their output and subsequently reducing their levels of engagement with the organisation. Conversely high levels of perceived procedural justice are an antecedent to organisational commitment and trust in managerial staff (Hadi et al., 2020; McFarlin and Sweeney, 1992). This is tempered where organisations are highly bureaucratic and controlling, clearly prescribing and limiting role behaviours; explicit levels of tight control and expressions of power sometimes militate against commitment to the organisation, employees feeling constrained and limited by the bureaucracy, and hence less trusted by the organisation. In other words, depending on the dictates of their role (i.e., the job demands), employees evaluate whether or not it is worth investing additional time and effort in a job depending upon the ways in which they perceive levels of organisational justice. Engagement is discretionary (not obligatory) and trust is a crucial and necessary antecedent to it occurring.

It is a self-evident truth that it is disengaged staff that are those employees actively looking for new jobs. Non-inclusive work processes that fail to inspire and support inclusivity at work are effectively promoting perceptions of injustice, labour turnover and inhibited engagement. Where organisations have strategies that actively foster a variety of inclusive ways of working then engagement and labour retention improve.

Case Snippet 8.1

Inclusivity Essential for Engagement

The international law company, Norton Rose Fulbright, with its global reach (it has more than 3,500 lawyers and associated staff based in Africa, Asia, Australia, Canada, Europe, Latin America, the Middle East, the UK and the USA) has successfully introduced a wide variety of inclusive measures that all help retain and engage staff. As part of its structure, the firm has created a Global and Inclusion Advisory Council, comprising regional CEOs and global directors alongside senior management. This vital top level of support sends a weighty message that diversity and inclusion are a crucial part of the strategy and culture, not to be ignored, but embraced and valued. The firm acknowledges that the more 'comfortable'

(Continued)

employees are at work the more likely they are to bring their 'whole-selves' to work and to be creative, engaged and remain with the firm. Its website points out to prospective employees that it expects

> ... you to be instrumental in shaping the growth of the business. You will become our most important asset. We shall want you to succeed in everything you do with us; and to feel valued – feel like you belong.

In other words, its strategy of inclusivity, made explicit to prospective and actual employees, is designed to facilitate work engagement and feelings of wellbeing. The improving year-on-year diversity figures are evidence of this and indicative of people feeling comfortable at work.

There is a range of in-house programmes to aid inclusivity. A number of different networking groups, aimed at providing employees with resources have been established, e.g., WiN (Women in Norton Rose Fulbright) and Early WiN - both support and run a number of internal events focusing on career progression; Pride - aims to create a more inclusive and accepting environment for LGBTQ individuals; Compass - a forum for learning about Islamic faith, culture and business; Origins - promotes ethnic and cultural awareness; Novel - increases awareness of social issues and perspectives surrounding diversity and inclusion through literature and dialogue; Advance - a resource group for social mobility; Shine - a disability discussion forum on, sharing experiences and advice while raising awareness of disabilities and health-related topics across the wider firm. All these groups provide networking opportunities and support helping participants meet like-minded individuals across the firm.

In April 2019, the firm replaced its Dignity at Work policy with a Respectful Behaviour one that set out, in detail, which behaviours the firm finds abhorrent and inappropriate. All employees and Partners have completed a mandatory e-learning training on Respectful Behaviour. NRF views diversity as being fundamentally 'about diversity of thought and ... believes that superior business performance requires tapping into these unique perspectives'. When its employees feel comfortable, they are, it thinks, more engaged, more productive and happier.

Sources: www.nortonrosefulbright.com/en/about/our-firm; www.nortonrosefulbright.com/en/careers; www.nortonrosefulbright.com/en/about/diversity-and-inclusion

---

As Macey et al. say,

> There is a need to treat people fairly, not just because people want to reciprocate, but because they will feel safe to use their energy without feeling that it will be used in vain on something unimportant, that credit that what they do will be taken by others, or more simply that they will be abused. (2009: 168–9)

Purcell (2013b: 244) meanwhile links levels of trust with the degree to which employees are able to voice their opinions and have their views sought, heard and valued (see Figure 8.2).

One of the antecedents of trust is an aspect of informational justice, namely the timely and appropriate sharing of information. Where there are open and transparent channels of workplace communication it is more than likely that employees will trust their colleagues and, as a consequence, show a greater propensity to become engaged with their work (Cohen-Charash and Spector, 2001; Kalay and Turkey, 2016; Qayyum et al., 2021). Communicating information about the organisation, job and tasks is crucial for two reasons: first, it lets employees know what to expect at work and why decisions have been made; but second, it is the very *act* of sharing and disseminating information that employees appreciate. When employees are 'kept in the loop' it increases their levels of trust in the organisation; when alternatively they are 'kept in the dark' their levels of trust decrease and with it their propensity to be actively engaged at the workplace. Corporate communicators know that it is possible to influence and persuade the workforce and that communication to employees may have an impact on their attitudes and values and subsequently on their behaviour. Accurate and targeted internal communication is an antecedent to employee engagement and following communication, where employees are able to enter into a meaningful dialogue with those in power, levels of engagement and trust escalate. The communication abilities of leadership teams are therefore recognised as important precursors of engagement, good communication facilitating engagement, poor communication leading to disenchantment/disengagement (Dajani and Zaki, 2015; MacLeod and Clarke, 2009; Men et al., 2021; Verma et al., 2021).

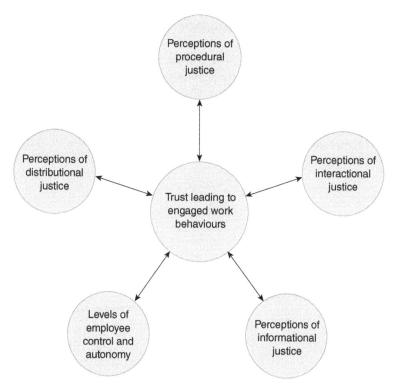

Figure 8.2 Positive employee perceptions of organisational justice enhance trust and enable engagement

Employee voice is a critical component of both interactional and informational justice. When voice is effective, according to MacLeod and Clarke, it is one of the empowering and essential ingredients that help to create an engaged employee; it occurs where 'employees' views are sought out, they are listened to and see their opinions count and make a difference. They speak out and challenge when appropriate. A strong sense of listening and of responsiveness permeates the organisation' (2009: 75).

Voice of course can be:

* *individual*, as when an employee discusses their role or task with a line manager, or completes an opinion survey
* *collective*, where voice is more likely to be indirect and via a representative on a consultative or negotiating committee

but the evidence is that, however it is enabled, voice is likely to improve reciprocal levels of trust and facilitate engagement for the individual with the employing organisation (see, e.g., Farndale et al., 2011; Kao et al., 2021). As Allen and Rogelberg put it, when

> … managers make their workgroup meetings relevant, allow for employee voice in their meetings where possible, and manage the meeting from a time perspective, employees appear poised to fully engage themselves in their work in general. (2013: 542).

John Purcell, in an article for the Involvement and Participation Association (2013a), elaborates on this when he points out that where there is deliberate, positive and active line-manager behaviour designed to promote and encourage employee voice (which occurs in organisations where there is a strong consultative infrastructure), then the predisposition and subsequent corollary for engagement is higher than when just one of these two antecedents is present. However, as previously noted, much of the engagement research is inconclusive, and the desire by managements to introduce engagement programmes is often a response to claims about engagement that specifically reflect the managerial and *unitarist* viewpoint, whereby employee engagement programmes are designed to 'trigger' engagement in order to gain the acceptance, and internalisation, of organisational goals. This perspective sits uncomfortably with the notion of employee voice where an individual employee, or group of employees, is able to safely express a view that might not accord with the established organisational goals (see Figure 8.3).

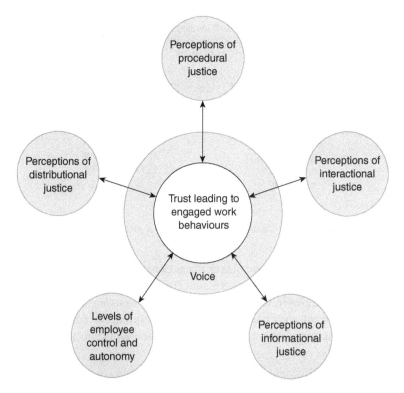

Figure 8.3 The importance of voice in employee perceptions of organisational trust leading to engagement

Case Study 8.2

Inclusivity Drives Engagement at Auto Trader (AT)

The UK and Ireland's largest 'digital marketplace' for vehicles, Auto Trader, has five separate offices, including three in Dublin, London and Manchester. It held its first annual employee network summit in 2021. This virtual, day-long, meeting brought together all of the various diverse networking groups within the company and, during the course of the day, analysed the results from the most recent engagement survey, retrospectively examined the company's financial performance, and developed a plan for the coming year, including a diary of employee engagement events (thereby avoiding holding activities at the same time). The meeting was so successful it has become an annual event.

Founded in 1975, in 2015 Auto Trader consolidated its 30 different offices into just three. At this time, its 800 (now 950) staff had to switch from paper-based work systems to a wholly digital environment. The company was concerned that resulting levels of staff engagement would fall and labour turnover increase. The changes impacted individual employees in different ways, resulting in a range of different employee experiences. The requirement for the management team to discover exactly what the workforce were feeling at this difficult and stressful time, led to the introduction of a new online engagement platform where the results could be analysed and acted on quickly.

Since that time, the company has continually strived to improve the ways to enhance and measure employee engagement. Priding itself on its collaborative culture AT set up a number of different employee networks to represent different staff groupings. These groups, catering for a range of interests, are run by employees and supported by the business (which provides guidance and governance). There are 12 distinct network groups embracing, amongst others, BAME, LGBT+, women, age, neurodiversity, community work, new starters and mental health first aiders. The groups are not mutually exclusive and employees can join more than one. Each group typically has around 100–200 members. The networks create clear objectives linked to both their own and the company's interests. Using data from employee surveys, as well as from the broad range of personal experiences within the group, they identify specific areas and topics that need addressing. The results are impressive, with most employees logging into specific networks on the company communication channel, Slack, on a daily basis. Part of the remit for each network is to raise awareness and improve the employee experience. This seems to be working; for example 93% of disabled employees, equalling the company average, said they were proud to work for AT.

Accurate information from the networks coupled with a mass of HR data has helped the company address areas that may have remained hidden. For example, in 2019 it became apparent that bisexual colleagues felt invisible at work. The LGBT+ network addressed this by publicising and showcasing bisexual employees, addressing misconceptions and encouraging open conversations. This raised awareness across the whole company and helped bisexual staff to feel included. The following year's engagement survey revealed an improvement in the ways bisexual staff felt towards work.

Sources: https://plc.autotrader.co.uk/who-we-are/about-us/; Autotrader, 2021

Summary

Employee engagement is a difficult concept about which to make accurate statements. It concerns the state of mind of an employee whereby they are actively involved with what they are working on such that they are fully engrossed in the task both mentally and physically. There are a number of predisposing factors that facilitate engagement and these include not only the personality of the employee but managerial styles, reciprocal levels of trust, job demands and job resources, levels of communication and an ability for the employee to influence the work processes by voicing opinions. Engagement may fluctuate over time, and sometimes occurs in short bursts of activity known as 'state work engagement'. Over-engagement can sometimes lead to exhaustion and mental burnout, while disengagement leads to low productivity, high absence levels and conflict. Where engagement is present it is likely that productivity will be sustained at a higher level and that innovation and creativity may occur. The concept is embraced by management who regard it as a way of ensuring higher levels of productivity than might otherwise have been achieved.

Review Questions

1   Is the effort to encourage employee engagement a manipulative managerial practice or an ethical way of treating employees? Justify your answer with references to organisational justice.
2   Why do some practitioners regard employee engagement as the 'philosopher's stone' in the employment relationship?
3   Employee voice only has a positive impact on workplace engagement when employees are able to influence decisions about their own work levels and practices. What academic evidence is there to back up this statement?

Revision Exercise 8.1

Make a list of the relevant academic arguments and research that underpin the 2021 comment by Kate Prichard, Head of Engagement and Leadership at Questback, that

> ... engaging staff has never been more vital - or more difficult ... new ways of working require new ways of listening, accelerating the pre-existing trend away from a single, annual employee engagement survey to more regular listening and engagement. The importance of feedback, two way communication and experience are now front of mind for everyone, whether employees, managers or HR teams. (Prichard, 2021)

Read the following information about SendGrid.

- Using academic reasoning to justify your answer, evaluate whether you think employee engagement is a reality at the company.
- How engaged might you feel if you worked for SendGrid?
- Why did you reach this conclusion?

Jim Franklin, CEO of SendGrid, an American company that provides email services for businesses and employs around 130 people, advocates an approach to a workplace culture that he says enables the company's employees to buy into the values of the organisation and become actively engaged *and* highly productive. The system known as 4Hs – honest, hungry, humble and happy – is, he says, integral to everything SendGrid does.

The employees are told that the company values honesty and endeavours to be transparent in everything it does, trusting its employees so that they in turn trust the organisation. *Honesty*, according to Franklin, is about not avoiding difficult conversations, being respectful but direct and facing up to and discussing sometimes unwelcome facts. To get the message across he uses sound bites – 'Trust First Trust: if you put trust out; you get trust back' is the organisational shorthand for showing that trust is reciprocal and necessary in a culture where employees carry a lot of delegated responsibility for front-line decision making.

Hungry, on the other hand, encapsulates the company's drive to achieve high standards and meet targets by expecting their workforce to take initiative: 'A lot of what happens at our company is bottom up. Want a new job? Create one'.

Humble indicates that this is a learning organisation where everyone has the opportunity to learn from one another and is prepared to consider divergent ways of doing things, willing to be challenged and accepting that occasionally they might be wrong. Consequently, he says, employees have a high degree of voice, they have been given the freedom to speak out and suggest things. Humility is also about giving credit to the team, instead of wanting the spotlight.

Happy refers to a general feeling that things will work out and a sense of being thankful for what you have. For example, Franklin says 'I cancelled our annual company trip to Mexico. The employee reaction was ... "That's cool. It was great while it lasted. Maybe we'll do it again down the road." (The trip is back on, by the way.) What I don't like is when benefits become entitlements.'

In addition to the 4Hs, Franklin says the following factors are important for engagement:

- knowing the big idea
- knowing exactly how your daily work influences it
- measuring progress toward that goal every day

and he explains that if an organisation is grappling with low engagement, the first step is to set clear values, the second to articulate them and the third and final step 'is to interview (and fire) based on them'.

(Continued)

Firing is not anathema to SendGrid: in early 2013, the company fired an employee who tweeted and blogged about two men sitting behind her at a conference when they were making what she felt were inappropriate remarks. (They were making jokes using 'double-entendre' around the words, commonplace amongst programmers, 'dongles' and 'forking'.) The company, and indeed the employee, received a lot of unwelcome and unpleasant publicity following which SendGrid put a statement on Facebook saying that the blogging employee's contract had been terminated and that 'while we generally are sensitive and confidential with respect to employee matters the situation has taken on a public nature. We have taken action that we believe is in the overall best interests of SendGrid, its employees, and our customers.'

Sources: ni Aodha, 2017; Koetsier, 2013; Steere, 2013

Relevant Articles for Further Reading

Fletcher, L. and Robinson, D. (2013) 'Measuring and understanding employee engagement', in C. Truss, K. Alfes, R. Delbridge, A. Shantz and E. Soane (eds), *Employee Engagement in Theory and Practice*. London: Routledge, pp. 273–90.

This provides a clear exposition of the concept of engagement and, importantly, how it is measured.

Pass, S., Watling, D., Kougiannou, N., Ridgway, M. and Abe, C. (2019) *Case Study Report: Exploring Employee Engagement in the Police Force*. Available at: http://irep.ntu.ac.uk/id/ eprint/38813/1/1236224_Pass_repl.pdf (accessed 1 August 2021).

This report, looking at engagement within the Police Force, covers many of the issues examined in this chapter and illustrates how engagement may (or may not) work in practice.

Purcell, J. (2014) 'Disengaging from engagement', *Human Resource Management Journal*, 24(3): 241–54.

The article provides an important, and critical look at the concept of engagement in relation to HRM.

Satata, D. B. M. (2021) 'Employee engagement as an effort to improve work performance: Literature review', *Ilomata International Journal of Social Science*, 2(1): 41–9.

A useful review of the engagement literature to date.

References

Alfes, K., Truss, K., Soane, E. C., Rees, C. and Gatenby, M. (2010) *Creating an Engaged Workforce*. London: CIPD.

Allan Lind, E. A. and Tyler, T. R. (1988) *The Social Psychology of Procedural Justice*. New York: Plenum.

Allen, J. A. and Rogelberg, S. G. (2013) 'Manager-led group meetings: A context for promoting employee engagement', *Group & Organization Management*, *38*(5): 543–69.

Autotrader (2021) *Making Diversity and Inclusion a Business Reality 2021*. Available at: https://plc. autotrader.co.uk/media/2312/making-diversity-and-inclusion-a-business-reality-2021-ennis-co-auto-trader.pdf (accessed 2 March 2022).

Baghdadi, N. A., Farghaly Abd-El Aliem, S. M. and Alsayed, S. K. (2021) 'The relationship between nurses' job crafting behaviours and their work engagement', *Journal of Nursing Management*, *29*(2): 214–19.

Blau, P.M. (1964) *Exchange and Power in Social Life*. New York: Wiley.

Brandl, B. (2021) 'Trust relationships in employment relationships: The role of trust for firm profitability', *International Journal of the Economics of Business*, *28*(1): 139–61.

Briner, R.B. (2014) 'What is employee engagement and does it matter? An evidence based approach', in D. Robinson and J. Gifford (eds), *The Future of Engagement: Thought Piece Collection*. Brighton: Institute for Employment Studies.

Brownhill, L. (2013) 'Employee engagement: Want to drive profits? Get your staff involved', *Business Reporter*. Available at: http://business-reporter.co.uk/2013/09/employee-engagement-want-to-drive-profits-get-your-staff-involved/ (accessed 24 February 2013).

Caza, A. (2012) 'Typology of eight domains of discretion in organisations', *Journal of Management Studies*, *49*(1): 144–77.

Chartered Management Institute (CMI) (2020) *Management Transformed: Managing in a Marathon Crisis*. Available at: www.managers.org.uk/wp-content/uploads/2020/11/management-transformed-managing-in-a-marathon-crisis.pdf (accessed 1 May 2022).

Choia, O.-K. and Chobc, E. (2019) 'The mechanism of trust affecting collaboration in virtual teams and the moderating roles of the culture of autonomy and task complexity', *Computers in Human Behavior*, *91*: 305–15.

Christian, M. S., Garza, A. S. and Slaughter, J. E. (2011) 'Work engagement: A quantitative review and test of its relations with task and contextual performance', *Personnel Psychology*, *64*(1): 89–136.

CIPD (2010) *Creating an Engaged Workforce*, Research Report, January. London: CIPD.

Cohen-Charash, Y. and Spector, P. E. (2001) 'The role of justice in organizations: A meta-analysis', *Organizational Behaviour and Human Decision Processes*, *86*(2): 78–321.

Cole, M. S., Walter, F., Bedeian, A. G. and O'Boyle, E. H. (2012) 'Job burnout and employee engagement: A meta-analytic examination of construct proliferation', *Journal of Management*, *38*(5): 1550–81.

Collins, J. C. and Rocco, T. S. (2018) 'Queering employee engagement to understand and improve the performance of gay male law enforcement officers: A phenomenological exploration', *Performance Improvement Quarterly*, *30*(4): 273–95.

Conte, J. M. and Landy, F. J. (2019) *Work in the 21st Century: An Introduction to Industrial and Organizational Psychology* (6th edn). Chichester: Wiley.

Costa, P. L., Passos, A. M., Bakker, A. B., Romana, R. and Ferrão, C. (2017) 'Interactions in engaged work teams: A qualitative study', *Team Performance Management: An International Journal*, *23*(5/6): 206–26.

Cropanzano, R. and Mitchell, M. S. (2005) 'Social exchange theory: An interdisciplinary review', *Journal of Management*, *31*: 874–900.

Dajani, D. and Zaki, M. A. (2015) 'The impact of employee engagement on job performance and organisational commitment in the Egyptian banking sector', *Journal of Business and Management Sciences*, *3*(5): 138–47. doi:10.12691/JBMS-3-5-1

Delbridge, R. (2007) 'Explaining conflicted collaboration: A critical realist approach to hegemony', *Organization Studies*, *28*(9): 1347–57.

Department for Business, Innovation & Skills (DBIS) (2013) *The 2011 Workplace Employment Relations Study (WERS) Transparency Data*. London: DBIS. Available at: www.gov.uk/government/publications/the-2011-workplace-employment-relations-study-wers-transparency-data (accessed 5 October 2015).

Direction, S. (2020) 'Determining the link between employee engagement and organizational effectiveness: South African company insights on the all-encompassing importance of good communication', *Strategic Direction*, *36*(8): 33–35.

Downey, S. N., van der Werff, L., Thomas, K. M. and Plaut, V. C. (2015) 'The role of diversity practices and inclusion in promoting trust and employee engagement', *Journal of Applied Social Psychology*, *45*(1): 35–44.

Edwards, P. (2003) *Industrial Relations Theory and Practice* (2nd edn). Oxford: Blackwell.

Eldor, L. (2017) 'Looking on the bright side: The positive role of organisational politics in the relationship between employee engagement and performance at work', *Applied Psychology*, *66*(2): 233–59.

Farndale, E., Van Ruiten, J., Kelliher, C. and Hope-Hailey, V. (2011) 'The influence of perceived employee voice on organisational commitment: An exchange perspective', *Human Resource Management*, *50*(1): 113–29.

Gallup (2021) *State of the Global Workplace*. Available at: www.gallup.com/workplace/349484/state-of-the-global-workplace.aspx (accessed 19 July 2021).

Gifford, J. and Young, J. (2021) *Employee Engagement: Definitions, Measures and Outcomes*, discussion report. London: Chartered Institute of Personnel and Development.

Guest, D. E. (2014) 'Employee engagement, fashionable fad or long term fixture', in C. Truss, K. Alfes, R. Delbridge, A. Shantz and E. Soane (eds), *Employee Engagement in Theory and Practice*. London: Routledge, pp. 221–35.

Hadi, S., Tjahjono, H. K. and Palupi, M. (2020) 'Study of organizational justice in SMEs and positive consequences: Systematic review', *International Journal of Advanced Science and Technology*, *29*(03): 4717–30.

Halbesleben, J. R. (2010) 'A meta-analysis of work engagement: Relationships with burnout, demands, resources, and consequences', in A. B. Bakker and M. P. Leiter (eds), *Work Engagement: A Handbook of Essential Theory and Research*. New York: Psychology Press, pp. 102–17.

Hearn, S. (2020) 'Employee engagement isn't just HR's responsibility', *Personnel Today*, 11 March. Available at: www.personneltoday.com/hr/responsibility-for-employee-engagement-hr/ (accessed 21 July 2020).

Jabeen, R. and Rahim, N. (2021) 'Exploring the effects of despotic leadership on employee engagement, employee trust and task performance', *Management Science Letters*, *11*(1): 223–32.

Jabutay, F. (2018) 'Antecedents and consequences of emotional dissonance among call center agents', *Kasem Bundit Journal*, *19*(June): 273–86.

John-Eke, E. C. and Akintokunbo, O. O. (2020) 'Conflict management as a tool for increasing organizational effectiveness: A review of literature', *International Journal of Academic Research in Business and Social Sciences*, *10*(5): 299–311.

John-Eke, E. C. and Gabriel, J. M. O. (2019) 'Corporate incivility and employee engagement', *West African Journal of Business*, *13*(1): 1595–3750.

Kahn, W. A. (1990) 'Psychological conditions of personal engagement and disengagement at work', *Academy of Management Journal*, *33*(4): 692–724.

Kalay, F. and Turkey, V. (2016) 'The impact of organizational justice on employee performance: A survey in Turkey and Turkish context', *International Journal of Human Resource Studies*, *6*(1): 1–19.

Kaltiainen J., Lipponen, J. and Petrou, P. (2018) 'Dynamics of trust and fairness during organizational change: Implications for job crafting and work engagement', in M. Vakola and P. Petrou (eds), *Organizational Change: Psychological Effects and Strategies for Coping*. London: Routledge.

Kao, K. Y., Hsu, H. H., Thomas, C. L., Cheng, Y. C., Lin, M. T. and Li, H. F. (2021) 'Motivating employees to speak up: Linking job autonomy, PO fit, and employee voice behaviors through work engagement', *Current Psychology*: 1–15.

Katili, P. B., Wibowo, W. and Akbar, M. (2021) 'The effects of leaderships styles, work-life balance, and employee engagement on employee performance', *Quantitative Economics and Management Studies*, *2*(3): 199–205.

Kaur, R. and Randhawa, G. (2020) 'Supportive supervisor to curtail turnover intentions: Do employee engagement and work–life balance play any role?', in *Evidence-based HRM: A Global Forum for Empirical Scholarship*. Available at: https://doi.org/10.1108/ebhrm-12-2019-0118 (accessed 18 August 2022).

Koetsier, J. (2013) 'Playhaven developer fired for sexual jokes after SendGrid marketer outs him on Twitter', *VentureBeat*, 20 March. Available at: http://venturebeat.com/2013/03/20/playhaven-developer-fired-for-making-sexual-jokes-after-sendgrids-developer-evangelist-outs-him-on-twitter (accessed 7 October 2015).

Kooij, D. T., Nijssen, H., Bal, P. M. and van der Kruijssen, D. T. (2020) 'Crafting an interesting job: Stimulating an active role of older workers in enhancing their daily work engagement and job performance', *Work, Aging and Retirement*, *6*(3): 165–74.

Kuijpers, E., Kooij, D. T. and van Woerkom, M. (2020) 'Align your job with yourself: The relationship between a job crafting intervention and work engagement, and the role of workload', *Journal of Occupational Health Psychology*, *25*(1): 1.

Laulié, L. and Morgeson, F. P. (2020) 'The end is just the beginning: Turnover events and their impact on those who remain', *Personnel Psychology*. Available at: https://doi.org/10.1111/PEPS.12422 (accessed 18 August 2022).

Leary, T. and Miller, M. (2021) 'The toxic relationship between laissez-faire leadership and employee burnout: No longer a well-kept secret', *International Leadership Journal*, *13*(2): 3–15.

Macey, W. H. and Schneider, B. (2008) 'The meaning of employee engagement', *Industrial and Organizational Psychology*, *1*(1): 3–30.

Macey, W. H., Schneider, B., Barbera, K. M. and Young, S. A. (2009) *Employee Engagement: Tools for Analysis, Practice, and Competitive Advantage*. Chichester: Wiley.

MacLeod, D. and Clarke, N. (2009) *Engaging for Success: Enhancing Performance Through Employee Engagement*. Available at: www.engageforsuccess.org/wp-content/uploads/2012/09/file52215.pdf (accessed 7 October 2015).

McFarlin, D. B. and Sweeney, P. D. (1992) 'Distributive and procedural justice as predictors of satisfaction with personal and organizational outcomes', *Academy of Management Journal*, *35*(3): 626–37.

Maslach, C., Jackson, S. E. and Leiter, M. P. (2017) *Maslach Burnout Inventory Manual* (4th edn). Menlo Park, CA: Mindgarden Press.

McGregor, D. (1960) *The Human Side of Enterprise*. New York: McGrawHill.

Men, L. R., Qin, Y. S. and Mitson, R. (2021) 'Engaging startup employees via charismatic leadership communication: The importance of communicating "vision, passion, and care"', *International Journal of Business Communication*. Available at: https://doi.org/10.1177%2F23294884211020488 (accessed 18 August 2022).

Mentari, R. R. and Ratmawati, D. (2020, February) 'Linking distributive justice and procedural justice to employee engagement through psychological contract fulfillment (a field study in Karmand Mitra Company Andalan, Surabaya)', in *3rd Global Conference On Business, Management, and Entrepreneurship (GCBME 2018)*. Paris: Atlantis Press, pp. 199–203.

MetLife UK (2022) *More Than 10 Million Brits Take Time Off Due To Burnout*, press release, 1 March. Available at: www.metlife.co.uk/about-us/media-centre/media-centre-archive/2022/march/10-Million-Brits-pull-sickie/ (accessed 3 April 2022).

Mishra, A. K. and Spreitzer, G. M. (1998) 'Explaining how survivors respond to downsizing: The roles of trust, empowerment, justice and work redesign', *Academy of Management Review*, 23(3): 567–88.

Newman, D. A., Joseph, D. L. and Hulin, C. L. (2010) 'Job attitudes and employee engagement: Considering the attitude "A-factor"', in S. L. Albrecht (ed.), *The Handbook of Employee Engagement: Perspectives, Issues Research and Practice*. Cheltenham: Edward Elgar, pp. 43–61.

ni Aodha, E., (2017) *Employee Engagement: The SendGrid Way*. Available at: https://sendgrid.com/blog/employee-engagement-the-4h-way/ (accessed 7 August 2021).

Peccei, R. (2004) 'Human Resource Management and the Search for the Happy Workplace'. Inaugural Addresses Research in Management Series. Erasmus Research Institute of Management.

Peccei, R. (2013) 'Employee engagement at work: An evidence-based review', in S. Bach and M. Edwards (eds), *Managing Human Resources* (5th edn). Chichester: Wiley, pp. 336–63.

Prichard, K. (2021) *Thriving at Work – New Ways to Engage Your People*. Available from: https://engageforsuccess.org/strategic-leadership/thriving-at-work-new-ways-to-engage-your-people/ (accessed 7 August 2021).

Purcell, J. (2013a) 'Employee voice and engagement', in C. Truss, K. Alfes, R. Delbridge, A. Shantz and E. Soane (eds), *Employee Engagement in Theory and Practice*. London: Routledge, pp. 236–40.

Purcell, J. (2013b) 'The future of engagement, speaking up for employee voice', Involvement and Participation Association. Available at: www.ipa-involve.com/news/the-future-of-engagement/ (accessed 4 November 2015).

Purcell, J. and Sisson, K. (1983) 'Strategies and practice in the management of industrial relations in Britain', in G. Bain (ed.), *Industrial Relations in Britain*. Oxford: Blackwell.

Qayyum, A., Shafi, M. Q., Naz, I. and Gul, Z. (2021) 'Linkage of organizational justice and employees cognitive work engagement: Power distance orientation matters. *Foundation University Journal of Business & Economics*, 6(1).

Rees, C., Alfes, K. and Gatenby, M. (2013) 'Employee voice and engagement: Connections and consequences', *The International Journal of Human Resource Management*, 24(14): 2780–98.

Robertson, I. T. and Cooper, C. L. (2010) 'Full engagement: The integration of employee engagement and psychological well-being', *Leadership & Organization Development Journal*, 31(4): 324–36.

Robinson, D. (2008) '"Employee engagement an IES perspective", presentation to the IES HR network', in D. MacLeod and N. Clarke, *Engaging for Success: Enhancing Performance through Employee Engagement*. Available at: www.engageforsuccess.org/wp-content/uploads/2012/09/file52215.pdf (accessed 7 October 2015).

Saks, A. M. (2008) 'The meaning and bleeding of employee engagement: How muddy is the water?', *Industrial and Organizational Psychology*, 1(1): 40–3.

Schaufeli, W. B. and Backer, A. B. (2010) 'Defining and measuring work engagement: Bringing clarity to the concept', in A. B. Backer and M. P. Leiter (eds), *Work Engagement: A Handbook of Essential Theory and Research*. New York: Psychology Press, pp. 10–24.

Schaufeli, W. B. and Salanova, M. (2011) 'Work engagement: On how to better catch a slippery concept', *European Journal of Work and Organisational Psychology*, 20: 39–46.

Schaufeli, W. B., Salanova, M., González-Romá, V. and Bakker, A. B. (2002) 'The measurement of engagement and burnout: A two-sample confirmatory factor analytic approach', *Journal of Happiness Studies*, 3(1): 71–92.

Schaufeli, W. B., Bakker, A. B. and Salanova, M. (2006) 'The measurement of work engagement with a short questionnaire: A cross-national study', *Educational and Psychological Measurement*, 66(4): 701–16.

Shantz, A., Alfes, K., Truss, C. and Soane, E. (2013) 'The role of employee engagement in the relationship between job design and task performance, citizenship and deviant behaviours', *The International Journal of Human Resource Management*, 24(13): 2608–27.

Sharma, A. (2021) 'Want engaged employees? Encourage human resource and enhance organizational connectedness', *Perception*, 6(1).

Shuck, B., Osam, K., Zigarmi, D. and Nimon, K. (2017) 'Definitional and conceptual muddling: Identifying the positionality of employee engagement and defining the construct', *Human Resource Development Review*, 16(3): 263–93.

Shuck, B., Kim, W. and Chai, D. S. (2021) 'The chicken and egg conundrum: Job satisfaction or employee engagement and implications for human resources', *New Horizons in Adult Education and Human Resource Development*, 33(1): 4-24.

Shimazu, A., Miyanaka, D. and Schaufeli, W. B. (2010) 'Work engagement from a cultural perspective', in S. L. Albrecht (ed.), *The Handbook of Employee Engagement: Perspectives, Issues Research and Practice*. Cheltenham: Edward Elgar, pp. 364–72.

Sonnentag, S., Dormann, C. and Demerouti, E. (2010) 'Not all states are created equal: The concept of state work engagement', in A. B. Backer and M. P. Leiter (eds), *Work Engagement: A Handbook of Essential Theory and Research*. New York: Psychology Press.

Steere, L. (2013) 'Creating employee engagement through culture and job design', *Lead Change Group*, 4 December. Available at: http://leadchangegroup.com/creating-employee-engagement-through-culture-and-job-design/ (accessed 7 October 2015).

Storey, J. (1987) *Developments in the Management of Human Resources: An Interim Report*, Warwick Papers in Industrial Relations. Coventry: Warwick University SIBS.

Tiny Pulse (2019) *The 2019 Employee Engagement Report: The End of Employee Loyalty*. Available at: www.tinypulse.com/hubfs/EE%20Report%202019.pdf (accessed 18 July 2021).

Tran, T. T. T., Watanabe, K., Imamura, K., Nguyen, H. T., Sasaki, N., Kuribayashi, K.,... and Kawakami, N. (2020) 'Reliability and validity of the Vietnamese version of the 9-item Utrecht Work Engagement Scale', *Journal of Occupational Health*, 62(62), e12157.

Tremblay, M., Cloutier, J., Simard, G., Chênevert, D. and Vandenberghe, C. (2010) 'The role of HRM practices, procedural justice, organizational support and trust in organizational commitment and in-role and extra-role performance', *The International Journal of Human Resource Management*, 21(3): 405–33.

van Wanrooy, B., Bewley, H., Bryson, A., Forth, J., Freeth, L., Stokes, L. and Wood, S. (2013) *Employment Relations in the Shadow of Recession*. Basingstoke: Palgrave Macmillan.

Van Wijhe, C., Peeters, M. and Schaufeli, W.B. (2013) 'Irrational beliefs at work and their implications for workaholism', *Journal of Occupational Rehabilitation, 23*: 336–46.

Verma, J., Bhattacherjee, S. B. and Kumari, R. (2021) 'Convergence of leadership styles and organisational ambidexterity in the perspective of employee engagement: A proposed framework', *International Journal of Business Competition and Growth, 7*(3): 262–83.

Victor, J. and Hoole, C. (2017) 'The influence of organisational rewards on workplace trust and work engagement', *SA Journal of Human Resource Management, 15*(1): 1–14.

Wang, J., Zhan, Y., Li, L., Wang, M. and Tian, Y. (2021) 'Correlation analysis between mental health and work engagement of nurses', *Chinese Journal of Practical Nursing*: 517–21.

Welbourne, T. M. (2011) 'Engaged in what? So what? A role-based perspective for the future of employee engagement', in A. Wilkinson and K. Townsend (eds), *The Future of Employment Relations: New Paradigms, New Developments*. Basingstoke: Palgrave Macmillan.

Yildiz, R. Ö., Baran, E., Ayaz, I. S. (2017) 'The effect of organizational trust on work engagement: An application on logistics personnel', *The International New Issues in Social Sciences, 5*(5): 139–58.

Zeijen, M. E., Peeters, M. C. and Hakanen, J. J. (2018) 'Workaholism versus work engagement and job crafting: What is the role of self-management strategies?', *Human Resource Management Journal, 28*(2): 357–73.

9

SHARING INFORMATION AND DECISION-MAKING: FROM EMPLOYEE INVOLVEMENT TO PARTNERSHIP

Learning Outcomes

By the end of this chapter, you should be able to:

- analyse definitions of employee involvement, participation and partnership and explain their importance for the employment relationship
- identify the aims underlying each system in order to understand their differences and how each relates to managerial styles and perspectives
- critically explore the relationship between involvement, managerial control and conflict reduction
- examine different approaches to employee involvement and evaluate a number of different employee involvement initiatives and mechanisms
- critically analyse the links between involvement and perceptions of workplace justice.

What to Expect

This chapter takes a critical look at the development of employee involvement, participation and partnership (EIP), linking these to employers' styles, perspectives and conflict reduction mechanisms. Employee workplace participation and involvement concerns the structures, mechanics and practices that give employees a chance to express opinions and/or participate in decision-making within their organisation (Lavelle et al., 2010). EIP is, as Wilkinson et al. point out (2020), rather an 'elastic' term, meaning different things to different people. The types, depth and range of employees' influence is not homogenous: some organisational arrangements merely provide employees with an opportunity to express opinions without real involvement in decision making, whereas others provide employees with a more significant say in organisational governance. A number of different definitions and models of EIP are critically explored together with relevant organisational practices and significant, relevant, legislative influences. The introduction of specific employee networks, aimed at improving inclusivity and involvement for targeted groups, is evaluated to determine whether or not such networks are tokenistic gestures towards inclusion or positive vehicles for employee involvement. The chapter explores employees' responses to EIP initiatives and how these might influence their perceptions of justice.

Encouraging Commitment Through Involvement and Participation

Over the years there have been several (usually) managerially instigated, designed and controlled schemes encouraging employees to voluntarily become committed to their workplaces and proactively work towards the organisation's objectives. Such schemes recognise that the employment relationship is not merely one comprising economic transactions; instead other, softer factors, social and psychological, are influential and in play. Higher levels of involvement are presumed to enhance employee levels of motivation, with motivated employees actively investing in, and committing to, organisations that provide them with increased levels of workplace satisfaction and opportunities to influence workplace decisions. For example, Chevalier et al. (2020) found that organisational commitment increased for those French police who received workplace training. Providing skills training and facilitating on-the-job learning expedites one of the ways to promote and enable the active involvement and commitment of employees, encouraging them to take more responsibility for their workplace activities, *apparently* for their own as well as the organisation's benefit (Abid et al., 2019; Boxall et al., 2015; Felstead et al., 2010; Varshney, 2020).

Sometimes involvement arrangements can be dictated or inspired by government initiatives (both voluntary and statutory); for example, the UK Labour government under Tony Blair emphasised and *encouraged* voluntary partnership approaches to managing the workforce, while European and UK legislation *requires* employers to consult with employees across a number of areas (e.g., when redundancies are possible). Unlike the USA, where no such consultative arrangements are legally required, China's Labour Contract Law stipulates that employers *have to* hold discussions with employees (or their representatives) when they intend to devise, revise, or change internal rules or policies that directly affect employees. Employees there, as with redundancy in Europe and the UK, are automatically consulted, *and by default involved*, in some employment practices that affect them. Indeed, the Chinese Government specifically encourages **employee participation** seeing it as a means of enhancing innovative practices (Zhou et al., 2019). The Varieties of Capitalism (VoC) literature is useful here because it provides an indication of how participative structures may be endemic in certain regions, and reviled in others, due to historic and or cultural influences (Barry et al., 2014: 523).

Sometimes the adoption of involvement practice is encouraged by non-governmental external parties like employers' associations and professional bodies. Such encouragement promotes involvement while, importantly, allowing employers the freedom to implement the mechanisms of involvement in ways that are commensurate with organisational culture, goals and managerial perspectives (Marchington, 2015a). At times involvement arrangements are prompted by prevalent managerial fashion; for example, HRM and high-commitment organisations place emphasis on the importance of managing human resources in ways that maintain competitive advantage by deploying a range of strategies, like employee involvement, to create congenial antecedents where everyone is (*supposedly*) aligned to, and working towards, the organisational goals. Yet participatory activity is more nuanced than this. When Zhou and his colleagues examined 183 Chinese companies they found that high performance workplaces, with **direct voice** mechanisms, encouraged general levels of employee participation; however, when direct voice practice was coupled with participation in corporate governance this led to even higher levels of employee involvement, commitment and participation (2019).

Williams points out that 'the term employee involvement can be applied to managerial initiatives that are designed to further the flow of communication at work as a means of enhancing the organisational commitment of employees' (2014: 25). Such measures include initiatives like **team briefing**, digital noticeboards, electronic newsletters and so on, that are specifically designed to regularly 'feed' employees information about their organisation, thereby enhancing their understanding of their own roles within the organisation and inducing higher levels of commitment, performance and flexibility. Conflict is, of course, deemed to be diminished, if not eliminated, by the facilitation of such positive employee behaviours and attitudes. Different initiatives, such as suggestion schemes and staff questionnaires, are designed, among other things, to elicit information from employees enhancing perceptions of organisational justice, improving the psychological contract, and possibly positively impacting productivity and innovation.

One of the *anticipated* results from the introduction of any of the involvement, participation and partnership initiatives is a committed, compliant workforce and an organisation where expressions of conflict are minimised, resistance to change reduced and subsequent levels of workplace flexibility and productivity improved. As Edwards pointed out at the end of the last century, 'it is becoming more commonplace to argue that, in the face of intensified competition, we are witnessing a shift away from adversarial approaches towards the generation of commitment at work' (1992: 361). In the UK, this shift has coincided with the decline of the trade union movement and a more individualistic unitary approach to the employment relation.

News Flash 9.1

Two Thirds of Companies Fail to Capitalise on Direct Employee Involvement

Of companies in Europe, the UK and Norway, 31% are failing to enable employees the opportunity to influence workplace decisions. They are therefore missing out on opportunities to enhance performance. This finding comes from the Fourth European Company Survey, which looked at a number of workplace practices including employee participation, from 21,869 human resources managers and 3,073 employee representatives in all 27 EU Member States and the United Kingdom during 2019.

Of establishments in the EU27, 94% use meetings between employees and their line manager as a way to engage with employees, although just over a third of these admit to the meetings being irregular. It was noticeable that Sweden (82%) and Austria (76%) were the countries in which regular employee/manager meetings were most prevalent – and Poland (42%) and Croatia (43%) were where such meetings were the least prevalent. Size was an important factor; smaller establishments were least likely to hold regular meetings.

Speaking about the survey results, Maria Jepsen, Deputy Director of Eurofound, said,

> Direct and indirect employee participation, facilitated by open and meaningful social dialogue, is crucial for both employees and companies. Not only can it boost performance and well-being, it can also provide pivotal decision-making structures when job losses or significant shifts in task allocation take place.

Source: Eurofound and Cedefop, 2020

As Hyman points out, all managerial strategies are 'routes to partial failure' (1987: 30) and it is unrealistic to see involvement strategies as a panacea for many of the adversarial behaviours within the employment relationship. The links between involvement mechanisms and increased performance are sometimes tenuous and, even when a correlation between the two can be proved, it does not necessarily mean that there is causation; as Yukl said, 'After 35 years of research on participation, we are left with the conclusion that participative leadership sometimes results in higher satisfaction, decision acceptance, effort, and performance, and at other times it does not' (1989: 86).

Despite the rhetoric, employee involvement with, and commitment to, an organisation does not always result in a compliant workforce; it may be that a committed workforce, emboldened by information and presented with the opportunity to speak out, may take the opportunity to articulate views that are unwelcome to the employer and anathema to those having to manage workforce expectations. Moreover when, on occasion, an employer indulges in the **deaf-ear syndrome** (Harlos, 2001) and ignores or disregards any employee input provided for under an involvement scheme, this may increase levels of employee cynicism and have a negative impact on morale and perceptions of justice, leading to increased rather than decreased levels of workplace conflict. Some participative initiatives may of course be merely ineffective, perhaps because they are operative in name only, perhaps because they have been poorly communicated to the workforce, perhaps because a controlling management culture inhibits and restricts participatory activities (Hickland et al., 2020), perhaps because there is no one willing, or able, to listen, or perhaps just because there is insufficient time for hard-pressed employees to take advantage of any opportunity to 'join in' effectively (see Wilkinson et al., 2018 for a useful discussion as to why some participatory voice mechanisms fail).

The form and type of employee involvement utilised by organisations is contingent upon: the legislation under which the organisation operates; the culture, sector, type and size of the organisation; whether or not there is a union presence; and the responses of the employees to such schemes. In Ireland, for example,

> workplace cooperation, and the idea that employees can be company stakeholders, goes against the grain of a deeply embedded cultural mind-set that employers should have unilateral authority to make decisions (Timming, 2007, cited by Dobbins, 2010: 499)

Whereas in many parts of Europe a more collectivist approach is adopted – here there is a pervasive 'social democratic' pattern, based on a social partnership between employers and employees, where strategies promoting employee participation are not so culturally alien. In a similar way the employment relationship found in public sector organisations is more likely to be one that encourages involvement, in part because it is more difficult for such organisations to go against the prevailing orthodoxy of the state under which they operate (Eurofound, 2013: 12). Often there may be situations where a number of different types of worker are deployed on site and not all of these individuals will respond to, or be included in, involvement and participation initiatives. Those who are agency workers or freelance workers, for example, may be excluded from the processes by the nature of their work and employment contracts. Such differences, where they result in inconsistent messages (or sections of the workforce being omitted from an involvement initiative), may have a potentially detrimental effect on levels of trust and perceptions of procedural, informational and interactional justice.

Employee involvement and participation are also contingent upon the personalities and abilities of the employees concerned; for example, managers may not want to share information even if the organisation has systems in place for this to happen. Similarly, employees may not want to (or may not be sufficiently skilled to) take advantage of all participatory initiatives on offer. The degree with which employers encourage involvement may also be dependent upon the skill sets held by their employees. Hosseini et al. (2022), studying knowledge workers in Iran, found that organisations facilitating workplace participatory decision-making for this category of skilled worker actually improved innovation and productivity. Occupational class theory suggests that employers want to retain and motivate higher-skilled employees, encouraging their discretionary effort, while retention and motivation are less important for those employees with lower skill levels (where the employer emphasis is more on hard management techniques and the ability to use labour flexibly). It follows from this that involvement strategies are more likely to be targeted at those employees exhibiting higher levels of skill (Zhou, 2009). To some extent this finding is countered by that of Jones et al. (2010), who found that even where employees are relatively low skilled, if they are operating in participatory workplaces, where their supervisors provide information and allow their involvement, then this can enhance the enterprise for which they are working. It is evident that, regardless of skill set, participatory structures may have a positive impact on productivity and innovation.

The Fifth European Working Conditions Survey found that levels of involvement through task discretion were particularly high in Estonia, Latvia, the Nordic countries and Malta, and much lower in Cyprus, Greece, Bulgaria, Romania and Slovakia; while overall, women had higher levels of task involvement, men had more influence at decision-making levels (Eurofound, 2013: 20, 21).

Employee Involvement, Participation and Partnership

Employee involvement and participation (EIP) activities may be arrayed along a continuum from individuals receiving a company newsletter and perhaps discussing their daily activities with a line manager, through to employee representatives participating in consultative forums, or negotiating with senior management, and at the highest level, employee representatives acting in partnership with the employer at strategic decision-making levels. In some circumstances there will be discussions between the state and employee representatives; these may occur where the state is the employer in question, or where the representatives are involved in tripartite strategic decisions impacting the ways in which the country operates. In the Netherlands, for example, discussions between the government and representative groups led directly to measures enabling and facilitating the employment of disabled persons (Bingham et al., 2013). Organisations may deploy none of these EIP mechanisms, a number that complementarily co-exist, or just one, depending on circumstances. Occasionally specific workplace changes may result in employers deploying one-off methods of involvement: for example, putting on an informative roadshow to explain changes in pension arrangements, or running a focus group around issues of relocation. However, it is quite common for organisations to use a range of involvement techniques of varying intensity and length that coexist within the same institutional environment (Marchington, 2015b). Peugeot UK, for example, has a comprehensive communications strategy deploying several involvement techniques that span the gamut, from internal flyers extolling the virtues of new models of car and providing an interesting and engaging intranet, through to directly involving employees and listening to their suggestions, while also involving indirect employee representatives with consultation and collective bargaining. As Wilkinson and Fay point out,

> participation can differ in the scope of decisions, the amount of influence workers can exercise over management, and the organizational level at which the decisions are made. Some forms are purposely designed to give workers a voice, but not more than a very modest role in decision-making, while others give the workforce a more significant say in organizational governance. (2011: 66)

The number of definitions for employee involvement are extensive, sometimes including participation, sometimes not, occasionally contradictory, frequently imprecise; as Cox et al. say (2009: 2150), employee involvement and participation (EIP)

... is both a problematic and loose term, covering an array of managerially determined and initiated practices intended variously to provide employees with information, enable a two-way exchange of views and/or opportunities to influence decision-making in the workplace. The plurality of form of EIP gives rise to differing degrees of scope, significance and impact reflected in the emphasis of definitions. These incorporate the notion of employees exercising 'some influence over their work and the conditions under which they work' (Strauss, 1998: 15) harnessing employee input 'to encourage commitment to organisational success' (Cotton, 1993: 14) or, more loosely, 'immediate personal involvement of organisational members' (Dachler and Wilpert, 1978: 12).

The UK Government considers the terms *employee participation* and *employee involvement* to be synonymous (Marchington et al., 1992), but others have argued that there are crucial differences between the categories depending on the amount of power management cedes to employees and the degrees of control and/or influence that each party has over the processes.

What Do Employee Involvement, Participation and Partnership Entail?

There are multiple ways that employers can create opportunities for employees to become involved with their organisations; these can be direct (e.g. in face-to-face communications between an employee and their line manager) or indirect (where a representative acts on behalf of the employee when dealing with the organisation). Marchington and Kynighou (2012) define three main areas of involvement and participation:

1   *Representative EIP*, where employees can make their views known to management through the intercession of representatives acting on their behalf on formal bodies such as health and safety committees or joint consultative committees (JCCs). Within the EU, European Works Councils would be examples of such formalisation, as would committees of management and employee representatives set up under the auspices of the Information and Consultation of Employees' Directive. Partnership arrangements too fall into this category (Hall and Purcell, 2012; Johnstone et al., 2009). In 2018 a revised UK corporate governance code put more emphasis on boards to include employees' views and concerns in key decisions. Research undertaken by the Involvement and Participation Association showed that 40% of the FTSE 350 companies complied with the new code by appointing a designated non-elected director to specifically represent workers' views, while 12% opted instead to establish an advisory panel and 16% introduced a combination of non-elected directors with a panel (Faragher, 2021).

2   *Direct EIP*, occurring when employers directly involve employees in formal, prearranged, two-way communication, such as team briefings, away-days, staff forums, attitude surveys, newsletters and so on; all of these mechanisms have, over the last 30 or so years, burgeoned in Western economies, particularly where HRM techniques have been adopted (Freeman et al., 2007) and where employers have attempted to talk directly to

employees (rather than relying on indirect trade union channels, where they have little control of the message and how it is being communicated). The ways in which direct EIP is actioned give line managers a crucial role: it is they who are responsible for the day-to-day workplace activities and it is they who are able to bypass/ignore employee opinions or give employees a regular opportunity to air their views and then to act on them (Cox et al., 2009; Helland et al., 2021; Lavelle et al., 2010).

3   *Informal EIP*, where employers interact with staff in ways that, although unplanned and unregulated, facilitate information exchanges (Marchington and Suter, 2013). Such exchanges include unplanned discussions that, when they occur, give employees a degree of power and the means to influence their day-to-day workplace environment (Strauss, 1998: 15). Informal interactions between supervisors and their teams are strongly linked to perceptions of organisational justice, particularly aspects of procedural and informational justice, and they may also be seen as a crucial part of the Budd (2004, 2010) triad of equity, efficiency and voice. Where there is a culture of trust and respect within the workplace, employees are more likely to engage in participatory activities both formally and informally. Informal interactions are often regarded as more important than formal structures (Schaufeli, 2014) for delivering employee involvement; however, it should be remembered that not all informal interactions are pleasant, joint exchanges, providing satisfactory involvement experiences – employees may, if not listened to, or if given information they do not want to hear, become less, not more, involved with the organisation and less inclined to participate further in influencing workplace decision making.

It is often, for example, within the informal arena that workplace bullying, racism or inappropriate sexism take place, leading to lack of trust, lower productivity, increased levels of sickness absence and a higher turnover of staff – all issues that are the opposite of the managerial aims behind the introduction of EIP.

In a number of organisations the word 'informal' is used to denote the first stage of a disciplinary process; in Tesco, for example, staff talk about 'having an informal' in ways that indicate it is actually part of the formal procedure for being disciplined. The way in which Marchington and Suter (2013) and Marchington and Kynighou (2012) use the phrase, however, has no formal connotations and should not be confused with regulated formal disciplinary processes.

Exercise 9.1

Informal interaction by its very informality is unregulated and therefore may lead to a range of contradictory and inconsistent behaviours that could, depending on circumstance, lead directly to perceptions of interactional and informational injustice.

- Analyse an incident where you think this could have occurred; explain how such inconsistencies have, or might have, led to perceptions of organisational injustice and a lack of trust.

The extent to which employees actually join in the mechanics and realities of workplace control depends upon the:

- number of decision-making powers that have been allocated to them – EIP initiatives may be resisted by managers who fear that sharing power and information might undermine their authority (Helland et al., 2021)
- range and depth of topics around which they are permitted to participate
- degree to which they want to engage with the participatory processes
- direction in which they can influence decisions
- the mechanisms deployed and the form of participation that the processes entail.

A distinction should be made between the levels of involvement where employees are without influence and those where they can actively have an impact on matters, whether operational or strategic, as opposed to being passive recipients of managerial dictat. It is the employer who, largely, is able to construct and implement the EIP structures and supporting mechanisms and therefore, importantly, it is the employer who has the power to control the ways in which involvement, participation or partnership programmes are proposed, adopted and run. It is moreover the employers who will largely promote, constrain or restrain the regulatory constitution under which such schemes operate. Consequently, it is important for any examination of EIP mechanisms to take account of the amount of power accorded to employees – and by the same token the amount of power relinquished by employers – whereby employees may, or may not, exert a degree of influence over organisational activities. Where there are forms of indirect collective representation, as when trade unions are involved with influencing and affecting the ways in which the work environment operates, it is a means of 'redressing the vulnerability of the individual employee in his/her dealings with the employer: a vulnerability inherent in the employment relationship itself and hence common, in varying degrees indeed, to all employees' (Hyman, 1997: 321).

Managerial commitment to involvement, in all its guises, is dependent upon the type of structures it would be willing to accept. To a great extent this will depend on its approach to the employment relationship generally, that is its frame of reference (e.g., unitarist or pluralist) (Fox, 1974) and on the dimension(s) of style it adopts or prefers (e.g., individualism or collectivism) (Purcell, 1987). British Telecom (BT), for example, is a pluralist organisation that adopts a number of collectivist, sophisticated modern, EIP mechanisms; in terms of employee involvement it has, however, for many years, run a *direct* involvement programme, part of which is an employee survey, the results of which influence the ways in which the company operates. Changes made at strategic and operational levels linked to the answers from the survey are fed back to the employees so they are aware of the part their views have played in influencing the company; in turn this feedback is thought to engender not just increasing participation in the survey but further employee commitment to BT.

Exercise 9.2

... employee participation and involvement are necessary conditions in the process of employee-work environment interaction. (Wilkinson et al., 2018: 861)

- Is this statement true? Justify your answer using academic and practical examples.

Employee Involvement

Involvement is occasionally used as a generic term for all forms of employee/employer communication (and potential interaction) that is intended to encourage employee commitment to an organisation. Sometimes, however, it is used in a more specific way to indicate managerial strategies and structures that are directed at the employee and designed as a one-way flow of information cascaded down to the employee and specifically calculated to help the employee understand the organisational goals and what they might do to help achieve those goals. As Kane pointed out, employees need to feel

> … connected as a part of a team. The best way to achieve this connection … is through good communications. So by communicating well, explaining what's going on, the reasoning for change and how changes may affect staff (through group talks, one-to-ones, emailing, etc.) employees will feel … involved in the process, and connected to the company. (2013: n.p.)

The environment, economic and sectoral influences on an organisation will all influence the type of involvement strategy and mechanisms deployed. It must be remembered that such involvement mechanisms do not stand alone and are usually integrated with other managerial activities, with the employee involvement aspects of any strategy acting as a crucial lubricant for the gaining of employee acceptance for managerially inspired workplace initiatives. The type and amounts of information given and to whom it is targeted will differ not just from organisation to organisation but often from one occasion to the next (see Figure 9.1).

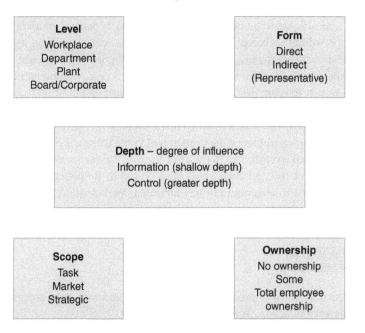

Figure 9.1 Analysing mechanisms for employee involvement and participation (based on Marchington and Wilkinson, 2008: 405-6)

Acas provides a useful definition suggesting that employee involvement is a:

> ... style of management and a range of activities that are designed to increase employees' understanding of the organisation, utilise their talents, enable them to influence decisions, and encourage their commitment to the goals of the organisation. (2010: 26)

A slightly more nuanced view of involvement, and one without acknowledgement of employee power and influence, comes from the employers' organisation, the CBI. It describes the purpose of employee involvement as being to

> ... promote business success through a combination of practices and systems designed to secure the maximum awareness and commitment of employees in an enterprise to its objectives. (CBI/EDG, 1991)

Both of these definitions signpost the alignment of the employee with the organisational goals and indicate a largely unitary perspective despite the fact that, under the Acas definition, employees are being asked to 'influence decisions'; actions which might, under other circumstances, be considered pluralist. Here the assumption behind both of these definitions is that the employer and employee want, and are working towards, the same thing, that is, business success and profitability under a managerial regime that remains unquestioned. Salamon (2000: 369) suggests that involvement is a means of enhancing the support and commitment of employees to the objectives and values of the organisation, while he sees participation as a way of providing employees with genuine opportunities to influence and contribute towards organisational decision making.

Involvement schemes burgeoned under the auspices of HRM. Teamworking, autonomous work groups, team briefing, and pick-and-mix development schemes such as 'cafeteria learning' as well as customer service initiatives, are all areas that have become part of the managerial lexicon promoting involvement. But despite numerous means of involvement it is unclear just how much real power has been ceded to employees and how much influence they are able to exert.

Marchington and Wilkinson (2005: 403–7) showed how **direct employee involvement** could be divided into a number of categories:

- *Downward communication* (top down) including, for example, in-house journals, employee reports, team briefings. Here management is in complete control of the information process – who receives the information, how and when it is delivered and crucially perhaps when information is withheld. This type of communication is not uncommon, with over 84% of managers in very small organisations and just under 80% of managers in very large organisations saying that they always discussed changes prior to implementation with their employees (see Table 9.1).
- *Upward problem-solving forms of involvement* are systems designed to utilise employee knowledge and opinions for the good of the organisation. Such schemes, often encouraging workplace collaboration, target individual employees or small groups of workers and include, for example, suggestion schemes, attitude surveys, employee engagement surveys, customer care programmes and schemes linked to total quality management (TQM) initiatives. For example, Ericsson, the global telecoms company, places huge importance on continuous improvement and the role that each employee

plays in this. At induction, each employee is given a booklet explaining how TQM works, why it is important and how they will be able to contribute to the process and be personally involved in Ericsson's future growth and prosperity.

- **Financial participation** occurs where employees are encouraged to feel part of the organisation via employee share ownership schemes, establishment-wide bonuses and/ or profit sharing arrangements, the assumption being that employees, feeling they have a stake in the business, work harder. Share ownership is frequently a standard component of the compensation and reward package provided to many employees, but shares and bonus payments may also be given to employees as a reward for sufficiently high levels of performance. Share ownership gives employees the right to receive both a share in the profits, and the right to receive financial information and vote on (i.e., participate in) the running of the company. Such rights are expected to encourage positive employee attitudes that could well lead to higher productivity and increased profitability (Rousseau and Shperling, 2003). At the beginning of the twentieth century, Webb pointed out that if an employee were made a shareholder it would 'stimulate his zeal and careful working and, as part owner of the capital' it would enable him to have a share in the responsibility for the company (1912: 232). The ideology behind providing financial involvement remains the same. A graphic example of this type of participation, and the reasoning behind its introduction, was evident when the HR Director of Railtrack explained to this author that he wanted every employee, watching a train go past on time, to think 'good, that's increased my profit'. Similarly, and more recently, Hugh Facey, the chairman of Gripple (manufacturers of wire joiners and tensioners) says that employee share ownership has been a positive influence for his organisation, with the 441 employees showing increased levels of attendance and innovation, and pointing out that, 'A sense of pride exists among all our staff and [share ownership] has allowed employees to take control of the destiny of the [organisation], thereby creating a culture of working together for the benefit of each other' (Hodge, 2014). In a laboratory experiment with 180 participants, Mellizo et al. (2011) found that those workers who voted to determine their own levels of reward performed better than those who had no say in how they were compensated for their efforts.
- *Task participation and teamworking* – of the four, this form of involvement is the one that is most integral to the way in which the day-to-day work is undertaken by employees; rather than the other arrangements, it is not an 'additional extra' bolted onto the employment package because fundamentally this form of involvement encourages individual workers to extend the range and type of tasks that are undertaken (e.g., job redesign, job enrichment and teamworking). Teamworking enables employees to experience what Friedman (1977) called *responsible autonomy* where they enjoy a degree of decision making 'for the good of the enterprise'. Here it could be argued that the employer relaxes control in order to maintain control, persuading employees, rather than coercing them, to determine the ways that they might enhance their own productivity and performance.

Task participation falls into two areas. **Vertical task-based participation** is where employees are 'up-skilled' so they can achieve more and where perhaps they are trained to take additional responsibility for managing their own tasks and workflows. **Horizontal task-based partici-pation** is where employees are given more control, so that with the same levels of skill they are able to exercise their own discretion over how they undertake their work in terms of the number and variety of tasks that they perform. Marchington points out that 'In some cases task-based participation may offer little more than a way in which to alleviate the boredom associated with repetitive routines, and at least offer the opportunity to do something different, if only for a short period of time' (2007: 234). The assumption, however, that employees will welcome such skill enhancement and increased responsibility levels may be misplaced as employees may resent these initiatives, viewing them not as additional opportunities for involvement but as ways of 'dressing up' work intensification.

Table 9.1   Data from WERS 2011

	Agree or strongly agree	Neither agree nor disagree	Disagree or strongly disagree	Total	Unweighted base: all workplaces
	%	%	%	%	
Workplace size					
5-9 employees	79.6	7.9	12.5	100	297
10-19 employees	80.6	9.4	10.0	100	378
20-49 employees	78.2	11.6	10.2	100	485
50-99 employees	81.5	11.1	7.4	100	387
100-499 employees	82.2	9.6	8.1	100	670
500 or more employees	82.9	8.1	9.0	100	461
Organization size					
Less than 100	84.7	8.2	7.1	100	714
100-999	72.4	14.2	13.3	100	525
1,000-9,999	71.3	10.2	18.5	100	747
10,000 or more	79.4	8.0	12.6	100	631

Source: Data from WERS 2011 - Department for Business, Innovation and Skills, 2013

Case Study 9.1

British Business Bank

The 100% UK government owned, but independently managed, British Business Bank began operating in 2014. It was specifically designed to help small businesses with a more diverse range of accessible finance options and support the UK's transition to a net zero economy. It neither lends, nor invests, money directly - instead, it works with over a hundred different partner organisations, like banks and leasing companies, to provide finance for enterprises that might otherwise find funding difficult. With a head office in Sheffield, and other offices based in some of the UK's major cities it is a thriving and growing company employing around 400 people.

(Continued)

From its inception the Bank regarded its employees as its greatest asset and wanted to involve them in the way the bank evolved, specifically in helping to create the new organisational values and culture. Creating workplace systems that were collaborative was important and, as Katie Hryschko (2017) said when she was HR director of the bank; 'Our senior team agreed to adopt a fully inclusive process that would foster collaboration and encourage the adoption of consistent working practices/ behaviours. Getting the entire organisation involved also meant every employee could have a sense of ownership'. She went on to explain how this important decision was the start of an iterative involvement process which grew from the initial creation of a 'Values Forum' (with representatives from all parts of the business), that produced a set of values and key words representing the Bank's culture that the *whole* organisation then voted to rank in order of importance. Following the vote *everyone* participated in briefing sessions and workshops helping to create a series of corresponding workplace behaviours that formed the bedrock of the way in which the firm continues to work at the time of going to press.

In 2016 the Values Forum evolved and widened its remit, becoming a 'Colleague Forum', the official channel through which the bank still listens to its employees. Made up of 12 representatives, elected from across the business, it engages with staff and keeps the senior management team informed about employees' views, needs and priorities. This representative platform:

- facilitates staff involvement
- provides a platform for strategic discussions
- enables employees to raise issues

and, where appropriate,

- agrees proposed ways to sustain or change the culture.

Employee Networks

Networks are groups set up specifically to aid particular clusters of people sharing a common interest. Occasionally they operate alongside organisations, for example, Stonewall, but, often, they are based internally, operating purely for the benefit of the sponsoring organisation. For example, BCLP, a global law firm, operates a scheme called Race for Change that encourages and helps aspiring black solicitors – those who eventually join the firm become part of an alumni network, sharing information and helping to mentor others. Similarly, Nestlé promotes separate affinity groups for veterans, military spouses, women in leadership, etc., that bring employees with similar experiences together to discuss their careers, access speakers, chat about daily problems, thereby enabling feelings of inclusivity, connection and involvement with the company. The aim behind such networks is to improve the employment relationship for those involved, by helping to raise their profile, reduce feelings of isolation, provide member mentoring and act as a conduit to the organisations as a whole for suggestions about training, etc. Successful networks help embed participants into an organisation, facilitating feelings of involvement, staff becoming committed and engaged with their work and colleagues. Where more than one network operates within an organisation it is not unknown for them to work together helping to enable an inclusive culture. As Patrick Briône, says,

> Networks also will do well to work in partnership with other staff groups, if these are present in the workplace. Often these groups can achieve more while working together, particularly when it comes to addressing difficult workplace issues that may have intersectional impacts and considerations. By working in partnership, these groups can also provide fuller support to those staff who bridge multiple categories. (2021: 7)

Different organisations regard networks in different ways. For some they are primarily vehicles for staff to just talk candidly with one another about their experiences within the organisation. For others, they are a means of ensuring inclusivity and these groups are placed prominently within the wider workforce. Sometimes of course networks are none of these things – sometimes they are more. For example, several prominent legal firms in the UK have developed very strong black networks, which help at recruitment level right through to the mentoring of senior staff. Where they operate successfully these groups have improved recruitment, labour retention, levels of commitment, motivation and feelings of involvement with the organisation.

Exercise 9.3

- Read the requirements from the European Union about consulting and informing staff (stated below) and evaluate whether or not these 'instructions' will make a real difference in the workplace. Ensure that your answer considers a number of possibilities such as size of organisation, culture, different managerial frames of reference and managerial styles.

A company that employs at least 50 people - including staff employed on fixed-term contracts - in an EU country (or at least 20 if it is a branch of a larger business), is legally obliged to:

- inform its staff about recent and probable developments in company activities and the economic situation of the company
- inform and consult staff about the current employment situation and its probable development
- inform and consult staff about possible substantial changes in work organisation or in contractual relations.

It must also make sure the information is provided in good time so that employee representatives have enough time to prepare for consultation on any related issues.

Employee representatives (and any experts assisting them) may not disclose to staff or third parties any confidential information you share with them.

Source: European Union, 2021

Employee Participation

Employee participation describes a variety of states, all of which relate to the degrees to which employers cede power to employees – ranging from minimal influence to equal power with management. In 1993, Ramsay pointed out that the introduction of employee participatory schemes involved the restructuring of authority relations in favour of the employee, while ten years prior to this Brannen remarked that:

> ... workers' participation is about the distribution and exercise of power, in all its manifestations, between the owners and managers of organisations and those employed by them. It refers to the direct involvement of individuals in decisions relating to their immediate work organisation and to **indirect involvement** in decision-making, through representatives, in the wider socio-technical and political structures of the firm. (1983: 16)

The American, Washington-based, company Steelscape, that manufactures metallic-coated and pre-painted steel for the construction industry, epitomises the way in which an employer, operating in a participatory way, has shared control with the employees. Here employees working in self-managed teams are able to effectively participate – and control – work processes in what were traditional areas of managerial expertise and prerogative. The Steelscape workforce is engaged in continuous process work (24/7), where the night shift employees have to make and take decisions without managerial support, so levels of participation are high. It is striking that in the areas of recruitment and selection, management has transferred a huge amount of discretionary control directly to the employees, specifically the recruitment and selection of new team members. It is the employees themselves, rather than representatives from HR or managers, who interview and select new members of staff. Since this process began, workplace conflict has decreased and productivity improved. The participation in this example is direct, with employees themselves involved in the running of parts of the enterprise.

Power ceded to employees to such a degree is unusual; it is far more common to find direct participation in the form of performance management and appraisals whereby tasks, activities, workflows and developmental requirements are discussed by employees (usually) with their line managers, the employees talking about how they performed in the past and having some say in how they would like to operate in the future. This balance between having to comply with managerial demands while being able to offer suggestions and determine one's own work patterns and flows has strong links with Edwards' (2003) notion of structural antagonism discussed in previous chapters. In times of economic uncertainty it is at this level of employee–line manager interaction that the participatory nature of performance management is at its weakest, joint discussions about how to move forward sometimes transforming into exhortations to do better, with coercive attempts to intensify work levels.

Participation can, of course, be undertaken through representatives (i.e., via indirect participation). Here the process of the employer sharing power is still evident. Stewart Johnstone concluded, from his research looking at workplace participation within a number of organisations in the financial service sector, that where there were representative mechanisms and structures enabling indirect workplace participation, employers 'need to accept the legitimacy of the representative body, and acknowledge the right of the body to question and to sometimes disagree' (2010: 205). Participatory activities therefore are those where employees, often through their representatives, have and use their ability to influence managerial judgements and pronouncements – as when they have the right to veto management decisions (e.g., the employees of the *Milwaukee Journal* in the USA are able to veto managerial decisions; Baker, 2006: 183) or when they are able to contribute to the decisions concerning the running of the organisation. Participation, both direct and indirect, is not always operative at a decision-making level. Sometimes employees and their representatives are asked their opinions, but such consultation does not empower them to do anything other than participate by expressing views that, when taken into consideration, are part of the processes influencing the final managerial decisions. A union presence is not always necessary for such joint consultation to occur. The WERS 2011 data (DBIS, 2013), for example, shows that 7% of workplaces with non-union representation had joint consultative committees. It is important to remember that participatory schemes are not mutually exclusive. It is not unusual for organisations to operate with several different means of participation simultaneously. For example, Credit Suisse has direct participation through its performance management system and indirect participation through both its staff council and its European works council.

Boxall and Purcell (2003: 162) explain that participation consists of a range of mechanisms that enable, and at times empower, employees directly and indirectly to influence and have an impact on decision making in the organisation for which they work. In the UK, the law requires employers to consult with their employees indirectly through representatives in the following circumstances:

- on matters of health and safety under the remit of a health and safety committee
- where there are collective redundancies
- when an organisation transfers the ownership of the organisation or part of the organisation
- if a trade union has statutory recognition, the representatives must be consulted about training issues and about specific director-level duties.

News Flash 9.2

Worker Directors Appointed at JD Wetherspoon

Following pressure from employees and shareholders in October 2021 the pub chain JD Weatherspoon, announced its intention to add workers to its eight-strong board of directors. More than 100 managers applied for the posts, and by Christmas of the same year the company had promoted four staff to its board of directors - two had full plc director status, and two became associate employee directors. Their appointments are initially for three years. Tim Martin, the pub chain's chairman, said,

(Continued)

A successful pub company depends primarily on gradual improvements, based on suggestions from employees ... Pub and area managers, and other members of pub teams, have always participated in weekly decision-making meetings, which distil suggestions from the 'front line' ... The appointment of employee directors will extend this approach to board meetings and will help to preserve the culture of the company for the future.

Sources: Ackerman, 2021; Goodley, 2021; Moss, 2021

Case Snippet 9.1

Direct Participation – Pringle Crisps

Pringle Crisps were invented by a team at Procter & Gamble and, in the early 1970s, were an immensely successful product with huge US sales. However, between 1975 and 1980 sales slumped and the losses for the company were enormous. Huge amounts of time, money and senior executive expertise were poured into resourcing a turnaround, to no avail. Towards the end of this period a very junior executive spoke to a long-serving employee who, amazed to be asked his opinion after 25 years with the parent organisation, provided a range of enthusiastic ideas for making the product successful once again. The result of this interchange was the setting up, by junior, not senior managers, of a system whereby customers and employees were asked about the product and the way forward. Team meetings, where open discussions were positively encouraged, provided forums for knowledge exchange and opinion sharing. The result of this participation was that in less than a year, packaging, pricing and product offering were all changed from the 'bottom up' and the company division concerned with Pringles moved into profit, subsequently selling its brand of crisps, with a range of different flavours, in over 140 countries. The Pringles part of Procter & Gamble (part of Kellogg's since 2012) has, since this experience, been open to listening to and (*sometimes*) acting on employee suggestions; for example, the idea of printing words on crisps with edible ink came from an employee who was not part of the product research team.

Source: Boehler, 2012

Case Snippet 9.2

Indirect Participation – Worker Directors, FirstGroup

FirstGroup, the UK-based transport firm, has had an employee director since the company was created in 1989. Workers in each division at FirstGroup elect their own employee director, and this group elects, from their ranks, the employee director for the main board. The employee director (who is a union member) also sits as an observer on the remuneration committee. Martin Gilbert, outgoing chair of FirstGroup, has said that 'the presence of employee directors on the FirstGroup board is invaluable'.

Source: Sweeney, 2014: 89

Case Snippet 9.3

Indirect Participation – Hewlett-Packard

Hewlett-Packard employs 320,000 people and is a global provider of software, solutions and services to a range of buyers from individual consumers through to governments, with large contracts in both the education and health sectors. It split into two companies at the end of 2015: HP Inc., the computer and printer business, and Hewlett-Packard Enterprise, selling servers, storage, networking software and technical services.

In the run-up to the split, Hewlett-Packard consulted the local works councils, aiming to operationalise the UK side of the division by the early autumn. Redundancies were inevitable and the employee representatives on the councils discussed the *impact* of the plans; that is, how to minimise disruption and manage job losses, rather than the company's intention to bifurcate.

Hewlett-Packard has been systematically reducing its workforce over the last few years, losing around 29,000 employees in its streamlining operation, 'Make it Better', with further reductions following on from this. The redundancy plans varied from country to country and were implemented following consultation with local works councils and employee representatives. Its relationship with its European Works Council is not always smooth – in 2012 the Council sued Hewlett-Packard, claiming that it failed to consult the Council about its plans. At this stage, the original works council agreement was discontinued, although eventually a new one was signed and the Council began to operate once more, in time to be involved in the discussions about resourcing plans for 2013/14. Since Brexit, the Hewlett-Packard European works council has moved its base from England to Ireland in order to remain within the ambit of the EU.

Sources: Kunert, 2013, 2014

Exercise 9.4

Evaluate, in terms of:

* power sharing
* organisational justice

the different methods of EIP in evidence in the three previous case snippets.

Categorising Participation

Over the last half century a number of authors have categorised participatory systems and mechanisms in different ways: some analyse it by looking at the effects such programmes have in terms of either **cognitive participation**, where shared information flows lead to higher levels of performance (Lawler et al., 1995), or **affective participation**, where, through involvement with workplace information and decision making, the employees achieve higher levels of personal satisfaction that may consequentially improve productivity (Miller and Monge, 1986). Geary and Sisson (1994) also divide participatory arrangements into two, talking about **consultative participation**, where management encourages employees to share their opinions (while retaining the sole right to make decisions), as opposed to **delegative participation**, where employers allow employees a degree of latitude, giving them increased levels of responsibility and autonomy over workplace decisions.

Stephens (1980: 3) also identifies two different forms of participation: the *transformational* and the *integrative*. **Transformational participation** is where, as a consequence of sociopolitical forces, there is a fundamental shift of power in favour of the employees so that they might eventually be empowered to control the organisation, and hence take part in a transfer of the prevailing social order from capital to labour. **Integrative participation** is a slightly different proposition. This is where employee pressure for increased amounts of control is resolved by permitting employees to have a degree of influence over their day-to-day operations by allowing them, usually through their representatives, to aid management in improving the general working conditions. Examples of this type of participation range from representatives on workplace forums, such as health and safety committees, through to activities on joint consultative committees or works councils, to perhaps working at national level on tripartite representative structures. For successful participation, the organisation concerned will be talking to employees and seeking their views – an essentially pluralist perspective.

Acas has suggested (2014: 24) that in order to make effective decisions employee representatives should:

- have open access to information – this encourages cooperation, efficiency and teamwork
- generate new and innovative solutions rather than falling back on what the group has done in the past
- test the proposed course against the yardstick of their aim or objective
- assess the consequences of making particular decisions
- play devil's advocate by challenging assumptions and promoting a thorough appraisal of any suggestions
- divide complex problems – for example, start with 'what?' to do and then move on to 'how?' and 'when?'
- reconsider decisions by ongoing reviews of relevant information
- feel ownership of and commitment to the decisions that are made
- be patient – developing trust can take time.

News Flash 9.3

Volkswagen: Further Investments in US Plants Unlikely

The Volkswagen Group (VW), operating in 29 different countries, and headquartered in Germany, has a history of employee involvement. Employees are represented by trade unions and a number of regional works councils together with a global works council made up of representatives from across the countries in which VW operates.

Brend Osterloh, the head of the Volkswagen works council, has declared that the company is very unlikely to make any future investments in the USA, particularly where anti-union attitudes prevail.

His comments follow the decision by the workers at the Volkswagen Chattanooga plant, who voted by 712 to 626 (57%) to reject union representation by the UAW: this despite Frank Fischer, the CEO of Volkswagen Chattanooga, claiming that they were enthusiastic about 'the idea of an American-style works council both inside and outside our plant'. The vote effectively stymied the operation of a wholly independent union at the plant *and* the subsequent formation and operation of a local Volkswagen works council. The Chattanooga VW factory is the only one in the company not to have a system of formal workplace employee representation. The vote by the workforce *not* to accept the union is important because US labour laws only allow the establishment of a works council in a company where the employees are represented by an *independent* union (that is one that is not seen as a *dependent* company union).

The company's global works council has repeatedly stated that it would oppose VW allocating new work to the plant if it remained out of line with the way in which the rest of the company operated, and for its part VW continues to show antipathy towards this decision by the global works council and its representatives.

Sources: Brooks, 2019; Cremer, 2014; Wright, 2014

Employee participation is a power-centred concept, often advanced by trade unions, and in some cases instituted through statutory regulation, which takes three principal forms: board level indirect representation; joint regulation – direct and indirect – of employment issues; and joint consultation – direct and indirect – where this allows for the meaningful consideration of employees' views about managerial proposals. Hyman and Mason used participation to

> … refer to State initiatives which promote the collective rights of employees to be represented in organisational decision-making, or to the consequence of the efforts of employees themselves to establish collective representation in corporate decisions, possibly in the face of employer resistance. (1995: 21)

This view epitomises what happens under European labour law, which provides a statutory right for employee representatives to give and receive business-linked information in order that they might influence, and sometimes co-decide, matters directly related to workplace practices and productivity. For example, the European Bank for Reconstruction and Development has a staff council whose remit includes:

- maintaining a channel of communication with management and HR
- providing EBRD staff with information about developments affecting their interests and ensuring as far as possible that EBRD management inform the staff about all such matters
- acting as the representative of staff with management and HR on all matters of common staff interest
- studying critical areas of management–staff relations, actual or potential, with a view to recommending solutions and identifying opportunities for improvement. (EBRD, 2022)

The EU Commission's report on Industrial Relations in Europe affirms that such types of employee influence on business matters is not just a means to share thinking but can successfully affect the ways in which a business operates:

> ... accumulating evidence from north-western Europe shows that well-functioning employee representation can play an important role in the modernisation and performance of a workplace. (Commission of the European Communities, 2006: 77, quoted in ETUI, 2014)

EIP rights are fundamental to the ways in which the EU promotes workplace social partnership. This is reflected in nearly 40 different EU Directives in the areas of employment law, company law and health and safety protection, all of which provide for some sort of workers' involvement. At the time of going to press the EU is debating a new framework that will rationalise its EIP legislation. Three of its current crucial measures promoting employee participation are:

- the European Works Councils Directive (1994, 2009/10)
- the European Company Statute (2001)
- Directive on the Information and Consultation of Employees (2002).

Disregarding its recommendations for financial participation, the EU promotes two main levels of employee participation: one below and one at board level. The implications for power sharing (and the consequent relinquishing of some organisational control) has, unsurprisingly, resulted in such arrangements being regarded by many unitarist organisations and neoliberal governments with at best suspicion, and at worst with outraged hostility (Davies, 1992). Although it is worth noting that, by operating in the overall interest of the organisation which they are part of, such bodies might be considered to be unitarist. Snook and Whittall (2013), for example, demonstrate how middle managers, using appropriate managerial skills such as communication, strategy, assertiveness and tact, were able to enhance works council processes and influence both company policy and strategy. Ultimately these managerial delegates, in their roles as European works council members, displayed a shared sense of identity, spanning national borders, by representing the interests of the whole of their respective workforces, not just the interests of their fellow managers.

These statutory rights are important because they ensure that where works councils are in operation they act as a check on the exercise of exploitative unilateral power by employers. In many European countries employee participation is realised via the mechanism of works councils (i.e., institutionalised bodies for representative dialogue and decision-making between employer and employee representatives). Management, employees or their representatives in European Community enterprises (or groups of enterprises) may initiate the process for setting up a European Works Council (EWC) if they operate in two or more separate European countries. A European Works Council has to be established if at least 100 employees from the same organisation operating in the minimum two EU member states ask for one. Should management fail to create a negotiating body with a remit to set up such a works council, a statutory EWC will be imposed.

Different countries of course promote, structure and regulate domestic works councils in different ways. France, for example, has statutory elected workers' councils, and similarly in Germany the Works Constitution Act (of 1972) provides for enforceable co-determination across areas such as pay, working time and holidays; the councils, operating at workplace levels, supplement the arrangements made by national level collective bargaining. In Belgium, however, such councils operate at a national level rather than local ones. The German system – regarded as a successful form of industrial democracy – was one of the influences behind the EU's 2002 Information and Consultation Directive (Hall, 2006). In the UK, the little-used Information and Consultation of Employees (ICE) Regulations (introduced in 2005) are relatively unheard of by employees, although they are designed to give employees – *upon request* and/or employer choice – the right to be:

- *informed* about the business's economic situation
- *informed* and *consulted* about employment prospects
- *informed* and *consulted* about decisions likely to lead to substantial changes in work organisation or contractual relations, including redundancies and transfers, *with a view to reaching agreement.*

The main requirements for employers of this directive are that:

- employers will have to *provide information* to representatives about the organisation's activities and economic situation
- employers will have to *consult* employee representatives on:
  - the 'situation, structure and probable development of employment'
  - future plans, particularly affecting jobs
  - substantial changes in work organisation or in contractual relations (e.g., redundancies, transfers) *with a view to reaching an agreement.*

This directive, deriving from Europe with its social partnership culture and history, fits uncomfortably with the current UK legislation, and to many the juxtaposition of the instruction to 'consult' followed by the phrase 'with a view to reaching agreement', is an implicit command to behave in a pluralist way and to negotiate.

Partnership

Partnership, as opposed to involvement and participation, describes the level of workplace activity that, while recognising the differences of interest between employer and employee, endeavours to reduce the contested elements within the employment relationship and gives weight to the need for employers and employees to work together for the good of the organisation. Partnership assumes shared interests and common goals with an emphasis on joint problem solving (often at a strategic level) necessitating high levels of information sharing, complete honesty and transparency and unconstrained channels of communication.

Implicit in the idea of partnership working is the suggestion that parties to the arrangement are working within a relationship where they are presumed equal, yet, as Heery (2002: 25) suggests, UK partnership agreements 'seem to represent union accommodation to an employer dominated process of reform' echoing what was said about power earlier on in this chapter.

Partnership, according to Guest and Peccei (2001: 16), requires three things

- a set of principles
- a set of practices
- a promise of benefits.

The *principles* are the values, prescribing appropriate forms of behaviour and practice, which under-pin any partnership agreement and are concerned with employer/employee rights and responsibilities stemming from notions of organisational justice, such as fair non-exploitative treatment, opportunities for employee contributions, fair compensation and benefits, and the requirement for both employees and employers to take responsibility for their actions. The *practices*, on the other hand, that might be found in organisations that observe partnership working may include:

- direct participation by employees in decisions about their own work
- direct participation by employees in decisions about personal employment issues
- participation by employee representatives in decisions about employment issues
- participation by employee representatives in decisions about broader organisational policy issues
- flexible job design with a focus on quality
- performance management
- employment security.

Guest and Peccei (2001: 32) also identify a range of areas of *potential benefit* stemming from partnership:

- enhanced employee attitudes and behaviour (in terms of contribution and commitment)
- an improved climate of employee relations (measured by labour turnover, retention, absence and conflict)
- better organisational performance (the business benefits of partnership being reflected in improvements in productivity, quality, innovation, sales and profits).

The rhetoric encompassing partnership ideals often emphasises a consensual, business-centric attitude towards organisational goals and aims, assuming that all parties to the partnership have the same degree of commitment to such principles and beliefs. For example, many NHS Foundation Trusts have partnership agreements specifying the potential benefits to everyone, ensuring high standards of employment practice within the Trusts, including the delivering of improved services to patients/service users.

In a similar, business-focused way the UK Department of Trade and Industry (DTI) (2001: 7) suggested that there were five routes to a successful partnership between employers and employees:

1 *Shared goals* – understanding the business that participants are engaged in.
2 *Shared culture* – agreed values binding the participants together.
3 *Shared learning* – continuously improving.

4   *Shared effort* – one business driven by flexible teams.
5   *Shared information* – effective communication throughout the company.

Case Snippet 9.4

Partnership on the Elizabeth Line

Aslef, the British train drivers' union, has a strong partnership with MRT Crossrail. They have worked together on a new rail link - the Elizabeth line - since 2014. Their collaboration included, for example, problem solving, shift rostering, exploring ways of improving diversity and importantly driver cab design, all of which helped to ensure a relatively positive employment relationship once the new line opened in May 2022. The success of the partnership is reflected in the staffing: 25% of drivers at MTR Crossrail are BAME compared to 5% of train drivers nationally, while Crossrail boasts just over double the percentage of female train drivers (12.5%) compared to the industry as a whole (6%). Before work on the line began there was already a strong foundation of working together on a range of procedures and structures like the drivers' functional council. The new partnership agreement has ratified and solidified this working together. Mick Whelan, general secretary of ASLEF, said:

> We have been involved with the Crossrail project all the way along the line. We welcome technology that makes our railways safer and we know, ... that there will be a driver on every train to ensure that the Elizabeth line service is modern, and efficient, and safe for passengers and for staff.

Sources: Creber, 2018; Dawson, 2018; Marius, 2021

Exercise 9.5

- With regard to the DTI routes to successful partnership arrangements, list:
  - the pluralist features
  - the unitarist features.
- Which features predominate?
- How problematic do you think the contradictory nature of partnership arrangements might be in practice?
- Analyse the importance of partnership arrangements in a contested employment relationship. Justify the reasoning behind your analysis.

The UK Department of Trade and Industry said that 'by working in partnership with their employees, and constantly assessing and re-assessing their progress along these five paths, companies have demonstrated that they are more aware of their customer's needs and more able to cope with the demands put upon them' (DTI, 2001: 7). This, of course, is a largely unitarist agenda clothed in pluralist rhetoric.

The attitudes towards partnership expressed by both Guest and Peccei and the DTI are not dissimilar to those expressed by Tzafrir and Dolan (2004) where harmony, reliability and concern engender trust between employers and employees (see Chapter 3), and indeed their categories also correspond to the earlier work by Whitener et al. (1998) who suggest that 'trust inducing' behaviours between supervisors and supervisees require:

- consistent behaviour (reliable and therefore predictable)
- behavioural integrity (truthfulness and keeping promises)
- sharing and delegation of control (sharing input into decision-making)
- communication (sharing accurate, timely, contextualised information)
- demonstrating concern (sensitivity towards each party's needs and interests, and acting empathetically).

Whether such consensual attitudes are sustainable in the long term is questionable. For example, a Cambridgeshire Local Authority had a partnership agreement with UNISON, where a large number of the shared attitudes and behaviours discussed above seemed present until the Authority planned redundancies, without informing the union at initial planning stages. This action strained the partnership, severely diminishing the levels of trust that the union representatives subsequently felt they had erroneously placed in their managerial counterparts. It took a long time for the partnership to 'get back on track' and for the parties to re-establish a good working relationship. It also, importantly, damaged the relationship between UNISON and its members who felt their representatives had let them down.

Exercise 9.6

Marchington and Cox (2007) use the words listed below on a diagrammatic escalator to show the potential way in which employee involvement might progress:

Communication

Co-determination

Consultation

Control

Information

- Draw an escalator/staircase and place these words where you think they will be most appropriate. In particular where would you put control?
- Why did you reach this conclusion?
- Do you think that control relates to the amount of power that a) management and b) employees exert? Why did you reach these conclusions?

Read the Marchington and Cox article and compare your positioning of the involvement categories on the escalator with theirs.

There are two contradictory perspectives from which partnership arrangements may be viewed: the first is that they are an essentially unitarist mechanism where all participants work as a single problem-solving unit; the second, a pluralist perspective, assumes differences in the interests, values, priorities and perspectives of the participants. Despite such differences, for any partnership arrangement to work there must be complete honesty between participants, yet within a contested employment relationship it is inevitable that such honesty will result in conflict – not to express this conflict would not only be dishonest but might also harm the representatives in the eyes of their respective constituents, who subsequently might reject the partnership arrangement. Consequently, under this pluralist perspective, partnership speaks more of adversaries than of partners, and partnership rhetoric about the 'joint ownership' of organisational concerns, issues and strategy is not an easy *modus operandi*. Strategic, problem-solving ways of operating are perhaps best described as pluralist in approach and unitarist in outcome.

Partnership is, regrettably, a term that carries with it *no precise* theoretical connotation. It is therefore difficult to disagree with. The imprecision of the term partnership and the ambiguity surrounding its interpretation and implementation, leads to confusion over what it is meant to stand for, that in turn leads to weakness of both academic analysis and workplace application. Consequently for many employers and employees the idea of partnership may seem vague and difficult to put into practice, yet for others it seems like an idea so good that it is hard to disagree with.

Exercise 9.7

Read Case Study 9.2.

- Evaluate the philosophy behind the company's way of working and analyse how it impacted upon perceptions of organisational justice.
- To what extent do you think there is a partnership between the owners and the workforce?
- Where does the power lie?

Case Study 9.2

Jump on Board (JOB)

Jump on Board is a UK manufacturing and retailing company specialising in making and selling skateboards. Since it began in the 1970s from a small workshop, based in the East End of London, with 20 dedicated employees crafting bespoke boards for a clientele of skateboarding fanatics, JOB has grown. It now employs around 800 staff, based on two sites, one in London, the other in Liverpool. The growth process has not been easy. It has been challenging to implement change effectively. At times it was difficult to switch the mindsets of the employees from creative (and individualistic) enthusiasts to a single team with the same goals and aspirations. As JOB grew from an intimate organisation into one operating globally, with commercial deadlines (and a reputation to protect), the employers, Steve and

(Continued)

Bob Benson, admit it was difficult to overcome workplace cynicism, resentment with the introduction of standardised processes, and mistrust in them as owners. It was not until 2019, when Sky Brown, the ten year-old British girl came third at the World Skateboarding Championship, that things began to change. As Steve said, 'The workforce suddenly realised they were part of something big and exciting. People came into work discussing her, her board, what she could achieve on it, and the technical merits of different types of wheelbase and thicknesses of veneer'.

The Bensons capitalised on the mood. They invited their workplace representatives from the GMB (London) and the Unite (Liverpool) unions to discuss a partnership agreement. Initially sceptical, the unions agreed to talks, partly because they saw an opportunity to improve wages, but also because they realised employee involvement might give everyone a say in the direction of the company. Site meetings for all staff - badged as 'Jump on Board for Partnership' - gradually changed the mood: suggestions were made, voted on and, after several months of dialogue, a shared vision for the future of both sites was produced.

The finally agreed principles underpinning the new agreement - *'Everyone* Jump on Board' - were that:

1   Everyone can participate, through their representatives, in the 'moving forward' strategic meetings,
2   Continuous improvement, as part of the culture, is nothing to fear.
3   Everyone, as individuals and/or team members, has the right to be innovative.
4   Training, upskilling and development is a right (not a privilege) for everyone.
5   Everyone has a responsibility to perform to their best ability.
6   Physical and mental safety at work is paramount.
7   Contribution and achievemssent will always be recognised.
8   JOB and the unions will continue to work in partnership for everyone's benefit; to this end they will work towards negotiating effective, collective agreements.

The process had to overcome initial scepticism but, because the union reps were involved, it was easier than it otherwise might have been. Change workshops, run by management and unions, ensured everyone knew the direction the company wanted to go in and how it intended to get there.

There were some early successes from the new style of working as people were happy knowing they could feed information and suggestions through to top management and be listened to. Following staff suggestions new designs were introduced and sold well. This improved morale and reinforced the feeling that everyone was working in partnership.

Yet not everything went smoothly. Ironically, the people who had to make the largest adjustments were the Bensons. Initially they made several decisions about increasing the sales volume to Canada and the USA without discussing the implications with the workforce. Indeed, when they recruited additional packers in the distribution section (and paid the minimum wage instead of the factory norm) there was uproar. A strike ballot was held, both unions said they would withdraw from the partnership agreement. Steve and Bob backed down. In early 2022 several staff were disciplined after they began, without authority, to work on innovative manufacturing processes for the wheel attachments. In their defence they cited the third partnership principle. Relationships between the union and management became fractious and the disciplinary charges were dropped.

The principles are now being discussed, clarified and possibly reformulated. The results will be subject to a workforce vote. Steve and Bob are wondering whether the partnership was such a good idea.

Summary

Whether involvement processes are targeted locally at individual employees or strategically enabling employee representation at higher levels, or whether they comprise single schemes or a mixture of involvement arrangements, both direct and indirect, the degree to which employee involvement contributes to organisational performance will crucially depend on the types of managerial philosophy (and style) in play and on whether the employees want to engage with the involvement processes. A number of factors influence the take-up and operation of EIP schemes, not least whether or not the government encourages or legislates for involvement (e.g., works councils in countries with social democratic traditions), and whether or not intermediary institutions, such as employers' associations, promote involvement activity. The schemes themselves may vary in scope and depth and whether the employer cedes sufficient power to the employees for the process to work (see Figure 9.1). Where EIP is offered in a half-hearted 'pseudo' way, or where line managers find the idea of worker participation unpalatable (Dundon and Wilkinson, 2021: 355), it is likely to lead to cynicism and perceptions of procedural and informational injustice; particularly where line managers are insufficiently trained in giving and receiving feedback potentially leading to perceptions of organisational injustice, particularly interactional injustice.

Review Questions

1 Distinguish between each of these terms: employee involvement, employee participation and partnership. To what extent and why might the differences between them be important from the point of view of a) the employer and b) the employee?
2 Which participatory activities do you think managers might need to deploy in order to minimise the incidence of conflict in their organisations? Why did you reach your conclusion?
3 Mellizo et al. (2011) found that individuals who voted to determine their own levels of reward performed better than those who did not vote; evaluate whether you think the findings from this participatory experiment could be applicable to a business organisation.
4 Discuss, with academic justification, whether or not partnership is ever possible in the contested employment relationship.

Revision Exercise 9.1

Charles et al. (2021) discovered, in their small study of 50 employees, that employee involvement in organisational decision making enhances productivity, increases commitment, and promotes creativity and innovation. The authors suggest that relationships between managers and employees should encourage consultation and the free flow of information, and thus they recommended that employees be involved in decision making because it encourages feelings of organisational ownership.

From your knowledge of the information in this chapter say whether you agree with their findings and justify, with academic reasons, why you reached your conclusion.

Revision Exercise 9.2

Critically discuss the following quote in the light of:

- different managerial styles
- employee perceptions of justice.

> Involving people varies from informing them of a decision, through to giving citizens full control. The difference between these levels is the relative balance of power and control between the participants and the instigators. (Richards et al., 2004: 3)

Revision Exercise 9.3

Analyse the differences between employee involvement, participation and partnership showing how employee:

- influence
- control
- involvement
- exercise of power
- intervention in decision making

might differ in each category.

    How might the allocations of each of the above affect employee perceptions of organisational justice?

Relevant Articles for Further Reading

Butt, A. N., Rehman, S. and Mushtaq, K. (2019) 'Role of communication and participation in promoting employees' openness to change: Mediating role of trust in supervisor', *Research*, 21(3): 560–75.

Looking at the employee–supervisor relationship in the Pakistan public sector, the authors show how trust in a supervisor, together with enhanced participation, helps alleviate resistance to organisational change.

Casey, C. and Delaney, H. (2019) 'The effort of partnership: Capacity development and moral capital in partnership for mutual gains', *Economic and Industrial Democracy*, 43(1): 52–71.

Following a partnership initiative in a large, multi-site company, with several unions, over a period of five years, Casey and Delaney show how tough it can be to introduce and maintain a positive momentum for participatory schemes. The processes of participation encourage collaborative employee behaviours such as tolerance, patience, mutuality and trust.

Dundon, T. and Wilkinson, A. (2021) 'Employee involvement and participation', in A. Wilkinson and T. Dundon (eds), *Contemporary Human Resource Management: Text and Cases*. London: Sage, pp. 345–62.

This is a comprehensive and critical look at current practices in EIP providing a range of examples that students will find helpful for putting the academic theory into practical context.

References

Abid, G., Contreras, F., Ahmed, S. and Qazi, T. (2019) 'Contextual factors and organizational commitment: Examining the mediating role of thriving at work', *Sustainability*, 11(17): 46–86.

Acas (2010) *A–Z of Work Handbook*. London: Acas. Available at www.acas.org.uk/media/pdf/0/0/A_to_Z_of_Work_(November_2010)-accessible-version-may-2012.pdf (accessed 30 November 2012).

Acas (2014) *Representation at Work*. London: HMSO.

Ackerman, N. (2021) 'Bar staff join JD Wetherspoon board as directors', *Evening Standard*, 20 December. Available at: www.msn.com/en-gb/news/uknews/bar-staff-join-jd-wetherspoon-board-as-directors/ar-AARZ5aK (accessed 20 December 2021).

Baker, C. E. (2006) *Media Concentration and Democracy: Why Ownership Matters*. Cambridge: Cambridge University Press.

Barry, M., Wilkinson, A., Gollan, P. J. and Kalfa, S. (2014) 'Where are the voices? New directions in voice and engagement across the globe', in A. Wilkinson, G. Wood and R. Deeg (eds), *The Oxford Handbook of Employment Relations: Comparative Employment Systems*. Oxford: Oxford University Press, pp. 522–40.

Bingham, C., Clarke, L., Michielsens, E. and Van de Meer, M. (2013) 'Towards a social model approach? British and Dutch disability policies in the health sector compared', *Personnel Review*, 42(5): 613–37.

Boehler, S. (2012) 'All you have to do is ask', in J. Miller and H. Alber (eds), *The New Heart At Work: Stories and Strategies for Building Self-esteem and Reawakening the Soul at Work*. Bloomington, IN: Trafford, pp. 103–5.

Boxall, P. and Purcell, J. (2003) *Strategy and Human Resource Management*. Basingstoke: Palgrave.

Boxall, P., Hutchison, A. and Wassenaar, B. (2015) 'How do high-involvement work processes influence employee outcomes? An examination of the mediating roles of skill utilisation and intrinsic motivation', *International Journal of Human Resource Management*, 26(13): 1737–52.

Brannen, P. (1983) *Authority and participation in industry*. London: BT Batsford Limited.

Briône, P. (2021) *A Guide to Establishing Staff Networks*. London: CIPD.

Brooks, C. (2019) 'Volkswagen Declares war against works council and German union', *Labor Notes*, 12 June. Available at: https://labornotes.org/blogs/2019/06/volkswagen-declares-war-against-works-council-and-german-union (accessed 12 February 2022).

Budd, J. W. (2004) *Employment with a Human Face: Balancing Efficiency, Equity, and Voice*. Ithaca, NY: Cornell University Press.

Budd, J. W. (2010) 'Theorizing work: The importance of conceptualizations of work for research and practice', paper presented at the 25th Cardiff Employment Research Unit Annual Conference, Cardiff Business School, 13–14 September. Available at: www.legacy-irc.csom.umn.edu/faculty/jbudd/research/cardiff2010.pdf (accessed 24 February 2013).

Charles, J., Francis, F. and Zirra, C. T. O. P. (2021) 'Effect of employee involvement in decision-making and organization productivity', *Archives of Business Research (ABR)*, 9(3): 28–34.

Chevalier, S., Huart, I., Coillot, H., Odry, D., Mokounkolo, R., Gillet, N. and Fouquereau, E. (2020) 'How to increase affective organizational commitment among new French police officers. The role of trainers and organizational identification.', *Police Practice and Research*, 21(6): 562–75.

Confederation of British Industry/EDG (1991) *Managing for Success: Launch Issue*, April. London: CBI/EDG.

Cotton, J. L. (1993) *Employee Involvement: Methods for Improving Performance and Work Attitudes*. Newbury Park: Sage.

Cox, A., Marchington, M. and Suter, J. (2009) 'Employee involvement and participation: Developing the concept of institutional embeddedness using WERS2004', *The International Journal of Human Resource Management*, 20(10): 2150–68.

Creber P. (2018) 'Alison Bell, HR director, MTR Crossrail', *HR Magazine*, 17 September. Available at: www.hrmagazine.co.uk/content/people/alison-bell-hr-director-mtr-crossrail (accessed 21 February 2022).

Cremer, A. (2014) 'VW workers may block southern US deals if no unions: Labor chief', *Reuters*, 19 February. Available at: www.reuters.com/article/2014/02/19/us-vw-usplant-idUSBREA1I0S820140219 (accessed 3 February 2015).

Dachler, P. and Wilpert, B. (1978) 'Conceptual dimensions and boundaries of participation in organisations', *Administrative Science Quarterly*, 23(1): 1–39.

Davies, P. L. (1992) 'The emergence of European labour law', in W. McCarthy (ed.), *Legal Intervention in Industrial Relations: Gains and Losses*. Oxford: Blackwell, pp. 313–59.

Dawson, S. (2018) 'MTR Crossrail and ASLEF: Partnership in Action', *IPA*. Available at: www.ipa-involve.com/blog/mtr-crossrail-and-aslef-partnership-in-action (accessed 21 February 2022).

Department for Business, Innovation and Skills (2013) *The 2011 Workplace Employment Relations Study (WERS) Transparency Data*. Available at: www.gov.uk/government/publications/the-2011-workplace-employment-relations-study-wers-transparency-data (accessed 3 October 2014).

Department of Trade and Industry (2001) *Partnerships With People: A Practical Guide*. Available at: www.dti.gov.uk/mbp/bpgt/m9m000002/m9m0000021.html (accessed 10 September 2001).

Dobbins, T. (2010) 'The case for "beneficial constraints": Why permissive voluntarism impedes workplace cooperation in Ireland', *Economic and Industrial Democracy*, 31(4): 497–519.

Dundon, T. and Wilkinson, A. (2021) 'Employee involvement and participation', in A. Wilkinson and T. Dundon (eds), *Contemporary Human Resource Management: Text and Cases*. London: Sage, pp. 345–62.

Edwards, P. (2003) *Industrial Relations Theory and Practice* (2nd edn). Oxford: Blackwell.

Edwards, P. K. (1992) 'Industrial conflict: Themes and issues in recent research', *British Journal of Industrial Relations*, 30: 361–404.

Eurofound (2013) *Work Organisation and Employee Involvement in Europe*. Luxembourg: Publications Office of the European Union.

Eurofound and Cedefop (2020) *European Company Survey 2019: Workplace Practices Unlocking Employee Potential*, European Company Survey 2019 series. Luxembourg: Publications Office of the European Union.

European Bank of Reconstruction and Development (EBRD) (2022) *The EBRD's Staff Council*. Available at: www.ebrd.com/who-we-are/ebrd-staff-council.html (accessed 20 February 2022).

European Trade Union Institute (ETUI) (2014) *Worker Interest Representation in Europe – Towards a Better Understanding of the Pieces of a Still Unfinished Jigsaw*. Brussels: ETUI. Available at: www.worker-participation.eu/content/view/full/1760 (accessed 5 June 2014).

European Union (2021) *Inform and Consult Staff*. Available at: https://europa.eu/youreurope/business/human-resources/employment-contracts/inform-consult-staff/index_en.htm (accessed 13 February 2022).

Faragher, J. (2021) 'FTSE 350 companies "could do better" on employee voice', *Personnel Today*, 25 May. Available at: www.personneltoday.com/hr/ftse-350-companies-could-do-better-on-employee-voice/ (accessed 12 February 2022).

Felstead, A., Gallie, D., Green, F. and Zhou, Y. (2010) 'Employee involvement, the quality of training and the learning environment: An individual level analysis', *International Journal of Human Resource Management*, 21(10): 1667–88.

Fox, A. (1974) *Beyond Contract: Work Power and Trust Relations*. London: Faber and Faber.

Freeman, R. B., Boxall, P. and Haynes, P. (2007) *What Workers Say: Employee Voice in the Anglo-American Workplace*. Ithaca, NY: ILR Press.

Friedman, A. (1977) 'Responsible autonomy versus direct control over the labour process', *Capital & Class*, 1(1): 43–57.

Geary, J. and Sisson, K. (1994) *Conceptualising Direct Participation in Organizational Change*. Luxembourg: The EPOC Project.

Goodley, S. (2021) 'JD Wetherspoon managers join board of directors for first time', *The Guardian*, 20 December. Available at: www.theguardian.com/business/2021/dec/20/jd-wetherspoon-area-managers-join-board-of-directors-for-first-time (accessed 20 December 2021).

Guest, D. E. and Peccei, R. (2001) 'Partnership at work: Mutuality and the balance of advantage', *British Journal of Industrial Relations*, 39(2): 207–36.

Hall, M. (2006) 'A cool response to the ICE Regulations? Employer and trade union approaches to the new legal framework for information and consultation', *Industrial Relations Journal*, 37(5): 456–72.

Hall, M. and Purcell, J. (2012) *Consultation at Work: Regulation and Practice*. Oxford: Oxford University Press.

Harlos, K. (2001) 'When organisational voice systems fail: More on the deaf-ear syndrome and frustration effects', *Journal of Applied Behavioural Science*, 31(3): 324–42.

Heery, E. (2002) 'Partnership versus organising: Alternative futures for British trade unionism', *Industrial Relations Journal*, 33(1): 20–35.

Helland, E., Christensen, M., Innstrand, S. T. and Nielsen, K. (2021) 'Line managers' middle-levelness and driving proactive behaviors in organizational interventions', *International Journal of Workplace Health Management*, 14(6).

Hickland, E., Cullinane, N., Dobbins, T., Dundon, T. and Donaghey, J. (2020) 'Employer silencing in a context of voice regulations: Case studies of non-compliance', *Human Resource Management Journal*, 30(4): 537–52.

Hodge, P. (2014) 'Employee ownership scheme boosts productivity at Gripple', *Employee Benefits*, 19 November. Available at www.employeebenefits.co.uk/benefits/share-schemes/employee-ownership-scheme-boosts-productivity-at-gripple/105895.article (accessed 5 May 2015).

Hosseini, E., Ardekani, S. S., Sabokro, M. and Salamzadeh, A. (2022) 'The study of knowledge employee voice among the knowledge-based companies: The case of an emerging economy', *Revista de Gestão*, 29(2).

Hryschko, K. (2017) 'A values-based approach to employee engagement', *HR Review*, 9 March. Available at: www.hrreview.co.uk/analysis/katie-hryschko-values-based-approach-employee-engagement/103581 (accessed 16 February 2022).

Hyman, J. and Mason, R. (1995) *Managing Employee Involvement and Participation*. London: Sage.

Hyman, R. (1987) 'Strategy or structure? Capital, labour and control', *Work, Employment and Society*, 11(1): 25–55.

Hyman, R. (1997) 'The future of employee representation', *British Journal of Industrial Relations*, 35(3): 309–36.

Johnstone, S. (2010) *Labour and Management Co-operation: Workplace Partnership in UK Financial Services*. Farnham: Gower.

Johnstone, S., Ackers, P. and Wilkinson, A. (2009) 'The British partnership phenomenon: A ten year review', *Human Resource Management Journal*, 19(3): 260–79.

Jones, D. C., Kalmi, P. and Kauhanen, A. (2010) 'How do high-involvement work processes influence employee outcomes? An examination of the mediating roles of skill utilisation and intrinsic motivation', *Industrial Relations*, 49(1): 1–21.

Kane, A. (2013) 'Keeping employees happy when communicating workplace change', *HR Review*, 10 July. Available at: www.hrreview.co.uk/blogs/blogs-hr-strategy-practice/alastair-kane-keeping-employees-happy-when-communicating-workplace-change/44947 (accessed 16 April 2014).

Kunert, P. (2013) 'HP: Yes, we plan to axe another 7,100 European staffers', *The Channel*, 24 October. Available at: www.channelregister.co.uk/2013/10/24/hp_job_cuts/ (accessed 29 April 2015).

Kunert, P. (2014) 'HP in talks with unions ahead of the Big Split-Up', *The Channel*, 27 April. Available at: www.channelregister.co.uk/2015/04/27/hp_calls_on_local_works_council_and_union_as_split_gains_pace/ (accessed 29 April 2015).

Lavelle, J., Gunnigle, P. and McDonnell, A. (2010) 'Patterning employee voice in multinational companies', *Human Relations*, 63(3): 395–418.

Lawler, E. E., Mohrman, S. A. and Ledford, G. E. (1995) *Creating High Performance Organizations*. San Francisco, CA: Jossey-Bass.

Marchington, M. (2007) 'Employee voice systems', in P. Boxall, J. Purcell and P. Wright (eds), *The Oxford Handbook of Human Resource Management*. Oxford: Oxford University Press, pp. 231–48.

Marchington, M. (2015a) 'The role of institutional and intermediary forces in shaping patterns of employee involvement and participation (EIP) in Anglo-American countries', *The International Journal of Human Resource Management*, 26(20): 2594–616.

Marchington, M. (2015b) 'Analysing the forces shaping employee involvement and participation (EIP) at organisation level in liberal market economies (LMEs)', *Human Resource Management Journal*, 25(1): 1–18.

Marchington, M. and Cox, A. (2007) 'Employee involvement and participation: Structures, processes and outcomes', in J. Storey (ed.), *Human Resource Management: A Critical Text*. London: Thompson, pp. 177–94.

Marchington, M. and Kynighou, A. (2012) 'The dynamics of employee involvement and participation during turbulent times', *The International Journal of Human Resource Management*, 23: 3336–54.

Marchington, M. and Suter, J. (2013) 'Where informality really matters: Patterns of employee involvement and participation (EIP) in a non-union firm', *Industrial Relations: A Journal of Economy and Society*, Special Issue: Employee representation in non-union firms, 52(s1): 284–313.

Marchington, M. and Wilkinson, A. (2005) 'Direct participation and involvement', in S. Bach (ed.), *Managing Human Resources: Personnel Management in Transition*. Chichester: Wiley, pp. 398–423.

Marchington, M., and Wilkinson, A. (2008) *Human Resource Management at Work* (4th edn). London: CIPD.

Marchington, M., Goodman, J., Wilkinson, A. and Ackers, P. (1992) 'New developments in employee involvement', *Employment Department Research Series*, 2.

Marius, C. (2021) 'Crossrail Elizabeth line trains will drive themselves when it opens in 2022', *My London*, 8 June. Available at: www.mylondon.news/news/zone-1-news/crossrail-elizabeth-line-trains-drive-20762488 (accessed 21 February 2022).

Mellizo, P., Carpenter, J.P. and Matthews, P.H. (2011) *Workplace Democracy in the Lab*, Discussion Paper Series No. 5460, Forschungsinstitut zur Zukunft der Arbeit. Available at: http://nbn-resolving.de/urn:nbn:de:101:201104113333 (accessed 5 May 2015).

Miller, K. I. and Monge, P. R. (1986) 'Participation, satisfaction and productivity: A meta-analytic review', *Academy of Management Journal*, 29(4): 727–53.

Moss, R. (2021) 'Weatherspoon appoints bar staff to board of directors', *Personnel Today*, 20 December. Available at: www.personneltoday.com/hr/wetherspoon-appoints-bar-staff-to-board-of-directors/ (accessed 20 December 2021).

Pateman, C. (1970) *Participation and Democratic Theory*. Cambridge: Cambridge University Press.

Purcell, J. (1987) 'Mapping management styles in employee relations', *Journal of Management Studies*, 24(5): 533–48.

Ramsay, H. (1993) 'Recycled waste? Debating the analysis of worker participation: A response to Ackers et al.', *Industrial Relations Journal*, 24(1): 76–80.

Richards, C., Blackstock, K. L. and Carter, C. E. (2004) 'Practical approaches to participation', *SERG Policy Brief No.1*. Aberdeen: Macaulay Institute.

Rousseau, D.M. and Shperling, Z. (2003) 'Pieces of the action: Ownership and the changing employment relationship', *Academy of Management Review*, 28(4): 553–70.

Salamon, M. (2000) *Industrial Relations: Theory and Practice*. Oxford: Pearson Education.

Schaufeli, W. (2014) 'What is engagement?', in K. Truss, R. Delbridge, K. Alfes, A. Shantz and E. Soane (eds), *Employee Engagement: Theory and Practice*. Abingdon: Routledge, pp. 15–35.

Snook, J. C. and Whittall, M. (2013) 'From "the best kept company secret" to a more proficient structure of employee representation: The role of EWC delegates with a managerial background', *Economic and Industrial Democracy*, 34(2): 355–78.

Stephens, E. H. (1980) 'Theoretical framework for the comparative study of workers' participation', in E.H. Stephens (ed.), *The Politics of Workers' Participation: The Peruvian Approach in Comparative Perspective*. London: Elsevier.

Strauss, G. (1998) 'An overview', in F. Heller, E. Pusić, G. Strauss and B. Wilpert (eds), *Organizational Participation – Myth and Reality*. Oxford: Oxford University Press, pp. 8–39.

Sweeney, E. (2014) *Making Work Better: An Agenda for Government*. London: The Smith Institute.

Timming, A. R. (2007) 'European works councils and the dark side of managing worker voice', *Human Resource Management Journal*, 17(3): 248–64.

Tzafrir, S. and Dolan, S. (2004) 'Trust me: A multiple item scale for measuring managers' "employee trust"', *Management Research*, 2(2): 115–32.

Varshney, D. (2020) 'Employees' job involvement and satisfaction in a learning organization: A study in India's manufacturing sector', *Global Business and Organizational Excellence*, 39(2): 51–61.

Webb, C. (1912) *Industrial Co-operation: The Story of a Peaceful Revolution*. London: Forgotten Books.

Whitener, E. M., Brodt, S. E., Korsgaard, M. A. and Werner, J. M. (1998) 'Managers as initiators of trust: An exchange relationship framework for understanding managerial trustworthy behaviour', *Academy of Management Review*, 23(3): 513–30.

Wilkinson, A. and Fay, C. (2011) 'New times for employee voice?', *Human Resource Management*, 50(1): 65–74.

Wilkinson, A., Gollan, P. J., Kalfa, S. and Xu, Y. (2018) 'Voices unheard: Employee voice in the new century', *The International Journal of Human Resource Management*, 29(5): 711–24.

Wilkinson, A., Dundon, T., Donaghey, J. and Freeman, R. (2020) 'Employee voice: Bridging new terrains and disciplinary boundaries', in A. Wilkinson, T. Dundon, J. Donaghey and R. Freeman (eds), *Handbook of Research on Employee Voice* (2nd edn). Cheltenham: Edward Elgar, pp. 2–18.

Williams, S. (2014) *Introducing Employment Relations: A Critical Approach*. Oxford: Oxford University Press.

Wright, R. (2014) 'Works councils at VW key for further US work', *Financial Times*, 19 February. Available at: www.ft.com/cms/s/0/8a5ceed0-99a3-11e3-b3a2-00144feab7de.html (accessed 3 February 2015).

Yukl, G. (1989) *Leadership in Organizations* (2nd edn). Englewood Cliffs, NJ: Prentice-Hall.

Zhou, Y. (2009) *British Employees' Organisational Participation: Trends, Determinants and Impact*. Berlin: VDM.

Zhou, Y., Fan, X. and Son, J. (2019) 'How and when matter: Exploring the interaction effects of high-performance work systems, employee participation, and human capital on organizational innovation', *Human Resource Management*, 58(3): 253–68.

10

EMPLOYEE VOICE: BEING HEARD AND MAKING A DIFFERENCE

Learning Outcomes

By the end of this chapter, you should be able to:

- express a critical understanding of the meanings given to voice and silence within the employment relationship
- identify the differences between direct and indirect voice and their links to the ways in which power is exercised
- critically evaluate alternative voice-enabling mechanisms in the light of different managerial perspectives
- show an awareness of the impediments to voice
- analyse the ways in which voice may, or may not, affect diversity
- critically review the impact that perceptions of justice might have on voice.

What to Expect

This chapter explores the different forms of voice, that is, direct and indirect, traditional and digital, looking at the ways in which different cultures, laws and organisations ignore or facilitate its operation. It examines some of the consequences, intended or otherwise, that arise from voice enactment. The ways in which employees might choose to remain silent and what this might mean for their organisations will be explored, as will some of the important links between diversity and voice. Different aspects of voice and the ways with which employees have an opportunity to 'have a say' are explored, alongside specific policies that encourage and enable voice.

Some practices are influential, either inhibiting or enhancing voice – such attitudes (inhibitors and enablers) towards voice are explored. Voice is often regarded as legitimate only when it accords with what the listener wants to hear; other antecedents, such as those associated with hard authoritarian regimes, are likely to muffle and suppress voice.

Voice – Definitions and Their Shortcomings

Employee voice is a rather elastic concept with a range of definitions and multitude of meanings, sometimes linked to employee involvement, sometimes not, and often, but not always, regarded as an essential ingredient for employee engagement and commitment to an organisation. Boxall and Purcell (2003: 162), for example, said that employee voice encompasses 'a whole variety of processes and structures which enable, and at times empower, employees directly and indirectly to contribute to decision-making in the firm', while in 2015 Mike Emmott, from the CIPD, defined voice as something that occurs where 'employees are encouraged, willing and able to make their opinions heard within the framework of an organisational culture based on mutual trust and respect' (Emmott, 2015). Neither of these definitions is completely satisfactory; it is not unknown, for example, for employees to express strong opinions to an employer by deliberately remaining silent, or by speaking out even when the definition's antecedents of 'mutual trust and respect' are absent. Detert and Burris add to the picture by defining voice as:

> the discretionary provision of information intended to improve organizational functioning to someone inside an organization with the perceived authority to act, even though such information may challenge and upset the status quo of the organization and its power holders. (2007: 869)

Oyetunde et al. meanwhile construe voice by looking at organisations' enabling infrastructures. They categorise employee voice

> … as mechanisms, structures and processes of voicing available to workers aimed at not just suggesting opinions, airing concerns or complaints, but initiating high-level participation and involvement in the decision-making process to influence not only employment terms but also work autonomy and other business issues. (2022: 144)

Detert and Burris crucially advance the notion of discretionary voice while both this and the Oyetunde definition are particularly important because they include the notion not just of employees challenging – and perhaps changing something – but of influencing those who hold the balance of power.

Freeman and Medoff (1984) took the work by Hirschman (1970), who looked at voice in terms of customers acting within competitive markets, and specifically applied it to the employment relationship. For them voice was associated with collective, indirect, representation where trade unions articulated the interests and concerns of their members to management (either through collective bargaining or via informal communication mechanisms) in an attempt to redress labour market inequalities, management often adjusting working practices following representation and negotiation (Wood, 2008: 154). On-site union representatives therefore enhance the ways and means by which collective voice is heard, their direct links with union members enabling them to understand and raise matters of concern (Bryson and Forth, 2010). Such indirect representative activity is associated with the managerially pluralist outlook that perceives collective bargaining between employers and employees as the legitimate way of settling differences in the workplace. For Wilkinson et al. however, a wider definition of employee voice applies – for them voice is all about

> ... how employees are able to have a say over work activities and decisions within the organizations in which they work, regardless of the institutional channel through which it operates. (2014: 6)

Their definition is sufficiently broad to cover both direct and indirect voice and the unitarist and pluralist perspectives, yet they do not really cover the issue of the silent voices that, by their very silence, speak volumes.

Employee voice, whether consensual or dissenting, directly expressed or indirectly communicated via representatives, is therefore in evidence on a scale ranging from:

- nothing because the organisation neither recognises nor inhibits voice
- silence (either due to assumed agreement or to a discretionary enacting of passive resistance)
- individual expressions of support, consent, or dissent
- the collective ways of influencing managerial behaviour via processes such as consultation and negotiation
- having a strategic input into the ways in which an organisation operates, or perhaps through expressions of palpable and very obvious protest.

Enabling mechanisms encouraging and facilitating voice take a variety of forms. As we saw in Chapter 9, scope, depth and breadth of the subjects discussed are all important, along with the ways in which employees react to the opportunities for speaking out. The notions of mutual trust and honesty – whether they are missing or present – are relevant in all these stages. Where they are present, positive perceptions of interactional and procedural justice are likely to encourage both voice and listening behaviours (Edezaro, 2022; Khaola and Musiiwa, 2021).

Evidence for the Concept of Employee Voice Within the Employment Relationship

Employees have been discussing work matters with their employers since at least the time of the medieval craft guilds and labourers' associations. (In the UK, for example, working conditions in the building industry were often better in the medieval period than in the seventeenth and eighteenth centuries, and strikes at this time were not uncommon, indicating that employees were prepared to withdraw labour as a means of voicing their discontent – Gimpel, 1976.) Yet the notion of 'employee voice' as a discrete concept only really became an issue for industrial/ employee relations scholars from the last part of the twentieth century where the emphasis was skewed towards the voices of the representatives of the relatively powerless (i.e., unions representing employees) rather than the voices of those with power (i.e., employers) (Kaufman, 2014; Kim et al., 2010). Much of the research and debate developed from the early work of Sidney and Beatrice Webb (see Chapter 1) and later took its lead from the seminal work of Freeman and Medoff (1984) on union voice and collective bargaining. Traditionally trade unions, as the representatives of employees, were regarded as the 'mouthpiece' of the workforce, broaching its concerns with management and becoming the 'go to' mechanism by which union members redressed workplace power imbalances. Consequently, the predominant academic work around the concept of employee voice for many years was based around mechanisms through which unions could counter, combat or constrain unilateral managerial dictat.

News Flash 10.1

'We Don't Want Our Company to Profit Off of Children Being in Concentration Camps'

571 employees at Wayfair, the USA online furniture business, were so appalled to learn that their company had arranged to sell beds for use in a children's detention centre on the USA/Mexico border that they sent a letter of complaint to their CEO, Niraj Shah, asking for the order to be rescinded and for the company to set up an ethical code of behaviour. They also, via social media messages, arranged a protest walk out.

The letter said:

> We believe that the current actions of the United States and their contractors at the Southern border do not represent an ethical business partnership Wayfair should choose to be a part of ... We believe that by selling ... products to BCFS or similar contractors we are enabling [child rights] violation and are complicit in furthering the inhumane actions of our government.

In response Wayfair said:

> No matter how strongly any one of us feels about an issue, it is important to keep in mind that not all employees or customers agree ... As a retailer, it is standard practice to fulfil orders for all customers ... it is our business to sell to any customer who is acting within the laws of the countries within which we operate.

Sources: Gajanan, 2019; Garrison, 2019

From the end of the last century, particularly since the decrease in union density, voice has been associated not just with union representation but with the wider workforce where it is seen as an essential ingredient for workplace democracy. For both employees and managements, voice is regarded as an 'intrinsic standard of participation – [where] participation in decision-making is an end in itself' (Budd, 2004: 23). Under the auspices of HRM, such participative democracy is evident where those employers who perceive employee contributions as essential to their competitive edge facilitate this 'edge' by evolving effective communication systems. Often these involve sharing information, having transparent workplace practices, consulting with employees, encouraging the workforce to participate in the processes of some decision making and providing for robust grievance procedures (Dundon et al., 2004; Paulet et al. 2021) – all of which, of course, promote employee voice. Whether this voice is actually effective and allowed to influence managerial decision making is a different matter. Mowbray et al. (2020) add to the debate by showing that in high performance workplaces line managers are integral to voice because it is they who create voice opportunities for their subordinates. Where voice arrangements are treated as central to, and part of, a bundle of HRM practices, there are links to higher levels of workplace productivity (Boxall and Purcell, 2011). Kornelakis et al. agree, proposing that 'both theory and empirical evidence suggest that certain inclusive workplace practices can have positive effects on productivity because they improve the organisational climate' (2018: 2). Interestingly Della Torre (2019), when looking at Italian employees, found that team voice (unlike union voice, which was positively linked to workplace productivity) showed no significant relationship with labour productivity.

Managerial perspectives – unitarist or pluralist – are useful to explain the rationale deployed by employers for their specific voice mechanisms. For the unitarist, voice is a way of allowing everyone in the organisation (assumed to be working towards identical goals) to have a way to be heard by exploiting discursive problem-solving techniques and *assuming agreement*. For the pluralist, voice is the means whereby workplace structures expedite the acknowledging of differing views prior to decision making, thereby seeming to share power (although often this is actually a way of maintaining power and keeping control). It is, however, not uncommon for some pluralist organisations to facilitate voice by supplementing union representation with a range of other types of workplace spokespeople, or by using complementary, direct and indirect systems of voice alongside one another, permitting non-union channels two-way communication to operate beside the union ones (Dundon and Gollan, 2007; Campolieti et al., 2013; Mowbray et al., 2019). There is international evidence showing a propensity for bargaining structures to co-exist in 'twin-track' systems: direct and indirect voice schemes; union and non-union voice mechanisms; collective bargaining alongside works councils and joint consultative committees (Brewster et al., 2007, 2019; Bryson et al., 2019). Heery points out that 'worker representation can, and should, assume a hybrid form, in which different institutions come together and reinforce and complement each other's efforts' (2010: 555). However, the power of non-union voices to be heard is limited; as Bellace et al. say, 'while workers in non-union firms strain to be heard, their voice is muted. They have had no role in creating the rules of the workplace, nor in the structuring of the grievance-arbitration process' (2021: 799).

In many organisations there is an historical legacy of acquisitions, mergers and changes of management personnel that result in a less than clear-cut division between managerial perspectives – unitary organisations, for example, may acquire pluralist ones, or vice versa. Similarly heads of division can change, leading to new appointments sometimes holding differing perspectives from previous role incumbents. When instances like this occur the employment relationship and its associated voice arrangements may be subject to a pragmatic muddling through (Sisson, 1995) and to the co-joining or adjacent operating of different practices. For instance, the management of a pluralist organisation, with collective **indirect voice** structures, may find itself in control of a new unitarist section with an infrastructure supporting direct voice and employee involvement. Where indirect, trade union collective voice mechanisms are found simultaneously at one company location, while other direct, non-union voice mechanisms are present at another location within the same organisation, it is known as **'double-breasting'** (Dundon and Wilkinson 2021; Gunnigle et al., 2009) – which Dundon et al. say

> ... is distinct from hybrid or dual union and non-union regimes in that the focus is not on comparative practices within sites, but rather across sites within the same company. The core of the approach means unionised workers have independent collective voice, while employees in non-union sites do not. (2014: 491)

The simultaneous use of two dissimilar types of voice arrangements at different locations can be a product of historical processes or may be part of a deliberate cost-cutting strategy to create different (lower-level) terms and conditions for parts of the workforce. In such circumstances inequitable access to voice mechanisms leads to perceptions of organisational injustice with consequential negative impacts on morale, productivity and turnover.

Employer Voice

Employer voice is taken as given as employers (and their managerial representatives) are able to direct and influence proceedings, voice opinions and communicate intentions because of the very positions that they hold. Where workplaces and working patterns are fragmented this is particularly so, in part because unions find it more difficult to coordinate activities where organisations operate on a number of different sites, particularly where employees have flexible work patterns and may work remotely. Employer voice is given legitimacy and weight by the authority conferred on employers and their representatives by their positions and status. Employers not only exercise their voices directly within their own organisations, but also, indirectly, through their associations and networks where they are able, for example, to influence/lobby governments and policy makers (Brandl and Lehr, 2019; Gooberman et al., 2018).

Recently there has been a burgeoning of **employee ownership schemes** whereby employees can own shares and take some of the responsibility for the direction of their organisations. Employee voice in such situations becomes, in theory, employer voice, although in larger organisations the shares are frequently held by a trust body acting for the employees and the individuals themselves have a limited *real* say in the day-to-day operation of their organisations. At John Lewis, for example, where the employees are partners in the organisation, their shares are held by a Trust, employee voice is indirect and collective via a number of workplace representatives. Individual employees have little voice outside of this arrangement. Where smaller 'mutual' organisations operate there is sometimes more opportunity for direct employee voice. For example, in December 2021, the publishing company, the Folio Society, sold the company, giving its employees 100% ownership. This – alongside the company works council and Folio Society Trust – gives all employees a stake *and a voice* in the business.

Exercise 10.1

[E]mployers are central to voice, [they] set the agenda and develop and maintain the culture and values that surround voice. (Holland, 2014: 135)

- Using academic references, discuss the ways in which this statement does (or does not) depict a crucial truth about the ways in which voice is facilitated at work.

News Flash 10.2

More Voice for Employees at Wool Mill

Employees at Melin Tregwynt, a family-owned woollen mill and shop in Wales, celebrated when, in April 2022, the Griffiths family handed the company over to them. The family created an employee ownership trust, thereby helping to preserve the traditional skills and knowledge built up since 1912. Now, via the trust, employees have a voice in the way the business is run. Family member Eifion Griffiths said, 'I am proud to be passing on the company to the new employee board who I know will take the business to new levels of growth'.

Source: Bird, 2022

Patterns of Voice

Voice, even if not consistently defined, is nevertheless a subject that continues to be studied and analysed. Categorised according to whether or not it is direct or indirect, initiated by management or the workforce, is token or leads to real influence in workplace decision making, it is an important aspect of the twenty-first century employment relationship. Within the UK there is a range of voice opportunities in operation. Smaller organisations are much less likely to deploy indirect voice mechanisms, while around one-third of all organisations, whatever their size, have no formal voice mechanisms, either direct or indirect. Workplace representation, and hence voice, varies within and across Europe, Australia, the USA and Asiatic countries. It is impacted and influenced by different legislative regimes and the degree to which such regimes support union presence and/or the right for time off work for representatives. Just one-third of

EU companies have an official employee representative body that benefits substantially from social dialogue (Eurofound, 2021: 30). In both the USA and Australia, for example, there is enabling legislation that gives worker representatives the right to negotiate on terms and conditions without external interference, thereby giving employees genuine voice where representation exists (Bogg and Novitz, 2012). In the USA, the rights for indirect representation are accorded to trade union bodies chosen by the relevant employees (Cox et al., 2011), while in Australia employees may nominate themselves to represent their own views, or choose another representative regardless of whether or not they are recognised union representatives. This free choice of a bargaining agent is designed to ensure that employee voice is unrestricted, that all voices have a chance of being heard (Creighton and Stewart, 2010).

Bryson et al. (2012) analysed the data from the 2009 European Company Survey and found that there were substantial variations, depending on sector, industry and workplace size, in the degrees to which employers accorded employees a voice. Indirect workplace representation (i.e., a works council or type of union representation) was present in nearly one-third of the workplaces surveyed, although between countries there was considerable variation – with Nordic countries showing that over 50% of workplaces facilitated some sort of indirect voice, while in countries such as Turkey and Portugal the rate was lower, often below 20%. Their analysis showed that employee representation was more prevalent in profitable industries, larger organisations/workplaces, and in the public sector (see also Conchon, 2011). Prouska et al. undertook some interesting comparative work looking at the context of voice in SMEs. They found, when comparing the UK with Thailand and Nigeria, that cultural context was all important. The need for respect, an aversion to challenging authority, and an awareness that speaking up might be career limiting were all relevant. For employees in Thailand the concept of voice was difficult, thus they were more prone to self-silence (2021: 21).

News Flash 10.3

'Show Your Face: Raise Your Voice'

The German union IG BCE launched a campaign in Summer 2020 called 'Show Your Face - Raise Your Voice', designed to promote workplace diversity and fight racism and right-wing extremism in the chemical sector. It encouraged everyone to speak out against prejudice in the workplace. To facilitate this IG BCE developed a new template for company agreements promoting defence against workplace discrimination. The template agreement requires management (and works councils) to 'oppose all forms of discrimination on the basis of, or because of, ethnic origin, gender, religion or belief, disability, age or sexual identity'. All decisions, agreements, actions and resolutions must therefore be based on the principle of non-discrimination, equal treatment and the promotion of equal opportunities.

IndustriAll Europe's General Secretary Luc Triangle said,

> IG BCE is setting a good example of what can be done concretely in the workplace to fight racism and discrimination. I hope this will inspire others in our movement to tackle racism in the workplace head-on.

Source: Husen-Bradley, 2020

Direct Voice

Where employees have the chance to contribute directly (i.e., without the intermediary of representatives) to discussions about workplace activities and decisions that impact upon them, it is known as 'direct' employee voice. Workplace mechanisms or practices that give employees the chance to *personally* express their opinions and/or contribute towards decision making within their organisation include such things as meetings between employees and their managers, working in teams, problem-solving in groups and appraisal practices. Sometimes employee opinions are collected formally, as with staff surveys, and at other times as part of the day-to-day workplace activity. Sometimes voice is semi-formal, as when the HR department at the UK National Probation Service has its weekly 'floor talk', which although concentrating on downward communication provides opportunities for upward feedback from staff. Occasionally voice is embedded in workplace procedure and elicited in a rather formal way; for example, employees at the Mini production plant, based in Cowley, are expected to submit at least three suggestions for improvement per year. To facilitate this the assembly lines in the factory are halted for 90 minutes' 'suggestion-making time'. Allowing employees to participate in decision making may help motivate them, encourage them to develop their skills, to engage in positive discretionary behaviours and thereby aid productivity (Eurofound, 2013). In a European-wide survey of company practice it was apparent that employee voice, resulting in joint workplace decision making, was more common in smaller establishments, with larger establishments more likely to inform its workforce about changes and initiatives without giving employees the chance to have their say (Eurofound, 2015).

In the current work environment 'knowledge' is an essential component (and exchanging ideas and information with work colleagues is crucial for organisations wishing to maintain a competitive edge). Trust, and the ways in which employees experience it, is necessary for there to be effective employee voice (Jiang and Luo, 2018). If employees have no trust in their management, or organisation, they will be less inclined to make use of direct voice mechanisms even when they are easily accessible. Voice is a matter of choice. In Britain, the gradual slide towards the individualisation of employment contracts is taking place at the same time as the diminishing of collective workplace trade union influence (particularly in the private sector). The number of employers facilitating mechanisms that promote direct employee voice is increasing, and non-union direct voice has replaced union representative voice as the main way for employees to exert their voice within the British private sector (Bryson et al., 2013; Charlwood and Forth, 2009; Dundon et al., 2004). Whether or not this trend towards divining and listening to employee opinion is a genuine attempt to allow employees workplace influence is a moot point: in the UK, for example, the incidents of job autonomy have increased but this has been coupled with higher levels of work intensity and increased job insecurity (van Wanrooy et al., 2013a, 2013b), neither of which indicate higher levels of employee influence. Where employment areas are 'up for discussion' these are often chosen by management, and where employees are given voice (e.g., where they can choose their own work patterns) voice is constrained by managerial parameters (Hales and Klidas, 2008: 89). Information from WERS 2011 (DBIS, 2013) showed that while levels of indirect voice, through collective bargaining, remained stable, there continued to be a significant number of workplaces where employees had no form of voice, although some mechanisms for voice, such as appraisals, particularly those linked to pay in the public sector, have increased (van Wanrooy et al., 2013a, 2013b). The availability of appraisals and other means of direct voice, such as the one-to-one meetings between line managers and their charges, does not automatically mean that employees will speak out as even those employees who are fully engaged with the work process may choose on occasion (as we saw earlier with Prouska et al., 2021 and workers from Thailand) to keep their opinions to themselves for reasons of self-preservation (Detert and Burris, 2007; Milliken et al., 2003; Xu et al., 2021). A study of hospital doctors in Ireland, by Creese and her colleagues (2021), exemplified this showing how a perceived inability to effect change, fear of reputational risk, lack of energy and time, and cultural norms all discouraged doctors from voicing concerns about working conditions. Sometimes the very powerlessness of employees results in their fear of authority and inability to speak out (Dai et al., 2022).

Case Snippet 10.1

Voice at the Go-Ahead Group plc

The Go-Ahead Group plc, employing 26,000 people in the UK, is a transport conglomerate with a number of operating companies in rail (such as Southeastern, Southern and Gatwick Express, London Midland) and bus transport (including Brighton & Hove, Go North East, Oxford Bus Company, Plymouth Citybus). The group not only conducts annual staff surveys but also listens to its numerous employees in direct and indirect ways. The majority of the employees are union members and have opportunities to express their opinions via their union representatives, but employees can also have their say electronically; for example, the 3,800 employees within the Southeastern rail company have access to, and regularly use, the company 'Workmate' site, which allows them to share information with colleagues and to discuss and ask questions about workplace issues. The company points out that 'if a member of staff posts a question, the site is accessed and monitored by all 3,800 employees who have the power and ability to instantly respond'. In a similar way the bus company Go-Ahead London has introduced an electronic forum, 'Have Your Say', where its 4,000 staff can post their opinions, give feedback and, importantly, ask questions – to which responses from managers and directors are expected within 48 hours of posting. Additionally Go-Ahead runs 'pulse feedback surveys' twice a year for employees at its HQ and bus companies. The staff comments from these, the company says, enable them to deliver timely improvements.

Source: Go-Ahead, 2011:16; 2022

Exercise 10.2

Read this quote from a Sodexo warehouse worker at the Simandou mine in Guinea:

> There is no shade where we work, everything is outside. We spend all day there; outside in the heat. We've asked and asked and asked for shade that we can rest in, but it's impossible. We'd like a place where we can rest after customers come with deliveries. They've never done anything about it.

What might this tell you about:

- the ways in which employee voice is perceived by the Sodexo management
- perceptions by the employees of interactional justice
- the impact of this incident on the levels of trust in their employer that Sodexo workers on this site might have?

Justify your answers with references to academic texts.

  Compare your analysis about Sodexo with the experience of employees at The Bridge – a small London-based charity promoting health and wellbeing, particularly for women. The CEO has encouraged employee voice: she says that she has an open-mind and an open-door policy. There are weekly meetings where everyone is invited, and full staff meetings every quarter where staff who would not normally be on site are paid to attend. Many staff suggestions have been implemented and, where they are not taken up, the reasoning behind the decision is explained. The CEO emphasises that listening to staff is imperative:

> The best thing about it is that once the staff realised that I'd listen to them and implement their suggestions, they keep coming up with new ones. Suggestions for altering the gym layout and improving the service to clients have been implemented. A particularly innovative example of a staff suggestion resulted in a programme for addressing food insecurity, where food was delivered to local people in need. It was developed from scratch and implemented successfully following Board approval. Currently everyone is looking at ways to improve inclusivity and we are all talking about ways of reducing our carbon footprint and enhancing our sustainability... when you don't listen to your staff and just implement change it causes resentment and reduces productivity: this happened when a previous manager, without consultation, removed bonus payments for additional personal training – the result: all personal training activity ground to a halt as did all discretionary effort and goodwill.

What might this tell you about:

- the ways in which employee voice is perceived by The Bridge management
- perceptions by the employees of interactional justice
- the impact that being listened to has on the levels of trust The Bridge workers might have in their employer?

Justify your answers with references to academic texts.

Sources: TransAfrica Forum (n.d.); Interviews with the CEO of The Bridge, Joy Grimshaw (8 June 2015 and 3 March 2022)

Indirect Voice

Indirect voice is the mechanism by which employees are able to let their employers know what they think and feel through the medium of a representative. Such agents of collective voice may be work colleagues or union representatives who have been elected to forums, councils, or committees, to represent a workplace constituency. Examples are health and safety representatives, and specific focus groups looking at certain areas of work processes, such as prospective office relocation. Different types of workplace councils and/or joint consultative/negotiating committees are sometimes stand-alone mechanisms for collective voice; occasionally they are used to replace or supplement a union voice by continuing to give employees a say within a proscribed range of topics but allowing the employers to retain power, making unilateral decisions following consultation. In the UK, where a trade union is recognised for negotiating or consultation processes, most frequently in the public sector, representatives will talk to/bargain with management both informally and formally to ensure that their members' views are passed on. However, indirect voice is not always simple. Atle Høie, the General Secretary of IndustriALL Global Union has pointed out that different countries receive (i.e., hear) and deal with indirect voice in different ways. For example, he explained that

> ... the Norwegian system is extremely flat. The shop stewards can walk into the CEO's office and have a rational discussion at any time. The employers in Norway see unionism as good because it gives them a counterpart and makes it easier for them to run their business. ... That's a trust structure that exists in the Nordic countries, partly in continental Europe and scattered in the UK, but in the rest of the world it doesn't exist. (IRGuru, 2022)

The degree of influence and power that representatives have differs from culture to culture, institution to institution and representative medium to representative medium. Union density across Europe has waned in the last 30 years. However this does not mean that the impact of collective bargaining has waned equally. For example, the overall density of German unions is rather lower than in Britain yet they have a greater impact with a large proportion of employees covered by industry wide collective bargaining arrangements (Parry et al., 2021).

As union density and influence wanes (see Table 10.1, and Figures 10.1 and 10.2) some feel that works councils may become a substitute mechanism replacing collective bargaining while enabling collective voice to continue despite the lack of union representation. Some, such as Heery (2010) feel that councils may reinvigorate union activity while others are convinced that the introduction of works councils may help reduce union power further (Cooper and Briggs, 2009), while Nienhueser (2009: 372) crucially argues that it is the power, or strength of representation, behind a works council that influences the quality and number of workplace agreements arising from council activity. In some circumstances, particularly in Europe, managers prefer to deal with works councils as they offer a more informal approach to workplace issues than their union counterparts. Certainly as a method of 'voice', works councils are perhaps more effective than employer-controlled and organised consultative committees or individual voice. Replacing union representation with non-union works council representation does not necessarily restrain and inhibit managerial power, although works councils are often as effective at limiting managerial actions as powerful unions. However, the picture is complicated.

Pulignano and Waddington (2020), when looking specifically at the operation of European Works Councils within multinational enterprises, found a lack of congruence between the EU legislative requirements and the operation of the councils. In only a few of the cases examined did managers inform and consult representatives in good time – enabling 'real' participation in strategic matters such as relocation.

Table 10.1 Trade union membership levels in employment 2000-2021

Year	Thousands		
	Male	Female	Great Britain all in employment
2000	3,947	3,461	7,175
2001	3,911	3,430	7,091
2002	3,789	3,511	7,038
2003	3,842	3,604	7,205
2004	3,764	3,599	7,101
2005	3,719	3,672	7,123
2006	3,661	3,728	7,123
2007	3,618	3,753	7,101
2008	3,534	3,731	7,019
2009	3,356	3,747	6,828
2010	3,194	3,702	6,657
2011	3,120	3,621	6,506
2012	3,159	3,651	6,557
2013	3,142	3,643	6,536
2014	3,094	3,668	6,514
2015	3,109	3,704	6,571
2016	3,042	3,535	6,370
2017	3,049	3,529	6,337
2018	3,021	3,648	6,410
2019	2,967	3,831	6,548
2020	3,004	3,893	6,654

Source: ONS, 2022

In the UK union membership increased between 2016–2020 as the numbers of union members rose in the public sector, particularly in education.

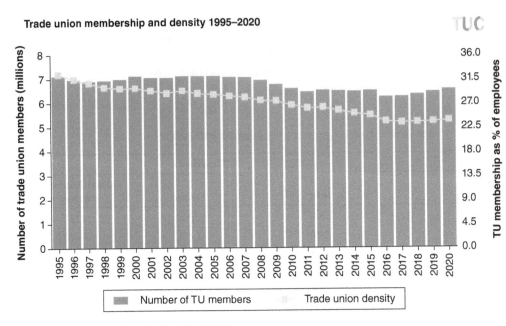

Figure 10.1   Trade union density 1995-2020

Source: TUC press release (27 May 2021) Good news, bad news and the same challenges - trade union membership statistics. Available at: https://www.tuc.org.uk/blogs/good-news-bad-news-and-same-challenges-trade-union-membership-statistics (Accessed 8 March 2022).

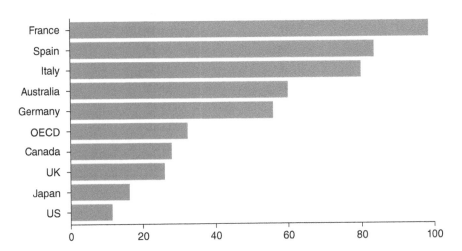

Figure 10.2   Distribution of employees with the right to bargain collectively 2017 or latest year

Source: From the Financial Times (19 January 2020) The upstart unions taking on gig economy and outsourcing. Bethany Staton. © The Financial Times Limited 2020. All Rights Reserved.

It is apparent that pervasive cultural, political and market economies will have a direct impact on whether indirect voice is effective; in both the UK, Europe and the USA, for example, poor job quality has been linked to weak unions and the absence of mechanisms, such as works councils, that help expedite collective voice (Garnero, 2021; Green et al., 2013: 757–58; Hermanns and Lenaerts, 2021; Holman, 2013a: 26; Jansen and Lehr, 2022), while union activities in countries that support social partnerships, such as Sweden and Denmark, are more likely to achieve higher levels of job quality (Holman, 2013b). Works councils themselves are difficult to generalise about as their formation, personnel and influence will depend on the context and statutory regulations in place where they are operating. Visser, in his 2011 work, shows that works councils are mainly found in Europe. Sometimes, such as in France and Spain, the councils operate in parallel with union collective bargaining arrangements; at others, where the 'councillors' are elected by the whole workforce, they are often the sole source of employee collective voice, as happens in the Netherlands and Belgium. Within the same country different systems may operate in different organisations or at different levels within the same organisation, so for example an organisational works council agreement may help set overall organisational strategy while enterprise union bargaining may supplement this. In Germany, for example, legislation separates union representation from works council representation – the works councils operating at establishment level and the unions negotiating externally at sector or industry wide levels. However, the personnel involved in both types of dialogue are not mutually exclusive, many union members acting as works council representatives (Aumayr et al., 2011).

Exercise 10.3

Nita Clarke, director of the Involvement and Participation Association, has said that 'The most efficient way of managing the workforce is still to listen collectively to them' (Blackhurst, 2015: 35).

* Evaluate this statement in the light of what you know about direct and indirect employee voice.

Collective Bargaining

Collective bargaining is a process whereby an employer (or an employer's representative) and a recognised trade union, or unions, negotiate about pay and other terms and conditions of employment (*substantive matters*) and the processes of employment, such as how to progress fairly prior to and during redundancy (*procedural matters*). Negotiations are carried out on behalf of a group of workers defined as 'the bargaining unit' (Acas, 2014: 4). The bargaining process itself may go smoothly – all parties reaching an agreement that is mutually acceptable – or turbulently, possibly resulting in stalemate, failure to agree, conflict, industrial action, or recourse to a third party to help reach a settlement. For bargaining to take place all the parties must be willing for it to occur. When this happens the employer is said to have recognised a trade union for bargaining purposes and a recognition agreement will be drawn up. Recognition agreements normally detail the employees who are covered by the arrangements (the bargaining unit), the areas that may be covered by bargaining (the scope of the agreement) and the parties who are recognised for bargaining purposes (the bargaining agents). Sometimes they include areas that may be discussed but not bargained about – and usually they contain provision for the process to be followed when agreement is unforthcoming.

The purpose of collective bargaining is to give employees an indirect say in matters at work, their representatives, participating on their behalf, jointly regulate the employment relationship. This institutionalises labour processes, simplifying the regulations/requirements for the pay-work-bargain, minimising the degrees of conflict and reducing the amount of time spent by management discussing terms and conditions with individual employees. As we have seen above, with regard to Germany, the processes of bargaining may occur at different levels.

National, industry or sector level

National or industry level bargaining occurs when employers' representatives negotiate with a number of union representatives to set industry minima (e.g., in the UK the banks and supermarkets bargain at national level). National agreements may be improved upon but *not* undercut by individual employers covered by the agreement. Governments sometimes negotiate at national level around areas of forthcoming legislation, although this is rare in the UK where lobbying, consultation and representation from interested parties is more usual. In Finland, for example, national level pay agreements, to which the government contributes alongside unions and employers' associations, result in recommendations that negotiators at industry level follow by negotiating and subsequently setting the minimum standard rates and basic conditions for each industry. These agreements are binding on all employers in that industry, whether or not they are members of the employers' organisation that was party to the negotiations. In Belgium, around 96% of employees in the private sector are covered by agreements made in national level negotiations that occur in the context of a government economic report which takes into account the state of the economies in its neighbouring countries, France, Germany and the Netherlands. Here the government has the power to intervene if the two sides cannot agree on a figure within the limitations set by the report. In Denmark, on the other hand, where over 80% of the workforce is unionised, employers and unions negotiate terms and conditions at industry level, although these are often supplemented by company level bargaining (ETUI, 2014a, 2014b).

Company or group level

Company level is where bargaining takes place between unions and a specific employer. The results are not industry wide, although some influential companies are benchmarked by others – their settlements, if not becoming the industry norm, influence levels of remuneration, smaller organisations benchmarking pay levels against them. The collective voice is therefore influential, even in organisations that do not recognise unions for bargaining purposes!

Where multinational organisations are in operation transnational collective bargaining is rare, in part due to these organisations decentralising non-strategic activities and devolving day-to-day responsibilities back to company/subsidiary levels, and in part due to trade union reluctance to operate across borders, and the lack of appropriate training for union representatives (Boni, 2012: 9–10).

Whether at a transnational or domestic level, company bargaining is important because:

- it encourages management to develop a more positive approach to managing the employment relationship, providing an awareness of the impact that certain decisions can have on perceptions of organisational justice, performance, turnover, productivity and so on
- it promotes partnership approaches between management and unions within the organisation
- the knowledge that they have a voice improves employee morale
- both sides are committed to, and responsible for, any agreements reached, giving the agreements legitimacy in the eyes of the workforce
- it requires management to address issues of communication
- negotiation skills are developed
- it is linked to local conditions
- it is linked to the organisation's specific strategy and culture
- it *may* enable the organisation to respond more closely to the labour market in which it is operating.

Plant or site level

Where a large organisation is split over a number of different sites or, as in manufacturing, has a different number of plants, then bargaining may occur at these levels. Such bargaining may supplement agreements made at a higher level or may stand alone. The disadvantage from the employers' view is that they may feel they are spending a disproportionate amount of time bargaining about working conditions, particularly if each bargaining group tries to negotiate for better conditions than those achieved by other groups. This can result in wages drift and increased levels of conflict. Where conditions between plants are perceived by employees as inequitable then the morale, productivity and the psychological contract may suffer.

Departmental or workshop level

Bargaining taking place at this level tends to be between shop stewards and individual supervisors. It is at this point that union representatives intercede, on behalf of their members, to affect and redress the day-to-day power imbalances at the workplace. It is sometimes considered to be taking place at the 'frontier of control' (Goodrich, 1975 [1920]) and is a crucial factor in the tensions influencing the levels of structural antagonism described by Edwards. Collective bargaining at this level is not, as may be supposed, mainly concerned with wage rates (although piece work is often the subject of bargaining at this level), but instead is concerned with working conditions, time allocation, flexibility, training, overtime, etc.

Exercise 10.4

- Analyse, using examples to illustrate your answer, why the different levels at which collective bargaining takes place might be important.

National v. Local Agreements

- National agreements are sometimes regarded as inflationary and contributing to higher levels of unemployment because less profitable companies cannot afford to meet their minimum terms and conditions – the same arguments are found around the implementation of the national minimum wage.
- National agreements are sometimes regarded as too restrictive and not responsive to local conditions – employers find that adjusting for local circumstances is difficult.
- Occasionally difficulties arise when the national level agreement links specific levels of performance to pay – this happens when an agreement fails to take into account different processes, machinery and cultures.
- Privatisation of some parts of an industry may have a disproportionate impact on industry agreements (e.g., NHS).

News Flash 10.4

Sector Wide Negotiations for London Bus Drivers?

In early 2015 London bus drivers, members of Unite, together with representatives from 18 different bus operating companies, including Arriva, Stage Coach and Metrobus, held talks at Acas about establishing a negotiating forum that would help eradicate the company by company pay negotiations. Discrepancies, resulting from competitive tendering for bus routes, had created pay disparities, providing different rates of pay for drivers doing the same jobs – many driving the same route but for different rates of pay. The union's London-based bus driver members were demanding a collective forum at which both sides could discuss 'sector wide negotiations' between their union, Unite, and their employers in order to eradicate the iniquitous disparity between pay awarded to drivers with identical training requirements and governed by the same regulations. At the time of the talks annual salary for the drivers ranged from £17,000 to £25,000 depending on the employing company.

A Unite spokesman said: 'we want, and are determined to achieve, a sector wide bargaining arrangement for all of our 25,000 members.'

Sources: Unite, 2014; www.bbc.co.uk/news/uk-england-london-29153713 www.unitetheunion. org/how-we-help/listofregions/londonandeastern/londoneasternnews/london-bus-drivers-rally-together-to-demand-fair-conditions/ (accessed 10 April 2015)

From a management viewpoint there are a number of advantages in having a national agreement:

- a collective response from employers stops one company being played off against another and acts as a check on escalating union demands targeting individual enterprises
- if working well national agreements stop lots of 'bites at the cherry'
- it is not time consuming for those not participating in the act of bargaining.

From a trade union point of view there are a number of advantages in having a national agreement:

- it saves time and resources
- it establishes minimum standards providing a common set of terms, conditions and rules and is therefore easier to regulate
- it reinforces the rate for the job encouraging adherence to spot salary systems (i.e. set rates) where they are stipulated
- it equalises trade union bargaining strength
- it increases bargaining power by using areas of high profit or labour market shortages as a minima.

There is, of course, constant tension within larger organisational groups about whether or not to centralise collective bargaining. Some of the positive things influencing the centralisation of this process are:

- corporate bargaining ensures consistency across plants
- it aids financial control and organisational change
- it helps organisationally mobile managers
- it helps regulate activities at a local level.

But this centralising process sometimes results in employees and managers feeling divorced from the process of influencing decision making. Centralised corporate bargaining is not:

- conducive to productivity bargaining and detailed work changes
- responsive to local variations in labour markets
- responsive to local variations in work practices.

Collective Bargaining Models

There are a number of different bargaining models, each affording employees, via their representatives, a potential opportunity to influence what they do at work, how they do it and, importantly, how they will be rewarded.

- The **Integrative Bargaining** Model is a problem-solving process used for averting conflict; the negotiators seek common solutions representing a win–win outcome. Each side attempts to reach a compromise in order that neither loses and that both can be seen to have gained. Such agreements are marked by cooperation. There is a concerted attempt to control conflict via bargaining, and hence perceptions of workplace power. Bargaining here focuses on workplace challenges and the process typically includes four stages: identifying the problem; searching for alternative solutions and their consequences; ordering preferred solutions; selecting and implementing a course of action. Within this model the issues bargained about may include such things as: preserving jobs while maintaining efficiency; increasing employee benefits at no cost to the employer; flexible working arrangements.

• The Distributive Model is a means of resolving conflict by competitive bargaining (**distributive bargaining**). Its purpose is to change the division of limited resources, each side trying to gain possession of the resources controlled by the other. It involves a win–lose situation; that is, because the issues being bargained over are finite, the end result will be a gain for one side, a loss for the other. The process sometimes involves coercion, transparent power struggles and an inability to avoid posturing. Within this model the issues bargained about may include such things as pay, conditions, staffing levels, timing, union rights.

• The **Mixed Bargaining** Model combines the two stages described above, that is, the distributive and integrative stages. Management/union negotiations present few 'pure conflict' situations; similarly the occasions resulting in total mutual gain are rare. The bargaining process may move from the distributive to the integrative, the latter solving the problems posed by the distributive process – collective bargaining is, after all, about reconciling divergent interests within a contested relationship.

• The **Intra-organisational Bargaining** Model refers to the stages before negotiations begin, where each side works out its position according to the needs and the expectations of their constituent groups. Negotiating groups are not always composed of individuals with homogenous thought processes and desires. Each person will have a different view as to how to proceed, what is and what is not an acceptable fall-back position, and what sanctions are acceptable to threaten/apply. These differences have to be thrashed out prior to the negotiations starting. This model also applies during adjournments to the negotiating process when the parties have to decide whether to modify or change their positions in the light of the negotiations so far.

Enabling Voice - UK Employers' Legal Obligations

Depending on the country concerned there is a variety of instances affected by legislation influencing when employers should consult and/or negotiate with, as well as inform and listen to, their employees. This is sometimes indirectly (via collective representation) and sometimes directly with individual employees. In countries such as Denmark there is little

legislation as it is presumed that collective bargaining will establish smooth working relationships at enterprise level. In the UK employment regulation is more pervasive. As we saw
in Chapter 4, within the UK when an employee starts work they will have spoken about, and
agreed to, the terms of their employment contract; such agreement requires an employee to
voice their consent to the conditions offered. In addition the Employment Rights Act 1996
requires employers to include in employees' written statements of terms and conditions
the details of how an employee might go about raising a grievance (i.e., how they might
voice/complain about a workplace issue) and where they might find the company grievance
procedure and the name or title of the person to whom employees can appeal if they want
redress for grievances (or appeal the decision of their grievance hearing). These requirements should ensure that all new employees have been given a chance to discuss and
agree their contract of employment, and know how to (and who to) voice any issues with
during their period of employment. Ideally the grievance process will follow the Acas *Code
of Practice on Disciplinary and Grievance Procedures* (2015), that suggests initial *informal* conversations as the first stage. Employees who remain unhappy are advised to put their complaint in writing and the employer is obliged to undertake any appropriate investigations:
hold a grievance meeting enabling the aggrieved employee (and accompanying companion
if requested) an opportunity to state their case and suggest how it might be solved; provide
an answer to the employee within a reasonable period of time; and provide the opportunity
for the employee to appeal the decision if they are unhappy. These basic rights attached to
the contract of employment together with the means by which employees are able to voice
any grievances are crucial, underpinning employee perceptions of justice and ensuring that
some of the imbalance of power between the primary parties to the employment relationship is redressed.

Additional legislation underpins and safeguards employees who may wish to speak up at
work. The UK whistleblowing legislation, regarded as a model of good practice and copied
by other European countries, is an example. The Public Interest Disclosure Act 1998 protects
employees who decide to speak out about practices at their workplace that they believe are
both in the public interest and are illegal, environmentally damaging, likely to damage the
health and safety of others, or where the organisation has deliberately covered up any of these
activities. This Act was amended in 2013 by the Enterprise and Regulatory Reform Act to make
it clear that the disclosure was to be in the public interest and to ensure that an employer
would be vicariously liable if the employee voicing concerns were victimised or harassed by
other employees because of the whistleblowing activity. This safeguard is not, however, failsafe;
some employees are still afraid to voice their concerns (Francis, 2014) and the Public Accounts
Committee has said that more protection should be offered to those individuals who choose
to whistleblow (Moss, 2014). When looking at whistleblowing in the Pakistan telecom industry
Khan et al. (2022) found that the more serious an offence, the greater the willingness of people
to voice concern, although speaking out was tempered by fears of reprisal. Fearing retaliation
following whistleblowing is more widespread.

News Flash 10.5

Whistleblowing Costs Include Career Damage and Mental Trauma

The UK All Parliamentary Party Group investigating whistleblowing has produced two separate reports looking at the state of whistleblowing in Britain. It collected over 600 pieces of evidence from whistleblowers and

> ... heard first-hand of the price they have paid: mental trauma and impact on whistleblowers and their families, loss and damage to careers, the cost of litigation, blacklisting and the use of NDAs to silence whistleblowers and cover up wrongdoing ... the evidence received over 20% of the disclosures relate to criminal activity; a further 30% relate to bullying in the workplace. (2019: 3)

Fear about potential negative outcomes that could occur after voicing concerns is real, and importantly has an inhibitory impact on voice.

Sources: APPG, 2019, 2020

Employers in the UK are required by legislation originating from the EU Acquired Rights Directive, known as Transfer of Undertakings (Protection of Employment) Regulations 2006, to share information and collectively consult with their employees formally before, during and after an occasion when a part of their business is transferred to another organisation, outsourced, or if the business changes hands. This gives affected employees a chance to say what they think about the transfer and how it might affect them; however, it does *not* give them the right to voice their objections to being transferred. It also means that where an organisation does not have indirect methods to consult with its employees, it must ensure that these are put in place. If an organisation recognises a union for bargaining and consultation purposes then the union representatives will be the required parties to the consultation; if there are no representatives and more than ten employees are affected, the employer must organise appropriate constituencies and representative elections. In such circumstances, the social partnership ethos pervasive in Europe that influences European legislation requires UK employers (post Brexit, at the time of going to press), to behave in a pluralist way, even if they are running a unitarist operation.

Such pluralist thinking affects other pieces of legislation enabling voice. The Health and Safety at Work Act 1974, amended in 1996 following a European Court ruling, requires employers to consult with union *and* non-union representatives about health and safety matters, while the UK redundancy legislation similarly makes explicit provision for representatives to be consulted about potential redundancy situations – with a view to reaching agreement. If fewer than 20 people are to be made redundant there is no requirement on employers to consult with their employees, and practices vary, some organisations ensuring consultation and others just informing employees about their intentions. Employers do, however, have a statutory duty to inform and *consult* the relevant employee representatives, within a 90-day period when they propose to make at least 20 employees redundant. In addition to this *indirect* consultation employers are obliged to talk *directly* with those individuals concerned, telling them why they have been selected and discussing possible alternative work. It is at this stage that employees are able to voice opinions that may affect the redundancy outcome; they can discuss whether or not they think the selection methods are fair, whether they should have been included in the redundancy pool, and any alternative suggestions for their redeployment or retraining. If such consultation is badly handled it has a detrimental impact on perceptions of procedural, interactional and distributional justice, not just for those employees at imminent risk of redundancy but also for those remaining with the organisation. Budd's notion of a balanced employment relationship, with equity, efficiency and voice all equally weighted is relevant here; where there is an imbalance, trust in the employer is likely to be diminished and, with it, employee morale (2004; Budd et al., 2010; Budd and Bhave, 2019).

In the same way that European Directives concerning the collective redundancies and transfers of undertakings influenced the UK statutory requirements, the 2002 EU Directive on informing and consulting employees resulted in the UK Information and Consultation of Employees (ICE) Regulations 2004 that introduced a statutory framework for workforce consultation. That is, for the first time UK employers had to, when requested, provide employee representatives with the opportunity to voice their opinions on specific workplace issues. The impact of the directive was small. Initially hostile, the unions (who disliked it, in part because they might have to share consultation, and therefore power, with non-union workplace representatives) were reluctant to utilise the provisions in the directive (Hall, 2005, 2006, 2010). Provided that there were no pre-existing consultation agreements, and that at least 10% of their employees asked for workplace consultation, the UK regulations require 40% of the relevant workforce to support implementing negotiations about the introduction of information and consultation agreements (this is regardless of whether or not the employer has a unitarist or pluralist perspective). Should negotiators fail to reach a bespoke agreement the employer is required to implement standard procedures obliging them to inform and consult elected representatives on a range of employment and business related issues. Longitudinal research, looking at 25 different organisations and their adoption of information and consultation (I&C) procedures found that union concerns were largely unfounded:

> In no case did management seek to derecognise unions in favour of the I&C body even where union membership was weak and the employer had sought to move beyond union-based representation. In every case but one, recognised unions were offered direct involvement in 'hybrid' I&C bodies, which in some cases reinforced the organisational security and representative role of unions with low membership. (Hall et al., 2015: 370)

Voice and Silence

Exercise 10.5

So far you have read about different forms of direct and indirect employee voice - yet expressing a view at work is sometimes difficult, sometimes an indication of powerlessness, sometimes an indication of indifference, and sometimes due to lack of an awareness about expressing an opinion in a workplace in an appropriate way.

How might:

- not expressing an opinion be a way of expressing voice?
- employee silence speak?
- withholding information actually express an opinion?
- a silent employee indicate acquiescence with a managerial viewpoint?

For a discussion about these issues, see van Dyne et al. (2003).

According to Knoll and van Dick, 'silence in organizations refers to a state in which employees refrain from calling attention to issues at work such as illegal or immoral practices or developments that violate personal, moral, or legal standards' (2013: 349). Yet the active withholding of an opinion about workplace-based issues need not necessarily be concerned with holding back moral viewpoints about incidents with which the employee disagrees. Deliberate silence may arise for a number of reasons; for example, it could be induced by feelings of self-preservation, or associated with cynicism around the processes associated with employee voice and its influence on managerial thinking, and occasionally feelings of powerlessness may inspire and contribute to silent choices. Sometimes speaking up at work can be risky, with many individuals, as we saw with whistleblowing, working in environments where they perceive it to be unsafe to speak up (Detert and Edmondson, 2011; Milliken et al., 2003). Yet deferential silence when linked to obedience to managerial authority might not be the result of fear, but of an acceptance of the cultural, legal-rational, legitimate authority of higher-ups, possibly acknowledging an employees' own inexperience or lack of knowledge (Kish-Gephart et al., 2009).

Van Dyne et al. (2003) categorise the silent withholding of work-related opinions and/or information into three different types of silence:

- **Acquiescent silence** where an employee feels unable to make a difference and therefore keeps their opinions to themselves, unlike *acquiescent voice* where the employee expresses support because they feel they have no option to do otherwise.
- **Defensive silence** where, based on fear of the consequences, an employee withholds information in order to protect themselves, unlike *defensive voice* where employees, in order to protect themselves, express ideas designed to shift the focus of attention elsewhere.
- **Prosocial silence** where the employee cooperates with the organisation by keeping quiet and benefitting the organisation, unlike *prosocial voice* whereby an employee deliberately expresses constructive solutions to problems based on cooperation with the organisation.

Such categorisation does not really take into account indirect voice, and how it might help anonymise a criticism but enable an employee to express an opinion by proxy.

It is apparent, from recent research that the ways in which managers encourage voice by consulting with employees and listening to their views has a direct influence on the degrees of silence exhibited by employees, those who see their voice as powerless remaining quiet and those who see it as influential deciding to speak out (Tangirala and Ramanujam, 2012; Willman et al., 2006). Defensive silence can eventually have a negative impact on the silent employees' levels of trust, morale, motivation, eventually leading to emotional exhaustion (Jahanzeb et al., 2018).

Even though the consequences of remaining silent may, on occasion, be life-threatening, employees sometimes remain quiet for the sake of preserving a good employment relationship and non-adversarial workplace atmosphere, as Bienefeld and Grote (2015) found when they researched the reasons behind air crews remaining quiet on safety issues even though this silence put the lives of passengers and air crew at risk.

Voice and Diversity

Green says that 'diversity issues should be at the heart of participatory democracy – allowing *all* employees to have a voice at work' (2015: 67). For diverse voices to be heard, a degree of management forethought is essential, particularly when the workforce comprises a variety of individuals, many engaged on different contracts, many working beyond their 60s, many balancing work with differing caring responsibilities and many falling into the LGBT (lesbian, gay, bisexual and transgender) and BAME (Black, Asian and Minority Ethnic) groupings. Falling birth rates and high life expectancy, coupled with a greater proportion of women and older people in the labour market – many choosing to work part time – have a direct impact upon the ways in which people are employed and deployed and, importantly, on the types of interaction and voice that they will find appropriate and beneficial. These changing patterns of employment, combined with lower trade union density, create a compelling argument for rethinking the ways that employers engage with, and listen to, their diverse workforces.

Case Study 10.1

Law Firm Successfully Promotes Diverse Voices

Latham & Watkins is the world's second largest law firm (by revenue), with offices in over 14 countries and around 3,000 employees. It is committed to promoting diversity and inclusion and listening to the many voices across the organisation. (In 2020, Latham & Watkins won the Diversity Innovation (Ethnicity Focus) Award at the *Legal Week* Innovation Awards.) As part of its inclusive strategy, it specifically encourages a number of separate affinity groups covering, for example women, parent lawyers and BAME employees. Its website points out that such groups, 'allow colleagues who share an affinity in terms of a particular life experience (or are in support of those that do) to come together, have a forum to air their voices, and share strategies for professional success'. Part of the company policy, specifically designed to promote inclusion, encourages the affinity groups to share their experiences and help educate

(Continued)

the rest of the organisation – which sometimes involves speaking out about contentious issues. For example, members of the Black Lawyers Group talk openly about workplace differences encountered by black employees; they discuss issues around the impact and prevalence of unconscious bias, and are not shy about airing potentially offensive, even if unintended, language. The affinity groups are not the only vehicle for voice that Latham & Watkins deploys as it also runs a number of mentoring schemes which ensure that staff are supported, listened to and understood. The promotion of voice activities, with employees sharing ideas, experiences, and feelings about the culture has increased retention, enhanced reputation and improved diverse recruitment.

Sources: Latham & Watkins, 2022; *The Lex 100*, 2019

Many academic and practitioner comments on (and analysis about) employee voice regard employees as a largely homogenous group, undifferentiated by whether they work full or part-time, work on standard or non-standard contracts, work remotely or on-site, and where particular differences (e.g., age, sex, race, class, disability, etc.) are 'conveniently' ignored (Bell et al., 2011; Syed, 2014). This homogenised approach, in many ways, misses the crucial point about voice: if employees are to be listened to, their *differences* may be important, and the ways of valuing and tapping into their opinions may require differentiated mechanisms and structures designed to ensure that their voices are not drowned by the concerns of the majority.

An example of how a specific grouping was given voice occurred between 2006 and 2010 (before the Coalition government introduced the Equality Act 2010) when the UK law required public sector employers to produce disability equality duty schemes. The government advice around their introduction used the pluralist social model of disability (Bingham et al., 2013), giving guidance under which employers were (supposed) to consult with disabled people, thereby giving them a platform from which to discuss their needs.

Within the UK health service many employers, such as the NHS Royal National Orthopaedic Hospital, followed this advice and specifically gave their disabled employees a voice (while some NHS employers concentrated on giving voice to just the users of their services). Here it is apparent that the legislation 'encouraged' employers to take into account the particular personal attributes of some employees and provide formal opportunities for these employees to have their say about their particular workplace issues. As a consequence employee voice in these establishments was not regarded as an undifferentiated chorus.

Exercise 10.6

Read Case Study 10.2 study below and, with respect to the town-hall meeting, analyse the:

- employees' reactions
- the senior staff reactions
- the HR Manager's thoughts.

Critically evaluate the role of power, and informational, procedural and distributional justice in relation to the employees' town-hall behaviours.

Case Study 10.2

Silence Voice and Inclusion

Company X is a large, multinational clothing company headquartered in the USA, with regional offices in Europe, India, and Hong Kong*.

After the murder of George Floyd in May 2020, and the subsequent renewed popularity of the Black Lives Matter movement, employees at Company X began to wonder how their workplace was going to get involved. Larger and smaller competitors had quickly released statements on their social media platforms condemning racism. Some also highlighted the steps their own organisations were taking, including diversity training and charitable donations.

Company X, however, remained silent on the issue. When pressed on this by some employees, the Head of HR sent an organisation-wide email, highlighting her own support for the movement, but pointing out that Company X did not want to get involved in a sensitive, political topic.

Many employees within the organisation were furious at the approach senior management took, voicing their concerns to line managers and through the company's suggestion box. The Head of the HR Department organised a town-hall meeting to allow employees to voice their thoughts and opinions in relation to the decision. She hoped this would allow the employees voice while keeping the issue in house.

When she arrived, the designated room was full of employees animatedly discussing the issue. Seeing her, however, they fell somewhat silent. After introducing herself and fellow senior managers she explained the reasoning for their decision in detail. Then she opened the floor for a discussion. A few people commented that they agreed with the decision, while one or two somewhat hesitantly voiced their opposition.

The Head of HR was confused – where was the anger she had heard about? Why was nobody speaking up?

Later, the other senior managers with her (the Head of Marketing and Head of Innovation) congratulated her on a well-chaired town-hall meeting, remarking that they were glad to put this issue to bed. The Head of HR, however, did not feel entirely comfortable with how the town-hall meeting had gone.

*The name of the company has been anonymised, and details have been changed, to retain confidentiality.

Ciáran McFadden

News Flash 10.6

Social Media in the Workplace

A CIPD report, examining social media in the workplace, alerted readers to the idea that, in order to offer sufficient ways and means of hearing a diverse range of employees, there needs to be a variety of methods by which employees can have their say and be heard by managements.

The report points out (p. 20) that:

individual differences in personality influence how likely employees are to speak up (Bishop, 2007). Having more channels of open communications and, therefore, more

(Continued)

opportunity to put forward an idea will increase the likelihood of lurkers becoming more active members. For example, in addition to organisation-wide initiatives such as surveys, organisations can consider building in opportunities for employee voice as part of formal performance reviews, as well as informal one-to-ones with managers, meetings and knowledge-sharing forums.

Sources: Bishop, 2007; Silverman et al., 2013

This 'nod' to voice across the diversity of employees is becoming more common. Some larger employers actively facilitate voice through tailored employee interest groups and networks. Kumra and Manfredi (2012) suggest that organisations enable diversity inspired networking groups to act as advocates for their membership base with management. Apart from indirect trade union forms of representation and individuals directly speaking to management, some larger organisations, such as IBM, have a number of different channels through which diverse groups can indirectly lobby the employer and express their voice; for example, IBM encouraged voice by setting up its network group EAGLE (Employee Alliance for Gay, Lesbian, Bisexual and Transgender Empowerment) that operates in over 30 countries, including Russia and India. Some organisations, such as TSB, approach diversity in a way that embraces all employees. TSB set up inclusion networks, and feedback from these is collected and acted upon via an executive sponsor from each of its five affinity groups – gender, ethnicity, LGBT, disability and new starters (Yarlagadda et al., 2015). However, many employing organisations do not have such groups, and where individuals feel uncomfortable about being open about themselves while at work, they are less likely to speak out as individuals or seek help via indirect representation. In order for employees to feel sufficiently empowered to voice their opinions, however, they need to feel assured that the workplace environment is safe for them to do so.

The risk with the targeted approach (where voice mechanisms are provided for differentiated groups), is partly that management have decided which groups it is appropriate to formalise, promote and recognise – possibly leaving sectors of the workforce underrepresented – and partly that individuals within such highlighted groups are identified by their distinctiveness, and it may be the very act of differentiation that inhibits individuals from speaking out about areas not specific to their distinguishing characteristics. As Fanshaw says, employers sometimes mistakenly ask 'questions to whole groups of people as if they all thought and felt the same just because they shared an overall identity, and then analysing the results as if they did' (2015), in effect analysing just part of the picture. The voice of any specific group will, by its very origins, often exclude information about wider organisational issues, remaining strictly within the parameters set by its original diversity identity. Another issue, perhaps not so widespread, is that different groups may find that they are vying for resources with, or ideologically opposed to, other groups within the same organisation, and despite workplace policies promoting diversity, conflict arises. For example, some American employers have had to manage workplace-based religious groups in conflict with workplace LGBT networks.

Despite employers efforts to create an inclusive workplace, not all individuals will be willing to voice their opinions in the workplace. Bowen and Blackmon showed in their research with gay and lesbian employees that employees evaluate how their colleagues might react before they proffer an opinion: 'individuals who differ from the majority fear ... marginalization, they may avoid speaking up on a wide range of organizational issues' (2003: 1399). If an employee trusts the organisation, and feels comfortable about how they think they are perceived by their co-workers and managers, they are more likely to pass on their opinions and speak out if necessary. Exercising organisational voice is discretionary, and employees who feel supported by an organisation that appreciates their difference are more likely to be attached to their workgroup and feel valued by their organisation, and hence are more likely to engage in organisational voice (Chattopadhyay, 1999). Stonewall found in its British research, where 50,070 people responded to its 2015 survey, that those employees who were disabled or Asian or Black *as well as* being either lesbian, gay or bisexual were more likely to disagree with the statement 'I feel able to be myself in the workplace' when compared to non-disabled, Asian or Black lesbian, gay and bisexual respondents (Ashok, 2015: 31), and one might surmise from this that such inability to be oneself at work inhibits accurate expressions of opinion, hindering not just employee voice but accurate impressions that the employer has of the working environment. Similarly Yarlagadda et al. (2015: 21) found that disabled workers in the NHS were more likely to be discriminated against by their line managers and colleagues, and one can infer from this that they would be less likely to speak out at work. Individuals experiencing discrimination or experiencing workplace isolation are unlikely to actively participate in voicing concerns linked to their differences, and their levels of trust and perceptions of organisational justice are likely to be low.

Exercise 10.7

What impact do you think legislation might have on the ways in which diverse groups feel able to exercise their voices within the workplace? Justify your answer with reference to academic texts.

Voice, Trust and Fairness

At its most fundamental, voice is associated with giving employees the opportunity to contribute to the ways in which their work is organised, undertaken and remunerated and for them to express their grievances should they think something unfair, or should they wish their superiors to address an inappropriate, unethical or illegal organisational practice. This firmly enmeshes voice within the spheres of the different aspects of organisational justice. The processes that allow employees to ask for better pay and conditions or articulate and pursue a grievance (appealing the decision if necessary) are basic tenets behind the perceptions of organisational justice and fairness. It follows therefore that when the ability for employees to voice concerns, opinions and requests at work is thwarted, their perceptions of injustice will increase and negatively impact their workplace performance and morale. Furthermore, where employees perceive that speaking up about their employment, or about the way the organisation is being run and managed, is a risk to their position (and that their actions might result in unfair retribution) they will be highly unlikely to voice their true opinions and/or whistleblow (Milliken et al., 2003; APPG, 2019, 2020).

Employees wanting to shine in the eyes of their managers and receive direct support and endorsement for their suggestions are likely to speak out if they think they will receive a sympathetic hearing but are unlikely to risk exposure by voicing their opinions if their managers are perceived to be unresponsive, critical and less open to suggestions, or if they presume that speaking out will be career limiting (Bari et al., 2020; Khan and Khan, 2021).

If employees are unhappy with and distrust the ways in which they are treated by management there will be poor levels of interactional justice (Bies and Moag, 1986), and as Roch and Shanock (2006) predict, their relationships with supervisors will be of low quality. Moreover, Kramer (1996) suggested that individuals with less power and authority are more aware of trust-related 'cues' associated with the employment relationship. Accordingly any perceived breaches of trust will be imbued, by less powerful employees, with greater importance than any real acts or expressions of trust. Consequently some supervisory behaviour will be interpreted through heightened trust-filters, and result in higher incidences of employees fearing to speak up and voice their concerns. Low-quality, low-trust relationships will tend, of necessity from an employee's point of view, to be low-voice relationships. Certainly, when a manager has to deliver unwelcome news, and the opportunities for voice are minimal, the managers may become a target of employee anger and retaliation (Tripp and Bies, 2009). To prevent such reactions it is sensible to allow employees a say in the process before any committal decisions are made, thereby encouraging perceptions of procedural justice (Bies and Shapiro, 1988; Folger and Greenberg, 1985; Greenberg, 1986), although if the outcomes are very negative, as when redundancies are announced, having a voice only partially negates the impact of the bad news (Bies, 2013).

The decisions that employees make about whether or not to speak out can be linked to social exchange theory; employees become willing to partake in relationships that benefit others with the proviso that there is a reciprocal obligation from the party with whom they are sharing information (Mushonga et al., 2014). Indeed, as Clapham et al. point out, where workplace relationships are interdependent but characterised by uncertainty, about both current and future concerns, 'the need for trust escalates as risk exposure increases' (2014: 57). If it becomes apparent that the other party (i.e., the manager/supervisor/employer) will not reciprocate, trust *and opportunities for mutual dialogues correspondingly diminish*, inhibiting and sometimes prohibiting voice exchanges. Employee voice occurs when people feel safe to express themselves, whereas **employee silence** may be the logical response to fears about the anticipated consequences that might restrict promotion opportunities, or reputational harm (Detert and Edmondson, 2005). Social exchange theory is similar to the notion of the psychological contract and Guest's model of fairness, trust and delivery of the deal (1997). In terms of reciprocal voice theories it can be seen that employees will be happy to contribute to discussions *if, and only if,* there is a trusting reciprocal relationship within which, by actively exposing their thoughts and voicing an opinion, there is going to be a positive, risk-free benefit to themselves.

The arena around voice, trust and perceptions of workplace fairness is complicated because employees may well feel comfortable voicing some opinions while withholding information about others. Often the *perceived* sincerity of management will determine the degree to which employees feel safe to communicate their own thoughts. Different managerial styles impact the ways in which employees trust their supervisory colleagues; in turn this affects whether or not they choose to respond to voice initiatives (Boxall and Purcell, 2011). Whether an employee chooses to exercise voice (or not) has a direct relationship with a number of the essential components that Folger and Bies (1989) identified for fair management, for example, employers must give adequate consideration to employee viewpoints and be truthful in any communication with their subordinates, treating them with courtesy and civility. Where this does not happen employee voice is likely to be muted at best and non-existent at worst. Where employees are operating within teams, or matrix systems, and engaging in a number of different social exchanges they may trust some people more than others, and this might impact the degree to which they allow themselves to share their thoughts publicly. It is in circumstances such as these, particularly where an employee might prefer anonymity, that indirect representation via a representative is regarded as a less risky way of communicating with management.

Summary

Employers choose how they listen to their employees. This choice is influenced by their managerial perspectives (i.e., whether they are unitarist or pluralist), culture and by the legislation within which they are operating. Organisations can facilitate voice directly, indirectly or not at all. Where unions are recognised they are not always the sole means for employee representation as sometimes there are hybrid practices in place enabling union and non-union representation alongside direct methods of facilitating dialogue between the employer and employees. The ways in which voice is organised will have a direct impact on the perceptions of organisational justice and on the levels of power ceded to employees around influencing workplace decisions. Silent employees may be 'sending a message' by non-verbal means. Specific arrangements for selective diverse groups of employees to use their voice are not uncommon, but employers should be aware of assuming that such groups speak with homogeneous voices.

Review Questions

1 To what extent and why does offering voice to discrete disadvantaged groups within the workforce improve perceptions of procedural justice?
2 Critically analyse whether employee silence should be accepted at face value.
3 Has the decline in union membership had a detrimental impact on the ways in which employees are able to voice their opinions at work?

Revision Exercise 10.1

Atzeni's (2010) article gives a first-hand account of how workers' voice in an Argentinian car factory first emerges in the form of collective action, is consolidated and then finally repressed. Using information from the article, analyse:

- the emergence of voice
- its links to organisational justice
- its links to mobilisation theory.

To what extent were the ways in which the employees expressed their discontent effective? Explain how you reached your conclusions.

Revision Exercise 10.2

Enabling voice at work leads to higher levels of conflict.
    Discuss this statement using academic justification for your answer.

Relevant Articles for Further Reading

Dundon, T., Marchington, M., Wilkinson, A., Martinez Lucio, M., Howcroft, D., Donaghey, J.,... and Carney, G. M. (2020) *Who Speaks For Whom At Work: Worker Voice and Social Dialogue*. Available at: www.ul.ie/sites/default/files/research/Case%2019%20-%20Worker%20voice%20 and%20social%20dialogue.pdf (accessed 22 August 2022).

This wide-ranging piece of research examines different forms of worker voice and how they link, or not, to equitable employment relationships and help support collaborative workplace partnerships.

Edezaro, P. O. (2022) 'Relationship between organizational justice, job satisfaction, perceived trust, employee voice, and organisational citizenship behaviour: The mediation role of organisational communication', *International Journal of Social Science and Education Research Studies*, 2(1): 22–8.

Looking specifically at Nigeria, this paper examines the relationship between employee voice, trust and organisational justice and how each relates to organizational citizenship behaviour.

Hickland, E., Cullinane, N., Dobbins, T., Dundon, T. and Donaghey, J. (2020) 'Employer silencing in a context of voice regulations: Case studies of non-compliance', *Human Resource Management Journal*, 30(4): 537–52.

It is not just employees who are silent, employers too can deliberately withhold information and circumvent regulatory requirements. Within the context of the EU Directive on informing and consulting employees this paper outlines three forms of employer silence: avoidance, suppression, and neglect.

Syed, J. (2020) 'Diversity management and missing voices', in A. Wilkinson, T. Dundon, J. Donaghey and R. Freeman (eds), *Handbook of Research on Employee Voice*. Cheltenham: Edward Elgar Publishing.

This book chapter, importantly, looks at the ways in which some voices within the workplace are missed and examines the ramifications of this particularly for diverse groups.

References

Acas (2014) *Representation at Work*. London: HMSO.

Acas (2015) *Code of Practice on Disciplinary and Grievance Procedures*. Norwich: TSO.

All Party Parliamentary Group (APPG) (2019) *Whistleblowing: The Personal Cost of Doing the Right Thing and the Cost to Society of Ignoring it*. Available at: https://docs.wixstatic.com/ugd/88d04c_9754e54bc641443db902cd963687cb55.pdf (accessed 15 March 2022).

All Party Parliamentary Group APPG (2020) *Making Whistleblowing Work for Society*. Available at: https://a02f9c2f-03a1-4206-859b-06ff2b21dd81.filesusr.com/ugd/88d04c_56b3ca80a07e4f5e8ace79e0488a24ef.pdf (accessed 21 October 2021).

Ashok, V. (2015) *Stonewall: Top 100 Employers 2015 – The Definitive Guide to the Best Places to Work for Lesbian, Gay and Bisexual Staff*. London: Stonewall.

Atzeni, M. (2010) 'Conflict and repression in an Argentinian car factory: A cycle of resistance from a worker's perspective', *Work Employment and Society*, 24(2): 366–74.

Aumayr, C., Demetriades, S., Foden, D., Scepanovic, V. and Wolf, F. (2011) *Employee Representative Structures at the Establishment Level*. Dublin: European Foundation for the Improvement of Living and Working Conditions.

Bari, M. W., Ghaffar, M. and Ahmad, B. (2020) 'Knowledge-hiding behaviors and employees' silence: Mediating role of psychological contract breach', *Journal of Knowledge Management*, 24: 2171–94.

Bell, M. P., Özbilgin, M. F., Beauregard, T. A. and Sürgevil, O. (2011) 'Voice, silence, and diversity in 21st century organizations: Strategies for inclusion of gay, lesbian, bisexual, and transgender employees', *Human Resource Management*, 50(1): 131–46.

Bellace, J., Minster, A., Scott, K., Kelly, E. L., Kochan, T. A., Sako, M. and Kaufman, B. E. (2021) 'Commentary on new theories in employment relations', *ILR Review*, 74(3): 798–826.

Bienefeld, N. and Grote, G. (2015) 'Silence that may kill: When aircrew members don't speak up and why', *Aviation Psychology and Applied Human Factors*, 2: 1–10.

Bies, R. J. (2013) 'The delivery of bad news in organisations: A framework for analysis', *Journal of Management*, 39(1): 136–62.

Bies, R. J. and Moag, J. S. (1986) 'Interactional justice: Communication criteria of fairness', *Research on Negotiation in Organizations*, 1(1): 43–55.

Bies, R. J. and Shapiro, D. L. (1988) 'Voice and justification: Their influence on procedural fairness judgements', *Academy of Management Journal*, 31: 676–85.

Bingham, C., Clarke, L., Michielsens, E. and Van de Meer, M. (2013) 'Towards a social model approach?: British and Dutch disability policies in the health sector compared', *Personnel Review*, 42(5): 613–37.

Bird, J. (2022) 'Melin Tregwynt marks 110 years with employee ownership deal', *Employee Benefits*, 14 April. Available at: www.employeebenefits.co.uk/melin-tregwynt-marks-110-years-with-employee-ownership-deal/ (accessed 12 May 2022).

Bishop, J. (2007) 'Increasing participation in online communities: A framework for human–computer interaction', *Computers in Human Behaviour*, 23(4): 1881–93.

Blackhurst, C. (2015) 'Where now for trade unions?', *Work*, 5: 28–35.

Bogg, A. and Novitz, T. (2012) 'Investigating voice at work', *Comparative Labor Law and Policy Journal*, 33(3): 323–54.

Boni, G. (2012) 'Introduction', in I. Schömann, R. Jagodzinski, G. Boni, S. Clauwaert, V. Glassner and T. Jaspers, *Transnational Collective Bargaining at Company Level: A New Component of European Industrial Relations?* Brussels: ETUI, pp. 7–18.

Bowen, F. and Blackmon, K. (2003) 'Spirals of silence: The dynamic effects of diversity on organizational voice', *Journal of Management Studies*, 40(6): 1393–417.

Boxall, P. and Purcell, J. (2003) *Strategy and Human Resource Management*. Basingstoke: Palgrave Macmillan.

Boxall, P. and Purcell, J. (2011) *Strategy and Human Resource Management* (3rd edn). Basingstoke: Palgrave Macmillan.

Brandl, B. and Lehr, A. (2019) 'The strange non-death of employer and business associations: An analysis of their representativeness and activities in Western European countries', *Economic and Industrial Democracy*, 40(4): 932–53.

Brewster, C., Wood, G., Croucher, R. and Brookes, M. (2007) 'Are works councils and joint consultative committees a threat to trade unions? A comparative analysis', *Economic and Industrial Democracy*, 28: 49–77.

Brewster, C., Croucher, R. and Prosser, T. (2019) 'Employee voice and participation: The European perspective', in P. Holland, J. Teicher and J. Donaghey (eds), *Employee Voice at Work*. Singapore: Springer, pp. 51–69.

Bryson, A. and Forth, J. (2010) *Union Organisation and the Quality of Employment Relations*. London: National Institute of Economic and Social Research.

Bryson, A., Forth, J. and George, A. (2012) *Workplace Social Dialogue in Europe: An Analysis of the European Company Survey 2009*. Dublin: Eurofound.

Bryson, A., Willman, P., Gomez, R. and Kretschmer, T. (2013) 'The comparative advantage of non-union voice in Britain, 1980–2004', *Industrial Relations: A Journal of Economy and Society*, 52(s1): 194–220.

Bryson, A., Freeman, R., Gomez, R. and Willman, P. (2019) 'The twin track model of employee voice: An Anglo-American perspective on union decline and the rise of alternative forms of voice', in P. Holland, J. Teicher and J. Donaghey (eds), *Employee Voice at Work*. Singapore: Springer, pp. 23–50.

Budd, J. W. (2004) *Employment with a Human Face: Balancing Efficiency, Equity, and Voice*. Ithaca, NY: Cornell University Press.

Budd, J. W. and Bhave, D. P. (2019) 'The employment relationship: Key elements, alternative frames of reference, and implications for HRM', in A. Wilkinson, N. Bacon, S. Snell and D. Lepak (eds), *The Sage Handbook of Human Resource Management*. London: Sage.

Budd, J.W., Gollan, P.J. and Wilkinson, A. (2010) 'New approaches to employee voice and participation in organizations', *Human Relations*, 63(3): 303–10.

Campolieti, M., Gomez, R. and Gunderson, M. (2013) 'Does non-union employee representation act as a complement or substitute to union choice? Evidence from Canada and the United States', *Industrial Relations*, 52(S1): 378–96.

Charlwood, A. and Forth, J. (2009) 'Employee representation', in W. Brown, A. Bryson, J. Forth and K. Whitfield (eds), *The Evolution of the Modern Workplace*. Cambridge: Cambridge University Press, pp. 74–96.

Chattopadhyay, P. (1999) 'Beyond direct and symmetrical effects: The influence of demographic dis-similarity on organizational citizenship behaviour', *Academy of Management Journal*, 42(3): 273–8.

Clapham, S. E., Meyer C. K., Caldwell, C. and Proctor, G. B. Jr. (2014) 'Trustworthiness, justice and the mediating lens', *Journal of Business and Behavioural Sciences*, 26(1): 55–74.

Conchon, A. (2011) 'Board-level employee representation rights in Europe: Facts and trends', Report 121. Brussels: ETUI, pp. 236–9.

Cooper, R. and Briggs, C. (2009) 'Trojan horse or vehicle for organizing? Non-union collective agreement making and trade unions in Australia', *Economic and Industrial Democracy*, 30(1): 93–119.

Cox, A., Box, D., Gorman, R. and Finkin, M. (eds) (2011) *Labour Law Cases and Materials* (15th edn). Westbury, NY: Foundation Press.

Creese, J., Byrne, J. P., Matthews, A., McDermott, A. M., Conway, E. and Humphries, N. (2021) '"I feel I have no voice": Hospital doctors' workplace silence in Ireland', *Journal of Health Organization and Management*, (35): 178–94.

Creighton, B. and Stewart, A. (2010) *Labour Law: An Introduction* (5th edn). Abingdon: Taylor and Francis.

Dai, Y., Li, H., Xie, W. and Deng, T. (2022) 'Power Distance Belief and Workplace communication: The mediating role of fear of authority', *International Journal of Environmental Research and Public Health*, 19(5): 29–32.

Davies, R. (2020) 'Why is understanding trade union membership from survey data harder than it might first seem?', UK Data Service, *Data Impact Blog*, 24 February. Available at: https://blog.ukdataservice.ac.uk/understanding-trade-union-membership/ (accessed 11 March 2022).

Della Torre, E. (2019) 'Collective voice mechanisms, HRM practices and organizational performance in Italian manufacturing firms', *European Management Journal*, 37(3): 398-410.

Department for Business, Innovation & Skills (DBIS) (2013) *The 2011 Workplace Employment Relations Study (WERS) Transparency Data*. London: DBIS. Available at: www.gov.uk/government/publications/the-2011-workplace-employment-relations-study-wers-transparency-data (accessed 5 October 2015).

Detert, J. R. and Burris, E. R. (2007) 'Leadership behaviour and employee voice: Is the door really open?', *Academy of Management Journal*, 50(4): 869–84.

Detert, J. R. and Edmondson, A. C. (2005) *Everyday Failures in Organizational Learning: Explaining the High Threshold for Speaking up at Work*, Harvard Business School Working Paper Series, no. 06–024. New York: Harvard University Press.

Detert, J. R. and Edmondson, A. C. (2011) 'Implicit voice theories: Taken-for-granted rules of self-censorship at work', *Academy of Management Journal*, 54(3): 461–88.

Dundon, T. and Gollan, P. J. (2007) 'Re-conceptualising non-union voice', *International Journal of Human Resource Management*, 18(7): 1182–98.

Dundon, T. and Wilkinson, A. (2021) 'Employee involvement and participation', *Contemporary Human Resource Management: Text and Cases*, 345.

Dundon, T., Wilkinson, A., Marchington, M. and Ackers, P. (2004) 'The meanings and purpose of employee voice', *International Journal of Human Resource Management*, 15(6): 1149–70.

Dundon, T., Cullinane, N., Donaghey, J., Dobbins, T., Wilkinson, A. and Hickland, E. (2014) 'Double-breasting employee voice: An assessment of motives, arrangements and durability', *Human Relations*, 19 June.

Edezaro, P. O. (2022) 'Relationship between organizational justice, job satisfaction, perceived trust, employee voice, and organisational citizenship behaviour: The mediation role of organisational communication', *International Journal of Social Science and Education Research Studies*, 2(1): 22–8.

Emmott, M. (2015) 'Voice: Pipe dream or philosopher's stone?', CIPD/London School of Economics: Voice and Value Conference, 16 April.

ETUI (2014a) *Collective Bargaining*. Available at: www.worker-participation.eu/National-Industrial-Relations/Countries/Belgium/Collective-Bargaining (accessed 2 July 2015).

ETUI (2014b) *Finland: Key Facts*. Available at: www.worker-participation.eu/National-Industrial-Relations/Countries/Finland (accessed 2 July 2015).

Eurofound (2013) *Work Organisation and Employee Involvement in Europe*. Luxembourg: Publications Office of the European Union.

Eurofound (2015) *Third European Company Survey – Overview report: Workplace Practices – Patterns, Performance and Well-being*. Luxembourg: Publications Office of the European Union.

Eurofound (2021) *Living and Working in Europe 2020*. Luxembourg: Publications Office of the European Union.

Fanshaw, F. (2015) 'Understanding diversity within diversity', *IPA-Involve*, June. Available at: www.ipa-involve.com/news/understanding-diversity-within-diversity/?utm_source=Adestra&utm_medium=email&utm_term= (accessed 4 June 2015).

Folger, R. and Bies, R. J. (1989) 'Managerial responsibilities and procedural justice', *Employee Responsibilities and Rights Journal*, 2(2): 79–90.

Folger, R. and Greenberg, J. (1985) 'Procedural justice: An interpretive analysis of personnel systems', in K. Rowland and G. Ferris (eds), *Research in Personnel and Human Resources Management*. Greenwich, CT: JAI, pp. 141–83.

Francis, R. (2014) 'Fear must not stop whistleblowers coming forward', *The Times*, 7 August.

Freeman, R. B. and Medoff, J. (1984) *What Do Unions Do?* London: Basic Books.

Gajanan, M. (2019) 'Wayfair employees plan walkout to protest the company selling beds to border detention facilities', *Time*, 25 June. Available at: https://time.com/5614072/wayfair-protest-border-detention-beds/ (accessed 1 March 2022).

Garnero, A. (2021) 'The impact of collective bargaining on employment and wage inequality: Evidence from a new taxonomy of bargaining systems', *European Journal of Industrial Relations*, 27(2): 185–202.

Garrison J. (2019) '"Shut down the concentration camps": Wayfair employees walk out, hundreds protest', *USA Today*, 26 June. Available at: https://eu.usatoday.com/story/news/nation/2019/06/26/wayfair-walkout-hundreds-protest-sales-migrant-detention-centers/1569622001/ (accessed 1 March 2022).

Gimpel, J. (1976) *The Medieval Machine: the Industrial Revolution of the Middle Ages*. London: Pimlico.

Go-Ahead (2011) *Moving With Our People: Corporate Responsibility Report 2011*. Available at: www.go-ahead.com/content/dam/go-ahead/corporate/documents/Sustainability%20Reports/PerformanceAndReports/2011/cr-2011.pdf (accessed 24 June 2015).

Go-Ahead (2022) *Who We Are, Sustainability, Better Teams, Staff Engagement*. Available at: www.go-ahead.com/sustainability/our-approach-sustainability/better-teams (accessed 2 March 2022).

Gooberman, L., Hauptmeier, M. and Heery, E. (2018) 'Contemporary employer interest representation in the United Kingdom', *Work, Employment and Society*, 32(1): 114–32.

Goodrich, C. L. (1975 [1920]) *The Frontier of Control*. London: Pluto, pp. 135–45.

Green, A-M. (2015) 'Voice and workforce diversity', in S. Johnstone and P. Ackers (eds), *Finding a Voice at Work?: New Perspectives on Employment Relations*. Oxford: Oxford University Press, pp. 67–91.

Green, F., Mostafa, T., Parent-Thirion, A., Vermeylen, G., Van Houtenmd G., Biletta, I. and Lyly-Yrjanainen, M. (2013) 'Is job quality becoming more unequal?', *Industrial and Labor Relations Review*, 66(1): 753–84.

Greenberg, J. (1986) 'Determinants of perceived fairness of performance evaluations', *Journal of Applied Psychology*, 71: 340–42.

Guest, D. (1997) 'Individualism, flexibility, and the psychological contract: The new orthodoxy in employee relations?', IPD/ESRC seminar, October.

Gunnigle, P., Lavelle, J. and McDonnell, A. (2009) 'Subtle but deadly? Union avoidance through "double breasting" among multinational companies', *Advances in Industrial & Labor Relations*, 16: 51–73.

Hales, C. and Klidas, A. (2008) 'Empowerment in five-star hotels: Choice, voice or rhetoric?', *International Journal of Contemporary Hospitality Management*, 10(3): 88–95.

Hall, M. (2005) 'Assessing the information and consultation of employees regulations', *Industrial Law Journal*, 34: 103–26.

Hall, M. (2006) 'A cool response to the ICE regulations? Employer and trade union approaches to the new legal framework for information and consultation', *Industrial Relations Journal*, 37: 456–72.

Hall, M. (2010) 'EU regulation and the UK employee consultation framework', *Economic and Industrial Democracy*, 31(4s): 55–69.

Hall, M., Purcell, J., Terry, M., Hutchinson, S. and Parker, J. (2015) 'Trade union approaches towards the ICE regulations: Defensive realism or missed opportunity?', *British Journal of Industrial Relations*, 53(2): 350–75.

Heery, E. (2010) 'Worker representation in a multiform system: a framework for evaluation', *Journal of Industrial Relations*, 52: 543–59.

Hermans, M. and Lenaerts, K. (2021) 'Equalizing effects of workplace-level trade union presence on quality of work', IREC Industrial Relations in Europe Conference 2021, 16–17 September, Firenze. Available from: lirias,kuleuven.be/3469408?limo=0 (accessed 7 March 2022).

Hirschman, A. O. (1970) *Exit, Voice, and Loyalty: Responses to Decline in Firms, Organizations, and States*. New York: Harvard University Press.

Holland, P. (2014) 'Employers and voice', in A. Wilkinson, J. Donaghey, T. Dundon and R. B. Freeman (eds), *Handbook of Research on Employee Voice*. Camberley: Edward Elgar, pp. 135–54.

Holman, D. (2013a) 'An explanation of cross-national variation in call-centre job quality using institutional theory', *Work, Employment and Society*, 27(1): 21–38.

Holman, D. (2013b) 'Job types and job quality in Europe', *Human Relations*, 66(4): 475–502.

Husen-Bradley, A. (2020) 'German chemical union IG BCE launches "Show Your Face: Raise Your Voice" campaign to fight racism & right-wing extremism in the workplace', *industriAll Europe*, 31 July. Available at: https://news.industriall-europe.eu/Article/484 (accessed 3 March 2022).

IRGuru (2022) *Interview with Atle Høie, General Secretary of IndustriALL Global Union*. Available at: https://irguru.online/interviews/atle-hoie/ (accessed 4 March 2022).

Jahanzeb, S., Fatima, T. and Malik, M. A. R. (2018) 'Supervisor ostracism and defensive silence: A differential needs approach', *European Journal of Work and Organizational Psychology*, 27(4): 430–40.

Jansen, G. and Lehr, A. (2022) 'On the outside looking in? A micro-level analysis of insiders' and outsiders' trade union membership', *Economic and Industrial Democracy*, 43(1): 221–51.

Jiang, H. and Luo, Y. (2018) 'Crafting employee trust: From authenticity, transparency to engagement', *Journal of Communication Management*, 22: 138–60.

Kaufman, B. E. (2014) 'Explaining breadth and depth of employee voice across firms: A voice factor demand model', *Journal of Labor Research*, 35(3): 296–319.

Khan, J., Saeed, I., Zada, M., Ali, A., Contreras-Barraza, N., Salazar-Sepúlveda, G. and Vega-Muñoz, A. (2022) 'Examining whistleblowing intention: The influence of rationalization on wrongdoing and threat of retaliation', *International Journal of Environmental Research and Public Health*, 19(3): 1752.

Khan, N. A. and Khan, A. N. (2021) 'Exploring the impact of abusive supervision on employee voice behavior in Chinese construction industry: A moderated mediation analysis', *Engineering, Construction and Architectural Management*. doi:10.1108/ECAM-10-2020-0829

Khaola, P. P. and Musiiwa, D. (2021) 'Bolstering innovative work behaviours through leadership, affective commitment and organisational justice: A three-way interaction analysis', *International Journal of Innovation Science*, 13(5): 610–26.

Kim, J., MacDuffie, J. P. and Pil, F. K. (2010) 'Employee voice and organizational performance: Team versus representative influence', *Human Relations*, 63(3): 371–94.

Kish-Gephart, J. J., Detert, J. R., Klebe Treviño, L. and Edmondson, A. C. (2009) 'Silenced by fear: The nature, sources, and consequences of fear at work', *Research in Organizational Behavior*, 29: 163–93.

Knoll, M. and van Dick, R. (2013) 'Do I hear the whistle …? A first attempt to measure four forms of employee silence and their correlates', *Journal of Business Ethics*, 113(2): 349–62.

Kornelakis, A., Veliziotis, M., & Voskeritsian, H. (2018). Improving productivity: the case for employee voice and inclusive workplace practices. *ETUI Research Paper-Policy Brief, 1*.

Kramer, R. M. (1996) 'Divergent realities and convergent disappointments in the hierarchic relation: Trust and the intuitive auditor at work', in R. M. Kramer and T. R. Tyler (eds), *Trust in Organisations: Frontiers of Theory and Research*. London: Sage, pp. 216–45.

Kumra, S. and Manfredi, S. (2012) *Managing Equality and Diversity*. Oxford: Oxford University Press.

Latham & Watkins (2022) *About Us: Diversity*. Available at: www.lw.com/aboutus/diversity (accessed 3 March 2022).

Milliken, F. J., Morrison, E. W., & Hewlin, P. F. (2003). An exploratory study of employee silence: Issues that employees don't communicate upward and why. *Journal of Management Studies*, 40(6), 1453-1476.

Moss, R. (2014) 'Whistleblowers need more protection', *Personnel Today*, 1 August.

Mowbray, P. K., Wilkinson, A. and Tse, H. (2019) 'Evolution, separation and convergence of employee voice concept', in P. Holland, J. Teicher and J. Donaghey (eds), *Employee Voice at Work*. Singapore: Springer, pp. 3–21.

Mowbray, P. K., Wilkinson, A. and Herman, H. M. (2020) 'High-performance work systems and employee voice behaviour: An integrated model and research agenda'', *Personnel Review*, 50(5): 1530–43.

Mushonga, S. M., Thiagarajan, P. and Torrance, C. G. (2014) 'Fairness in the workplace: The mediating role of trust in the relationship between supervisory justice and work outcomes', *SAM Advanced Management Journal*, 79(3): 17.

Nienhueser, W. (2009) 'The effects of different types of works councils on bargaining outcomes: Results of an empirical study', *Economic and Industrial Democracy*, 30(3): 372–400.

Office National Statistics (ONS) (2022) *Trade Union Membership Statistics 2020*. Available at: www.gov.uk/government/statistics/trade-union-statistics-2020 (accessed 8 March 2022).

Oyetunde, K., Prouska, R. and McKearney, A. (2022) Voice in non-traditional employment relationships: A review and future research directions', *The International Journal of Human Resource Management*, 33(1): 142–67.

Parry, E., Morley, M. J., & Brewster, C. (2021). Contextual approaches to human resource management: An introduction. *The Oxford Handbook of Contextual Approaches to Human Resource Management*, 1-25.

Paulet, R., Holland, P. and Bratton, A. (2021) 'Employee voice: The missing factor in sustainable HRM?', *Sustainability*, 13(17): 9732.

Prouska, R., McKearney, A., Opute, J., Tungtakanpoung, M. and Brewster, C. (2021) 'Voice in context: An international comparative study of employee experience with voice in small and medium enterprises', *The International Journal of Human Resource Management*, 33: 3149–74.

Pulignano, V. and Waddington, J. (2020) 'Management, European Works Councils and institutional malleability', *European Journal of Industrial Relations*, 26(1): 5–21.

Roch, S. G. and Shanock, L. R. (2006) 'Organizational justice in an exchange framework: Clarifying organizational justice distinctions', *Journal of Management*, 32(2): 299–322.

Silverman, M., Bakhshalian, E. and Hillman, L. (2013) *Social Media and Employee Voice: The Current Landscape*, CIPD Research Report. Available at: www.cipd.co.uk/binaries/social-media-and-employee-voice_2013-current-landscape-.pdf (accessed 22 June 2015).

Sisson, K. (1995) 'Change and continuity in British industrial relations: "Strategic choice or muddling through?"', in R. Locke, T. A. Kochan and M. Piore (eds), *Employment Relations in a Changing World Economy*. Cambridge, MA: MIT Press, pp. 33–58.

Syed, J. (2014) 'Diversity management and missing voices', in A. Wilkinson, J. Donaghey, T. Dundon and R B. Freeman (eds), *Handbook of Research on Employee Voice*. Camberley: Edward Elgar.

Tangirala, S. and Ramanujam, R. (2012) 'Ask and you shall hear (but not always): Examining the relationship between manager consultation and employee voice', *Personnel Psychology*, 65(2): 251–82.

The Lex 100 (2019) 'Latham Watkins global affinity groups', *The Lex* 100, 20 November. Available at: www.lex100.com/2019/11/20/latham-watkins-global-affinity-groups/ (accessed 3 March 2022).

TransAfrica Forum (n.d.) Voices for Change: Sodexo Workers from Five Countries Speak Out. Available at: http://news.emory.edu/special/workforce_and_labor/documents/transafrica_report.pdf (accessed 23 June 2015).

Tripp, T. M. and Bies, R. J. (2009) *Getting Even: The Truth about Workplace Revenge – and How to Stop it*. San Francisco, CA: Jossey-Bass.

TUC (2021) *Good News, Bad News and the Same Challenges – Trade Union Membership Statistics*, press release, 27 May. Available at: www.tuc.org.uk/blogs/good-news-bad-news-and-same-challenges-trade-union-membership-statistics (accessed 8 March 2022).

Unite (2014) *London Bus Drivers Take to the Streets to Demand Decent Wages*. Available at: www.unitetheunion.org/news/london-bus-drivers-take-to-the-streets-to-demand-decent-wages/ (accessed 10 April 2015).

Van Dyne, L., Ang, S. and Botero, I. C. (2003) 'Conceptualizing employee silence and employee voice as multidimensional constructs', *Journal of Management Studies*, 40(6): 1359–92.

van Wanrooy, B. V., Bewley, H., Bryson, A., Forth, J., Freeth, S., Stokes, L. and Wood, S. (2013a) *The 2011 Workplace Employment Relations Study: First Findings*. Available at: www.gov.uk/government/uploads/system/uploads/attachment_data/file/175479/13–535-the-2011-workplace-employment-relations-study-first-findings1.pdf (accessed 23 July 2013).

van Wanrooy, B., Bewley, H., Bryson, A., Forth, J., Freeth, L. and Wood, S. (2013b) *Employment Relations in the Shadow of Recession*. Basingstoke: Palgrave.

Visser, J. (2011) *ICTWSS: Database on Institutional Characteristics of Trade Unions, Wage Setting, State Intervention and Social Pacts in 34 Countries between 1960 and 2007*. Amsterdam: Institute for Advanced Labour Studies, AIAS, University of Amsterdam.

Wilkinson, A., Dundon, T., Donaghey, J. and Freeman, R. B. (2014) 'Employee voice: Charting new terrain', in A. Wilkinson, J. Donaghey, T. Dundon and R. B. Freeman (eds), *Handbook of Research on Employee Voice*. Camberley: Edward Elgar.

Willman, P., Bryson, A. and Gomez, R. (2006) 'The sound of silence: Which employers choose no employee voice and why?', *Socio-Economic Review*, 4(2): 283–99.

Wood, S. (2008) 'Job characteristics, employee voice and well-being in Britain', *Industrial Relations Journal*, 39(2): 153–68.

Xu, Z., Yang, F. and Peng, J. (2021) 'How does authentic leadership influence employee voice? From the perspective of the theory of planned behavior', *Current Psychology*, 1–19.

Yarlagadda, R., Dromey, J. and Fanshawe, S. (2015) 'Diverse voices: engaging employees in an increasingly diverse workforce', IPA and astar-fanshawe seminar, London, 2 June.

11

FLEXIBILITY AND FAIRNESS IN THE EMPLOYMENT RELATIONSHIP

Learning Outcomes

By the end of this chapter, you should be able to:

- be familiar with the links between flexible and hybrid working practices and employee perceptions of fairness
- describe the nature of, and reasons for, the development of flexible working arrangements
- critically analyse the ways in which organisations may flexibly deploy their workforce
- assess the benefits of flexible and hybrid working from both an employee's and an employer's point of view
- identify the positive and negative ways in which the psychological contract and levels of trust may be affected by the introduction of non-standard working patterns.

What to Expect

Flexible working implies that work is performed without set boundaries around working spaces, schedules, and contracts. This chapter looks at the range of flexible working options open to employers and employees and the impact that their deployment might have on perceptions of justice and levels of trust, particularly where such flexibility is imposed rather than desired. The pros and cons of flexible working, from the perspectives of all involved, are explored and the negative and positive impacts of flexibility on a diverse workforce are discussed.

The range of meanings attributed to flexibility are examined covering, as Swan and Fox point out, not just organisational constructions, such as flexible production methods and matrix working, but also a number of practices:

> ... such as functional flexibilities, numerical flexibilities, temporal and spatial flexibilities such as tele-work, virtual work and e-work, flexible pay, flexible contracts and flexible terms and conditions. [.... Flexibility has been used] to describe the ideal type of worker subjectivity and embodiment, sometimes referred to as a 'mindset' or 'capability', that fits in with or supports these other forms of flexibility. (2009: 149)

Much initial academic discussion about flexibility centred on operational requirements and an organisation's associated staffing needs (numerical flexibility). Later the emphasis moved towards *spatial* and, particularly, *temporal* flexibility (remote working, working from home, reduced hours, etc. for those whose jobs allow working off-site) with benefits for employees (Soga et al., 2022; Wheatley 2021), and concurrently for employers in terms of productivity, and the retention of valued employees (Australian Government, 2021; Choudhury et al., 2021; Pokojski et al., 2022), and these will each be explored.

Flexible Work Patterns: What Are They and Who Benefits?

Non-standard work patterns are often referred to as 'flexible' and can be described as alternative work options allowing work to be undertaken outside the temporal and/or spatial boundaries of standard, conventional working patterns (Klindzic and Marić, 2019). Flexible working is a way of working where employers may require, or employees may request and undertake, ways of working where the length of the time spent working (i.e., temporal) and/or the place at which the work is undertaken (i.e., spatial) is atypical. Flexible work patterns provide degrees of elasticity around where and when an individual might work and for how many hours at a time. They are sometimes known as **hybrid working patterns**, when an employee combines working on and off site, typically in an office and at home. This became prevalent around the Covid pandemic when employees had been 'locked down' at home and virtual ways of working became the norm. In the lockdown of April 2020, for example, nearly half of all those in employment in the UK worked from home, and, of these, 86% did so purely as a result of the pandemic. Similarly in the USA, 70% worked from home during the pandemic as opposed to 20% prior to it (Brand, 2022). The mushrooming of homework during the pandemic did a lot to dissolve attitudes of mistrust. For sceptical employers it was an eye opener – employees did not take advantage of the lack of supervision, work tasks were completed and levels of communication maintained (Galanti et al., 2021). For most employees the opportunity to work in home surroundings without a commute was beneficial, as was the feeling that they were trusted to work effectively in this way (Ramos & Prasetyo, 2020). There was a downside for many women however as they bore the brunt of simultaneously combining childcare responsibilities with working (Mooi-Reci and Risman, 2021) – in the USA for example, where mothers with young children worked fewer hours, the gender-gap in work hours grew by 20–50% (Collins et al. 2021). The ways in which flexible/hybrid work systems are introduced and operated have a big impact on employee perceptions of fairness and hence on the ways in which the employment relationship functions.

Flexibility is a crucial part of the process by which human resource departments can accommodate staff requests for alternative working patterns and, importantly, adjust staffing levels to the requirements of an organisation. Its introduction helps overcome problems of inadequate forecasting of staffing and aids the organisation in adapting to any unforeseen dips, or increases, in work and the subsequent demands for more or less labour. For example, in 2009 the GMB and Unite trade unions signed an agreement with Jaguar Land Rover enabling the 15,000 employees across the West Midlands and Merseyside to have security of employment (i.e., no redundancies) in exchange for increased labour mobility/flexibility, a four-day week and a pay freeze (Logan, 2009). If managed well, flexible processes can lead to increased efficiency and cost reductions, with the possible spin-off of increased employee morale and productivity.

'Flexibility' is a broad and ambiguous term that can refer to a number of different processes, not all of them mutually compatible; consequently it can mean different things to different people, sometimes causing confusion and resentment. Types of flexibility are as varied as the attitudes expressed and the many contradictions within workplaces.

Flexibility for the Employee

For employees, flexibility may result in increased job variety and opportunities for personal development that may enrich their work experience. The possibility of working off-site and 'remotely' from home, although not suitable for all occupations, e.g., firefighters, is often advantageous, with some positive outcomes including 'improved work–life balance', 'less travelling/avoid rushhour', 'get more work done', 'enjoy work/happier', 'improved health/less stress' and 'more time with family' – particularly for those with caring responsibilities (Tipping et al., 2012; Wheatley, 2017; Bainbridge and Townsend, 2020). Flexible working gives more opportunity for employees to behave in autonomous ways when deciding how and when to apportion their time (Eurofound, 2020) and works well for those who cannot work full or standard hours (e.g., those needing regular medical treatment such as dialysis) to continue in employment (Woodhams and Corby, 2007; Bingham et al., 2014).

Where work patterns are flexible an individual's employment relationship with their employer is affected by how and why such patterns have been established. Employer-introduced flexible work patterns may be perceived as *inflexible* work patterns by the workforce on whom they have been imposed. Just *who* benefits from such arrangements may have implications for the employment relationship; for example, where an employee requests and then works for a reduced number of hours, perhaps improving their work–life balance, they are likely to view their employer more favourably than an employee who suffers an imposed reduction in their working hours. Just how flexible work patterns are initiated and regulated has important implications for labour turnover. Stavrou and Kilaniotis, in their 2010 international study, found that where flexible work patterns were created collaboratively between the employer and employee, as is, they suggest, the practice in Nordic countries, then labour turnover figures were lower. However, where flexible work patterns had been established solely by the employer, as in many Anglo-American cases, then labour turnover was higher. This finding can be contrasted with that of McNall et al. (2010) who found positive links between labour retention and family-friendly homeworking in the UK.

News Flash 11.1

Homeworking on the Rise

CIPD research, looking at 12 organisations in depth and surveying more than 1,000 different employers, found that:

- 65% of organisations reported that home working has either increased productivity (28%) or had no impact on productivity (37%). Nearly a third (28%) of employers reported a *decrease* in productivity and surprisingly 7% didn't know the impact on productivity.
- Employers expect the proportion of their workforce that regularly works from home to double to 37% of the workforce on average post-pandemic, compared to the pre-pandemic incidence average of 18%.
- The main benefits associated with homeworking are reported to be a better work-life balance (61%), greater collaboration (43%), greater ability to focus with fewer distractions (38%) and IT upskilling (33%).
- The biggest challenges reported by employers include the unsuitability of jobs to be done from home (48%), reduced wellbeing among staff (47%), reduced staff interaction (36%) and the effectiveness of line management of home-based workers (33%).

Peter Cheese, CIPD CEO, said,

> ... if supported and managed properly, home working can be as productive and innovative as office working and we can give more opportunity for people to benefit from better work-life balance. This can also help with inclusion and how we can create positive work opportunities across our economies ... Employers will also have to redouble efforts to introduce flexible working arrangements for staff unable to work from home otherwise they will increasingly have a two-tier workforce of those who have opportunity to benefit from home working and flexibility and those who don't.

Source: CIPD, 2020

Employee commitment to an organisation and the subsequent use of discretionary effort is often linked to levels of *personal control* around how time is apportioned (Kelly and Moen, 2007), although such autonomy may not always be positive. Llave and his colleagues investigated IT workers in the UK and 27 European countries, and found evidence of what they termed an *autonomy paradox*, whereby workers with high levels of autonomy found working flexibly actually led to an intensification of work (Eurofound, 2020: 25). Putman et al. (2013) looked at both men and women employed in a 'results-only work environment', where output rather than time was important, and found that this type of working positively influenced turnover behaviour and the intention to stay with the organisation. Yet not all employees grasp the opportunity of flexible work when it is offered – this happens particularly where employers offer flexibility yet make it clear that they think less of those taking up the offer, often assuming they are less committed and uninterested in career progression (Leslie et al., 2012; Putman et al., 2013).

Individual employees' perceptions of how those other than themselves perceive flexibility are important. Some *employees* fail to request flexible working because they perceive that it will harm their standing within the organisation. There is some evidence that flexible work is linked to cultural norms and expectations; for example, Peretz et al. (2018) in a wide-ranging global study found that telework is strongly linked to power distance and flexitime to gender egalitarianism. Some *employers* fail to offer flexible working because they mistrust employees, suspecting they will 'game' the system. Similarly, the flexible activities themselves may be perceived in different ways as while what some *employee*s would call a 'tightening-up' of work practices and an increased workload, some *employers* would call 'flexibility'. Roberts (2008) distinguishes between the 'customisation' of work resulting in benefits for the employee and 'flexibility' of work benefitting the employer. In a similar vein Gash (2008) differentiates between *chosen* and *constrained* part-time working. Kelliher and Anderson (2010) found that where employees voluntarily opted to work flexibly, either remotely or in patterns of reduced hours, their levels of both organisational commitment and job satisfaction were higher than for employees working non-flexibly, although the levels of work intensified. (Such intensification often occurs in organisations that are becoming more 'boundaryless', with technologically enabled jobs expanding in space and time, and here, paradoxically, the flexibility for employees sometimes evaporates with a concomitant increase in stress and employee unhappiness – Moen and Huang, 2010.)

Employers have a duty of care towards their employees, so they should not expose them to excessive numbers of hours at work. Too much time spent working is positively correlated to poor health (Sparks et al., 1997). Indeed this work corroborated a body of research evidence, some dating back to the 1950s, indicating that individuals working non-traditional or staggered hours may be prone to higher levels of stress. Over half a century ago two American researchers, Breslow and Buell (1960), found positive correlations between long hours and heart disease. Their study discovered that individuals aged 45 or under who, rather than working 40 hours a week, worked more than 48 hours a week, doubled their risk of dying from heart problems. Shift work, a form of flexible working, can on occasions affect blood sugar levels, metabolic rates, sleep patterns, emotional states, accuracy and even blood temperature. Demir et al. (2003) unsurprisingly discovered that nurses working night shifts had lower levels of energy and higher levels of exhaustion than their day-working counterparts. Although in an earlier comprehensive study of research around hours, shift patterns, stress, absenteeism and efficiency, Ian Brooks (1997) concluded that whether or not nurses worked a rotating rather than a permanent shift pattern seemed to have an impact on their stress/health levels – not all shift patterns were equally bad; permanent shift patterns were not detrimental to health, whereas rotating patterns were correlated to higher levels of stress and so on. But, interestingly, these findings were strongly influenced by whether or not the nurses had a *voice* in the patterns they worked. Those able to choose their patterns, or with a degree of influence about when they worked, were less prone to suffering detrimental side effects, foreshadowing subsequent research about collaborative decision making and flexible work patterns. The impact of 'having a say' is clearly associated with the positive psychological wellbeing of the employees concerned and as such has links to Budd's (2004, 2010) essential three elements of an optimal employment relationship: equity, efficiency and voice. Brooks' findings notwithstanding, shift patterns, on the whole, are regarded by medical practitioners as predictors of mental and physical ill health. Such studies have implications for employers who may be liable for employee ill-health directly linked to working long hours.

Exercise 11.1

- In what ways do you think that flexibility at work decreases stress levels? Why did you say this? Back up your answer with academic references.
- In what ways do you think that flexibility at work increases stress levels? Why did you say this? Back up your answer with academic references.

Exercise 11.2

Explain the reasons that *might* lie behind these findings about home working in the list below (taken from an Office of National Statistics report looking at homeworking between 2011 and 2020 – ONS, 2021). Justify your thinking.

- Employees who mainly worked from home were less than half as likely to be promoted than all other employees between 2012 and 2017, when controlling for other factors.
- Employees who mainly worked from home were around 38% less likely on average to have received a bonus compared with those who never worked from home between 2013 and 2020, when controlling for other factors.
- People who completed any work from home did 6.0 hours of unpaid overtime on average per week in 2020, compared with 3.6 hours for those that never work from home.
- There is considerable regional variation in homeworking, not all of which is explained by differences in the types of industries that operate in each region.

Managerial Styles and Flexibility From the Employers' Point of View

The ways in which flexibility is introduced will depend heavily on the managerial style of the workplace. Hard and soft managers approach the ways in which they deal with the 'resources' (people) at their disposal very differently. The managerial style that deploys labour in the most cost-efficient way, using whatever methods it can to reduce labour costs, will primarily use numerical flexibility. A softer, more collaborative approach, will involve employees, take their requirements into account and encourage employee development. Whether or not there is a union presence is often crucial to the way systems are perceived, introduced and run. The TUC advocates a partnership approach between managers and unions to clarify the details, while Acas recommends consultation between individuals and their managers prior to the introduction of flexible work systems. Looking at flexible workplaces through the eyes of Tzafrir and Dolan (2004) (see Chapter 3), it is apparent that in workplaces exhibiting 'harmony' where employees and employers are in accord over an issue, 'reliability' where the employer's practices match their rhetoric, and 'concern' where the employer (and managers) have empathy with their workforce, there is likely to be a higher degree of trust around the deployment of staff in flexible ways (than when harmony, reliability and concern are missing) and the psychological contract and perceptions of organisational justice are likely to be positive.

Three different types of flexibility were traditionally associated with employment: numerical, financial and functional.

- **Numerical flexibility** refers to the ways in which employers deploy their employees. Hard employers often have a 'pick and mix' approach to resourcing, in particular they 'pick up' and 'put down' those people who are considered expendable. Recruitment here follows the peaks and troughs of the business cycle and staff who cannot be used are discarded until required. For example, hop-pickers in Kent are only employed by hop-growers when the crop requires harvesting – at other times of the year they have to find employment elsewhere. Similarly, many firms use agency workers to 'cover' for absent staff, and companies often hire people on temporary or short-term contracts in order to fulfil specific projects or short-term tasks. Sometimes staff are employed on zero-hours contracts that often require them to work as-and-when required without a set pattern of days or hours to their employment and often with short-notice changes.
- **Financial flexibility** is not concerned with work patterns but with payment patterns. It relates to the ability of employers to decide how they choose to manage the remuneration mix of their workforce. (Pensions, health care, share options, paying monthly or weekly, commission on sales, whether or not to give a bonus, etc.; all are part of the numerous options available to employers who can choose and adopt the schemes most suited to their type of workplace and the ways in which they wish to motivate their employees.)
- **Functional flexibility** is concerned with the ways in which people are deployed within the workplace. Employees may be required to be multi-skilled, possibly working across departmental boundaries, or mono-skilled, perhaps undertaking monotonous repetitive work. Functional flexibility can cover a range of different working options. Branham (1989, in particular pp. 62–72) discusses a number of different types of flexibility including the flexibility of training, and points out that some organisations strategically use training to multi-skill their workforce in order to ensure functional flexibility for the optimum number of people to undertake the largest number of tasks. This emphasises that the point of flexibility is to build an environment that encourages positive attitudes towards flexibility so that employees undertake work without reference to (irrelevant) job demarcations.

Under functional flexibility the mix of skills and the ways in which they are deployed is influenced by managerial styles and approaches. The soft approach often involves the employees in contributing to, or even making, some of the management decisions, particularly those about job redesign, and ensures that changes are accompanied by the appropriate staff development and training. Significant effort is often put into communication, consulting and informing the affected employees to aid acceptance of both the need for change and their possible redeployment. Care is taken to ensure that employees buy into changes. A hard philosophy would make the decisions about how and where people worked without necessarily considering the implications for the people themselves. Unitary and pluralist managerial frameworks are apparent here. The pluralists acknowledge possible conflicts of interest and expect different perspectives on flexibility from the affected employees, while the unitarists expect compliance for the good of the organisation.

These different types of flexibility are not mutually exclusive. Where an organisation operates functional flexibility and employs those capable of doing a number of tasks, this can often result in their being managed in a numerically flexible way. Broadcast journalists, for example, are trained to undertake their main occupation – journalism – while also managing to film, edit and record their stories and, as such, are often deployed by organisations using hard HRM and numerical flexibility, with the subsequent negative impact on employee morale and engagement.

Flexible Working and Pluralist Approaches

There is some evidence that in countries where there is high union density (and importantly where social partnerships and collective bargaining are the norm) working time is arranged and regulated in a balanced way and not in a way that prioritises the needs and requirements of employers (Berg et al., 2004, 2014; see also Stavrou et al., 2010). In Sweden, for example, where union membership is high (68% – ETUI, 2016), the Working Hours Act places limits on the amount of overtime that individuals may work in a year, and provides for a standard working week of 40 hours. The EU, with its ethos of social partnership, has introduced a number of directives generating regulatory standards governing the working hours and practices that apply across the EU countries. For instance, the directives covering working time (introduced in 1993) and part-time work (introduced in 1997) set minimum standards for average weekly working hours, annual paid holidays and ensure that those working part-time are treated no less favourably than their full-time counterparts. The pervasive more even-handed approaches to the employment relationship in these countries results in enabling legislation that may be enhanced by individual collective arrangements improving on the statutory minimum requirements, as is evident in the Netherlands and some parts of Germany. This is in contrast to where, for example, union influence is much less strong. In this situation the working practices involving flexibility and workforce deployment tend to be driven by management strategy and an individualistic approach (such as in the USA), where little regulatory legislation, coupled with the need for workplace flexibility, is sometimes implemented to the detriment of employees. In Russia, under the Soviet regime, flexible working in the form of shift work and/or **annualised hours** was commonplace, but since 'two decades of post-communist development have mostly extinguished the Soviet traditions of organised labour [that] have not been replaced by new forms like independent trade unions' (Gurkov et al., 2012: 1295), companies sometimes use flexible work practices, in the form of partial employment as a means of avoiding layoffs; such partial working includes unpaid leave and imposed part-time working. Such flexibility, as this study points out, is not always by mutual consent – in 2009, 40% of employees in the competitive sectors were compelled to take '[voluntary] holidays' by the initiative of the employers (Gurkov et al., 2012).

In many ways the Gurkov study bears out the findings of Berg, showing that countries with collective perspectives have better flexible regulations. Where collective perspectives are weaker, employees may suffer from employer-led flexibility initiatives.

News Flash 11.2

Working Time: Court Imposes Daily Record-keeping Across EU

In May 2019, the highest court of the European Union, the European Court of Justice, ruled that all employers must now track the working time and attendance of their employees. EU Member States are now required to compel employers to undertake systematic detailed and accurate tracking of employee working time, although each State is free to define how to implement such a system. The Court pointed out that the change was necessary because:

> In the absence of a system enabling the duration of time worked each day by each worker to be measured, it is not possible to determine, objectively and reliably, either the number of hours worked and when that work was done, or the number of hours of overtime worked, which makes it excessively difficult, if not impossible in practice, for workers to ensure that their rights are complied with.

The ruling is important because it overrides the various separate national laws in each member state. Every EU employer must, as before, meet the minimum standards defined in the EU directive (and be compliant with the national legislation that's been implemented based on this directive) and track the time and attendance of each of their employees. This ruling brings the situation in EU closer to that in the USA, where all businesses are required to track employees' working time in order to be compliant with the regulations set out by The Fair Labor Standards Act.

Source: Court of Justice of the European Union, 2019

The Flexible Firm

One of the most often quoted conceptual models depicting the ways in which flexibility is linked to the labour market and utilised within different organisations is the Atkinson and Meagre

(1986) model of the **flexible firm**. This model is a useful descriptive tool (see Johnstone, 2019) helping to explain how some organisations work; however it is of little predictive use and increasing technologically enabled working makes it less universally applicable.

The model describes the ways in which people are deployed and treated within an organisation. Those who are regarded as essential to the enterprise are depicted at the core (**core workforce**), or centre, of the organisation. Such 'vital' people are well-treated, trained, receive lots of relevant communication, and are rewarded with good remuneration packages and career prospects. Surrounding this group is the **peripheral workforce**. The further these individuals are from the central core of employees the less crucial they are to the organisations' success. So for example, part of the layer next to the core employees would include part-time employees or those on temporary contracts. Further out yet again are the groups undertaking outsourced tasks or those under the control of sub-contractors.

According to the model the further from the central core, the more easily the groups can be replaced and the less responsibility the organisation has for their wellbeing and training. An individual's position on the model is linked to the type of flexibility required, so the core employees are often associated with functional flexibility and managed in a soft way, while the peripheral employees are associated with numerical flexibility and managed in a hard way.

Exercise 11.3

● To what extent and why might lack of trust and/or conflict arise between those employees at the core and those at the periphery in this model – how might technology play a part here? Justify your answer with reference to academic arguments.

The model is limited – there are a number of gaps where certain categories of employee are not included. It does not, for example, cover those who are *essential* to an organisation but who are temporally or spatially separated from it, like those working non-standard hours from home. Organisations that have embraced technology – and hence have evolved interrelated networks of virtual tasks undertaken by people at all levels of the organisation, from the strategic to the operational – do not fit neatly into the categories; this is especially so where roles and tasks undertaken are constantly changing. Furthermore the model's categorisation could be misleading as terms such as 'part-time work' can cover a range of working practices and hours. Where matrix structures are in operation, the same individuals could be perceived to be simultaneously both core and peripheral. The model does not acknowledge the impact that external forces, such as skill shortages or legislation, can have on the positioning and importance of employees. It could be argued that the model, although a useful starting point, is limited as an explanatory tool for flexible organisational practice, not just because it assumes static working patterns but also because the labour market is portrayed as unchanging and therefore without major influence. Some commentators have disregarded the model because it was initially based on too small a sample to be representative (Penn, 1992).

Certainly in those organisations exhibiting an increase in the take-up of multiple work patterns a clear and unambiguous distinction between the core and peripheral workforce is not always apparent. An Industrial Society survey around flexible working practices found that of the 516 respondent organisations, just under half had flexible working operating at *all levels* of the organisation, while 7–8% said that flexible working was mainly *limited to senior staff* (Bingham, 2001). Where senior staff are operating flexibly it is unlikely that these people are regarded as part of a peripheral workforce. This then raises questions about the applicability of the Atkinson and Meagre model in all situations. The model, it appears, is occasionally rather too simplistic to be regarded as a comprehensive explanatory tool for flexible organisational practice.

The static nature of the Atkins and Meagre model, with its assumption of fixed categories of areas of work, also fails to take into account formal and informal networks of employees, their spheres of influence and, importantly, the potential such influence has for impacting on the ways in which an organisation operates.

Different Types of Flexible Working Patterns

Part-time Work

Part-time work usually refers to work where the number of hours worked each week is 30 or under. According to Kossek and Lautsch (2018), part-time employment improves recruitment and retention for upper-level jobs but disproportionately hurts lower-level employees. Within the EU and the UK, part-time workers should be treated no less favourably than their full-time counterparts: this means that they are entitled to the same hourly rates of pay, that their holiday and pension arrangements should be pro-rata, and that they should have the same access to training and promotion as their full-time colleagues. (In the UK this is covered by the Part-time Workers (Prevention of Less Favourable Treatment) Regulations 2000 and its 2002 amendment.) Sometimes pro-rating can be confusing; for example, if a part-time worker works additional hours they will not be entitled to overtime payments until they have worked the same number of hours as a full-time employee. Employee benefits, such as gym membership, access to office equipment and so on, should be available in proportion to the amount of time worked compared with someone who is employed full-time in the same organisation, although it is not always practical to 'divide' a benefit and it may therefore be denied to those who work part-time. It is, however, up to the employer to justify this. On occasions, the easiest way of dealing with this lack of identical behaviour is to translate the missing element into its monetary equivalent. Sometimes the ways in which part-time workers are treated compared to their full-time colleagues can lead to their feeling excluded and 'hard done by'. Such perceptions of organisational injustice are not just to do with money and notions of distributional injustice – they could be to do with the culture of the organisation, the ways in which information is disseminated, the allocation of work and perceptions of procedural injustice. Training for part-time staff too is sometimes problematic because their commitments outside work can make attendance at training events difficult.

Shift Work

Shift work is where workers formally replace one another within a 24-hour period. Some organisations operate on a continuous shift system so that the organisation is manned 24-hours a day. The emergency services – police, fire and ambulance – are examples of this. For some heavy manufacturing processes (e.g., foundry work, steel making, etc.), it is efficient for the operators to have the equipment running for sustained periods of time, and shift work enables them to do this. There are a variety of shift work patterns: sometimes employees are contracted to work fixed shifts, yet others may be employed on a rotating shift basis, alternating their work patterns on a weekly or fortnightly basis. For example, the continental shift system is a continuous three-shift system that rotates the times of the hours that employees work, so employees could be required to work for three nights then two mornings then two afternoons. Some organisations operate split-shift systems where shifts are split into different parts to best cover peak periods. This happens, for example, in the passenger transport industry. It is not unknown for changes in shift patterns to be introduced to help avoid redundancy. For example, at the end of 2018, in response to redundancy threats at the Dundee Michelin tyre factory, the Unite union proposed a two-phase plan, combining voluntary redundancy with a move from a five-set shift rotation to four-set shifts in the first year followed by the option of further voluntary redundancies and a move to a three-set shift pattern if more action was required. If employers operate a shift system they have to ensure that it complies with the working time regulations and is applied fairly so that it does not disadvantage particular groups of employees. The London Underground, for example, endeavoured to change the shift patterns of drivers, but it was deemed to have behaved in a discriminatory way because single-parent females were unable to work the new shifts due to their caring responsibilities (*London Underground* v. *Edwards* [1998] IRLR 364, [1999] ICR 494 CA).

News Flash 11.3

Hybrid Working Tops-up Flexible Options

Starting in October 2021, Princes, the UK food and drink manufacturer, launched two new flexible working options for its 500 employees.

- The introduction of new core working hours of 10am to 4pm Mondays to Thursdays and 10am to 3pm on Fridays
- Employees are now able to opt for a hybrid model, working two days remotely and three days in the office.

The initiative, part of the company's Smart Working project, tops-up its already existing flexible working practices, including annualised hours, continental shift patterns (for its manufacturing employees), together with staggered start and finish times, compressed hours, part-time working and job shares.

Source: Wickens, 2021

Flexitime

Flexitime is where individual employees may choose how they arrange the hours that they work. Their contracts of employment dictate the minimum hours they are expected to work but within this they can decide their working pattern. Some workplaces have a system of core hours, when employees are expected to be present, and flexi-hours of which they must work a minimum. Sometimes this involves *time off in lieu*, which is where employees agree with managers to take time off at a mutually agreed time to make up for additional hours that have been worked previously. The system must be managed carefully to ensure that, for example, not everyone takes Monday morning or Friday afternoon off, but employees working under such a system have flexibility to adjust their working hours around outside commitments, such as medical appointments and caring responsibilities. Employers using the system usually discover that their absence and turnover figures go down and productivity rises – as does morale and commitment to the organisation.

Job-sharing

Job-sharing is a system whereby two people with permanent, part-time, positions fill one job, splitting the tasks, responsibilities, hours, remuneration and benefits between them according to how many hours they each work.

There are a variety of ways of job-sharing depending upon the job being shared. Sometimes the job is divided in a way such that each participant has their own tasks and responsibilities, and sometimes, where the two are interchangeable, each picks up where the other has left off. In this latter scenario there is usually a handover period when both parties are at work simultaneously. The communication processes here must be robust. The system works well providing there is sufficient coordination between the two sharers and that the partners are well matched; there are occasionally problems when one partner is suitable for, and receives, promotion while the other does not. The system is common in retailing, teaching, local authorities, and in the utilities as well as being widespread in some professions – doctors and solicitors often finding it a useful way to ensure a healthier work–life balance.

Annualised hours

Annualised hours arrangements are used to achieve a more even match between the work needed and the availability of employees by redistributing the hours worked by staff to coincide with actual levels of organisational need. Where there are obvious peaks and troughs in the demand for labour this makes sense. Employees agree to work for a set number of hours a year arranged to coincide with work requirements. For example, in 2000 the motor company Peugeot UK negotiated an agreement with the manufacturing unions whereby some employees were contracted to work a set number of hours a year (1,666 hours) plus an additional 200 hours to be worked within the year whenever the company required – this cut down the need for overtime payments. In return the company agreed to guarantee the workforce up to 200 hours of full pay should lay-offs occur. Sometimes the arrangements are not so evenly balanced with employees required to work at times convenient for the organisation with little choice around the arrangement of hours. On occasions schemes fail because the hours allowance is unrealistic and is used too quickly at the beginning of the year, leaving the company to either employ additional labour or pay additional overtime.

Compressed Working Week (CWW)

Under a Compressed Working Week system workers cover their normal working hours, but over fewer working days. Sometimes, as with Japanese Microsoft workers, productivity increases under such a system. Proponents of CWW claim employees' work–life balance improves, yet a study in New Zealand found a four-day working week was actually detrimental to the health of those subject to this system; workers becoming stressed when they were unable to fulfil all of their duties in a shorter time frame (Miller, 2022). In June 2022 over 3,000 employees in 70 British organisations began a six-month trial to assess the feasibility of a four-day working week. Depending how it is organised, a CWW can lead to increasing the hours worked during each day, using the time saved to extend the weekend period. Different organisations arrange the working hours in different ways – sometimes the daily increase in hours is slightly less and the additional day-off occurs not weekly but fortnightly – this is sometimes known as a 'nine-day-fortnight' and is not uncommon in local authorities and the NHS.

News Flash 11.4

Iceland: Four-day Work Week Trial a Success

Between 2015 and 2019, Iceland ran two large-scale trials of a shortened four-day working week, with no reduction in pay, for over 2,500 public sector workers. Initiated by the Reykjavik City Council and the Icelandic national government, the project was deemed a success, researchers claiming 'transformative positive effects' benefitting employees and employers. Productivity remained the same or improved across most of the workplaces and worker wellbeing increased, with decreased levels of stress and improved work-life balance.

Between 2019 and 2021 Icelandic unions built on these positive outcomes and negotiated permanent reductions in working hours, with approximately 86% of Iceland's entire working population now either covered by shorter weeks or gaining the right to shorten their working hours.

Source: Haraldsson and Kellam, 2021

Hybrid working/remote working/teleworking

Employees spend all or part of their week working away from the employer's premises, usually from home in hybrid, remote or teleworking work patterns. It requires a degree of trust on the part of the manager who has to accept that an 'out of sight' employee is neither an 'out-of-the-loop' employee nor one that is liable to take advantage of the situation and work less hard or fewer hours. Indeed the reverse is true: there is a danger that employees working from home are likely to be more productive but at risk to their health because they take fewer breaks and do not always use ergonomically acceptable equipment even if they have it. There is some evidence that in the UK, the working day of homeworkers is longer but more broken up than for those who work away from home, with a variety of start times and more frequent and lengthy breaks (Martin, 2021). When the AA introduced homeworking it found that productivity increased significantly – this was partly due to employees putting in excessive hours and not 'switching off' from tasks associated with work. Prior to the Covid pandemic, when homeworking was less prevalent, research in the USA by Elsbach et al. (2010) looking specifically at the physical presence of employees in the workplace concluded that time spent physically at the workplace led to positive perceptions about commitment, loyalty and ability. They suggested that employers 'be particularly aware of the pitfalls of combining such work arrangements with performance evaluations that encourage managers to rely ... in part on passive face time' (2010: 754). It remains to be seen whether the increased prevalence of homeworking and increase in hybrid working will affect perceptions. Good homeworking policies will include information about health and safety and details about how to stay in touch with the workplace.

Zero-hours and key-time contracts

Under this system employees work for only those hours when there is work for them to do. These types of contracts of employment do not specify either the minimum or maximum number of hours that an employee is expected to work. The TUC declares that zero-hours contracts hand the employer total control over their workers' hours and earning power. This means that workers never know how much they will earn each week, and their income is 'subject to the whims of managers' (TUC, 2022). Zero-hours contracts may be exploitative; for example, some fast-food employers at the beginning of this century required their employees to be at work but only paid them for the time they actually spent serving customers. If no customers were served, no work was deemed to have taken place, so no money was paid. These contracts were sometimes used in residential children's homes when care workers were required to sleep at work, but only paid for any time spent attending to wakeful children. If none of the children woke up, no pay was forthcoming. Zero-hour contract work has increased and data from the Office of National Statistics shows that over one million workers are now on zero-hours contracts (ONS, 2022). In its 2022 analysis of the ONS data, the TUC suggest that zero-hours contract work 'tightens grip of structural racism' on the UK labour market and deepens gender inequalities. Its analysis reveals black, minority and women are twice as likely to be on zero-hours contracts as white men (4.7% compared to 2.4%). White women are more likely than white men to be on zero-hours contracts (3.6% compared to 2.4%). Overall, BAME workers are significantly overrepresented on zero-hours contracts compared to white workers (4.3% compared to 3%).

News Flash 11.5

Zero-hours Contracts

Working flexibly sometimes means working for several employers at different times. The CIPD has pointed out that although employees on zero-hours contracts have the explicit right not to be sacked if they work for someone else in their spare time, some zero-hours contracts *require individuals to be* available for work when it is offered. This provision goes against the spirit of the legislation as it could prevent someone on a zero-hours contract from working for another employer. In other words, by keeping themselves available, even though there is no guarantee of work, zero-hours employees could be discouraged or prevented from accepting other work.

Source: CIPD, 2021: 17

Voluntary reduced work time

Some employees find that it is practical for them to reduce their working hours. Some organisations are happy for this to occur, although, as with other working patterns, the decisions as to who is and who is not allowed to reduce their hours should not be arbitrary and there should be consistency across the organisation. It is good practice to allow those employees on reduced hours the opportunity to revert to full-time work if requested. When hours are reduced it is usual for remuneration and benefits to be reduced pro-rata at the same time.

Term-time working

Term-time working is when a person is on a full contract but has unpaid leave of absence during the school holidays. Many retail establishments use this, replacing employees who have taken unpaid time-off to be with school-aged children with students who want to work at holiday times.

Sabbaticals

Some organisations, notably academic ones, reward their staff by allowing them to take a break from their day-to-day duties and instead devote paid time-off to study or research to enhance their professional development. Some larger consultancies, such as PriceWaterhouseCoopers, encourage staff to take sabbaticals to help them recharge their batteries, update their learning and increase the organisational knowledge pool. Other organisations grant extended periods of leave, calling such breaks 'sabbaticals' even though there is no requirement to link activities during such breaks to work-related issues.

Organisations offering such 'perks' should ensure that the processes are transparent and seen to be fair. Where the allocation is linked to length of service, it should not indirectly discriminate against women who have taken time out away from the workforce, nor should it contravene age discrimination legislation. Organisations must ensure that there is consistency in the way sabbaticals are allocated – if this is not apparent the employment relationship between the organisation and those *not* receiving sabbaticals will suffer, particularly if these employees have to 'cover' for their absent colleagues. The processes have to ensure fairness to those on sabbatical and to those remaining behind. Some policies, although they may not specify what is to be undertaken when on sabbatical, do specify what is *not* to be done; the policy at the *Guardian* newspaper, for example, specifically excludes those on sabbatical from undertaking paid work for other organisations.

Outsourced labour

There will be occasions when an organisation will find it expedient *not* to use its own employees but to contract an external person or organisation to do the work instead. This often will cover things such as building work, security services, IT back up, cleaning and maintenance. Such a solution may be used to cover a period of staff shortages, when the work is of a short-term nature only, or when specific skills not generally available to the employer are required. Sometimes where these tasks are usually undertaken 'in-house', there may be potential employee relations problems. Occasionally agency staff work alongside permanent employees, each doing the same work but for different rates of pay. This occurs in the NHS, where agency nurses, on a different rate of pay, work alongside those directly employed by an NHS trust. In the car industry, for example, employees on the production line sometimes work alongside those who have been brought in from the outside for a specific period of time. When their terms and conditions differ significantly it causes problems, particularly when the 'external' workers are not members of the recognised unions and not subject either to the collective agreements or union discipline. Where, to save costs, organisations outsource functions or departments that were previously undertaken in house, this may have a detrimental impact on the employment relationship, particularly where it has resulted in redundancies and/or the newly outsourced workforce receives lower remuneration than the previous job incumbents.

Exercise 11.4

Read Case Study 11.1 about Lou's Electrical Repairs and answer the following questions:

- What do you think Lou will discover when he returns from France about the need for labour flexibility in his establishments?
- What recommendations would you make regarding the use of people resources at Lou's? What was the academic justification behind your answer?
- What are the implications of your recommendations for the employment relationship for the staff in all of Lou's establishments? If the recommendations are not implemented and things remain the same, describe the state of the psychological contract.

Case Study 11.1

Lou's Headache: Lou's Electrical Repairs

Background

Lou's Electrical Repairs is a repair company dealing, in the main, with audio visual equipment, mostly television and some white goods. It has one repair workshop, and a retail outlet used both by customers needing repairs and those wanting to purchase secondhand goods and basic electrical equipment. Recently Lou, the owner, has set up 'Lou@yourservice.com' – this is an emergency repairs service employing four electricians who make home visits to diagnose faults and repair goods. These four are served by an office manager and a couple of administrators who operate from an office over a local garage. When the electricians need parts and equipment they get them from the workshop storeroom at cost price. Historically the workshop, the retail outlet and now Lou@yourservice.com have all operated autonomously, each as a separate cost centre, each making independent decisions and each reporting separately to Lou, who now lives abroad for nine months of the year.

Retail outlet

The success of this outlet has been based on good friendly and informed service coupled with operating atypical hours to serve its loyal customer base. Traditionally opening from 9 a.m. to 8 p.m. Tuesday to Saturday and on a Sunday until 5 p.m., the shop has maintained a steady growth in the sale of secondhand goods, although recently the repair workshops have expressed fears that sales may have been at the expense of referring repairs to the workshop. The eight sales staff receive a basic salary and 0.1% commission for each £250 taken in sales. The busiest times are between midday and 2 p.m., after 4 p.m. on weekdays and Sunday morning. Two of the sales staff are women who work each morning from 9 a.m. until 1 p.m.; the other six of the sales staff work full-time from 1 p.m. until 8 p.m. each day apart from Sunday when they work from 11 a.m. until 5 p.m.. These are all men, one of whom also acts as store manager and is responsible for the day-to-day running of the shop. Increasingly, although he is supposed to leave at 8 p.m. with the others, he is finding that he finally locks up at around 9.30 p.m. during the week and 8 p.m. on Sunday.

Recently there has been a degree of confusion as staff have begun to informally swap hours in order to accommodate out-of-work commitments. This has caused problems when allocating the commission payments and highlighted the fact that those who work in the mornings have fewer opportunities for increasing their take-home pay.

Workshop

The workshop is open from Monday to Friday, from 8 a.m. until 6 p.m.. When their goods need servicing customers either take them to the shop or bring them to the workshop. Those taken to the retail outlet are collected each evening by the foreman, Joe, and the goods are then repaired over the next few days. Objects for repair that are taken to the retail outlet on a Sunday are not picked up until the following Tuesday, while the items that the customers bring in for repair are checked in at the workshop reception and are dealt with in order of arrival. The reception desk is run by a female (pregnant) receptionist who is also responsible for ordering parts, maintaining stock levels and ringing customers for authorisation if the cost of repair exceeds an agreed amount. If she is away from the desk the customer must wait. At check-in the receptionist confirms details and gives a general estimate of the time the repair may take. This is sometimes time consuming as people would often like to drop the item and arrange then and there when they can pick it up. The receptionist with only a vague idea of how long each repair might take is generous when giving an 'expected ready by' date. This sometimes causes problems as the customers try to negotiate earlier pick-up times. Around 65% of customers bring in their repairs before 10 a.m. The receptionist is also responsible for collecting payment for the repairs and returning the goods to the customers. These early customers also prefer to pick up their repaired goods first thing in the morning.

The ten repair staff (seven men and three women) are full-time, and paid at an hourly rate of £11.50 - they all start at 8 a.m. and put in overtime until 6 p.m. as it is expected. The foreman, Joe, works longer hours but does not like to claim payment for this as he feels he should be able to do the job in his allotted hours.

Lou@yourservice.com

About two-thirds of the bookings are taken by telephone; the rest are electronic requests. All calls are taken by one of the two part-time assistants. One assistant works four hours in the morning (8 a.m.-12 noon), the other works four hours in the afternoon (2.30-6.30 p.m.). The office manager covers for the lunch-time period and at other times when the incoming requests for help are peaking. Phone calls take priority: all e-mail requests for help are logged and dealt with when the phones are quiet. As business increases, it is becoming difficult for the electricians to respond to calls in an efficient way - sometimes they are sent from one end of town to the other several times in a day. The lack of systematic planning and the time wasted in travelling from one job to another is beginning to erode their trust in the office staff. They have taken to calling one another on their mobile phones, comparing notes and rearranging the jobs depending on the geographical areas that they are in. On occasions this has led to customers being left without a visit or the electricians calling at houses when no one is at home. When customers subsequently ring to complain the office staff become confused because, as far as they are concerned, the jobs have been allocated and should have been completed. When there is a glut of calls or emails the staff are expected to work additional hours. As the repair electricians rearrange the schedules, such requests are becoming more frequent. The office manager is finding that he is starting work earlier and earlier and leaving later and later. This is becoming a problem as his wife, recently diagnosed with heart problems, has to rest a lot and he is often left to make sure the children get off to school on time and to cook for them in the evening.

Recently Lou received a number of letters of complaint about late repairs. When he rang both the shop and workshop he found, to his annoyance, that it was impossible not to speak to 'voice mail' - similarly his email request for a chat remained unanswered. Irritated, he has returned from France to discover at first-hand what is going on.

Flexibility: Gender and Family-friendly Practices

'First comes love, then comes marriage, then come flex-time and a baby carriage' (Wilson, 2010). This ditty, submitted as part of the evidence in an American legal case against Novartis, was allegedly said by a supervisor to justify his reluctance to employ young women. It epitomises the attitude of many employers who, when faced with the opportunity to employ women with caring responsibilities, would prefer not to do so as it could lead to requests to work non-standard hours. High income, union presence and being a woman are all linked with better access to arrangements for flexible work (Wels, 2021) although, for women, much of the flexibility arises from part-time opportunities. Although flexible work practices improve the opportunities for women joining the workforce (and staying economically productive) following childbirth (Chung and Van der Horst, 2018) there is an under-utilisation of flexible-work policies, particularly at managerial level. Ambivalent or negative national and/or workplace cultures, including different degrees of, 'management support, organisational time expectations, career consequences, gendered perceptions of policy use and co-worker support' (McDonald et al., 2007: 603) all discourage workforce participation. Even when legislation promotes flexible working to enable greater female participation in paid work, the reality may be different. For example, in Japan, where the economic growth rate is falling in line with the aging population, women have been encouraged to enter the labour market (Steinberg and Nakane, 2012). Consequently, since the end of the last century, the Japanese government has targeted women, changing the Labour Standards Law to promote 'discretionary' or flexible work, enabling employees to choose the arrangement of the hours that they work. Despite this encouragement, the uptake of such discretionary working is not widespread, and rigid corporate structures discourage the take-up of alternative flexible-work patterns (Kingston, 2013: 191; Berg et al., 2004).

Individual employees use a number of different strategies in order to ensure that work does not conflict with the amount of time required for their other activities. Women, rather than men, are more often responsible for housework and childcare (Van der Lippe et al. 2018), they are more likely to experience work/family conflict, even if women choose to work from home (Van der Lippe et al., 2018). Where families or couples are involved this often necessitates one partner withdrawing from the labour force (or working reduced hours); however, such strategies often reinforce gender inequality because it is women who are more likely to reduce work hours or leave paid employment altogether (Kelly et al., 2011; Moen and Huang, 2010).

UK employees have the right to request flexible working and can request changes to the hours they work, the times at which they work and the place at which they work. (This right of course may not alter the ways either employees or employers behave because employees might be unaware of their rights and, where requests are made, flexibility might be declined.) A number of studies have looked at whether or not practices promoting a healthier work–life balance are linked to higher levels of efficiency and productivity. Clarke and Holdsworth (2017: 2) found that flexible workers actively 'craft' their work environments to improve their own efficiency (and also the effectiveness of their colleagues) and were more focused in their work effort. In their study of an Italian workplace Angelici and Profeta (2020) found evidence that flexibility around time and place of work increased the productivity of workers, improving their wellbeing and work–life balance. Sometimes productivity increases not because of a healthier work–life balance but because the employee is so grateful for the flexibility that they over-compensate by putting in additional working hours (Lott, 2018). In contrast men opting for flexible working for family reasons are more likely to be lauded for their 'sacrifice' than their female counterparts (Munsch, 2016: Gerstel and Clawson, 2018).

Table 11.1   Reasons for not wanting a full-time job

Reasons	United Kingdom, Jan-Dec 2018			
	Male		Female	
	population	percentage	population	percentage
Insufficient child-care facilities	3,000	1.6	84,000	5.9
Earn enough part-time	34,000	20.2	156,000	10.8
Another reason	43,000	25.4	197,000	13.7
Financially secure - work because want to	53,000	31.6	215,000	14.9
Domestic commitments prevent full-time	9,000	5.4	229,000	15.9
Want to spend more time with family	27,000	15.9	558,000	38.8

Source: Office for National Statistics (2019) - Annual Population Survey

Masuda et al. (2012) point out that managers with access to flexible work arrangements are more satisfied with their jobs, more likely to remain with their organisation and less prone to experiencing work family conflict, i.e., they have a healthy work–life balance. Data about working time patterns from Eurofound's fifth European Working Conditions Survey (EWCS) (based on interviews with more than 38,000 respondents in 34 countries) found that 'around 80% of EWCS respondents report that their working time fits well or very well with their family or other social commitments outside work' (Eurofound, 2012: 2).

Employees, whether they are working in standard or non-standard ways, should be treated in fair, consistent and ethical ways by their employers. Crucially the unhealthy nature of an imbalanced work–life culture falls under the health and safety umbrella. Long hours, stressed employees coping with commitments outside work that clash with those inside work, are detrimental to the employment relationship, the psychological contract and levels of trust.

Flexibility: Power, Conflict and Trust

Employees who have the ability to alter their work schedules to suit their individual preferences are said to have a higher degree of *control* over their circumstances than is denied to those individuals whose employers may unilaterally change their hours and place of work (Berg et al., 2004). Employees who have a large degree of autonomy over their own working periods, pace and place, allowing them greater degrees of personal control, exhibit lower levels of conflict between work and outside commitments; such a delegation of power from the employer, ceding control to the individual employee, has a direct and positive impact on the employment relationship, levels of workplace commitment and intention to remain with an organisation (Kelly et al., 2011; Richman et al., 2008).

Not all managers, however, approve of flexible working practices. In the UK there is an undercurrent of disapproval that surrounds flexible working. Around half (48%) of the 1,026 managers surveyed by the Institute of Leadership and Management in 2012 said that some flexible work arrangements caused resentment within teams; 15% of the manager respondents said they personally felt resentment towards colleagues working flexibly; and one-third (31%) reported hearing colleagues make disparaging remarks about those working flexibly (ILM, 2013). In such situations employees requesting more flexibility in their working hours, or place of work, can be regarded as unnecessarily bothersome by their employers – if only because the administrative burden of who is doing what, when and where can be quite daunting for a company used to everyone working homogenously. Previously mentioned research findings by both Leslie and Putman are both relevant here (Leslie et al., 2012; Putman et al., 2013).

Perceptions of injustice are sometimes created where an organisation purports to offer flexible working but imposes barriers to its adoption by perhaps 'keeping quiet' about its availability or ensuring that the practicality of the offer is unsuitable for those seeking to adopt a flexible work pattern. The ILM survey mentioned above found one-third of managers said that despite their organisation having flexible work policies in place it was not fully embraced at organisational level. Interestingly one-third of the managers surveyed said they would like to work flexibly but felt too inhibited to request it.

In such circumstances the reality of the workplace for employees fails to match with the rhetoric of the organisation, damaging the psychological contract. Employees denied flexibility show decreased levels of motivation which may lead to higher levels of absenteeism and an increase in labour turnover. In such an environment, where the *reality* of the employment relationship is at odds with the claims of the employer, it fosters a lack of trust (see Tzafrir and Dolan's 2004 components of trust, discussed in Chapter 3).

Similarly, levels of distrust and damaged psychological contracts may be in evidence where employers manage in a hard way and alter the times and ways that staff are deployed. The act of unilaterally deploying staff flexibly, according to the changing needs of the organisation, may leave employers open to the accusation of abusing their power and breaching the employment contracts of those concerned – for employees being asked to fit in with the peaks and troughs of business, for example, can disrupt carefully constructed timetables facilitating alternative care for those with childcare/domestic responsibilities.

The perception of employer-initiated flexibility and its implications for the working lives of employees can be sufficient to disrupt smooth employee relations. For example, in July 2003 British Airways ground staff, based at Heathrow, caused an enormous amount of disruption to the company, and its flying customers, when they took part in a two-day unofficial strike triggered by the simultaneous introduction of electronic swipe cards with changes in working practices. The cards, designed to register the times employees began and finished work, were perceived as a threat, the strikers believing that their introduction would permit the collection of electronic data that would provide information that could subsequently be used to impose a flexible regime – with working patterns requiring employees to work when it was busy and be sent home when it was not. The implications for carers who needed regular hours were sufficient to trigger a strike.

Some companies are attempting to address the work–life imbalance particularly as there is evidence that long working hours are detrimental to health, and a joint World Health Organisation and ILO study (2021) covering 194 countries showed that, in 2016, working long hours contributed to 745,000 deaths from stroke and heart disease. Health problems, such as heart disease linked to long hours, have caused companies, such as LinkedIn, Mozilla and Bumble specifically to introduce additional weeks of holiday, where the whole company shuts down, as part of their duty of care to employees. In 2002 the construction company Heery International evolved a two-pronged approach to tackling long hours. Where on occasions it had to cancel employee holidays, it offered staff double the missed days off in lieu. Coupled with this it introduced a flexi-card scheme where each employee receives three cards a year each entitling them to take three hours off work at short notice.

Exercise 11.5

- Within Heery International, what impact do you think cancelling an employee's holiday will have on both the employment relationship and the psychological contract of each of the following:
  - the manager who has to do the cancelling
  - the employees who have their holidays cancelled
  - the rest of the workforce who witness it happening?
- How effective do you think the three-card system is for those employees with caring responsibilities?
- Critically analyse the situation at Heery International by using information that you gleaned about fairness and trust in Chapter 3.

Flexibility in the workplace may, therefore, be contentious. Some employees may regard the ways in which managers choose to deploy available labour, together with employee work patterns that are flexible rather than fixed, with suspicion. Furthermore if unwelcome flexibility is imposed on employees or given to some but not all, it may be perceived as unfair or unjust. Similarly when flexibility is denied it may result in higher levels of absence and lowered morale. Hughes and Bozionelos (2007) found this to be the case when they examined the attitudes of male bus drivers, and Dousin et al. (2021) suggest, from their study of Malaysian nurses, that introducing flexible work practices might reduce labour turnover.

Two recent events – the Covid 19 pandemic and the Ukraine–Russian war – have impacted the take up of flexible work patterns. During the pandemic more people worked from home, helping to detoxify any impression that this pattern of working was inefficient and impractical. Post pandemic, the experience increased the demand for a number of different non-traditional working patterns that is unlikely to diminish. For those organisations not granting such demands it is likely that perceptions of injustice and higher labour turnover will result. The increased cost of fuel and energy, arising from the war, raised the cost of travel, making working from home more desirable and increasing the demand for remote work. It is likely that many employers acceding to these demands will then be asked to contribute toward rising domestic fuel bills, and again, where such requests are denied, or only partially met, this too is likely to increase perceptions of injustice and intentions to leave.

Flexibility: Points to Consider for Maintaining an Harmonious Employment Relationship

- *Introducing flexible working.* This process, particularly in the initial stages, can be fraught with difficulties as suspicion of change, together with the perceptions of the parties involved, may precipitate conflict, mistrust and low morale.
- *Negotiating flexibility.* Whether with individuals or with representatives this can be time-consuming and, if not handled with an awareness of the holistic picture of the organisation, could lead to discrepancies in approach and outcome.
- *Consistency of approach.* When different groups are treated in different ways it can lead to indirect/direct discrimination. If this is serious it could result in one or more of the following:
  - industrial action
  - a rise in the number of grievances brought against the organisation
  - discrimination claims brought before tribunals
  - requests for union recognition.

  Groups of employees without regular domestic commitments may regard the flexible opportunities offered to, and taken up by, others unfair. This perception could lead to higher absence levels, lower productivity and higher turnover figures.

- *Communications.* Managers must ensure that those workers who are not in constant attendance at the main workplace are kept informed about issues on a regular basis.

  It is very easy to leave certain groups out of the communication loops; for example, team briefings should not always be held on the same day of the week if some employees never attend work on that day.

  Gossip and rumour management is essential. Transparency of treatment and openness about different working patterns prevents resentment building up against those who often work remotely or work non-standard hours.

- *Fairness of treatment between groups.* Care should be taken with the way in which groups outside the core are treated. Such groups of peripheral workers may receive less or no training, be excluded from communication loops, have lower commitment, morale and productivity because of their position in the hierarchy.

  Perceptions of fairness and equity are important; individuals will compare their own positions with that of others, and if they distinguish levels of treatment that they find unwarranted or unfair this will have a direct impact on the employee relations within the workplace. The results of this could lead to higher levels of conflict, less cooperation and a lack of commitment.

- *Mis-matched value systems.* Workers who are not part of the core of the organisation may hold values and beliefs that are incompatible with that of the main employer. This can be awkward if, for example, those not indigenous to the organisation behave in unacceptable ways (e.g., racist or bullying behaviour).

All of these bulleted points have an impact on the psychological contract and on the perceptions of fairness experienced by employees. It is therefore crucial to have sufficient transparency around flexible work processes and equity between the ways in which flexible work is communicated about – and subsequently allocated to individuals – in order to avoid increased levels of workplace conflict.

Summary

This chapter explored the different ways in which flexibility is used in the workplace and the impact that it might have on the morale, productivity, health and wellbeing of those subject to its regimes. The ways in which flexibility is introduced are important and will have a direct influence on employees' perceptions of organisational justice, particularly procedural justice (concerning how it is done), distributional justice (how the work is allocated, who is allowed flexibility, etc.) and informational justice. Where flexibility is mishandled or dealt with in an inconsistent way there is a greater potential for gendered imbalances, conflict and lack of trust.

Review Questions

1   Read the following quote from Berg et al. and discuss, using academic justification, whether or not there can ever be a balance between the needs of the employer and employee where the control of working time is central to an outcome.

Convenient flexibility for the employer may not be in the interest of the employee, and schedules that allow workers to respond to personal or family matters on short notice can cause significant organisational problems for firms. The extent to which the interests of either group are served by these arrangements is determined largely by the degree to which employees or employers have control over their working time. The ultimate goal of policy in this area is to find flexibility arrangements with some form of shared control that serve the interests of both groups or that at least promote the interests of one without harming those of the other. (2004: 333)

2   What happens when different groups requesting flexibility are treated in different ways - can this lead to indirect/direct discrimination? Give examples.

3   Do peripheral workers have lower commitment, morale and productivity because of their position in the hierarchy? Justify your answer.

4   Is work-life balance just trendy rhetoric? Does one have to become a peripheral worker to achieve it? Why did you say this?

5   How does flexibility impact on the psychological contract?

6   How does the introduction of hybrid working have an impact on the ways in which employees perceive justice?

Revision Exercise 11.1

The following scenario with its associated questions is designed to help you apply the knowledge of flexible working that you have gained from reading this chapter. If you answer all of the questions you should gain some insight around the pros and cons of flexible working from the standpoint of both the employer and the employee and an awareness of the difficulties surrounding the introduction of flexible work.

Cutting the Coat According to the Cloth!

Costas Botzia and his partner Phytos Annand have run a small clothing company, C&P, for the last 30 years. Based in an industrial area of a large city, they employ 267 full-time women to cut, sew and dispatch garments to the retail trade. A further 60 people do the same type of work but on a part-time basis. A team of 26 undertakes the additional work of designing, marketing and selling the goods, and of course managing the business above line-manager level. There is a security staff of ten, all male, who work a continuous shift system. Not many of the employees have been with the company for more than a few years. A typical employee profile would be to begin as a school leaver, stay a few years and then leave to start a family (many of these would like to continue with the company; however, the opportunities for part-time work that is compatible with their domestic commitments are rare). The age profile of the workforce ranges from 17 to 56, with a concentration at either end of the spectrum; all live within a four-mile radius of the workplace, although on occasions, when traffic is heavy, this distance seems greater.

When Costas and Phytos started the company they endeavoured to ensure its success by aggressive pricing, competitive 'low' wages and, on occasions, buying up rival companies. One of these companies recognised the National Union of Tailors and Garment Workers (part of the GMB since 1991), and the two partners continued to negotiate with the national officials of the union because, if truth be told, they found it easier dealing with the union officials, who, unlike their members, not only knew the law better than the partners, but were sensitive to market conditions and the company position. In private the partners expressed a preference for coping with employee relations in this way – it was undoubtedly less hassle than dealing with a series of individual employees, some of whom, they felt, could possibly be litigious, and each, certainly, would have their own unique, possibly inflated, perceptions both of what the company could afford and of their own worth.

In recent months, the company has been hit by falling demand – possibly due to a flood of cheaper imported fashion goods from the Baltic countries, increased costs for wages, petrol and pension contributions to name but a few. A series of exploratory talks between the union and the partners have begun. These have been quite wide-ranging, looking at a number of different areas such as cost cutting, labour redeployment, outsourcing and the potential for altering workflows and processes.

Today the group is meeting to discuss the possible impact that flexible work could have on the situation. Present at the meeting are Costas and Phytos, the chief operations manager Barry, a national union official Pete, and two lay representatives Deirdre and Ted.

Questions

Think about how you would construct robust arguments for the following scenarios between the senior partners and the union representatives.

1   Union representatives putting the case for flexible work to a sympathetic management.
2   Union representatives putting the case for flexible work to an unsympathetic management.
3   Management putting forward the case for flexible work to a sympathetic union side.
4   Management putting forward the case for flexible work to an unsympathetic and suspicious union side.

If you are working in a group, each of these scenarios may be undertaken as separate role plays.

Revision Exercise 11.2

Requests for Flexible Working

Imagine you are the HR Manager, Sabreen Awan, in a long-established medium-sized toy manufacturing company based on three separate sites in the Northeast of England. You have received the following memo from one of the site managers, Cillian O'Sullivan, and after considering the relevant legal and practical implications behind the requests you need to compose an appropriate reply, one that addresses all of the issues he raises. What would you say?

To: HR Manager, Sabreen Awan

From: South Site Director, Cillian O'Sullivan

Reference: 243COSFlex

_____

Message

Dear Sabreen

I have had requests regarding flexible working from a few of my admin/clerical staff and I have agreed to them all, even though it was a bit inconvenient and some staff are grumbling that it has left them working additional hours to make up work for their newly flexible colleagues. My problem is that some of the factory hands are now requesting the same flexibility and, as they are already working shifts on the production line, this is causing me a headache. One, in particular, is asthmatic and reacts badly to some of the production processes, but, as he needs the money, refuses to switch to a different section of the plant.

I would be very grateful for your suggestions, and sooner rather than later as the unrest is spreading.

Best wishes

Cillian

Relevant Articles for Further Reading

Choudhury, P., Foroughi, C. and Larson, B. (2021) 'Work-from-anywhere: The productivity effects of geographic flexibility', *Strategic Management Journal*, 42(4): 655–83.

Investigating American employees who switched from a working-from-home scheme to a work-from-anywhere programme (that is, one that offered employees *both* temporal and geographic flexibility), the authors show that the change resulted in a 4.4% increase in output.

Klindzic, M. and Marić, M. (2019) 'Flexible work arrangements and organizational performance: The difference between employee and employer-driven practices', *DruštvenaIstraživanja/Journal for General Social Issues*, 28(1): 89–108.

Looking at Croatian companies, the paper examines the differences between employer and employee led flexible working practices. The findings show that performance was higher in the employee-driven rather than the employer-led arrangements of flexible work practices.

Ryan, L. and Wallace, J. (2019) 'Mutual gains success and failure: Two case studies of annual hours in Ireland', *The Irish Journal of Management*, 38(1): 26-37.

Examining the introduction of annualized hours in two different Irish companies, the article shows the reasons behind the failure of one scheme and the success of the other.

References

Angelici, M. and Profeta, P. (2020) *Smart-working: Work Flexibility Without Constraints*, CESifo Working Paper No. 8165. Available at: https://ssrn.com/abstract=3556304 or http://dx.doi.org/10.2139/ssrn.3556304 (accessed 23 March 2022).

Atkinson J. and Meagre, N. (1986) *New Forms of Work Organisation*, IMS Report 121. Brighton: IMS.

Australian Government (2021) *Working From Home*, Research paper, Productivity Commission, Australia.

Bainbridge, H. T. and Townsend, K. (2020) 'The effects of offering flexible work practices to employees with unpaid caregiving responsibilities for elderly or disabled family members', *Human Resource Management*, 59(5): 483–95.

Berg, P., Appelbaum, E., Bailey, T. and Kalleberg, A. L. (2004) 'Contesting time: International comparison of employee control of working time', *Industrial and Labor Relations Review*, 57(3): 331–49.

Berg, P., Kossek, E. E., Misra, K. and Belman, D. (2014) 'Work–life flexibility policies: Do unions affect employee access and use?', *Industrial and Labor Relations Review*, 67: 111–37.

Bingham, C. (ed.) (2001) *Flexible Work Patterns*, Managing Best Practice No. 85. London: The Industrial Society.

Bingham, C., Michielsens, E. and Clarke, L. (2014) 'Managing diversity through flexible-work arrangements: Management perspectives', *Employee Relations*, 36(1): 49–69.

Brand, A. (2022) 'Covid-19 2 years in, a statistical breakdown', *HR Review*, 23 March. Available at: www.hrreview.co.uk/hpm/covid-19/covid-19-two-years-on-a-statistical-breakdown/141208?utm_source=rss&utm_medium=rss&utm_campaign=covid-19-two-years-on-a-statistical-breakdown&gator_td=%2fB70E15Me0NuCr%2fqvXnN%2fKrNDk1K4%2fQvfKbHuQPgxJAPl3ZiMP7F68z1zzJmV8U7DKC8hMN7mvQ3Ui8X63LFKiWknxqBa%2bCrEe1RjiKnqgWoMLGsPqu6r2QOM8Dzd8WewWk3GTZkjSwjar801Rr4ECFedJm5%2bJn7Fbip3YeZLWf4k3KYsQsEykSIZoE4SHrzbgwytdjGpeTPhmAXEOFgQOdxKM3hOKawbe%2bu3nrJge0%3d, (accessed 23 March 2022).

Branham, J. (1989) *Human Resource Planning*. London: Institute of Personnel Management.

Breslow, L. and Buell, P. (1960) 'Mortality from coronary heart disease and physical activity of work', *California Journal of Chronic Diseases*, 11: 615–25.

Brooks, I. (1997) 'The lights are bright? Debating the future of the permanent night shift', *Journal of Management Medicine*, 11(2): 58–70.

Budd, J. W. (2004) *Employment with a Human Face: Balancing Efficiency, Equity, and Voice*. Ithaca, NY: Cornell University Press.

Budd, J. W. (2010) 'Theorizing work: The importance of conceptualizations of work for research and practice', presentation at the 25th Cardiff Employment Research Unit Annual Conference, Cardiff Business School, 13–14 September. Available at: www.legacy-irc.csom.umn.edu/faculty/jbudd/research/cardiff2010.pdf (accessed 24 February 2013).

Chartered Institute of Personnel and Development (CIPD) (2020) *Embedding New Ways of Working Post-Pandemic*. Available at: www.cipd.co.uk/knowledge/work/trends/working-post-pandemic (accessed 23 August 2022).

Chartered Institute of Personnel and Development (CIPD) (2021) *Zero-hours Contracts: Understanding the Law, Guide 2021*. Available at: www.cipd.co.uk/Images/zero-hours-contracts-guide-web-2021_tcm18-10706.pdf (accessed 21 March 2022).

Choudhury, P., Foroughi, C. and Larson, B. (2021) 'Work-from-anywhere: The productivity effects of geographic flexibility', *Strategic Management Journal*, 42(4): 655–83.

Chung, H. and Van der Horst, M. (2018) 'Women's employment patterns after childbirth and the perceived access to and use of flexitime and teleworking', *Human Relations*, 71(1): 47–72.

Clarke, S. and Holdsworth, L. (2017) 'Flexibility in the workplace: Implications of flexible work arrangements for individuals, teams and organizations', *Business and Management*. Available at: file:///D:/Users/Admin/Downloads/flexibility-in-the-workplace-implications-of-flexible-work-arrangements-for-individuals-teams-and-organisations.pdf (accessed 26 March 2022).

Collins, C., Landivar, L. C., Ruppanner, L. and Scarborough, W. J. (2021) 'COVID-19 and the gender gap in work hours', *Gender, Work & Organization*, 28: 101–12.

Court of Justice of the European Union (14 May 2019), *Member States Must Require Employers to Set up a System Enabling the Duration of Daily Working Time to be Measured*, press release No. 61/19, 14 May. Available at: https://curia.europa.eu/jcms/upload/docs/application/pdf/2019-05/cp190061en.pdf (accessed 23 March 2022).

Demir, A., Ulusoy, M. and Ulusoy, M. F. (2003) 'Investigation of factors influencing burnout levels in professional and private lives of nurses', *International Journal of Nursing Studies*, 40: 807–27.

Dousin, O., Collins, N., Bartram, T. and Stanton, P. (2021) 'The relationship between work–life balance, the need for achievement, and intention to leave: Mixed-method study', *Journal of Advanced Nursing*, 77(3): 1478–89.

Elsbach, K. D., Cable, D. M. and Sherman, J. W. (2010) 'How passive "face time" affects perceptions of employees: Evidence of spontaneous trait inference', *Human Relations*, 63(6): 735–60.

ETUI (2016) *Worker-Participation EU*. Available at: www.worker-participation.eu/National-Industrial-Relations/Countries/Sweden/Trade-Unions (accessed 2 June 2022).

Eurofound (2012) *Working Time and Work–Life Balance in a Life Course Perspective*. Dublin: Eurofound.

Eurofound (2020) *Telework and ICT-based Mobile Work: Flexible Working in the Digital Age, New forms of employment series*. Luxembourg: Publications Office of the European Union.

Gash, V. (2008) 'Preference or constraint? Part-time worker's transitions in Denmark, France and the United Kingdom', *Work, Employment and Society*, 22(4): 655–7.

Gerstel, N. and Clawson, D. (2018) 'Control over time: Employers, workers, and families shaping work schedules', *Annual Review of Sociology*, 44: 77–97.

Galanti, G., Guidetti, G., Mazzei, E., Zappala, S., & Toscano, F. (2021). Work From Home During the Covid-19 Outbreak: The Impact on Employees' Remote Work Productivity, Engagement, and Stresse. *Journal of Occupational and Environmental Medicine*, Vol. 63, No. 7.

Gurkov, I., Zelenova, O. and Saidov, Z. (2012) 'Mutation of HRM practices in Russia: An application of CRANET methodology', *The International Journal of Human Resource Management*, 23(7): 1289–1302.

Haraldsson, G. and Kellam, J. (2021) *Going Public: Iceland's Journey to a Shorter Working Week*. Available at: autonomy.work/wp-content/uploads/2021/06/ICELAND_4DW.pdf (accessed 23 March 2022).

Hughes, J. and Bozionelos, N. (2007) 'Work–life balance as source of job dissatisfaction and withdrawal attitudes: An exploratory study on the views of male workers', *Personnel Review*, 36(1): 145–54.

Institute of Leadership & Management (2013) *Flexible Working: Goodbye Nine to Five*. London: ILM.

Johnstone, S. (2019) 'Employment practices, labour flexibility and the Great Recession: An automotive case study', *Economic and Industrial Democracy*, 40(3): 537–59.

Kelliher, C. and Anderson, D. (2010) 'Doing more with less? Flexible working practices and the intensification of work', *Human Relations*, 63(1): 83–106.

Kelly, E. L. and Moen, P. (2007) 'Rethinking the clockwork or work: Why schedule and control may pay off at work and at home', *Advances in Developing Human Resources*, 9(4): 487–506.

Kelly, E. L., Moen, P. and Tranby, E. (2011) 'Changing workplaces to reduce work–family conflict schedule control in a white-collar organization', *American Sociological Review*, 76(2): 265–90.

Kingston, J. (2013) 'Demographic dilemmas, women and immigration', in J. Kingston (ed.), *Critical Issues in Contemporary Japan*. London: Routledge, pp. 189–200.

Klindzic, M. and Marić, M. (2019) 'Flexible work arrangements and organizational performance: The difference between employee and employer-driven practices', *DruštvenaIstraživanja/Journal for General Social Issues*, 28(1): 89–108.

Kossek, E. E. and Lautsch, B. A. (2018) 'Work–life flexibility for whom? Occupational status and work–life inequality in upper, middle, and lower-level jobs', *Academy of Management Annals*, 12(1): 5–36.

Leslie, L. M., Park, T. Y. and Mehng, S. A. (2012) 'Flexible work practices: A source of career premiums or penalties?', *Academy of Management Journal*, 55(6): 1407–28.

Logan, G. (2009) 'Jobs saved at Jaguar Landrover as staff agree pay freeze and short week', *Personnel Today*, 5 March. Available at: www.personneltoday.com/hr/jobs-saved-at-jaguar-land-rover-as-staff-agree-pay-freeze-and-short-week/ (accessed 6 November 2015).

Lott, Y. (2018) 'Does flexibility help employees switch off from work? Flexible working-time arrangements and cognitive work-to-home spillover for women and men in Germany', *Social Indicators Research*, 151(2): 471–94.

Martin, J. (2021) *Homeworking Hours, Rewards and Opportunities in the UK: 2011 to 2020, Office of National Statistics*. Available at: www.ons.gov.uk/releases/homeworkingintheukhoursopportunitiesandrewards (accessed 24 March 2022).

Masuda, A.D., Poelmans, S.A., Allen, T.D. et al. (2012) 'Flexible work arrangements availability and their relationship with work-to-family conflict, job satisfaction, and turnover intentions: a comparison of three country clusters', *Applied Psychology*, 61(1): 1–29.

McDonald, P., Pini, B. and Bradley, L. (2007) 'Freedom or fallout in local government? How work-life culture impacts employees using flexible work practices', *The International Journal of Human Resource Management*, 18(4): 602–22.

McNall, L., Masuda, A. and Nicklin, J. (2010) 'Flexible work arrangements, job satisfaction and turnover intentions: The mediating roles of work to family enrichment', *Journal of Psychology*, 144: 61–81.

Miller, S. (2022) 'Thousands of British workers begin trial of 4-day workweek', *SHRM*, 8 June. Available at: www.shrm.org/resourcesandtools/hr-topics/benefits/pages/thousands-of-british-workers-begin-trial-of-four-day-work-week.aspx#:~:text=More%20than%203%2C300%20workers%20at,trial%20of%20a%20shorter%20workweek. (accessed 12 June 2022)

Moen, P. and Huang, Q. (2010) 'Customizing careers by opting out or shifting jobs: Dual-earners seeking life-course "fit"', in K. Christensen and B. Schneider (eds), *Workplace Flexibility: Realigning 20th-century Jobs to 21st-century Workers*. New York: Cornell University Press, pp. 73–94.

Mooi-Reci, I. and Risman, B. J. (2021) 'The gendered impacts of COVID-19: Lessons and reflections', *Gender & Society*, 35(2): 161–7.

Munsch, C. L. (2016) 'Flexible work, flexible penalties: The effect of gender, childcare, and type of request on the flexibility bias', *Social Forces*, 94(4): 1567–91.

Office National Statistics (ONS) (2019) *Table 5, Reasons for not wanting a full-time job* Jan – Dec 2018, Available at: www.ons.gov.uk/employmentandlabourmarket/peopleinwork/employmentandemployeetypes/articles/labourmarketeconomiccommentary/january2019 (accessed 4 November 2022)

Office of National Statistics (2021) *Homeworking Hours, Rewards and Opportunities in the UK: 2011 to 2020*. Available at: www.ons.gov.uk/employmentandlabourmarket/peopleinwork/labourproductivity/articles/homeworkinghoursrewardsandopportunitiesintheuk2011to2020/2021-04-19#characteristics-and-location-of-homeworkers (accessed 24 March 2022).

Office of National Statistics (2022) *EMP17: People in Employment on Zero Hours Contracts*. Available at: www.ons.gov.uk/employmentandlabourmarket/peopleinwork/employmentandemployeetypes/datasets/emp17peopleinemploymentonzerohourscontracts (accessed 29 March 2022).

Penn, R. (1992) 'Flexibility in Britain during the 1980s: Recent empirical evidence', in N. Gilbert, R. Burrows and A. Pollert (eds), *Fordism and Flexibility*. London: Macmillan, pp. 66–86.

Peretz, H., Fried, Y. and Levi, A. (2018) 'Flexible work arrangements, national culture, organisational characteristics, and organisational outcomes: A study across 21 countries', *Human Resource Management Journal*, 28(1): 182–200.

Pokojski, Z., Kister, A. and Lipowski, M. (2022) 'Remote work efficiency from the employers' perspective – what's next?', *Sustainability*, 14(7): 4220.

Putman, L. L., Myers, K. K. and Gailliard, B. M. (2013) 'Examining the tensions in workplace flexibility and exploring options for new directions', *Human Relations*, 67: 413–440. Available at: www2.deloitte.com/au/en/pages/human-capital/articles/examining-the-tensions-workplace. html (accessed 13 October 2015).

Ramos, J. P., & Prasetyo, Y. T. (2020). *The Impact of Work-Home Arrangement on the Productivity of Employees during Covid-19 Pandemic in the Philippines: A Structural Equation Modelling Approach.* ICIBE 2020: 2020 The 6th International Conference on Industrial and Business Engineering, 135–140.

Richman, A. L., Civian, J. T., Shannon, L. L., Jeffrey Hill, E. and Brennan, R. T. (2008) 'The relationship of perceived flexibility, supportive work–life policies, and use of formal flexible arrangements and occasional flexibility to employee engagement and expected retention', *Community, Work and Family*, 11(2): 183–97.

Roberts, E. (2008) 'Time and work–life balance: The roles of "temporal customization" and "life temporality"', *Gender Work and Organization*,15(5): 430–53.

Soga, L. R., Bolade-Ogunfodun, Y., Mariani, M., Nasr, R., and Laker, B. (2022) 'Unmasking the other face of flexible working practices: A systematic literature review', *Journal of Business Research*, 142: 648–62.

Sparks, K., Cooper, C., Fried, Y. and Shirom, A. (1997) 'The effects of hours of work on health: A meta-analytic review', *Journal of Occupational and Organisational Psychology*, 70: 391–408.

Stavrou, E. and Kilaniotis, C. (2010) 'Flexible work and turnover: An empirical investigation across cultures', *British Journal of Management*, 21(2): 541–54.

Stavrou, E., Spiliotis, S. and Charalambous, C. (2010) 'Flexible working arrangements in context: An empirical investigation through self-organizing maps', *European Journal of Operational Research*, 202(3): 893–902.

Steinberg, C. and Nakane, M. (2012) *Can Women Save Japan?*, IMF paper. Available at: www.imf. org/external/pubs/cat/longres.aspx?sk=40048.0 (accessed 13 October 2015).

Swan, E. and Fox, S. (2009) 'Becoming flexible: Self-flexibility and its pedagogies', *British Journal of Management*, 20: S149–59.

Tipping, S., Chanfreau, J., Perry, J. and Tait, C. (2012) *Report of the 4th Work–life Balance Employee Survey.* London: BIS.

TUC (2015) 'Work life balance', 5 June. Available at www.tuc.org.uk/workplace-issues/work-life-balance/04-homeworkers/home-working-increase-despite-recession-says (accessed 13 October 2015).

TUC (2022) Press Release: BME women twice as likely to be on zero-hours contract as white men, available from: www.tuc.org.uk/news/tuc-bme-women-twice-likely-be-zero-hours-contracts-white-men (Accessed 29 March 2022)

Tzafrir, S. and Dolan, S. (2004) 'Trust me: A multiple item scale for measuring managers' "employee trust"', *Management Research*, 2(2): 115–32.

Van der Lippe, T., Van Breeschoten, L. and Van Hek, M. (2018) 'Organizational work–life policies and the gender wage gap in European workplaces', *Work and Occupations*, 46(2): 111–48.

Wels, J. (2021) 'The contribution of labour unions in fostering access to flexible work arrangements in Britain', METICES Discuss Paper, 1: 23.

Wheatley, D. (2017) 'Employee satisfaction and use of flexible working arrangements', *Work, Employment and Society*, 31: 567–85.

Wheatley, D. (2021) 'Workplace location and the quality of work: The case of urban-based workers in the UK', *Urban Studies*, 58(11): 2233–57.

Wickens, Z. (2021) 'Princes launches new flexible working initiatives', *Employee Benefits*. Available at: https://employeebenefits.co.uk/princes-launches-flexible-working-initiatives/ (accessed 23 March 2022).

Wilson, D. (2010) 'Novartis bias suit to begin', *New York Times*, 7 April. Available at: www.nytimes.com/2010/04/07/business/07gender.html (accessed 18 January 2014).

Woodhams, C. and Corby, S. (2007) 'Then and now: Disability legislation and employers' practices in the UK', *British Journal of Industrial Relations*, 45(3): 556–80.

World Health Organisation and ILO (2021) *Long Working Hours Increasing Deaths From Heart Disease and Stroke*. Available from: www.who.int/news/item/17-05-2021-long-working-hours-increasing-deaths-from-heart-disease-and-stroke-who-ilo, (accessed 29 March 2022).

12

EQUITABLE REWARD AND THE EMPLOYMENT RELATIONSHIP

Learning Outcomes

By the end of this chapter, you should be able to:

- identify the impact and influence that different systems of reward have on the employment relationship
- critically evaluate different methods of wage determination
- examine reward systems in the light of equity.

What to Expect

Pay is at the epicentre of the employment relationship; it is the lubricant that ensures interaction – positive or negative – between the employer and employee – too little, or too much, upsets the balance between the two. This chapter provides an opportunity for you to analyse and evaluate the impact that the different methods of rewarding people at work have on the employment relationship; in particular it discusses what reward (of which pay is a part) is actually designed to achieve and how this conveys messages about management values to the workforce. A number of theories, e.g., expectancy, exchange, agency and target theories are explored in the light of different payment systems, while the ways in which different types of **reward management** influence and impact organisational behaviour and perceptions of trust are examined.

The Value of Reward in the Workplace

Reward systems within organisations are designed to attract, motivate and retain staff (Chiang and Birtch, 2020). Systems that fail on any, or all, of these three levels are dysfunctional, inhibiting optimum performance and the efficient achievement of organisational goals. On occasion inadequate or inappropriate rewards result in lower productivity, high labour turnover, conflict and sometimes, negative publicity. Conflict directly stemming from employee perceptions about inadequate reward can lead to strike action which, in turn, is detrimental to the company, the customers and any potential investors who may be deterred from investing by the negative publicity (Maungwa, 2021: VI).

The amount that people get paid, how they get paid and how frequently they get paid in return for the work they do is crucial to the ways in which employees view their employer. It often determines which job they take, which jobs they remain in and their attitudes to their co-workers. The wage they receive is, more often than not, tied into their own perceptions of self-worth and the degree of job satisfaction that they receive. As Kessler points out, pay is 'a central concern of most employees and a key pillar of the employment relationship' (2003: 331). The different elements that make up a reward package, not just the amount of pay, but the benefits such as pensions, the opportunities for training and development as well as the work–life balance all become vitally important as soon as someone is employed (Turnea and Prodan, 2020: 79). The amount of pay that an employer decides to offer is influenced by a number of different things ranging from legislative restrictions to fashion; it is not always linked to the specific job being undertaken nor to the person undertaking the job and his or her levels of competence and performance. Reward systems are important because they provide powerful signals about the ways in which employees are regarded. (To offer someone 'peanuts', for example, signals that you, as an employer, hold them in little regard.) Similarly managers, by making pay contingent upon the ways in which *they* define levels of performance, symbolise and signal that it is they who are in control (Beer, 1984; Godard, 2020). The method chosen to reward can therefore reinforce managerial requirements, signposting behaviours management would like to encourage (and highlighting those less desirable behaviours it would like to restrict). Whether it is determined by the board, by HR, by a line manager or by negotiation, for better or worse the centrality of the pay–work bargain determines the nature of the employment relationship.

News Flash 12.1

Employees Say Salary Is Their Top Priority

A survey conducted in June 2020 by SDWorx, looking at 5,683 employees in five European countries found that 649 UK employees claimed that salary packages topped their list when it comes to career management. This was closely followed by the importance given to what jobs actually entail. Job security was third on their list. Interestingly the survey found that, on average, only 46% of employees check their monthly pay slips. This percentage is even lower in the Netherlands (40%), France (39%) and Belgium (37%). For German and British employees, just over half of all employees check their pay slips monthly.

Sources: SDWorx, 2021; Sharma, 2021

Employers and Reward

Employers use rewards for a variety of purposes; for example, a monetary reward is often used as 'bait' to attract someone into a job. Once an individual has been attracted, and then embedded (some would say 'ensnared') within the organisation, pay can be used to reward past performance, stimulate future performance and to encourage the maintenance or improvement of existing levels of performance. How employers decide to pay their employees is affected by a number of factors, including the country in which the organisation is operating in, the labour market, legislative constraints, the skills required and importantly the managerial style in operation and whether or not the components of a reward system are unilaterally or consensually decided.

Rewards received by employees from their employers do not have to be monetary; other forms of rewarding behaviour are available. The health of the psychological contract sometimes depends on the reward of 'recognition' that employees receive for their work – and this can be as simple as a 'thank you' from their manager, or as complex as the internal satisfaction gained after being empowered to accomplish a task and allowed to make mistakes. As Bratton and Gold say, 'Reward refers to a package of monetary, non-monetary and psychological payments that an organisation provides in exchange for a bundle of work related behaviours' (2012: 361). Non-financial rewards for an employee often lead to higher levels of intrinsic satisfaction and hence to an improved psychological contract. Examples of such intangible rewards have both an internal and external dimension (Sisson, 2010: 77). Extrinsic rewards are seen where there is the opportunity for social contact and a public recognition of worth, while intrinsic rewards are those where perhaps an individual is allowed to develop their levels of expertise and personal growth, perhaps by holding, and being recognised for having, a particular level of responsibility and influence. It is clear that training, development, communication and job design all play an important part in the ways in which organisations reward members of their workforce. As Edwards says,

> ... what goes on within the employment relationship is crucial, not only in terms of the pay that is earned but also the condition under which it is earned: the degree of autonomy the employee is granted, the safety of the work environment, the opportunity for training and development, and so on. (2003: 2)

The approaches that organisations adopt when rewarding their staff are crucial. There is some academic evidence that the introduction of a clear strategy, linking reward to organisational objectives affects behaviour, values and performance, resulting in an increased competitive edge (Tenhiälä and Laamanen, 2018; Trevor, 2010; Trevor and Brown, 2012). Yet formal strategies, by their very nature, tend to be subverted by expediency and the day-to-day requirements of an organisation. As Trevor and Brown say,

> ... there remain unavoidable obstacles to the ability of management to implement pay systems aligned to strategic goals. These obstacles impose fundamental limitations on the strategic applications of pay. (2012: 21)

Where however a formal strategy is implemented, care has to be taken that the right things are being encouraged. Digital Equipment Corporation, for example, withdrew its system of sales-commission for its sales reps because, although the commission resulted in a higher volume of sales, it also led to a disproportionately higher level of customer dissatisfaction. Similarly, financial services mis-selling in the early part of last century was due to inappropriate behaviour that was inadvertently encouraged by the system of rewards and inducements offered by a number of companies. In the same vein Mervyn King, when Governor of the Bank of England, talked about the dangers of 'morally hazardous' employee behaviour that was *stimulated and encouraged* by the bonus and reward systems operating in a banking sector that relied on insurance to cover costly mistakes (King, 2007: 8). Such behaviour was part of the mix that led to the unfortunate and inappropriate consequences around the economic crash in 2008.

On the whole, where they are in place, reward systems – whether or not they are formally linked to a **reward strategy** – 'should' encourage organisational performance and, if working well, help boost levels of performance while simultaneously obtaining and retaining the types of employees an organisation requires. In theory, reward systems are designed specifically to encourage behaviour that contributes directly to the achievement of the organisation's goals. Whether an organisation is in the not-for-profit or profit sector will have an impact on the way reward packages are configured, the not-for-profit organisations often providing better fringe benefits to compensate for the lower levels of pay regardless of levels of performance (Campos et al., 2017; Chen et al., 2013; Dickson et al., 2014).

Yet the reality of reward in practice is slightly different from the theoretical assumptions. Many payment systems evolve over time in *ad hoc* and inconsistent ways, responding to individual events and the immediate needs of an organisation. Over time, therefore, the rewards that people receive may be disconnected from the areas of performance that they were originally intended to encourage. Changes to the system are not always well received and this of course may have a detrimental impact on the employment relationship. It is because reward is so central to employees' wellbeing that this occurs. Kessler emphasises 'the importance of pay to employees', suggesting that it

> … is liable to lend a considerable degree of risk to managerial attempts to alter accepted and established pay-performance relationships with demoralisation and other dysfunctional organisational effects a potential outcome. (2003: 331)

Case Snippet 12.1

Paying Everyone the Same Is a Bad Idea

When the London-based online psychotherapy company, Spill, started up with five employees everyone was given the same salary (£36,000). This was regarded as equitable and a good idea that fostered goodwill amongst the staff. Yet within a short time this egalitarian idea had become a nightmare. It was impossible to operate successfully. Some staff worked longer hours than others but still received the same pay and discontent began to bubble up. Then, as the company needs grew, taking on a software developer and some sales workers and clerical staff became imperative. It was at this time that problems around the level of pay began in earnest. The software developer was difficult to recruit as the salary was deemed too low. The sales staff wanted more and to improve their basic £36,000 with commission, while Spill was inundated with responses to the advertisements for the clerical jobs because £36,000 was regarded as exceptionally high.

After a year, the equal pay system was scrapped and replaced with a transparent structure of pay grades based on seniority and technical expertise. The CEO, Calvin Benton, says that now,

> ... there are no rumours over who is being paid what. That has helped produce harmony in the office. And if you are in the therapy business, it's important to have harmony in your own workplace.

Source: Howell, 2021

There is a range of different conceptual and theoretical perspectives linked to the ways in which employees are rewarded. Because pay is discussed within a number of different academic fields (e.g., economics, occupational psychology, sociology and industrial relations, to name a few), the associated theories occasionally conflict with one another, rely on differing assumptions, or emphasise different aspects of reward. Where, for example, someone with a grounding in strategic HRM might look at pay emphasising the way in which it fits into an overall reward package aligned to company goals, an economist might view it solely in relation to the labour market and movements of wage rates across time.

Some of the most prevalent theories on which many organisations draw when compiling (or rationalising) their reward practices are detailed below. They are not mutually exclusive and organisations may well utilise more than one theory when implementing reward strategies:

- **Goal theory** and **expectancy theory** – whereby employees are provided with an incentive designed to elicit and encourage the behaviour desired by the organisation (see Frömer et al., 2020; Heckhausen, 2018; Locke and Latham, 2020; Porter and Lawler, 1968; Vroom, 1982). Here the theoretical underpinning is from occupational psychology and the assumption is that employees, so long as they think the desired reward is worth the effort, and have a clear **line of sight** between what is being asked and what is being offered in return, will willingly, without compulsion, do what is requested. Employees are motivated by goals, particularly if they help set them – the tougher they are to achieve, the more motivating they become. Rewards designed to encourage performance are more likely to work as motivators if the reward is clearly and closely linked to the effort of the individual or the team and if there is the smallest possible time lag between the reward and the effort made to achieve it. The Porter and Lawler model takes this further: if an employee can see the reward as a goal and it is something that they want then they will work towards it and achieve intrinsic and extrinsic satisfaction from their performance towards those goals. This of course is provided that their role allows for this – and that they have the skills and abilities required. The problems occur when the incentive does not produce the required behaviours, where, for example, employees find ways of achieving the rewards on offer but deviate from the types of performance the organisation requires or where other factors moderate and militate against such instrumental behaviour.

- **Principal–agency theory** – whereby employees are seen as agents who receive a basic rate of pay that may be enhanced by the employer (the principal) by the agents furthering the amount of effort they put into their work. At its simplest the theory covers payment systems that provide for annual increments to a pay spine, thereby rewarding agents (employees) for the length of time spent with the organisation. The theory assumes that the interests of the agents and principals do not necessarily coincide, the agents wanting more money and the principals more effort – conflict between the two is an ever-present possibility. **Piecework**, commission, bonus payments, profit sharing systems and **gainsharing** all fall into this category, with piecework and gainsharing used to encourage additional performance at the lower end of the salary scale and bonus payments and profit sharing more often geared to those on executive levels of pay. In all of these examples, employees are aware that increased rewards are achievable if they manage to perform to a set of required standards. The systems work when both agents and principals are happy with the pay–work bargain that they have struck and if employees know what to expect in return for their performance. If bonus payments, for example, are awarded in an arbitrary way it can damage the employment relationship for those who perceive such payments either unfair or unachievable or both. Wright says that a 'criticism of the theory is that it tends to overemphasise efficiency and neglect the institutional context' (2004: 15).

- **Target theory** *or* **tournament theory** – whereby a level of competition is introduced to incentivise top management. The winner does not necessarily take all, but the process of competition is deemed good for the organisation and for a few 'high flyers'. However, it can lead to high employee turnover at the higher end of an organisation if the levels of reward are not matched by employee expectations. It can also lead employees ineligible for such high payments feeling disgruntled, relatively 'hard done by' and experiencing increasing perceptions of inequity (Pepper et al., 2015). One of the problems associated with this system is that those eligible for reward are occasionally tempted to spend a disproportionate amount of time attempting to thwart their counterparts – often deploying tactics that are inimical to organisational goals. Yet tournament theorists argue that this system of pay promotes competition and provides incentives in such a way that those employees deemed best rise above their colleagues (Connelly et al., 2014; Fredrickson et al., 2010).

- **Social exchange theory** – based around notions of reciprocity, this theory deploys the notion of the **wage–effort bargain** that states that employees proportionally regulate their workplace output in direct relation to the wage that they expect to receive for their work (Baldamus, 1961; Gouldner, 1960; Joyce, 2020) and as such it has links with the psychological contract and with notions of fairness. Conflict is inherent in this approach to reward because the interests of management require a cost-effective approach towards encouraging employees to be as productive as possible; employees, on the other hand, would like the highest possible return for their efforts. Frequent negotiation is endemic with this method of remuneration; discussions around the degrees of effort required, and the ways in which employees might be deployed to best effect, form a constant and time-consuming backdrop to regulating the employment relationship. Where an employee restricts output as a direct result of their negative perceptions about the level of an anticipated reward, this has a damaging impact on the employment relationship and may result in increased levels of workplace conflict. The notion of the wage–effort bargain is, however, particularly attractive to those responsible for setting levels of reward because of the apparent motivational link between pay and increased productivity; consequently it has been a formative and vital ingredient in the development of pay and reward practices over the years (Perkins and White, 2008). It is particularly pertinent when pay negotiations are undertaken at a collective rather than individual level and therefore may currently be less applicable to the UK. Apart from the propensity to encourage repeated wage negotiations, one of the main disadvantages of using the concept of the wage–effort relationship for the rationale behind a payment system is that effort is influenced by a range of factors, not just by perceptions about reward, and therefore may either decrease or increase in response to factors that are nothing to do with the expected levels of remuneration.

- **Exchange theory**, *sometimes called* **efficiency wage theory** – whereby employees exchange their labour in return for payment. This economically based theory is one in which employees are regarded as instrumentally motivated, and where the employers may, particularly when they need to ensure continuity of production and a stable skill set, be forced to concede to levels of pay higher than they would like and, as a consequence, might view the workforce in terms of core and periphery employees (see Chapter 11 on Flexibility). On occasion the employer may pay more than the market rate for an employee in order to avoid unnecessary replacement costs. Problems occur when employees perceive that the pay received is worth less than the effort expended, thereby inducing perceptions of distributional injustice and conflict ensues.

- **Justice theory** – this, as we saw in Chapter 3, concerns *equity theory* (Adams, 1963; Greenberg, 1987) whereby employees evaluate their workplace reward in relation to: first, the amount of effort that they need to expend in order to receive the desired reward; and second, how they compare themselves with others in a similar situation – are their peers, for example, working less hard for a higher reward? This process involves employees looking at whether the amount they receive is fair in relation to others (*distributional justice*), whether the way in which the organisation decides on, and organises, the payment structure is processed fairly (*procedural justice*) and whether the way in which their supervisors interact with them and communicate pay decisions is fair (*interactional and informational justice*). The degree to which employees have a say in the targets they are supposed to reach and how this is managed is important here, as Tepper et al. say, 'Decision making is said to be procedurally just when those affected have an opportunity to influence decisions and when they are treated with neutrality, trustworthiness and respect' (2006: 103). How employees perceive their own worth in relation to others is subjective; it is not unknown for individuals to overestimate (or underestimate) both their own contribution and the pay of others (Guest, 1992). Such subjectivity can lead to inaccurate perceptions of distributional injustice and damage the levels of trust between employer and employee.

- *Human relations school* – evolved from the theories of Elton Mayo (O'Connor, 1999) and regards employees in an holistic way, recognising that employees are influenced by social interactions and that their motivation may not be solely affected by monetary concerns. Work is not always a solitary activity and employees behave in ways that are shaped by the need for inclusion and social acceptance – accordingly informal group norms may affect and manipulate productivity levels.

- *The Marxist school* – views the ways in which the employers (capital) 'buy' and then deploy the employees' efforts (labour) for a specified amount of work; here the effort (and therefore the employee) is no more, no less, than a commodity to be bought and sold (there are clear links with hard HRM here). The employees have little choice as in order to satisfy their requirements for food, shelter and so on, they must seek out an employer who will pay them. The relationship between the employer and employee is therefore a product of class relationships, the labour market merely reflecting the social structure and distribution of power in any given society. Those analysing payment systems from this perspective have to take into account

> ... the complex inter-relationship between the structure of in-equality, the prevailing standards of occupational worth ... and the institutions of class power and political control. Any explanation which excludes consideration of such factors among the determinants of pay and attitudes to pay is incomplete. (Hyman, 1974: 171)

In practice of course many organisations utilise a combination of reward mechanisms that could be analysed using a number of different theoretical approaches. Not all practitioners involved with payment setting are consciously aware of the theoretical implications behind their payment/ reward systems; instead their employees may just be paid according to the market rate, or perhaps in compliance with legislation. The result of such activity is often a haphazard payment system (it could not realistically be called strategic) that may not always be internally consistent, and may, in certain circumstances, lead to inequity and potential discrimination. The employment relationship in such situations is unlikely to be healthy and conflict free.

Influences Affecting Reward

Pay, according to Mahoney (1989), should reflect three elements: job, person and performance. It is not, however, quite as simple as this. An organisation has to balance what it does in relation to the external labour market. Yet while doing this the organisation still has to reward and motivate its workforce while maintaining an internal consistency of behaviour that ensures required staffing levels as well as an overall perception of fairness. Cultural differences too impact on the ways in which rewards might be received; a reward designed to achieve a specific outcome in one country may not have the same effect in another (Chiang et al., 2016; Becton and Field, 2009). While some rewards targeted at improving individual behaviours may not be as effective in cultures that are of a more collective nature it follows therefore that reward strategies and practices need to be tailored to different cultural arrangements (Aoki and Rawat, 2020). Often companies state that they aim to be externally competitive and internally equitable (Armstrong and Brown, 2006). If an organisation is unsuccessful in this and a clear sense of injustice prevails, people are quite likely to reduce their contribution to the organisation.

A number of authors, for example Armstrong, Brown and Perkins, have suggested that managers contemplating implementing a different system of employee reward should answer the following questions:

- Where is the organisation going?
- How can it help employees to get there and maintain its position?
- How can it involve employees and ensure employee interaction with the process?
- What sorts of competencies, values and behaviour does it want to encourage?
- How can the reward system encourage desired behaviour and values without enabling dysfunctional outcomes?

Cox, in particular, points out that 'employee involvement in pay system design and implementation is critical to ensuring acceptance and effectiveness' (2000: 372).

Armstrong (2000), in a rather prescriptive way that writes employees out of the script and bizarrely assumes each organisation comprises a single culture, stresses that a competent reward strategy is frequently linked to the goals of the organisation, enabling and enhancing such goals, and as such the system often specifically:

- provides for the integration of reward policies and processes with key strategies for growth and improved performance
- underpins the organisation's values, especially those concerned with innovation, teamwork, flexibility, customer service and quality
- fits the culture and management style of the organisation as it is or as it is planned to be
- drives and supports desired behaviour at all levels by indicating to employees what types of behaviour will be rewarded, how this will take place and how their expectations will be satisfied
- provides the competitive edge required to attract and retain the level of skills the organisation needs
- enables the organisation to obtain value for money from its reward practices. (2000: 233)

News Flash 12.2

Spain Takes First Step Towards Gender Pay Equality

The Spanish government has made a move towards tackling gender pay inequality. In October 2020 it passed a law requiring anyone employing more than 50 staff to provide their pay figures, alongside a remuneration report and equality plan evaluating their current position on gender equality and how they plan to improve it.

Irene Montero, the minister of equality for the Spanish government, said:

> The wage gap between men and women continues to be above 20% in Spain and as a feminist government we will do everything possible to close that gap. Hence the

(Continued)

importance of the two royal decrees approved by the Council of Ministers today ... (this is) a vaccine against inequality.

Yolanda Díaz, the minister of labour and social economy for the Spanish government, said:

By being effective, these equality plans place the role of women far beyond equal pay: we are talking about the main role they will play in the 21st-century business.

Source: Pratt (2020)

A number of factors influence how reward is managed within an organisation. Not least amongst these is the ability and awareness of the top management and the importance it accords to reward. Reward strategy is influenced initially by an organisation's ability and willingness to pay its employees at a certain level, and this may be influenced by the country and sector within which an organisation is operating, together with the organisation's size and culture. Global and local competition for goods, markets and skills will affect the organisation and its ability to reward staff appropriately. The smaller an organisation the more probable it will be that executive pay will be clustered at the lower end of the spectrum (Atkinson and Meager, 1994: 11). The historical ways and means of rewarding people will be important, as will be the management style and whether or not employees have some sort of say, either individually or collectively, in their own pay determination.

The legislation impacting on the organisation will have an important influence on reward levels. For example, in the interests of fairness the EU introduced a number of restrictions on hours of work and levels of pay to which the member countries are supposed to adhere. In the UK, a minimum wage was introduced in 1999. According to the UK Office for National Statistics (2021), the Annual Survey of Hours and Earnings shows that there were 1,084,000 employee jobs, with employees aged 16 years and over who were paid *below* the National Minimum Wage or National Living Wage in April 2021. (From April 2016, a mandatory National Living Wage (NLW) for workers aged 25 and over was introduced, initially set at £7.20p/h) The NLW applies to all workers aged 23 and over and will be further reduced to 21 by 2024. To help enforce the new regulations the government set up a new team in HMRC to prosecute employers who deliberately fail to pay workers the wage they are due. Penalties for non-payment are 200% of arrears owed, although these will be halved if paid within 14 days. The maximum penalty is currently (2022) £20,000 per worker. An investigation by HM Revenue and Customs (HMRC) found that a total of £2.1 million was owed to more than 34,000 UK workers because of NLW violations taking place between 2011 and 2018:

- 47% wrongly deducted pay from workers' wages, including for uniform and expenses
- 30% failed to pay workers for all the time they had worked, such as when they worked overtime
- 19% paid the incorrect apprenticeship rate.

In the 2020 to 2021 UK tax year, HMRC assisted over 155,000 workers to recover more than £16 million in pay owed to them. It also issued more than £14 million in penalties to firms not complying with the law (DBEIS, 2021). Some employer excuses for incorrect payments were breathtakingly naïve, for example, claiming that the law did not apply to them or that staff did not deserve that amount of money, one employer saying, 'I thought it was okay to pay young workers below the National Minimum Wage as they are not British and therefore do not have the right to be paid it' (HMRC, 2021).

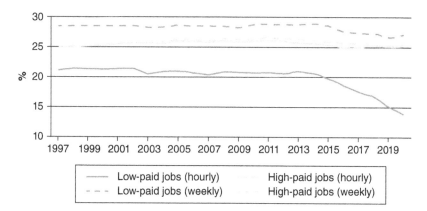

Figure 12.1   The proportion of low-paid employee jobs based on hourly pay fell to a record low of 15.1% in 2020

News Flash 12.3

Ocado Drivers Now Being Paid Way Below the Minimum Wage

Since Ocado Zoom began to use a new delivery partner, Ryde, in June 2021 the pay for delivery drivers has plummeted. Their pay prior to Ryde's involvement had been guaranteed at £14 an hour. This has now been reduced to £5 a hour. Alex Marshal, the president of the Independent Workers of Great Britain, has demanded that Ocado bring these drivers back 'in house', particularly as the Ocado group profits had doubled to £73.1m in the same year that Ryde took over responsibility for the drivers.

Source: Wall, 2021

Within an organisation there will be concerns about skill shortages and the availability of potential staff, coupled with internal and external pay relativities that may impact on existing differences between different internal pay levels. Employees' perceptions of such differentials are occasionally the cause of disputes about pay and sometimes result in 'wages drift'. (Wages drift occurs when the levels of pay creep upwards over time as an organisation adjusts its pay differentials – sometimes as a result of employee pressure linked to perceptions of distributional justice, rather than in response to a planned reward strategy.)

Employers need to decide whether or not they are going to create a reward system that is sufficiently flexible to respond to all of the above, while at the same time they need to decide whether they are going to pay for:

- productivity: the amount produced
- potential: work that might be achieved, for example, employing a graduate with no work experience
- time: the amount spent working – measured in anything from hours to years
- performance: the ways in which an employee achieves the desired results
- knowledge and skills
- individual or team performance.

As Chiang and Birtch say:

> To be effective, when designing and implementing reward-performance practices, managers must be cognizant of a range of context specific and confounding forces that could potentially influence the performance implications of different types of rewards. (2012: 562)

See Figure 12.2 for influences that affect an employee's reward package.

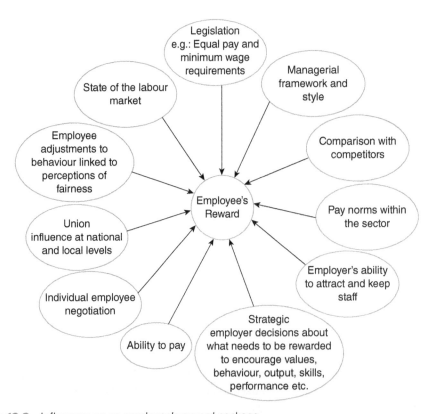

Figure 12.2   Influences on an employee's reward package

Once in place of course it is essential that both employees and those responsible for managing them should understand the system, with the links between effort and reward clearly identified. However, the entire exercise is pointless if the employees do not value the rewards on offer.

Perhaps a simplistic way of looking at the reward process is to ignore the complexity of organisational arrangements and structures (see Figure 12.3). This model shows that reward structure consists of a number of components where the final delivery of the reward itself follows from the structure and type of the payment system in operation (e.g., whether or not it is negotiated or unilaterally imposed) which itself is derived from the organisational values and underlying philosophy.

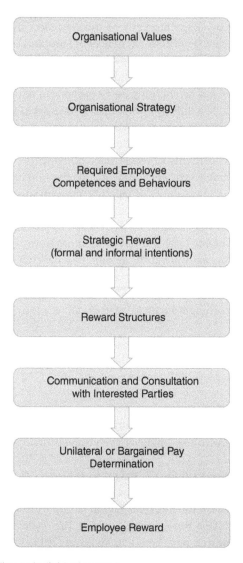

Figure 12.3   Stages leading to individual reward

Consensual Methods of Determining Reward

Pay determination is not always subject to unilateral managerial prerogative. Pay is the most likely aspect of the employment relationship to be affected by, and conditional on, collective bargaining. Pay bargaining itself institutionalises the distributional conflict within organisations and its outcomes reflect the balance of power between the bargaining parties. Bargaining can occur at numerous levels (company, sectoral, regional, national, etc. – see Chapter 10) and be undertaken by a range of different participants (employers, unions, governments) who are subject to different legislative systems and cultures, making comparisons between different national systems of pay determination problematic. The ways in which wage-related statistics are collected and the types of taxation imposed further increase the difficulties of comparison (see Chapter 2).

The outcomes of company wage negotiations usually reflect the economic conditions that those companies face. A recent trend across a number of European countries – notably Denmark, Finland, France, Germany, the Netherlands, Spain, Sweden and the UK – has been for collective agreements to permit a degree of latitude for individual employees, allowing them to personalise their collectively negotiated pay by choosing how a proportion of their own remuneration package is configured, for example a different proportion to be used as holiday or pension contributions (Ligthart et al., 2021; Arrowsmith and Marginson, 2009).

It is important to note that the introduction of standard pay packages where managers have the discretion to tweak the contents to reflect the requirements of individual employees, and indeed of individual departments with recruitment and retention issues, is a trend that is becoming increasingly apparent. The capability of tailoring a system to suit individual needs is something that employees may appreciate When this occurs employees may perceive Variable Pay Schemes as potentially fairer than standardised pay systems, provided that they are procedurally robust and deliver an acceptable level and distribution of returns (Arrowsmith and Marginson, 2011: 57). Unions though are wary about the amount of independent action managers take over pay because such activity reduces their influence and power, possibly leading to cases of indirect discrimination and perceptions of unfairness. Bechter et al. found when studying variable pay systems and collective bargaining from all EU States that,

> the institutional structure of collective bargaining matters: variable pay systems thrive under company and multi-level collective bargaining, while their implementation is hindered under national-level collective wage bargaining. (2021: 443)

This 'green light' facilitating individual remuneration preferences alters the balance of power between the negotiators, giving a degree of control back to the individual employee by according them a direct relationship with the employer even though their pay is subject to a negotiated agreement.

Because trade unions have traditionally sought to reduce levels of managerial pay discretion and have, as a consequence, bargained about the pay that is associated with jobs, but not with that associated with the job holders, the individualisation of pay structures impacts upon their levels of influence (Heery, 2000). This is not to say, however, that collective bargaining has no influence on levels of **performance pay**. West and Mykerezi (2011) found, when looking at teachers' remuneration, some evidence that collective bargaining affects the design of performance pay arrangements. In particular, unions were found to encourage teacher bonuses if they were based on additional qualifications or duties, but discouraged bonuses that directly rewarded improvements in students' test scores.

Within the UK the level of bargaining about pay has decreased from its peak in the twentieth century, when it covered around four-fifths of employees By 2019 the Labour Force Survey showed that only just under 27% of employees were covered by collective bargaining, although the Annual Survey Hours Earnings for the same year suggests that many more than this had their pay set with regard to an agreement affecting more than one employee, i.e., through collective bargaining. In Europe where union density is higher, particularly where there is a culture of social partnership and where works councils are more widespread, collective bargaining about pay, as with other terms and conditions, is more prevalent. Industries where there is a low union density have higher instances of low pay (D'Arcy, 2018). In 2018 a report written by Jack Dromey for The Institute for Public Policy Research suggested that the UK government should alter its somewhat hostile approach to unions and encourage sectoral and firm-based collective bargaining in order to improve wages.

In the UK there is a growing divide between the public and private sectors concerning the ways in which pay is determined. In both there is an emphasis on the individual performance of employees, but pay determination within the public sector is primarily regulated by collective bargaining (pluralist) while in the private sector the system is one that is predominantly unitary, and based firmly on managerial discretion. Where collective bargaining in the private sector occurs, it tends to be in the larger organisations (van Wanrooy et al., 2013: 79). Collective pay bargaining between union and employer representatives can occur at a number of different levels; it may, for example, be conducted at industry level, where minimum levels are agreed (organisations within the sector sometimes improve upon these base-level conditions), or at enterprise or establishment level. On occasions, employers who are not party to the bargaining machinery will nevertheless follow, or better, a bargained settlement from elsewhere to ensure that their pay rates remain competitive. (Chapter 9 on employee voice gives more detail about the different levels of bargaining.)

Trade union negotiating power is not, however, the only way in which employees have a voice in pay determination. The Low Pay Commission (LPC), established under the National Minimum Wage Act 1998, annually gathers pay data through both research and consultation (including visits, discussions with workers, businesses and representative bodies), and makes recommendations to the government so that the minimum wage may be set at the appropriate rate. The commissioners are people who are chosen specifically because they have knowledge of, or experience or interest in:

- trade unions or matters relating to workers
- employers' associations or matters relating to employers generally
- independent areas – with other relevant knowledge or experience, for example, academic experts in labour markets (Low Pay Commission, 2014).

This means that, although bargaining is not in evidence, the employees do have a voice and representation in the process of pay determination.

Similarly there are a number of pay review bodies in the UK that make recommendations to the government about pay levels for specific groups of public sector workers, such as those in the armed forces or the police. These bodies, the first of which was established in 1971, are used to make recommendations for the remuneration levels of groups that have limited bargaining power, such as nurses, senior civil servants and judges. The government need not of course accept the recommendation; in 2013, for example, it placed a cap on the levels of increase that could be received by doctors and dentists (NHS England, 2014: 3).

The Low Pay Commission and the Pay Review Bodies are independent of the Government but part of the machinery of the state. Other groups not similarly affiliated may also have an influence on pay levels and working conditions allowing employee representation. For instance religious or community groups will, on occasion, intercede and make representations to an employer on behalf of employees in order to influence a decision about pay. The campaign for the London living wage, for example, was initiated in April 2001 by the London branch of Citizens UK, a broad alliance of different community, union and faith groups. (This group followed the example of a similar American community alliance grouping that had secured the first living wage, setting a new floor for wages paid via government funding in Baltimore – Neumark et al., 2012.) The London group argued that addressing low pay, with its direct impact on health, education and family life, was a *moral* issue that needed to be addressed by employers. The argument for the living wage is, however, presented as one that makes sound business sense.

The London Citizens UK group, now part of the Living Wage Foundation which operates nationwide, has persuaded over 8,362 employers – including Google, Linklaters, and Nestlé – to agree to implement the living wage. (From April 2023 the UK Living Wage stood at £10.90 p/h, while the London Living Wage was set at £11.95 p/h from September 2022.)

Exercise 12.1

- Discuss the following quotation in relation to what you know about those mechanisms for pay determination that incorporate employee voice but exclude collective bargaining:

  As collective bargaining has diminished, transparency has reduced and hence the opportunity for employers to obscure the detail of pay decisions has increased. (White, 2009: 23)

- Read the next section of this chapter on perceptions of fairness and then revisit the answer you gave for this question. What would you add to improve your response?

Reward and Perceptions of Fairness

The concept of fairness when applied to wages is inevitably a concept which requires comparisons. It is not possible to decide whether someone is fairly paid until one knows what other people are paid. Differentials and relativities lie at the very heart of the concept of equity as applied to wage determination. (Robinson, 1973: 7)

Fairness is a subjective and value-laden concept, so the meaning of fairness in relation to reward is also complex and subjective. The notion therefore of a 'fair day's pay for a fair day's work' can mean different things depending upon the perspective of the person using the phrase. As we have seen, the pay–work bargain is the key element in the employment relationship. This concept, elaborated by Farnham and Pimlott (1995), determines that every employment contract consists of two elements: an agreement on the rate of pay (either per unit of time or per unit of output) – *a pay rate bargain* – and an agreement about the work to be done in exchange – *an effort bargain.* If the pay–work bargain is managed badly, rewards insufficiently or is perceived to be delivering unfairly, there will be knock-on effects on recruitment, retention, morale and productivity. Similarly a too generous system will impact on the bottom line, reducing the potential value added to the organisation by the workforce and adversely affecting overall profitability. Where there is only limited information about levels of pay within an organisation, affected employees are likely to be distrustful, fearing malevolent exploitation by the employer (Montag-Smit and Smit, 2021).

Part of the sensitivity surrounding perceptions about pay concerns the ways in which people see themselves in relation to others. Human nature is such that comparisons are inevitable. Employees view their own levels of reward in the light of the rewards that they think are received by others and then decide whether they are being paid in ways that are compatible with:

- the amount of effort they put in, and
- the amount of effort and reward that others achieve.

This awareness of one's position in relation to others is particularly important where employees are paid for their performance. There are extremely strong elements of distributive and procedural justice that influence employees' perceptions of the rewards that they receive.

Burawoy (1979), in a thought-provoking study of machine-shop workers, discovered an informal culture of game-playing that was influenced by employee perceptions about the extent to which the wages paid were deemed appropriate. Where there was an assumption of underpayment, the employees played workplace games leading to significant underproduction; where there was a perception of overpayment, the workforce played competitive games resulting in higher productivity. The finding that employees alter their output in direct relation to their attitudes towards their levels of reward was borne out by Greenberg (1990), who noted that the level of theft rose when employees suffered a pay cut of 15% – corresponding levels of theft did not increase for those employees whose pay was unaffected. Workers will sometimes deliberately restrict their output fearing their higher productivity will become the 'new norm,' ratcheting up future work expectations without a corresponding rise in income. Cardella and Depew (2018: 182) found that workers restrict their output when productivity is evaluated at the individual level but not when productivity is evaluated collectively at the group level unless there is communication between group members. Perceptions about pay play an important part in the ways in which employees view both the *actual rewards* received and the *ways* in which such rewards are delivered. Employee perceptions of their own level of reward more often than not involve comparisons with others (equity theory: Adams, 1963). This perception determines whether or not individuals regard the level of reward that they receive as being fair. Blau, when looking at pharmaceutical managers, argued there were five different points of comparison (referents) that employees used to evaluate reward fairness:

- comparison with family and friends – *social* referents
- comparison of actual reward against what is needed – *financial* referents
- comparison of current reward levels with past reward levels – *historical* referents
- comparison of reward with that received by others in the same organisation – *organisational* referents
- comparison of own reward with reward received by others outside the organisation – *market* referents. (1994: 1253)

News Flash 12.4

Pay: Fairness Creeping up the Agenda Following Black Lives Matter

A third of all employers consider the fairness of their reward practices, says the CIPD in its reward fairness research, published in the spring of 2021. It collected data from 420 reward professionals from the private (67%), public (15%) and voluntary (16%) sectors supplementing the results with focus group discussions.

Of those surveyed a quarter had either taken action to improve reward fairness or planned to do so. Their activities included:

- conducting an equal pay audit
- carrying out a gender pay gap review
- making their appraisal processes clearer
- reviewing their performance-related pay system.

In addition, in response to Black Lives Matter, 19% have, or intend to, change their reward systems by a variety of means, some examples of which include:

- ethnicity pay gap reporting
- the introduction of **new pay** policies
- creating a race equality action plan
- setting up race employee networks for employees to share concerns and receive support
- unconscious bias training
- reviewing their current spending on benefits to ensure fairness.

Within the private services sector, 58% of professional services firms - those involved with legal, financial, technology activities - were more likely to see their reward policies and outcomes as fair after reviewing them in response to BLM; while retail, hospitality, catering, leisure and cleaning firms (36%) were less likely to do so.

Source: CIPD, 2021

Employee perceptions are important for managers deciding on a pay strategy; if for example the decision is made to be a low-wage employer, this runs the risk that employees will perceive them as unfair, perhaps leading to higher turnover, lower productivity and a damaged employee relationship. Employees are not passive; if the perception is one of 'negative equity' and unfairness this is directly correlated to lack of satisfaction at work and a poor psychological contract. The converse is true: when employees perceive that their level of pay is greater than that of their comparators then their pay level satisfaction increases (Dreher, 1981; Miceli and Jung, 1991; Rice et al., 1990). A study by Schulz et al. places an interesting nuance on fairness awareness as they found that employees can construe pay inequality as fair *if* it reflects greater managerial contributions and responsibilities, but that this acceptance can turn to perceptions of unfairness and mistrust if the inequality becomes excessive (2022: 725).

News Flash 12.5

One in Five Workers Are Banned From Discussing Their Pay

A poll of 2,700 workers by the TUC/GQR found that nearly a fifth of UK workers are prohibited from discussing their earnings with colleagues. Over half of the sample were not given information about co-workers' pay and half were unaware of the pay of senior managers in their organisations. Just 18% reported that their workplace had a pay policy where salary details were officially available to everyone.

Frances O'Grady, the TUC's general secretary, commented that,

> Pay secrecy clauses are a get out of jail free card for bad bosses. They stop workers from challenging unfair pay, allow top executives to hoard profits and encourage discrimination against women and disabled people. Talking about pay can feel a bit uncomfortable, but more openness about wages is essential to building fairer workplaces.

(N.B. The Equality Act 2010 already places restrictions on pay secrecy clauses, making them unenforceable if an employee discusses pay in order to find out if they are being paid less than colleagues for discriminatory reasons.)

Source: TUC, 2020

There is a basic assumption in much of the academic and practitioner literature that reward has the ability to motivate employees to behave in ways that they might not otherwise want to. This legacy comes from the instrumentalist school that propounded the view that individuals could be encouraged to accomplish a number of things *if* the inducements, usually monetary, were right. This perception is frequently elaborated upon by additional explanations based on the psychological processes involved in motivation. These are concerned with peoples' perceptions of their working environment and the ways in which they interpret it. Equity theory (in particular Adams, 1963), goal theory and expectancy theory all fit in here.

Perhaps one of the most quoted of the motivational theorists, Hertzberg (1968) argued, amongst other things, that money has more influence in terms of demotivation than motivation. (If pay is wrong and perceived to be unfair then the recipients are more likely to feel and express discontent; when it is right other factors, such as achievement, motivate.) Such discontent has its roots in perceptions of unfairness. As Brown says:

> [p]ay deserves more respect as a source of disincentive than of incentive. The most ingenious of bonus schemes and the best of supervision are of little use if the underlying pay structure is felt unfair. Consequently, the prudent personnel manager devotes far less time to devising new pay incentives than to tending old notions of fairness. (1989: 252–53)

The demotivational aspects of badly constructed payment systems are apparent particularly when the system in use is out of line with current practice. Some payment systems have changed because of legislation – in theory women are no longer paid less than men merely because they are women – but other practices have continued, often perpetuating feelings of inequity and occasionally unjustified inadequacy. For example, in the 1920s and 1930s managers would measure and rate the ways in which individual employees worked on what was called the 'graphic rating scale'. Typically this would rate workers at the top end of the scale as '*inspiring*'; in the middle they were either '*favourable*' or '*indifferent*'; at the lower end they were '*unfavourable*'; while the bottom rating was a ghastly '*repellent*'. Such language, one would have thought, is hardly conducive to encouraging improvements in performance. Yet Armstrong and Baron, when undertaking research in 1998 for the then IPD, found these categories still in use. Systems that ranked employees along these lines and then gave some form of merit pay had moved with the times only marginally (perhaps calling the system 'performance management') and one can only speculate about the state of the psychological contract of those receiving the lowest rankings. Since that time the rhetoric associated with remuneration has changed. Much is now associated with performance management and appraisal systems with their concomitant links to training and development.

Exercise 12.2

The *Daily Telegraph* has suggested that it might link some elements of its journalists' pay to the popularity of their articles. It wants to investigate the use of a system which scores stories published online according to how many subscriptions they drive (and how many clicks they get). These individual scores will then be linked to levels of reward.

The possibility of this system being adopted has distressed staff who fear it will impact what they write and how they write it, possibly inhibiting the serious coverage of some topics while enhancing the less serious 'showbiz' type of article. The Editor, Chis Evans, has pointed out that this idea is still embryonic but said, 'It seems only right that those who attract and retain the most subscribers should be the most handsomely paid'. Deputy Editor Mike Adamson told *Press Gazette*,

All that's been said is that if we could use the analytics to find a fairer way of rewarding the best journalism then that's what we might do. It's not a plan, it's a question at this stage. All journalists are rewarded according to a perception of their value to the publisher that they work for anyway and they always have been. If we could find a better way of doing that, we should consider it.

- Do you think this plan will work? Give reasons for your answer supported by academic evidence.

Sources: Bland, 2021; Ponsford and Tobitt, 2021

Different Types of Payment Systems

There is a range of different payment systems that can be used to reward employees. *Time-based* methods provide an employee with a wage that may be paid hourly/weekly/monthly/annually – in its simplest form it is not dependent on anything other than the time spent working for the employer; for example, a shop assistant receiving the minimum wage receives payment based on the number of hours worked that is unrelated to productivity; similarly someone receiving an annual increment on top of their basic salary receives this because they have worked an additional year and for no other reason.

Incentive-based systems are designed to inspire an employee to work harder: the more they produce the greater the reward. Thus a car sales representative may receive commission payments linked to the number of sales achieved. Incentive payments can either be linked to specified targets or to actual output. Incentives take a variety of forms: bonus schemes are geared towards encouraging an individual to perform in a specific way over a period of time, while piecework or 'payment by results' links pay to specific amounts produced, and typically there is a high degree of managerial control, although there is also a degree of employee autonomy because output can be self-regulated. Such a system can lead to constant negotiation and renegotiation about the targets to be achieved as well as about the pace and timing of the work. Conflict is frequent, as too are injuries. Bender et al. (2012) looked at the experiences of over 30,000 piecework employees from across Europe and found that just under 15% had suffered from a workplace injury (commonly back and musculoskeletal). They suggest that pieceworkers are 5% more likely to be injured at work than their non-piecework colleagues. Interestingly they also found evidence of 'blood-in-pocket syndrome' – this is where employees working under collective incentive schemes that are based on group output hide injuries sustained at work so as not to jeopardise piecework payments for their workmates.

Piecework is not as prevalent in the UK as it used to be, in part because of changes in the types of work done (technology is important here) and the ways in which it is accomplished, with more teamworking and greater flexibility, but in part because piecework was contentious, leading to constant mini disputes, taking up a disproportionate amount of managerial time. Arrowsmith and Marginson quote a union official who, when discussing the switch away from piecework to one where employees were paid a daily rate, explained that,

… if production stopped, the pressure would come from the shopfloor to the managers – 'where is the work, where is the work, where is the work?'; under the daywork system, the pressure is reversed … It really puts more and more responsibility on management to make sure that there are the logistics, supply line and the number of operators required. (2010: 307)

Other sorts of incentive pay include:

- *Gainsharing* – an infrequent system of reward, rare in the UK but more common in the USA, whereby employees work towards gaining a set of points linked to specific targets. Such points are translated into payments, usually quarterly. This system is usually applied to manual workers and often used to change aspects of a workplace culture, so for example a group could gain points by reducing levels of absence and improving attendance.
- *Bonus payments based on profits* – generated by the organisation or section within the organisation. These can take a number of different forms, for example, profit sharing or employee share-option schemes (ESOPs). Profit-based pay is part of an employee's pay that is formally linked to the profits of the business in which the employee works. There is a clear distinction between the objectives that lie behind schemes that share profits and those that reward employees with shares. Those schemes that offer shares are designed to:
  - encourage long-term commitment
  - be a more tax-efficient way of rewarding employees, depending on legislation.
- *Profit-sharing schemes* – designed to:
  - encourage an increased awareness and interest in company performance
  - help employees to benefit from company profitability
  - ensure that labour costs are responsive to organisational performance.

But such schemes are not without their problems:

  - they cannot be used to reward differential individual performance, particularly as many schemes are multifactorial
  - the reward offered is usually small and infrequent
  - employee involvement and influence is often illusory
  - there are problems setting the level at which payments may be triggered.

- *Individual pay based on assessment of performance* (performance related pay – PRP or merit pay) – regarded by many as an equitable payment system because it recognises achievement and differentiates rewards according to individual skill and contribution. As Isaac says:

the challenge for performance related pay is to establish a pattern of pay which is seen as fair by employees, which uses reasonably objective measures of performance, which can stand the strain of change, which sustains the object of the system, is not too large a portion of the pay packet and is not too costly to administer. If a 'conventional' view of fairness is maintained in relation to PRP, the net returns may not be sufficient for the majority of employees. (2001: 111)

The problem, of course, with assessing someone's performance is that the assessment is frequently subjective and based on a range of assumptions, some of which may not be conscious. Added to this ambiguity over assumptions that may, or may not, be relevant when appraising staff in order to influence pay levels, is the CIPD's 2007 finding that front line managers 'do not have the skills, attitudes, and knowledge to manage performance based rewards' in part because they are removed from the initial reward processes set by HR departments.

Where salary is dependent upon an individual negotiating their own levels of increase, research from Bowles et al. (2007) and Kray and Thompson (2005) indicates that women are more hesitant than men in initiating negotiations about salary, and that behaviour linked to salary negotiation is considered inappropriate for women. Bowles et al. (2007) showed that those women who, unlike their male counterparts, negotiated for higher pay were regarded less favourably than their male peers. Furthermore during appraisal itself,

> women still are not given equal consideration based on their skills and abilities, because of the expectations that they are ill-equipped to do traditionally man's work. They still are punished when they step out of line with the 'shoulds' and 'should nots' prescribed for their gender … And they still are the recipients of multiple reactions rooted in bias – serious and trivial, subtle and obvious, intentional and unintentional – the total of which are … detrimental to their advancement. The consequence is a failure to utilize human resources in the most effective way possible. (Heilman, 2012: 135)

Neunsinger has pointed out that during the first part of the twenty-first century in the majority of Western countries, despite the gender **pay gap** narrowing, women 'earn on a global average between 40–90% of men's wages' and worryingly that the gap is no longer closing but opening up (2018: 121). In the UK, the gender pay gap has been gradually decreasing over time, falling by approximately a quarter among full-time employees and by just over one fifth among all employees. In 2020, the gap among full-time employees fell to 7.4% from 9.0% in 2019, while among all employees it fell to 15.5%, from 17.4% in 2019. Interestingly because women fill more part-time jobs, which in comparison with full-time jobs have lower hourly median pay, the gender pay gap is higher for all employees than for each of full-time employees and part-time employees (ONS, 2021). Care must be taken when looking at these figures because over the period covered many employees will have been on reduced wages as they were furloughed due to the Covid pandemic.

Exercise 12.3

- Is reward under a performance management system always equitable?
- Can groups be left behind?
- Describe how it might be possible that subjective factors influence perceptions and consequent ratings of performance. Justify your answers using academic theories.

There are indeed a number of problems with performance-related pay:

- It is a questionable motivator – the less able employees will not respond well to the possibility of rewards that they do not expect to receive.
- There is difficulty in measuring some performance objectively.
- Poorly conducted assessments can reduce morale.
- It can encourage people to focus too narrowly on those tasks that give them 'brownie points'.
- Undue emphasis on the individual results in a potential weakening of teamwork.
- It can lead to upward drift in pay out of step with productivity increases.
- Handled badly it can damage the psychological contract and lead to conflict.
- It can damage the employment relationship if its execution is regarded as unfair.

Summary

This chapter has presented an overview of reward management, highlighting how payment systems are value laden and subjective. The perspectives of those instituting them, as well as of those in receipt of, or indeed analysing them, have an impact on the ways in which schemes are regarded. In particular whether or not a scheme is perceived as fair, and distributively just, will be dependent on a range of subjective factors. When designing a payment system organisations need to bear a number of different factors in mind:

- They need to look at the external factors that may influence pay and balance these against any internal criterion they wish to apply while being aware of the impact that the final decision may have on perceptions of equity.
- There has to be a decision about whether the system is to be simple – this may lead to rigidities and employee relations problems in future years – or whether it is to be a more complex but flexible system. The danger here is that, although flexibility is appealing, organisations have to ensure that they do not indirectly discriminate against certain sectors of their workforce with the corresponding effects on productivity, morale and labour turnover.
- Employers have to decide whether to have one or several concurrent pay systems; should, for example, there be harmonisation of conditions or should there be a continuation of the traditional differences between blue- and white-collar employees? If the differences persist then this might lead to arguments about differentials and a 'them and us' culture.
- Consideration should be given to the issues linked to equity and fairness. Is the balance between effort and reward reflected accurately? Are employee expectations of fairness and transparency likely to be met? Are any differentials between pay bands proportional to the value added to the organisation by the individuals concerned?

- Importantly there has to be consistency of aim. It is no good, for example, rewarding individual effort while simultaneously expecting strong cohesive team performances – the two are incompatible.
- Getting a reward structure wrong may lead to a damaged employment relationship with high turnover, increased levels of conflict, a rise in absence, demotivated and demoralised employees.

Review Questions

1 Discuss the various ways that payment systems can impact upon on the employment relationship and analyse the effect of each on the notions of equitable justice.
2 Is conflict about pay inevitable? Why did you reach your conclusion?
3 Explain why a reward strategy may seem desirable in principle yet is barely in evidence in practice.
4 To what extent is pay strategy tied to the 'market rate' consistent with both an 'ability to pay' and 'reward for performance'? What are the implications of such a policy for the employment relationship and the psychological contract?
5 Linking your answer to appropriate reward theories, discuss whether it is possible to be simultaneously internally and externally equitable in terms of employee reward.

Revision Exercise 12.1

Read the scenario below about the reduction in pay for workers employed by Pret a Manger. What does it tell you about:

- equity theory
- perceptions of justice
- the impact of both of these on the employment relationship?

The majority of staff working for Pret a Manger earn the legal minimum wage of £8.91 per hour. In April 2021 staff were informed that the £1 per hour pay increase, given to staff following a positive mystery shopper experience, would temporarily be reduced to 50p an hour. At the beginning of August this change was made permanent. However, following employee complaints, this decision was quickly reversed although a separate perk – paid breaks – will not be reinstated as the company is struggling (sales have fallen by 60% year-on-year and more than 3,000 jobs have been lost following the closure of 74 sites).

Source: Crush, 2021

Revision Exercise 12.2

Gender pay gaps tend to be slightly wider among highly educated men and women than among their less educated counterparts, though a handful of countries (e.g., Greece, Korea and Turkey) show wider gender pay gaps among low-skilled men and women. Table 12.1 shows the wage differences between men and women from a variety of different countries over the period 2016-2020.

- What do the figures tell you about the wage gap over time in each different country?
- What impact do you think these differences might have on perceptions of equity if you are:
  - Male and Canadian?
  - Female and Colombian?

Table 12.1

Location	The Gender Wage Gap (%)				
	2016	2017	2018	2019	2020
Australia	11.53846	11.66419	11.71429	14.15788	9.86386
Canada	18.22115	18.17322	18.51852	17.60714	16.11253
Czech Republic	16.02343	15.61401	15.12741	14.71433	12.37286
Ireland*			8.284024		
France *			11.8238		
Japan	24.60129	24.51809	23.53737	23.48001	22.51857
Korea	36.66667	34.61738	34.10731	32.48044	31.48475
Mexico	16.49225	11.11111	14	18.75	9.612403
New Zealand	7.769231	7.150838	7.869693	6.50845	4.581467
Norway	6.306306	5.494761	5.129369	4.367867	4.813864
Slovakia	13.89918	15.04004	15.66208	13.86985	11.01447
Sweden	8.169935	7.348243	7.142857	7.575758	7.418398
Great Britain	16.79654	16.5341	16.31042	16.09981	12.27787
USA	18.14208	18.17216	18.91059	18.47071	17.6525
Colombia	7.091751	7.692308	5.787926	4	-0.11403

*not all figures are available

The gender wage gap is defined as the difference between median earnings of men and women relative to median earnings of men.

Source: OECD (2021) Available at: https://data.oecd.org/earnwage/gender-wage-gap.htm (Accessed 21 August 2021)

Relevant Articles for Further Reading

Dromey, J. (2018) *Power to the People*. Available at: www.ippr.org/files/2018-06/cej-trade-unions-may18-.pdf (accessed 1 July 2021).

This provides a wealth of information about pay and makes a strong case for government encouraging the collective voice influencing pay decision making.

Garbers, Y. and Konradt, U. (2014) 'The effect of financial incentives on performance: A quantitative review of individual and team-based financial incentives', Journal of Occupational and Organizational Psychology, 87(1): 102–37.

This article demonstrates how equitably distributed rewards lead to higher performance and suggests that managers should design appraisal and feedback processes for individual team members and the team as a whole.

Montag-Smit, T. A. and Smit, B. W. (2021) 'What are you hiding? Employee attributions for pay secrecy policies', Human Resource Management Journal, 31(3): 704–28.

Pay secrecy, according to this research can lead to lack of trust and ill will towards the employing organisation.

References

Adams, S. (1963) 'Towards an understanding of inequity', *Journal of Abnormal and Social Psychology*, 67(4): 422–36.

Aoki, N. and Rawat, S. (2020) 'Performance-based pay: Investigating its international prevalence in light of national contexts', *The American Review of Public Administration*, 50 (8): 865–79.

Armstrong, M. (2000) *Strategic Human Resource Management: A Guide to Action* (2nd edn). London: Kogan Page.

Armstrong, M. and Baron, A. (1998) *Performance Management: The New Realities*. London: IPD.

Armstrong, M. and Brown, D. (2006) *Strategic Reward: Making it Happen*. London: Kogan Page.

Arrowsmith, J. and Marginson, P. (2009) *Wage Flexibility*. Dublin: Eurofound. Available at: www.eurofound.europa.eu/docs/eiro/tn0803019s/tn0803019s.pdf (accessed 14 January 2014).

Arrowsmith, J. and Marginson, P. (2010) 'The decline of incentive pay in British manufacturing', *Industrial Relations Journal*, 41(4): 289–311.

Arrowsmith, J. and Marginson, P. (2011) 'Variable pay and collective bargaining in British retail banking', *British Journal of Industrial Relations*, 49(1): 54–79.

Atkinson, J. and Meager, N. (1994) 'Running to stand still: The small business in the labour market', in J. Atkinson and D. J. Storey (eds), *Employment, the Small Firm and the Labour Market*. London: Tavistock.

Baldamus, W. (1961) *Efficiency and effort: An analysis of industrial administration*. London: Tavistock Publications.

Bechter, B., Braakmann, N. and Brandl, B. (2021) 'Variable pay and/or collective wage bargaining? Complements or substitutes?', *ILR Review*, 74(2): 443–69.

Becton, J. B. and Field, H. S. (2009) 'Cultural differences in organizational citizenship behavior: A comparison between Chinese and American employees', *International Journal of Human Resource Management*, 20: 1651–69.

Beer, M. (ed.) (1984) *Managing Human Assets*. London: Simon and Schuster.

Bender, K. A., Green, C. P. and Heywood J. S. (2012) 'Piece rates and workplace injury: Does survey evidence support Adam Smith?', *Journal of Population Economics*, 25(2): 569–90.

Bland, A. (2021) 'Daily Telegraph plans to link journalists' pay with article popularity', *The Guardian*, 15 March. Available at: www.theguardian.com/media/2021/mar/15/daily-telegraph-plans-link-journalists-pay-article-popularity?CMP=Share_iOSApp_Other (accessed 21 March 2021).

Blau, G. (1994) 'Testing the effect of level and importance of pay referents on pay level satisfaction', *Human Relations*, 47(10): 1251–62.

Bowles, H. R., Babcock, L. and Lai, L. (2007) 'Social incentives for gender differences in the propensity to initiate negotiations: Sometimes it does hurt to ask', *Organizational Behavior and Human Decision Processes*, 103(1): 84–103.

Bratton, J. and Gold, J. (2012) *Human Resource Management Theory and Practice* (5th edn). Basingstoke: Palgrave.

Brown, W. (1989) 'Company pay policies: The art of getting change on the cheap', Shirley Memorial Lecture, Manchester, 18 May, Mimeographed, pp. 14–16, cited in J. E. Isaac (ed.) (2001), 'Performance-related pay: The importance of fairness', *Journal of Industrial Relations*, 43: 111.

Burawoy, M. (1979) *Manufacturing Consent: Changes in the Labor Process under Monopoly Capitalism*. Chicago, IL: University of Chicago Press.

Campos, M. M., Depalo, D., Papapetrou, E., Perez, J. J. and Ramos, R. (2017) 'Understanding the public sector pay gap', *IZA Journal of Labor Policy*, 6(7). doi:10.1186/s40173-017-0086-0

Cardella, E., & Depew, B. (2018). Output restriction and the ratchet effect: Evidence from a real-effort work task. *Games and Economic Behavior*, 107, 182-202.

Chen, X., Ren, T. and Knoke, D. (2013) 'Do nonprofits treat their employees differently? Incentive pay and health benefits', *Nonprofit Management and Leadership*, 20 December.

Chiang, F. F. and Birch, T. A. (2012) 'The performance implications of financial and non-financial rewards: An Asian Nordic comparison', *Journal of Management Studies*, 49(3): 538–70.

Chiang, F. F. and Birch, T. A. (2020) 'Reward Management', *Labour*, 148.

Chiang, F. F., Lemański, M. K. and Birch, T. A. (2016) 'The transfer and diffusion of HRM practices within MNCs: Lessons learned and future research directions', *The International Journal of Human Resource Management*, 28(1): 234–58. doi:10.1080/09585192.2016.1246461

CIPD (2007) *Reward Management Annual Survey Report 2007*. London: Chartered Institute of Personnel and Development.

CIPD (2021) *Reward Management Survey*. Available at: www.cipd.co.uk/Images/reward-management-fairness_tcm18-91389.pdf (accessed 5 May 2021).

Connelly, B. L., Tihanyi, L., Crook T. R. and Gangloff, K. A. (2014) 'Tournament theory: Thirty years of contests and competitions', *Journal of Management*, 40(1): 16–47.

Cox, A. (2000) 'The importance of employee participation in determining pay system effectiveness', *International Journal of Management Reviews*, 2(4): 357–75.

Crush, P. (2021) 'Pret a Manger in bonus U-turn', *Employee Benefits*, 17 August. Available at: https://employeebenefits.co.uk/pret-a-manger-u-turn/?ID=zqjqf~qhnq99~n9th9j~W4ik~Ky0g k&utm_campaign=Employee%20Benefits%20Weekly-200821-DE&utm_medium=email&utm_ source=email&utm_content=newsletter (accessed 20 August 2021).

D'Arcy, C. (2018) *Low Pay Britain 2018*. Available at: www.resolutionfoundation.org/app/uploads/2018/05/Low-Pay-Britain-2018.pdf (accessed 4 June 2021).

Department for Business, Energy and Industrial Strategy (DBEIS) (2021) *National Living Wage And National Minimum Wage: Government Evidence On Compliance And Enforcement 2019/20*. Available at: https://assets.publishing.service.gov.uk/government/uploads/system/uploads/attachment_data/file/964235/nmw-enforcement-compliance-report-2019-2020.pdf (accessed 22 August 2021).

Dickson, M., Postel-Vinay, F. and Turon, H. (2014) 'The lifetime earnings premium in the public sector: The view from Europe', *Labour Economics*, 31: 141–61.

Dreher, G. (1981) 'Predicting the salary satisfaction of exempt employees', *Personnel Psychology*, 34(3): 579–89.

Dromey, J. (2018) *Power to the People*. Available at: www.ippr.org/files/2018-06/cej-trade-unions-may18-.pdf (accessed 1 July 2021).

Edwards, P. K. (2003) 'The employment relationship and the field of industrial relations', in P. K. Edwards (ed.), *Industrial Relations: Theory and Practice* (2nd edn). Oxford: Blackwell.

Farnham, D. and Pimlott, J. (1995) *Understanding Industrial Relations*. London: Cassell.

Fredrickson, J. W., Davis-Blake, A. and Sanders, W. M. G. (2010) 'Sharing the wealth: Social comparisons and pay dispersion in the CEO's top team', *Strategic Management Journal*, 31: 1031–53.

Frömer, R., Lin, H., Wolf, C. D., Inzlicht, M. and Shenhav, A. (2020) *When Effort Matters: Expectations of Reward and Efficacy Guide Cognitive Control Allocation*. doi: 10.1101/2020.05.14.095935

Godard, J. (2020) 'Labor and employment practices: The rise and fall of the new managerialism', in B. Bowden, J. Muldoon, A. M. Gould and A. J. McMurray (eds), *The Palgrave Handbook of Management History*. Cham: Palgrave Macmillan, pp. 913–33.

Gouldner, A. (1960) 'The norm of reciprocity: A preliminary statement', *American Sociological Review*, 25(2): 161–78.

Greenberg, J. (1987) 'A taxonomy of organizational justice theories', *Academy of Management Review*, 12(1): 9–22.

Greenberg, J. (1990) 'Employee theft as a reaction to underpayment inequity: The hidden cost of pay cuts', *Journal of Applied Psychology*, 75: 561–8.

Guest, D. (1992) *Motivation for Results – Incentives Now*. London: Personnel Management Publications.

Heckhausen, H. (2018) 'Motivation as a function of expectancy and incentive', in H. Heckhausen (ed.) *Motivation and Action*. Cham: Springer, pp. 113–61.

Heery, E. (2000) 'Trade unions and the management of reward', in G. White and J. Drucker (eds), *Reward Management: A Critical Text*. London: Routledge.

Heilman, M. E. (2012) 'Gender stereotypes and workplace bias', *Research in Organizational Behavior*, 32: 113–35.

Hertzberg, F. (1968) 'One more time: How do you motivate employees?, *Harvard Business Review*, Jan.–Feb.: 53–62.

HMRC (2021) *HMRC Reveals Absurd Excuses For Not Paying National Minimum Wage*. Available at: www.gov.uk/government/news/hmrc-reveals-absurd-excuses-for-not-paying-national-minimum-wage (accessed 21 September 2021).

Howell, J. (2021) 'CEO Secrets: "We tried paying everyone the same salary. It failed"', *BBC News*, 27 January. Available at: www.bbc.co.uk/news/business-55800730 (accessed 28 January 2021).

Hyman, R. (1974) 'Inequality, ideology and industrial relations', *British Journal of Industrial Relations*, 12(2): 171–90.

Isaac, J. E. (2001) 'Performance related pay: The importance of fairness', *The Journal of Industrial Relations*, 43(2): 111–23.

Joyce, S. (2020) 'Rediscovering the cash nexus, again: Subsumption and the labour–capital relation in platform work', *Capital & Class*, 44(4): 541–52.

Kessler, I. (2003) 'Pay and performance', in B. Towers (ed.), *The Handbook of Employment Relations Law and Practice* (4th edn). London: Kogan Page, pp. 331–51.

King, M. (2007) 'Turmoil in financial markets: What can central banks do?', paper submitted to the Treasury Committee, London. Available at: www.bankofengland.co.uk/publications/Documents/other/treasurycommittee/other/paper070912.pdf (accessed 2 April 2014).

Kray, L. J. and Thompson, L. (2005) 'Gender stereotypes and negotiation performance: An examination of theory and research', *Research in Organizational Behavior*, 26: 103–82.

Ligthart, P.E., Poutsma, E. and Brewster, C. (2021) 'The development of financial participation in Europe', *British Journal of Industrial Relations*.

Locke, E. A. and Latham, G. P. (2020) 'Building a theory by induction: The example of goal setting theory', *Organizational Psychology Review*, 10(3–4): 223–39.

Low Pay Commission (2014) *Terms of Reference*. Available at: www.gov.uk/government/organisations/low-pay-commission/about/terms-of-reference (accessed 15 February 2014).

Mahoney, T. A. (1989) 'Multiple pay contingencies: Strategic design of compensation', *Human Resource Management*, 28(3)A: 337–47.

Maungwa, M. R. (2021) 'Effects of labour unrest on the share returns of the JSE Top 40 companies', *Doctoral dissertation, North-West University (South Africa)*.

Miceli, M. and Jung, I. (1991) 'Predictors and outcomes of reactions to pay for performance plans', *Journal of Applied Psychology*, 76(4): 508–21.

Montag-Smit, T. A. and Smit, B. W. (2021) 'What are you hiding? Employee attributions for pay secrecy policies', *Human Resource Management Journal*, 31(3): 704–28.

Neumark, D., Thompson, M. and Koyle, L. (2012) 'The effects of living wage laws on low-wage workers and low-income families: What do we know now?', *IZA Journal of Labor Policy*, 1(1): 1–34.

Neunsinger, S. (2018) 'The unobtainable magic of numbers: Equal remuneration, the ILO and the International Trade Union Movement 1950s–1980s', in E. Boris, D. Hoehtker and S. Zimmerman (eds), *Women's ILO: Transnational Networks, Global Labour Standards and Gender Equity, 1919 to Present*. Leiden: Brill, pp. 121–48.

NHS England (2014) *The Review Body on Doctors' & Dentists' Remuneration: Review for 2014, General Medical Practitioners and General Dental Practitioners*. Available at: www.england.nhs.uk/wp-content/uploads/2013/09/ddrb-evid.pdf (accessed 6 November 2015).

O'Connor, E. (1999) 'Minding the workers: The meaning of human and human relations in Elton Mayo', *Organization*, 6(2): 223–46.

OECD (2021) *Gender Wage Gap (Indicator)*. doi: 10.1787/7cee77aa-en

Office for National Statistics (2021) *Low and High Pay in the UK: 2021*. Available at: www.ons.gov.uk/employmentandlabourmarket/peopleinwork/earningsandworkinghours/bulletins/lowandhighpayuk/2021 (accessed 21 May 2022).

Pepper, A., Gosling, T. and Gore, J. (2015) 'Fairness, envy, guilt and greed: Building equity considerations into agency theory', *Human Relations*, 68(8): 1291–1314.

Perkins, S. J. and White, G. (2008) *Employee Reward: Alternatives, Consequences and Contexts*. London: CIPD.

Ponsford, D. and Tobitt, C. (2021) 'Telegraph's proposed pay incentives for reporters are about subscriber satisfaction not clickbait', *Press Gazette*, 16 March. Available at: https://pressgazette.co.uk/cash-for-clicks-telegraph/ (accessed 21 March 2021).

Porter, L. W. and Lawler, E. E. (1968) *Managerial Attitudes and Performance*. Homewood, IL: Irwin.

Pratt, L. (2020) 'Spanish government introduces law for businesses to disclose gender pay gap figure', *Employee Benefits*, 13 October. Available at: https://employeebenefits.co.uk/spanish-government-pay-gap-law/ (accessed 13 October 2020).

Rice, R., Phillips, S. and McFarlin, D. (1990) 'Multiple discrepancies and pay satisfaction', *Journal of Applied Psychology*, 75(4): 386–93.

Robinson, D. (1973) 'Differentials and incomes policy', *Industrial Relations Journal*, 4(1): 4–20.

Schulz, F., Valizade, D. and Charlwood, A. (2022). The effect of intra-workplace pay inequality on employee trust in managers: Assessing a multilevel moderated mediation effect model. *Human Relations*, 75(4), 705-733.

SDWorx (2021) *Show Your Employees What They Really Earn*. Available at: www.sdworx.co.uk/en/blog/payroll/show-your-employees-what-they-really-earn (accessed 4 June 2021).

Sharma, M. (2021) 'Salary is highest priority for employees, new research finds', *Employee Benefits*, 15 January. Available at: www.hrreview.co.uk/hr-news/salary-is-highest-priority-for-employees-new-research-finds/130631 (accessed 4 June 2021).

Sisson, K. (2010) *Employment Relations Matters*, University of Warwick, UK. Available at: http://digitalcommons.ilr.cornell.edu/articles/29/ (accessed 12 October 2013).

Tenhiälä, A. and Laamanen, T. (2018) 'The contingent effects of strategic orientation and pay system design on firm performance: Right on the money?', *Strategic Management Journal*, 39(13): 3408–33.

Tepper, B., Duffy, M. K., Henle, C.A. and Schurer Lambert, L. (2006) 'Procedural injustice, victim precipitation and abusive supervision', *Personnel Psychology*, 15(1): 101–23.

Trevor, J. (2010) *Can Pay be Strategic: A Critical Exploration of Strategic Pay in Practice*. Basingstoke: Palgrave McMillan.

Trevor, J. and Brown, W. (2012) 'The limits on pay as a strategic tool: Obstacles to alignment in non-union environments', *British Journal of Industrial Relations*, 52(3): 553–78.

TUC (15.01.2020) *One in Five Workers are Banned from Discussing their Pay, TUC Poll Finds*, press release, 15 January. Available at: www.tuc.org.uk/news/one-five-workers-are-banned-discussing-their-pay-tuc-poll-finds (accessed 3 June 2021).

Turnea, E. S. and Prodan, A. (2020) 'The relative influence of total reward on retention of human resources', *Revista de Cercetare si Interventie Sociala*, 69.

Van Wanrooy, B., Bewley, H., Bryson, A., Forth, J., Freeth, S., Stokes, L. and Wood, S. (2013) *Employment Relations in the Shadow of Recession: Findings from the 2011 Workplace Employment Relations Study*. Basingstoke: Palgrave Macmillan.

Vroom, V. H. (1982) *Work and Motivation*. Malabar, FL: Krieger.

Wall, T. (2021) 'Ocado drivers paid less than £5 an hour', *The Observer*, 22 August: 1–2.

West, K. L. and Mykerezi, E. (2011) 'Teachers' unions and compensation: The impact of collective bargaining on salary schedules and performance pay schemes', *Economics of Education Review*, 30(1): 99–108.

White, G. (2009) 'Determining pay', in G. White and J. Drucker (eds), *Reward Management: A Critical Text* (2nd edn). London: Routledge.

Wright, A. (2004) *Reward Management in Context*. London: CIPD.

13

FAIRNESS
IN PRACTICE

Learning Outcomes

By the end of this chapter, you should be able to:

- use the different facets of fairness and organisational justice when analysing aspects of the employment relationship
- critically evaluate workplace situations in the light of power, equity theory and trust
- competently analyse and evaluate the importance of employee voice (direct and indirect) and its links to perceptions of fairness
- critically examine the role of the line manager and how this links with the use of power, the engendering of trust and efficient organisational performance
- be critically aware of how fairness (or lack of it) leads to expressions of conflict and influences the ways in which conflict is managed.

What to Expect

This chapter can be used for revision purposes, as it sets fairness at work into context, consolidating information and salient issues derived from all of the preceding chapters. It also explores some of the practical aspects, such as redundancy, of managing a contested employment relationship in an equitable way. Fairness, voice, power and notions of trust will be examined in the light of practical examples drawn from the workplace, and a number of case studies and exercises encourage analysis and reflection around the notions of equity within the practicalities of managing employment.

—┤Exercise 13.1├—————————————————————————————

Consider the questions below, and justify your answers with reference to academic concepts and models from previous chapters.

● What factors, do you think, might influence employees' judgements of fairness in the workplace?
● How might managers counteract the feelings that some people are being treated unfairly? To what extent, and why, does this matter?

_____

Fairness in Context

Legal, social, cultural and economic environments all play a part in shaping behaviour, expectations, values and perceptions. Employee attitudes, behaviours and ways of looking at things are influenced by all of these factors *and*, importantly, by the organisations that they work for and the countries that they work in. Organisations too function in, and are influenced by, their legal, economic and social environments – which in turn influence the ways that they treat their employees. In addition, the increasing use of a range of digital technologies, particularly machine learning technologies, has impacted the ways in which work is structured and controlled (Joint Research Centre, 2019) creating many jobs where workers are isolated, without voice and with little recourse to worker representation (Meacham and Tava, 2021).

The employment relationship is symbiotic with employers and employees needing and reacting to one another. Employee/worker behaviour does not 'stand alone' as organisations have a direct impact and influence on the quality of workers' perceptions, behaviours and subsequent patterns of work. Such perceptions (and ensuing attitudes and behaviours) will themselves have an impact on colleagues, other workers and upon the subsequent actions of the organisation. The cultural mores and values experienced by workers will influence the ways in which their employing organisations are regarded, in particular whether the job requirements and working environment are fair. Similarly, the prevailing employment legislation, together with the degree of publicity it receives, will influence employee expectations of employer behaviour. (However, if unemployment is high and opportunities scarce it may be that individuals will 'put up with' illegal terms and conditions of employment that, in other circumstances, they would not – precarious workers are often forced by circumstances to take whatever jobs they can.) Whether individuals like the ways in which their organisation operates will have an impact on their subsequent beliefs and actions. If, for example, someone is happy at work and regards the organisation as a 'just' one, then this will engender feelings of wellness; if however the employing organisation is seen as unjust, then this is an antecedent to the employee/worker experiencing feelings of suffering and withdrawal. These feelings could be expressed in a number of different ways: unauthorised absenteeism, for example, represents behavioural withdrawal, while expressing an intention to resign represents an attitudinal withdrawal, while feelings of alienation and dislocation from the work process represent psychological withdrawal from the employing organisation (Milić, 2021; Yu et al., 2021).

Case Study 13.1

Bulgarian Kitchen Hand Physically and Verbally Abused

Mr Mustafa employed Mr Dimov, a Bulgarian with very little English, in both of his adjoining restaurants. Taking advantage of his vulnerable position (no family and little English) he paid him £300 a week in cash. Dimov took no holiday and received no holiday pay. As there was no written contract he was unaware both of his rights, and what his pay should have been. Dimov worked in one of the establishments during the day and the other in the evening seven days a week. This made washing his only work tee-shirt difficult and he had to leave work if he needed to attend to personal matters such as having a haircut or going to the bank. The tribunal heard that he worked for a consecutive period of at least two years during which time he was harassed, underpaid and overworked.

In November 2019 Mr Dimov had had enough of being shouted at – called 'donkey', 'gypsy', 'f***ing Bulgarian', 'idiot', 'f***ing c**t' 'pig' (on one occasion pushed against a wall and held by the throat) – and he resigned. After contacting ACAS in January 2020, he brought a tribunal claim against Mr Mustafa.

The tribunal had some difficulty in working out what had happened over his period of employment, in part because much of the paperwork (employment contract and some payslips) was missing and partly because the witnesses and defendant were not always credible and changed their accounts of what happened. Mr Dimov's credibility was helped when Mr Mustafa lost his temper on several occasions during the hearing.

On 12 April 2022 the Tribunal found in favour of Mr Dimov: his employer had been exploitative, hostile, degrading, humiliating and offensive, failing to pay the national minimum wage and holiday pay and harassing him verbally and physically.

Source: Dimov v Mustafa T/a Mambocino/Riverside Fish and Steakhouse and Gastro Erith Trading Ltd. ET2301194/2020

Budd (2004, 2010) has pointed out that an optimum employment relationship requires a *balance* between equity, efficiency and voice. *Efficiency*, relating to the ways in which resources are deployed, is an important objective within the employment relationship because of the clear implications for economic value and prosperity – yet efficiency, as seen in Case Study 13.1, can come at a cost to employees/workers. This is perhaps even more evident when it is driven by algorithmic management. Despite the constraints and demands of efficiency, those who work are morally, and in many societies legally, entitled to equitable, fair treatment at work, together with opportunities to voice their opinions and to be listened to by their employer. Crucially, Budd maintains that equity and voice are critical objectives of the employment relationship, even when they do *not* directly improve efficiency. What matters therefore is striking a balance between all three of these objectives. Where employees are treated in ways that they perceive to be equitable and fair then the levels of trust in management and commitment to the organisation are correspondingly high. According to Tzafrir and Dolan (2004), such trust becomes apparent when the elements of harmony, reliability and concern are present. *Harmony* relates to a set of values shared by those within the workforce and *reliability* is an indication that employees can expect management to show consistency between the rhetoric of what it says it is going to do and the practice of what it actually does do. *Concern* is where there is evidence of self-interest being balanced against the interest of another, often involving a degree of empathetic awareness. Levels of trust and employee perceptions of organisational justice are interlinked and interdependent, each impacting upon and reinforcing the other. Indeed, where there is a breach in the psychological contract this is negatively related to reduced trust in management often leading to workplace resignations (Manolopoulos et al., 2022; Megeirhi et al., 2020; Yang et al., 2020). Trust is an outcome of the social exchange between an employer and an employee/worker and it underwrites the manifestations of employee behaviours such as loyalty, workplace discretionary behaviours and commitment to the employing organisation (Aryee et al., 2002; Yu, 2021). If an employee perceives an organisation to be one that operates with a high level of justice this will lead to their perceiving the organisation as trustworthy; this perception, in its turn, influences employee behaviour (Blau, 1964). However, if an injustice becomes apparent employees' levels of trust toward the organisation are diminished, resulting in negative employee attitudes and behaviours (Abela and Debono, 2019; Thomas et al., 2003). Workplaces that exhibit both Budd's and Tzafrir and Dolan's concepts are likely to be those where the employees perceive them to be 'decent', fair places to work.

Exercise 13.2

- Read Case Study 13.2 and then analyse a) Mr Kelly's and b) his colleagues' experiences in the light of Tzafrir and Dolan's essential components of trust.
- Do you think the Tribunal decision was fair to both Mr Kelly *and* the colleagues he treated inappropriately?
- Why did you reach this conclusion?

Case Study 13.2

Sainsbury's Dismissal of Racist Worker Accused of Groping Staff Deemed Unfair

Mr Kelly had worked for Sainsbury's for a number of years, and initially he was well regarded and seen worthy of training for promotion. Unfortunately, due to memory problems and child-like behaviour patterns following a car accident, his performance began to deteriorate, and he was unable to continue with the company's management training programme. However, he remained employed by Sainsbury's. In 2010 he was disciplined for using inappropriate language to female colleagues. Later, in 2015, he received an informal warning and was told to 'know your audience' after he called a colleague a 'yummy mummy' and asked for her phone number.

Complaints against Mr Kelly began to accrue. In April 2020 another colleague formally complained, alleging he had called her 'bitch' and 'whore', as well as groping her and rubbing her shoulders. The store manager interviewed a number of staff and decided *no* action should be taken. This was appealed by the complainant. Her appeal was upheld. It was reinvestigated by a store manager from another Sainsbury's branch, who decided Kelly should face disciplinary action. When interviewed Kelly had no memory of the incident.

Later an anonymous letter was sent to Sainsbury's claiming Kelly had asked a colleague about her bra size, regularly used inappropriate and explicit language, and stood behind women - including customers - and rubbed their shoulders. But, as there was no firm evidence substantiating this complaint, the manager took no action. Yet this was not the end of the matter; the accuser phoned the company's whistleblowing hotline and consequently the case was reopened, and an investigation undertaken. During the investigation Mr Kelly was suspended and more colleagues gave evidence against Mr Kelly. One, a lady of Pakistani ethnic origins. said that Mr Kelly had touched her on her hips, her shoulder and her back. Claiming he had, over a period of four years 'said stuff' to her about her 'butt', sent her a weird video on Facebook, and had referred to her as 'Bin Laden's mistress'. At a disciplinary hearing in July 2020, Mr Kelly was told he would be dismissed due to unacceptable behaviour out of line with company values and policy.

Mr Kelly appealed, claiming the evidence was false and that Sainsbury's 'had no regard to his health and wellbeing'. Furthermore, he said he had struggled to remember anything since his car accident and that he had a 'child-like' nature. The manager conducting the appeal hearing suggested it would have been unreasonable to expect the investigating manager to take the car accident into account as it had happened 16 years previously and upheld the decision to dismiss Kelly.

Mr Kelly took the case to an employment tribunal that upheld his complaint (21 February 2022), finding that Kelly's behaviour arose as a consequence of his disability caused by his car accident, and that Sainsbury's had treated him unfavourably by subjecting him to disciplinary proceedings and then dismissing him without taking into account his disability and poor memory. Sainsbury's manager and HR department had not, it said, investigated the full contents of Mr Kelly's file and the psychologist's reports following the car accident. The tribunal pointed out that,

A proportionate approach would have entailed seeking an update of the medical evidence it already held on file, either via Occupational Health or going directly to a psychiatrist seeking information on the extent to which Mr Kelly's behaviour would have been explained by his head injuries, what steps might be taken to prevent such behaviour and what chances there would have been of those steps being successful. (para. 106.4)

Accordingly, the tribunal found that he was unfairly dismissed and discriminated against.

Source: Mr C Kelly v Sainsbury's Supermarkets Ltd, ET 3315272/2020

Fairness and Power

The balance of power, and the ways in which power is exercised in the employment relationship, is a crucial element in the ways in which an employee regards their work environment, and in particular whether or not they regard the employing organisation as a just one. In spite of the power at their disposal an employer (or an employee) may decide against using the power available to them. It is not unknown for individuals to occasionally refrain from deploying power for the purposes of their own self-interest to the detriment of others (Edwards and Wajcman, 2005: 118–20). Power when restrained (for reasons other than self-interest) in favour of the employee usually results in positive perceptions about the employer. When, of course, power is not constrained and is used in an inappropriate way, such as when a line manager uses their power to sexually exploit someone in their department, then this is regarded negatively. (Richard Edelmann, the author of *Interpersonal Conflicts at Work* [2009], suggests that rebutting a sexual relationship with an insistent senior colleague has the potential for unpleasant repercussions, pointing out that such a potentially exploitative situation concerning unequal participants is more than likely to be problematic – Allen, 2006.) A less extreme example of use of exploitative power would be where an employer, knowing someone is desperate to keep their job because of their financial commitments, asks them to work for longer hours.

The following three case snippets are examples of different uses of power. The first two show how those in an organisation might exert power, and the last gives an indication of the way in which skilled employees may be able to exert some control over their terms and conditions.

Case Snippet 13.1

False Accusation

Writing in *The Guardian*, Misa Han describes how her employer, noticing that she had logged onto Facebook for 10 minutes while at work, 'threatened to sue me for "stealing" company time unless I worked the following week, unpaid. I obliged reluctantly and did so because I prided myself in having good work ethics, and was mortified that my 10-minute Facebook interlude had supposedly turned me into a slacker'.

Source: Han, 2014

Case Snippet 13.2

Personal Blackmail

Helen Marks, an HR professional at the Derbyshire Healthcare NHS Foundation Trust, was friendly with the chairman of the Trust, Alan Baines. They often lunched together discussing both work and personal matters. Just before Helen got married Mr Baines confessed his love for her. When she returned from her honeymoon Mr Baines intimated that he wanted their relationship to become sexual. Mrs Marks did not, and she made this plain. Things deteriorated, Mr Baines sent her a number of abusive texts, including one calling her a 'whore', and accused her of having an affair with a colleague. Then, to her surprise, she was accused of bullying, suspended and escorted from the building. She resigned and successfully claimed for constructive dismissal and sexual harassment at an Employment Tribunal.

Source: Crowson, 2015

Case Snippet 13.3

Retaining Good Workers

Skilled staff are often difficult to replace so employees who have the skills that employers need are in a better position to ask for the terms and conditions of employment that specifically suit their personal circumstances. A number of organisations are endeavouring to ensure that they retain skilled employees while remaining consistent in their treatment of the rest of the workforce. For example, the NHS has a myriad different contract types in order to attract nurses back into the profession after a career break, while companies wanting to retain financial and accountancy staff are finding they have to adjust their salary scales so that these staff receive the market rate.

Bewley and Forth (2010) in their analysis of the 4,010 responses to the UK Fair Treatment at Work Survey 2008, found that a range of things influenced whether or not someone was likely to be on the receiving end of adverse treatment from an employer. These included:

- the skills, temperament and abilities of the employees themselves
- the type of employing organisation, including whether there was a union presence
- the type of job
- the external labour market
- whether an organisation was in a healthy position within its own product market.

They argued that if a combination of these things created a situation where the balance of power was tilted in the favour of the employer then this would, *ipso facto*, increase the likelihood of the employees being treated in an unfavourable way. However, if the balance favoured the employee then the likelihood of unfavourable treatment decreased. They suggested that when the imbalance of power

> ... tips in the favour of the employer, this creates an opportunity for the employer to shape the employment relationship in their favour. This may usually be done with the employee's explicit approval (i.e. through negotiation) or with the employee's implicit consent if the outcome is seen as reasonable in the circumstances. However, employers may sometimes act unilaterally in ways which do not meet with the employee's approval. The opportunities for the employer to do so are accentuated by the indeterminacy of the labour contract, which typically fails to specify, in full, the rights and responsibilities of either party, thereby creating uncertainties over the precise behaviours and outcomes which are expected on either side. (Bewley and Forth, 2010: 5)

Chapters 4 and 5 discuss different types of contracts of employment, and it is apparent that the old Master–Servant regulations from which the current contract legislation originates, influences and prescribes the ways that employees/workers allow their employers to control their working time and effort, often with little room for discretion. The very imprecision of contracts often ensures that unscrupulous organisations exert disproportionate, unwarranted, levels of power legitimately. Such power, particularly when it is deployed in inappropriate ways, may, or may not, be tempered by the presence of a trade union. Despite the decline in union membership and the trend towards fewer collective bargaining arrangements, the presence of trade unions exerts a positive influence on the employment relationship: where they are recognised, their agents, acting as a countervailing power, help improve terms and conditions and provide employee representation for workplace difficulties (Bryson and Forth, 2010a, 2010b). Perhaps unremarkably, where they are not recognised unions still have the ability to indirectly influence some employers – who choose to act in fair and reasonable ways precisely to prevent possible union incursion into their workplaces.

Fairness and Justice at Work: A Recap

Otaye and Wong (2014) suggest that being aware of unfairness within, and by, organisations is becoming a key subject for both scholars and practitioners. Getting fairness wrong, they suggest, costs companies billions each year; while those organisations getting it right and treating their employees with fairness, integrity and sensitivity are more likely to reap the benefits of higher levels of commitment, productivity and, it can be inferred, a happier, less conflict-ridden employment relationship.

News Flash 13.1

Employees Hiding Reasons for Absence Linked to Mistrust in Employers

In the August and September of 2019 an international health insurance provider, Aetna, surveyed 3,520 employees across the USA, UAE, UK and Singapore and found that two in five office workers had little or no trust in their organisation's ability to treat their mental health as a priority, thereby exposing a gap between what employers promise and what they achieve when it comes to mental health support. Four years earlier research by AXA PPP healthcare revealed that 23% of employees claim not to tell their line manager the real reason for their absence when calling in sick because they're afraid of being judged; another 15% said they're afraid they won't be believed.

An online survey of 1,000 senior business managers, MDs, CEOs and owners, together with another online survey of 1,000 other (non-exec) employees, was undertaken in February 2015 by market researcher OnePoll. The findings indicate employers, seemingly, are not particularly sympathetic in their attitudes towards illness: 78% of managers believed that suffering from a migraine does not warrant time off work; 58% of the senior managers polled disagreed that flu was a serious enough reason for an employee to be absent from work; with 61% viewing back pain as an insufficiently serious reason to stay off work. Astonishingly, where elective surgery, such as a knee replacement operation or cataract surgery, was concerned, only 35% of employers accepted this as a valid reason for absence from work.

Sources: Aetna, 2022; Marsh, 2015

The academic concepts linked to organisational justice specifically focus on how employees determine fair treatment within their organisations and how their perceptions (which may or may not match reality) influence aspects of positive, through to negative, work-related behaviours; that is, from positive attitudes and performance resulting in organisational citizenship behaviour, compliance, engagement and loyalty to negative, non-compliant behaviours, ranging from mild insubordination, high levels of absence and sabotage, through to employees deciding to leave the organisation.

The ways in which people experience work lead them to make value judgements about the organisation that employs them. A survey looking at 2,000 office workers in the UK and USA found that of those surveyed 'the vast majority of workers are hesitant to report misconduct due to the lack of confidence in their employers to deal with the matter appropriately' (Vault Platform, 2022). These findings were not dissimilar to the 2013 CIPD Employee Outlook Survey (Sparrow et al., 2013), that questioned 2,067 employees and asked, among other things, whether the respondents had, in the previous year, come across anything in the workplace, or their professional life, that they thought was particularly unfair: 41% said they had. Just under 60% felt that workplace procedures and regulations were applied inconsistently, and just under half felt that the rewards and resources were inappropriately and unfairly distributed. Furthermore in terms of communication, 49% of respondents thought that the policies specifically designed to ensure fairness were unclear to many people within their organisation. Sixty-four per cent of respondents thought that there was inadequate consultation with those who would be affected by the implementation of decisions. There were a certain number of areas where perceptions of unfairness were particularly high, especially:

- pay – especially where it had been frozen and where it was related to long hours for what was perceived to be inadequate reward; pay was also regarded as unfair in comparison with senior management pay/bonuses
- workload – above all, how it was distributed
- bullying/victimisation/harassment
- favouritism
- forced redundancy/redundancy procedures
- promotion decisions. (Sparrow et al., 2013: 5)

A number of academic studies (e.g., Colquitt et al., 2005) chart and analyse the ways in which employees make judgements about fairness and outcomes (organisational justice) when considering their interactions with their employing organisation, and those within it, splitting organisational justice into a number of categories:

- *Distributive justice* is concerned with perceptions about decisions around the allocation of resources, and normally refers to comparative thoughts about pay, promotion, benefits, training, status and rewards (Adams, 1965). Individuals are therefore focused on whether or not they are receiving their 'just deserts'. Distributive justice can be split into three: *personal equity*, where an individual compares their reward with the effort and skills that they put into their work; *internal equity*, where an individual compares their own remuneration with pay rates and jobs across their employing organisation; and *external equity*, where their own jobs and rates of pay are compared with similar jobs and levels of pay provided outside the organisation (Milkovich et al., 2014).

- *Procedural justice* addresses the perceptions of fairness that employees have about the ways an organisation makes workplace decisions and how it carries out those decisions in practice. Employees evaluate whether or not the way an organisation does things (i.e., its procedures) are designed without bias and applied consistently, with the availability of a mechanism to correct any decisions that are flawed. Managers and decision makers are judged on whether or not they are using accurate (and timely) information to make their decisions (Thibaut and Walker, 1975). For example, police officers report higher satisfaction levels with a police force's complaints process when any investigation of a complaint against them has been undertaken in a procedurally fair manner regardless of the outcome (De Angelis and Kupchik, 2007).
- *Interactional justice* relates to the ways in which people interact with one another at an interpersonal level and concerns their perceptions about manners and whether or not they, or their colleagues, have been treated with dignity, politeness and respect, and been given an opportunity to proffer their own opinions (Bies and Moag, 1986; Colquitt et al., 2013). Bies and Moag talk about interactional justice in terms of employees' feelings of fairness concerning how they are treated, typically by their supervisor – such perceptions are particularly important when line managers have to hold difficult conversations with their subordinates, perhaps disciplining them or discussing potential redundancies. This type of justice is especially important within the constraints of what Goodrich (1920) called the *frontier of control* and the ways in which supervisors use their abilities to both constrain and empower their supervisees. (See Edwards, 2003, on structural antagonism.)
- *Informational justice* focuses on the adequacy of the information presented, evaluating whether or not it can, to the employees' satisfaction, describe and justify any decisions affecting the employees in a timely and appropriate manner (Greenberg, 1990, 1993). A recent study of 515 business leaders across the USA, UK, Netherlands, Germany and the Nordic countries found that over a quarter (28%) said that confusion at work – specifically unclear goals and expectations – repeatedly contributed to employees wasting time and missing organisational targets (Lewis, 2015).
- *Natural justice* is the process that has evolved through case law to ensure due process, ensuring fairness by protecting against the arbitrary exercising of power. Employees have a right to advance notice of any allegations and evidence against them; they should be given the opportunity to challenge allegations and evidence before any decisions are reached and have the right to answer any accusations, as well as the write to appeal a decision. In the UK employees have the right to be accompanied by their representative should they so wish during any formal disciplinary hearings.

Exercise 13.3

Information Briefing at Horlicks

- Read the extract below and identify where the company utilised aspects of organisational justice described above.

When Martin Swain joined the Berkshire drink manufacturer and supplier, Horlicks, as an HR Manager, there was no formal way of regularly imparting information to employees. The company worked a continuous shift system, 24/7 with most of those responsible for communicating with the workforce employed from 9 a.m. to 5 p.m. Monday to Friday. There was no formal system of letting people know what was going on if they were not working on the conventional standard day shifts. Rumour, gossip and misinformation were rife.

Martin introduced a system of monthly team briefing and everyone, via trained representatives, receives core information supplemented with relevant local details – any questions that employees might have are answered within ten days. This, Martin says, has increased motivation and performance levels, in part because there is a greater level of individual knowledge within teams. Getting senior managers to share relevant and meaningful information (together with appropriate training for the briefers) were key to the system working effectively.

Source: Bingham, 2000

Many studies of employee experiences of justice regard justice, and its effects, as products of discrete daily events and encounters that are responsible for shaping employees' momentary values and behaviours *in situ* (Cropanzano et al., 2001; Liao and Rupp, 2005; Mayer et al., 2007). Yet it is often the cumulative effect of day-to-day interactions in a climate of either high or low justice that influences the attitudes and subsequent actions of employees. Colquitt et al. (2001) conducted a meta-analytic review of 183 justice studies from the last quarter of the twentieth century and concluded that the four different dimensions to justice within the workplace – distributive, procedural, interpersonal and informational justice – were interrelated with employee perceptions of one aspect of justice often affecting their perceptions of the other aspects. The interrelationships of these perceptions affect organisational outcomes such as: the levels and quality of engagement and job satisfaction; organisational commitment; evaluation of authority at a positive level; withdrawal of discretionary effort; mild insubordination; sabotage; and leaving the organisation at the negative end of the spectrum.

Whitman et al. (2012) also undertook a slightly smaller meta-analytic examination of 66 studies and deduced that employee perceptions of interactional justice were most strongly related to organisational citizenship behaviour and cohesion, while perceptions of distributive justice were strongly linked with organisational performance, particularly productivity and customer satisfaction. Interestingly they found that these relationships were influenced by the overall strength of the culture of justice within the organisation *and* by the place within the organisational hierarchy that was held by the unit under investigation. One might surmise from this, for example, that an employee working in an HR department might expect to be treated with high levels of interactional justice while someone on the shop floor might have lower expectations and therefore their subsequent perceptions would be tempered. Cultural influences, as well as departmental ones, also play an important part in how different aspects and perceptions of justice impact on employee behaviours. Jiang (2015), in a cross-cultural study, found that distributive justice interacted with procedural justice to influence positive employee commitment in Australia, but not in South Korea and China. In Australia levels of employee trust also influenced the relationship between positive employee commitment and perceptions of distributive justice but had no impact on the relationship between employee commitment and procedural justice. In South Korea and China, however, perceptions of organisational trust had no bearing on employee commitment/loyalty to the organisation. Over time, Schneider (1987) suggested that attitudes to justice by employees in the same work group gradually coalesce, in part because any new employees who have divergent perceptions around justice will leave the organisation with only those employees who interpret events in similar ways remaining.

Exercise 13.4

Read the extract below, then answer the following question:

- What does this small quotation tell you about Jessica's perceptions of organisational justice and the culture of her employing organisations?

  In the summer of June 2014, the Dublin based newspaper *The Journal* published a number of workplace bullying experiences related by some of its readers. One woman, Jessica, who claimed to have been systematically bullied by a female boss, said about the perpetrator that she 'spread rumours about people ... [would] call us names both to our face and behind our backs, [would] tell us that none of us were any good at our jobs and were failures and [she] routinely commented on people's appearance. ... it was in the public sector, where there was really a clear anti-bullying policy and 'full commitment to dignity in the workplace'. It turns out that while the policy articulated very laudable principles, in practice (even after multiple complaints from the team) nothing was done, which gave her even more confidence that she was untouchable.' Jessica then left her job and took up a position in the private sector where she was happier.

Source: Finn, 2014

Injustice, Justice and Conflict

Workplace irritants that develop into outright antagonism and expressions of conflict can arise at a number of levels. Hebdon and Noh (2013) suggest that expressions of conflict in the workplace are the outcome of a number of things including worker dissatisfaction and the subsequent worker resistance to control; this is particularly so when the dissatisfaction is the result of perceptions of unfair or unjust treatment. The employment relationship is a contested relationship because the parties to the relationship have divergent concerns and differing interests, their differences in perception and attitudes often resulting in workplace friction. As Hyman says, there are four sources of conflict: 'imbalances of power between employees and employers, inequalities of income, fears around job security and insufficient or negligible control over work processes' (1972: 109). All of these are linked to the perceptions and expectations that employees have around fairness, and all of them are managed in ways that are usually consistent with managerial styles and frameworks utilised by the employing organisation.

The imbalance of power between employees and employers has already been discussed but, taking each of the three remaining categories (Hyman, 1972) in turn, we can see how justice-linked conflict might arise and be contained in practice. From the point of view of the employees, the fairer their perception of the solution the more likely it is to be acceptable.

Inequality of income

Inequality of income is strongly linked to perceptions of distributional justice and Adams' equity theory (1965). The CIPD (2022: 22) Reward survey of 2,557 employees discovered that just under half said their employer had *not* told them about the reward-linked benefits on offer. This links to informational injustice; if employees don't know what's being provided (or why, or indeed how to access benefits) they won't fully appreciate what an employer is offering. This lack of transparency could have an effect on employees' perceptions about their pay and benefits and importantly of their views around distributional justice, perhaps impacting on whether they perform well and/or remain with the organisation. In an earlier, 2014–2015, CIPD survey, covering respondents from 525 organisations, looking at aspects of transparency, the authors explained that:

> [s]ome strong opinions on pay transparency were evident among our panel, with a clear view that greater transparency may be morally desirable but the reality of managing it is far from straightforward. There was acknowledgement that concealment of pay information can create mistrust so, at least in theory, if good pay decisions are being made, it should be possible to treat employees as grown-ups and explain them. ... The overall view was that while many organisations have internal equity issues, this is largely due to the human factor; people make decisions so they will not be perfect. Even with systems such as **job evaluation** in place, pay is based on human judgement. There was also a view that greater pay transparency could lead to employee confusion and anxiety (CIPD, 2015: 25).

These CIPD reports encapsulate some of the aspects strongly linked to perceptions of equity and distributional justice. The next case snippet and exercise illustrate how the ways in which organisations reward their workforces can be perceived to be inequitable. For managers there are always dilemmas, not just around how much they reward people but of how much transparency is appropriate – will, for example, the act of publicising pay rates lead to staff making comparisons and feeling unjustly rewarded?

Case Snippet 13.4

Inequality (Women's Pensions)

In two-thirds of British industries women have built up workplace pensions worth less than half as much as men (TUC, 2022). TUC General Secretary Frances O'Grady pointed out that: 'Women face a whopping pension gap ... at current rates of progress, it could take more than fifty years to close'.

(Continued)

The TUC says that in manufacturing, wholesale and retail, and other service activities, women aged between 45 and 64 have less than a fifth (19%) of the pension wealth of male colleagues. In administration and support services the average woman in this age group has built up almost no pension wealth and has a pension pot a hundred times smaller than the average man in this industry.

This gender pensions income gap is due to:

- unequal caring responsibilities – it is harder for women to build up a workplace pension as they are more likely to take time out of work, or work part-time, to look after children
- gaps in pensions auto-enrolment that mean employers do not have to enrol low paid workers into a workplace pension
- over time women earn less than men because of gender pay inequalities
- historic differences in National Insurance have left women with lower state pensions on average.

Unless these disparities in pension wealth are tackled the TUC says the gender pension gap will persist.

Prospect Senior Deputy General Secretary and TUC President Sue Ferns point out that between 2015-16 and 2022 the gender pension gap has reduced by just 2.8 percentage points.

If progress continues at this rate, it could take 54 years to close. Gender parity would not happen until 2076.

The TUC is calling on ministers to take urgent action to close the gap more quickly.

Source: TUC, 2022

Exercise 13.5

Read the piece below about the sackings of P&O employees.

- What was the conflict about?
- Analyse how many aspects of organisational justice are apparent in the perceptions of the striking employees and evaluate, on the available evidence, whether or not they had a good case for asking for reinstatement.
- Evaluate the likely morale of the remaining staff and of the replacement agency workers.

Unexpectedly, and with no warning, on 17 March 2022, 800 staff at P&O Ferries were told, via a very short Zoom call, that, with immediate effect, it was their last day of employment, and henceforth they would no longer work for the company. The call lasted a few minutes and ended with the staff at all levels, from captains to deck hands, being made redundant. Legally an employer making more than 100 staff redundant is required to give 45 days' notice; additionally, staff should be alerted to their risk of redundancy and consulted formally about possible alternatives to dismissal. As this did not happen staff are eligible to claim unfair dismissal at an employment tribunal.

As compensation for the short notice, P&O provided three months of counselling through its employment assistance programme and offered the sacked workers 'enhanced' compensation as long as they signed – and adhered to – the terms of a settlement agreement within two weeks. P&O

claimed it needed to replace the sacked employees with cheaper agency workers to remain finan-cially viable. It specifically said that it did not consult with the unions, or staff, as they would not have agreed to the proposals.

There was a public outcry about the inhumanity and illegality of the abrupt sackings, particularly when there were reports of workers in handcuffs being escorted off their ships by security staff. The RMT union threatened legal action and said P&O Ferries should honour existing contracts of employ-ment. The Government initially demanded an immediate reinstatement of the affected employees, with the Transport Secretary, Grant Shapps suggesting that the government might be forced to make it illegal for ferry companies operating from UK ports to pay less than the minimum wage. At the time of the sacking the UK minimum wage was £8.91 per hour for workers over 23 compared to the average hourly rate of £5.50 for the replacement agency staff, in line with international maritime standards. The new arrangement would, the company explained, use one crew instead of two and pay staff for the actual time they worked, plus holidays, instead of 'giving full-pay for working 24 weeks a year'. A P&O spokesman welcomed the government's threat to introduce a minimum wage increase for *all* seafaring workers as this would ensure 'a level playing field when it comes to pay and conditions on British ferry routes'.

The TUC general secretary, Frances O'Grady, said,

P&O must not be allowed to get away with its scandalous and unlawful treatment of staff. Firms who behave like corporate gangsters deserve far more than a slap on the wrist.

Sources: BBC News, 2022; Jones, 2022

Fears around job security

Fears around job security and redundancy are perhaps inevitable in twenty-first century work-places in an era of austerity and abundant precarity. Job security is an important component of employee wellbeing. In countries where there are schemes providing income replacement to help unemployed workers find jobs, this is mitigated slightly, although in countries with stricter employment protection legislation this increases the negative effect (Morgan and O'Connor, 2022). When job security is threatened, mental health and the psychological contract are dam-aged, which jeopardises the smooth running of the employment relationship. Employees who are worried about their future employment may be fearful because of impending redundancy or dismissal and, depending upon circumstances, this might be arbitrarily imposed and unjustified, or the result of justifiable managerial action.

In reality each disciplinary and redundancy situation is an exercise in fairness. Employers must not make assumptions, pre-judge a situation or show any bias. If these occur it will have a direct, negative impact on the perceptions of the employees concerned and on others in the organisation who are not affected but aware of the situation.

A contract of employment involves mutual obligations for both the employer and employed. If circumstances are such that the obligation is broken, dismissal can be the outcome. In the UK the Employment Rights Act 1996 (s.6) sets out the conditions under which employers may terminate an employee's employment. As we have seen in Chapters 4 and 7, employers must tell employees where they might find, and access, the discipline and grievance rules for the organisation. These regulations or procedures will explain what is permitted or prohibited at work, and should provide examples of the sorts of behaviour that are disallowed, as well as explaining the stages that a disciplined employee might expect to go through should they be suspected of breaking the rules. Telling an employee where they might find the regulations and what is and what is not acceptable workplace behaviour, together with the procedure itself, is designed to ensure natural justice. Not all organisations provide fair regulations and ways of dealing with employees under discipline. Line managers should be trained in how to undertake the disciplinary process fairly. Dealing with workplace transgressions should be transparent and timely and a thorough investigation around the alleged infringement should be undertaken. (It is unfair, for example, not to tell an employee what they have been accused of and to leave an employee with an accusation hanging over them for an inordinate amount of time – although they will need sufficient time to prepare an answer to any allegations, once they know about the evidence against them and have access to witness statements.) Employees need to be given the opportunity to have someone with them and to be given the right to appeal the decision.

Exercise 13.6

Analyse the scenario below.

- Say whether you think the CEO behaved according to the rules of natural justice.
- If you were the HR manager at the organisation, how would you have advised the CEO to proceed?

At the end of the day, two receptionists working for a London-based organisation were expected to make sure no one was left in the building and then lock up and secure the building for the night. On one occasion they failed to notice that someone was still in the building and had not signed out. The receptionists, assuming the building was empty, forged the signature and locked the building. The intruder alarm went off when the person who was locked in tried to leave. The police and CEO were summoned to the building to free the unfortunate 'prisoner'. Incensed, the CEO accused the receptionists of gross misconduct and, in a heated phone call to each, fired them that evening.

Employees can be disciplined for either poor conduct (e.g., bad timekeeping, being rude to customers, etc.) or because they are deemed not to be sufficiently capable and have failed to reach the standards required to undertake their work properly. The Acas code (2015) recommends that an informal conversation with the employee should be the necessary first stage in the disciplinary process. This gentle 'hand-on-the-tiller' may be all that is required to prevent any further breaches and conflicts with their line manager. However, if informality fails, a more formal approach is required.

The formal disciplinary process requires that:

1   There is an investigation to establish the facts around the case – sometimes the employee is suspended on full pay while this takes place.

2   The employee is notified about the accusation in writing.

3   A meeting is held with the accused, who has the right to be accompanied.

4   A decision is made and the employee informed of the outcome, which is:

   i   there will be no penalty, *or*

   ii   they will receive a first written warning; if, following this process, an employees' conduct improves there will be no further action; if, however, it remains poor, Stages 1–4 will be repeated – continued poor performance will lead to a final written warning, *or*

   iii they will receive a final written warning – if their conduct remains poor, Stages 1–4 will be repeated – continued poor performance will lead to dismissal, *or*

   iv   they are to be dismissed following due process.

5   The employee has the opportunity to appeal the decision with a manager who has not previously been involved.

In *British Homestores* v. *Burchell* [1980] ICR 303 EAT, the Employment Appeals Tribunal (EAT) made some important observations that are useful pointers to the ways in which natural justice can be guaranteed, prior to a decision to dismiss, suggesting that an employer must ensure that they have a genuine belief based on reasonable grounds, after a reasonable investigation, that the employee did commit the alleged infraction of the regulations. The difficulty with this is the fact that what is perceived as reasonable by one person may not be reasonable for another. The EAT advice had to be broad in order to be applicable across the board, because different organisations will have different requirements and different ranges of resources at their disposal.

When redundancies occur, the ways in which the redundancy has been managed will have an impact on the employees. If the process is deemed necessary, and is regarded as fair and appropriately handled, transparent and unbiased, this mitigates against some of the more unpleasant side effects on employees, such as loss of self-esteem and depression. Where the process is seen as unfair and poorly managed, depression is more likely to occur (Arzuaga and Gandolfi, 2022; van Eersel et al., 2021). Employees working for organisations where jobs are being lost are acutely aware of how the processes of shedding labour are being undertaken. For those at risk of redundancy there is a heightened sense of injustice if the processes are deemed to be biased, arbitrary and handled in ways that exclude consultation. For those not at risk, but aware of what is happening to others, the sense of distributive, procedural and informational justice is very important. López-Bohle et al. in an interesting study looking at Chilean workers who 'survived redundancy' say that it is

> ... crucial that justice should be an important issue in the downsizing process, and that the company should develop actions that reflect the perception of procedural justice throughout the process. ... it is useful to simultaneously consider procedural justice and stress reactions in a downsizing process, since neither are independent variables (2021: 596)

If aspects of justice are absent, then those employees surviving redundancies are likely to show less trust and lower levels of engagement than they had prior to the downsizing.

One of the ways employers manage to keep their employees on-side during the redundancy process is to abide by the legislative requirements and ensure that all of the procedures facilitating redundancy are adhered to.

Exercise 13.7

The Acas website (www.acas.org.uk) provides a lot of guidelines around redundancy. Look at what it has to say, and download the booklet about handling large-scale redundancies. After you have read it, look at the example below of a redundancy policy from Company XXX. This large organisation, based on two sites within the UK (with 830 employees in total), has an in-house staff association but no specific redundancy procedure, just this policy.

- Indicate where the company might be lacking.
- Do you think there is evidence of procedural and distributional justice? Give academic justification for your answers.

Company XXX Redundancy Policy

It is the Company's policy to take all reasonable steps to avoid making employees redundant. When redundancy is unavoidable the Company will seek to handle the redundancy in a fair and consistent manner. The individual concerned will be given reasonable paid time off work during working hours for the purposes of looking for new employment, irrespective of length of service.

Redundancy Selection Criteria

The HR manager will define the group of employees from which selection is to be made. The Company will endeavour to offer suitable alternative employment to staff whose post is to become redundant.

If appropriate, volunteers for redundancy will be sought in the first instance in order to avoid, as far as possible, compulsory redundancy. It is management's right to decide whether it is appropriate for a particular employee to leave under voluntary redundancy.

Where no other suitable selection criteria (e.g., special skills, timekeeping, attendance, warnings, appraisal reviews) are identified, employees will be selected for compulsory redundancy on the basis of the 'last-in-first-out' principle, with the employee with the shortest continuous employment being selected first.

Consultation will take place as soon as possible with the individuals concerned (even if consultation has already taken place with appropriate representatives) and within the statutory time limits. Employees will be informed of the reasons for the redundancy proposal and be given the opportunity to comment or make representations prior to the final decision to dismiss. Part of the consultation will include discussing steps to avoid dismissal; that is, any alternative work that may be offered and the acceptability to the employee, for example in terms of nature of work and grade and so on.

Notice Period

As much notice as possible of dismissal on grounds of redundancy will be given. As a minimum the Company will give the statutory or contractual period (whichever is the longer) of notice of termination of employment.

Dependent on the circumstances, the HR manager will determine whether or not the employee is required to work the period of notice.

All employees required to work their period of notice will be granted a reasonable amount of paid time off work to look for new employment in accordance with employment law or to make arrangements for training. This time off will be agreed initially with the employee's line manager.

An employee who is given notice due to redundancy will receive a written statement outlining the reason for the redundancy and detailing the calculation of any redundancy payment due.

Redundancy Payments

Employees with at least 2 years' continuous service will normally qualify for redundancy payment. The number of weeks' pay used in assessing the amount of redundancy payment due is determined by the employee's continuous years of service (up to a maximum of 20 years) and their age when those years were being worked:

- 1.5 week's pay for each year of employment during which the employee was aged 41 or over but had not reached age 60
- 1 week's pay for each year of employment during which the employee was aged 22–40 inclusive
- 0.5 week's pay for each year of employment during which the employee was aged 18–21.

N.B. Only complete years of service count.

A week's pay is the basic weekly wage or salary under the contract of employment. Where earnings vary, the amount is the average weekly earnings (excluding non-contractual overtime) during the 12 weeks before termination.

Insufficient or negligible control over work processes

This affects the ways in which employees interact with their immediate colleagues and line manager. Not being able to have a say in how they do their work, and perhaps not having any control over the speed and timing of their actions, can lead to perceptions of powerlessness and injustice, sometimes leading to conflict. The introduction of digital, self-managing, self-learning algorithms to control elements of work processes may exacerbate such feelings of powerlessness and inhibit worker solidarity and resistance (Meacham and Tava, 2021). When an employee feels powerlessness, due to a lack of control, this can result in a resigned acceptance of the situation until a new job can be found. The DTI defined a worker who was vulnerable as:

> someone working in an environment where the risk of being denied employment rights is high and who does not have the capacity or means to protect themselves from that abuse. Both factors need to be present. A worker may be susceptible to vulnerability, but that is only significant if an employer exploits that vulnerability. (2006: 25)

Employee vulnerability can occur at many different levels within an organisation and may, or may not, be related to the pay they receive and whether or not they are unionised: although it is notable that contingent work frequently restricts worker security, involvement, voice, representation and power (Wilson and Ebert, 2013). The literature on vulnerable, precarious workers tends to concentrate on those at the lower end of the occupational hierarchy (e.g., see Bretones, 2020), but emotions connected to lack of control at work need not only apply to these individuals. Where employers take advantage of employees, or even where they do not, but an employee perceives that they are being used in a way that is unwarranted, this leads to perceptions of injustice and unfairness. To counteract the power imbalance between employers and employees and give employees a degree of control, legislation provides a number of rights; for example, it limits the number of hours that an employee might be required to work and gives the right to a minimum wage, although it should be noted that these rights are not helpful for those workers who either do not know about them or who feel powerless to exercise them.

Case snippet 13.5

Exploitation (Insecure Workers)

The TUC has produced reports on vulnerable and insecure workers (2008, 2019) that examined how insecure and vulnerable workers were treated. These people are often 'invisible': cleaners, night porters, homeworkers, and so on. Compared to permanent UK employees, insecure workers in casual employment are more likely to have higher levels of anxiety and depression and be young, non-white and employed in elementary occupations, with little job satisfaction and low job security (2019: 54). The extracts below give a flavour of how some individuals find themselves working in unacceptable ways but are unable to alter the situation because they need the work.

> On an average day Angela starts work at 6am and gets a 40-minute unpaid break at 9am. She then works from 9:40am through till 1:15pm, despite her contractual hours ending at 12:45pm. There were previously two cleaners working at Angela's office but she is now the only one and has to do the work previously done by two people within the same number of hours: 'It's all left to me, so it is a little bit stressful thinking that I've got to do everything and don't want to get myself into trouble for not doing the work'. (2008: 22)

> [A supermarket worker on a zero hours contract] I am literally at their mercy for these shift patterns. In quite a big way because .... you feel like, a bit jet lagged sometimes. Sometimes you don't know what day it is because I'm not doing a structured Monday to Friday, nine-to-five job, I'm doing lates, earlies, middles, here and there. I think it affects your mental health too, to be honest, because you just don't know when you're coming and going, really' (2019:36).

The 2019 report talks about younger workers not being given work if they refused the sexual favours of older supervisory staff. The ways in which employees actually experience work leads them to trust/distrust their supervisors, colleagues and indeed the organisation they are working for. High levels of trust lead to workplace engagement, while conversely, low levels of workplace trust engender disengagement. Where work is controlled by the means of artificial intelligence, rather than by individuals, there is evidence showing this is detrimental to trust levels and to the psychological contract, 'detracting from the very nature of decent work' (Braganza et al., 2021: 485). Little engagement was evident from the workers covered by the TUC reports who were subject to the needs of their bosses with no *reciprocal* acknowledgement of their requirements.

Where there is no trust, no perceptions of justice and no subsequent engagement, the employment relationship will be damaged. In high-performance workplaces where the intensity of work has the potential to create ever higher levels of demoralised employees, where cynicism and lack of trust are prevalent (Appelbaum, 2013: 120; see also Han et al., 2020), it is likely that employees will exhibit less engagement with the work processes plus higher levels of insecurity, fuelled by the employer's concentration on the bottom line and the employee's perceptions of organisational injustice. The web of interactions between the intentions and goals of the employing organisation, through to its managerial practices, the work itself and the ways in which the employee perceives them all, have a direct impact on the ways in which employees perform (Macky and Boxall, 2007) and those employees who feel insecure are less likely to be engaged with the work process and vice versa.

Voice Mechanisms and the Perceptions of Fairness

The four main types of organisational justice surround the ways in which employees are allowed a voice at work. In particular, distributive justice influences the ways in which employees view the outcomes of voice interactions – particularly those where negotiation and consultation have been concerned. Similarly, procedural justice, where employees have views on how the processes of negotiation or consultation might have been managed, are important. There is of course the danger that where specific groups or units are asked for their views and opinions, those not asked will perceive the process as unfair, particularly if they are affected in negative ways by the outcome. Where there has been an element of negotiation people are more willing to accept an agreement *provided* they assessed the process as fair; similarly, better joint outcomes are achieved when more collaborative negotiation processes are used (Hollander-Blumoff and Tyler, 2008). When employees are given, and then take, the opportunity to express their voice during a negotiation, this will lead to more positive evaluations of the decision-making process and to judgements of fairness in the outcome (Lind et al., 1990; Tyler, 1987). Rasak et al. (2019) have highlighted the lack of voice, particularly representational voice, for those subject to flexible working patterns and casual insecure work. Although they were looking specifically at Nigeria, this unfair block on voice opportunity still holds true for other insecure casual workers unable to access and associate with representational groups.

Interestingly, where voice is enabled, yet negotiation fails, and mediation is used, this actually improves the trust levels between managers, employees and their representatives (Currie et al., 2017).

The greater the variety of ways that employees can express themselves at work and have a say in what goes on the more likely it is that the perceptions of justice associated with this will lead to levels of trust and benefits to the organisation, ranging from increased output to declining absenteeism (Sisson, 2000). Where organisations promote a culture where employees can speak up, Meidav (2021) found that they are more likely to feel their concerns will be heard, and issues dealt with internally, to the benefit of everyone.

As noted previously, legislation has a direct impact on the way in which the employment relationship is regulated, and where employee voice (direct and indirect) is concerned, this is no exception. For example, the requirement to consult employee representatives 'with a view to reaching agreement' about redundancies has been enshrined in UK legislation since 1975; and, although little used, the ICE Regulations (Acas, 2005) provide a mechanism for employees to be informed about upcoming business decisions within the organisation for which they work (organisational justice). Chapter 10 looked at a variety of voice mechanisms and, if operated well, these help perceptions of fairness at work. Sometimes, of course, employees speak to their organisation by their very silence, and depending on the issue, such silence may be a product of mistrust and perceptions of the different forms of organisational injustice. Boodoo et al. (2020) examined the ways in which 786 employed people in the USA reacted to experiences of perceived organisational injustice. Interestingly, although perhaps not surprisingly, they found that in cases of interactional injustice people were more likely to leave work than in instances of distributional justice, where they were more likely to voice their discontent to the appropriate manager.

Exercise 13.8

- Does giving someone a say at work improve the levels of fairness in an organisation? Give the academic reasoning behind your answer.

Holding the Front Line Via Fairness: The Importance of Line Managers

The ways in which managers manage are constricted, influenced and motivated by a number of things, including the variety of capitalism and country in which they are operating, the culture and type of organisation, their own personalities and of course legislative requirements and fashionable notions of current effective managerial practice. It could be assumed that the managerial role requires the occupant to behave in an ethical and fair way when undertaking managerial duties – after all, managers are typically well educated, responsible for those they supervise, able to manage complex tasks, capable of motivating their teams and creating effective working environments (Delmestri and Walgenbach, 2005). To achieve all this fairly by behaving justly, without bias, should be second nature to them. It is, of course, for some; for others, it is legislative restrictions that help steer them in the appropriate direction and ensure that they achieve fair process via legal compliance. There will always be a tension for line managers when they have to decide how much individual workplace discretion they allow their teams in relation to how much they impose 'hands-on' direct supervision. The ways in which such structural antagonism is played out will have a direct bearing on the ways in which members of their teams perceive the four main aspects of organisational justice. Other influences too, such as unconscious bias, will impact on the ways in which line managers undertake their role. In particular their own values and perceptions of organisation justice will impact their actions. The managerial framework and style of the organisation – and indeed the frameworks and styles of the managers themselves –

will be important. Are they authoritarian, or do they take a softer approach to management? Do they consult and listen to employees and/or their representatives or merely dictate using command and control techniques? Do they say one thing yet do another? These issues have all been covered in previous chapters. The ways in which line managers operate will have a direct impact on the employment relationship and the ways in which employees and potential employees perceive the organisation. If it is regarded as a fair place to work, for example, the organisation could become an employer of choice, and the employees may be involved and engaged with the work processes and happy to use discretionary effort. If a workplace is not perceived as fair, it will probably experience high levels of labour turnover, recruitment difficulties, and occasional threats about being taken to court. By ensuring that line managers are trained and equipped to manage in a way that perpetuates high levels of perceived organisational justice, the rights of employees will be safeguarded and the workplace will be a happier place.

Revision exercise 13.1

Read Case Study 13.3 by Julius Nyiawung, about Dunnes Stores Ireland. Critically evaluate with a focus on the ways in which organisational justice is perceived and the nature of the employment relationship within the company. (A large number of the aspects about the employment relationship covered in the book are to be found within this case study; critical analysis of it will provide useful revision.)

Case study 13.3

In Pursuit of Decency and Fairness in Dunnes Stores Ireland – 30 Years and Counting

Dunnes Stores (or Dunnes) is a privately owned Irish multinational with retail (grocery and drapery) outlets in Ireland, the UK and Spain. Dunnes is headquartered in Dublin and operates more than 100 outlets, employing over 10,000 workers in the Republic of Ireland. Retail is often operated by technology that enables employers to adjust work rotas, including just-in-time scheduling, to respond to business needs. As such, working and operating in retail is just part of the precarious landscape.

In the last 30 years, Dunnes has variously come to public attention in relation to low pay and precarious working terms and conditions, including poor pay, low hours contracts and job insecurity. These, and the fact that Dunnes workers have engaged in strike actions because the retailer sold South African products during the apartheid years, and the fact that Dunnes have a long-standing policy of not engaging directly with trade unions, depict a complex context wherein the issue of decency and fairness for workers is contentious in the company.

Most workers in Dunnes are represented by the retail workers union (Mandate) and the Services, Industrial, Professional and Technical Union (SIPTU). While the Irish Constitution guarantees the right of people to join a union, the national industrial relations acts accord employers the right not to

(Continued)

recognise one (this scenario is often referred to, locally, as 'an Irish solution to an Irish problem'). In the backdrop of poor pay and working terms and conditions in the 1990s, sustained pressure from customers and workers pushed the 'efficiency-seeking' management of Dunnes to sign a collective bargaining agreement with the trade union Mandate in 1996, but in the years that followed, successive managers have adopted union avoidance and substitution initiatives, including sacking of trade union shop stewards and unilaterally altering hours of work. This anti-union approach by Dunnes Stores has led to the non-implementation, till date, of most of the provisions of the 1996 agreement. So, work in Dunnes is set in a context of a just over 30-year-old turbulent relationship between management and workers and their trade unions.

In a characteristic unitarist approach, especially in the last 20 years, Dunnes neither negotiates with individual workers nor with trade unions. In recent years however, this managerial posture has pushed workers to seek alternative sources of power by turning to 'society' to put pressure (through the 'Decency for Dunnes Workers' campaign on virtual and physical platforms) on Dunnes Stores to improve working hours, minimally use temporary and fixed contracts, increase pay and recognise and work with trades unions. Ireland being a liberal market economy with minimal or no interventions in the employment relationship by the state, the most government ministers and opposition politicians have done is to plead with Dunnes to cooperate with the voluntary procedures operated by the state's dispute resolution bodies to try to manage the numerous pursuits/conflicts, by employees, regarding decent and fair work in the company. Dunnes Stores has often boycotted conflict mediation sessions at the workplace relations commission leaving trade unions with little option than to ballot for strike action.

Julius Nyiawung

Sources: www.eurofound.europa.eu/publications/article/2015/ireland-strike-at-dunnes-stores-for-higher-pay-and-better-job-security; https://mandate.ie/category/decency-for-dunnes-workers/; www.irishtimes.com/news/sacked-dunnes-union-activist-reinstated-1.773321

Relevant Articles for Further Reading

Acas (2015) *Code of Practice on Discipline and Grievance Procedures*. London: TSO. Available at: www.acas.org.uk/media/pdf/f/m/Acas-Code-of-Practice-1-on-disciplinary-and-grievance-procedures.pdf (accessed 16 October 2015).

A useful/essential read, written clearly and designed for practitioners.

Boodoo, M. U., Frangi, L., Gomez, R. and Hebdon, R. (2020) *How do Employees Respond to Workplace Injustice? New Insights from Ranked Ordinal Employee Preferences*. Available at: https://ssrn.com/abstract=3634539 (accessed 26 August 2020).

This takes a critical look at the ways in which perceptions of injustice are dealt with by employees – placing their actions on a continuum depending on the type of injustice experienced.

Smith, A. and Elliott, F. (2012) 'The demands and challenges of being a retail store manager: "Handcuffed to the front doors"', *Work, Employment and Society*, 26(4): 676–84.

This article provides a good insight into an imperfect work environment – aspects of justice, trust and the psychological contract are apparent.

Xu, X. M., Du, D., Johnson, R. E. and Lu, C. Q. (2021) 'Justice change matters: Approach and avoidance mechanisms underlying the regulation of justice over time', *Journal of Applied Psychology*, 107(7): 1070–93.

The authors examine what happens when justice perceptions and behaviours change over time. They show how, when justice alters, the impact affects employee behaviour, they either become more, or less, disengaged with work depending upon the ways in which the justice is revised.

References

Abela, F. and Debono, M. (2019) 'The relationship between psychological contract breach and job-related attitudes within a manufacturing plant', *SAGE Open*, 9(1): 2158244018822179.

Acas (2005) *The Information and Consultation of Employees Regulations (ICE)*. London: Acas. Available at: www.acas.org.uk/index.aspx?articleid=1598 (accessed 17 October 2015).

Acas (2015) *Code of Practice on Discipline and Grievance Procedures*. London: TSO. Available at: www.acas.org.uk/media/pdf/f/m/Acas-Code-of-Practice-1-on-disciplinary-and-grievance-procedures.pdf (accessed 16 October 2015).

Adams, J. S. (1965) 'Inequity in social exchange', in L. Berkowitz (ed.), *Advances in Experimental Social Psychology*, Vol. 2. San Diego, CA: Academic Press, pp. 267–99.

Aetna (2022) *Rhetoric Verses Reality*. Available at: www.aetnainternational.com/content/dam/aetna/pdfs/aetna-international/Explorer/tackling-polarized-perceptions.pdf (accessed 30 April 2022).

Allen, A. (2006) 'Work ardour', *People Management*. Available at: www.cipd.co.uk/pm/peoplemanagement/b/weblog/archive/2013/01/29/workingardour-2006–08.aspx (accessed 24 October 2014).

Appelbaum, E. (2013) 'The impact of new forms of work organization on workers', in G. Murray, J. Belanger, A. Giles and P-A. Lapointe (eds), *Work and Employment in the High Performance Workplace*. London: Routledge, pp. 120–40.

Aryee, S., Budhwar, P. S. and Chen, Z. X. (2002) 'Trust as a mediator of the relationship between organizational justice and work outcomes: Test of a social exchange model', *Journal of Organizational Behavior*, 23(2): 26'7–85.

Arzuaga, S. and Gandolfi, F. (2022) Theoretical perspectives on downsizing: The long-term effect and impact of repeat downsizing', *Journal of Management Research*, 21(2): 76–85.

BBC News (2022) 'P&O Ferries given deadline to reemploy sacked workers', *BBC News*, 28 March. Available at: www.bbc.co.uk/news/business-60895833 (accessed 7 May 2022).

Bewley, J. and Forth, J. (2010) *Vulnerability and Adverse Treatment in the Workplace, Employment Relations Research Series*. London: Department for Business Innovation and Skills.

Bies, R. J. and Moag, J. S. (1986) 'Interactional justice: Communication criteria of fairness', *Research on Negotiation in Organizations*, 1: 43–55.

Bingham, C. (ed.) (2000) *Team Communication*, Managing Best Practice No 72. London: The Industrial Society.

Blau, P. M. (1964) *Exchange and Power in Social Life*. New York, NY: Transaction.

Boodoo, M. U., Frangi, L., Gomez, R. and Hebdon, R. (2020) *How do Employees Respond to Workplace Injustice? New Insights from Ranked Ordinal Employee Preferences*. Available at: https://ssrn.com/abstract=3634539 (accessed 26 August 2020).

Braganza, A., Chen, W., Canhoto, A. and Sap, S. (2021) 'Productive employment and decent work: The impact of AI adoption on psychological contracts, job engagement and employee trust', *Journal of Business Research*, 131: 485–94.

Bretones, F. D. (2020) 'Migrant workers, hazards and vulnerability', in F. D. Bretones and A. Santos (eds), *Health, Safety and Well-being of Migrant Workers: New Hazards, New Workers*. Cham: Springer, pp. 9–22.

Bryson, A. and Forth, J. (2010a) 'The regional labour market in the UK', in P. Dolton, C. Rosazza-Bondibene and J. Wadsworth, *The Labour Market in Winter: The State of Working Britain*. Oxford: Oxford University Press.

Bryson, A. and Forth, J. (2010b) *Union Organisation and the Quality of Employment Relations*. London: TUC.

Budd, J. W. (2004) *Employment with a Human Face: Balancing Efficiency, Equity, and Voice*. Ithaca, NY: Cornell University Press.

Budd, J. W. (2010) 'Theorizing work: The importance of conceptualizations of work for research and practice', presentation at the 25th Cardiff Employment Research Unit Annual Conference, Cardiff Business School, 13–14 September. Available at: www.legacy-irc.csom.umn.edu/faculty/jbudd/research/cardiff2010.pdf (accessed 24 February 2013).

CIPD (2015) *Reward Management, Annual Survey Report, 2014–2015*. London: CIPD.

CIPD (2022) *Reward Management Survey, Focus on Employee Benefits*. London: CIPD.

Colquitt, J. A., Conlon, D. E., Wesson, M. J., Porter, C. O. and Ng, K. Y. (2001) 'Justice at the millennium: A meta-analytic review of 25 years of organizational justice research', *Journal of Applied Psychology*, 86: 425–45.

Colquitt, J. A., Greenberg, J. and Zapata-Phelan, C. P. (2005) 'What is organizational justice? A historical overview', in J. Greenberg and J. A. Colquitt (eds), *Handbook of Organizational Justice*. Mahwah, NJ: Erlbaum, pp. 3–56.

Colquitt, J. A., Scott, B. A., Rodell, J. B., Long, D. M., Zapata, C. P., Conlon, D. E. and Wesson, M. J. (2013) 'Justice at the millennium, a decade later: A meta-analytic test of social exchange and affect-based perspectives', *Journal of Applied Psychology*, 98(2): 199–236.

Cropanzano, R., Byrne, Z. S., Bobocel, D. R. and Rupp, D. E. (2001) 'Moral virtues, fairness heuristics, social entities, and other denizens of organizational justice', *Journal of Vocational Behavior*, 58: 164–209.

Crowson, I. (2015) 'Chairman of Derbyshire health trust "called employee a whore"', *Derby Telegraph*, 25 July. Available at: www.derbytelegraph.co.uk/Chairman-health-trust-tried-violate-dignity/story-27479646-detail/story.html (accessed 31 July 2015).

Currie, D., Gormley, T., Roche, B. and Teague, P. (2017) 'The management of workplace conflict: Contrasting pathways in the HRM literature', *International Journal of Management Reviews*, 19(4): 492–509.

De Angelis, J. and Kupchik, A. (2007) 'Citizen oversight, procedural justice, and officer perceptions of the complaint investigation process', *Policing: An International Journal of Police Strategies and Management*, 30(4): 651–71.

Delmestri, G. and Walgenbach, P. (2005) 'Mastering techniques or brokering knowledge? Middle managers in Germany, Great Britain and Italy', *Organization Studies*, 26(2): 197–220.

DTI (2006) *Success at Work: Protecting Vulnerable Workers, Supporting Good Employers. A Policy Statement for this Parliament.* London: Department of Trade and Industry.

Edelmann, R. J. (2009) *Interpersonal Conflicts at Work.* Chichester: Wiley.

Edwards, P. and Wajcman, J. (2005) *The Politics of Working Life.* Oxford: Oxford University Press.

Edwards, P. K. (2003) 'The employment relationship and the field of industrial relations', in P. K. Edwards (ed.), *Industrial Relations: Theory and Practice.* Oxford: Blackwell, pp. 1–36.

Finn, C. (2014) 'Bullied: Your stories of bullying in the workplace', *The Journal*, 18 July. Available at: www.thejournal.ie/readme/bullying-in-work-665391-Jun2014/ (accessed 30 July 2015).

Goodrich, C. L. (1920) *The Frontier of Control.* New York: Harcourt, Brace and Howe.

Greenberg, J. (1990) 'Organizational justice: Yesterday, today, and tomorrow', *Journal of Management*, 16: 399–432.

Greenberg, J. (1993) 'The social side of fairness: Interpersonal and informational classes of organizational justice', in R. Cropanzano (ed.), *Justice in the Workplace: Approaching Fairness in Human Resource Management.* Hillsdale, NJ: Erlbaum, pp. 79–103.

Han, J., Sun, J. M. and Wang, H. L. (2020) 'Do high performance work systems generate negative effects? How and when?', *Human Resource Management Review*, 30(2): 100699.

Han, M. (2014) 'When your boss turns into Big Brother, surveillance has grave consequences', *The Guardian*, 17 February. Available at: www.theguardian.com/commentisfree/2014/feb/17/when-your-boss-turns-into-big-brother-surveillance-has-grave-consequences (accessed 6 January 2015).

Hebdon, R. and Noh, S. C. (2013) 'A theory of workplace conflict development: From grievances to strikes', in G. Gall (ed.), *New Forms and Expressions of Conflict at Work.* Basingstoke: Palgrave Macmillan, pp. 26–47.

Hollander-Blumoff, R. and Tyler, T. R. (2008) 'Procedural justice in negotiation: Procedural fairness, outcome acceptance, and integrative potential', *Law & Social Inquiry*, 33: 473–500.

Hyman, R. (1972) *Strikes.* London: Fontana.

Jiang, Z. (2015) 'The relationship between justice and commitment: The moderation of trust', *Asia-Pacific Journal of Business Administration*, 7(1): 73–88.

Joint Research Centre (2019) *The Changing Nature of Work and Skills in the Digital Age*, JRC117505. Luxembourg: Publications Office of the European Union. Available at: https://op.europa.eu/en/publication-detail/-/publication/508a476f-de75-11e9-9c4e-01aa75ed71a1/language-en (accessed 17 April 2022).

Jones, L. (2022) 'P&O Ferries says sacking U-turn would cause collapse', *BBC News*, 29 March. Available at: www.bbc.co.uk/news/business-60913206 (accessed 7 May 2022).

Lewis, G. (2015) 'Unclear goals and expectations contribute to wasted time at work, say employees', *People Management*, 4 September. Available at: www.cipd.co.uk/pm/peoplemanagement/b/weblog/archive/2015/09/04/unclear-goals-and-expectations-contribute-to-wasted-time-at-work-say-employees.aspx?utm_medium=emailandutm_source=cipdandutm_campaign=pm_dailyandutm_term=655485andutm_content=pm_daily_040915–3353–3214—-20150904175844-Unclear%20goals%20and%20expectations%20contribute%20to%20wasted%20time%20at%20work%2C%20say%20employees (accessed 4 September 2015).

Liao, H. and Rupp, D. E. (2005) 'The impact of justice climate and justice orientation on work outcomes: A cross-level multifoci framework', *Journal of Applied Psychology*, 90(2): 242.

Lind, E. A., Kanfer, R. and Earley, P. C. (1990) 'Voice, control, and procedural justice: Instrumental and non-instrumental concerns in fairness judgments', *Journal of Personal Social Psychology*, 59: 952–9.

López-Bohle, S. A., Chambel, M. J. and Diaz-Valdes Iriarte, A. (2021) 'Job insecurity, procedural justice and downsizing survivor affects', *The International Journal of Human Resource Management*, 32(3): 596–615.

Macky, K. and Boxall, P. (2007) 'The relationship between "high-performance work practices" and employee attitudes: An investigation of additive and interaction effects', *International Journal of Human Resource Management*, 18(1): 537–67.

Manolopoulos, D., Peitzika, E., Mamakou, X. J. and Myloni, B. (2022) 'Psychological and formal employment contracts, workplace attitudes and employees' turnover intentions: Causal and boundary inferences in the hotel industry', *Journal of Hospitality and Tourism Management*, 51: 289–302.

Marsh, J. (2015) 'Nearly a quarter of employees fear boss' judgement for calling in sick', *HR Review*, 3 September. Available at: www.hrreview.co.uk/hr-news/wellbeing-news/nearly-quarter-employees-fear-boss-judgement-calling-sick/59007?utm_source=cc-HRreview_Daily+News+A&utm_medium=Email&utm_content=Untitled4&utm_campaign=HRreview+Daily+News+-+A+list+-+THU-+V4&affiliates=28&hraffiliate=2&_ccCt=wurl9ybH27Hc9bmpC8Ef25%7eNLlKsXXsRqFA5Xk_DYHBLD%7ex248iCcgvEpac7Mb3d (accessed 3 September 2015).

Mayer, D., Nishii, L., Schneider, B. and Goldstein, H. (2007) 'The precursors and products of justice climates: Group leader antecedents and employee attitudinal consequences', *Personnel Psychology*, 60(4): 929–63.

Meacham, D. and Tava, F. (2021) 'The algorithmic disruption of workplace solidarity', *Philosophy Today*, 65(3): 571–98.

Megeirhi, H. A., Ribeiro, M. A. and Woosnam, K. M. (2020) 'Job search behavior explained through perceived tolerance for workplace incivility, cynicism and income level: A moderated mediation model', *Journal of Hospitality and Tourism Management*, 44, 88–97.

Meidav, N. (2021) 'Ethical behavior is the antidote to toxic culture', *Strategic HR Review*, 20(2): 44–50.

Milić, K. (2021) 'The relationship between the perception of justice in the organization and the intention to leave the organization: Meta-analysis', *Civitas*, 11(1): 68–117.

Milkovich, G. T., Newman, J. M. and Gerhart, B. A. (2014) *Compensation* (11th edn). New York: McGraw-Hill.

Morgan, R. and O'Connor, K. J. (2022) 'Labor market policy and subjective well-being during the great recession', *Journal of Happiness Studies*, 23(2): 391–422.

Otaye, L. and Wong, W. (2014) 'Mapping the contours of fairness', *Journal of Organizational Effectiveness: People and Performance*, 1(2): 191–204.

Rasak, B., Ake, M., Asamu, F. and Ganiyu, R. (2019) 'Casual Work Arrangements (CWAs) and its effect on right to freedom of association in Nigeria', *International Journal of Innovative Legal & Political Studies*, 7(1): 1–17.

Schneider, B. (1987) 'The people make the place', *Personnel Psychology*, 40: 437–53.

Sisson, K. (2000) *Direct Participation and the Modernisation of Work Organisation*. Dublin: Eurofound.

Sparrow, P., Wong, W., Otaye, L. and Bevan, S. (2013) *The Changing Contours of Fairness: Can we Match Individual and Organisational Perspectives?* London: CIPD.

Thibaut, J. W. and Walker, L. (1975) *Procedural Justice: A Psychological Analysis*. Hillsdale, NJ: Lawrence Erlbaum.

Thomas, D. C., Au, K. and Ravlin, E. C. (2003) 'Cultural variation and the psychological contract', *Journal of Organizational Behavior*, 24(3): 451–71.

TUC (2008) *Hard Work, Hidden Lives: The Full Report of the Commission on Vulnerable Employment*. London: TUC. Available at: www.vulnerableworkers.org.uk/files/CoVE_full_report.pdf (accessed 16 October 2015).

TUC (2019) *Living on the Edge, Experiencing workplace insecurity in the UK*. London: TUC. Available at: www.tuc.org.uk/sites/default/files/insecure%20work%20report%20final%20final.pdf (accessed 2 April 2022).

TUC (2022) *Gender Pensions Gap Means Retired Women go the Equivalent of Four and Half Months Each Year Without a Pension*, press release, 22 May. Available at: www.tuc.org.uk/news/gender-pensions-gap-means-retired-women-go-equivalent-four-and-half-months-each-year-without (accessed 5 June 2022).

Tyler, T. R. (1987) 'Conditions leading to value-expressive effects in judgments of procedural justice: A test of four models', *Journal of Personal Social Psychology*, 52: 333–44.

Tzafrir, S. and Dolan, S. (2004) 'Trust me: A multiple item scale for measuring manager–employee trust', *Management Research*, 2(2): 115–32.

van Eersel, J. H., Taris, T. W. and Boelen, P. A. (2021) 'Grief reactions, depression, and anxiety following job loss: Patterns and correlates', *European Journal of Psychotraumatology*, 12(1): 1905348.

Vault Platform (2022) *The Trust Gap: Expectation vs Reality in Workplace Misconduct and Speak-Up Culture*. Available at: https://vaultplatform.com/the-trust-gap-thanks/?submissionGuid=018a4bd4-9b9a-4b32-9ca5-70342b4ea955 (accessed 28 April 2022).

Whitman, D. S., Caleo, S., Carpenter, N. C., Horner, M. T. and Bernerth, J. B. (2012).'Fairness at the collective level: A meta-analytic examination of the consequences and boundary conditions of organizational justice climate', *Journal of Applied Psychology*, 97: 776–91.

Wilson, S. and Ebert, N. (2013) 'Precarious work: Economic, sociological and political perspectives', *The Economic and Labour Relations Review*, 24(3): 263–78.

Yang, C., Chen, Y., Roy, X. Z. and Mattila, A. S. (2020) 'Unfolding deconstructive effects of negative shocks on psychological contract violation, organizational cynicism, and turnover intention', *International Journal of Hospitality Management*, 89: 102591.

Yu, H., Yang, F., Wang, T., Sun, J. and Hu, W. (2021) 'How perceived overqualification relates to work alienation and emotional exhaustion: The moderating role of LMX'. *Current Psychology*, 40: 6067–6075.

Yu, T. W. (2021) The effects of organizational justice, trust and supervisor–subordinate guanxi on organizational citizenship behavior: A social-exchange perspective. *Management Research Review*. Available at: https://doi.org/10.1108/MRR-03-2021-0238 (accessed 30 April 2022).

GLOSSARY

Acas Advisory, Conciliation and Arbitration Service. Independent body promoting harmonious employment relationships, providing advice and helping resolve workplace conflict through conciliation, mediation and arbitration.

Acquiescent silence Employees' submissive acceptance of managerial/organisational rules, processes and suggestions.

Affective participation Employee involvement practice that leads to higher levels of personal satisfaction possibly leading to improved productivity.

Agonism A principle suggesting that the contested nature of the employment relationship is one in which each side has a moral duty to recognise the legitimacy of the other, refuting its ideas *without* wanting to destroy it.

Algorithmic management Computer generated formulas that automatically make decisions and predictions based on data sets, models and simulations, without any human intervention.

Alternative dispute resolution A range of processes where parties in dispute try to solve a difference without recourse to the courts and in so doing retain control over the outcome, but use a neutral third party to assist them in defining the issues of difference, finding common ground and, ultimately, reaching a settlement.

Annualised hours A system whereby an employee's total hours for the year are divided so that the employees' working time is arranged to fit in with the demands of the organisation, often accommodating seasonal peaks and troughs up to the annual maximum number of hours.

App-work Work controlled by algorithm.

Arbitration A process whereby a dispute is decided by an independent third party.

'At-will' employment principle Prevalent in the USA this principle enables an employer to end an employee's employment without notice or warning. Its use is often justified by employers who point out that an employee is equally free to leave their employment.

Balance of power This relates to the relative power that parties to the employment relationship have over one another.

BRICS countries Brazil Russia, India, China and South Africa.

Burnout A stress syndrome characterised by emotional exhaustion, depersonalisation and reduced personal accomplishment.

Ca'canny   The policy of deliberately limiting output at work.

Calculus-based trust   Occurs when employees make a rational calculation about the costs and benefits of trusting another individual and then decide, on the basis of this assessment, how much trust to invest in that individual.

Chartered Institute of Personnel and Development (CIPD)   The UK professional body for those involved in personnel and human resource management. A source of advice and guidance about HRM issues.

Closed shop   A place of work where employees must belong to an agreed trade union in order to work there. It is illegal in the UK.

Coercive Power   The use of threats or intimidation by an employer towards an employee in order to effect obedience.

Cognitive participation   Shared information leads to higher performance

Collective bargaining   A voluntary process of negotiation between representatives for both the employer and the employees that sets terms and conditions of employment for those they represent.

Collectivism   A way of managing that recognises the right of employees to have a say in what goes on at work and to be represented as a group in order to express their views and make their interests known to management.

Collective power   Where a group of cooperating individuals acts together to oppose the way an organisation operates.

Competence   The observable, demonstrable, measurable and evidence-based ability to perform the activities of a job role, to a defined standard, within a given context.

Competency-based pay   Remuneration linked to the skill and expertise of the employees under the scheme.

Competency framework   Identification of a set of behaviours required by employees to achieve business objectives; can also profile top performers in the organisation.

Concern   An awareness and consideration of another's position and point of view.

Conciliation   The practice of bringing together the parties to an employment dispute with an independent third party who helps them to settle their differences.

Conflicted collaboration   The simultaneous inter-dependence and disconnection between parties to the employment relationship resulting in both coercive and collaborative experiences for workers (Delbridge, 2007).[1]

---

[1]Delbridge, R. (2007) 'Explaining conflicted collaboration: A critical realist approach to hegemony', *Organization Studies*, 28(9): 1347–57.

Connectivism   Coordinated local groupings of individuals united to protest about an issue.

Consultative participation   Management encourage employees to share their own opinions (management retaining the sole right to make decisions).

Contest-based crowdwork   Many people simultaneously undertake a task but only one result is chosen and paid for.

Contingent work   See precarious work.

Contract of employment   Formal legally binding agreement governing obligations and rights in the work relationship.

Contract of service   A contract between an employer and an employee stipulating the tasks to be undertaken and the remuneration and benefits that an individual can expect.

Convergent employment practices   Describes a process whereby national systems of employment are becoming similar i.e. converging, and hence becoming more liberal over time).

Coordinated Market Economies (CMEs)   A variety of capitalism identified by Hall and Soskice (2001)[2] and exemplified by the economies of Germany, Denmark and Japan where employers consolidate and arrange employment activities by non-market mechanisms, such as multi-employer collective bargaining, with a stakeholder-based framework of social dialogue.

Core workforce   As part of the workforce that is crucial to an organisation's ability to function effectively, it comprises those employees whose skills are vital, who are not easily replaced and who are managed by soft HRM.

Crowdwork   A large number of individuals each separately contributing a small amount of work to complete a larger task, e.g., analysis of a large data set.

Deaf-ear syndrome   A state of selective deafness when the listener ignores information that they find unwelcome (Harlos, 2001).[3]

Defensive silence   An employee's deliberate decision not to speak out about something at work in order to protect their own position.

Delegative participation   Employers allow employees a degree of increased responsibility and autonomy over workplace decisions.

Dependent stakeholders   Low paid individuals without power and whose work is required as a commodity.

---

[2]Hall, P. A. and Soskice, D. (eds) (2001) *Varieties of Capitalism: The Institutional Foundations of Comparative Advantage.* New York: Oxford University Press.

[3]Harlos, K.P. (2001) 'When organizational voice systems fail more on the deaf-ear syndrome and frustration effects', *The Journal of Applied Behavioral Science*, 37(3): 324–42.

Deregulation Freedom of the marketplace, removing legal restrictions on the business operation.

Direct employee involvement The mechanisms and processes whereby employees are provided with information about their work, and the organisation for which they work, in order that they might have a greater understanding about – and commitment to – the employer.

Direct voice The act of an employee communicating with an employer without using an intermediary representative.

Discipline Management action against an employee who has not met expected standards of behaviour or performance.

Discretionary behaviour Voluntary employee activity for the good of the organisation that is freely undertaken and not proscribed.

Dissensus The opposite of consensus, here differences between parties are accepted and such recognition helps avoid/prevent exploitation.

Distributive bargaining Negotiations used to decide the distribution of a fixed resource, such as money.

Distributive justice Employee perceptions concerning whether or not resources have been allocated in a fair way.

Divergent employment practices International systems of employment becoming less like one another over time.

Double-breasting An organisation that simultaneously operates parallel *union* and non-union companies.

Dysfunctional management Poor decision-making or other behaviour (e.g., bullying) which generates problems such as poor standards of conduct or unethical behaviour.

Efficiency A way of working that maximises productivity/profitability.

Efficiency wage theory An economically based theory sometimes called exchange theory. It describes the process where employers exchange payment in return for employees' labour. There is an assumption that employees are primarily motivated by money. On occasion the employer may pay more than the market rate to an employee in order to avoid unnecessary replacement costs.

Egoist A frame of reference where employers and employees each separately puts themselves first.

Employee commitment A positive attitude and loyalty shown towards the employing organisation.

Employee engagement Management initiatives to gain employee co-operation/commitment through a range of direct and indirect activities with the organisation.

Employee involvement   Managerial initiatives that are specifically designed to improve communication with, and to, employees in order that their understanding of the organisational goals (and the part that they as individuals play in meeting these goals) becomes explicit and generates levels of awareness that lead to greater employee commitment and enhanced employee contributions.

Employee ownership schemes   There are three types of employee ownership schemes:

- Individual (direct) employee ownership where employees own the majority of shares in their company.
- Collective (indirect) employee ownership where the shares are held collectively, often through a trust, on behalf of the employees.
- A combination of individual and collective share ownership.

Employee participation   A process that involves employees directly, or indirectly through their representatives, in workplace decision-making processes.

Employee silence   The withholding of information by employees.

Employee voice   Employee views, which can perhaps influence plans and workplace decisions, are given, sought-out and listened to by management.

Employer association   An organisation of employers generally from the same sector/industry that provides professional and employment information and help, negotiates on behalf of its members, and on occasion lobbies to promote the interests of its constituents.

Equal pay   Legal obligation to give the same pay for work of equal value to women and men alike.

Equity   Fairness.

Evolutionary perspective   A linear way of looking at employment that assumes working conditions improve over time.

Expectancy theory   A process theory of motivation which argues that people will direct their effort to behaviours which they can expect to lead to desired outcomes, e.g., where extra effort can lead to a desirable bonus (Vroom, 1982).[4]

Expert power   An individual's skills and knowledge accord them leadership authority that is respected because of their expertise.

Express terms of contract   Explicit terms contained in a contract of employment.

Facilitation   A process in which a neutral person helps a group work together more effectively; it is sometimes used as a form of alternative dispute resolution.

Family-friendly policies   Policies on flexible working (e.g., hours, place of work) to enable employees to juggle job and family commitments.

---

[4]Vroom, V. H. (1982) *Work and Motivation*. Florida: Robert E. Krieger Publishing Company.

Financialisation   Managerial concentration on financial aspects (for example, pleasing shareholders) at the sometimes long-term detriment to other workplace issues.

Financial flexibility   The ability of an employer to choose which method of remuneration is going to be deployed in order to achieve the best results for the organisation.

Financial Participation   A way of motivating employees to work harder by providing them with a sense of ownership through the provision of shares, or similar profit-sharing schemes.

Flashmob unionism   Technologically enabled, spontaneous collective action.

Flexible (cafeteria) benefits   Benefits (e.g., loans, vouchers, gym membership) offered to allow employees some choice in the makeup of their remuneration package so it is more suited to their individual needs/circumstances.

Flexible firm   A concept devised by Atkinson and Meager (1986)[5] describing an adaptive organisation which has numerical, functional and financial flexibility regarding staffing arrangements with a limited core group of employees and a larger periphery group comprising those with less job security.

Flexible work patterns   Non-standard ways of working that alter the way in which the hours of work are organised, for example term-time working, compressed working weeks, job-sharing.

Frame of reference   The ideology through which a situation is viewed.

Functional flexibility   The deployment of a workforce in such a way that the skills of the employees are used effectively over a broad range of tasks in order to adjust to production and technological demands – often the same employees performing a variety of functions depending upon need.

Furlough   A process where employees are temporarily laid off but remain on their organisations' pay roll.

Gainsharing   A motivational payment system in which employees receive points that reward specific behaviours; the points are then translated into payments.

Gig work   Income-earning work occurring outside of standard, long-term employer–employee relationships.

Goal theory   As with expectancy theory, this suggests that providing employees with a motivational target will elicit their desired productive behaviour.

Graded salary structure   A sequence or hierarchy of pay levels (grades) into which jobs that are broadly comparable in value/size are placed.

Grievance   A formal complaint by an employee that is processed through a set of procedures.

---

[5]Atkinson, J. and Meager, N. (1986) *New Forms of Work Organisation*, IMS Report 121, Brighton.

Hard HRM   A way of managing that treats the workforce as a resource that needs to be controlled in order to achieve the best possible profit and competitive advantage.

Harmony   A collective identity and a set of values shared by those within a workforce.

Horizontal task-based participation   Employees are given more control but have the same skill set.

Human Capital theory   Employers are able to pick the cheapest workers (i.e., human capital) who have access to all labour markets and are paid in proportion to their productivity.

Human Resource Management   The holistic and strategic approach used to manage a workforce so that it is aligned with organisational goals. It recognises that individuals are uniquely important to organisational success and give a competitive advantage.

Hybrid working pattern   A flexible working pattern, usually weekly, where employees balance working from home with working in the office.

Identification-based trust   Occurs where individual employees identify with one another's intentions and have developed complete mutual understanding and trust in one another.

Implied terms of contract   Terms of an employment contract that are not explicit but still binding such as common law duties, e.g., to pay wages.

Indirect involvement   Where employees receive and provide information to management via representatives.

Indirect voice   Where employees are able to 'have a say' – and be listened to – through the medium of their representatives.

Individualism   Occurs where employees are regarded as separate entities, and are dealt with as such.

Industrial pluralist perspective   A way of looking at the work environment that recognises the imbalance of power between the parties to the employment relationship, acknowledging that different groups will hold different values and perspectives and that negotiation may help to manage conflict between groups.

Informational justice   A perception experienced by employees when the amount of information provided to them is sufficient for them to undertake a task well, understand why the task is necessary and how it fits into the overall scheme of things (Colquitt, 2001).[6] Where information is deliberately withheld or perhaps where an employer makes decisions without fully briefing the workplace this is known as informational injustice and it leads directly to employee disquiet and lack of trust.

Insecurity   A lack of job and workplace security often leading to poor health and financial difficulties.

---

[6]Colquitt, J. A. (2001) 'On the dimensionality of organizational justice: A construct validation of a measure', *Journal of Applied Psychology*, 86(3): 386.

Integrative bargaining   A way of negotiating where the final outcome leads to positive results for all of the participants.

Integrative participation   Employees are allowed a degree of influence over their day-to-day operations by letting them, usually through their representatives, to aid management in improving the general working conditions (Stephens, 1980: 3).[7]

Intellectual capital   Argument that human knowledge can be valued as an asset.

Interactional justice   A perception by an individual or group that they are being accorded respect and dignity and communicated with in a fair way.

Intra-organisational bargaining   A process prior to negotiations where the individuals comprising each side separately discusses their respective position(s) and reach decisions about their corresponding negotiating positions.

Job evaluation   Systematic process for defining the relative values of jobs in an organisation.

Justice theory   posits that employees adjust their output according to the rewards they expect to receive in relation to: a) the amount of effort that they need to expend; and b) the fairness behind the ways in which an organisation organises and processes its payment system.

Key Performance Indicators (KPIs)   Quantifiable measurements of the issues an organisation regards as critical to its success such as labour turnover, return on investment, etc. KPIs differ from organisation to organisation.

Key Result Areas (KRAs)   A focus on elements of the job deemed critical for success in the overall job.

Legal power   The use of rules and regulations to gain an advantage.

Legitimate Power   This is exhibited when someone's position within the organisation gives them the authority to make decisions and control the activities of others.

Liberal Market Economies (LMEs)   A variety of capitalism identified by Hall and Soskice (2001)[8] and exemplified by the economies of the USA and UK where employers rely on market forces to influence the pay and skills of their workforce.

Line of Sight   In the design of pay schemes where employees can clearly see that effort can lead directly to reward.

Mainstreaming   Incorporating issues to do with equality into all aspects of organisational strategy and policy.

Management style   The preferred way managers deal with their staff ranging from autocratic to democratic participative.

---

[7]Stephens, E. H. (1980) 'Theoretical framework for the comparative study of workers' participation', in E.H. Stephens (ed.), *The Politics of Workers' Participation: The Peruvian Approach in Comparative Perspective*. London: Elsevier.

[8]Hall, P. A. and Soskice, D. (eds) (2001) *Varieties of Capitalism: The Institutional Foundations of Comparative Advantage*. New York: Oxford University Press.

Managerialist perspective A unitarist way of looking at employment that assumes conflict can be managed by using the appropriate processes and procedures.

Managerial Styles The preferred way that managers deal with their staff ranging from autocratic through to democratic/participative.

Mediation A form of alternative dispute resolution in which a third party helps others to reach an acceptable solution.

Mixed bargaining Negotiations where the outcomes are a mixture of distributive and integrative bargaining.

Mobilisation Where groups coalesce around a specific grievance in order to address, and redress, the areas of complaint.

Natural justice The principles prescribing a way of proceeding that is fair; decreeing that individuals should know about the standards and behaviour expected from them and that, should an allegation be made against them, they have the right to be told about it, and to answer the accusation prior to a decision being reached by a fair and unbiased hearing. Individuals should, in such circumstances, be told about their right of appeal. In addition the Employment Rights Act 1999 requires that workers:

Have the opportunity to be accompanied by a friend/colleague/trade union representative

Be given the outcome of the hearing in writing.

Negotiation A process of bargaining between two or more parties.

Neo-corporatist perspective A way of looking at something, deriving from political exchange theory. Based on voluntary tripartite social partnerships it assumes that the intensity, degree and frequency of conflict will be in direct response to the amount of power that the labour movement can exert in relation to the amount of restraint that the state and associated institutions are able to bring to bear against it.

Neoliberalism A philosophy that regards market forces as all important and as a consequence promotes economic liberalisation, deregulation, fiscal austerity, decreased state spending and privatisation.

Neo pluralism A perspective that emphasises the importance of cooperation between employers and workers, such that it will be for the good of society as a whole.

New pay Notion that internal equity is less important than market value in supporting business objectives (Zingheim and Schuster, 2000).[9]

---

[9]Zingheim, P.K. and Schuster, J.R. (2000) 'Total rewards for new and old economy companies', *Compensation & Benefits Review*, 32(6): 20–23.

Organisational justice Employees' perceptions about the fairness and consistency with which they are treated when they compare themselves with others (Greenberg, 1987).[10]

Partnership An arrangement based on problem solving and consensus where workplace representatives and management work together.

Pay gap The difference in the average rate of pay between one group and another.

Peer review A formal review process whereby co-workers honestly evaluate one another's performance.

Performance appraisal Assessment of past and current work performance with a focus on improvement – the resulting evaluation may be tied to an increased level of remuneration.

Performance pay Pay that depends on performance, competence or contribution.

Peripheral workforce Non-essential workers/employees that are easily replaced.

Personal power Where an individual understands how an organisation works and uses it to their own benefit.

Picketing The act of standing outside a workplace/organisation in order to dissuade others from entering – often used in conjunction with strike activity.

Piecework Work where a fixed payment is made for each unit (piece) produced, or action performed, regardless of the time it takes.

Platform work Work that is arranged through a technology-enabled virtual platform that facilitates the matching of a flexible workforce with jobs.

Pluralist perspective A way of analysing workplace relationships that recognises the legitimacy of often conflicting values held by different groups within the workplace. Conflict is regarded as inevitable.

Power The authority (or ability) to direct, control or influence the behaviour of others.

Primary parties Those who pay for work and those who provide it in the labour market: for example, employers and employees.

Precarious work Work that is poorly paid, offers no job security, is of uncertain duration, and often falls outside the remit of employment legislation. The workforce rather than the employer bears the risks associated with the work. Sometimes referred to as contingent work (USA).

Principal–agency theory A theory in which employees are seen as agents who receive a basic rate of pay that may be enhanced by the employer (the principal) by the agents increasing the amount of effort they put into their work.

---

[10]Greenberg, J. (1987) 'A taxonomy of organizational justice theories', *Academy of Management Review*, 12(1): 9–22.

Procedural injustice   A perception that the process or processes by which something has been undertaken was in some way unfair or unjust.

Prosocial silence   The deliberate keeping quiet by an employee in order to benefit the organisation.

Psychological contract   An unwritten set of beliefs, perceptions, expectations and informal reciprocal obligations between an employer and an employee; distinguishable from the formal written contract of employment which identifies mutual duties and responsibilities.

Radicalist   A frame of reference where an employment relationship is regarded as one whose sole purpose is to satisfy the interests of the dominant class.

Radical perspective   A way of seeing situations through a lens that puts the differences between capital and labour at the heart of the interactions between employers who are committed to extracting as much value as possible out of their workforces and employees who react to this and resist such pressures in order to achieve a greater degree of control over their workplace experiences.

Redundancy   Official notification and the process of losing a current job. Legal termination may be because of the disappearance of a job, or reduction in work or change of location of employer's activities.

Referent power   Respect and authority conferred on someone because they are respected and often regarded as inspirational.

Relational relationship   A relationship in which the parties engage with one another at an emotional level.

Reliability   A term used to denote the way in which organisations actually do what they purport to do – if an organisation says one thing and does another it is likely that the employees will not trust it.

Resource-based view of the firm   The notion that an organisation's resources (e.g. people) are a key source of competitive advantage and that the aim should be to maximise resources to create and dominate future opportunities for the organisation.

Reward management   Strategy designed to reward (e.g., pay) employees fairly, consistently and in relation to their value for the organisation.

Reward strategy   Development of objectives for the longer term in order to implement rewards and support business goals.

Reward Power   Persuading others to behave at work in exchange for something that they want.

Secondary parties   Representative actors in the employment relationship who are management, union or staff association representatives whose role is to act for – and present the views of – the primary parties to the employment relationship.

Secondary picketing   The picketing by employees of one organisation of the premises of another organisation that has important trade links with their employer but is not otherwise involved in the dispute in question. It is illegal in the UK.

Social exchange theory   Proposes that individuals behave in ways that are calculated to maximise personal advantage: thus good treatment at work is likely to elicit commitment and productivity, conversely, poor treatment is likely to engender a lack of commitment and poor productivity.

Social movement unionism (SMU)   A conscious and deliberate union strategy to combat injustice by mobilising their membership (sometimes by collaborating with other social groupings).

Social partnership   A multi-party arrangement often involving employers, trade unions and the state working together for the common good. Social partnership is usually concerned with areas of economic and social policy.

Socially irresponsible HRM   HRM systems that do nothing about in-work poverty.

SOE   State-owned enterprise.

Soft HRM   A way of managing where the employees are considered to be a crucial resource for a company's growth and profitability; as a consequence they are treated well, receive timely and relevant information and their skills are developed.

Sophisticated modern constitutionalist managerial style   A pluralist managerial style in which conflict is managed by negotiation and by a reliance on rules and procedures.

Sophisticated modern consulter managerial style   A pluralist managerial style in which conflict is managed by asking the opinions of and negotiating with employee representatives.

Sophisticated paternalist managerial style   A unitarist managerial style in which the employees are managed in a soft HRM way to encourage their identification with and commitment to the organisation for which they work.

Spot salary structure   Single rate of pay for the job instead of a grade or range of pay.

Stakeholders   Individuals or groups of individuals who are involved with an organisation and have an interest in how it operates/performs.

Standard modern managerial style   A pluralist managerial style where the management negotiates with employee representatives on a 'fire-fighting' basis.

State work engagement   Sporadic bursts of engagement (Sonnentag et al., 2010).[11]

Strike   An expression of collective employee power that involves the withdrawal of labour in order to put pressure on management.

---

[11]Sonnentag, S., Dormann, C. and Demerouti, E. (2010) 'Not all states are created equal: The concept of state work engagement', in A. B. Backer and M. P. Leiter (eds), *Work Engagement: A Handbook of Essential Theory and Research*. New York: Psychology Press.

Structural antagonism The implicit tension found as a result of the managerial requirement to tell others what to do while simultaneously allowing them sufficient freedom to choose how they undertake their tasks.

Symbolic power A pervasive ideology within an organisation that confirms an individual's subservient position and leads to acquiescent behaviours.

Target theory Sometimes known as tournament theory, it advances the idea that introducing and encouraging elements of competition between senior staff will enhance productivity.

Taylorist Scientific Management Focus on using rational scientific procedures in management with simple effort/reward systems such as payment for goods produced (piecework) in manufacturing (F. W. Taylor 1856–1917).

Team briefing A process that ensures regular (usually face to face) communication takes place between management and employees.

Theory X managers Managers who assume that people dislike work and therefore will not be committed to the organisation – and consequently that they must be continually controlled and coerced in order for them to work effectively.

Theory Y managers Managers who assume that people will be committed to the organisation and exercise self-direction – and consequently that they will work without prompting towards achieving organisational objectives.

Third parties Parties not directly involved in the day-to-day employment relationship – often 'agents of the State'. Such parties will include the legislature, law enforcers and the courts. Other external third parties that may become involved in the relationship may do so in a lobbying capacity – for example, Stonewall – while yet others such as ACAS and the Citizens Advice Bureau may act as advisors, mediators, conciliators or arbiters.

Total reward An integrated strategic rewards framework (pay, benefits, etc.) to attract, retain, motivate and satisfy employees.

Tournament theory Sometimes known as target theory, this is a system of pay that incentivises top management by introducing a level of competition – regarded as an effective motivator for high-flying employees, it can lead to dissatisfaction and high turnover when staff do not receive the reward they think they are due.

Traditionalist managerial style A unitarist, hard managerial style in which the employees are treated as units of production by an authoritarian management.

Transformational participation Sociopolitical forces create a fundamental shift of power in favour of the employees enabling their eventual control of the organisation, thereby altering the prevailing social order (Stephens, 1980: 3).[12]

---

[12]Stephens, E. H. (1980) 'Theoretical framework for the comparative study of workers' participation', in E.H. Stephens (ed.), *The Politics of Workers' Participation: The Peruvian Approachin Comparative Perspective*. London: Elsevier.

Transactional relationship   A relationship in which the parties evaluate, on a quid pro quo basis, exactly what they will or will not do in order to achieve the desired outcome.

Transparency   Reward policies and practices which are open, clear, well communicated and easily understood by employees.

Trust   A belief that an organisation, group or individual is reliable and honest and keeps to their word.

Union density   The unionised workforce expressed as a percentage of potential membership.

Unitarist perspective   A way of perceiving workplace relations that assumes everyone has the same values and beliefs and is working towards the same goals. Conflict is regarded as anathema.

Varieties of Capitalism (VOC)   Different approaches to managing labour and capital; see also *Coordinated Market Economies and Liberal Market Economies*.

Varieties of Unionism (VOU)   Different union approaches to collective organisation and representation.

Vertical task-based participation   Employees are up-skilled in order to be able to take additional responsibility.

Voice   The ability to speak out and be heard at work.

Wage-effort bargain   An arrangement by which employees proportionally regulate their workplace output in direct relation to the wage that they expect to receive for their work.

Working to rule   Protest behaviour by employees where they work without undertaking any discretionary behaviour and stick to strict interpretations of their contracts of employment and workplace regulations – unlike strike behaviour the employees remain at work and receive payment.

Work–life balance   The need to deal with equally or balance the competing demands of job and private life (e.g., family caring commitments).

Works councils   A formal group comprised of employee representatives and their managerial counterparts that meets to negotiate terms and conditions of employment. Councils can be at local, national or sectoral level and are common across Europe.

INDEX

absenteeism 63, 163, 165, 240, 354, 400, 419
absorption 227, 230, 231, 237, 238
academic perspectives on conflict 161–5
Acas 175–6, 212, 216, 267, 276, 339, 429
    Code of Practice on Disciplinary and Grievance Procedures (2015) 198, 203, 313, 414
  redundancy 416
Ackers, P. 67
acquiescent silence 316, 429
Adams, S. J. 70
Adamson, Mike 386–7
adversarial pluralism perspective 195
Aetna 406
affective participation 275–6, 429
Age Concern 108
agonism 21
aircraft cabin crew 156
Airtasker 142
algorithmic management 138, 139–40, 429
algorithms 124, 125, 127, 132
  Amazon's recruitment app 138
  automatic regulation 136–7
  data protection and privacy 137
  discrimination 137
  dissatisfaction with 136
  impact on employment relationship 139–41
  legal challenges to 138
All-Party Parliamentary Groups (UK) 133–4, 314
Allen, J. A. and Rogelberg, S. G. 246
alternative dispute resolution (ADR) 214–16, 429
Amazon 80
  case study 138
  trade union discrimination 140
American Jobs Plan 7
Andersson et al. 41
Angelici, M. and Profeta, P. 352
Annand, Phytos 357
annual leave 117, 135, 205
Annual Survey of Hours and Earnings (ONS, 2021) 376
annualised hours 340–1, 345–6

App Drivers and Couriers Union (ADCU) 133, 137
app-work 132, 429
apps 132, 139–40
Arafat, Laurn 169
arbitration 215, 429
Armstrong, M. 375
Armstrong, M. and Baron, A. 386
Arriva 172
Arrowsmith, J. and Marginson, P. 387–8
Aslef (case study) 281
Associated Biscuits 167–8
Atkinson J. and Meagre, N. 341–3
at-will employment principle 50, 51, 113, 429
austerity 36, 47, 153, 174, 413
Australia 36, 157, 392
  employee trust 409–10
  employee voice 300
  employment contracts 103
  workplace conflict 173
Australian Abrasives 24
Austria 142, 262
Auto Trader (case study) 246–8
autocratic unitarism perspective 195
automation 171–2
autonomy 17, 80, 135, 139, 234, 245, 247, 353
autonomy paradox 336

Baccaro, L. and Howell, C. 43
Baillot, Jean-Louis 99
Baines, Alan 404
balance of power 2, 429
BAME 3–4
bargaining *see* collective bargaining
Barnet, R. J. and Muller, R. E. 39
Barry, M. and Wilkinson, A. 20
Bates, Jennifer 80
Bauman, Z. 129
BCLP 270
Bechter et al. 380
behavioural engagement 229
Belgium 279, 307, 308

Bender et al. 387
Bennett, T. 216
Benson, Steve and Bob 283–4
Benton, Calvin 371
Berlin Brandenburg Airport 75–6
Better.com 163
Bewley, J. and Forth, J. 405
beyond contract working 96
Biden, President Joe 7
Bies, R. J. and Moag, J. S. 408
Bilimoria, Lord Karan 3
binding terms
    employees 102
    employers 102
Bingham, C. A. 2
Black Lives Matter (BLM) 172, 384
Blackard, K. 216
Blair, Tony 258
BLAPA 4
Blau, G. 383–4
blood-in-pocket syndrome 387
Bolton, S. C. and Boyd, C. 156
bonus payments 388
Botzia, Costas 357
Bowden, Justin 110
Bowen, F. and Blackmon, K. 320–1
Bowles et al. 389
Bowsy 131
Boxall, P. and Purcell, J. 273, 294
Brandl, B. 242
Branham, J. 339
Bratton, J. and Gold, J. 369
Bray et al. 21, 195
breaches of contract 107, 108
Breslow, L. and Buell, P. 337
BrewDog 162, 195
Brewley, H. and Forth, J. 2
bricklaying 171–2
BRICS countries 33, 429
Briner, R. B. 226–7
Briône, Patrick 271
British Airways 72, 354
British Business Bank (case study) 269–70
British Gas 109–10, 157
British Homestores v. *Burchell* (1980) 415
British Telecom (BT) 265
Brockner et al. 192
Brodie, D. 103
Bronfenbrenner, Kate 157
Brooks, Ian 337–8
Brown, Sky 284
Brown, W. 386
Brownhill, Louise 226
Bryson, A. 79

Bryson et al. 300
Budd, J. W. 68–70, 111, 141, 315, 338, 401
bullying 15, 74, 80–1, 108
Burawoy, M. 383
Burberry 169–70
burnout 156, 233, 234, 236, 429
bus drivers 38, 172, 190, 310

C&P 357
ca'canny 171, 429
Cadbury 79
calculus-based trust 62, 430
call centres 63, 117, 193, 234
Cambridgeshire Local Authority 282
Canada 18, 41, 78, 209, 231, 306, 392
Canadian Union of Postal Workers
    (CUPW) 128
Capita plc 81
capital platform work 131
capitalism 47, 154
Cardella, E. and Depew, B. 383
Caza, Aran 230
CBA v. *Barker* (2013) 103
CBI (Confederation of British Industry)
    3–4, 267
Charlwood, Andy and Pollert, Anna 174
Chartered Institute of Personnel and
    Development (CIPD) 229–30, 319–20,
    336, 348, 384, 389, 430
    Employee Outlook Survey (2013) 407
    report (2010) 231, 232, 239
    report (2020) 15, 160, 232
    Reward survey (2022) 411
Chartered Management Institute survey
    (2020) 233
Cheese, Peter 336
Chemical Industries Association (CIA) 9
Chen et al. 128–9
Chevalier et al. 258
Chevron 33
Chiang, F. F. and Birch, T. A. 378
China 102
    economy 33–4, 36
    employee participation 259
    employment contracts 113
    gig workers 140
    'iron rice bowl' system 44
    Labour Contract Law 258–9
    marketisation of SOEs 44
    organisational trust 410
CIPD *see* Chartered Institute of Personnel
    and Development (CIPD)
Citizens Advice Scotland (CAS) 188
Citizens UK 381–2

Clapham et al. 322
Clarke, Nita 307
Clarke, S. and Holdsworth, L. 352
Coalition government 202, 318
Codagnone et al. 129–30
coercive power 15, 189–91
cognitive participation 275, 430
collaborative pluralism perspective 195
collective bargaining 9, 306, 307–12,
    380, 381, 430
  bargaining unit 307, 308
  company or group level 308–9
  departmental or workshop level 309
  models
    distributive bargaining 312
    integrative bargaining 311–12
    intra-organisational bargaining 312
    mixed bargaining 312
  national v. local agreements 310–11
  plant or site level 309
collective power 16
collectivism 11, 172, 430
Colquitt et al. 409
Colvin, A. J. S. 209
Commonwealth Bank 103
communication
  flexible working 356
  workplace 245
company level bargaining 308–9
compassionate leave 204, 205
competence 14, 368, 430
compliance 191–2
  constitutional mechanisms 191
  consultative mechanisms 191
Compressed Working Week
    (CWW) 346
concern 401–2
  trust and 64
conciliation 67, 215, 430
conflict 19, 21, 151–2
  academic perspectives on 161–5
    evolutionary 161–2
    industrial pluralist 163
    managerial 162–3
    neo-corporatist 163–4
    neoliberal 162
    radical 164–5
  addressing 196–201
    good practice 198
    regulation 196–7, 199–200, 201
  alternative dispute resolution 214–16
  in a capitalist environment 173
  causes and inevitability of 152–5
  cooperation 195

demographics 174
disciplinary measures 159–60
divergent and convergent interests 155–9
expressions of 167–74
  collective 167, 170, 171
  defiance 167–8
  dissent 170, 171
  individual 167, 170, 171
  mobilisation theory 169–70
  sabotage 167–8, 169
financial cost of 172–3, 187
flexible working 353–5
justice and injustice 410–11
legal restrictions 204–5
legislation 201–2
management of 188, 200
managerial styles 189–92
  coercion 189–91
  compliance 191–2
performance management 192–4
procedures 205–10
  types of 210–11
restrictions on employers 203–4
rights 155
smaller businesses 159–60
sources of 154
strategies for reducing 194–6, 201
trade unions 197
tribunal system, UK 175–6
trust 159–60, 194–6
UK expressions of 159–60
conflicted collaboration 239, 430
conflicts of interest 154
conflicts of right 154
Conlon, Valerie 166
connectivism 172
consensual variation 106, 107
Conservative government 189
constitutionalists 24
consultative participation 276
consultative unitarism perspective 195
consulters 24
contest-based crowdwork 132, 430
contingent work see precarious work
contract for service 94, 96
contract law 203
contract of employment see
    employment contracts
contract of service 94, 96
Contracts of Employment Act (1963) 95
control 13, 156
convergence 43–7
convergent employment practices 43, 430
Cooke, Hannah 156

cooperation, perspectives of 195
coordinated market economies
    (CMEs) 47, 431
COP26 (Glasgow, 2021) 157
  bin strike 158–9
Corbyn, Jeremy 158
core workforce 342, 431
Cosla 158
Costa et al. 231–2
Covid-19 pandemic 35, 36, 81–2, 355
  Sri Lankan taskforce 164
  strikes 173
Cox, A. 375
Coxall v. *Goodyear GB Ltd* (2002) 76
Crédit Agricole SA 155
Credit Suisse 273
critical perspective/radicalism 195
Croatia, employee/manager meetings 262
Crocodile Tears Tour 172
crowdwork 125, 132, 431
crowdworkers 140–1
Crowley, M. and Hodson, R. 162
Croydon, Emma 199
custom and practice 102

Daily Telegraph 386–7
Dalton, K. and Bingham, C. 44
Dancey, Nikki 82
Dawson, T. 16
deaf-ear syndrome 260, 431
Debenhams Retail Ireland 165–6
decent work 34
decision-making *see* employee involvement,
    participation and partnership (EIP)
dedication 227, 230, 237
defensive silence 316, 317, 431
defiance 165, 166, 167
  covert 167
  overt 167
delegative participation 276
Demir et al. 337
Denmark 173, 308, 312–13
Deny, R. 8
Department for Business, Energy and
    Industrial Strategy (BEIS) 124
Department of Trade and Industry
    (DTI) 280–1
departmental level bargaining 309
dependent stakeholders 3, 431
Detert, J. R. and Burris, E. R. 294
Deutsche Bank 80
Díaz, Yolanda 376
Dietz, G. and Fortin, M. 69
Digital Equipment Corporation 369–70
digital labour platforms 130

digital platforms 130, 133–4
  see also platform work
Digital Regulation Cooperation Forum
    (DRCF) 134
dinobabies 153
direct EIP 260, 263–4, 265, 272, 273, 274
direct employee involvement 267–8, 431
direct voice 295, 297, 298, 301–3, 431
direct voice mechanisms 259
Direction, S. 228
disability 175, 244, 318
discipline procedures 105, 210, 414–15, 431
discretionary behaviour 96, 230, 431
discretionary voice 294
dissensus 21
dissent 170, 171
distributional justice 125, 132, 242, 245, 247,
    315, 373, 377, 411
distributive bargaining model 312, 431
distributive justice/injustice 70, 73, 243,
    407–8, 409, 419, 432
divergence 43–7
divergent employment practices 217, 432
diversity 317–21
  case study 317–18
  targeted approach 320
Dix et al. 187
double-breasting 298, 432
Dousin et al. 355
downward communication 267
Dreamtouch Mattresses Ltd 104
Dromey, Jack 381
Duggan et al. 131–2, 139
Dundon et al. 298
Dunnes Stores (case study) 421–2
Duran-Palma, Fernando (case study) 44–6
duty of care 75–6
Dyson 34

East of England Ambulance Service 75
Edelman 'Trust Barometer' (2019) 66
Edelmann, R. J. 404
EDF (Electricité de France) 18
Edwards, Paul 21–2, 66, 81, 259,
    272, 369
Edwards, Ron 157
efficiency, Budd's framework 68–70, 111,
    141, 315, 338, 401
efficiency wage theory 373, 432
effort bargain 383
egoist frame of reference 18
Egypt 167
Elizabeth Line (case study) 281
Elsbach et al. 346–7
Emmott, Mike 294

employee commitment 12, 258–62, 265
employee engagement 196, 225–6,
    248, 432
  Auto Trader (case study) 246–8
  definitions 226–9
  discretionary behaviour 230
  employee behaviour 227–8, 229
  employee performance 226–7
  employment relationship 238–42
  engagement paradox 232–6
  engendering 232
  managerial concern for 231–2
  measures of 237–8
  processes 240
  responsibility for 231
  Tiny Plus report (2019) 228
  trust 239, 242–6
  voice 242–6
employee involvement, participation
    and partnership (EIP) 258, 285
  activities 262
  commitment 258–62, 265
  communication 266
  definitions 262–3
  direct EIP 263–4, 265
  direct employee involvement 267–8
  employee networks 270–1
  Eurofound survey (2020) 260
  influence and power 265
  informal EIP 264
  involvement 266–9, 432
    definitions 267
  Ireland 261
  mechanisms 266
  participation 272–3
    case studies 273–5
    categorising 275–9
    statutory regulation 277, 278
  partnership 279–84
  personalities and abilities 261
  representative EIP 263
  rights 278
  workplace control 264–5
employee ownership schemes 298, 432
employee participation 259, 261, 263,
    272–3, 277, 278, 432
employee share-option schemes
    (ESOPs) 388
employee silence 322, 432
employee voice 17, 52, 293–4, 323, 432
  collective bargaining 307–12
  definitions 294–5
  direct voice 259, 297, 298, 301–3
  diversity and 317–21
  efficiency and equity 68–9

employee ownership schemes 298
  enabling voice 312–17
  escalator 282
  evidence for concept 295–8
  fairness and trust 69–70
  indirect voice 295, 297, 298, 300, 303–7
  managerial perspectives 297–8
  national, industry or sector level 308
  organisational trust 247
  patterns of 299–303
  silence and 316–17, 322
  trade unions 296
  trust and engagement 242–6
  trust and fairness 321–3
  UK employment regulation 313
  workplace democracy 297
employees
  autonomy 17
  disciplinary processes 414–15
  empowerment 17
  exerting power 157
  interests of 17, 21
  vulnerability 417–18
  see also work
employer associations 8–9, 432
employer voice 298–9
employers
  duty of care 75–6, 337
  interests of 17, 21
  relocation, threat by 157
  reward systems 369–71
  see also work
Employment Act (2002) 105, 202, 204
employment contracts 65, 94–118, 413–14
  Australia 103
  China 102, 113
  contract changes
    advice for employers 110–12
    impact on employment
      relationship 105–9
    poorly handled 109–10
  discretionary behaviour 96
  dissatisfaction 100
  evolution of 95
  Finland 104
  flexibility 96, 97
  Germany 98
  Italy 98
  Japan 113
  legislation 94–5
  nature of 94
  Portugal 111
  power imbalances 98–100
  property rights 95–6
  Russia 105

temporary work 97–8
termination 113–15
terms 101–5
  United Kingdom 114
  United States 113
  wording of 94–5
employment rates 37
employment relations
  case studies 50–3
  context 32–7
  convergence versus divergence 43–7
  definition 2
  employer associations 8–9
  frames of reference 18–22
  globalisation and 38–42, 49
  human resource management
      (HRM) 11–12
  influences on 10
  institutions 9
  interests 16–17
  management 7–8
  managerial styles 23–5
  participants 3–4
  power and control 156
  power imbalances 12–16
  trade unions 5–7, 47–9
  UK employment market, changes
      in 10–11
Employment Relations Act (1999) 4, 203–4
employment relationships (ER) 49, 65
  case study 50–2
    local and national practices 50–1
    power and authority 50
    voice and engagement 52
  conflict 201
  high-trust 83
  low-trust 83
Employment Rights Acts (1996, 1999) 95, 197,
      203, 313, 413–14
employment termination 51
empowerment 17
engagement see employee engagement
Engaging for Success (MacLeod and
      Clarke) 226
Enterprise and Regulatory Reform Act
      (2013) 313
equal pay 103, 433
Equality Act (2010) 203, 385
equity 17, 433
  Budd's framework 68–70, 111, 141,
      315, 338, 401
equity theory 373, 411
Esterson, Bill 34
ethical decision-making 8

Euro Zone 36
Eurofound 260
European Association of Craft, Small
      and Medium-sized Enterprises 9
European Bank for Reconstruction and
      Development 277
European Commission (EC) 278
European Convention on Human Rights 34
European Court of Human Rights
      (ECHR) 114, 204
European Court of Justice 341
European Economic and Social
      Committee 133
European Union (EU) 271
  Directive on platform workers 136
  EIP rights 278
  levels of employee participation 278
  working hours and practices 340
European Working Conditions Survey
      (Fifth) 262
European Working Time Directive 207
Evans, Chris 386
evolutionary perspective on
      conflict 161–2
exchange theory 226, 373
expectancy theory 371, 433
expert power 14–15, 433
express terms 101, 104, 111, 433
external equity 407–8
extrinsic rewards 369

Facey, Hugh 268
facial recognition systems 137
facilitation 215, 433
Factory Act (1961) 207
Fager, Hanna 43
fair work 109
fairness 399
  case studies 401, 402–3, 421–2
  in context 400–3
  employee voice 321–3
  evaluation of 383–4
  flexible working 356
  inequality of income 411–13
  job security 413–17
  justice and 406–10
  law and 67–8
  line managers 420–2
  organisational justice 70
  pay 382
  perceptions of 65, 66, 69–72, 419–20
  power and 403–6
  reward 382–7
  trust 63–4, 65–7, 321–3, 402

unfairness 407
voice 419–20
work processes 417
family-friendly policies 80, 351–3, 433
Fanshaw, F. 320
Farnham, D. 196
Farnham, D. and Pimlott, J. 383
Federation of International Employers
  (FedEE Global), 8–9
feminist perspective 161
Feng, J. and Xie, P. 215
Ferns, Sue 412
financial flexibility 339, 433
financial participation 268
financialisation 7–8
Finland 104, 308
fire and rehire 109
  Tesco 112
FirstGroup (case study) 274
Fitzgerald, I. and Hardy, J. 41
Flanders, A. 13, 20
flashmob unionism 172
flexible firm model 341–3, 433
flexible working 333–4, 357, 433
  benefits 335–7
  case study 350–1
  definitions 334
  employees' perceptions of 337
  gender and family-friendly
    practices 351–3
  impact of 335–8
  important consideration 356–7
  managerial styles 338–40
  pluralist approaches 340–1
  power, conflict and trust 353–5
  reasons for requesting 353
  types of 345
    annualised hours 340–1, 345–6
    Compressed Working Week
      (CWW) 346
    financial flexibility 339
    flexitime 337, 345
    functional flexibility 339–40
    hybrid working 346–7
    job-sharing 345
    key-time contracts 347
    numerical flexibility 339
    outsourced labour 349
    part-time work 343
    remote working 346–7
    sabbaticals 348–9
    shift work 337–8, 344
    teleworking 346–7
    term-time working 348

voluntary reduced work time 348
zero-hours contracts 96, 347–8
working from home 334, 335, 336,
  338, 346–7
flexitime 84, 337, 345
Foley, Kevin 165–6
Folger, R. and Bies, R. J. 71, 197–8, 322
Folger, R. and Greenberg, J. 191
Folio Society 299
Foodora 142
forced labour 34
Ford UK 209
Foreign and Commonwealth Office
  (UK) 192
Forret, M. and Love, M. S. 73
4Hs 249–50
Fox, A. 13, 18, 23, 83, 189, 191, 193
frames of reference 18–19, 433
France 42, 278, 307, 308, 392
  disciplinary action 160
  rights of gig workers 135
  rights of platform workers 141–2
France Télécom (Orange) 82–3
Franklin, Jim 249–50
freelance workers 94, 261
Freeman, R. B. and Medoff, J. 294–5
Frege, C. and Kelly, J. 32, 48
Freie ArbeiterInnen-Union 142
French, J. R. P. and Raven, B. 14–15
Friedman, A. 268
frontier of control 16, 156, 309, 408
Frost & Sullivan 169
fuel prices 35–6
functional flexibility 339–40, 433
furloughed workers 35, 433

gainsharing 372, 388, 433
Gallie et al. 78
Gallup 231, 237
Garcia-Perez et al. 97
Garg, Vishal 163, 196
Garment and Textile Workers' Union
  (GATWU) 39–40
Gasparri et al. 48
GATT (General Agreement on Tariffs
  and Trade) 38
Geary, J. and Sisson, K. 276
gender equality/inequality 160, 192,
  334, 347
  flexible working 351–3
  pay 375–6, 389, 392
  pensions 411–12
General Confederation of Greek Workers 153
Germany 33, 36, 42, 98, 142, 307, 308

employment contracts 98
employment termination procedure 51
Works Constitution Act (1972) 279
gig economy
  app-work 132
  business model 127–8
  capital platform work 131
  crowdwork 132
  definition 124
  strikes 143
gig work 124–5, 434
  algorithms 125
  characterisation 124
  transactional nature of 140
gig workers 124–5
  algorithmic management 139–40
  legal rights and protections 135, 136
  self-employment 132–3, 135
Gilbert, Martin 274
globalisation 10, 38–42, 49
  three Ps 38
GMB 81–2, 110, 142, 335
  Crocodile Tears Tour 172
GMB Scotland 158
Go-Ahead Group plc (case study) 302
goal theory 371
Godard, J. 161, 163, 173
Gokaldas Exports (case study) 39–40
Goodrich, C. L. 408
Gospel, H.F. and Palmer, G. 209
governments
  as employers 17
  employment framework 17
  see also Coalition government;
    Conservative government;
    Labour government
Gowans, Rob 188
graphic rating scale 386
Greece 35, 36, 37, 153
Green, A.M. 317
Green, Helen 80
Green, Joseph 213–14
Greenberg, J. 383
grievance procedures 105, 169, 170,
    203, 210, 297, 313, 322, 434
grievances
  distrust of co-workers 170
  employee rights 206, 207, 313
  management time 174
  mobilisation of employees 169, 435
  voice mechanisms 209–10
Griffiths, Eifion 299
Grimshaw, J. 303
group level bargaining 308–9

Guest, D. E. and Isaksson, K. 97
Guest, D. E. and Peccei, R. 280
Guest, David 77, 97, 227
Gurkov et al. 340–1

H&M 39–40
Hadrian X 171
Haiti 36
Hall et al. 315
Han, Misa 404
hard HRM 12, 40, 434
harmony 401, 434
  trust and 64
Harris, Lynette 201
health and safety 52–3
Health and Safety at Work Act
    (1974) 204, 314
Hearn, S. 231
Hebdon, R. and Noh, S. C. 152, 410
Heery, E. 279, 297, 304
Heery International 355
Heilman, M. E. 389
Hertzberg, F. 386
Hewlett-Packard (case study) 275
high-performance workplaces 83
hire and fire conditions 106
Hirschman, A. O. 294
Hoel, H. and Cooper, C. L. 80
Hoffman, Christy 49
Høie, Atle 304
horizontal task-based participation
    268–9, 434
Horlicks 409
Hosseini et al. 261
Hryschko, Katie 270
Hughes et al. 169
Hughes, J. and Bozionelos, N. 63, 190, 355
human capital theory 40, 434
human relations school 373–4
human resource management
    (HRM) 11–12, 434
  hard 12, 40
  socially irresponsible 40
  soft 12, 40
Huws et al. 132
hybrid working patterns 334–5, 346–7
  see also flexible working
Hyman, J. and Mason, R. 277
Hyman, Richard 47, 69, 154, 156, 165,
    260, 374, 410

IBM 153, 320
ICE Regulations 279, 315
Iceland 346

identification-based trust 62, 434
IG BCE 300
Ikea France 99
imbalances of power *see* power imbalances
implied terms 101–2, 104, 111, 434
incentive-based payment systems 387
income, inequality of 411–13
incorporated terms 104
Independent Workers Union of Great Britain
    (IWGB) 143
India 36
indirect EIP 263, 266, 272, 273, 274–5
indirect involvement 272, 434
indirect voice 295, 297, 298, 303–7, 434
individualism 11, 434
induction 199
industrial pluralist perspective on
    conflict 163, 434
IndustriALL 49
industry level bargaining 308
inflexible work pattern 335
informal employment 47
informal VIP 264
informally dominated market economy 47
information sharing 245
    see also employee involvement,
        participation and partnership (EIP)
informational justice/injustice 71, 245,
    246, 373, 408, 411, 434
injustice 70–1
insecurity, work 10
    increasing prevalence of 128–9
    platform work and 127–9
Institute of Leadership and Management
    survey (2012) 354
institutions 9
integrative bargaining model 311–12
integrative participation 276, 435
interactional justice/injustice 70–1, 73, 246,
    373, 408, 435
interests 16–17, 21
internal equity 407
International Labour Organisation (ILO) 34
intra-organisational bargaining model 312
intrinsic rewards 369
involvement *see* employee involvement,
    participation and partnership (EIP)
Involvement and Participation
    Association 263
involvement practice 259
Ireland 32–3, 131, 302, 392
    employee involvement 261
    employee relations dispute 165–6
    'Iron rice bowl' system 44

Isaac, J. E. 388
Ishmael, A. and Alemoru, B. 81
Italy 40–1, 41–2, 98
    employment contracts 98
ITUC Global Rights Index 155
IUF 52–3

Jabutay, F. 234
Jaguar Land Rover 335
Japan 36, 392
    employment contracts 113
    women labour force 352
JD Weatherspoon 273–4
Jepsen, Maria 260
Jiang, Z. 409
job demands 234
job evaluation 411, 435
job resources 234
job satisfaction 229
job security 413–17
    see also redundancy
job-sharing 345
Johan Sverdrup oil field 6
John Lewis 298–9
Johnstone, Stewart 272–3
joint action 196
Jones et al. 261
Jordan et al. 72
Jump on Board (case study) 283–4
Just Eat 133
justice 70–1
    distributional 125, 132, 242, 245, 247, 315,
        373, 377, 411
    distributive 70, 73, 243, 407–8, 409,
        419, 432
    fairness and 406–10
    informational 71, 245, 246, 373, 408,
        411, 434
    injustice and conflict 410–11
    natural 197–8, 199
    organisational justice 70, 245, 407,
        419, 436
    procedural 71, 73, 78–9, 243, 373, 408, 409,
        419, 437
justice theory 373

Kahn-Freund et al. 99
Kahn, W. A. 227, 242
Kane, A. 266
Karojisatsu 16
Karoshi 16
Kaufman et al. 18–19
Kellogg (case study) 235
Kelly, John 169, 173

Kessler, I. 370
Keune, M. and Pedaci, M. 142
key-time contracts 347
Khan et al. 313
Kim, M. and Beehr, T. A. 69
Kim, Pauline 137
Kim, W. C. and Mauborgne, R. 70, 73, 208
King, Mervyn 370
King v Sash Windows Workshop (2017) 135
Knoll, M. and van Dick, R. 316
knowledge-based trust 62
Kolb, D. M. and Putnam, L. L. 152
Kossek, E. E. and Lautsch, B. A. 343
Kostal 100
Kramer, R. M. 322

Labour government 189, 258
labour platforms 130
labour power 13
labour process theory 145
Lancashire Textile Manufacturers'
    Association 9
Latham & Watkins (case study) 317–18
law *see* legislation
leave
    annual 34, 117, 135, 205
    compassionate 204, 205
    maternity 51, 77, 103, 204, 205
    menstrual 210–11
    parental 43, 204
    sick 157, 170, 171
Leeds Council 74
legal power 16
legislation
    employee relations 32–3
    employment 67–8, 314
    employment contracts 94–5
    fairness 67–8
    main UK Acts 202
    Master and Servant Acts 95
    maternity leave 51, 103
    platform work 133–8
    redundancy 415–17
    strikes 204–5
    workplace conflict 201–2
    see also individual Acts
legitimate power 15–16
Lemons, M. and Jones, C. 73–4
Levinson et al. 77
Lewicki, R. J. and Benedict Bunker, B. 62
Lewis, J. D. and Weigert, A. 62
LGBT employees 160, 242, 244, 248, 317, 320
liberal market economies (LMEs) 47, 435
Ligeika, Remy 49–51

Lind, Allan 194
line managers 8, 420–2
line of sight 371, 435
Lionbridge 130
Living Wage Foundation 382
local agreements 310
location-based applications 130
lockdowns (Covid-19) 334
London Underground 344
Longley, Sue 53
López-Bohle et al. 415
Lou's Electrical Repairs (case study) 350–1
Low Pay Commission (LPC) 381, 382
Lukes, S. 14

Macey et al. 231, 233, 244
Macey, W. H. and Schneider, B. 229
Machuel, Denis 52–3
MacLeod, D. and Clarke, N. 226
Mahoney, T. A. 374
Malaysia 197, 232
Malik v. *BCCI* (1998) 103
management 7–8
    collectivism 11
    individualism 11
management styles 110
managerial action 196
managerial perspective on conflict 162–3
managerial prerogative 24, 49, 380
managerial styles 23–5, 67, 435
    flexible working 338–40
    workplace conflict 189–92
        coercion 189–91
Mandate 165–6, 421, 422
Marchington, M. 269
Marcus, Anton 164
markets perspective/egoism 195
Marks, Helen 404
Marley Tiles Ltd 81–2
Martin, Tim 273–4
Marxist school 374
Masuda et al. 353
maternity leave 51, 77, 103, 204, 205
matrix working 10, 323, 330, 342
Mayo, Elton 373–4
McGregor, Douglas 238
McNall et al. 336
mediation 215, 216, 435
    techniques 196
Melin Tregwynt 299
Menegatti, E. 97
menstrual leave, paid 210–11
Mentari, R. R. and Ratmawati, D. 242
Merrill Lynch 100

MetLife UK 236–7
Metropolitan Council (case study) 212–13
micro-tasking crowdwork 132
migration 41–2
Miller, Maria 200
Mishra, A. K. and Spreitzer, G. M. 234
mixed bargaining model 312, 435
MNCs (multinational corporations) 33
mobile labour markets 130
mobilisation 48, 435
    theory 169–70
Modern Slavery Act (2015) 34
Montero, Irene 375–6
Moore, S. and Read, I. 159
Morgan, W. B. and King, E. B. 77
Mowbray et al. 297
MRT Crossrail (case study) 281
Mulholland, Kate 63
multidimensional engagement 230
mutual trust and confidence 103,
    107, 108

national agreements 310, 311
National Insurance Act (1946) 96
national level bargaining 308
National Living Wage (NLW) 376–7
National Minimum Wage
    (NMW) 376–7
natural disasters 35–6
natural justice 197–8, 199, 408,
    415, 435
negotiation 215–16, 436
Nelson et al. 171
neo-corporatist perspective 163–4, 436
neo-pluralism 21
neoliberal perspective on conflict 162
neoliberalism 32, 43, 436
Nestlé 270
Netherlands 307, 308
    employee involvement 262
    rights of gig workers 135
networks 270–1
Neunsinger, S. 389
new pay 384, 386, 436
New Zealand 33, 392
News International 24
Nienhueser, W. 304
Norlander et al. 140
Norton Rose Fulbright
    (case study) 243–4
Norway 304, 392
numerical flexibility 339
nurses 190–1
nursing profession 156

Ocado 377
occupational class theory 261
Office of National Statistics (ONS) 96,
    173, 174, 305, 338, 347, 389
O'Grady, Frances 106, 190, 385, 411, 413
oni joshi 16
Oni-Ojo et al. 215
online labour markets 129–30
organisational justice 70, 245, 407,
    419, 436
organisational trust 247, 410
Osterloh, Brend 277
Otaye, L. and Wong, W. 406
outsourced labour 349
outsourcing 127
Oyetunde et al. 294

P&O Ferries 412–13
parental leave 43, 204
Paresashvili et al. 154
part-time work 343
Part-time Workers (Prevention of Less
    Favourable Treatment) Regulations
    (2000) 343
participation 272–3
    case studies 273–5
    categorising 275–9
    statutory regulation 277, 278
    see also direct EIP; employee involvement,
        participation and partnership (EIP);
        indirect EIP
partnership(s) 21, 279–84, 436
    benefits 280
    between employers and employees 280–1
    between supervisors and supervisees 282
    case studies 281, 283–4
    contradictory perspectives 283
    definition 279
    honesty 283
    practices 280
    principles 280
Pasquier et al. 172
pay
    bargaining 380–1
    fairness 382
    gender equality/inequality 375–6, 389, 392
    living wage 376–7, 382
    minimum wage 376–7, 381
    motivational theory 385–6
    payment systems 387–90
    performance-related 380–1, 388–90, 436
    review bodies 381–2
    reward and 368, 370–1, 374
    secrecy clauses 385

transparency 411
variable pay schemes 380
see also reward
pay gap 384, 389, 392, 436
Pay Review Bodies 381–2
pay-work bargain 383
Peccei, Richard 234
peer review 215
pensions 411–12
Peretz et al. 337
performance appraisal 191, 436
performance management 192–4
　care or coercion 193
performance pay 380–1, 388–90, 436
peripheral workforce 343, 436
personal equity 407
personal power 16
personal role engagement 229
Pesole et al. 130
Peugeot UK 262, 345–6
Pfeiffer, S. and Kawalec, S. 140–1
picketing 14, 143, 158, 166, 436
piecework 372, 387–8, 436
Pimlico Plumbers 135
plant level bargaining 309
platform businesses 126
　multinationals 127
platform work 124, 129–30, 436
　Accountability for Algorithms Act,
　　proposed 134
　employment plus pattern 129
　insecurity and 127–9
　legislation 133–8
　power and worker representation 141–2
　rights of workers 135
　status of employees 134–5
　types of 131–3
　see also algorithms; gig economy;
　　gig work; gig workers
pluralist frame of reference 18, 20–1,
　297, 436
Poland
　employee/manager meetings 262
　strikes 173
Pollert, A. and Charlwood, A. 209–10
Pool, M. 7
Porter, L. W. and Lawler, E. E. 371
Portugal 300
　employment contracts 111
power 13–14, 436
　abuse of 15
　case studies 404–6
　collective 16
　decision making 14

'to do' 14
dominance 14
economic position 16
fairness and 403–6
flexible working 353–5
legal 16
manipulative 14
'over' 14
personal 16
platform work and worker
　representation 141–2
positional 16
sharing 272–3
sources of 15–16
　coercive 15
　expert 14–15
　legitimate 15–16
　referent 15
　reward 15
symbolic 16, 438
technical 16
trade unions 13
workplace conflicts 155–9
power imbalances 12–16, 405
　employment contracts 98–100
　fairness 410–11
precarious work 10, 40, 123–4,
　125–7, 437
　defining 129
　factors for growth of 128
precarious workers 125–7
precariousness, study of 129
precarity at work 125
precarity from work 125
Pret a Manger 391
PriceWaterhouseCoopers 348–9
primary parties 3, 436
Princes 344
principal-agency theory 372, 437
Pringles (case study) 274
procedural justice/injustice 71, 73, 78–9,
　243, 373, 408, 409, 419, 437
procedures, workplace 205–10
　types of 210–11
Procter & Gamble (case study) 274
profit-based pay 388
profit-sharing schemes 388
prosocial silence 316, 437
Prouska et al. 300
psychological contract 77–9, 82, 97, 117,
　140, 141, 190, 209, 226, 233, 236, 239,
　354, 369, 386, 402
　relational 77
　transactional 77

Public Interest Disclosure Act (1998) 313
Purcell, John 246
Putman et al. 336–7

Qatar 41

radical perspective 164–5, 437
radicalist frame of reference 18, 21–2
Ramsay, H. 272
Rand 107
Random House group 130
Rasak et al. 419
RATP 38
reasonableness 13, 65, 101, 102, 107, 108,
    110, 111, 198, 199, 405, 415
redressing the balance 64
redundancy 10, 192, 203–4, 275,
    315, 437
  Acas 416
  consultation 314–15
  contract termination 113
  fairness 192
  fears about 413–15
  procedures for 415–17
referent power 15
Reid, Susan 64–5
relational contract 77
Relational Quality Index 19
reliability 401, 437
  trust and 64
remote working 346–7
representative EIP 263
resolution gap 200–1
responsible autonomy 268
retained pay 112
reward 367, 390–1
  banks 370
  CIPD survey (2022) 411
  components of 379
  consensual methods of
      determining 380–2
  employers 369–71
  fairness, perceptions of 382–7
  influences 374–9
  management 368, 369
  non-financial 369
  pay 368, 370–1, 374
  power 15
  theories of 371–4
  trade unions 380–1
  value of 368
  see also pay
reward management 367, 437
reward power 15

reward strategy 370, 437
rights, employment 3
Rix, Mick 142
RMT 208, 413
Roberts, E. 337
Roberts, Yvonne 109
Robinson, D. 382
robots 171–2
Romania 44
Roper et al. 80
Rousseau, D. 77
Royal National Orthopaedic
    Hospital 318
Russia 105
  employment contracts 105
Ryanair 4, 111
Ryde 377

sabbaticals 348
sabotage 167–8, 169
Sainsbury's (case study) 402–3
Saks, A. M. 229, 236
Salamon, M. 267
Sanches, Valter 40
Sapsford, D. and Turnbull, P. 173
Schaufeli et al. 227
Schneider, B. 410
Schneider Electric 43
Schulz et al. 83, 385
Scottish Fair Work Convention 109
Searle, R. H. and Rice, C. 63–4
secondary parties 3, 437
Secretly Group Union 48
sector level bargaining 308
self-employment 132–3, 135
Selfridges 74
SendGrid 249–50
Sewell et al. 193
sexual harassment 200
Shantz et al. 238–9
Shapps, Grant 168, 413
share ownership 268
sharing information 245
    see also employee involvement,
        participation and partnership (EIP)
shift work 337–8, 344
Shrewsbury Pickets' 14
Shuck et al. 227, 229
sick leave 157, 170, 171
silence 316–17, 322
Singapore 51
site level bargaining 309
Slee, T. 144
Smith, Gillian 108

Snook, J. C. and Whittall, M. 278
Sobolewski, Edward 169
social exchange theory 322, 372–3
social media 170, 296, 319–20
social movement unionism (SMU) 48
Social Partnership Programmes
    (Ireland) 32–3
social partnerships 8, 32–3, 47, 164, 261, 278,
    279, 307, 438
socially irresponsible HRM 40, 438
Sodexo 302–3
    case study 52–3
SOEs (state-owned enterprises) 44, 438
soft HRM 12, 40, 438
Sonnentag et al. 231
sophisticated modern constitutionalist
    managerial style 24, 438
sophisticated modern consulter managerial
    style 24, 438
sophisticated paternalist managerial
    style 24, 438
Sorenson, Jessica 172
South Korea 410
Spain 97, 210–11, 307
    gender pay equality 375–6
    strikes 173
    temporary contracts 102
Spill (case study) 370–1
spot salary structure 311, 438
Sri Lanka 164
staff associations 24
stakeholders 3, 438
standard modern managerial style 24, 438
Starnes, Chip 72–3
state engagement 229
state, the
    neoliberal work practices 32–3
    regulation 196
state work engagement 231, 438
statutory rights 106
statutory terms 104
Stavrou, E. and Kilaniotis, C. 335
Steelscape 272
steelworkers 167
Stephens, E. H. 276
Steyn, Lord 101, 103
Stiles et al. 78–9
Stonewall 321
Storey et al. 97
Storey, John 12
Streeck, W. 39
strikes 438
    ballots 205
    British Airways 72

British Gas 109–10
bus drivers 38, 172
COP26 (Glasgow, 2021) 158–9
Debenhams Retail Island 165–6
delivery drivers 133, 143
financial cost of 172–3
Greek workers 153
international comparative statistics 173
Johan Sverdrup 6
legal restrictions 204–5
loss of working days 172–3, 174
Marley Tiles Ltd 81–2
refuse collection workers 157, 158
Shrewsbury pickets 14
Stuart 143
Transport for London (TfL) 208
structural antagonism 21, 66, 239, 438
Strutton, Brian 4
Stuart (company) 143
Suff, R. 175
suicides, in the workplace 82–3
Swain, Martin 409
Swan, E. and Fox, S. 334
Sweden 392
    employee/manager meetings 262
    Working Hours Act 340
symbolic power 16, 438

target theory 372
task participation 268–9
Tayfur, O. 43
Taylorism 130, 438
team briefing 259, 439
teamworking 268
teleworking 346–7
temporary work 97–8
Tepper et al. 373
term-time working 348
Tesco 264
    case study 74–5
    fire and rehire case 112
Thailand 300
The Bridge 303
theory, teaching of 44–6
Theory X managers 238, 439
Theory Y managers 238, 439
Thibaut, John and Walker, Lauren 71
third parties 3, 439
three Ps 38
time-based payment systems 387
time off in lieu 345
Tiny Plus report (2019) 228
Tjosvold, D. 161
Tomlinson, Amy 236–7

Tomprou, M. and Lee, M. K. 77
Torre, Della 297
tournament theory 372, 439
Trade Union and Labour Relations
    (Consolidation) Act 1992 204–5
Trade Union Congress of Nigeria (NTUC) 33
trade unions 5–7, 47–9
  agreements with employers 207
  Amazon 140
  common aims 5
  cultural factors 45–6
  decline 7, 152, 259
  density 7, 39, 47, 304, 306, 439
  employee voice 296
  fairness 79
  gig workers and 141
  globalisation and 38–9
  grass roots mobilisation 48
  institutional factors 45–6
  membership 6–7, 11
  membership levels in employment 305
  pay bargaining 380
  power 13
  representatives 5–6
  reward systems 380–1
  Ryanair dispute 4
  social movement unionism (SMU) 48
  strikes 6
  types of 47
  varieties of unionism (VOU) 47–8
  voice 6
  workplace conflict 197
  see also individual trade unions
traditionalist managerial style 23–4, 439
trait engagement 229
transactional contract 77
Transfer of Undertakings (Protection of
    Employment) Regulations (2006) 314
transformational participation 276
transparency 74, 411, 439
Transport for London (TfL) 208
Trevor, J. and Brown, W. 369
Triangle, Luc 300
tribunal system, UK 175–6
tripartite partnership 164
tripatism 164
trust 61–85, 439
  calculus-based trust 62
  case study 74–5
  concern 64
  definition 62
  duty of care 75–6
  earned 78
  employee engagement 239, 242–6

  employee voice 242–6, 321–3
  equity, efficiency and voice 68–9
  fairness and 63–4, 65–7, 321–3, 402
  flexible working 353–5
  harmony 64
  high-performance workplaces 83
  identification-based trust 62
  increased workloads 80–1
  knowledge-based trust 62
  perception of 62
  perceptions of fairness, justice and
    injustice 70–4
  psychological contract 77–9
  reliability 64
  swift trust 62
  values 62–3
  workplace conflict 159–60, 194–6
TSB 320
tube strikes (London) 208
TUC 106, 339, 347, 412, 418
TUPE regulations 81
Turkey 36, 105, 300
Tzafrir, S. S. and Dolan, S. 64, 282,
  339, 401

Uber 127, 130, 135, 137,
  139, 140
  recognition of GMB 142
Ukraine-Russia conflict (2022-23)
  35, 355
unfair dismissal 198
UNI Global Union 155
Unilever 46
Unions New South Wales
  (UNSW) 142
UNISON 213, 282
unitarist frame of reference 18, 19–20,
  297, 439
Unite 310, 335, 344
United Arab Emirates (UAE) 103
United Bank Limited v. *Akhtar*
  (1989) 111
United Kingdom (UK)
  economic growth rate 36
  employee participation 273
  employment contracts 96, 114
  employment legislation 314
  employment market 10–11
  employment regulation 313
  flexible working 352
  Information and Consultation of
    Employees (ICE) Regulations
    279, 315
  involuntary temporary work 97

legislation 202
National Living Wage
    (NLW) 376–7
National Minimum Wage
    (NMW) 376–7
strikes 173, 174
tribunal system 175–6
unpaid overtime 189–90
workplace conflict 172–3
workplace mediation and
    conciliation 216
United States of America
    (USA) 41, 392
employee voice 300
employers' power 157
employment contracts 113
employment termination
    procedure 51
workers' rights 154–5
workplace conflict 173
unpaid overtime 189–90
upward problem-solving 267–8
USDAW 112
Utrecht work engagement scale
    (UWES) 237–8

value systems 356
Van Buren et al. 21
Van Dyne et al. 316
Varfell Farms 42
variable pay schemes 380
varieties of capitalism
    (VoC) 47, 259
varieties of unionism
    (VoU) 47–8
Verdi 76
vertical task-based participation
    268, 439
Victim Support 64–5
Vida 142
voice 68
    Budd's framework 68–70, 111, 141,
        315, 338, 401
    collective 246
    of employees see employee voice
    fairness 419–20
    individual 246
    of trade unions 6
Volkswagen Group
    (VW) 276–7
voluntary partnerships 258
voluntary reduced work time 348
Volvo 43
vulnerability 417–18

wage-effort bargain 372–3, 439
wages drift 377
Wajcman, J. 161
Walmart 190
Wayfair 296
web-based platforms 130
Webb, Christian 114, 268
Webb, Sidney and Beatrice 5
Welbourne, T. M. 232–3
wellbeing 75, 125, 210, 229, 236, 242,
    244, 303, 338, 352, 370
Whelan, Madeline 166
Whelan, Mick 281
whistleblowing 313, 314
Whitener et al. 282
Whitman et al. 409
Wilkinson, A. and Fay, C. 262
Wilkinson et al. 295
Williams, S. 259
Wizz Air 157
Wollard, Karen 64
women
    inequality see gender
        equality/inequality
    negotiating pay 389
    pensions 411–12
Women and Equalities
    Committee 200
work
    health and 337–8, 355, 406
    long hours 100, 190,
        337, 355
    working time and attendance 341
    see also flexible working
Work and Families Act
    (2006) 204
work engagement 230
work-life balance 63, 440
work processes 417
worker representation 141–2
workers 94–5
    definition 95
    insecure 418
    vulnerable 417–18
    see also employees
workers' rights 155
working from home 334, 335, 336,
    338, 346–7
    see also flexible working
working time and attendance 341
Working Time Regulations
    (1998) 204
working to rule 157, 439
Working Washington 140

Workplace Employee Relations Surveys
    (WERS) 159, 174, 195–6, 200, 240–1,
    269, 273, 301
Works Councils 104, 142, 277, 278–9, 304–5,
    307, 440
    European 202, 263, 275,
        278, 305
workshop level bargaining 309
World Economic Forum (2020) 124
World Trade Organisation (WTO) 38
written statements 105

Xiao, Q. and Cooke,
    F. L. 44

Yarlagadda et al. 321
Yhou et al. 259
Yukl, G. 260

Zara 154–5
zero-hours contracts 96, 118, 339,
    347–8, 418
Zoom 10, 163, 196